Research & Education Association

The Best Teachers' Test Preparation for the

FTCE

Elementary Education K-6

Anita Price Davis, Ed.D.
Professor Emerita
Converse College, Spartanburg, S.C.

And the Staff of
Research & Education Association

Visit our Educator Support Center at:
www.REA.com/teacher

The competencies presented in this book were created and implemented by the Florida Department of Education. For further information visit the FTCE website at *www.fl.nesinc.com.*

Research & Education Association
61 Ethel Road West
Piscataway, New Jersey 08854
E-mail: info@rea.com

The Best Teachers' Test Preparation for the Florida FTCE Elementary Education K–6 Test

Published 2009

Copyright © 2006 by Research & Education Association, Inc.
All rights reserved. No part of this book may be reproduced
in any form without permission of the publisher.

Printed in the United States of America

Library of Congress Control Number 2006923804

ISBN-13: 978-0-7386-0146-5
ISBN-10: 0-7386-0146-2

REA® is a registered trademark of
Research & Education Association, Inc.

About the Author

Dr. Anita Price Davis is The Charles A. Dana Professor Emerita of Education and was the Director of Elementary Education at Converse College, Spartanburg, South Carolina, before retiring in 2005. Dr. Davis earned her B.S. and M.A. from Appalachian State University and her doctorate from Duke University. She also received a postdoctoral fellowship to Ohio State University for two additional years of study.

Dr. Davis had worked more than 36 years at Converse College, where she served as the faculty advisor for Kappa Delta Epsilon, a national education honor organization. She also worked 5 years as a public school teacher.

Dr. Davis has received wide recognition for her work, including a letter of appreciation from the U.S. Department of the Interior, inclusion in *Contemporary Authors*, and a citation of appreciation from the Michigan Council of the Social Studies. She has authored/coauthored 23 funded grants for Converse College. She has served as a mentor and was a two-time President of the Spartanburg County Council of the International Reading Association. The state of South Carolina twice named her an outstanding educator, and she was twice a nominee for the CASE U.S. Professor of the Year.

Dr. Davis has authored, co-authored, and edited more than 80 books. She has written two college textbooks titled *Reading Instruction Essentials* and *Children's Literature Essentials*. Dr. Davis has published several history books and is also the author of more than 80 papers, book reviews, journal articles, and encyclopedia entries.

About Research & Education Association

Founded in 1959, Research & Education Association is dedicated to publishing the finest and most effective educational materials—including software, study guides, and test preps—for students in middle school, high school, college, graduate school, and beyond.

REA's Test Preparation series includes books and software for all academic levels in almost all disciplines. Research & Education Association publishes test preps for students who have not yet entered high school, as well as for high school students preparing to enter college. Students from countries around the world seeking to attend college in the United States will find the assistance they need in REA's publications. For college students seeking advanced degrees, REA publishes test preps for many major graduate school admission examinations in a wide variety of disciplines, including engineering, law, and medicine. Students at every level, in every field, with every ambition can find what they are looking for among REA's publications.

REA's practice tests are always based upon the most recently administered exams and include every type of question that you can expect on the actual exams.

REA's publications and educational materials are highly regarded and continually receive an unprecedented amount of praise from professionals, instructors, librarians, parents, and students. Our authors are as diverse as the fields represented in the books we publish. They are well-known in their respective disciplines and serve on the faculties of prestigious high schools, colleges, and universities throughout the United States and Canada.

Today, REA's wide-ranging catalog is a leading resource for teachers, students, and professionals.

We invite you to visit us at *www.rea.com* to find out how "REA is making the world smarter."

Acknowledgments

We would like to thank REA's Larry B. Kling, Vice President, Editorial, for supervising development; Pam Weston, Vice President, Publishing, for setting the quality standards for production integrity and managing the publication to completion; Christine Reilley, Senior Editor, for project management and preflight editorial review; Diane Goldschmidt, Senior Editor, for post-production quality assurance; Barbara McGowran for copyediting the manuscript; Christine Saul, Senior Graphic Artist, for cover design; and Jeff LoBalbo, Senior Graphic Artist, for post-production file mapping.

We also gratefully acknowledge the team at Aquent Publishing Services for typesetting and indexing the manuscript.

CONTENTS

FTCE

Florida Teacher Certification Examinations
Elementary Education K–6

Review

Passing the Examination

About This Book

REA's *The Best Teachers' Test Preparation for the Florida FTCE Elementary Education K–6 Test* is a comprehensive guide designed to assist you in preparing to take the Florida Teacher Certification Examination required for teaching at the elementary level, kindergarten through grade 6. To enhance your chances of success in this important step toward your career as a teacher in Florida elementary schools, this test guide:

- identifies some of the important information and its representation on the FTCE: K–6;
- summarizes the content for a quick review;
- provides sample questions in the actual test format;
- suggests tips and strategies for successfully completing standardized tests;
- presents an accurate and complete overview of the FTCE: K–6;
- provides two practice tests for rehearsal before the test date;
- replicates the format of the FTCE: K–6;
- represents the types and the levels of difficulty of the questions that appear on the test; and

- supplies the correct answer and detailed explanations for each question on the two practice tests. (This enables you not only to identify correct answers but also to understand why they are correct and, just as important, why the other answers are incorrect.)

The guide is a result of studying many resources. The editors considered the most recent test administrations, other test guides, and professional standards; they also researched information from the Florida Department of Education, professional journals, textbooks, and educators.

In addition to guiding your preparation for certification, recertification, out-of-field certification, or multiple certifications, this REA test prep is a valuable resource for college and university personnel and in-service trainers. They will find the book helpful as they construct help sessions and recommend resources for a test candidate. The guide may even suggest topics or content to include in a college course syllabus.

Although our book is intended to help you succeed on the FTCE: K–6, you should not consider it a replacement for any college course, a duplicate of the test, or a complete source of subject matter to master. Like knowledge itself, the FTCE: K–6 can change.

This book includes the best test preparation materials based on the latest information available from test administrators. The number and distribution of questions can vary from test to test. Accordingly, prospective examinees should pay strict attention to their strengths and weaknesses and not depend on specific proportions of any subject areas appearing on the actual exam.

About the Test

Who Must Take the FTCE: K-6?

Individuals take the FTCE: K–6 to obtain a temporary certificate (nonrenewable and valid for three school years) or a professional certificate (Florida's highest educator certificate, renewable and valid for five school years). To obtain either certificate, a prospective teacher must demonstrate mastery of subject matter knowledge, as indicated by a passing score on the FTCE: K–6.

People taking the test include (1) individuals seeking initial teacher certification in Florida, (2) educators with temporary certificates who want professional certificates, and (3) educators who are making changes in their teaching career. You are eligible to take the test if you are:

* enrolled in a college or university teacher preparation program at the bachelor's or master's degree level,
* teaching with provisional certification, or
* making a change in your teaching career.

What If I Do Not Pass the Test?

If you do not achieve a passing score on the FTCE: K–6, you should not panic! Instead, as a serious test taker, plan to retake the test after waiting at least 31 days. The waiting period enables you to do additional work to improve your score on the next test. Remember, a low score on the FTCE is not an indication that you should change your plans about a teaching career.

Who Designs the Test?

The Florida Department of Education, together with the Evaluation Systems group of Pearson Education, Inc., develops and administers the FTCE: K–6. The test reflects modifications the Florida Legislature has made to the program of testing required for teacher candidates, who must demonstrate mastery of subject matter in areas covered by the certification.

A committee developed the FTCE: K–6. The specialists on the committee came from within the state and included teachers, supervisors, and college faculty with expertise in the content areas. Recommendations by professional organizations, content area experts, and teachers' unions assisted in the selection of committee members.

The committee identified the information for inclusion on the FTCE: K–6 and validated the content. To develop the test, the committee used reviews of the literature, surveys of and interviews with teachers, pilot tests, and their own expertise. They designed and implemented a validation process to ensure that the content and difficulty level of the test are appropriate.

When Should I Take the FTCE: K-6?

Most candidates for teacher certification take the test just before or after graduation. Some institutions have rules about the dates by which students must have taken and passed the examination. Consult the rules of the college where you are enrolled to determine if any stipulations exist.

The Florida Department of Education establishes the tests you must take for certification and the deadlines by which you must complete the tests for certification purposes. For instance, if you have a temporary certificate, it is good for only three years; if you do not take and pass the required FTCE: K–6 within the period that the Florida State Department sets, your certificate can lapse.

Computer-based tests are offered throughout the year in many locations; you simply schedule an appointment at a testing center. Paper-based tests are offered about six times per year at fixed times and locations. In addition, a test candidate who has a disability and cannot take the test under standard testing conditions can request special accommodations. A disabled test-taker needs to check with the Florida Department of Education about rules for requesting special arrangements.

Several Web sites, phone numbers, and addresses help you stay up-to-date with information about the FTCE: K–6. You can contact the Florida Department of Education as follows:

325 West Gaines Street, Suite 1514
Tallahassee, FL 32399-0400
Phone: (850) 245-0505
Web site: http://www.fldoe.org/asp/ftce

The FTCE Home Page: *www.fl.nesinc.com*

Is There a Registration Fee?

To take the FTCE: K–6, you must pay a registration fee. Payment must be by personal check, money order, cashier's check, or credit card (Visa or MasterCard). Cash is not accepted. For information on the current test rules, regulations, and fees, contact the Florida Department of Education or go to the Web sites listed above.

How to Use This Book

The following sections outline ways you can use this study guide and take the practice tests to help you prepare for the Florida Teacher Certification Examination: K–6.

How Do I Begin Studying?

1. Review the organization of this test preparation guide.
2. Follow the "FTCE: K–6 Study Schedule" presented at the end of this chapter. The schedule is for a seven-week independent study program, but you can condense or expand the schedule according to the time you have available.
3. Take the Diagnostic Test.
4. Score the Diagnostic Test according to the directions in the section of this chapter titled "Scoring the FTCE: K–6."
5. Review the section of this chapter titled "Format of the FTCE: K–6," which provides the format of items on the sample test and a replica of the real test.
6. Review the suggestions for test-taking presented later in this chapter.
7. Pay attention to the information about the competencies and skills, content, and topics on the test.
8. Spend time reviewing those topics that seem to warrant more study.
9. Take the Practice Test and study those competencies that your test scores indicate need more review.
10. Follow the suggestions presented later in this chapter for the day before and the day of the test.

Thoroughly studying the subject area reviews in Chapters 2 through 6 of this guide will reinforce the basic skills you need to do well on the exam. Taking the practice tests under timed, simulated testing conditions will help you become familiar with the format of the FTCE: K–6 and the procedures involved in taking the actual test.

When Should I Start Studying?

It is never too early to start studying for the FTCE: K–6. (Actually, you started preparing when you began your first college course and internship.) The earlier you begin using this guide, however, the more time you will have to sharpen your skills. Do not procrastinate! Cramming is not the most effective way to study; it does not give you the time you need to think about the content, review the competencies, and practice the test. It is important, however, to review the material one last time the night before the test administration.

Format of the FTCE: K–6

The FTCE: K–6 requires all morning and most of the afternoon to complete; test takers get a lunch break between the two parts. The morning test is about 135 minutes, and the afternoon test is 125 minutes. The total test-taking time is, therefore, 260 minutes (4 hours, 20 minutes). Adding the tutorial time and the lunch break, the total examination period is 330 minutes. The FTCE: K–6 is the only subject area test that you cannot take on the same day as another test, for instance the Professional Education Test.

You should have plenty of time to complete the FTCE: K–6 during the examination period, but you will need to be aware of the amount of time you spend on each question. You do not want to find you have run out of time before you finish all the questions. Although speed is not very important, a steady pace is necessary when answering the questions. Using the practice tests will help you set your pace.

Each of the roughly 223 questions has four answer options: A, B, C, and D. Individual test items require levels of thinking, ranging from simple recall to evaluation, analysis, and problem solving. The questions, however, are all in multiple-choice format. To complete the FTCE: K–6 in the allotted 260 minutes, you should allow yourself about one minute for each test question.

Format of Questions on the FTCE: K–6

There are several types of questions on the FTCE: K–6. The types are (1) scenario; (2) direct question, command, and sentence completion; (3) graphs and maps; (4) graphics; and (5) word problems. Following are definitions of each type of question and examples for practice.

1. **Scenario.** You must examine a case study, scenario, or problem and answer the question, diagnose the problem, or suggest the best course of action from the provided options.

i. A student describes an analysis of a recent presidential address for the class. The teacher replies, "You have provided us with a most interesting way of looking at this issue!" The teacher is using

 (A) simple positive response.

 (B) negative response.

 (C) redirect.

 (D) academic praise.

ii. While waiting for students to formulate their responses to a question, a student blurts out an answer. The teacher should

 (A) ignore the answer entirely.

 (B) respond immediately to the student's answer.

 (C) silently acknowledge the student's response and address the response after someone else has answered the question.

 (D) move on to another question without comment.

2. **Direct question, sentence completion, and command.** The examinee must choose the option that best answers the question, best completes the sentence, or best responds to the command given. With the direct question, there is actually a question mark as punctuation in the question stem. The examinee answers the question.

iii. Which of the following is a trait of effective professional development?

 (A) A continuous plan of lifelong learning

 (B) Activities developed solely by the principal

 (C) A one-hour stand-alone workshop

 (D) A totally theory-based program

iv. What is one way of incorporating nonperformers into a discussion?

 (A) Ask a student to respond to a previous student's statement.

 (B) Name a student to answer a question.

(C) Only call on students with their hands raised.

(D) Allow off-topic conversations.

3. With the sentence completion, there is a portion of the sentence omitted. The test-taker chooses the best answer to finish the statement declaratory sentence.

v. Teachers convey emotion through

(A) body language, eye contact, and verbal cues.
(B) verbal contact and cues.
(C) voice levels.
(D) the way they listen.

4. With the command, the word *you* is understood. The test-taker is given a direction to follow.

vi. Identify the type of traditional literature that serves to explain why a phenomena or phenomenon occur(s).

(A) Fable
(B) Fairy tale
(C) Myth
(D) legend

5. **Graph or map.** Identify or interpret a graph or map by choosing the response that best answers the question.

vii. The following graph shows sales totals for each region of the state in thousands of dollars; the graph shows the totals by yearly quarters.

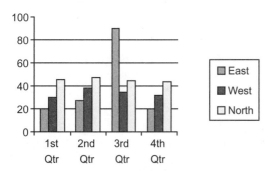

The region with the largest total sales for the year is

(A) the east.
(B) the north.
(C) the west.
(D) the south.

6. **Graphics.** Choose the response that best answers a question about a number line, a geometric figure, a chart, a graph of lines or curves, or a table–but not the typical maps and graphs of the previous question type.

viii. Troubled by what seems to be an increase in gang-type activity among increasingly younger children, Bill wants to find out what his students think and know about gangs. He wants to learn the most he can about the students' thinking on this topic in the least amount of time. He wants all students to have the chance to share what they think and know, yet he also wants to maximize interaction among students. The students will spend the entire morning reading, talking, and writing a group report about this subject. Which of the following seating arrangements would best help Bill meet his objectives?

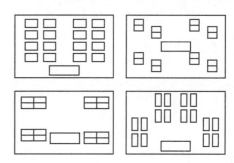

(A) The upper-left diagram
(B) The lower-left diagram
(C) The upper-right diagram
(D) The lower-right diagram

7. **Word problem.** Apply mathematical principles to solve a real-world problem.

ix. Examine the following addition problems worked by an elementary school student. Analyze what error pattern the student's work is exhibiting. If the student worked the problem 88 ± 39 using the error pattern exhibited here, what answer would the student give?

$$\begin{array}{cccc} 74 & 35 & 67 & 56 \\ +56 & +92 & +18 & +97 \\ \hline 1,210 & 127 & 715 & 1,413 \end{array}$$

(A) 127   (C) 51
(B) 131   (D) 1,117

Answers

i.   Academic praise (D) is composed of specific statements that give information about the value of the object or about its implications. A simple positive response (A) does not provide any information other than the praise, such as the example, "That's a good answer!" There is nothing negative (B) about the teacher's response. A redirect (C) occurs when a teacher asks a student to react to the response of another student. The correct answer is (A).

ii.   If the teacher ignores the answer entirely (A) or moves on to another question (D), it devalues the student's response. If the teacher responds immediately to the digression (B), the disruptive behavior has been rewarded. The correct answer is (C).

iii.   Effective professional development is not a one-time workshop, nor can it be satisfied within a specified amount of time (C). To effect growth in children, teachers must grow and develop as well (A). This learning must extend throughout the teacher's career and beyond. In addition, effective professional development relies on meeting the needs of those involved and therefore cannot be dictated solely by one individual (B). Finally, in addition to being theory and research-based, the learning gained from professional development activities must be practical and applicable (D). Otherwise, the learning cannot be used at the school site, and the training is rendered useless. The correct answer is (A).

iv.   Nonperformers are students who are not involved in the class discussion at that particular moment. Asking students to respond to student statements (A) is the only option that describes a way of incorporating nonperformers into a class discussion.

v.   Even without saying a word, teachers can communicate a variety of emotions with their body language, eye contact, and verbal cues (A). Smiles, verbal cues (such as the intonation of voice), movement, posture, and eye contact with students can convey enthusiasm. Body language can even convey that teachers are actively listening to their students by maintaining eye contact and leaning into the conversation.

vi.   A myth (C) is an explanation for something that a person does not understand; examples are stories about why a rabbit has a short tail, why the camel has a hump, and why there are certain patterns (constellations) in the night sky. A fable (A) is a story that teaches a moral and that may have animals acting like people. A fairy tale (B) is a story that often has stereotyping, magic, and good winning out over evil. A legend (D) often has some elements of truth, but the person, place, or thing becomes exaggerated. For example, there is a fountain in St. Augustine, but it does not provide eternal youth; there was a lumberjack, but he did not have a blue ox and was not a giant (Paul Bunyan). (C) is the best answer.

vii.   To figure out the answer to any question involving the bar graph, you need to look at the graph carefully. The numbers on the left of the graph in this question are in increments of 20, which would be $20,000; these large increments make it difficult to get a precise answer. The first reaction is that the east might be the correct answer. The largest bar is in the color for the east. If you look more closely, however, you see that during the first quarter, the sales in the east were $20,000; sales were about $28,000 during the second quarter. The third quarter sales in the east (A) amounted to about $90,000; added to the $20,000 for the fourth quarter, you get a total of about $148,000. The totals for the north (D) were $42,000, $42,000, $42,000, and $42,000; this gives a total of $168,000. The sales for the west (C) are $30,000, $38,000, $37,000, and $25,000; that gives a total of $130,000. The reader has no idea of sales figures for the south (D).

viii.   Placing the students in small groups in which they meet face to face (B) will allow Bill to maximize the students' interaction while giving each student the maximum opportunity to speak. Placing students in the traditional rows facing the front discourages student interaction and minimizes each student's opportunities to speak (A). Although placing students in pairs maximizes each student's opportunity to speak, it limits the sources of interaction; each student can share thoughts with only one other student (C). In contrast, a group of four allows the student to interact as part of three dyads, two triads, and a quadrant. When placing the students in cooperative groups, it is wise to arrange the desks within the physical space of the classroom in such a way that each group's talking does not distract the members of other groups (D).

ix.   You should note that the student is failing to carry in both the ones and tens places. 56 + 97 is being treated as 5 + 9 and 6 + 7. The two answers are then combined for a total of 1,413. Choice A presents the correct answer to the addition problem and therefore does not exhibit the error pattern. Choice C exhibits switching from addition to subtraction (9 – 8 = 1) and (8 – 3 = 5). Also, the child subtracts the top number from the bottom one in the first step. In choice B, the child subtracts 8 from 9, and also 3 from 8, and then adds to the 8 in the tens place. Only choice (D) illustrates the pattern of recording the sum and not carrying.

Content of the FTCE: K–6

The FTCE: K–6 comprises five subject areas, with competencies (areas of content knowledge) under each subject:

- Language Arts: 5 competencies
- Mathematics: 6 competencies
- Social Science: 5 competencies
- Music, Visual Arts, Physical Education, and Health: 9 competencies
- Science and Technology: 9 competencies

The Florida Department of Education has identified skills related to each competency. These competencies and skills are the basis for the FTCE: K–6. The reviewer can use these competencies and skills as an inventory of information to consider when preparing to take the test. The subject area reviews, competencies, and skills in Chapters 2 through 6 of this guide can help one prepare for the FTCE: K–6.

Computer-Based Testing

Computer-based tests are available as alternatives to the traditional pencil-and-paper tests. Test candidates can take the computer-based tests at flexible times throughout the year; they are comparable in length and in difficulty to the paper-and-pencil tests. Like the traditional FTCE: K–6, the computer-based tests use only multiple-choice questions. You can preview and review questions and change your answers while taking the test. Immediately after you complete the computer-based tests, unofficial score reports appear on your monitor; you should receive official score reports by mail in about a month. To register for computer-based tests, you can go to *www.fl.nesinc.com*.

Minimal computer skills are necessary to take the test. However, you should be comfortable with the Windows platform; able to use a mouse; and familiar with the skills of scrolling, dragging, clicking, and double-clicking. Before you take the computer-based examination, you can complete an on-line short tutorial. The tutorial shows you how to move through the test, mark answers, change responses, and review questions throughout the test.

About the Subject Area Reviews in This Book

The subject area reviews in Chapters 2 through 6 of this book will help you sharpen the basic skills you will need when you take the FTCE: K–6. In addition, the reviews provide you with strategies for attacking the test questions. Each teaching area has its own chapter; subtopics in each chapter include the competencies within the subject area and information on the skills within the competencies.

Your education has already provided much of the information you need to score well on the FTCE: K–6. Education classes and internships have given you the know-how to make important decisions about situations that teachers face. The reviews in this book will help you fit the information you have already acquired into specific competency components. Reviewing class notes and textbooks and using the competency and skill reviews in this book will provide excellent preparation for passing the FTCE: K–6. Each subject area review includes a competency statement and a list of the associated skills.

Another important part of the book is the two practice tests that will help develop your test-taking skills. Although the review sections and the practice tests will help prepare you for the FTCE: K–6, this guide is not an all-inclusive source of information or a substitute for course work. The sample test items cannot be exact representations of questions that actually appear on the test.

Scoring the FTCE: K–6

How Do I Score the Practice Tests?

There are about 223 questions on the FTCE: K–6. The exact number of questions necessary for a passing score varies with different administrations of the test and with different numbers of test questions on the test. A passing score on the FTCE: K–6 is about 65 percent. In other words, if the test you take has 223 questions, you need to answer roughly 145 questions correctly to achieve a passing score. The passing score for each of the practice tests in this guide is also 65 percent.

If you do not achieve a passing score on the practice tests, you should review completely the detailed explanations for the questions you answered incorrectly. Pay particular attention to the questions you answered incorrectly, note the types of questions you missed, and reexamine the corresponding review section. After further study, you might want to retake the practice tests.

When Will I Receive My Score Report for the FTCE: K–6?

Unofficial score reports are available through the FTCE website after 5:00 p.m. on the day of the test. Official score reports are issued approximately 2 weeks after each computer-based test, and approximately one month after each paper-based test. The Bureau of Educator Certification will receive an electronic copy of the score report. A copy of the score report will go to one Florida college or university and/or one school district if you so requested. Additional copies are $10.00 each.

Studying for the FTCE: K–6

Choose a study time and study place that suit the way you live and learn. Some people set aside a certain number of hours every morning to study; others choose to study at night before going to sleep. Busy test candidates study at random times during the day: while waiting in line for coffee, while eating lunch, or between classes. Only you can determine the study plan that is best for you.

It is important to study consistently and to use your time wisely. After you work out a study routine, stick to it. It is crucial not to wait until the last minute and not to cram.

When you take the practice tests in this book, observe the time constraints and try to simulate the conditions of the actual test as closely as possible. Turn off the television, the phone, and the radio. Sit down at a table in a quiet room, free from distraction.

After you complete a practice test, calculate your score. Keeping track of your scores will enable you to gauge progress and discover general weaknesses in particular sections.

Reviewing thoroughly the explanations to the questions you answered incorrectly and noting the reasons for the correct answers will help you gain mastery. Give extra attention to the review sections that cover areas of difficulty you have noted, and gradually build skills in those areas.

It is important to concentrate on just one problem area at a time; a good way to do this is by studying the questions you missed and the explanations of why those answers are inappropriate. Study the corresponding chapter for additional information. Giving extra attention to competencies and skills related to your areas of weakness is an effective learning tool and will help increase your knowledge and confidence in subject areas that initially gave you difficulty.

Using note cards to record facts and information for future review is a good way to study and keep the information at your fingertips in the days to come. You can easily pull out the small note cards and review them at random moments: during a coffee break or meal, on the bus or train as you head home, or just before falling asleep. Using the cards gives you essential information at a glance, keeps you organized, and helps you master the materials. Ultimately, you gain the confidence you need to succeed.

Before the Test

If the test center is not located in a familiar area, you might want to make a trial run to ensure that you do not get lost and that there are no detours. It is always a good idea to check your registration slip to verify the time and place. Before leaving for the test center, be sure you have your admission ticket and two forms of identification. Both forms of identification must be valid, unexpired, and printed in English. The first must be government-issued and have a photograph and signature (e.g. driver's license, state-issued ID, US Military ID, or passport). The second form of identification must have either a photo or signature (e.g. Social Security card or student ID). You may not enter the test center without proper identification.

It is helpful to arrive at the test center early. This allows you some time to relax, and avoid the anxiety that might come with a late arrival.

You should plan what to wear ahead of the test day. It is important to dress comfortably and in layers; that way you can remove a sweater or add a jacket if the room is too hot or too cool. Dressing in layers ensures that the room temperature will not divert your concentration while taking the test.

What to Take (and What Not to Take) to the Test Center

If you are taking the paper-based test, you must supply your own pencils. It is a good idea to bring several sharpened No. 2 pencils with erasers because the test monitors will not provide any at the test center. You do not want to have to get up during the test to sharpen a pencil; another test taker may forget a pencil and may ask you to share so it is best to have a supply on hand. Also, you must bring blue- or black-ink ball-point pens.

You should wear a watch to the test center. However, you cannot wear a watch that makes noise because it can disturb the other test takers. The computer will indicate the total time for the session; when you know how many questions are in the exam and how many minutes are in the morning or afternoon session, you can gauge time accurately for each question.

As an added precaution in the paper-based test, be sure to check the page numbers very quickly. One test taker's booklet was incorrectly stapled, and she did not realize it until she was three pages from the end of the test. It would be better to realize this at the beginning of the test than when your time is almost up.

You cannot bring cell phones, electronic devices, paper, dictionaries, textbooks, notebooks, calculators, briefcases, or packages. Food, drinks, cigarettes, and other smoking implements must also remain at home.

During the Test

The FTCE: K–6 requires 260 minutes to administer. You will have a lunch break during the test. To maintain test security, test takers and the proctor must follow certain procedures. Once you enter the test center, you must follow all the rules and the instructions that the proctor gives. Test takers who do not do so risk dismissal from the test and having their test scores canceled.

During the paper-based test, after distributing the testing materials, the proctor will give the directions for filling out the answer sheet. It is important to fill out the sheet carefully because the information you provide will appear on the score report. Once the test begins, you should be sure to fill in answers darkly and neatly, mark only one answer per question, and completely erase unwanted answers and marks.

Test-Taking Tips

REA's *The Best Teachers' Test Preparation for the FTCE: Elementary Education K–6* will acquaint you with the test and help alleviate test-taking anxieties. Listed here are ways you can get ready to take the FTCE: K–6, and perhaps other tests as well.

Tip 1. Become comfortable with the format of the FTCE: K–6. Use the practice tests, simulate the conditions under which you will be taking the actual test, try to stay calm, and pace yourself. In fact, after simulating the test only once, you will boost your chances of doing well and will be able to sit down for the actual FTCE: K–6 with much more confidence.

Tip 2. Read all the possible answers. Even if the first response appears to be the correct answer, the savvy test taker will read all the choices and not automatically assume that the first is the best answer. Read through each choice to be sure that you are not making a mistake by jumping to conclusions.

Tip 3. Use the process of elimination by going through each answer to a question and discarding as many of the answer choices as possible. For instance, if you eliminate two of the four answer choices, the chances of getting the item correct have increased because you have only two choices left from which to make a guess—a 50-50 chance of choosing the correct answer.

Tip 4. Never leave a question unanswered. It is better to guess than to leave a question blank on the FTCE: K–6.

Tip 5. Work quickly and steadily when taking the test. The actual test consists of roughly 223 questions, and you will have 260 minutes to complete the test. Therefore, you will need to work at a constant pace over a long period of time. Wearing a watch and referring to the time occasionally will help you gauge the time left. You will need to allow about a minute for each question.

Tip 6. Do not focus on any one question too long.

Tip 7. Take the practice tests in this guide to help you learn to budget the precious time allotted for the test session.

Tip 8. Study the directions and the format of the FTCE: K–6. Familiarizing yourself with the directions and format of the test will not only save time but also alleviate anxiety and the mistakes caused by being anxious.

Tip 9. During the paper-based test, you should constantly check the answer sheet to be sure that the number beside the answer bubble matches the number beside the question in the test booklet.

Tip 10. Enter your answers carefully. The paper-based FTCE: K–6 is a multiple-choice test graded by machine. If you skip a bubble or enter an answer twice, the rest of the answers on the answer sheet may be incorrect and may affect your score seriously.

Tip 11. Make a note of any question for which you had to guess. If you have extra time, you can always re-check those questions you marked. Do not, however, make stray marks on the answer sheet.

FTCE: K–6 Study Schedule

The following study schedule allows for thorough preparation to pass the FTCE: K–6. The course of study suggested here is seven weeks, but you can condense or expand your preparation program to match the time you have available for study. In any case, it is vital that you adhere to a structured plan and set aside ample time each day to study. Depending on your timeframe, you might find it easier to study throughout the weekend and during the week. No matter what timetable you plan, the more time you devote to studying for the FTCE: K–6, the more prepared and confident you will be on the day of the actual test.

Week 1. Take the diagnostic exam. The score will indicate your strengths and weaknesses. Make sure that you take the test under simulated exam conditions and observe the time guidelines. After taking the test, score it and review the explanations, particularly for the questions you answered incorrectly.

Week 2. Review the explanations for the questions you missed, and choose the review sections in the chapters that will provide information in your areas of weakness. Useful study techniques are to highlight key terms and information; to take notes on the material in the review sections as you work; and to put new terms and information on note cards to help you retain the information.

Weeks 3 and 4. Reread the note cards you created in preparation for the test, look through your college textbooks, and read over your class notes from past courses. In addition, you may find it helpful to re-read the competencies and skills that the test emphasizes; a summary of this information is in the review sections of this guide. This is the time to consider any other supplementary materials that your counselor or the Florida State Department of Education suggests. (Be sure to review the Web site for the Florida Department of Education at *http://www.fldoe.org/.*)

Week 5.   Begin to condense your notes and findings. A structured list of important facts and concepts—based on the FTCE: K–6 competencies and skills and written on index cards—will help you as you review for the test.

Week 6.   Have a relative, friend, or colleague quiz you using the index cards you created the previous week. Take the practice test, adhering to the time limits and replicating actual testing conditions as closely as possible. Review the explanations for both the incorrectly and correctly answered questions.

Week 7.   Review your areas of weakness using study materials, references, and notes. This is a good time to retake the practice test.

After the Test

When the time is up, the proctor will dismiss you from the test center. You are then free to go home and relax—a well-deserved treat!

FTCE

Florida Teacher Certification Examinations
Elementary Education K–6

Diagnostic Test

Answer Sheet

1. Ⓐ Ⓑ Ⓒ Ⓓ
2. Ⓐ Ⓑ Ⓒ Ⓓ
3. Ⓐ Ⓑ Ⓒ Ⓓ
4. Ⓐ Ⓑ Ⓒ Ⓓ
5. Ⓐ Ⓑ Ⓒ Ⓓ
6. Ⓐ Ⓑ Ⓒ Ⓓ
7. Ⓐ Ⓑ Ⓒ Ⓓ
8. Ⓐ Ⓑ Ⓒ Ⓓ
9. Ⓐ Ⓑ Ⓒ Ⓓ
10. Ⓐ Ⓑ Ⓒ Ⓓ
11. Ⓐ Ⓑ Ⓒ Ⓓ
12. Ⓐ Ⓑ Ⓒ Ⓓ
13. Ⓐ Ⓑ Ⓒ Ⓓ
14. Ⓐ Ⓑ Ⓒ Ⓓ
15. Ⓐ Ⓑ Ⓒ Ⓓ
16. Ⓐ Ⓑ Ⓒ Ⓓ
17. Ⓐ Ⓑ Ⓒ Ⓓ
18. Ⓐ Ⓑ Ⓒ Ⓓ
19. Ⓐ Ⓑ Ⓒ Ⓓ
20. Ⓐ Ⓑ Ⓒ Ⓓ
21. Ⓐ Ⓑ Ⓒ Ⓓ
22. Ⓐ Ⓑ Ⓒ Ⓓ
23. Ⓐ Ⓑ Ⓒ Ⓓ
24. Ⓐ Ⓑ Ⓒ Ⓓ
25. Ⓐ Ⓑ Ⓒ Ⓓ
26. Ⓐ Ⓑ Ⓒ Ⓓ
27. Ⓐ Ⓑ Ⓒ Ⓓ
28. Ⓐ Ⓑ Ⓒ Ⓓ

29. Ⓐ Ⓑ Ⓒ Ⓓ
30. Ⓐ Ⓑ Ⓒ Ⓓ
31. Ⓐ Ⓑ Ⓒ Ⓓ
32. Ⓐ Ⓑ Ⓒ Ⓓ
33. Ⓐ Ⓑ Ⓒ Ⓓ
34. Ⓐ Ⓑ Ⓒ Ⓓ
35. Ⓐ Ⓑ Ⓒ Ⓓ
36. Ⓐ Ⓑ Ⓒ Ⓓ
37. Ⓐ Ⓑ Ⓒ Ⓓ
38. Ⓐ Ⓑ Ⓒ Ⓓ
39. Ⓐ Ⓑ Ⓒ Ⓓ
40. Ⓐ Ⓑ Ⓒ Ⓓ
41. Ⓐ Ⓑ Ⓒ Ⓓ
42. Ⓐ Ⓑ Ⓒ Ⓓ
43. Ⓐ Ⓑ Ⓒ Ⓓ
44. Ⓐ Ⓑ Ⓒ Ⓓ
45. Ⓐ Ⓑ Ⓒ Ⓓ
46. Ⓐ Ⓑ Ⓒ Ⓓ
47. Ⓐ Ⓑ Ⓒ Ⓓ
48. Ⓐ Ⓑ Ⓒ Ⓓ
49. Ⓐ Ⓑ Ⓒ Ⓓ
50. Ⓐ Ⓑ Ⓒ Ⓓ
51. Ⓐ Ⓑ Ⓒ Ⓓ
52. Ⓐ Ⓑ Ⓒ Ⓓ
53. Ⓐ Ⓑ Ⓒ Ⓓ
54. Ⓐ Ⓑ Ⓒ Ⓓ
55. Ⓐ Ⓑ Ⓒ Ⓓ
56. Ⓐ Ⓑ Ⓒ Ⓓ

57. Ⓐ Ⓑ Ⓒ Ⓓ
58. Ⓐ Ⓑ Ⓒ Ⓓ
59. Ⓐ Ⓑ Ⓒ Ⓓ
60. Ⓐ Ⓑ Ⓒ Ⓓ
61. Ⓐ Ⓑ Ⓒ Ⓓ
62. Ⓐ Ⓑ Ⓒ Ⓓ
63. Ⓐ Ⓑ Ⓒ Ⓓ
64. Ⓐ Ⓑ Ⓒ Ⓓ
65. Ⓐ Ⓑ Ⓒ Ⓓ
66. Ⓐ Ⓑ Ⓒ Ⓓ
67. Ⓐ Ⓑ Ⓒ Ⓓ
68. Ⓐ Ⓑ Ⓒ Ⓓ
69. Ⓐ Ⓑ Ⓒ Ⓓ
70. Ⓐ Ⓑ Ⓒ Ⓓ
71. Ⓐ Ⓑ Ⓒ Ⓓ
72. Ⓐ Ⓑ Ⓒ Ⓓ
73. Ⓐ Ⓑ Ⓒ Ⓓ
74. Ⓐ Ⓑ Ⓒ Ⓓ
75. Ⓐ Ⓑ Ⓒ Ⓓ
76. Ⓐ Ⓑ Ⓒ Ⓓ
77. Ⓐ Ⓑ Ⓒ Ⓓ
78. Ⓐ Ⓑ Ⓒ Ⓓ
79. Ⓐ Ⓑ Ⓒ Ⓓ
80. Ⓐ Ⓑ Ⓒ Ⓓ
81. Ⓐ Ⓑ Ⓒ Ⓓ
82. Ⓐ Ⓑ Ⓒ Ⓓ
83. Ⓐ Ⓑ Ⓒ Ⓓ
84. Ⓐ Ⓑ Ⓒ Ⓓ

85. Ⓐ Ⓑ Ⓒ Ⓓ
86. Ⓐ Ⓑ Ⓒ Ⓓ
87. Ⓐ Ⓑ Ⓒ Ⓓ
88. Ⓐ Ⓑ Ⓒ Ⓓ
89. Ⓐ Ⓑ Ⓒ Ⓓ
90. Ⓐ Ⓑ Ⓒ Ⓓ
91. Ⓐ Ⓑ Ⓒ Ⓓ
92. Ⓐ Ⓑ Ⓒ Ⓓ
93. Ⓐ Ⓑ Ⓒ Ⓓ
94. Ⓐ Ⓑ Ⓒ Ⓓ
95. Ⓐ Ⓑ Ⓒ Ⓓ
96. Ⓐ Ⓑ Ⓒ Ⓓ
97. Ⓐ Ⓑ Ⓒ Ⓓ
98. Ⓐ Ⓑ Ⓒ Ⓓ
99. Ⓐ Ⓑ Ⓒ Ⓓ
100. Ⓐ Ⓑ Ⓒ Ⓓ
101. Ⓐ Ⓑ Ⓒ Ⓓ
102. Ⓐ Ⓑ Ⓒ Ⓓ
103. Ⓐ Ⓑ Ⓒ Ⓓ
104. Ⓐ Ⓑ Ⓒ Ⓓ
105. Ⓐ Ⓑ Ⓒ Ⓓ
106. Ⓐ Ⓑ Ⓒ Ⓓ
107. Ⓐ Ⓑ Ⓒ Ⓓ
108. Ⓐ Ⓑ Ⓒ Ⓓ
109. Ⓐ Ⓑ Ⓒ Ⓓ
110. Ⓐ Ⓑ Ⓒ Ⓓ
111. Ⓐ Ⓑ Ⓒ Ⓓ
112. Ⓐ Ⓑ Ⓒ Ⓓ

Diagnostic Test

TIME: 130 minutes (2 hours and 10 minutes) for 112 questions.

> In this section, you will find examples of test questions similar to those you are likely to encounter on the FTCE.

1. When reading, the semantic cueing system refers to

   (A) the meaning system of language.
   (B) the structural system of language.
   (C) the letter-sound relationships in written language.
   (D) the social and cultural aspects of language.

2. When reading, the syntactical cueing system refers to

   (A) the meaning system of language.
   (B) the structural system of language.
   (C) the letter-sound relationships in written language.
   (D) the social and cultural aspects of language.

3. When reading, the phonological cueing system refers to

   (A) the meaning system of language.
   (B) the structural system of language.
   (C) the letter-sound relationships in written language.
   (D) the social and cultural aspects of language.

4. When reading, the pragmatic cueing system refers to

   (A) the meaning system of language.
   (B) the structural system of language.
   (C) the letter-sound relationships in written language.
   (D) the social and cultural aspects of language.

5. Literacy is a person's ability to

   (A) hop and skip.
   (B) read and write.
   (C) encode and be pragmatic.
   (D) comprehend and engage.

The figure below represents an economy that produces vehicles. That economy is presently producing 12 vans and zero cars. Use the figure to answer questions 6 and 7.

Production Possibilities Curve

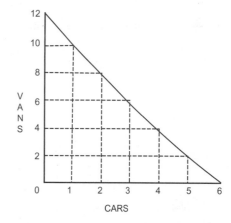

6. The opportunity cost of increasing the production of cars from zero units to two units is the loss of production of _____ of vans.

   (A) 1
   (B) 2
   (C) 3
   (D) 4

7. This is an example of _____ opportunity costs per unit for cars.

(A) constant
(B) increasing
(C) decreasing
(D) zero

8. The United States Constitution defines the powers of the United States Congress and the states. The Tenth Amendment to the Constitution reserves powers to the states, while Article I, Section 8, delegates powers to the federal government. Some powers are shared concurrently between the states and the federal government. Which of the following powers are concurrent powers?

I. Lay and collect taxes
II. Regulate commerce
III. Establish post offices
IV. Borrow money

(A) I and II
(B) II and III
(C) III and IV
(D) I and IV

9. The United States has a two-party system, while several European governments have a multiparty system. Which of the following statements is true about political parties in the United States but not true about political parties in multiparty European governments?

(A) Political parties form coalitions to advance their policy initiatives through Congress.
(B) Single-member district voting patterns clearly identify candidates for seats in political offices.
(C) Parties provide candidates for office and organize campaigns to get the candidate elected.
(D) Political parties are linked to religious, regional, or social class groupings.

10. The Pacific Northwest receives the greatest annual precipitation in the United States. Which of the following statements best identifies the reason this occurs?

(A) The jet stream moving south from Canada is responsible for pushing storms through the region.

(B) The region's mountains along the coast cause air masses to rise and cool, thereby reducing their moisture-carrying capacity.
(C) Numerous storms originating in Asia build in intensity as they move across the Pacific Ocean and then dump their precipitation when they reach land.
(D) The ocean breezes push moisture-laden clouds and fog into the coastal region, producing humid, moist conditions that result in precipitation.

11. Six employees at a circuit board factory—strangers to each other—are chosen to compose a new work team. To encourage these six workers to get to know each other better, management has asked each worker to arrange a short, one-on-one introductory meeting with each of the other team members. How many one-on-one meetings will there be?

(A) 12
(B) 36
(C) 15
(D) 18

12. The distance from Tami's house to Ken's house is 3 miles. The distance from Ken's house to the Soda Depot is 2 miles. Which of the following statements are true?

I. The greatest possible distance between Tami's house and the Soda Depot is 5 miles.
II. The greatest possible distance between Tami's house and the Soda Depot is 6 miles.
III. The shortest possible distance between Tami's house and the Soda Depot is 1 mile.
IV. The shortest possible distance between Tami's house and the Soda Depot is 2 miles.

(A) I and III
(B) I and IV
(C) II and III
(D) II and IV

13. Which inequality describes the allowable speeds indicated by the following speed limit sign?

```
75 MPH
MAXIMUM

40 MPH
MINIMUM
```

(A) $75 \le x \le 40$
(B) $75 < x > 40$
(C) $40 \le x \le 75$
(D) $40 < x > 75$

14. Which types of graphs or charts would be appropriate for displaying the following information?

Favorite Lunch Foods of 40 Surveyed 6th Graders

Pizza	18
Chicken nuggets	12
Macaroni and cheese	4
Tacos	4
Hamburgers	2

    I.   Bar graph
   II. Pie (circle) chart
  III. Scatter plot
  IV. Broken-line graph

(A) I and II
(B) III and IV
(C) I and III
(D) II and IV

15. Which of the following illustrates the distributive property?

(A) Multiplying 23 by 16 gives the same product as multiplying 16 by 23.
(B) The numbers 65, 70, and 12 can be added together in any order, and the sum will always be the same.
(C) The sum of 102 and 9 is the same as the sum of 9 and 102.
(D) The product of 3 and 42 is the same as the sum of the products 3×2 plus 3×40.

16. You have stepped into an art museum and are drawn to a painting you know nothing about. To appreciate the painting, it is helpful to

    I.   know all the details of the artist's intentions and motivations.
   II. study the clues in the artwork for potential meaning.

  III. determine the cultural significance of every visual clue in the painting.
  IV. consider the art elements and principles in the work of art.

(A) I and II
(B) I and III
(C) II and IV
(D) III and IV

17. Which of the following statements is most true regarding the materials of visual art?

(A) Industrial innovations in art-making materials have improved art in the past 150 years.
(B) The use of uncommon materials in art making has improved art in the past 150 years.
(C) The use of unusual materials in art making has changed the way in which we view art.
(D) Industrial innovations in art-making materials have had little influence on visual art.

18. Which of the following is an important reason why music should be included in every child's daily classroom activities?

(A) The imagination, creativity, and aesthetic awareness of a child can be developed through music for more creative living in our mechanized society.
(B) Students need an opportunity to stay current with today's popular music culture.
(C) Making and listening to music is part of our cultural experience and provides opportunities for personal aesthetic growth.
(D) Participating in creatively planned musical activities helps build a child's self-esteem and understanding of others.

19. Pitch is the relative _____ of a musical sound.

(A) duration, or length
(B) loudness or softness
(C) highness or lowness
(D) rhythm

20. A pyramid represents the pattern of progression from simple to complex activities in creative drama.

Using the base of the pyramid for the simplest activities and the tip for the most complex, which of the following patterns correctly represents this progression?

(A) Story dramatization, story creation, improvisation, pantomime, beginning activities

(B) Improvisation, pantomime, beginning activities, story dramatization, story creation

(C) Beginning activities, improvisation, pantomime, story dramatization, story creation

(D) Beginning activities, pantomime, improvisation, story creation, story dramatization

21. A teacher interested in improving the comprehension skills of students should

I. teach students to decode well.
II. allow time during the day to read and reread selections.
III. discuss the selections after reading to clarify meaning and make connections.
IV. tell jokes.

(A) I and II
(B) I, II, and IV
(C) I, II, and III
(D) All of the above

Use the following information to answer questions 22–24.

An experiment is planned to test the effect of microwave radiation on the success of seed germination. One hundred corn seeds will be divided into four sets of 25 each. Seeds in group 1 will be microwaved for 1 minute, seeds in group 2 for 2 minutes, and seeds in group 3 for 10 minutes. Seeds in group 4 will not be placed in the microwave. Each group of seeds will be soaked overnight and placed between the folds of water-saturated newspaper.

22. Among the seeds available at the store, no single package contained enough seeds for the entire project; most contained about 30 seeds per package. Which of the following is an acceptable approach for testing the hypotheses?

I. Purchase one packet from each of four different brands of seed, one packet for each test group.
II. Purchase one packet from each of four different brands of seed, and divide the seeds from each packet equally among the four test groups.
III. Purchase four packets of the same brand, one packet for each test group.
IV. Purchase four packets of the same brand, and divide the seeds from each packet equally among the four test groups.

(A) I and II
(B) II and IV
(C) III and IV
(D) IV only

23. During the measurement of seed and root length, it is noted that many of the roots are not growing straight. Efforts to manually straighten the roots for measurement are only minimally successful because the roots are fragile and susceptible to breakage. Which of the following approaches is consistent with the stated hypothesis?

(A) At the end of the experiment, straighten the roots and measure them.

(B) Use a string as a flexible measuring instrument for curved roots.

(C) Record the mass instead of length as an indicator of growth.

(D) Record only the number of seeds that have sprouted, regardless of length.

24. In a presentation of the results of this experiment, which of the following could be used to show the data that confirm or refute the hypothesis?

I. A single bar graph, with one bar for each test group indicating the number of days until the first seed sprouts
II. A pie chart for each test group showing the percentage of seeds in that group that sprouted
III. A line graph plotting the total number of sprouted seeds from all test groups versus time (experiment day)
IV. A line graph plotting the number of germinated seeds versus the minutes of time exposed to the microwave

(A) I only
(B) II only
(C) II and IV
(D) III and IV

25. A hot-air balloon rises when propane burners in the basket are used to heat the air inside the balloon. Which of the following statements correctly identifies the explanation for this phenomenon?

(A) Heated gas molecules move faster inside the balloon, and their force striking the inside causes the balloon to rise.
(B) Hot gas molecules are themselves larger than cool gas molecules, resulting in the expansion of the gas.
(C) The amount of empty space between gas molecules increases as the temperature of the gas increases, resulting in the expansion of the gas.
(D) The combustion of propane releases product gases that are lighter than air and are trapped in the balloon, causing it to rise.

26. A marble and a feather are both released at the same time inside a tube that is held at very low pressure (a near vacuum). Which of the following correctly links the observation to explanation?

(A) The marble falls faster because it is heavier.
(B) The marble falls faster because it has less air resistance.
(C) Both fall at the same rate because there is no air resistance in a vacuum.
(D) Both fall at the same rate because the forces of gravity are different in a vacuum.

Read the following passage and answer the question that follows.

The police believed that Dollree Mapp was hiding a person suspected in a crime. The police went to her home in Cleveland, Ohio, knocked, and requested entry. Mapp refused. After more officers arrived on the scene, police forced their way into Mapp's house. During their search of the house, the police found pornographic books, pictures, and photographs. They arrested Mapp and charged her with violating an Ohio law against possession of pornographic materials. Mapp and her attorney appealed the case to the Supreme Court of Ohio. The Ohio Supreme Court ruled in favor of the police.

Mapp's case was then appealed to the Supreme Court of the United States. Mapp and her attorney asked the Court to determine whether or not evidence obtained through a search that violated the Fourth Amendment was admissible in state courts. The U.S. Supreme Court, in the case *Mapp v. Ohio,* ruled that evidence obtained in a search that violates the Fourth Amendment is not admissible. The majority opinion states, "Our decision, founded on reason and truth, gives to the individual no more than that which the Constitution guarantees him, to the police officer no less than that to which honest law enforcement is entitled, and, to the courts, that judicial integrity so necessary in the true administration of justice."

27. The majority opinion best illustrates which of the following features of judicial proceedings in the United States?

(A) Due process of law
(B) A fair and speedy trial
(C) Judicial review
(D) The exclusionary rule

28. Which of the following statements best defines the role of the World Trade Organization?

(A) It resolves trade disputes and attempts to formulate policy to open world markets to free trade through monetary policy and regulation of corruption.
(B) It is an advocate for human rights and democracy by regulating child labor and providing economic aid to poor countries.
(C) It establishes alliances to regulate disputes and polices ethnic intimidation.
(D) It regulates trade within the United States to eliminate monopolistic trade practices.

29. The drought of the 1930s that spanned from Texas to North Dakota was caused by

I. overgrazing and overuse of farmland.
II. natural phenomena, such as below-average rainfall and wind erosion.
III. environmental factors, such as changes in the jet stream.
IV. the lack of government subsidies for new irrigation technology.

(A) I and II
(B) II and III
(C) I and III
(D) II and IV

30. What does it mean that multiplication and division are *inverse operations*?

(A) Multiplication is commutative, whereas division is not. For example, 4 × 2 gives the same as 2 × 4, but 4 ÷ 2 is not the same as 2 ÷ 4.
(B) Whether multiplying or dividing a value by 1, the value remains the same. For example, 9 × 1 equals 9; 9 ÷ 1 also equals 9.
(C) When performing complex calculations involving several operations, all multiplication must be completed before completing any division, as in 8 ÷ 2 × 4 + 7 − 3.
(D) The operations "undo" each other. For example, multiplying 11 by 3 gives 33. Dividing 33 by 3 then takes you back to 11.

31. One day, 31 students were absent from Pierce Middle School. If that represents about 5.5% of the students, what is the population of the school?

(A) 177
(B) 517
(C) 564
(D) 171

32. Which of the following are equivalent to 0.5%?

I. One-half of 1%
II. 5%
III. 1/200
IV. 0.05

(A) I and III
(B) I and IV
(C) II and III
(D) II and IV

33. The primary and most efficient energy source of the body comes from

(A) proteins.
(B) fats.
(C) complex carbohydrates.
(D) simple sugars.

34. Which of the following is a locomotor skill?

(A) Bouncing
(B) Catching
(C) Throwing
(D) Leaping

35. Which is *not* a principle of aerobic conditioning?

(A) Requires oxygen
(B) Continuous and rhythmic
(C) Burns protein for energy
(D) Uses major muscle groups

36. Dr. Kenneth Goodman developed the notion of miscue analysis. This is a system for examining how a child's oral reading of a passage varies from

(A) singing the same passage.
(B) encoding the passage from a dictation.
(C) the printed text.
(D) diagrams of the sentences.

37. You have just finished reading all but the ending of a story. If you were going to ask the children to finish the story as a writing activity, what would you do next?

(A) Have the children complete a worksheet about the vocabulary words.
(B) Ask them to diagram the first sentence.
(C) Ask the children to form small groups and talk about what might happen next.

(D) Have them complete a Venn diagram of the story so far.

38. Which of the following describes best practice in writing instruction?

(A) Instruct students in writing, and give them time to write.

(B) Have students complete worksheets about writing.

(C) Have students copy famous speeches.

(D) Have students create a mural of a story and label all the characters.

39. Each month, a teacher kept track of the number of books as well as the genre of the books the students read during free-reading time in school. The teacher constructed the following graph from the data for October and May of the same year. This teacher completed a unit on fairy tales in April. What conclusions could be reached from the data shown in the graph?

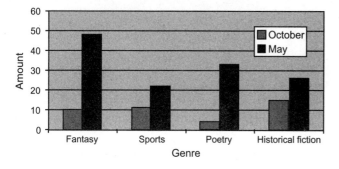

Genres of Selected Books

I. These children are reading more titles during free-reading time.

II. Completing a fairy tale unit created interest in the fantasy genre.

III. These children need to complete more worksheets.

IV. These children are participating in an accelerated reading program.

(A) I, II, and III

(B) I, II, III, and IV

(C) None of the above

(D) I and II

40. Which of the following would be considered a primary source in researching the factors that influenced U.S. involvement in the Korean War?

I. The personal correspondence of a military man stationed with the Fifth Regimental Combat Team in Korea.

II. A biography of Harry S Truman by David McCullough, published in 1993.

III. A journal article about the beginning of the Korean War by a noted scholar.

IV. An interview with Secretary of Defense George Marshall.

(A) I and II

(B) II and IV

(C) II and III

(D) I and IV

41. Which of the following statements is *not* true?

(A) Infectious diseases are caused by viruses, bacteria, or protozoans.

(B) Cancers and hereditary diseases can be infectious.

(C) Environmental hazards can cause disease.

(D) The immune system protects the body from disease.

42. Which of the following types of pollution or atmospheric phenomena are correctly matched with their underlying causes?

I. Global warming—carbon dioxide and methane

II. Acid rain—sulfur dioxide and nitrogen dioxide

III. Ozone depletion—chlorofluorocarbons and sunlight

IV. Aurora borealis—solar flares and magnetism

(A) I and II

(B) II and III

(C) I and IV

(D) I, II, III, and IV

Use the figure below to answer questions 43 and 44.

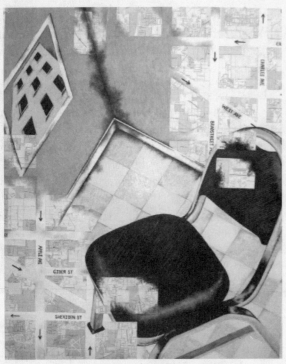

Student Work by Sara Goodrich

43. The technique of gluing imagery to a two-dimensional surface, as shown in the figure, is referred to as a

    (A) montage.
    (B) etching.
    (C) collage.
    (D) assemblage.

44. In the figure, the chair is the focal point of the drawing. Why?

    (A) It is large, frontal, and drawn in high contrast.
    (B) It is highly simplified and minimally detailed.
    (C) It is asymmetrically balanced in the drawing.
    (D) It is drawn in three-point perspective.

45. Which line on the following chart best matches the source of information with the historical question being asked?

Line	Historical Research Question	Source of Information
1	How many people were living in Boston during the time of the American Revolution?	Historical atlas
2	What role did Fort Mackinaw fulfill during the American Revolution?	Encyclopedia article
3	How did the average temperatures and snowfall during the winter of 1775–1776 compare with previous winters?	Historical almanac
4	When was the first U.S. treaty signed, and what were the terms of the treaty?	Government publication

(A) Line 1
(B) Line 2
(C) Line 3
(D) Line 4

46. Which of the following is an example of a question or task requiring synthesis (from Bloom's *Taxonomy*)?

    (A) Here are five words. Write a sentence using these five words and adding any other words you might need.
    (B) Describe how Columbus, in his search for the New World, ended his journey in the Caribbean islands.
    (C) Compare Freud's theory of psychosexual development to Erikson's theory of psychosocial development.
    (D) Diagram the sentence written on the board.

47. A teacher plays a piece of music for her music appreciation class, telling the students that it is an example from the Romantic period. She plays the piece again and asks the students to describe the piece. After students describe the music, she asks them to define *romantic*. The teacher is engaging her students in

(A) inductive reasoning.
(B) deductive reasoning.
(C) oral interpretation.
(D) evaluation.

48. To help a student who has very creative and sophisticated ideas improve his or her spelling (and thus his or her grades in English class), a teacher might suggest that

(A) the student try typing the next paper on a word processor, using a spell checker.
(B) the student use simpler words that are easier to spell.
(C) the student write each misspelled word on the last paper 20 times.
(D) spelling errors not count against the student on papers.

49. An English teacher wants to challenge his students to think critically. He has been teaching about the parts of speech. He writes the following sentence on the board, "The man ran down the street." He asks a student to identify the part of speech of the word *down*. The student says that *down* is an adverb telling where the man ran. The teacher should respond

(A) "No, *down* is not an adverb."
(B) "Yes, *down* does tell where the man ran."
(C) *"Down* is a preposition, and "down the street" is a prepositional phrase."
(D) "Well, *down* does tell where the man ran, which is what adverbs do. But in this case, *down* is part of the phrase "down the street." Do you want to change your answer?"

50. A teacher writes this question on the board: "How do you know if someone is intelligent or not?" The class then is assigned to research the question and develop a list of all the traits and characteristics that define or describe someone who is intelligent. Through this exercise, the teacher has

(A) led her students through an activity of developing criteria against which a judgment can be made.
(B) led her students through an activity of gathering examples.
(C) led her students through an activity of testing if someone is intelligent or not.

(D) engaged her students in a creative-thinking activity.

51. Which of the following is an example of a question or task requiring application thinking skills according to Bloom's *Taxonomy*?

(A) Demonstrate how to fill the printer tray with paper.
(B) What kind of paper is needed to fill the printer tray?
(C) Describe how to load the printer tray with paper.
(D) If the printer does not print after loading the paper tray, what could be the problem?

52. Why is it a good idea for a social studies teacher to give students options and allow them to make choices?

(A) Some teachers dislike telling students what to do.
(B) Some teachers like to give students various options so they can exercise their decision-making skills.
(C) Teachers know that different students are motivated and stimulated by different tasks.
(D) Students deserve a break from all the rules and regulations in most classes.

53. Which of the following requires the higher-order thinking skill, according to Bloom's *Taxonomy*?

(A) Demonstrate how to change the printer cartridge.
(B) State what kind of cartridge the printer needs.
(C) Describe how to change the printer cartridge.
(D) If the printer does not print after the cartridge has been changed, figure out what the problem is.

54. Harmony results when a melody is accompanied by

I.   a rhythm instrument.
II. a guitar.
III. another instrument or singer playing or singing the melody.
IV. another instrument playing chords.

(A) I and II
(B) I and III
(C) II and III
(D) II and IV

55. Which of the following tenets of the atomic theory is *not* correct?

(A) Elements comprise extremely small particles called atoms.
(B) All atoms of a given element are identical, with the same size, mass, and chemical properties.
(C) The atoms of one element are different from the atoms of all other elements.
(D) Compounds are composed of more than one atom from one or more elements.

56. Which of the following observations explains the area of geologic instability surrounding the Pacific Ocean known as the "Ring of Fire"?

(A) Similarities in rock formations and continental coastlines suggest that the earth's continents were once one landmass.
(B) The earth's plates collide at convergent margins, separate at divergent margins, and move laterally at transform-fault boundaries.
(C) Earthquakes produce waves that travel through the earth in all directions.
(D) Volcanoes form when lava accumulates and hardens.

57. The earth's moon is

(A) generally closer to the sun than it is to the earth.
(B) generally closer to the earth than to the sun.
(C) generally equidistant between the earth and the sun.
(D) closer to the earth during part of the year, and closer to the sun for the rest of the year.

58. Which of the following is the best definition of *earth science*?

(A) Study of the planet Earth compared with other planets in the solar system

(B) Study of Earth's living organisms
(C) Study of Earth's natural systems and structures
(D) Study of the structure and composition of Earth

59. The large intestine is part of the _____ system.

(A) digestive
(B) respiratory
(C) endocrine
(D) circulatory

60. The normal number of chromosomes in a human cell is

(A) 52.
(B) 108.
(C) 30.
(D) 46.

61. In an ecosystem, an example of a producer is a

(A) fungus.
(B) maple tree.
(C) wolf.
(D) rock.

62. An example of a fungus is

(A) bacteria.
(B) algae.
(C) protozoa.
(D) yeast.

63. A material with definite volume but no definite shape is called a

(A) plasma.
(B) gas.
(C) liquid.
(D) solid.

64. An acidic solution can have a pH of

(A) 13.
(B) 10.
(C) 9.
(D) 5.

65. Which equation could be used to answer the following question?

Together, a pen and a pencil cost $2.59 (ignoring tax). The pen cost $1.79 more than the pencil. What was the cost of the pencil?

(A) $x = (2.59 - 1.79)$
(B) $2.59 = x - 1.79$
(C) $2.59 = x + (x + 1.79)$
(D) $x = 2.59 - 1.79$

Use the figure below to answer the question that follows.

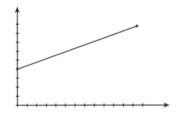

66. Which of the following situations might the graph illustrate?

I.   The varying speed of an experienced runner over the course of a 26-mile race
II.   The number of households a census taker still has to visit over the course of a week
III. The value of a savings account over time, assuming steady growth
IV.   The changing height of a sunflower over several months

(A) I and II
(B) III and IV
(C) II, III, and IV
(D) I, III, and IV

67. Light is refracted when it passes across a boundary between media with different densities. This can occur between solids, liquids, or gases or even because of differences within the same phase. The longer wavelengths of light are refracted less than the shorter wavelengths. Which of the following correctly places the colors of the visible spectrum in order from lowest extent of refraction to highest?

(A) Blue-Violet, Green, Orange, Yellow, Red
(B) Blue-Violet, Green, Yellow, Orange, Red
(C) Red, Yellow, Green, Orange, Blue-Violet
(D) Red, Orange, Yellow, Green, Blue-Violet

68. Around the time of World War II, the chemical industry developed several new classes of insecticide that were instrumental in protecting U.S. soldiers from pest-borne diseases common to the tropic regions they were fighting in. These same insecticides found widespread use at home to increase production of many agricultural crops by reducing the damage from insects like cotton weevils and grasshoppers. While farmers continued to use the same levels of insecticide, over time the insect population began increasing. Identify the best explanation for this observation.

(A) Insecticides, like most chemicals, lose their potency when stored.
(B) The insect population was increasing to reach the carrying capacity of a given ecosystem.
(C) The initial doses of pesticide were too low to kill the insects effectively.
(D) Insects with a tolerance to insecticide survived the initial doses and lived to produce insecticide-resistant offspring.

69. Under the right conditions of temperature and pressure, any type of rock can be transformed into another type of rock in a process called the rock cycle. Which of the following processes is *not* a part of the rock cycle?

(A) The drifting and encroachment of sand at the edge of a desert
(B) The melting of rock beneath the surface to form magma
(C) The erosion of sedimentary rocks to form sand
(D) The eruption of a cinder cone volcano

70. Mr. Nelson's class has just returned from seeing a children's theater production at a nearby university. Now Mr. Nelson plans to ask his students to discuss what they have seen. In preparation for this, he plans to model the types of responses

desired. Which of the following should he use as examples?

I.   I liked the play.
II. I liked the play because the characters reminded me of people I know.
III. I liked the play because the theater was big.
IV. I liked the play because sometimes the story was funny and sometimes it was sad.

(A) I only
(B) II and IV
(C) I and III
(D) IV only

71. Which of the following best describes a major difference between a state government and the federal government?

(A) State governments have more responsibility for public education than the federal government.
(B) State governments are more dependent on the personal income tax for revenue than is the federal government.
(C) State governments are more dependent on the system of checks and balances than is the federal government.
(D) State governments are subject to term limits, whereas federal government representatives serve unlimited terms.

72. Which of the following were major causes of the Great Depression?

I.   Hoarding money greatly reduced the money supply, resulting in higher prices on consumer goods.
II. The gold standard limited the amount of money in supply, reducing money circulation and causing a drop in prices and wages.
III. The Smoot-Hawley Tariff Act increased tariffs, which resulted in increased prices for consumer goods.
IV. The stock market crash reduced the values of companies, causing them to raise the prices of consumer goods.

(A) I and II
(B) II and III
(C) III and IV
(D) I, II, and III

Use the figure below to answer the question that follows.

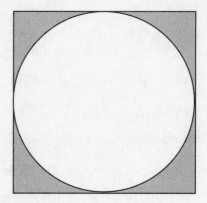

73. What is the approximate area of the shaded region, given the following?

> The radius of the circle is 6 units
> The square circumscribes the circle

(A) 106 square units
(B) 31 square units
(C) 77 square units
(D) 125 square units

74. How many lines of symmetry do all nonsquare rectangles have?

(A) 0
(B) 2
(C) 4
(D) 8

Use the figure below to answer the question that follows.

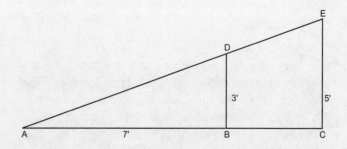

75. The figure is a sketch of a ramp. Given that the two ramp supports (DB and EC) are perpendicular to the ground and the dimensions of the various parts

are as noted, what is the approximate distance from point B to point C?

(A) 4.7 feet
(B) 4.5 feet
(C) 4.3 feet
(D) 4.1 feet

76. Bemus School is conducting a lottery to raise funds for new band uniforms. Exactly 1,000 tickets will be printed and sold Only one ticket stub will be drawn from a drum to determine the single winner of a big-screen television. All tickets have equal chances of winning. The first 700 tickets are sold to 700 different individuals. The remaining 300 tickets are sold to Mr. Greenfield. Given this information, which of the following statements are true?

I. It is impossible to tell in advance who will win.
II. Mr. Greenfield will probably win.
III. Someone other than Mr. Greenfield will probably win.
IV. The likelihood that Mr. Greenfield will win is the same as the likelihood that someone else will win.

(A) I and II
(B) I and III
(C) II and IV
(D) III and IV

77. We may be told to "gargle with saltwater" when we suffer from a sore throat. Which of the following phenomena would be used to explain this advice?

(A) Lowering of vapor pressure
(B) Increasing osmotic pressure
(C) Increasing boiling point
(D) Decreasing freezing point

78. In announcing the Emancipation Proclamation, Lincoln's immediate purpose was to

(A) free black slaves in all the slave states.
(B) free black slaves in only the border slave states that had remained loyal to the Union.
(C) let the southern states know that whether or not they chose to secede from the Union,

slavery would not be tolerated by his administration once he took office.
(D) rally northern morale by giving the war a higher moral purpose than just preserving the Union.

79. In its decision in the case of *Dred Scott v. Sanford*, the U.S. Supreme Court held that

(A) separate facilities for different races were inherently unequal and therefore unconstitutional.
(B) no black slave could be a citizen of the United States.
(C) separate but equal facilities for different races were constitutional.
(D) affirmative action programs were acceptable only when it could be proven that specific previous cases of discrimination had occurred within the institution or business in question.

80. The Declaration of Independence was primarily the work of

(A) Thomas Jefferson.
(B) George Washington.
(C) Benjamin Franklin.
(D) James Monroe.

81. Which of the following vitamins is *not* fat soluble?

(A) Vitamin D
(B) Vitamin C
(C) Vitamin E
(D) Vitamin K

82. Of the following, which test does *not* measure muscular strength and endurance in children?

(A) Pull-ups
(B) Flexed arm hang
(C) Grip strength test
(D) Sit-and-reach test

83. Dance can reflect the religion of a culture by

I. offering adoration and worship to the deity.
II. appealing to the deity for survival in war.
III. asking the deity for success in the hunt.
IV. miming the actions of planting and harvesting crops.

(A) I and II
(B) I and III
(C) II, III, and IV
(D) I, II, III, and IV

84. Which of the following do the dances known as the waltz, Lindy Hop, and the twist have in common?

(A) They became popular in the nineteenth century.
(B) They are forms of "swing" dance.
(C) They reflect changes in the social attitudes of their times.
(D) They are danced by couples touching each other.

85. Identify the incorrect statement from the following.

(A) Heredity is the study of how traits are passed from parent to offspring.
(B) The chemical molecule that carries an organism's genetic makeup is called DNA.
(C) Sections of the DNA molecule that determine specific traits are called chromosomes.
(D) The genetic makeup of an organism is altered through bioengineering.

86. Which of the following forms of energy is not renewable?

(A) Hydrogen cell
(B) Geothermal
(C) Nuclear
(D) Hydroelectric

87. To move a heavy book across a tabletop at a constant speed, a person must continually exert a force on the book. This force is primarily used to overcome which of the following forces?

(A) The force of gravity
(B) The force of air resistance
(C) The force of friction
(D) The weight of the book

88. Ms. Gitler is selecting books for the classroom library. In addition to student interest, which of the following would be the most important considerations?

(A) The books should be at reading levels that match the students' independent reading abilities.
(B) All books should have a reading level that is challenging to the students.
(C) The books should include separate word lists for student practice.
(D) A classroom library is not appropriate for students at such a low reading level.

89. Matt earned the following scores on his first six weekly mathematics tests: 91%, 89%, 82%, 95%, 86%, and 79%. He had hoped for an average (mean) of 90% at this point, which would just barely give him an "A–" in math on his first report card How many more total percentage points should Matt have earned over the course of those six weeks to qualify for an "A–"?

(A) 87
(B) 3
(C) 90
(D) 18

90. Which of the following best explains why the boiling point of water is reduced and cooking times are increased at high altitudes?

(A) At high altitudes, there is greater atmospheric pressure than at sea level.
(B) At high altitudes, there is less oxygen than at sea level.
(C) At high altitudes, the vapor pressure of water is reduced because of the reduced atmospheric pressure.
(D) At high altitudes, water boils at a lower temperature because of the reduced atmospheric pressure.

91. The fourth-grade students in Ms. Alvarez's class are studying Native Americans. Ms. Alvarez wants to strengthen her students' ability to work independently. She also wants to provide opportunities for the students to use a variety of print and media resources during this unit of study. Ms. Alvarez plans to begin the unit by leading the class in a brainstorming session to formulate questions to guide their research about Native Americans. Which of the following criteria should guide Ms. Alvarez as she leads the brainstorming session?

(A) The questions should emphasize the factual content presented in the available print materials.

(B) The questions should emphasize higher-order thinking skills, such as comparison, analysis, and evaluation.

(C) The questions should reflect the interests of the students.

(D) The questions should include all of the fourth-grade objectives for this unit.

92. Ms. Alvarez has collected a variety of print and media resources for the students to use in their research. Which of the following would probably be the best way to motivate students to research the questions they have prepared?

(A) The teacher should assign two to three questions to each student so that all the questions are covered.

(B) The teacher should allow individual students to select the questions they would like to research.

(C) The teacher should select three key questions and assign them to all the students.

(D) The teacher should assign one topic to each student and then provide the students with additional information.

93. Ms. Gitler teaches 26 third graders in a large inner-city school. About one-third of her students participate in the ESL program at the school. Ms. Gitler suspects that some of the students' parents are unable to read or write in English. Four of the students receive services from the learning resource teacher. At the beginning of the year, none of the students read above the 2.0 grade level, and some of the students did not know all the letters of the alphabet. Which of the following describes the instructional strategy that is most likely to improve the reading levels of Ms. Gitler's students?

(A) An intensive phonics program that includes drill and practice work on basic sight words

(B) An emergent literacy program emphasizing pattern books and journal writing using invented spelling

(C) An instructional program that closely follows the third-grade basal reader

(D) Ensuring that all the students participate in the school's ESL program and receive services from the learning resource center

Use the figure below, which shows a sequence of calculator keystrokes, to answer the question that follows.

| 1 | 8 | 2 | X | 1 | . | 0 | 3 | X | 1 | . | 0 | 4 | = |

94. The sequence of keystrokes would be useful for finding which of the following values?

(A) The total distance an automobile travels if it covers 182 miles one day but only 1.03 and 1.04 miles over the next two days

(B) The amount of money in a savings account after the original deposit of $182 earns 3% and then 4% simple annual interest over two years

(C) The total distance an automobile travels if it covers 182 miles one day, 103 miles the next day, and 104 miles the third day

(D) The amount of money in a savings account after the original deposit of $182 grows by $1.03 and $1.04 in interest over two days

95. The Silk Road did not connect to which of the following countries?

(A) China
(B) Greece
(C) Iran
(D) India

96. The characteristics of fascism include all of the following *except*

(A) democracy.
(B) totalitarianism.
(C) romanticism.
(D) militarism.

97. The industrial economy of the nineteenth century was based on all the following *except*

(A) the availability of raw materials.
(B) an equitable distribution of profits among those involved in production.
(C) the availability of capital.
(D) a distribution system to market finished products.

98. Examine the elementary school student's work shown here. Analyze the error pattern that the student is making. If the student worked the problem 88 plus 39, which incorrect answer would the student give (assuming the use of the error pattern exhibited here)?

74	35	67	56
+56	+92	+18	+97
1,210	127	715	1,413

(A) 127
(B) 131
(C) 51
(D) 1,117

99. At the end of each week, Ms. Axtel takes a few minutes to write in her journal. She makes written comments about the lessons she taught that week, as well as the students' response to those lessons. She also includes comments about how to change or revise the lessons in the future. This practice indicates that Ms. Axtel is

(A) concerned about process writing.
(B) a reflective practitioner.
(C) keeping notes for her formal evaluation.
(D) is a habitual journal writer.

100. The needle on the dial depicted here points most nearly to which reading?

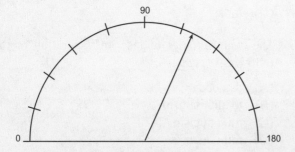

(A) 108
(B) 128
(C) 114
(D) 117

Mr. Drake is teaching his first-grade class about animals. Answer questions 101–103 related to Mr. Drake's teaching practices.

101. Mr. Drake is using the whole language method in his first-grade class. Before reading a story to the students, Mr. Drake tells them what he expects them to learn from the story. What is his reason for doing this?

(A) The students should know why the instructor chose this text particular book.
(B) It is important for teachers to share personal ideas with their students to foster an environment of confidence and understanding.
(C) Mr. Drake wants to verify that all students are on-task before he begins the story.
(D) Mr. Drake is modeling a vital prereading skill to teach it to the young readers.

102. Mr. Drake has a heterogeneously grouped reading class. He has the students in groups of two—one skilled reader and one remedial reader—reading selected stories to one another. The students read the story and question each other until they feel that they both understand the story. By planning the lesson this way, Mr. Drake has

(A) set a goal for his students.
(B) condensed the number of observations necessary, thereby creating more time for class instruction.
(C) made it possible for another teacher to use the limited materials.
(D) used the students' strengths and weaknesses to maximize time, materials, and the learning environment.

103. Before reading a story about a veterinary hospital, Mr. Drake constructs a semantic map of related words and terms using the students' input. What is his main intention for doing this?

(A) Demonstrate a meaningful relationship between the concepts of the story and the prior knowledge of the students
(B) Serve as a visual means of learning
(C) Determine the level of understanding the students will have at the conclusion of the topic being covered
(D) Model proper writing using whole words

104. How many ten thousands are in 1 million?

(A) 100

(B) 10

(C) 1,000

(D) 10,000

105. Which of the following data can the owner of twin Siamese cats use to determine the cost of cat food for 7 days for the two cats?

   I.   Cost of a can of cat food

   II.   Volume of a can of cat food

   III. Number of cans of cat food eaten each day by one cat

   IV. Weight of the cat food in one can

(A) I and II

(B) I and III

(C) I and IV

(D) III and IV

106. Which of the learners indicated are capable of conserving information; that is, which learners can recognize information as being the same even though its context changes?

(A) Nursery school and kindergarten children

(B) First- and second-grade children

(C) Third- and fourth-grade children

(D) Fifth- and sixth-grade children

107. Read the following nursery rhyme, and then choose the group of syllables that would occur on the beat.

> Little boy blue come blow your horn,
> The sheep's in the meadow, the cow's in the corn.
> Where is the boy who looks after the sheep,
> He's under the haystack, fast asleep.

(A) Lit, boy, come, your, the, in, dow, cow's, corn, where, the, who, ter, sheep, under, hay, a

(B) Lit, blue, blow, horn, sheep's, mea, cow's, corn, where, boy, aft, sheep, un, hay, fast, sleep

(C) Lit, blow, sheep's, cow's, where, aft, under, fast

(D) Little, the, where, he's

108. Reading and then dramatizing a story, using that story as the basis of a puppet play, scripting the story and performing it in the classroom, and then attending a performance of the story done as a play by a theater company illustrates which of the following concepts?

(A) Teachers should work with material until they find the correct way to use it with students.

(B) There are multiple ways to express and interpret the same material.

(C) Plays are more interesting than classroom dramatizations.

(D) Students learn less as audience members than as participants in drama activities.

109. A student portfolio

(A) contains artwork by a student.

(B) is used to compare the work of all students in the class.

(C) is graded on a scale.

(D) contains documents and/or products to show the student's progress.

110. What is the narrative report approach?

(A) Students describe how they feel they are doing.

(B) The teacher writes a formal report card.

(C) the teacher provides parents with a written assessment of the student's progress.

(D) Parents and the teacher discuss the student's attitudes about learning.

111. Ms. Ramirez, an art teacher, is concerned about her student's academic performance. Ms. Ramirez may discuss the student's permanent record with the

(A) student's parents or legal guardians, current teachers, and school administrators.

(B) parents only.

(C) school administrators only.

(D) school administrators and parents only.

112. When are students more likely to score higher on a music test?

(A) When the questions are multiple choice

(B) When they are not coached by a teacher

(C) When they are familiar with the test format and content

(D) When the format is always changing

Answer Key

1. (A)	29. (A)	57. (B)	85. (C)
2. (B)	30. (D)	58. (C)	86. (C)
3. (C)	31. (C)	59. (A)	87. (C)
4. (D)	32. (A)	60. (D)	88. (A)
5. (B)	33. (C)	61. (B)	89. (D)
6. (D)	34. (D)	62. (D)	90. (D)
7. (A)	35. (C)	63. (C)	91. (C)
8. (D)	36. (C)	64. (D)	92. (B)
9. (B)	37. (C)	65. (C)	93. (B)
10. (B)	38. (A)	66. (B)	94. (B)
11. (C)	39. (D)	67. (D)	95. (B)
12. (A)	40. (D)	68. (D)	96. (A)
13. (C)	41. (B)	69. (A)	97. (B)
14. (A)	42. (D)	70. (B)	98. (D)
15. (D)	43. (C)	71. (A)	99. (B)
16. (C)	44. (A)	72. (B)	100. (C)
17. (C)	45. (C)	73. (B)	101. (D)
18. (C)	46. (A)	74. (B)	102. (D)
19. (C)	47. (A)	75. (A)	103. (A)
20. (D)	48. (A)	76. (B)	104. (A)
21. (C)	49. (D)	77. (B)	105. (B)
22. (D)	50. (A)	78. (D)	106. (D)
23. (D)	51. (A)	79. (B)	107. (B)
24. (C)	52. (C)	80. (A)	108. (B)
25. (C)	53. (D)	81. (B)	109. (D)
26. (C)	54. (D)	82. (D)	110. (C)
27. (D)	55. (B)	83. (D)	111. (A)
28. (A)	56. (B)	84. (C)	112. (C)

Diagnostic Test

Detailed Explanations of Answers

1. (A)

Semantic cueing involves using the meaning of the text and the context to figure out an unknown word. The genre of the selection, the illustrations, the reader's knowledge of the topic of the selection, and the context of the written words can provide semantic cues as the reader tries to unlock an unknown word.

2. (B)

Syntactic cueing involves using the reader's grammatical knowledge of spoken and written language to figure out the significance of an unknown word in a text.

3. (C)

Phonological cueing involves using the knowledge of matching written symbols with their sounds. This cueing strategy has limitations: it can be used effectively only for words where the letter patterns are known by the reader, and the reader must know how to analyze an unknown word.

4. (D)

The pragmatic cueing system involves using the understanding that people use language differently in different contexts. This knowledge may help a reader to correctly interpret a text.

5. (B)

The most basic definition of *literacy* is the ability to read and write.

6. (D)

If you look at the intersection of the production of zero cars (that is, the y-axis) with the production

possibilities curve, you can see that the production of zero cars allows for the production of 12 vans. The straight line drawn upward from 2 on the x-axis (that is, the production of 2 cars) intersects the production possibilities curve at 8 on the y-axis (vans). Thus, the loss of production is 12 − 8 = 4 vans.

7. (A)

Scarcity necessitates choice. Consuming or producing one commodity or service means consuming or producing less of another commodity or service. The opportunity cost of using scarce resources of one commodity or service instead of another is graphically represented as a production possibility curve.

8. (D)

Both state and federal governments have the power to lay and collect taxes and to borrow money. Article I, Section 8, of the Constitution establishes the powers of Congress, whereas the Tenth Amendment to the Constitution (the last amendment within the Bill of Rights) sets forth the principle of reserved powers to state governments. Reading state constitutions will show that states also possess the power to lay and collect taxes.

9. (B)

Multiparty systems use an electoral system based on proportional representation. Therefore, each party gets legislative seats in proportion to the votes it receives. In the United States, the candidate who receives a plurality of the votes is declared the winner.

10. (B)

The region's mountain ranges are the main reason for both the high precipitation and varied climate.

11. (C)

There are several methods available to determine the answer. Making a sketch is a classic approach to mathematical problem solving, which is helpful here. You could draw six *x*'s, representing the six workers, as follows:

Then you could connect each *x* with all other *x*'s, counting the number of connecting lines as you add them. The connecting lines represent individual meetings, as shown here:

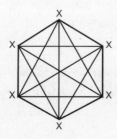

In the figure, there are 15 connecting lines, so there were 15 meetings. (Be sure to count the outermost lines forming the hexagon.)

Here is another approach: Worker number 1 must have had five meetings. Once she completed her fifth meeting, she was done with her meetings and could be considered out of the picture for the moment. Worker number 2 also had five meetings, but you should not count the one he had with worker number 1; it is already accounted for in the first worker's tally of five meetings. So worker number 2 had only four more new meetings. Worker number 3 had five meetings, but you should not count the first two; she had only three more new meetings. Continuing the pattern for all six workers, you see that you need to add together 5, 4, 3, 2, and 1 meetings. This again gives the correct answer of 15 meetings.

12. (A)

Drawing a sketch with dots marking the possible locations of the two houses and the Soda Depot is a good idea. You can start with dots for the two houses, using inches for miles, as shown here:

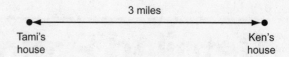

If you then draw a dot representing the Soda Depot 2 miles (inches) to the right of Ken's house, as in the figure that follows, you see that the greatest possible distance between Tami's house and the Soda Depot is 5 miles.

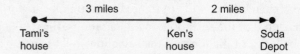

If you draw the Soda Depot dot to the left of Ken's house, as in the figure below, you see that the Soda Depot could be as close as 1 mile to Tami's house but no closer. Only statements I and III, then, are true.

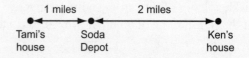

13. (C)

Each combined inequality can be seen as the combination of two single inequalities. Inequality A, for instance, can be seen as the combination of the following two single inequalities:

$$75 \le x$$
$$x \le 40.$$

The meaning of a single inequality is often made clearer if you transpose the statement, placing the variable on the left. That is,

$$75 \le x.$$

means the same thing as

$$x \le 75.$$

Therefore, combined inequality A says that x (the speeds that vehicles may drive at) is greater than or equal to 75 mph and less than or equal to 40 mph.

You can separate combined inequalities B and D into individual inequalities in the same way. Combined inequality B, $75 < x > 40$, means the same as

$$x > 75$$

and

$$x > 40.$$

That means that drivers have to drive faster than 75 mph! That doesn't match what the sign says. Combined inequality D, $40 < x > 75$ means the same as

$$x > 40$$

and

$$x > 75.$$

That's the same as combined inequality B. The correct answer is C, $40 \leq x \leq 75$, because that combined inequality means the same as

$$x \geq 40$$

and

$$x \leq 75.$$

That is, vehicles can travel at or faster than 40 mph but no faster than 75 mph.

14. (A)

A bar graph works well here. The height of each of five bars would be determined by the number of votes for each lunch food. A circle or pie chart could also be used. The 18 votes for pizza give the fraction 18/40, so pizza would be assigned 45% of the area of a circle chart, or

162°. The same approach would tell us the appropriate size of each lunch food's slice of the pie chart. A scatter plot illustrates the relationship between sets of data. A broken-line graph generally illustrates change over time. Neither is appropriate for illustrating the given data.

15. (D)

In simple notation form, the distributive property is as follows:

$$a\,(b + c) = (a \times b) + (a \times c)$$

This means that when multiplying, you may have some computational options. Consider choice D. The distributive property allows us to break 42 down into the convenient addends 2 and 40. You can then separately multiply each addend by 3. Thus, 3×2 equals 6, and 3×40 equals 120. We can then (courtesy of the distributive property) add those products together to get 126. Therefore, only choice D is illustrative of the distributive property.

16. (C)

You would want to study the clues in the artwork for potential meaning and consider the art elements and principles in the work of art. The more you know about the context in which the artist worked, the more you can appreciate the work itself. Not everything will be immediately evident, so you will want to assume the role of detective.

17. (C)

The use of uncommon materials has dramatically changed the criteria by which we assess visual art.

18. (C)

This question is focused on large-scale objectives. Therefore, it is important to look for the choice that best reflects the objectives. Choice C is the best answer because it covers all three of the objectives in at least a minimal way. Choice A is the second-best choice because it deals with several of the objectives, but the focus on creativity keeps it from being the best choice. Choices B and D are not good choices because they do not deal with all of the objectives.

19. (C)

This question focuses on a specific and very basic musical concept, pitch. Choice C is the only correct answer. Choice D is another basic concept, rhythm, and choice A refers indirectly to it. Choice B is incorrect because it refers directly to the basic concept of dynamics.

20. (D)

In creative drama, activities build on one another. Establishing a foundation of skill-building activities is the norm. Beginning activities are warm-ups. These are used to introduce a session and to help players become comfortable with one another. Pantomime activities are next; these help children to develop nonverbal communication abilities and to clearly express ideas without speaking. Without these experiences, players too often rely only on voice for sharing ideas and for characterization.

Because improvisations can be done with or without speaking, they follow pantomimes. When students incorporate dialogue into their improvisations, they have a better understanding of how an actor uses voice and body as artistic tools. Improvisations also help students learn to think quickly and creatively.

Story creation is next. There are multiple ways of creating stories. These can be done using unison or individual play and in pantomime or with dialogue. The result can be simple or complex stories. To successfully engage in story creation, students should understand characterization and plot. They should be experienced at using imagination and ensemble play.

Story dramatization is the most complex creative drama activity because it incorporates skills developed at lower levels. Players engage in individual rather than unison play. Story dramatizations are often student-directed activities based on original stories or stories from literature. These require an investment of time if believable characterizations are to result. Engaging in story dramatizations encourages an understanding of both drama and literature. If one were to construct a hierarchy of creative drama activities, story dramatization would be at the top.

21. (C)

Teaching effective comprehension is a process that takes time and practice. It seems obvious that students cannot comprehend a text if they cannot decode it. It also seems obvious that, if you want students to get better at reading, they need time to read. Students also need time and input, usually in the form of conversation, to make connections between what they read and what they already know.

22. (D)

The experiment requires a control of all variables other than the one identified in the hypothesis—exposure to microwave radiation. Seeds from different suppliers may be different; for example, one brand might be treated with a fungicide, whereas another brand is not treated or is treated with a different fungicide. While it is likely that choice III might be acceptable, without confirming that all packages are from the same year and production run, the four packages could be significantly different from each other. The best solution is to randomly divide the available seeds equally between the four test groups. Choice II also allows the experiment to compare the germination rates between the different brands, but only if the seeds from each packet are isolated within each test group and the number of seeds is large enough to create a statistically significant sample.

23. (D)

The hypothesis is to evaluate seed germination as a function of microwave irradiation. Recording the overall growth or length of the seed root, although interesting, is not included in the stated hypothesis. Choice C would be a good approach if the hypothesis were to relate seed growth to some variable, as it would more accurately reflect the growth of thicker or multiple roots in a way that root length might not measure.

24. (C)

Choice I will not reflect the success of seed germination overall, one seed in a given sample may germinate early. Reporting the time until the last seed germinates would also not be useful. Choice III combines the number of all the sprouted seeds, losing the differentiation of the test groups. Choices II and IV maintain the distinction between test groups and indicate the overall success rate of the germination.

25. (C)

The gas molecules themselves do not expand when heated, but the spaces between them increases as the molecules move faster. The expanding hot air leaves the balloon body through the opening at the bottom. With less air in the balloon casing, the balloon is lighter. The combustion products of propane are carbon dioxide (molar mass 44 g/mol), which is heavier than air, and water (molar mass 18 g/mol), which is lighter.

26. (C)

The upward force of air resistance partially counteracts the force of gravity when a feather falls in air. In a vacuum or near vacuum, this force is dramatically reduced; therefore, the feather and both objects will fall at the same rate. The effect can be modeled without a vacuum pump by comparing the falling of two papers, one crumpled to reduce air resistance and the other flat.

27. (D)

Due process is the legal concept that every citizen is entitled to equal treatment under the law. The excerpt illustrates one aspect of due process, the exclusionary rule. The exclusionary rule is applied when evidence is seized in violation of due process. So the most correct choice is the exclusionary rule.

28. (A)

The main purpose of the World Trade Organization is to open world markets to all countries to promote economic development and to regulate the economic affairs among member states.

29. (A)

Overgrazing, overuse of farmland, and a lack of rainfall caused the drought of the 1930s.

30. (D)

It is true that multiplication is commutative and division is not, but that is not relevant to their being inverse operations. Choice A does not address the property of being inverse. Choice B also contains a true statement, but again, the statement is not about inverse operations. Choice C gives a false statement. In the example shown in choice C, the order of operations tells you to compute $8 \div 2$ before performing any multiplication. As noted in choice D, the inverseness of two operations indeed depends on their ability to undo each other.

31. (C)

One way to arrive at the answer is to set up a proportion, with one corner labeled x:

$$\frac{31}{x} = \frac{5.5}{100}$$

To complete the proportion (and to find the answer), you can cross-multiply 31 and 100, giving 3,100, which you then divide by 5.5, giving approximately 564.

32. (A)

The value 0.5 is equivalent to 5/10 or ½. That means that 0.5% (which is one way to read the original numeral) is the same as one-half of 1%, so choice I is correct. One-half of 1% cannot be the same as 5%, so choice II cannot be correct. The value 1/200 is equivalent to 0.5%. Here is why: 1% is equivalent to 1/100; therefore, half of 1% (0.5%) is 1/200, so choice III is correct.

33. (C)

Complex carbohydrates are the most efficient energy source for the body. Although the other choices provide some energy, they are not nearly as efficient as complex carbohydrates.

34. (D)

Leaping is the only locomotor skill listed. Bouncing (A), catching (B), and throwing (C) are manipulative movements.

35. (C)

Choices A, B, and D are principles of aerobic conditioning; choice C is not.

36. (C)

Miscue analysis is designed to assess the strategies that children use in their reading. Goodman was interested in the processes occurring during reading. He believed that any departure from the written text could provide a picture of the underlying cognitive processes. Readers' miscues include substitutions of the written word with another, additions and omissions of words, and alterations to the word sequence.

37. (C)

Small-group discussion is the next step in the writing process.

38. (A)

There is a direct relationship between what is taught in school and what is learned in school. Also, if you want children to improve in writing, they need time to write.

39. (D)

After the teacher taught the unit on fairy tales, the interest in reading—especially books on fantasy—increased. The number of titles increased. There is no indication that worksheets (III) are needed or that the students are using—or necessarily need to use—an accelerated reading program (IV). This teacher's data suggests a successful literacy program.

40. (D)

Both the personal correspondence of a military man stationed with the Fifth Regimental Combat Team in Korea and an interview with Secretary of Defense George Marshall are primary sources because they involve correspondence or testimony from individuals who were actually involved in the Korean War.

41. (B)

Diseases caused by viruses, bacteria, or protozoans that invade the body are called infectious diseases. These disease-causing organisms are collectively referred to as germs. Cancers and hereditary diseases are not infectious.

42. (D)

Because all the choices are correctly matched, D is the correct answer.

43. (C)

The artwork is a collage. A montage (A) is a composite picture that brings together several different pictures and superimposes them one on another so that a blended whole is made; the parts are still discernable. An assemblage (D) is a collection or a whole that results from the fitting together of parts. An etching (B) is a print made from a glass or metal plate on which drawings or designs have been etched through the action of acid on lines made with a special needle.

44. (A)

The drawing is large, frontal, and drawn in high contrast (A). It has many details and is not highly simplified; therefore, choice B is not the correct answer. Because there is no asymmetrical balance, choice C is not correct. The drawing is not in three-point perspective (D).

45. (C)

Historical almanacs contain yearly data of certain events, including the time at sunrise and sunset along with weather-related data and statistics. A historical atlas is a collection of historical maps that may or may not include population data. Historical population data may best be found in government publications on the census. An encyclopedia article would contain a factual summary of the colonial period and the American Revolution; however, the article might not include an analysis of the role of Fort Mackinaw during the American Revolution because encyclopedias attempt to give overviews rather than interpretations or analysis. A secondary source on Michigan during the colonial period might better address that question. Information on when the first treaty was signed and the terms of the treaty would most likely appear in a history book.

46. (A)

Putting together or arranging elements to make a whole pattern or product is synthesis. Choices B, C, and D are examples of tasks requiring analysis, not synthesis.

47. (A)

Inductive reasoning involves making generalizations based on a particular fact or example. Students would use deductive reasoning (B) if they were to discuss the characteristics of romance and then compose a musical piece encompassing those characteristics. Oral interpretation (C) is a type of dramatic speech, and evaluation (D) involves judging the quality or merits of a work or product.

48. (A)

New technologies can be helpful to students in many ways. Choice B would stifle the student's creativity and result in less sophisticated writing. Choice C has not been proven effective as a technique to help students improve their spelling. Choice D means that the teacher would not be applying standards of good writing in evaluating the student's work.

49. (D)

In choice D, the teacher gives the student appropriate feedback and avoids simply stating the answer, giving the student a chance to think about the correct answer. The other choices are only partially correct.

50. (A)

The students have developed criteria against which they can decide or judge if someone is intelligent. The students were gathering characteristics, not examples (B), and the students have yet to test their criteria (C). Instead of creative thinking (D), in this activity, students are engaged in critical thinking.

51. (A)

Demonstrate is a word used to show application or that the student has learned to apply knowledge to perform a task. The other choices deal with other aspects of Bloom's *Taxonomy*: choices B and C with the knowledge and comprehension levels, respectively, and choice D with analysis.

52. (C)

Different students respond differently to different kinds of stimuli. Choices A and B state basically the same idea in different words. Choice D is incorrect

because even when teachers plan an activity that is different from the norm, an instructional principle or rationale should be behind the activity.

53. (D)

The task described in choice D requires analysis of the situation or problem. Choice A requires application, the level below analysis; choice C requires comprehension, the level below application; and choice B requires knowledge, the lowest level in Bloom's *Taxonomy*.

54. (D)

This question focuses on a basic musical concept, harmony. Harmony is the performance of two or more different pitches simultaneously. Therefore, when looking at the answer choices provided, it is good to begin by eliminating those that have nothing to do with pitch. A rhythm instrument (I) is a nonpitched instrument in almost all cases, so choices A and B are eliminated. Because two or more different pitches must be performed simultaneously to have harmony, choice III can also be eliminated, because there are two performers but not two different pitches. That eliminates choice C and leaves choice D as the correct answer.

55. (B)

Not all atoms of an element are identical in mass, which is primarily the sum of the protons and neutrons. Isotopes—atoms with the same atomic number and thus the same element—vary only in the number of neutrons. The atomic masses listed in the periodic table represent the weighted average of the naturally occurring isotopes for each element. For example, most carbon atoms have a mass of 12 atomic mass units (amu), and less than 1 percent have a mass of 14 amu. The average atomic mass of carbon is thus 12.011 amu.

56. (B)

Expansion occurring on the ocean floor along the mid-Atlantic ridge creates pressure around the edges of the Pacific plate; this expansion creates geologic instability where the Pacific plate collides with the continental plates on all sides. Careful! Just selecting a true statement will not yield a correct response. The response must answer the question. Choices A and D may be true, but they do not account for the instability that is constant at the Ring of Fire. Choice C is accurate, and earthquakes do produce waves, but the waves do not account for the instability typical at the Ring of Fire.

57. (B)

The moon is much closer to the earth than to any other planet or the sun.

58. (C)

Earth science is the study of Earth—its natural systems and structures. It is not a study of Earth in comparison with other planets in the solar system (A) or a study of living organisms (B); and earth science is more than just a study of the structure of Earth (D).

59. (A)

The large intestine is part of the digestive system. It is not a part of the respiratory system, which includes the lungs (B); the endocrine system, which includes the glands (C); or the circulatory system, which includes the heart (D).

60. (D)

This question is an example of the sentence completion question. Only one answer is the correct one; the other choices—52 (A), 108 (B), and 30 (C)—are incorrect.

61. (B)

A fungus (A) does not produce anything, nor does a wolf (C) or an inanimate rock (D). Only one answer (B) is appropriate for this sentence completion question.

62. (D)

Fungi form a large group of very simple plants without chlorophyll; they get their food from that produced by other plants and animals. An example of a fungus is yeast. Bacteria (A) are one-celled microorganisms without chlorophyll, can be seen only with a microscope, and multiply by division. Algae (B) contain chlorophyll and have no true root, stem, or leaf; they are not fungi. Protozoa (C) are one-celled, often microscopic, animals.

63. (C)

A liquid has definite volume, but it does not have a definite shape; because it satisfies the required definition, choice C is the correct answer. Plasma is the fluid part of the blood, lymph, milk, or intramuscular liquid; it does have volume, so choice A cannot be the correct answer. A gas is a fluid form of a substance that can expand indefinitely and completely fill its container; choice B is not the correct answer. A solid has definite volume and definite shape, so choice D cannot be the right answer.

64. (D)

An acid has a pH value of 0 to 7; an alkaline has a pH from 7 to 14. The only possible choice that indicates an acid is D, a pH of 5. The other pH numbers indicate an alkaline state.

65. (C)

The total price of the two items in the original problem is given as $2.59, hinting that choice B or C may be correct. (In both cases, $2.59 is shown as the sum of two values.) Examine the right side of choice C: Notice that one value is $1.79 higher than the other. That is, in choice C, x could stand for the price of the pencil, and $(x + 1.79)$ could stand for the price of the more expensive pen. Hence, choice C is the correct answer. None of the other equations fit the information given.

66. (B)

One way to approach the problem is to examine each scenario for reasonableness. Although a runner continually increases the distance covered in a marathon, the runner's mile-by-mile pace is not consistent, and the graph would not always move upward; thus choice I is not consistent with the graph. The number of households a census taker has left to visit decreases with each visit, so choice II does not work either. Both choices III and IV are examples of steady growth, so both match the graph.

67. (D)

Most elementary students remember placing the colors of the visible spectrum in order from lowest extent of refraction to highest by memorizing the mnemonic device: ROY G. BIV. Red light is refracted less, having a longer wavelength. This is the basis for our observation of a red sunrise or red sunset as light passes through more of the atmosphere than at midday. The high number of particles in a polluted or particulate-laden atmosphere leads to intense red sunsets as the more refractive blue wavelengths are refracted away from view. Differences in refraction are also the basis of TV commercials for sunglasses with yellow lenses that improve the clarity of vision. As light from an object passes through the lens of the eye, the blue wavelengths are refracted more and may be focused before reaching the retina, and the longer wavelengths are focused on the retina. Multiple images within the eye lead to the perception of a blurred image. Yellow glasses that filter out the blue wavelengths eliminate one image and give the perception of sharper, clearer vision for the wearer.

68. (D)

Early doses of pesticide were strong enough to kill most of the insects. The few that survived, perhaps because of some genetic trait, had a slightly higher tolerance to the poison. When these pesticide-tolerant insects reproduced, they passed the tolerance to their offspring. Higher doses of pesticide are initially effective, but again, a few individuals survive with tolerance to that new level. Control of pest populations generally requires access to various pesticides that work through different mechanisms and are applied so as to minimize buildup of tolerance in the insect population.

69. (A)

The physical movement and accumulation of sand is not part of the rock cycle. No transformation of rock

type is involved in choice A. It is the only one of the choices that has nothing to do with rock formation. This is one example of a question that requires the test taker to choose an answer that is a negative.

70. (B)

In offering criticism of the play, students should give opinions that reveal not only how they feel about what they saw but also the reasons for their opinions. In other words, they should be able to support their judgments based on their personal aesthetic. Choices II and IV are supported opinions that show an appreciation for the theatrical elements of character and plot. These choices also reveal connections to the viewer's emotions and life experiences. Choice I is an unsupported opinion and is, therefore, incorrect. Choice III is a response to the theater building in which the play was presented rather than a response to the play, and it is the latter that Mr. Nelson wants his students to give.

71. (A)

The responsibility for public education belongs to the state governments. The federal government has often passed legislation to regulate and provide funds for public education, but the main responsibility for establishing and regulating education resides with the state governments.

72. (B)

A limited money supply and rising prices were major causes of the Great Depression. The money supply was most affected by the gold standard, and the Smoot-Hawley Tariff Act further affected consumer prices.

73. (B)

First, it is helpful to view the shaded area as the area of the square minus the area of the circle. With that in mind, you simply need to find the area of each simple figure, and then subtract one from the other. You know that the radius of the circle is 6 units in length. That tells you that the diameter of the circle is 12 units. Because the circle is inscribed in the square (meaning that the circle fits inside of the square touching in as many places as possible), you see that the sides of the square are each 12 units in length. Knowing that, you compute the area of the square to be 144 square units (12×12). Using the formula for finding the area of a circle (πr^2), where $\pi = 3.14$, you get approximately 113 square units ($3.14 \times 6 \times 6$). Then subtracting 113 (the area of the circle) from 144 (the area of the square) gives you the answer of 31 square units.

74. (B)

If you can fold a two-dimensional figure so that one side exactly matches or folds onto the other side, the fold line is a line of symmetry. The following figure is a nonsquare rectangle with its two lines of symmetry shown.

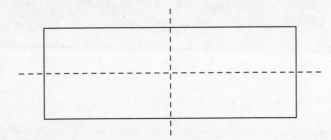

One might think that lines drawn from opposite corners are lines of symmetry, but they are not. The two halves would be the same size and shape, but they would not fold onto each other. Note that the question asked about nonsquare rectangles. Squares (which are rectangles) have four lines of symmetry.

75. (A)

To answer the question, you must recognize that triangles ADB and AEC are similar triangles, meaning that they have the same shape. Therefore, the corresponding angles of the two triangles are the same, or congruent, and the corresponding sides of the two triangles are proportional. Given that, you can set up the following proportion, where x is the distance from point A to point C:

$$\frac{3}{7} = \frac{5}{x}$$

Solving the proportion by cross-multiplication, you see that the length of segment AC is about 11.7. Knowing that the length of segment AB is 7 feet, you subtract to find the length of BC ($11.7 - 7 = 4.7$).

76. (B)

Statement I is true because the winner could be Mr. Greenfield and it could be someone else. Statement II is not true, even though Mr. Greenfield bought many more tickets than any other individual. He still has a block of only 300; there are 700 ticket stubs in the drum that aren't his. This tells us that statement III is true. Finally, statement IV is false. Do not confuse the true statement "all tickets have an equal chance of winning" with the false statement that "all persons have an equal chance of winning."

77. (B)

Salt is a strong electrolyte that completely dissociates in solution. When this solution is in contact with a semipermeable membrane, like the inflamed cells in the throat, water moves across the membrane from the side with lowest solute concentration to the side of higher solute concentration. In the case of the sore throat, water from inside the inflamed cells moves out toward the higher concentration (salt water) and the throat cells shrink because of the loss of water. All the choices are colligative properties, meaning they are a function of the number, but not the nature, of particles in solution.

78. (D)

Lincoln's immediate purpose in announcing the Emancipation Proclamation was to rally flagging northern morale. Lincoln waited until after a major Union victory, at Antietam in 1862, so he could not be charged with making the announcement as an act of desperation. He recognized that the costs of the war had reached a point where preserving the Union would not be a powerful enough reason to motivate many Northerners to continue the war. Framing the war as a war against slavery would mobilize powerful abolitionist forces in the North and perhaps create an atmosphere of a "holy crusade" rather than one of using war to resolve a political conflict. Although the Emancipation Proclamation had the announced purpose of freeing the slaves, Lincoln himself indirectly stated that freeing the slaves was a means to a greater end, preserving the Union. In a statement released before the Emancipation Proclamation, Lincoln asserted, "If I could save the Union without freeing any slave I would do it, and if I could save it by freeing all the slaves I would do it. . . . What I do about slavery, and the colored race, I do because I believe it helps to save the Union."

79. (B)

In the 1857 case *Dred Scott v. Sanford*, the Supreme Court held that no black slave could be a citizen of the United States. It was in the 1954 case *Brown v. Board of Education of Topeka* that the court held separate facilities for the races to be unconstitutional (choice A). The reverse—choice C—was the court's holding in the 1896 case *Plessy v. Ferguson*. Affirmative action was limited—choice D—in the 1970s and 1980s.

80. (A)

The Declaration of Independence was primarily the work of Thomas Jefferson. Americans associate many names—George Washington and Benjamin Franklin, in particular—with freedom, but it was Thomas Jefferson who did most of the writing. James Monroe (1758–1831) was only 16 at the time.

81. (B)

Vitamin C is water soluble; the remaining choices are fat soluble.

82. (D)

Pull-ups for boys (A), flexed arm hang for girls (B), and the grip strength test (C), are all tests to measure muscular strength and endurance. The sit-and-reach test measures flexibility.

83. (D)

Dance can reflect the religion of a culture in many ways because of its deep historical roots in religious tradition.

84. (C)

The waltz, Lindy Hop, and twist each reflect changes in social attitudes of their time. The couples do not touch each other in the twist; therefore, choice D is not correct. The dances were popular in the twentieth century, not the nineteenth century, so choice A is also incorrect. Because all three of the dances were not "swing" dances, choice B is not correct.

85. (C)

This question requires the test taker to find the incorrect statement. Chromosomes are not the parts of the DNA molecule that determine specific traits; therefore, choice C is the incorrect statement and the correct answer. Genes are the sections of the DNA molecule that determine specific traits.

86. (C)

Nuclear energy is nonrenewable. Nuclear energy has potential advantages in providing large quantities of energy from a small amount of source material, but the process of radioactive decay is nonreversible.

87. (C)

The force of friction between the book and the table is the primary force that must be overcome to move the book. An experiment to study these frictional forces could keep all other variables (size and weight of the book, speed of travel) constant while measuring the force needed to move the book using a spring scale. Various experiments could change the surface of the book by covering the book with wax paper, construction paper, or sandpaper.

88. (A)

By selecting books for the classroom library that match students' independent reading abilities, the teacher is recognizing that each student must improve his or her reading ability by beginning at his or her own level and progressing to more difficult materials. Choice B is incorrect because books that are challenging will most likely be frustrating to at least some of the students.

Choice C is incorrect because the presence or absence of separate word lists should not be a determining factor in selecting books for a classroom library. Choice D is incorrect because all children need access to a classroom library regardless of their reading abilities.

89. (D)

Adding up Matt's scores, you get 522. Multiply 90 by 6 to compute the number of total points it would take to have an average of 90 (90 × 6 = 540). Subtracting the points Matt earned from the points he needed to earn an "A–", you find that he was 18 points shy of his goal.

90. (D)

A liquid will boil when its vapor pressure, which depends on temperature, is equal to the atmospheric pressure above the liquid. At high altitudes, the atmospheric pressure is lower; thus, water will boil at a lower temperature. The boiling point of water is only 100°C at 1 atmosphere pressure (760 torr). In Leadville, Colorado, elevation 10,150, when the atmospheric pressure may be as low as 430 torr, the boiling point of water may be 89°C. The lower temperature increases cooking times.

91. (C)

The use of instructional strategies that make learning relevant to individual student interests is a powerful motivating force that facilitates learning and independent thinking. Choices A and B are both important factors to consider during a brainstorming session of this type, but both factors should influence the teacher only after the student interests have been included. Choice D indicates a misunderstanding of the situation described. The students are setting the objectives for the unit as they brainstorm questions.

92. (B)

Choice is an important element in motivating students to learn. Choice A is contradictory to the stated purpose of the activity. The students proposed the questions, so covering all the questions should not be a problem. Choice C is incorrect because the students have chosen

what they consider to be key questions; the teacher should select different or additional key questions. Choice D is a possibility, but only if there is a specific reason why all the students should not research all the questions.

93. (B)

An important way to teach children to read, regardless of grade level, is to use a program of emergent literacy that includes pattern books and journal writing with invented spelling. Choice A is incorrect; although an intensive phonics program that includes drill and practice seatwork on basic sight words may be effective with some students, it is not the most effective way to teach all students to read. Choice D is incorrect because an ESL program is intended to provide assistance only to students who are learning English as a second language. Additionally, the learning resource teacher should provide assistance only to students who have been identified as having a learning disability that qualifies them to receive services. An instructional program that closely follows the third-grade basal reader (choice C) may not meet all the needs of the students who are below grade level.

94. (B)

The keystrokes indicate multiplication, and only choice B involves multiplication. Multiplication is hidden within the concept of interest. One way to compute a new savings account balance after interest has been earned is to multiply the original balance by (1 + the rate of interest). In this case, that is first 1.03 and then 1.04. The keystrokes match that multiplication.

95. (B)

The Silk Road was a transcontinental trade route that branched out over a vast area, including western China (A) northern Iran (C), northern India (D), and eventually the Sahara. This question contains a qualifier (*not*), so the correct answer is Greece (B).

96. (A)

Democracy is the correct answer because it is the antithesis of the authoritarianism of fascism. Indeed, the totalitarian, romantic, militaristic, and nationalistic characteristics of fascism were, in large part, a reaction against the perceived inadequacies of democracy.

97. (B)

The industrial economy of the nineteenth century was not based on an equitable distribution of profits among all those who were involved in production. Marxists and other critics of capitalism condemned the creed of capitalists and the abhorrent conditions of the industrial proletariat. Raw materials, a constant labor supply, capital, and an expanding marketplace were critical elements in the development of the industrial economy.

98. (D)

You should notice that the student is failing to carry in both the ones and tens places. For instance, 56 + 97 is being treated as 5 + 9 and 6 + 7; the two solutions are then combined for a total of 1,413. Choice A is the error-free solution to the problem and is therefore eliminated. Choice C exhibits switching from addition to subtraction (9 − 8 = 1) and (8 − 3 = 5). Also, the child subtracts the top number from the bottom one on the first step. In choice B, the child subtracts 8 from 9 and 3 from 8 and then adds to the 8 in the tens place. Only choice D illustrates the pattern of recording the sum and not carrying.

99. (B)

The correct response is Choice B. Maintaining a written journal about both events in the classroom and student responses is a technique used by reflective practitioners in order to review and evaluate their personal growth as professionals. Choice A is incorrect because journal writing may or may not indicate a concern about process writing. Additionally, journal writing alone is not the same as process writing. Choice C is incorrect because the purpose of the journal is much broader, even though the instructor may use some of her journal entries in her formal evaluation. Choice D is incorrect because it is too simplistic. If Ms. Axtel were a habitual journal writer, she would be writing about a variety of topics, not just emphasizing those related to teaching.

100. (C)

You should first count the number of spaces on the dial. There are 10 spaces. Five spaces equals 90 units, and 90 divided by 5 is 18 units; each space is worth 18 units. The needle points to about halfway between the marks numbered 6 and 7. Thus, one-third of 18, plus 6 times 18, is 114. Choice (C) is the correct reading.

101. (D)

Comprehension is shown when the reader questions his or her intent for reading. For example, a person might be reading a story to find out what terrible things will befall the main character. The rationale for choosing a book may be an interesting bit of information (A), but it is not a major topic of discussion with the students. Sharing personal information (B) creates a certain bond but is not directly relevant to the question. It is also important that all students are on-task before the beginning of a lesson (C), but that is a smaller part of the skill modeled in choice D.

102. (D)

When a mixed-level pair read together, the remedial student receives instruction and the skilled student receives reinforcement. It uses alternative teaching resources, the students themselves, to enhance the learning environment. A certain goal, comprehension, has been set (A) but is not the most likely outcome. The teacher will need to observe fewer groups (B), but it is unlikely that the time needed to work with all groups will change as long as quality is to be maintained. Although reading in pairs, each student should have a book, and it would be impractical to permit another teacher to use the books while one teacher is using them (C).

103. (A)

By mapping out previous knowledge, information already known can be transferred to support new information. Although words on the board are visual (B), that is not the underlying motive. Semantic mapping done at the beginning of a story tests how much prior knowledge the students have about the topic at the outset, not at the conclusion (C). The activity does model proper use of words (D), but that is not the main intent of the exercise.

104. (A)

You know that 10,000 contains four zeros and can be expressed in exponential notation as 10^4. One million contains six zeros and can be expressed in exponential notation as 10^6. Thus, 10^6 divided by 10^4 is 10^2 or 100. You could calculate the long division of 10,000 into 1 million, but that is the laborious way to solve this problem.

105. (B)

You are challenged to analyze which data you would need to calculate the cost of feeding two cats for 7 days. If you calculate the cost for one cat for 7 days and then double that, you will have an approximate cost for two cats. The total cost for one cat is the cost of a can of food times the number of cans of food eaten each day by one cat, times 7 days.

106. (D)

To employ teaching techniques effectively, it is important to understand when a child is ready for that technique. Most children are not able to conserve information until fifth or sixth grade. Some children will begin conserving information earlier, so choice C could be considered partially correct but is not the best choice.

107. (B)

This question relates to the difference between the concept of steady beat and the concept of rhythm. Choices B and C are both good answers, but the best answer is B because each of the syllables listed falls on a strong pulse (i.e., the beat) when spoken or sung. Choice C is made up of words that fall on the beat but highlights larger segments encompassing multiple beats. Choice D highlights the beginnings of lines with no regard for the beat, and choice A likewise has no regard for the beat.

108. (B)

One of the virtues of using drama or theater with young people is that it challenges them to think independently and creatively. Many questions posed in drama or theater have no one right answer or interpretation. Using the same material in a variety of ways offers the following advantages: (1) information is presented through multiple channels, thereby increasing opportunities for knowing; (2) using different types of dramatic activities broadens both the appeal of and the learning opportunities inherent in the material; (3) multiple formats increase opportunities to engage students and to address their learning styles; (4) and students can see that there are various ways of creating meaning and expressing ideas. Choice A is incorrect because there may not be only one correct way to use material. Exploring content is one way to move students beyond the obvious and encourage them to use higher-level thinking skills. Choice C is incorrect because it requires a value judgment based on personal preference; it is not grounded in fact. Likewise, choice D is incorrect because it reflects a value judgment that is without substance. Some students may learn more by directly participating in activities; some may learn more by watching a performance. Both creative drama activities and theater performances are educationally sound undertakings.

109. (D)

A portfolio keeps a collection of dated samples of a student's work over time. The student can have a single portfolio for all subjects or separate portfolios for specific subjects. The work contained in a portfolio then becomes an accurate representation of the student's progress. It may contain artwork by a student but is not limited to artwork (A). It is not used to draw comparisons among students (B), nor is a portfolio graded on a scale (C).

110. (C)

Teachers compose narrative reports which describe a student's strengths, weaknesses, behaviors, progress, and any other information to supplement the information that is conveyed in a report card. They can be used if a parent cannot attend a parent-teacher conference, for example. Choice A is incorrect because it is the teacher, not the student, who describes how the student is performing. It is not a formal report card (B) but is used to supplement the information on the report card. Choice D is also incorrect because narrative reports can be used as an alternative to parent–teacher conferences.

111. (A)

A student's permanent record, which is a file containing all aspects of a student's background, should be discussed with the student's parents, legal guardians, teachers, and school administrators. It is a highly personal and comprehensive student record. It may be discussed with the student's parents (B) or the school administrators (C) but is not limited only to school administrators and parents (D). Teachers also have the right to discuss the student's record.

112. (C)

Students perform better on tests when they are familiar with the test content and test format. It does not matter if the test contains a particular type of question (A), as long as the students know what to expect. Students have greater success in testing situations when their teacher coaches them; therefore, choice B is not correct. Students perform poorly when the test format changes frequently (D).

Language Arts

Competency 1: Knowledge of Emergent Literacy

Six test items relate to this competency.

Definition of Emergent Literacy

Marie M. Clay (1966) coined the term *emergent literacy* in her unpublished 1966 doctoral dissertation, *Emergent Reading Behavior* (University of Auckland, New Zealand). She defined *emergent literacy* as the stage during which children begin to receive formal instruction in reading and writing and the point at which educators and adults expect them to begin developing an understanding of print.

Today, educators use the term to describe the gradual development of literacy behavior, or the stage in which students begin learning about print. Educators usually associate emergent literacy with children from birth to about age 5. During the emergent literacy period, children gain an understanding of print as a means of conveying information. It is essential that they should develop an interest in reading and writing in this stage (Tompkins 2006).

Some educators suggest that reading readiness or emergent literacy is a **transitional period**, during which a child changes from a nonreader to a beginning reader; others suggest that reading readiness/emergent literacy is a stage (Clay 1979). The Southern Regional Education Board's Health and Human Services Commission (SREB 1994) cautions that children go through emergent literacy at individual rates.

Some **transmission educators** suggest that if a child is not ready to read, the teacher should get the child ready. Others declare that the teacher should not begin formal reading instruction until the child is ready. Most reading readiness advocates take the position that there are certain crucial factors that a teacher or parent should consider in deciding if a child is ready to read (Davis 2004).

Skill One
Identify the Content of Emergent Literacy

An important part of emergent literacy is the skill of identifying print concepts, which involves being able to identify the parts of a book, indicating the directionality of print, and recognizing the connection between spoken and written words.

Parts of Books

Clay (1985) developed a formal procedure for sampling a child's reading vocabulary and determining the extent of a child's print-related concepts. For instance, her assessment checks whether a child can find the title of a book, show where to start reading it, and locate the last page or end of the book. These components may differ from those typically considered essential before children can begin to read, like discriminating between sounds and finding likenesses and differences in print (Finn 1990; Davis 2004). A teacher or parent might hand a book to a child with the back of the book facing the child and in a horizontal position. The adult would then ask questions like, "Where is the name of the book?" "Where does the story start?" "If the book has the words *the end,* where might I find those words?" (Davis 2004).

Directionality of Print

Another part of the skill of identifying concepts of print is being able to indicate the directionality of print. The reader in American society must start at the left side of the page and read to the right. This skill is not inborn but rather comes through observation or through direct instruction. Some societies do not write from left to right. For instance, in ancient Greek society, writing followed the same pattern as a person would use when plowing: the reader would start at the top of the page and read to the right until the end of the line, turn, drop down a line, read that line to the left, turn, drop down a line, read that line to the right, and so on. Other languages, like Hebrew, require the reader to begin at the right and read to the left. Japanese writing is generally vertical (Davis 2004).

To teach left-to-right direction, the teacher can place strips of masking tape on the child's desk, study center, or table area. One strip goes where the left side of the book or writing paper would be and one strip where the right side of the book or writing paper would be. The child colors the left side green and the right side red. The teacher helps the child use this device as a clue to remember on which side to begin reading or writing and reminds the child that *green* means "go" and *red* means "stop." Ideally, the teacher should use similar strips on the chalkboard or poster paper to model writing from left to right (Davis 2004).

Children can also remember on which side to begin reading by holding up their hands with their thumbs parallel to the floor. The left hand makes the shape of the letter *L*, for "left," the side on which to begin reading; the right hand does not make the *L* shape. Another way a teacher can help children who are having trouble distinguishing left from right, or which side to begin reading and writing, is to point to sentences while reading from a big book or writing on the board; observing the teacher do this can help children master print directionality. Books that are 18 × 12 inches or larger are designed for this purpose and are effective with groups of children. Teachers or parents can also model directionality by passing their hands or fingers under the words or sentences as they read aloud (Davis 2004).

Teachers can use games like Simon Says or songs like "The Hokey Pokey" to give children practice in the skills of distinguishing left from right. In another instructional game, each child holds a paper plate like a steering wheel, and the teacher calls out directions like "Turn the wheel to the left" and "Turn your car to the right." As the children "drive" their cars, the teacher observes whether they are turning the wheel in the correct direction (Davis 2004).

Voice-to-Print Match

Being able to recognize the connection between the spoken word and the written word is important to developing reading and writing skills. During the emergent literacy period, children should begin to understand that the printed word is just speech written down. Shared reading (discussed in more detail under "Skill Two: Identifying Strategies for Developing Concepts of Print") can help children gain this understanding. As the adult reads aloud, the children join in with words, phrases, repetitions, and sentences they recognize. They begin to make the connection between the printed word and the spoken word and between phonemes and graphemes. **Phonemes** are the speech sounds; **graphemes** are the written symbols for the speech sounds. These voice-to-print relationships are important to reading (Davis 2004).

Skill Two

Identify Instructional Methods for Developing Emergent Literacy

Skill Three

Identify Common Difficulties in Emergent Literacy Development

Skill Four

Identify Methods for Prevention of and Intervention for Common Emergent Literacy Difficulties

Emergent literacy research cautions that in pre-school and kindergarten programs, teachers should avoid isolated, abstract instruction and tedious drills. Teachers should avoid programs that tend to ignore and repeat what the children already know. Programs that focus on skills and ignore experiences often place little importance on reading as a pleasurable activity and ignore early writing—important components of whole language (Noyce and Christie 1989).

Developmentally Appropriate Classrooms, Materials, and Curriculum. The SREB (1994) states that the classroom, materials, and curriculum should be developmentally appropriate. **Developmentally appropriate** is a concept with two dimensions: individual appropriateness and age appropriateness. **Individual appropriateness** recognizes that each child is unique. Ideally, schools and teachers respect and accommodate individual differences, which include growth, interest, and styles. **Age appropriateness** implies that there are sequences of growth and change during the first nine years that a teacher must consider when developing the classroom environment and experiences. In general, the age-appropriate skills considered necessary for reading—during the reading readiness period and beyond—are visual discrimination, auditory discrimination, and left-to-right direction (Davis 2004).

Reading Aloud. The U.S. Department of Education recognizes that "parents are their children's first and most influential teachers" (Bennett 1987, 5). The department further notes that "what parents do to help their children learn is more important to academic success than how well-off the family is" (Bennett, 7). After reviewing many studies, the department reports, "The best way for parents [and adults] to help their children become better readers is to read to them—even when they [the children] are very young. Children benefit most from reading aloud when they discuss the stories, learn to identify letters and words, and talk about the meaning of words" (Bennett, 7). The department also found that "children whose parents simply read to them perform as well as those whose parents use workbooks or have had training in reading . . . . Kindergarten children who know a lot about written language usually have parents who believe that reading is important and who seize every opportunity to act on that conviction by reading to their children" (Bennett, 7)

Jim Trelease (1985) reinforces that parents and teachers should read aloud regularly to children. The reasons Trelease cites for reading aloud include "to reassure, to entertain, to inform or explain, to arouse curiosity, and to inspire" (68). Trelease also explains that reading aloud to a child can strengthen writing, reading, and speaking skills and the child's entire civilizing process. Another important reason for reading to children while they are young is that at that age, children want to imitate what they hear and see adults do. In his book, *The Read-Aloud Handbook*, Trelease suggests stories and books ideal for reading aloud.

The SREB (1994) recommends that schools help parents to become actively involved in their children's education and that schools adopt formal policies to improve communication between parents (or caregivers) and schools.

Shared Reading. At the emergent literacy level, the students and the teacher "share" the tasks involved in reading and writing. Teachers are practicing "shared reading" when they read big books (18 × 12 inches) with their classroom. Parents are practicing shared reading when they read aloud to their children. At this early stage, the adult is doing most of the reading, but the child follows as the adult reads and chimes in for the reading of familiar words, repeated words, and/or repeated phrases. An upper-grade teacher can also use shared reading when students are reading a difficult book that they may not fully comprehend; if they were to read independently; the teacher can read portions aloud, and the students can follow along and read silently (Tompkins 2006).

In 1969, R. G. Heckleman developed his **Neurological Impress Method (NIM)**, an approach that adults had probably been using with children for generations. He advocates that the teacher sit slightly behind the reader; the teacher and the learner hold (share) the book jointly and read aloud together whenever possible. The teacher should slide a finger along each line and follow the words as the two say the words together. Heckleman reports significant gains in children with whom the method was used. Susan Partridge (1979) reports that the results of the NIM have been favorable. Jimmie Cook and his colleagues (1980) also report, "The NIM helps." In 1978, Paul Hollingsworth suggested using a wireless system to make it possible to use the NIM with several students at one time. Marie Carbo (1978) suggests using "talking books" or the recorded book to teach reading. Her method is like NIM, except the child has a recording instead of a one-on-one tutor during the reading. Heckleman, however, emphasizes that human contact is essential to the enjoyment and success of the NIM plan.

Environmental Print. Our environment is rich with words. People see signs advertising everything from fast foods to fast cars. Television shows display many words, and newspapers and magazines depend on words to sell their products and to communicate their messages. Around swimming pools, playgrounds, recreation centers, and movie theaters are printed signs and cautions to help ensure the safety of customers and users. Becoming aware of these environmental words is important to children. They should begin to notice and try to recognize these important words at an early age. Noting the signs and words around them will help children feel comfortable with words and make them aware of the importance of reading in our society.

Anita P. Davis and Thomas R. McDaniel (1998) identified words that they considered essential for physical safety, social acceptability, and the avoidance of embarrassment. Some of these "essential words" are *exit, danger, high voltage, stop, beware, keep out,* and *no trespassing.* Being able to read these words is vital. Davis and McDaniel advocate that teachers and adults help children notice and master these words in their environment.

Edward Dolch (1960) identified the most frequently used vocabulary words from preprimer level to grade 3.

Listing the words by grade in the Dolch Word List, the author recommends teaching them to primary children to develop their reading vocabulary. Because Dolch advocates teaching the beginning reader to read the words quickly and to "pop" them off immediately, many teachers call the words the "Popper Words."

Language Experience Approach. The language experience approach (LEA) attempts to facilitate students' language development through the use of experiences, rather than with printed material alone. After an event or experience in which the learners in the class participate, the students make a written record of it as a group (with the help of the teacher). In this way, each student can see that

- what I say, I can write;
- what I can write, I can read; and
- what others write, I can read.

The LEA can be a part of many levels of teaching. Even high school classes often have the teacher at the board recording information that the class offers about something read or experienced as a group.

Competency 2: Knowledge of Reading

Skill One
Identify the Processes, Skills, and Phases of Word Recognition That Lead to Effective Decoding

Skill Two
Identify Instructional Methods for Promoting the Development of Decoding and Encoding Skills

Skill Three
Identify the Components of Reading Fluency

Students are preparing for reading when they work with letters and their sounds, the parts of words, and picture and context clues.

Phonological Awareness. Increased phonological awareness occurs as children learn to associate the roughly 44 speech sounds in the English language with their visual representation. Children learn to pronounce these 44 sounds as they begin to talk. Because English comprises only 26 letters, it obviously is not a phonetic language; that is, there is no one-to-one correspondence between letters and sounds. The 26 letters are combined in many different ways to reproduce the needed sounds.

Children in the early grades create **invented spellings** when they try to write by applying their understanding of spelling rules. They soon realize that it is difficult to write and to decode many common words. As children progress through the grades, their spellings usually become more conventional (Tompkins 2006).

Phonics. The most commonly used method of teaching reading in the United States from colonial times through the 1920s was the phonics method. Other reading methods—the sight word method, modified alphabet approach, and the whole language approach, for example—came into being after the 1920s. However, phonics is still an important part of reading instruction in the United States.

The phonics method of teaching reading emphasizes the association between the grapheme (the written symbol) and the phoneme (the speech sound). The phonics method attempts to relate spelling rules to the process.

William Holmes McGuffey and Rudolf Flesch were proponents of the phonics method. McGuffey produced his series of reading books in 1836. The readers used phonics while teaching morals to students; it was a cultural force, not just a reading textbook. By 1920, sales of McGuffey readers had reached 122,000,000. In 1955, Flesch wrote *Why Johnny Can't Read—And What You Can Do About It* to warn parents that the reason many children cannot read is that the schools are not using the phonics approach.

Phonics is, of course, a skills-based approach. There are several **advantages of the phonics method** that are readily apparent. One important advantage of the phonics method is that it gives children tools for decoding, or figuring out how to read and pronounce words that they do not know immediately. Because the phonics approach involves phoneme–grapheme associations, auditory learners—those who learn best through the sense of sound—often prefer to read using phonics. Auditory learners can usually hear a sound and associate it easily with its printed symbol. Using phonics with auditory learners is an evident advantage. A third advantage of this method with its emphasis on sound–symbol relationships is that phonics readers can often transfer their skills to spelling. Spelling involves associating sounds with letters; it is the opposite of phonics, which associates symbols with sounds. A final advantage is that phonics readers are often good spellers (Davis 2004).

At its January 1997 meeting, the board of directors of the International Reading Association (IRA) passed a position statement titled "The Rule of Phonics in Teaching Instruction." The key assertions were that phonics is an important aspect in beginning reading instruction, primary teachers value and teach phonics, and effective phonics is integrated into the total language arts program (IRA takes a stand on phonics, 1997).

There are, however, **disadvantages to the phonics method**. A major disadvantage of phonics is that visual learners may not read well by this method. A second disadvantage of the method is that the rules do not hold true all the time. In his now-classic study, Theodore Clymer (1963) reports that he found few phonic generalizations that held true in more than 50 percent of the cases in the primary grades. Four years later, however, Mildred Hart Bailey (1967) found in her study of phonic rules that 27 of the 45 generalizations identified by Clymer held true in 75 percent of the words appearing most often in reading materials for grades 1 through 6.

A third disadvantage of the phonics method is that some students are confused when they learn a phonics rule and then encounter frequent exceptions; inconsistencies pose a problem for them. Some educators, though not all, note a fourth disadvantage to the phonics method; they believe that there is no basis for the view that there are subskills, such as phonics, that students need in order to read; they see the skills as mythical (Davis 2004).

To help children learn phonics, many teachers find certain **techniques for teaching** the method helpful.

Students should have opportunities to practice the phonics rules and generalizations in context; instructors should make every effort to illustrate the transfer of the phonics rules and generalizations to everyday materials and to other subjects. **Analytic phonics** (using phonics in context with actual materials), as opposed to **synthetic phonics** (phonics taught in isolation from meaningful books and materials, often using worksheets), seems to be the more helpful technique.

Teachers can introduce a phonics rule or generalization as it appears, but such an **incidental approach** does not ensure that all students meet and practice the most frequently encountered phonics rules. A structured, systematic, sequential program of phonics helps ensure that readers have at their disposal an arsenal of skills to decode new words and spell the words correctly. Such a plan of presenting the rules and regulations of phonics can help eliminate gaps in students' word attack skills (Davis 2004).

Marie Carbo (1993), nationally known for her work with reading styles, recognizes the importance of making available phonics instruction in any reading program. She particularly warns, "a good whole language program does include phonics."

In *Becoming a Nation of Readers* the Commission on Reading (1986) stressed that phonics is an essential strategy for beginning reading. Teachers should use a systematic approach and present the skills in meaningful sentences, passages, and materials, not just as words in isolation.

A word of caution for teachers of phonics is that in the beginning, students may read slowly. When students begin to commit high-frequency words to memory, however, reading speed and, in turn, comprehension will increase (Davis 2004). The young child begins recognizing letters and their sounds. These skills will help the child with reading and spelling. Another technique that will help the child in attacking unknown words is analyzing the structure of the words, or structural analysis (Davis 2004).

Word Structure. Breaking a word into its parts, or syllables, is called **structural analysis**. By dividing a word into its syllables and sounding out these smaller parts, student are often able to pronounce longer, unknown words that they previously did not recognize. There are many rules for dividing words into syllables; some of these rules often hold true, but some of the rules do not. As mentioned earlier, Bailey (1967) found in her study of phonics rules that 27 of 45 syllabication rules hold true in 75 percent of the words a child frequently encounters in grades 1 through 6.

Children do not work with all the rules for structural analysis in the early years. Usually, children work mainly with adding word endings to words that are already a part of their sight vocabulary or word families. Some of the endings that children encounter first are the suffixes *-ed*, *-s*, *-es*, and *-ing* (Davis 2004). Fry (1980) says that six suffixes cause a large percentage of the variants: *-ed*, *-s*, *-er*, *-ly*, *-est*, and *-ing*.

Young children are constantly encountering new words. Even though some texts try to limit the new words a child meets at a given time (**controlled vocabulary**), most children do not experience such a protected environment. All the words a child sees may not be those in the list of sight words the child already knows. It is important for the child to have some word attack skills to decipher new, unknown words.

Separating the prefix and/or the suffix from the root word is an example of structural analysis. After separating these word parts, the child may be able to sound out the word. Examples include *un-tie*, *re-peat*, and *sing-ing* (Davis 2004).

Another important rule for separating words into parts is the compound word rule. With this rule, the child divides a compound word into its parts. The child and the teacher can work together to sound out each part. Examples include *cow-boy* and *foot-ball* (Davis 2004).

Two essential rules for structural analysis are the v/cv and the vc/cv rules. Teachers introduce these rules and encourage the students in the later stages of reading development to employ these attack skills. To use the rules successfully, the child must first determine if each letter in a word is a vowel (v) or a consonant (c). The child can write the label over each letter in the word.

Looking for the v/cv or vc/cv pattern, the child separates the word at the appropriate place. Examples of the v/cv rule are *o-ven* and *bo-dy*. Examples of the vc/cv rule are *sum-mer* and *ig-loo* (Davis 2004).

Some rules of structural analysis, such as the following, are complex, useful, and best for older readers (Davis 2004):

1. When *-le* comes at the end of the word and a consonant comes before it, the consonant goes with the *-le*, as in the word *pur-ple* and *bub-ble*. (An exception to this rule is when the word contains a *ck*, one would not separate the *c* and the *k*, as in the word *pick-le*.)

2. *Ed* forms a separate syllable if *d* or *t* comes before the *-ed*, as in *skidd-ed* and *mist-ed*.

Context Clues. As children progress in their skills and confidence, teachers might encourage them to use picture clues and previously read materials to predict what word would make sense. To help children make their predictions, the teacher can give them a clue, like the first sound of the word. Another way a teacher can provide context clues is to mask words or portions of words with a "magic window"—a sturdy piece of cardboard with a small rectangle cut out of the center. This allows the teacher to single out a letter or syllable for the children to consider. The teacher can also cover up words or parts of words on a transparency sheet on the overhead (Combs 2006).

The technique of using all the language cueing systems together is important to comprehension. The following are the three major types of language cues:

Syntactic cues. Attention to syntax can increase **comprehension**, or understanding. These cues include grammatical hints; the order of words; word endings; and the way the words function, or work, in a phrase, sentence, or passage.

Semantic cues. Semantics can include "hints" within the sentence and from the entire passage or text that help the reader determine the meaning. Semantic cues, then, are meaning clues.

Phonemes and graphemes. The phonemes (sounds) and graphemes (written letters) are crucial to reading and writing. A child who does not know the word *phone* but knows that the letters *ph* often sound like the letter *f* and knows that the sound of a phone is a ring may be easily able to figure out the word in the sentence "I heard the phone ring."

Again, through demonstration, invitation, and discussion, the teacher can help children confirm or correct as they read, monitor understanding during the reading process, and review and retain information after the reading is complete (Davis 2004).

Views about reading and the stages vary from source to source. Most sources agree that it is imperative that teachers **scaffold**, or support, children of all ages. Scaffolding involves demonstrating, guiding, and teaching; the amount of support the teacher provides should depend on the instructional support needed and the individual child. Five stages that mark scaffolding are—moving from greatest to the least as students assume more and more responsibility—the modeled, shared, interactive, guided, and independent levels of support (Tompkins 2006).

Martha Combs (2006) notes three stages of development:

1. **Emergent reading stage.** A child at this stage is making the transition from speaking to writing and reading, with support from others. Reading might involve predictable books that initially are at the child's frustration reading level, but as the child practices, the books are at the child's instructional level and eventually at the independent level. Shared reading and interactive writings, which the child composes and the teacher records, provide practice and build confidence.

2. **Developing reading stage.** At this stage, the child—usually on a middle-first- to late-second-grade level—becomes more independent in reading. The child's texts should include many decodable words—words that follow a regular pattern and have a predicable sound, such as *man, tip,* and *me.* By practicing decoding skills while reading, the child gains confidence.

3. **Transitional reading stage.** A child who is a transitional reader usually has an instructional reading level of second grade or beyond. Ideally, the child spends much time with independent-level and instructional-level materials. The teacher is still there to help the child, but the child can refine old skills and practice new skills.

Reading Strategies

Looking at strategies used by proficient readers helps teachers make skillful choices of activities to maximize student learning in subject area instruction. Anne Goudvis and Stephanie Harvey (2000) offer the following list:

Activating prior knowledge. Readers pay more attention when they relate to the text. Readers naturally bring their prior knowledge and experience to reading, but they comprehend better when they think about the connections they make between the text, their lives, and the larger world.

Predicting or asking questions. Questioning is the strategy that keeps readers engaged. When readers ask questions, even before they read, they clarify understanding and forge ahead to make meaning. Asking questions is at the heart of thoughtful reading.

Visualizing. Active readers create visual images based on the words they read in the text. These created pictures enhance their understanding.

Drawing inferences. Inferring is when the readers take what they know, garner clues from the text, and think ahead to make a judgment, discern a theme, or speculate about what is to come.

Determining important ideas. Thoughtful readers grasp essential ideas and important information when reading. Readers must differentiate between less important ideas and key ideas that are central to the meaning of the text.

Synthesizing information. Synthesizing involves combining new information with existing knowledge to form an original idea or interpretation. Reviewing, sorting, and sifting important information can lead to new insights that change the way readers think.

Repairing understanding. If confusion disrupts meaning, readers need to stop and clarify their understanding. Readers may use a variety of strategies to "fix up" comprehension when meaning goes awry.

Confirming. As students read and after they read, they can confirm the predictions they originally made. There is no wrong answer. One can confirm negatively or positively. Determining if a prediction is correct or not is a goal.

Using parts of book. Students should use book parts—like charts, diagrams, indexes, and the table of contents—to improve their understanding of the reading content.

Reflecting. An important strategy is for students to think about, or reflect on, what they have just read. Reflection can be just thinking, or it can be more formal, such as a discussion or writing in a journal.

While providing instruction in a subject area, the teacher needs to determine if the reading material is at the students' level of reading mastery. If not, the teacher needs to make accommodations either in the material itself or in the manner of presentation.

Skill Four

Identify Instructional Methods for Developing Reading Fluency

An instructor can teach reading strategies explicitly to students in a carefully orchestrated manner. First, the teacher should model the strategy, explain it, and describe how to apply successfully the strategy. It helps if the teacher "thinks aloud" while modeling the strategy for students. Second, the teacher should practice the strategy with the students. It is important to scaffold the students' attempts and support their thinking by giving feedback during conferencing and classroom discussion. In this case, it helps if the students "think aloud" while practicing the strategy. Third, the teacher should encourage the students to apply the strategy and should give them regular feedback. Fourth, once the students clearly understand the strategy, they should apply it on their own in new reading situations. While monitoring students' understanding of the subject matter, the teacher should become aware of students' thinking as they read and as they detect obstacles and confusions that derail their understanding. The teacher can suggest, teach, or implement strategies to help students repair meaning when it breaks down.

Teachers need to be explicit about teaching students to be aware, to check for understanding, and to use reading comprehension strategies to make meaning. To monitor and repair their understanding, teachers should explicitly teach students to do the following (Goudvis and Harvey 2000):

- Track their thinking through coding with sticky notes, writing, or discussion.
- Notice when they lose focus.
- Stop and go back to clarify thinking.
- Reread to enhance understanding.
- Read ahead to clarify meaning.

- Identify and articulate what is confusing or puzzling about the text.
- Recognize that all of their questions have value. (There is no such thing as a stupid question.)
- Develop the disposition to question the text or author.
- Think critically about the text and be willing to disagree with its information or logic.
- Match the problem with the strategy that will best solve it.

Depending on the situation, instructors may use these strategies across the curriculum in any subject area. In addition, the effective teacher can use graphic organizers such as these:

- Double-entry journals, in which the student enters direct quotes from the text (with page number) in the left column and enters "thinking options"—such as "This is important because," "I am confused because," "I think this means,"—in the right column.
- Venn diagrams (two overlapping concentric circles), in which the student compares two items or concepts by placing specific criteria or critical attributes for one in the left circle, for the other in the right circle, and attributes or characteristics that are shared by the two in the overlapping section in the center.
- Webs, in which the student charts out a concept or section of text in a graphic outline. The web begins with the title or concept written in the middle of the page and branches moving out in web fashion; students will note specific bits of information on the branches or strings of the web. Arrows or lines in other formats can make connections from one bit of information to another.

These and many other graphic organizers can help students gain understanding of a text by making it visual and more concrete. As students manipulate information in writing, they have a better opportunity to deal with it effectively and more concretely (Barry 2005).

Skill Five

Identify Instructional Methods and Strategies to Increase Vocabulary Acquisition Across the Content Areas

Vocabulary instruction is important to the teaching of the language arts and other subjects. Teachers identify important vocabulary words in their units and often single those words out for their students to study.

Vocabulary study is more than memorizing definitions, however. Effective teachers employ many strategies to increase the vocabulary of their students. They post new words on a "word wall" as reminders of the new vocabulary words. They develop lessons about idioms, the use of dictionaries and glossaries, multiple meanings of words, antonyms, synonyms, homonyms, figurative meanings, word parts, and other word study techniques.

Effective instruction includes making connections to the background of the students. Repeating vocabulary words and using them in meaningful sentences, as well as encouraging independent reading, will enhance students' vocabulary development (Tompkins 2006).

Combs (2006) reminds educators that children acquire vocabulary best when the teacher explains the meaning of new words in context. Children should have ample opportunities to review and use newly acquired vocabulary words, especially in other contexts. Shared reading is particularly useful in vocabulary development.

Skill Six

Identify Instructional Methods to Facilitate Students' Reading Comprehension

A teacher might encourage higher-level thinking skills in the classroom through activities like mapping or webbing; study plans like the SQ3R discussed earlier; puzzles, riddles, and "think-alouds"; and programs like the Tactics for Thinking program (which provides activities for all levels of comprehension) adopted by South Carolina.

Mapping and Webbing. Story mapping or webbing helps students think about a reading passage and its structure. Some typical devices in good narrative fiction and which might be useful on a story map include setting, stylistic devices, characters, and plot A class reading Wilson Rawls's *Where the Red Fern Grows* (1961/1976) created the following story map.

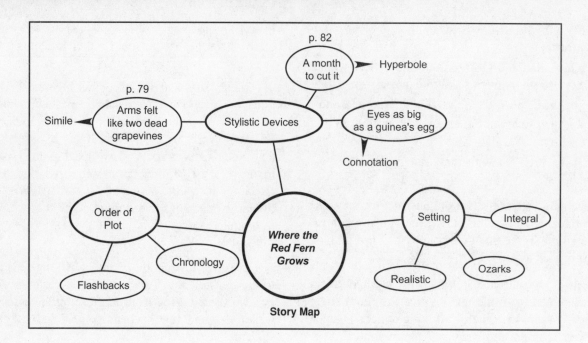

Story Map

Study Plans. The teacher might acquaint students with several plans to help them read content materials. Many of these plans already exist, and the teacher and the students can simply select the plan(s) that works best for them with various subjects. Students may use **mnemonic devices**, or memory-related devices, to help them remember the steps in reading a chapter effectively. Students often use plans like the following SQ3R plan when reading text in content areas:

Survey. Before reading a passage or an entire section of the text, the student should look over the assigned page or chapter and consider some questions. Are there illustrations, charts, or diagrams? What are some of the chapter headings? Are some words in bold type?

Question. The student may wish to devise some questions that the chapter will probably answer. If an assigned chapter has questions at the end, the student can look over the questions before reading the chapter; the questions serve as a guide to the text.

Read. The student now reads the passage to answer the questions at the end of the chapter or to answer the questions that the student developed before reading the chapter.

Recite. The student attempts to answer orally or in writing the student-developed questions or the questions at the end of the chapter.

Review. The student reviews the material to "double-check" the answers given in writing or orally at the previous step.

Vacca and Vacca (1989) express doubt that most students actually use a study plan. Even though an instructor may try to teach the "formula" for reading and studying a passage by having a class memorize the steps, practice the procedure several times, and view the formulas as a lifelong activity, Vacca and Vacca contend that a study system "evolves gradually within each learner" and that the SQ3R plan is difficult even for junior high school students (227). They suggest that students need to become "text smart" and learn to preview, skim for the main idea, and organize information through mapping or outlining.

Other reading authorities disagree. Richardson and Morgan (1990) suggest that students can use the SQ3R plan by fifth or sixth grade. Gunning (1996) reminds teachers that SQ3R has been around since the 1930s; he describes the method as "a widely used and effective study strategy incorporating five steps." (319) Michaelis and Garcia (1996) suggest that students can create their own self-directed reading strategies. They cite PROVE as an example:

Purpose. Establish a purpose or set up questions to guide your reading.

Read. Read the passage to try to achieve the purpose or answer the questions.

Organize. Outline; place details under main ideas.

Vocabulary. Note any new vocabulary or concepts that you master.

Evaluate. Evaluate to determine if you achieved your purpose.

Puzzles, Riddles, and "Think-Alouds." Students can practice their thinking skills by solving puzzles and riddles alone, in small groups, or as a class with the teacher helping in the modeling process. Here are some puzzles that encourage students to think:

1. A truck heading to Chicago is loaded with ice cream. At a tunnel in a mountain, a sign announces the height of the tunnel is 12 feet, 3 inches. The truck driver knows the truck is 12 feet, 4 inches. To get to Chicago, the trucker would have to make a 75-mile detour to avoid the tunnel. The trucker knows that the ice cream will melt in another hour. How can the truck driver get through the tunnel?

2. Twelve elementary school teachers meet at a party. If each teacher shakes hands with every other teacher, how many handshakes will occur at the party?

3. As I was going to St. Ives, I met a man with seven wives. Each wife had seven sacks. Each sack had seven cats. Each cat had seven kittens. Sacks, cats, kits, wives. How many were going to St. Ives?" (This is an old nursery rhyme.)

Tactics for Thinking. Developed by Robert J. Marzano and Daisy E. Arredondo (1986) for the South Carolina schools, Tactics for Thinking implements the teaching of thinking skills from grades K through 12. The program asserts that thinking-skills development should be part of the classroom and teacher directed. Components include elaboration, synthesizing, goal seeking, and deep processing.

Skill Seven
Identify Essential Comprehension Skills

Comprehension skills include the ability to identify supporting details and facts, the main idea or essential message, the author's purpose, fact and opinion, point of view, inference, and conclusion. To help students develop these skills, teachers can consistently emphasize meaning in the classroom and should focus on the four levels of comprehension: literal, interpretive, critical, and creative.

The **literal level of comprehension**, the lowest level of understanding, involves **reading the lines**, or reading and understanding exactly what is on the page. Students may give back **facts** or **details** directly from the passages as they read. For example, a teacher works with students as they make their own play dough, and use the recipe to practice **authentic reading** (Davis 2004). The teacher might question the students on the literal level as they mix their ingredients. Here are some sample questions:

> **Factual question.** How much salt do you add to the mixture?
>
> **Sequence question.** What is the first step in making the play dough?
>
> **Contrast question.** Do you add more or less salt than you did flour?

The **interpretive level of comprehension**, the second highest level of understanding, requires students to **read between the lines**. At this level, students must explain figurative language, define terms, and answer interpretive or inferential questions. **Inferential questions** require the students to **infer**, or figure out, the answers. Asking students to figure out the **author's purpose, the main idea** or **essential message, the point of view, and the conclusion** are examples of inferential questions. Inferential questions may require students to draw conclusions, generalize, derive meaning from the language, speculate, anticipate, predict, and summarize. All such questions are from the interpretive level.

Here are some examples of interpretive questions the teacher could ask at the cooking center while students are making play dough:

> **Contrast.** How is the dry measuring cup different from the liquid measuring cup? Why are they different?
>
> **Deriving meaning.** What does the term *blend* mean?
>
> **Purpose.** What is the purpose of making play dough at home? Why would you want to make play dough instead of buying it?

Cause and effect. Why do the directions say to store the play dough in a covered, airtight container?

The **critical level of comprehension** requires a high level of understanding. The students must judge the passage they have read. The critical level is one of the two highest of the levels of understanding; it requires students to **read beyond the lines**. Having students determine whether a passage is true or false, deciding whether a statement is a fact and opinion, detecting propaganda, or judging the qualifications of the author for writing the passage are examples of using the critical level of comprehension. Here are some examples of questions the teacher could ask students as they make play dough to encourage their thinking and understanding at the critical and creative levels:

Checking author's reputation. The recipe for the play dough comes from a book of chemistry experiments. A chemist wrote the book. Do you think that a chemist would be a good person to write about play dough? Why, or why not?

Responding emotionally. Do you prefer to use the play dough we made in class or the play dough that the local stores carry?

Judging. Do you think that the recipe for play dough that is on the recipe card will work? Why, or why not?

The **creative level of comprehension** is at the highest level of understanding. As with the critical level of comprehension, the student must **read beyond the lines**. The student must often make judgments about other actions to take. Answers may vary among the students. The teacher may not want to stifle creativity by saying one action is better than another. For instance, a teacher may suggest that after making a batch of cookies a student finds that the baked cookies do not fit in the cookie jar; the teacher may ask, "What can the student do?"

Answers may include, "Donate the extras to the first-graders." "Give some to the teacher." "Share with my little sister." "Put them in a plastic storage bag." All these answers are creative; the teacher should not judge one as better than another.

Skill Eight
Identify Appropriate Classroom Organizational Formats for Specific Instructional Objectives

Skill Nine
Identify Appropriate Uses of Multiple Representations of Information for a Variety of Purposes

Charts, tables, graphs, pictures, and print and nonprint media are examples of materials writers use to present information. Richard and Jo Anne Vacca (1989) report that it is not unusual to find as many as 500 or more graphic aids in a single textbook. Because printing a book is expensive, the reader should immediately realize that the representations are there as more than trimmings. Their purpose is to present information and to encourage interpretation.

A graphic can expand a concept, serve as an illustration, support points, summarize data, organize facts, add a dimension to the content (for example, a cartoon adds humor), compare information, demonstrate change over time, or furnish additional information. Through graphics, the reader can interpret, predict, and even apply information with some observation. The questions that teachers use can make a difference in the ability of students to focus on and clarify the information derived from graphics.

Many students initially skip over graphic aids or just notice their presence without even reading them. These students may not have been taught how to use multiple representations of information. Even students who have some training in the use of graphic information may not be able to transfer that knowledge to other content areas or may have trouble going from print to graphic and back to print.

Adults can help students use multiple representations of information by using open-book and guided reading. A teacher can demonstrate how to use a chart or graph by using an overhead projector. Pausing a video that presents a chart or graph gives the teacher a chance to demonstrate how to use the graphic. Even a graphic that appears uncomplicated may challenge a reader's interpretive skills. Many inferences may be necessary for even the simplest aid. Modeled reading may be an effective technique to use.

Pictures and other graphics can arouse interest and stimulate thinking. Additionally, graphics can add clarity; prevent misunderstandings; show step-by-step developments; exhibit the status of things, events, and processes; and demonstrate comparisons and contrasts (Vacca and Vacca 1989).

Skill Ten
Identifying Strategies for Developing Critical Thinking Skills

Critical thinking skills include analysis, synthesis, and evaluation.

Bloom's *Taxonomy*

Bloom describes six levels of comprehension in his *Taxonomy*. The teacher may wish to develop questions at each level to increase comprehension, develop a series of questions for though and discussion, or prepare a test (Krathwohl, Bloom, and Masia 1964).

1. **Knowledge level.** Students give back the information that is on the page.
2. **Comprehension level.** Students show that they can give the meaning of terms, idioms, figurative language, and other elements of written material.
3. **Application level.** After reading a story about how a class raised money for playground equipment, the students discuss some ways that they might improve their own playground.
4. **Analysis level.** Students examine the parts or components of a passage. For example, students might examine a menu and locate food groups, or they might identify terms in a word problem to determine the operations they should use.
5. **Synthesis level.** Students move from specifics to generalities. For instance, the class might develop a solution to the overcrowding problem suggested in a story, or students might construct a platform for the main character to use if she should run for class officer in the school described in another story.
6. **Evaluation level.** Students, judge if a passage is fact or opinion, true or false, biased or unbiased.

Assessing Comprehension

A frequent device for assessing comprehension is the use of oral or written questions. A question may be **convergent**, which indicates that only one answer is correct, or **divergent**, which indicates that more than one answer is correct. Most tests, however, include a combination of question types.

Another device for checking comprehension is a **cloze test**, a passage with omitted words the test taker must supply. The test maker must decide whether to require the test taker to supply the exact word or to accept synonyms. Passing scores reflect which type of answer is acceptable. If meaning is the intent of the exercise, the teacher might accept synonyms and not demand the surface-level constructs, or the exact word.

The speed at which a student reads helps determine comprehension, *up to a point*. The faster that a student reads, the better that student comprehends, *up to a point*. The slow reader who must analyze each word does not comprehend as well as the fast reader. It is possible, however, to read too fast. Most students have had the experience of having to reread materials. For example, a student reading a physics chapter in preparation for a test might read more slowly than when reading a novel but not slowly enough to note every important detail.

A teacher might ask students to read a passage and record their reading times. Then the teacher might give the students a quiz on the passage. After scoring the quizzes, the teacher could meet with each student to discuss the student's reading speed and its relation to the quiz grade. For students who received low quiz scores, the teacher could assign another passage and attempt to have the student slow down, or perhaps even accelerate, the speed of reading.

Skill Eleven
Identify Instructional Methods to Teach a Variety of Informational and Literary Text Structures

Informational writing and literary text commonly use several patterns of organization or structure: descriptive writing, ordered list, sequence, cause and effect, comparison, contrast, chronological order, and problem and solution.

To set the scene for a novel or to describe a place in a geography text, for example, a writer often uses

descriptive writing. Typically, the writer of fiction describes a time and the characteristics of the setting. The time can be thousands of years in the future, for example, as long as the writer makes the setting believable for the reader. Descriptions should encourage readers to feel some kind of connection to the information. Descriptive writing is usually in paragraph form and differs from the ordered list or sequence (Combs 2006).

The **ordered list** is typical in content area textbooks. Using an ordered list, the author can present facts and information more quickly and concisely than is possible using the paragraph format. Text clues of an ordered list structure are numbers, bullets, or letters or word clues like *first* and *second* (Combs 2006).

Sequence organization can occur in both fiction and nonfiction writing. A writer can organize a sequence to suit the purpose of the text—for instance, in alphabetical order, order of occurrence, or geographical placement, among others. A reader who quickly determines the sequence can gain understanding (comprehension) of the material more easily. A perceptive reader watches for word clues like *first*, *next*, *before*, *after*, and *last* (Combs 2006).

Cause-and-effect writing does not necessarily have to progress from cause to effect; a writer might decide that presenting the effect and then discussing the cause is the most effective way to present the material. In a social studies text, for instance, the writer might mention the American Revolution first and discuss the causes afterward; an alternative structure, however, would be to give the causes first and then indicate the effect: the American Revolution. Teachers can guide students to watch for key words that indicate the cause and effect structure, including *because, resulting in, why, as a result, therefore, if . . . then, cause,* and *effect*.

Comparison writing occurs when the writer explains the similarities between two or more things. The reader can often identify this type of writing by looking for cue words such as *alike, same as,* and *similar to*.

Sometimes it is helpful for the writer to use a structure that **contrasts** things or indicates how they are different. The cue words that a reader can watch for include *different from, on the other hand,* and *opposite of*.

History books, biographies, and many narratives relate their information in the order in which they happened, or **chronological order**. Watching for words like *first, next, then,* and *last* may cue students that the arrangement is chronological, beginning at the start of the action.

Some writers structure their material according to a **problem-and-solution** organization. The writer can state the problem and then either offer several solutions or present the best answer for the reader (Combs 2006; Tompkins 2006).

Summary

Benjamin Bloom gives a taxonomy of six levels of understanding: knowledge, comprehension, application, analysis, synthesis, and evaluation. Tests to indicate the level of comprehension include both cloze tests and tests with convergent and/or divergent questions. A focus on reading speed is often helpful for students to see how fast they read might affect comprehension. A teacher might encourage higher-level thinking skills in the classroom through activities like mapping and webbing; study plans; puzzles, riddles, and "think alouds"; and programs like Tactics for Thinking.

Competency 4: Knowledge of Literature*

Six test items relate to this competency.

Words are some of the most powerful and important things I know . . . . Language is the tool of love and the weapon of hatred. It's the bright red warning flag of danger—and stone foundation of diplomacy and peace.
—Anonymous

*Note: Due to changes in the competencies incorporated by the Florida Department of Education in 2006, the skills of Competency 3 became part of Competency 2.

The potency of language is evident in its utility and diverse forms. Without language, humankind would be incapable of conceptualizing ideas. Literature provides a forum to express the versatility of language. The art of literature paints language in many forms, including novels, poetry, and essays. Reading offers the opportunity to employ language—and in different ways.

Skill One

Identify Characteristics and Elements of a Variety of Literary Genres

Literary genres include prose, novels, short stories, poetry, plays or drama, and personal narratives or essays.

Prose

Students are sometimes confused about what prose is. Basically, **prose is not poetry**. Prose is what people write and speak most of the time in everyday conversation: unmetered, unrhymed language. This does not mean, however, that prose does not have its own rhythms. Language, whether written or spoken, has cadence and balance. Certainly prose can have instances of rhyme or assonance, alliteration, or onomatopoeia. Language is, after all, **phonic**. Furthermore, prose can be either **fiction** or **nonfiction**. A novel or short story is fiction; an autobiography is nonfiction. Although a novel or short story may have autobiographical elements, most readers regard an autobiography as entirely factual.

An initial question is, "Why do people write prose?" The answer depends, in part, on the writer's intent. Generally, a writer chooses the novel as the medium to tell a rather long story, filled with many characters and subplots; interlaced with motifs, symbols, and themes; with time and space to develop interrelationships and to present descriptive passages. If a writer wants to present a story in a more compact, less complex form, the novella or the short story may be the genre of choice.

Novels

Most literary handbooks define a **novel** as an extended fictional prose narrative. The term *novel* comes from the Italian word *novella*, meaning "tale, or piece of news." In most European countries, the word for novel is *roman*, short for *romance*; this term could also apply to long narrative set in verse, like Malory's *Morte d'Arthur*. Associated with "legendary, imaginative, and poetic material" and tales "of the long ago or the far away or the imaginatively improbable," novels were the early romances; these realistic novels were "bound by the facts of the actual world and the laws of probability" (Harmon and Holman 2002, 354).

The novel has, over some 600 years, developed into many special forms. Classifications by subject matter include the detective novel, the psychological novel, the historical novel, the regional novel, the picaresque novel, the Gothic novel, the stream-of-consciousness novel, the epistolary novel, and so on. These terms, of course, are not exhaustive or mutually exclusive. Furthermore, depending on the conventions of the author's time, style, and outlook on life, the modes include **realism**, **romanticism**, **impressionism**, **expressionism**, **naturalism**, or **neoclassicism.** According to Harmon and Holman (2002), a novel is "a rather long story, filled with many characters and subplots, interlaced with motifs, symbols, and themes, with time and space to develop interrelationships and to present descriptive passages" (359).

Analyzing novels is a bit like asking the journalist's six questions: what? who? why? when? where? and how? The "what" is the story, the narrative, the plot, and subplots. The most important of these questions, however, is why. The critic's job is to discover why the author of a piece of writing chose to include in it the ideas and words the reader sees.

As the reader charts the novel's events, the "change which structures the story" should emerge. There are many events in a long narrative, but generally only one set of events comprises the "real" or "significant" story.

However, subplots often parallel or serve as counterpoints to the main plot line and enhance the central story. Minor characters sometimes have essentially the same conflicts and goals as the major characters, but the consequences of the outcomes seem less important. Sometimes the parallels involve reversals of characters and situations, creating similar yet distinct differences in the outcomes. Nevertheless, seeing the parallels makes understanding the major plot line less difficult.

Sometimes a writer divides the novel into chapters—named or unnamed, perhaps just numbered. Alternatively, the writer might divide the novel into books or parts, with chapters as subsections. Readers should take their cue from these divisions, because the writer must have had some reason for them. Readers should take note of what happens in each larger section, as well as within the smaller chapters. Whose progress is the story following? Is the writer using foreshadowing to prepare the reader for what and event of occurrence that follows? What causal or other relationships are there between sections and events? Some writers, such as John Steinbeck in *The Grapes of Wrath*, use **intercalary** chapters, which alternate between the "real" story (the Joads) and peripheral or parallel stories (the Okies and migrants in general). A reader should look for the pattern of such organization and try to see the interrelationships of alternating chapters.

Of course, plots cannot happen in isolation from **characters**, the "who" element of a story. The interplay of plot and characters determines, in large part, the **theme**: the why of the story. It is sometimes difficult to distinguish between a mere topic and a genuine theme or thesis or between a theme and contributing motifs. A **topic** is a phrase, such as "man's inhumanity to man" or "the fickle nature of fate." A theme, however, turns a phrase into a statement: "Man's inhumanity to man is barely concealed by 'civilization'" or "Man is a helpless pawn, at the mercy of fickle fate." Although many writers deal with similar topics, such as the complex nature of true love, their themes vary widely, from "True love will always win out in the end" to "Not even true love can survive the cruel ironies of fate."

An illustration of the relationship between plot, character, and theme is evident in a familiar fairy tale. In "The Ugly Duckling," the structuring story line is "Once upon a time there was an ugly duckling, who became a beautiful swan." In this case, the duckling did nothing to merit either his ugliness or his eventual transformation, but he did not curse fate. Lonely and outcast, he only wept and waited. When he became beautiful, he did not gloat; he eagerly joined the other members of his flock, who greatly admired him. The theme is, "Good things come to him who waits," or "Life is unfair—you don't get what you deserve, nor deserve what you get." What would happen to the theme if the ugly duckling remained an ugly duckling? "Some guys just never get a break"?

By changing events (plot elements) at any point, a writer can also change the theme. If one of the ugly

stepsisters in "Cinderella" disguised herself at the wedding behind the bridal veil, the Prince would be dismayed when she lifted the veil for the kiss. The new theme might now be, "Virtue is not its own reward."

Skilled writers often employ motifs to help unify their works. A **motif** is a story detail or element that repeats throughout the work; it may even become symbolic. The Nancy Drew books are ready examples of the use of motifs. Lonely roads, ticking clocks, shadows, and empty houses are familiar to most readers of this series–or other mystery books. These motifs, or details, work in concert to help convince the reader that the detective is doing all she/he can to "get to the bottom" of the problem.

Motifs can also become symbolic. The humming engine of the roadster returning again to civilization signals, "It's over. Finished." Motifs in the hands of a skillful writer are valuable devices. In isolation, and often magnified, a single motif can become a controlling image with great significance. In William Golding's *Lord of the Flies*, wise Piggy loses one of the lenses in his glasses and later is without specs at all. This loss of sight is symbolic of a loss of insight and wisdom in the midst of the chaos on the island.

The **setting** is the where and the when of the story. Setting indicates the place and the time of day, time of year, or period; the setting is the dramatic moment and the precise intersection of time and space for the story. Setting is also the atmosphere: positive or negative ambiance, calm, chaotic, Gothic, romantic. The question for the reader to answer is whether the setting is essential (integral) to the plot or theme or whether it is incidental; that is, could this story or theme have been told successfully in another time and/or place (backdrop)? For instance, could the theme in *Lord of the Flies* have "worked" if the boys were not on an island? Could they have been isolated in some other place? Does it matter to the theme whether the "war" they are fleeing is World War II, World War III, or some other conflict? It is evident that the four elements of plot, character, theme, and setting are intertwined and largely interdependent.

The final question, how, relates to an author's **style**. Style involves

- language (word choice);
- syntax (word order, sentence type and length);

- the balance between narration and dialogue;

- the choice of narrative voice (first-person participant or third-person observer with limited omniscience);

- use of descriptive passages; and

- other aspects of the actual words on the page that are basically irrelevant to the first four elements: plot, character, theme, and setting.

Stylistic differences are easy to spot among such diverse writers as Jane Austen, whose style is—to today's reader—very formal and mannered; Mark Twain, whose style is very casual and colloquial; William Faulkner, whose prose often spins on without punctuation or paragraphs far longer than the reader can hold either a thought or a breath; and Ernest Hemingway, whose dense but spare, pared-down style has earned the epithet, "Less is more."

Short Stories

Differing from traditional short fiction, such as the parable, fable, and folktale, the modern short story has its emphasis on character development through scenes rather than summary, through showing rather than telling. Gaining popularity in the nineteenth century, the short story generally is realistic and presents detailed accounts of the lives of middle-class people. This tendency toward realism dictates a probable plot, with causality fully in operation. Furthermore, the characters are human, with recognizable human motivations, both social and psychological. Setting—time and place—is realistic rather than fantastic. As Edgar Allan Poe stipulated, the elements of plot, character, setting, style, point of view, and theme all work toward a single unified effect.

However, some writers stretch the boundaries and add elements of nonrealism—such as the supernatural and the fantastic—into their stories; they sometimes switch back and forth between realism and nonrealism and confuse the reader who expects conventional fiction. Some of Poe's short stories are not, strictly speaking, realistic. However, if readers approach and accept this type of story on its own terms, they will be better able to understand and appreciate it more fully. Unlike the novel, which has time and space to develop characters and interrelationships, the short story must rely on flashes of insight and revelation to develop plot and characters. The "slice of life" in a short story is of necessity much narrower than that in a novel; the time span is much shorter and the focus much tighter. To

attempt anything like the panoramic canvas available to the novelist would be to view fireworks through a soda straw: occasionally pretty, but ultimately not very satisfying or enlightening.

The elements of the short story are those of the novel. Because of the concentration of the material in a short story, the author's choice of point of view may be especially significant. A narrator may be objective and present information without bias or comment. Hemingway frequently uses the objective third-person narrator; he does not directly reveal the thoughts or feelings of the characters. Hemingway presents scenes dramatically—that is, with a great deal of dialogue and very little narrative. The third-person narrator may, however, be less objective and may directly reveal the thoughts and feelings of one or more of the characters. Depending on how complete the narrator's knowledge of the characters' psychological and emotional makeup may be, the narrator may be fully or only partially omniscient.

The least objective narrator is the first-person narrator, who presents information from the perspective of a single character who is a participant in the action. Such a narrative choice allows the author to present the discrepancies between the writer's and reader's perceptions and those of the narrator. One reason the choice of narrator and the point of view from which the storyteller relates the story is immensely important in a short story is that the narrator reveals character and events in ways that affect the reader's understanding of theme. The initiation story frequently employs the first-person narrator. Truman Capote's narrator in "A Christmas Memory" identifies himself as follows:

> The person to whom she is speaking is myself. I am seven; she is sixty-something. We are cousins, very distant ones, and we have lived together—well, as long as I can remember. Other people inhabit the house, relatives; and though they have power over us, and frequently make us cry, we are not, on the whole, too much aware of them. We are each other's best friend. She calls me Buddy, in memory of a boy who was formerly her best friend. The other Buddy died in the 1880's, when she was still a child. She is still a child (Capote, 4).

Buddy's characterizations of his friend are self-revelatory. The two are peers, equals, despite their vast age difference. They are both totally unselfish, enjoying the simple activities mandated by their economic circumstances. They are both "children." Capote tells the story in present tense; he makes the memories from the first paragraphs seem as "real" and immediate as those from many years later. Buddy's responses from the early years are as true to his seven-year-old's perspective as are those when he, much older, has left home.

Poetry

Opening a book to study for an examination is perhaps the worst time to read poetry or to read about poetry; above all, the reader should enjoy poetry. Poetry should be "reading for pleasure."

Poetry was the "current language" for students growing up in the Elizabethan or Romantic eras. In those worlds, people were more apt to take the time to sit down, clear the mind, and let poetry take over. Because the meaning of a poem typically does not come across in a nanosecond, many modern students find reading poetry very frustrating. Sometimes it takes years for a poem to take on meaning; the reader simply knows that the poem sounds good, and it provokes an unexplained emotional response. With time, more emotional experience, further reading about similar experiences, and more life, the reader comes to a meaning of that poem that satisfies for the time being. In a few more years, the poem may take on a whole new meaning.

Reasons for Writing Poetry. An important first step in learning to appreciate poetry is to answer the question, "Why do people write poetry?" An easy answer is that the poet wishes to convey an experience, an emotion, an insight, or an observation in a startling or satisfying way, often one that remains in the reader's memory for years. Why not use a straightforward sentence or paragraph? Why wrap up that valuable insight in fancy words: rhyme, verse, meter, symbolism, and all the other seeming mumbo-jumbo that explicators of poetry use? Why not just come right out and say it as "normal people" do?

Poetry is not just a vehicle for conveying meaning. Poetry can provide intellectual stimulus. One of the best ways of studying a poem is to consider it as a jigsaw puzzle: an integral work of art that can be taken apart piece by piece (word by word), analyzed scientifically, labeled, and put back together again into a whole with the meaning complete.

Poems help the reader see things from a different perspective. For example, William Wordsworth's poem "Daffodils" presents the reader with a unique description of a common flower:

> Continuous as the stars that shine
> And twinkle on the Milky Way, They stretch'd
> in never-ending line
>   Along the margin of a bay: Ten thousand
> saw I at a glance, Tossing their heads in sprightly dance.

If poets enhance our power of sight, they also awaken the other senses as powerfully. In "Snake," the reader can hear Emily Dickinson's serpent in the repeated *s* sound, or sibilance, of the lines.

> A narrow fellow in the grass Occasionally rides; You may have met him, did you not? His notice sudden is.
>   The grass divides as with a comb, A spotted shaft is seen; And then it closes at your feet And opens further on.

Poets write, then, to awaken the senses. They have crucial ideas, but the words they use are often more important than the meaning.

Children love poetry: nursery rhymes, ball-game rhythms, jump-rope patterns. Even with no idea of the meaning of the words (like "Little Miss Muffet sat on a tuffet"), a child can respond to their sounds and the pattern they form.

Adults, too, read poetry for that sense of sound and pattern; with more experience, the poetry reader gains a sense of pleasure in recognizing poetry forms, like the sonnet and the rondelle. Even greater enjoyment comes from watching a poet's and/or poem's development, tracing themes and ideas, analyzing maturity in growth of imagery, noting use of rhythm, and recognizing stylistic devices. To the novice reader of poetry, a poem can speak at a particular time and become an experience in itself; for instance, Alfred Lord Tennyson's "Crossing the Bar" may give a reader comfort at a time of death. The reader may see death through another's eyes; the experience may seem similar and help the reader to re-evaluate, view a universal human response to grief, and feel encouraged to deal with the grief.

More important than ideas and sense awakening is the poet's appeal to the emotions. It is precisely this aspect of poetry that disturbs many students. Modern society tends to block out emotions; many people need reviews to tell them if they enjoyed a film and a critic's praise to judge whether a play or novel is worth their time. They hesitate to laugh at something in case it is not the "in" thing to do. They certainly do not cry, at least not in front of others.

Poets write to overcome that blocking of emotion. Very often it is their own blocking that they seek to alleviate but that is not to say that poetry immediately makes readers laugh, cry, love, hate. The important fact about the emotional release in poetry is that poets help readers explore their own emotions, sometimes by shocking them, sometimes by drawing attention to balance and pattern, sometimes by cautioning readers to move carefully in the inner world.

Many poets might paraphrase Lord Byron, who claimed that he had to write or go mad. The writer and the reader of a poem enter into a collision, each helping the other to find significance in the human world, to find safety in a seemingly alien world.

Poets may offer nothing really new. Instead, they may reveal old truths about human emotions that readers can begin to restructure, reading past their own experiences in light of the poets' and reevaluating their worldview. Just as a car manual helps the owner understand the workings of a particular vehicle, a poem helps readers understand the inner workings of people.

That last point might lead the poetry reader to ask the question, "Why read poetry?" Perhaps a good drama, novel, or short story would provide the same emotional experience, but a poem is much more accessible. Besides being shorter than other genres, poems have

a unique directness that hinges purely on language. Poets can say in one or two lines what may take novelists and entire works to express. For example, these lines from "Ode on a Grecian Urn" by John Keats are memorable:

"Beauty is truth, truth beauty"—that is all
Ye know on earth, and all ye need to know

When readers study these lines, reflect on them, and interpret them, the lines linger in their memories with more emphasis than do passages from George Eliot's *Middlemarch*, or Ibsen's *The Wild Duck,* which endeavor to make the same point.

Poetry is perhaps the oldest art and has been a part of people's lives through the years. Like the ancient listeners who thrilled to Homer's poetry and the tribes who chanted invocations to their gods, today's generation listens to pop song lyrics and finds itself, sometimes despite itself, repeating certain rhythmic lines. An advertisement that listeners chuckle over—or say they hate—has a way of repeating itself as listeners use the catchy phrase or snappy repetition. Both lyricists and advertisers cleverly use language and play on people's ability to pick up on a repeated sound or engaging rhythm or inner rhyme.

On reading a poem, a person's brain works on several levels: it responds to the sounds, the words themselves and their connotations, the emotions, and the insights or learning of the world being revealed. This mental process makes poetry a good training ground—a boot camp—for learning how to read literature in general. All the other genres have elements of poetry within them. A person who learns to read poetry well will be a more accomplished reader, even of car manuals.

Perhaps the best response to reading poetry comes from a poet, Emily Dickinson. She claimed that reading a book of poetry made her feel "as if the top of [her] head were taken off!"

Elements of Poetry. Children reading or learning poetry in school refer to each section of a poem as a **verse**. In fact the word *verse* has a different meaning. Perhaps the origin of *verse* was the original Latin word *versus*, meaning "row or line." Perhaps its etymology was the notion of turning, or *vertere*, meaning "to move to a new idea." In modern use, *verse* often bears with it the connotation of rhyme, rhythm, and meter; the word *verse* also refers to the positioning of lines on the page.

A **stanza** is a grouping of lines with a metrical order. Often, a poem has a repeated rhyme, called the *rhyme scheme*. Letters represent the repeating sounds, and the group of letters represent the rhyme scheme. For example, the following excerpt from Lord Byron's "Stanza" has a definite rhyme scheme and has the letters beside the appropriate lines:

> When a man hath no freedom to
> fight for at home,   *a*
> Let him combat for that of his neighbors;   *b*
> Let him think of the glories of Greece and
> of Rome,   *a*
> And get knocked on the head for his labors. *b*

The rhyme scheme is simple: *abab*. Why such a simple, almost sing-song rhyme? The simplicity reinforces the **tone** of the poem: sarcastic, cryptic, and cynical. There is almost a sneer behind the words "And get knocked on the head for his labors." It is as if the poet sets out to give a lecture or at least a homily along the lines of "Neither a lender nor a borrower be" but then undercuts its seriousness. The **irony** of the poem rests in the fact that Byron joined a freedom-fighting group in Greece and died, not gloriously, but of a fever.

Types of Rhymes. There are several types of rhymes. The most common is the **end rhyme**, which has the rhyming word at the end of the line. The rhyming word brings the line to a definite stop but sets up the verse for a rhyming word in another line later on. For instance, in "Stanzas," "home . . . Rome" is a perfect end rhyme. **Internal rhyme** includes at least one rhyming word within the line. The purpose of internal rhyme can be either to speed the rhythm or to make it linger. Byron uses internal rhymes mixed with half rhymes, as in "combat for that." **Slant rhyme**, sometimes referred to as half, off, near, or approximate rhyme, often jolts a reader who expects a perfect rhyme. Poets use slant rhyme to express disappointment or a deliberate

letdown. **Masculine rhyme** uses one-syllable words or stresses the final syllable of polysyllabic words, giving the feeling of strength and impact. **Feminine rhyme** uses a rhyme of two or more syllables; the fact that the stress does not fall on the last syllable gives a feeling of softness and lightness.

Free and Blank Verse. When the lines of a poem are unrhymed and varying in metrical pattern, the verse is **free verse**—or to use the French term, *vers libre*. Although the lines of blank verse are also unrhymed, it has a strict rhythm: iambic pentameter (as discussed later). Free verse, which some readers call "modern" poetry, has added to its so-called obscurity because without rhyme and rhythm, poets often resort to complicated syntactical patterns, repeated phrases, awkward cadences, and parallelism. Robert Frost preferred not to use free verse; he compared writing free verse to playing tennis without a net (*http://ssl.pro-et.co.uk/home catalyst/RF/bio.html*). He suggested that free verse is easier than rhymed and metrical verse. Such a claim for the artistry and hard work behind a poem introduces perhaps the most difficult of the skills for a poet to practice and a reader to learn: meter.

Meter and Rhythm. **Meter** refers to the pattern or measure of stressed or accented words within a line of verse. When studying meter, a student should note where the stresses fall on syllables; if a verse does not have stressed syllables, the poet wrote it that way for a reason. A typical rhythm is the rising and falling rhythm of **iambic rhythm**. A line of poetry that alternates stressed and unstressed syllables is **iambic meter**. A line of poetry with 10 syllables of rising and falling stresses is **iambic pentameter**; both William Shakespeare and John Milton used iambic pentameter in their blank verse. The basic measuring unit in a line of poetry is called a **foot**.

More important than memorizing the terminology of poetry is being able to analyze why the poet has used the terms in the particular context of the poem. For example, Shakespeare did not want the lyrical fall and rise of the iamb for his witches around the cauldron; he wanted to suggest the gloom and mystery of the heath in *Macbeth*. A poet will abruptly change the pattern of a poem only for a good reason. If the poet subtly moves from a disruptive meter into a smooth one, the reader will want to analyze what is going on in the meaning. If the poet is doing "a good job," then the rhyme, rhythm, and meter work together in harmony to make the poem an integral whole. This time the Greeks provide the definition of the word *meter*, from *metron*, meaning "measure."

Types of Poetry. When reading for pleasure, it is not vital to recognize that a poem is a sonnet or a villanelle. In discussing a poem, however, it is useful to know what "breed" you are dealing with, because the form may dictate certain areas of rhyme or meter and enhance the meaning. The pattern or design of a poem is its **form**, and even the strangest, most experimental poetry will have some type of form to it. Some poets even try to match the **shape** of the poem to the subject. Such visual poems are not just fun to look at and read, but the shape adds to the subject and helps the reader appreciate the poet's worldview.

There are two forms of poetry. **Open form**, which developed from free verse, has no rules regarding number of lines, rhyme scheme, or meter. That does not imply, however, that the poet used little skill or craft when writing an open-form poem. In contrast, **closed form** is immediately recognizable because it has a set number of lines, rhyme scheme, and meter. The poet using closed form must not deviate from the recognized form. Among the types of closed-form poetry are the sonnet, couplet, epic, ballad, narrative, lyric, elegy, ode, villanelle, sestina, epigram, aubade, and blank verse.

The most easily recognized closed form of poetry is the **sonnet**. The sonnet always has 14 lines, but there are two types of sonnets: the Petrarchan or Italian and the Shakespearean or English. The Petrarchan sonnet is organized into two parts: the first eight lines make up the **octave**, and the next six lines are the **sestet** (meaning "a turn or shift"). Typically, the **octave** sets up a problem or a proposition, and the sestet gives the answer or resolution after a turn or shift. The Shakespearean sonnet organizes the 14 lines into three groups of four lines and an ending group of two rhyming lines called a couplet.

The **couplet** is itself a closed form of poetry that many poets have found useful. It is a two-line stanza that usually rhymes with an end rhyme. If the couplet is firmly end-stopped and written in iambic pentameter,

it is known as a **heroic couplet**, because it was used in the English translations of the great classical or heroic epics like *The Iliad* and *The Odyssey*.

An **epic** has vastness of size and range. The translation is usually in couplets. The meter is regular with equal line lengths because originally the performer sang the epic poems aloud or chanted them to the beat of drums. Long before movies or television, epic poems were a common form of entertainment, and audiences, who had heard the stories many times before, would cue the bards or singers who forgot their lines. The subjects of most epics are the great deeds of heroes, like Odysseus (Ulysses). The one great English epic, *Paradise Lost* by Milton, deals with the story of Adam and Eve and the Fall.

The **ballads** are much simpler in structure and theme. The earliest poems children learn are often ballads. Some folk or popular ballads, usually anonymous, date from the fifteenth century; families and regions handed them down through generations until some scribe finally wrote them down. Many ballads were the creations of simple folks who could not read or write. These stories in song often revolve around love and hate, lust and murder, lovers, knights, and the supernatural. As with the epic, and for the same reason, repetition plays a major role in the ballad; a repeated refrain can hold the entire poem together. The form gave rise to the **ballad stanza**: four lines rhyming *abcb*, with lines 1 and 3 having eight syllables and lines 2 and 4 having six. Poets who later created **literary ballads** kept the same pattern. Samuel Taylor Coleridge's "The Rime of the Ancient Mariner" has all the ballad elements, which come together as he reconstructs an old folk story.

Early poetry was in the form of **narrative**. The "father of English poetry," Geoffrey Chaucer, told stories within a story in the *Canterbury Tales*. The Elizabethans turned to love and the humanistic battle between love of the world and love of God. Wordsworth and Coleridge marked a turning point not only by using "the language of men" in poetry but also by moving away from the narrative poem to the **lyric**. The word *lyric* comes from a Greek term that means "a story told by a poet playing on a lyre." Wordsworth moves from story to emotion, often "emotion recollected in tranquillity," as in his "Daffodils." Very often the poet seems to be musing aloud.

Part of the lyric "family" is the **elegy**, a lament for someone's death or the passing of a love or concept. The most famous is Thomas Gray's "Elegy Written in a Country Churchyard," which mourns not only the passing of individuals but of a past age and the wasted potential within every human being, no matter how humble.

Often *ode* and *elegy* become synonymous, but an **ode**, also part of the lyric family, is usually longer, dealing with more profound areas of human life than simply death. Keats's odes are perhaps the most famous and most beloved in English poetry.

More specialized types closed-form poetry also need mentioning. For example, the **villanelle**, a courtly love poem structure from medieval times, builds on five three-line stanzas (**tercets**), with the rhyme scheme *aba*, followed by a four-line stanza (**quatrain**), which ends the poem as *abaa*. As if this were not pattern and order enough, the poem's first line appears again as the last line of the second and fourth tercets, and the third line appears again in the last line of the third and fifth tercets. The first and third lines appear yet again as rhyming lines at the end of the poem. Some of the old villanelles can be so stiff in their pattern that the meaning is inconsequential. The most famous and arguably the best is Dylan Thomas's "Do Not Go Gentle into That Good Night." The poem stands on its own with a magisterial meaning of mankind raging against death; when the reader appreciates the structure, the rage is even more emphatic because it is so controlled. It is a poem well worth finding for "reading for pleasure." In James Joyce's novel *A Portrait of the Artist as a Young Man*, writing a villanelle on an empty cigarette packet turns the young boy, Stephen Dedalus, who dreams of being an artist, into a poet, a "real" artist.

The most difficult of all closed forms is said to be the **sestina**. Also French, this "song of sixes" was sung by medieval troubadours. The poet presents six six-line stanzas, with six end words in a certain order, and then repeats those six words in any order in a closing tercet.

An **epigram** is short, even abrupt, a little cynical, and always to the point. Alexander Pope mastered the epigram, as did Oscar Wilde centuries later. Perhaps at some stage we have all written another closed form of poetry, the **doggerel**—rhyming poetry that becomes horribly distorted to fit the rhymes, not through skill but the opposite. In contrast, a **limerick** is very skilled: five lines using the rhyme scheme *aabba*. Elementary students should be familiar with Edward Lear's limericks, like "There Once Was a Man with a Beard." His limericks display fine poetry. Another specialized type of closed-form poetry is the **aubade**. Originally a song or piece of music sung or played at dawn, the aubade often revolves around the subject of lovers at dawn, or the poet composed it at dawn, the very time when poetic inspiration is extremely high.

Although the name suggests open form, **blank verse** is in fact closed-form poetry, which is unrhymed iambic pentameter. True open-form poetry is often arranged randomly on the page, not confined by any rhyme pattern or meter. The words might appear as though they were spilled onto the page, and readers might feel that the poet is addressing them directly, as if the poet is cornering them in a room or simply chatting over the kitchen table. With lines breaking at any point and dashes darting in and out, the poet seems to be talking to the audience with all the "natural" breaks of the speaking voice.

Open-form poets can employ rhyme, but sometimes it seems as if the rhyme has slipped into the poem quite easily; there is no wrenching of the word to force the rhyme. Many open-form poems have internal rhyme as poets play with words and convey the sensation that they are thinking aloud. Open-form poetry is usually thought of as "modern," at least post–World War I, but Emily Dickinson's use of space on the page, her direct address to the reader, and her use of the dash clearly mark her as an open-form poet, even though she lived from 1830 to 1886.

Drama

Students begin reading plays even in first-grade readers. By upper-elementary and middle school, most students are familiar with Freytag's pyramid, which is used to illustrate the structure of a five-act drama (and is also widely used to analyze fiction). The stages specified in the pyramid are **introduction** or exposition, **complication**, **rising action**, **climax**, **falling action**, and **denouement** or conclusion. Satire in drama is also common.

Essay

The genres of novels, short stories, poetry, and drama require from the reader a different kind of involvement than does the essay. Rather than presenting a story from which the reader may discern meaning through the skillful analysis of character, plot, symbol, and language, the essay presents a relatively straightforward account of the writer's opinion on a specific topic. Depending on the type of essay, the reader may become informed (expository essay), provoked (argumentative essay), convinced (persuasive essay), enlightened (critical essay), or acquainted with the writer (narrative, when the writer illustrates a point with a personal story—autobiographical or fictitious). "Competency 5: Knowledge of Writing" addresses writing types, like the essay, in more detail.

Satire

Satire, properly speaking, is not a genre at all but rather a mode of writing. Writers of various genres—poetry, drama, fiction, and nonfiction—use satire. It is less a product than a perspective that the reader must try to understand through critical thinking. Satire is a manifestation of the writer's attitude (tone) and purpose.

Satire mainly exposes, ridicules, derides, and denounces vice, folly, evil, and stupidity; those qualities manifest themselves in persons, groups, ideas, institutions, customs, and beliefs. Although satirists have many techniques at their disposal, only two types of satire are available—gentle or harsh; the type depends on the author's intent, audience, and methods.

Knowing the meaning of the terms *romanticism, realism*, and *naturalism* can help in understanding the role of satire in literature. **Romanticism** sees the world idealistically, as perfectible, if not already perfect. **Realism** sees the world as it is, with healthy doses of both good and bad. **Naturalism** sees the world as imperfect, with evil often triumphing over good. The satirist is closer to the naturalist than to the romantic or realist; both the satirist and the naturalist focus on what is wrong with the world, intending to expose the foibles of humans and their society. The difference between the satirist and the naturalist lies in their techniques. The naturalist is very direct and does not necessarily employ humor; the more subtle satirist uses humor, even when writing on very serious topics. For instance, people plagued with overpopulation and starvation are not, on first glance, material for humor. Many works have treated such conditions with sensitivity, bringing attention to the plight of the world's unfortunate. Steinbeck's *Grapes of Wrath* is such a work. Satirical writers, on the other hand, call readers' attention to matters they believe are repulsive, despicable, or destructive by using exaggeration (**hyperbole**) and cutting or even cruel remarks at the expense of their subjects. **Irony** is perhaps the satirist's most powerful weapon. The basis of irony is inversion or reversal, doing or saying the opposite or the unexpected.

A classic satirical novel is Jonathan Swift's *Gulliver's Travels*. Swift vigorously attacks aspects of religions, governments, and the prevailing intellectual beliefs of their respective societies. Satire is also evident in two adaptations of the biblical story of King Solomon, who settled the dispute between two mothers regarding an infant. King Solomon advocated cutting the baby in two and dividing it between the two women. The rightful mother protested and promptly received the child. The story is meant to attest to the king's wisdom and understanding of parental love.

In Mark Twain's *The Adventures of Huckleberry Finn* (1884/1991), Huck has some difficulty persuading the runaway slave Jim that Solomon was wise. Jim insists that Solomon, having fathered "'bout five million chillen,'" was "'waseful. . . . He as soon chop a chile in two as a cat. Dey's plenty mo'. A chile er two, mo' er less, warn't no consekens to Solcrmun, dad fetch him!'" (321). Twain not only ridicules Jim's ingenuousness, as he does throughout the novel but also deflates time-honored beliefs about the Bible and its traditional heroes, as he did earlier in the novel in an account of Moses and the "bulrushers." Although Twain's satirical tone is fairly mild, his serious intent shows through.

Skill Two

Identify the Terminology and Appropriate Use of Literary Devices

Categorizing Narrative Fictional Literature for Children

Based on its content, narrative fictional literature for children is either traditional or modern in form. **Traditional** literature consists of ancient stories and comprises seven types, each with a set structure. People handed these stories down for many years by word of mouth. Later others, like Joel Chandler Harris, the Grimm brothers, and Charles Perrault, recorded the stories for other generations. The categories of **modern** literature can overlap some of the categories of traditional literature and include additional forms of literature.

Seven Types of Traditional Literature

The seven types of traditional fiction are parables, fables, fairy tales, folktales, noodlehead tales, myths, and legends. Each has certain characteristics which set it apart from the others.

Parables. The **parable** is a story that is realistic and has a moral. The story is didactic because it teaches a lesson. Unlike the fable, the parable could be—but is not necessarily—true. Jesus often taught with parables. One of his best known parables is "The Prodigal Son." He used other parables, like "The Good Samaritan," "The Lost Coin," and "The Seeds on Rich and Fallow Ground."

Fables. The **fable** is a nonrealistic story with a moral. The fable often has animals as main characters. **Aesop**, a Greek slave supposedly born around 600 BCE, is often associated with the fable. Whether he actually lived and whether he actually developed the fables, however, is debatable. Charlotte Huck, Susan Hepler, and Janet Hickman, noted children's literature authorities and the authors of *Children's Literature in the Elementary School* (1993), assert that the fables were actually in Greek literature as early as 800 BCE. Some of the best-known fables are probably "The Fox and the Crane," "The Fox and the Crow," and "The Fox and the Grapes." Fables about animals behaving as humans are often classified as **beast tales**.

Translators changed Aesop's fables from Greek to Latin to English. William Caxton was the first to publish the fables in English in 1484.

Fairy Tales. Although not every **fairy tale** has a fairy among its list of characters, the element of magic is a necessary element of this type of traditional children's literature. Most fairy tales follow a certain pattern and may present an "ideal." For instance, fairy tales like "Cinderella," "Snow White," and "Rapunzel" convey a message about the "proper" woman. According to these tales, the ideal woman is beautiful, kind, and long suffering; she waits for her prince to come and save her from any disappointment or disaster that may occur.

Charles Perrault recorded French fairy tales in the 1600s. It was not until the 1800s that Jacob and Wilhelm Grimm recorded German fairy tales, Joseph Jacobs recorded British fairy tales, Peter Asbjornsen and Jorgen Moe recorded Scandinavian fairy tales, and Aleksandr Nikolaevich Afanas'ev recorded Russian fairy tales.

Some writers, like Nathaniel Hawthorne, use the term *wonder tales* to refer to stories with magical elements. Examples of the magic often appear in the characters of witches, wizards, magical animals, and talking beasts. The use of the "**magic three**" is another frequent feature of the fairy tale; for instance, there are often three wishes, three attempts at achieving a goal, or three siblings.

Another characteristic of the fairy tale is that the listener or reader knows that good will always wins over evil. A youngster may be frightened by witches, wicked ogres, and evil forces, but the child knows that the protagonist of every fairy tale manages to "live happily ever after."

Stereotyping is another characteristic of the fairy tale. As soon as the storyteller says the word *stepmother*, for instance, the listener knows that the woman is wicked. Likewise, the mere mention of a setting in the woods conveys feelings of fear, impending doom, and evil. The word *prince* brings to mind a young, handsome man on a white horse, and the princess is usually the youngest in the family, beautiful, soft spoken, kind, inactive, and waiting for her prince to come. The female in the fairy tale is often a direct contrast to the assertive female of the folktale.

Folktales. **Folktales** use the language of the people. The stories rarely have morals but are solely for entertainment, with humor often playing a major role. In the 1600s and 1700s, early residents of the Appalachian Mountains brought many of the fairy tales of England,

Scotland, and Ireland with them when they immigrated to the "new" country; the mountain residents adapted the tales to their new way of life. For example, the fairy tale "Cinderella" became the folktale "Ashpet" (Chase, 1948). The quiet, passive Cinderella became the hardworking, smart, active Ashpet, a character more like the women who had to work hard helping the men tame the harsh mountain territory. The German fairy tale "The Bremen Town Musicians" (Grimm 1968) became "Jack and the Robbers" in another mountain folktale (Chase 1943).

Noodlehead stories are folktales with a humorous bent. These stories feature one or more characters whom the reader or listener can outsmart. The humor of the story is in the ridiculous antics of a character that makes the listener or reader feel superior. *Epaminondas and His Auntie* (Bryant 1938) is an example of a noodlehead story.

The humor in folktales may be coarse, and the diction is often that of the particular group of people who originated the tales. Richard Chase collected many of the Appalachian folktales. He transcribed the tales on paper and told them in personal appearances, on records, and on tapes for the public. He was always careful to use the mountain dialect. His *Jack Tales* (1943) and *Grandfather Tales* (1948) are among his best-known works.

Likewise, other cultures around the world have their own unique folktales and fairy tales. For instance, Perrault's French tale of "Cinderella" is "Tattercoats" in Jacobs's collection (1959). In the British version of the story, the prince falls in love with a dirty, ragged girl, not a beautiful, well-dressed figure at the ball. The Norwegian version of the tale in *East o' the Sun and West o' the Moon* (Asbjornsen and Moe 1946) features Cinderlad rather than Cinderella. The Jewish folktale of *Zlateh the Goat* (Singer 1966) tells of the survival of a young boy and his goat in a snowstorm.

Myths. **Myths** are stories that attempt to explain things the teller does not understand. Greeks and Romans used myths and their associated heroes and heroines to explain thunder, fire, and the "movements" of the sun. Norse myths, too, explain phenomena—especially those associated with the frost, snow, and the cold climate of the north. Likewise, Native American myths answer questions such as why the rabbit does not have a tail and why the constellations exist. (Sometimes these Native American myths are mistakenly called legends). Another name for these explanations is pourquoi (French for "why") tales. Most cultures have their own myths.

Legends. **Legends** are stories—usually exaggerated—about real people, places, and things. George Washington, for instance, was a real person. However, not all the stories about him are true. Because there were no silver dollars minted during the American Revolution, it would have been impossible for him to have tossed a silver dollar across the Potomac. Paul Bunyan may have actually been a logger or lumberjack; it is doubtful that he owned a blue ox or had a pancake griddle large enough that his cook could tie hams on his feet and skate on it. The careful reader of literature realizes that although they are generally part of traditional literature, legends are currently springing up about modern figures, animals, and places.

Classifying Modern Literature

One way of classifying modern literature is simply to decide if a book is realistic or fanciful. There are times, however, when a more discrete classification method is in order. In such cases, modern fiction can be classified into four categories: novels, romance, confession, and Menippean satire.

Novels. **Novels** are realistic stories of events that could really happen. A novel has a realistic setting and realistic characters. A novel could happen on any planet, in any city, or in any country—as long as the author can convince the reader that the setting is real. Anyone can serve as a main character—as long as the author can convince the reader that the character is believable.

Romances. A **romance**, on the other hand, presents an idealized view of life. The story may—or may not—involve love, but a romance always contains fantasy. The characters and the setting are idealizations of real life. An ocean cruise in a romance book might, therefore, involve characters who are young, good looking, and rich, possibly possessing all the qualities of the elite. The weather would, of course, be clear and pleasant for the entire cruise.

Confessions. In a **confession**, one character reveals personal thoughts and ideas. This particular character is a **round character**, whom the reader knows in detail. In Laura Ingalls Wilder's books, for example, the reader knows exactly what the main character, Laura, is thinking; the reader, however, does not know what Mary (Laura's sister) is thinking. The confession allows the reader to view only one character, in this case.

Menippean Satires. A **Menippean satire** allows the reader to see the world through the eyes of another. In Roald Dahl's *Charlie and the Chocolate Factory* (1972), the reader sees the world through Charlie's eyes. The desire for candy becomes almost overpowering for the reader, just as it does for Charlie. A person's outlook on candy, and even life itself, could change as a result of reading *Charlie and the Chocolate Factory*.

Plot

The **plot** of a book is the story line and is usually the element that holds the reader's attention. The plot has a definite order, involves conflict, and has a pattern and structure.

Order: Chronological, Flashback, or Foreshadowing. The events of the plot can occur either randomly or in **chronological**, or sequential, order. In some books or stories, the plot carries the reader from the present to events in the past (**flashback**). The plot may carry the reader to and from the past once or several times. There may even be a hint of the future or of what is to come (**foreshadowing**). For example, in *Where the Red Fern Grows* (Rawls 1961/1976), readers find themselves drawn into the past with the main character living in the Ozark Mountains.

Conflict. There must be **conflict**, or unsettled issues, in the plot to keep the reader interested. The conflict can be with self, others, society, or nature. Of course, *Robinson Crusoe* (Defoe 1719/1972) is an excellent example of conflict with nature. In *Gulliver's Travels* (Swift 1726/1945), the protagonist encounters conflict with the Lilliputians, small people though they are. Vera and Bill Cleaver present a family of children who are fighting society and its rules to remain together in *Where the Lilies Bloom* (1969). Jerry Renault, the main character in *The Chocolate War* (Cormier 1974/1977) faces conflicts with himself (Am I strong enough to refuse to sell the chocolates that the rest of the school is selling?), with others who try to force him to sell, and with society, because the entire school community is at odds with him for not selling candy to support the school.

Pattern: Suspense, Cliffhanger, Foreshadowing, Sensationalism, Climax, or Denouement. A book or story that has **suspense** keeps the reader in doubt or uncertainty as to the outcome until the end. For instance, in *The Island of the Blue Dolphins* (O'Dell 1960), the reader does not know until the end of the book whether the main character, Karana, will stay on the island.

A book in which each chapter ends in an exciting, unsolved event designed to keep the reader turning the page is a **cliffhanger**. Many examples of cliffhangers are evident in television and movie lineups. The Batman television series originally aired on Tuesday and Thursday nights; the viewer had to wait until the Thursday night episode to find out the outcome. Of course, soap operas are excellent examples of cliffhangers, as were the Saturday radio serials that were especially popular in the 1940s.

Foreshadowing gives a clue or a hint as to what will occur. In the movie *Jaws*, there was an auditory clue as to when the shark would appear; on the one occasion when the music did not precede the shark's appearance, the audience received a shock. In *The Chocolate War*, the narrator uses foreshadowing and gives the reader a hint of what is to come: "They shouldn't have picked Frankie Rollo for an assignment, of course" (Cormier 1974/1977, 130).

Sensationalism occurs when a series of exciting events occur. "Hansel and Gretel" is an example of sensationalism in traditional literature. The evil stepmother sends the father out into the woods to abandon the children; they find their way back; the father takes them out again; the birds eat the crumbs and the children become lost; the witch takes them captive; Hansel pushes the witch in the oven. Many action movies, like *Raiders of the Lost Ark*, also contain elements of sensationalism.

The **climax** is the highest point of interest in a book or story. At the climax, the reader says, "Ah-ha! Now I am sure of the outcome of the conflict!" Sometimes a story has a **false climax** that leads readers to believe they have their questions answered, only to find that the story has new twists and turns. In "Hansel and Gretel," some readers think the conflict is resolved when the children find their way home after their father leaves them in the forest the first time. However, the questions raised in the story are not answered until later in the story.

The **denouement** is the ending of the book. There are two types of endings: open and closed. An **open denouement** occurs when readers do not have answers to all their questions. A **closed denouement** occurs when readers have answers to all their questions. Each story in Howard Garis's volume titled *Uncle Wiggly's Adventures* (1912/1915) contains an open ending, which keeps the reader turning the pages. For instance, this is the how the first story ends:

> But then, all of a sudden, a harsh voice cried out: "Ha! Now I have you! I was just wishing someone would come along with my dinner, and you did! Get in there, and see if you can find your fortune, Uncle Wiggly!"
>
> And with that a big, black bear, who had been hiding in the stump, pushed Uncle Wiggly into a dark closet, and locked the door! And there the poor rabbit was, and the bear was getting ready to have him for dinner.
>
> But don't worry, I'll find a way to get Uncle Wiggly out. And in case we have ice cream pancakes for supper, with strawberry jam pudding sauce, I'll tell you, in the next story, how Uncle Wiggly got out of the bear's den, and went fishing. (14)

The open endings of some horror movies are what keep viewers attending numerous sequels. *Friday the 13th*, *Nightmare on Elm Street*, *Halloween*, and *I Know What You Did Last Summer* are some examples. Of course, the *Rocky* series is also a good example of movies with open denouements, and television soap operas are notorious for their open endings. The American public waited a whole summer to find out "Who shot J. R." when the last episode of *Dallas* had an unsettled ending. The open endings of *The Borrowers* by Mary Norton (1953) and *The Indian in the Cupboard* by Lynne Banks (1980) kept many readers eager for the sequels to those books.

Structure: Progressive or Episodic. Plots are either progressive or episodic. If a novel has a **progressive** plot, the reader must finish the book or story to find the answers to the questions in the plot. For instance, to find out who created the statue in *From the Mixed-up Files of Mrs. Basil E. Frankweiler* (Konigsburg 1967), readers are forced to read every page (unless, of course, they cheat and skip to the end).

Robert Newton Peck's *Soup* series (beginning with *Soup*, published in 1974) contains chapters, each of which is a complete story, or episode, in itself. The chapters in *Soup*, therefore, are **episodic**.

Setting

As with picture books, the **setting**—the time and place where a story or book occurs—is important to juvenile literature. An essential element of the setting is its believability. The plot and the setting together make up the structure of the story.

A setting may be either backdrop or integral. A **backdrop** setting is not essential to the text. The setting in many of the Nancy Drew books is a backdrop setting because the plot could have happened in almost any American city. Most backdrop settings are **figurative**, meaning they serve as illustrations.

An **integral** setting is essential to the plot. Rawls's novel *Summer of the Monkeys* (1977) has an integral setting: the Ozark Mountains. This novel's setting is also **literal**, meaning the story could actually occur where the author sets it. Rawls's description of the novel's mountain setting gives readers the feeling they are reading a biography:

> It was in the late 1800s, the best I can remember. Anyhow—at the time, we were living in a brand-new country that had just been opened up for settlement. The farm we lived on was called Cherokee land because it was smack dab in the middle of the Cherokee Nation. It lay in a strip from the foothills of the Ozark Mountains to the banks of the Illinois River in northeastern Oklahoma. (9–10)

Characterization

As important as the plot and action might be, the **characters** make many books live on for many years. It is Tom Sawyer, Long John Silver, Meg, Beth, Jo, and Amy who help make *Tom Sawyer, Treasure Island,* and *Little Women* classics; the characters have withstood the test of time.

Characters can be **round** (fully developed, described, or revealed) or **flat** (undeveloped). In addition, characters are either dynamic or static. A **dynamic** character undergoes some kind of change in the course of the story, becoming more fully revealed as the plot develops. **Static** characters do not change in significant ways—that is, in ways that relate to the plot that is structuring the novel. Even though a character dies—that is, changes from alive to dead—that character is static unless the death is central to the narrative.

Major characters are protagonists or antagonists. The terms come from the Greek word *agon*, meaning "struggle." The **protagonist** struggles for someone or something; the **antagonist** is the enemy or the rival struggling against the protagonist. In "The Three Little Pigs," for instance, the wolf is the antagonist fighting against the pigs, who are the protagonists trying hard to keep their homes and each other safe from the wicked wolf.

Characters are **stock** if they exist because the plot demands them. For instance, the ball scene in "Cinderella" must include many men and women who do nothing more than attend the dance; these party-goers are stock characters. A Western novel, with a gunman who robs a bank, may have several stock characters: the banker's lovely daughter, the tough but kindhearted barmaid, the cowardly white-shirted citizen who sells out the hero to save his own skin, and the young freckle-faced lad who shoots the bad guy from a second-story hotel window.

A character can be a **stereotype**, without individual characteristics. For instance, in many fairy tales, the oldest daughter is ugly and mean, while the youngest daughter is beautiful—outside and inside. A sheriff in a small southern town, a football player who is all brawn, a librarian clucking over her prized books, or the cruel commandant of a prisoner-of-war camp might all be stereotypic.

Characters often serve as **foils** for other characters, serving to help the reader see the novel's other characters more clearly. A classic example is in Mark Twain's *The Adventures of Tom Sawyer* (1876/1989). Tom is the romantic foil for Huck Finn's realism. In Harper Lee's *To Kill a Mockingbird* (1960/1982), Scout serves as the naive observer of events that her older brother, Jem, comes to understand from the perspective of the adult world.

Some characters are **allegorical**, standing for qualities or concepts rather than for actual personages. In C. S. Lewis's *The Lion, the Witch, and the Wardrobe* (1950/1988), the Lion stands for good.

Revealing Characters. Writers use a variety of means to reveal characters to the readers. The writer may **tell about the character**. For instance, here is a description of the dog Lassie, the main character in Eric Knight's *Lassie Come Home* (1938/1966):

> Greenall Bridge was like other Yorkshire villages. Its men knew and understood and loved dogs, and there were many perfect ones that walked at men's heels; but they all agreed that if a finer dog than Sam Carralough's tricolor collie had ever been bred in Greenall Bridge, then it must have been long before they were born. (11)

Another effective device is to **describe the character in the character's surroundings**. In the following passage from *Never Cry Wolf*, Farley Mowat (1963/1984) gives readers a feeling of what it might be like to be an Eskimo:

> This country belonged to the deer, the wolves, the birds and the smaller beasts. We two were no more than casual and insignificant intruders. Man had never dominated the Barrens. Even the Eskimos, whose territory it had once been, had lived in harmony with it. The little group . . . was the last of the inland people, and they were all but swallowed up in this immensity of wilderness. (126)

The writer might also **show the character in action**. The following excerpt from *To Kill a Mockingbird* (Lee

1960/1982) describes Atticus, the lawyer and father, in action when a rabid dog enters their neighborhood:

> Atticus pushed his glasses to his forehead; they slipped down, and he dropped them in the street. In the silence, I heard them crack. Atticus rubbed his eyes and chin; we saw him blink hard . . . . With movements so swift they seemed simultaneous, Atticus's hand yanked a ball-tipped lever as he brought the gun to his shoulder. (96)

The **speech**, or dialect or diction, of a character can aid the author in revealing the character. The language of the gang members in *Durango Street* (Bonham 1965/1975) helps to disclose Tojo's and Rufus's attitudes:

> Tojo smiled. "Esscuse me, brothers. I meant bloods."
> Rufus rocked his head. "That's all right, greaseballs—Esscuse me: I mean Spanish-Americans."
> "Mexicans," Tojo snapped.
> "Sure, man," Rufus said. "Well, if you beans change your minds, you know where to find us. But don't come into Durango unless you're ready to talk business. Adiòs, huh?" (105)

The author often **reveals the thoughts of a character** to inform the reader about the character. Billie Jo in Karen Hesse's 1998 Newbery Award winner *Out of the Dust* expresses her thoughts in her diary: "From the earliest I can remember I've been restless in this little Panhandle shack we call home, always getting in Ma's way with my pointy elbows, my fidgety legs" (4).

A **character's appearance** can help the reader to understand the character. Dori Sanders uses this device in her book *Clover* (1991):

> They dressed me in white for my daddy's funeral. White from my head to my toes. I had the black skirt I bought at the six-dollar store all laid out to wear. I'd even pulled the black gross-grain bows off my black patent leather shoes to wear in my hair. But they won't let me wear black. (1)

What others say about the character gives the reader additional insight into the character. S. E. Hinton uses this device in *The Outsiders* (1967/1983) to tell the reader about Dallas:

> He had quite a reputation. They have a file on him down at the police station. He had been arrested, he got drunk, he rode in rodeos, lied, cheated, stole, rolled drunks, jumped small kids—he did everything. I didn't like him, but he was smart and you had to respect him. (13)

What others say to the character is another way of revealing the character to the reader. In *Brighty of Grand Canyon* (Henry 1953/1967), Uncle Jim—a prospector—speaks to the burro as if it were a human. The reader comes to believe that the burro can understand. When a mountain lion cuts Brighty, Uncle Jim explains how he is helping the burro:

> "I've an idee!" he crowed, eyes twinkling in triumph. He took out his pocketknife and pierced the denim just above one knee. Then he cut his way around the pants leg and stepped out of it. "Y'see, boy," he said, "if we hide yer cuts, you can't pick at 'em so easy, and they'll heal nice and clean." (57–58)

Sometimes the author gives the reader **information about the character**. Mary Mapes Dodge in *Hans Brinker* (1963) gives the reader an idea of the time, the place, and the character Hans by her description:

> These queer-looking affairs [homemade skates] had been made by the boy Hans. His mother was a poor peasant woman, too poor even to think of such a thing as buying skates for her little ones. Rough as these were, they had afforded the children many a happy hour upon the ice; and now as with cold, red fingers our young Hollanders tugged at the strings—their solemn faces bending closely over their knees—no vision of impossible iron runners came to dull the satisfaction glowing within. (1–2)

The **reactions of a character to others** and the **reactions of others to the character** can help the reader gain insight into both characters. Anne's reactions to Marilla and Marilla's reactions to Anne help the reader to know both characters in the classic *Anne of Green Gables* (Montgomery 1908/1935):

> "Will you please call me Cordelia?" she [Anne] asked eagerly.
>
> "*Call* you Cordelia! Is that your name?" [Marilla]
>
> "No-o-o, it's not exactly my name, but I would love to be called Cordelia. It's such a perfectly elegant name."
>
> "I don't know what on earth you mean. If Cordelia isn't your name, what is?"
>
> "Anne Shirley," reluctantly faltered forth the owner of that name, "But oh, please do call me Cordelia. It can't matter much to you what you call me if I'm only going to be here a little while, can it? And Anne is such an unromantic name."
>
> "Unromantic fiddlesticks!" said the unsympathetic Marilla. "Anne is a real good plain sensible name. You've no need to be ashamed of it." (34)

Whatever method the writer chooses to reveal a character, a careful writer will avoid stereotyping. **Stereotyping** is typecasting a character by such characteristics as the character's nationality, religion, size, or age. Gender, too, has been a way of stereotyping characters in children's books. Traditionally, fewer female than male characters have appeared in books for children. The female characters who have been portrayed usually have poorer reasoning skills and lead a more placid existence than the males. Many female characters depend on males to rescue them and are more passive than their male counterparts. Davis and McDaniel (1999) report some gains for girls in the way that Caldecott Award–winning picture books depict female characters, but the researchers were perplexed that books awarded the Caldecott in the 1950s included more female characters than did books from the supposedly more "liberated" decades that followed.

Some teachers who discover stereotyping in a juvenile book may wish to exclude it from the required reading lists for their classrooms. Other teachers may make a point of including such books as a way of helping students become aware of stereotyping and indicating to students the weaknesses of such pigeonholing.

Theme

The **theme** is the main point of the book. The three most common themes in traditional literature are the survival of the unfittest theme, the picaresque theme, and the reversal of fortune theme. These themes are also found frequently in modern juvenile literature as well. Whether **implicit** (suggested) or **explicit** (stated), the reader should immediately recognize these common themes.

The **survival of the unfittest** theme appears in *Gulliver's Travels* and *Robinson Crusoe*, two books that were published in the 1700s for adults but have become classics for children. In the satire *Gulliver's Travels* and the religious writing *Robinson Crusoe*, Gulliver and Crusoe face many life-threatening situations; in reality they probably should not have survived. Yet, with the survival of the unfittest theme prevailing, they manage to endure.

The **picaresque** theme features a roguish character (*picaro* is Spanish for "rogue"). Typically lowborn but clever, the rogue wanders in and out of adventures at all social levels. Punctuated by broad humor and satire, the picaresque theme was nonetheless had the serious intent of ridiculing social elitism. Examples of picaresque novels are *Don Quixote* by Miguel de Cervantes, *Tom Jones* by Henry Fielding, and *Moll Flanders* by Daniel Defoe.

The **reversal of fortune** theme, which focuses on the changing circumstance of a character or characters, is a frequent feature of modern juvenile literature. *Heidi* is an example of a book in which the main character goes to live in the mountains with her grandfather, finds herself in the city with a foster family, and then goes back to the mountains with her friend to live with Grandfather. Not only is Heidi's fortune reversed, but also the fortune of her crippled friend is changed by the healing mountain air, fresh food, and proper exercise.

Style

Another criterion for evaluating juvenile fiction is the writing style of the author. There are many devices that the writer can employ to enhance the flow of the words, make the writing more appealing, and clarify the meaning. These stylistic devices include denotation, connotation, irony, humor, figurative language (similes, metaphors, personification), alliteration, consonance, assonance, onomatopoeia, rhythm, imagery, hyperbole, understatement, allusion, word play (pun), parody, and diction. All these stylistic devices appear in Homer Hickam Jr.'s autobiography *October Sky* (1999), the story of some West Virginia high school students who manage to launch their own rockets in the late 1950s and pursue their life dreams.

Denotation. The **denotation** of a word is its precise meaning. Denotation is evident throughout *October Sky*, which seems logical because as a scientist, Hickam would use accurate, clear descriptions and would say precisely what he means. Homer uses denotation when he describes Emily Sue's family and where they live:

> Emily Sue lived in a house built on the side of a nearly vertical mountain across the creek and not more than a hundred yards from Big Creek High School. Her father owned a big scrap yard in War [the name of a town], and her mother was the third-grade schoolteacher at War Elementary. (232)

Connotation. The **connotation** of a word is the impression or feeling a word gives beyond its exact meaning. Sometimes the reader must have some prior knowledge to understand the term. For example, Homer's statement that "Mr. Turner was a banty-rooster type of man" (94) gives a unique impression of Mr. Turner. However, a reader with no previous experience with a banty rooster may not get much insight into the character of the man.

Irony. **Irony** is the incongruity between what one expects and what actually happens. When Homer uses a telescope to try to look at his own town of Coalwood, he is unable to do so—an unexpected happening:

> I went back to the telescope and tried to use it to look at Coalwood, but discovered I couldn't focus it close enough. I thought how ironic it was that Jake's telescope could see stars a million light-years away, but not the town it was in. Maybe I was that way myself. I had a clear vision of my future in space, but the life I led in Coalwood sometimes seemed to blur. (162)

Humor. **Humor** is precise and exacting; it is *funny*! When Homer wears his Sunday shoes to the creek, his mother punishes him:

> For punishment, she dictated that the next week I had to go to church in my stocking feet. It didn't take long before everybody in town got wind of what I was going to have to do. I didn't disappoint, walking down the church aisle in my socks while everybody nudged their neighbor and snickered. The thing was, though, I had picked out the socks, and my big toe poked through a hole in one of them. Mom was mortified. Even the preacher couldn't keep a straight face. (49)

Figurative Language. **Figurative language** includes the use of similes, metaphors, and personification. It is a way of adding information and description to the writing and of encouraging the reader to think about the text. All the details are not "spoon fed" to the reader.

A **simile** is a description that uses *like, than,* or *as*. In describing Jake Mosby, the new junior engineer, Homer remarks, "'He's got more money than Carter's got little liver pills'" (145). Homer overhears a secretary tell some other women that "'He looks just like Henry Fonda'" (146). Homer's mother notes that on one occasion Jake is, "'drunk as Cooter Brown'" (146). This figurative language brings imagery to the mind of the reader, requires the reader to think, and adds information to the description.

Using a **metaphor** is calling something by a different name. Jake calls the *McDowell County Banner* "'a grocery-store rag'" (154). Homer calls the rocket fuel "rocket candy" because of its sweet odor (181). He also refers to a cord as "a thick electrical umbilical" (199).

Personification is giving human characteristics to inanimate objects. For instance, Homer states that the "big golden moon hovered overhead" (53). Later he says that "a shuttle car darted in, its crablike arms sweeping up the coal thrown out" (199).

Alliteration. Alliteration is the writer's use of repeated sounds. In Homer's description of riding the bus to school on a snowy morning, he uses the repetition of the *s* sound, certainly fitting for the *slippery, snowy season*:

> Cresting the top of Coalwood Mountain, we were faced with a steep, straight stretch followed by a series of curves that dipped and turned. Jack slipped into a low gear and we trundled slowly through them, coming out at a short straight stretch that bottomed out into a wide inside curve, a rocky cliff looming over it. (228)

Consonance. Consonance, like alliteration, is the repetition of sounds—in this case, consonant sounds. The short, staccato sound of the hard *c* builds tension when Homer reports that the mining town is about to experience change that may result in the loss of jobs and company housing for Coalwood residents: "In May, the company announced that its big new coal-preparation plant in Caretta was complete, and all the coal from both the Coalwood and Caretta mines would henceforth be loaded into coal cars over there" (148).

Assonance. Assonance is the repetition of vowel sounds. The Rocket Boys work to build a blockhouse for protection while they watch their rocket launchings. They chant as they work. The use of similar vowel sounds (and final consonant sounds) is necessary for the chant's rhyming pattern:

> "I'm not the carpenter or the carpenter's son," he chanted as we sawed and drove nails, "but I'll do the carpentryin' until the carpenter comes."

> "Anybody here ever pour concrete?" I asked the group.

> "I'm not the concrete pourer or the concrete pourer's son . . . ." came back the cheerful chorus of replies. (139–140)

The school fight song also uses assonance: "On, on, green and white . . . . We are right for the fight tonight! Hold that ball and hit that line, every Big Creek star will shine. We'll fight, fight, fight for the green and white" (133–134).

Onomatopoeia. Onomatopoeia is a stylistic device in which the word that the writer uses imitates the sound. Cartoons often use onomatopoeic words like *pow, bop, splat,* and *pop* in their sound effects; sometimes the words even appear on the screen.

October Sky contains many instances of onomatopoeia. For instance, Homer wonders if *Sputnik* will "zip along or dawdle" and notes that his father "plopped on his hat" (37). Later, Homer remarks that Roy Lee growled an "'Ughhhh'" (133) and that his father's "door banged open and I heard him thumping down the stairs . . . . At the bottom of the stairs he started to cough, a racking, deep, wet hack (54).

Rhythm. The **rhythm**, or flow or cadence, of the words can help create a **mood**, or feeling, in the reader. When Homer and the Rocket Boys attempt to launch their first rocket, the sentences and thoughts that follow the "blast off" are short and choppy—almost staccato—evoking the tension and excitement the boys felt. These brief sentences and concise thoughts are in marked contrast to Hickam's typical style of longer, more descriptive sentences.

> Wooden splinters whistled past my ears. Big clunks of the fence arced into the sky. Burning debris fell with a clatter. A thunderous echo rumbled back from the surrounding hollows. Dogs up and down the valley barked and house lights came on, one by one. People came out and huddled on their front porches. (45)

The reader senses the tension subsiding when Hickam returns to his more usual style of longer, less stressful sentences:

Later, I would hear that a lot of them were wondering if the mine had blown up or maybe the Russians had attacked. At that moment, I wasn't thinking about anything except a big orange circle that seemed to be hovering in front of my eyes. When I regained some sensibility and my vision started to come back, the circle diminished and I started to look around. (45)

Imagery. Imagery is a description of the smells, feelings, sounds, or sights of a person, place, thing, or event. Hickam employs imagery to describe many of the places and events surrounding the activities of the Rocket Boys. Particularly important are his descriptions of the town of Coalwood and how the town appeals to the many senses of its inhabitants:

> Every weekday, and even on Saturday when times were good, I could watch the black coal cars rolling beneath the tipple to receive their massive loads and then smoke-spouting locomotives straining to pull them away. All through the day, the heavy thump of the locomotives' steam pistons thundered down our narrow valleys, the town shaking to the crescendo of grinding steel as the great trains accelerated. Clouds of coal dust rose from the open cars, invading everything, seeping through windows and creeping under doors. Throughout my childhood, when I raised my blanket in the morning, I saw a black, sparkling powder float off it. My socks were always black with coal dirt when I took my shoes off at night. (2)

Hickam's description of Buck, a football player, employs the senses of seeing, smelling, hearing, and feeling:

> "You really are a little sister, ain't you?" He pulled his face in close to us, his chin prickly with whiskers. There was a brown chewing-tobacco stain in the lower left corner of his mouth. I could smell its sweetness on his breath. (93)

Hyperbole. A **hyperbole** is an exaggeration. Hickam makes use of many of these in *October Sky*. Here is one example: "There was. . .a huge flash in the Hickams' yard and a sound like God Himself had clapped his hands" (Hickam, 44). Another exaggeration

occurs when Homer found out that the Russians had sent the dog Laika into space. Homer begins to consider the size of his dog, Poteet:

> Mom saw me and came outside. "What are you doing to that dog?"
>
> "I just wondered how big a rocket it would take to put her into orbit."
>
> "If she don't stop peeing on my rosebushes, she's going into orbit, won't need any rocket," Mom said. (40)

Understatement. Whereas a hyperbole exaggerates or embellishes to the maximum, an **understatement** is a comment that minimizes. For example, Homer remarks that "I did as I was told with the enthusiasm of a prisoner going to his own beheading" (48). Dreaming about the girl he secretly loves, Homer says, "'I wonder if I crawled over there and kissed her feet if she'd pet me on the head?'" (29).

Allusion. An **allusion** is a reference to a historical, literary, or otherwise generally familiar character event that helps make an idea understandable. Hickam employs this device when he refers to the family pets with the names Daisy Mae (a character in a comic strip popular in the 1950s) and Lucifer (another name for the devil). The pet's names give the readers a hint of the "characters" of the animals. Homer mentions that he "got barely a glimpse of J. Fred Muggs" on the *Today Show* before a snowball hit the window. The allusion to the chimpanzee cohost of the morning television show that began in the late 1950s helps set the time frame of the upcoming events of the story.

Word Play. Hickam makes use of a **word play**, or a pun, when he describes Homer losing a wheel off his wheelbarrow and telling his mother "that I'd spotted some great flower dirt up in the mountains and would've brought Mom some home with me 'if this blame ol' 'wheelbare' hadn't fallen apart!'" (47).

Parody. A **parody** is an imitation of something else. While the Rocket Boys work, they mimic singers of the time:

> We went through the parts we could remember of "Be-Bop-a-Lulu," "The Great Pretender,"

"Blueberry Hill," and "That'll Be the Day." . . . Roy Lee . . . gave us a solo rendition of the Everly Brothers' "All I Have to Do Is Dream" (139)

At another point in *October Sky*, the principal announces that the football team will not be able to compete for the year and that there will be a concentrated curriculum and more homework than ever. The principal calls the cheerleaders to the front and tries to make the occasion into a happy pep rally—a parody.

Diction. Diction is the language of the people. Hickam frequently employs diction as he informs the reader of the words of the people of Coalwood.

"We ought to just shoot that damn Sputnikker down." There was a pause while the men all thoughtfully spat tobacco juice into their paper cups, and then one of them said, "Well, I'll tell you who we oughta shoot. Makes me madder'n fire"—he pronounced the word as if it rhymed with tar—"them damn people up in Charleston who's tryin' to cheat Big Creek out of the state champs. I'd like to warp them upside the head." (32)

Homer's mother states that his dad "'would have a hissy'" (51), and Roy Lee tells Homer to "'Have at it'" (37) when Homer says he plans to build a rocket. Quentin, unlike most of the residents of the West Virginia town, speaks in his own dialect: "'O'Dell,'" Quentin replied, in all sincerity, "'I'm worried that your insatiable cupidity will ultimately prove to be something less than a virtue for our club'" (105).

Symbolism

Symbolism is the use of one person, place, or thing to represent another. A common symbol in juvenile literature is the loss of an animal to represent the death of childhood; this symbol appears in *Old Yeller* (Gipson 1956), *The Yearling* (Rawlings 1938), *The Biggest Bear* (Ward 1952), and *Where the Red Fern Grows* (Rawls 1961/1976).

Authenticity

An essential element in juvenile books is **authenticity**. Even though the juvenile book might be fiction,

it is essential that the elements of the book be believable and convincing. This means that the components (setting, characters, diction, details) must be accurate for the time and place—or at least believable to the reader. A story may, for example, take place on the planet Mars, but as long as the facts, setting, and characters are valid, the story meets one criterion of good literature.

Summary

Juvenile fiction can be categorized as modern or traditional fiction. Under each of these broad categories are several types of literature. For instance, traditional literature includes parables, fables, fairy tales, folktales, noodlehead tales, myths, and legends; modern fiction includes novels, romance, confession, and Menippean satire.

One important element of fiction is the plot and its order (chronological, flashback, foreshadowing); conflict; pattern (suspense, cliffhanger, foreshadowing, sensationalism, climax, denouement); and structure. Another important element is the **setting** (the time and place), which may be one of two types: backdrop (figurative) or integral (literal).

Character revelation is one of the necessary elements of a good juvenile novel. There are many ways to reveal the character. Most authors use more than one method. The characters may be round or flat, dynamic or static. The characters, however, should not be stereotypical.

The theme may be implicit or explicit. The three main types of theme in children's literature are survival of the unfittest, picaresque, and reversal of fortune.

One of the essential elements in good writing is the use of stylistic devices. Some of the common stylistic devices used in good juvenile books are denotation, connotation, irony, humor, figurative language (similes and metaphors), personification, alliteration, consonance, assonance, onomatopoeia, rhythm, imagery, hyperbole, understatement, allusion, word play, parody, diction, symbolism, and authenticity.

Literary Terms

Apostrophe. The direct address of someone or something that is not present. Many odes begin with an address to the person or object to which the ode is written to. For instance, Keats's "Ode on a Grecian Urn" begins, "Thou still unravish'd bride of quietness."

Bathos. Deliberate anticlimax to make a definite point or draw attention to a falseness. Perhaps the most famous example is from Alexander Pope's "Rape of the Lock": "Here thou, great Anna! whom three realms obey, Dost sometimes counsel take— and sometimes tea."

Enjambment. The running on of the sense and structure of one line of poetry into the next. Usually, the endings of lines are rhymed, so there is an end stop. In more modern poetry, without rhyme, run-on lines often occur to give a speedier flow, the sound of the speaking voice, or a conversational tone.

Oxymoron. A form of paradox in which contradictory words are used next to each other; for example, "painful pleasure" and "sweet sorrow."

Paradox. A situation, action, or feeling that appears to be contradictory but on inspection turns out to be true or at least make sense. "The pen is mightier than the sword" at first glance is a contradiction of reality. One can hardly die by being stabbed by a pen, but in the larger worldview, the words of men, such as death warrants and legislation granting acts of war, do kill.

Pun. A play on words, often for humorous or sarcastic effect. Many of Shakespeare's comedies draw on punning.

Sarcasm. Harsh verbal irony. It has been termed the "lowest form of wit" but can be used to good effect in the tone of a poem.

Syntax. The ordering of words into a particular pattern.

Tone. The voice or attitude of the speaker. Remember that the voice need not be that of the poet. A poet often adopts a particular tone for a purpose. The reader's task is to determine whether the tone is angry, sad, conversational, abrupt, wheedling, cynical, affected, satiric, or something else.

Skill Three

Identify and Apply Professional Guidelines for Selecting Multicultural Literature

Literature for children is a window through which to view the world. For this reason, children's literature that

is truthful will reflect the diversity of the world's peoples—young and old, rich and poor, male and female. According to Denise Ann Finazzo (1997), guidelines for selecting literature should ensure that the content enables the reader to recognize

- the likenesses and differences of various groups;
- the contributions of all citizens of the Earth;
- the sense of pride that all people have as members of a family, a community, and a world;
- the need to understand ourselves and others; and
- the opportunity that words can give us to view others and ourselves realistically and objectively.

The oral tradition of the many cultures of the world is rich. With the advent of moveable type, more of the fables, fairy tales, parables, folktales, and myths became available in print. Researching the origin of this traditional literature reveals the varied cultures of the world and the many variations on each tale. In China, for example, Cinderella's slipper is of fur, not glass, and Red Riding Hood is Lon Po Po. Other stories are just as culture specific but are often still recognizable as variants.

Multiculturalism and Cultural Pluralism

Their Impact on Society and Children's Literature. According to Finazzo (1997), **cultural pluralism** "recognizes that in diversity lies strength and in acceptance of different races, ethnicities, languages, and cultures [lies] understanding and growth" (00). **Multiculturalism**, by contrast, "speaks to the issue of many cultures combining to form a better society" (00).

Multiculturalism reflects both assimilationism and pluralism. **Assimilationism** is a view that promotes a "national culture" and considers microcultures as deficient until they become part of the national culture. **Pluralism** suggests that a functional society should recognize and accept microcultures as they are (Finazzo 1997). The teacher who subscribes to multiculturalism combines some elements of both pluralism and assimilationism into the curriculum and does not take extreme or radical stands on either issue.

Finazzo (1997) suggests that an educator promotes multiculturalism in the classroom by emphasizing

- the diversity in American culture;
- the influence of cultures on society;

- the many various cultures in the world; and

- the origins of rhymes, stories, games, and riddles.

Children's literature of the current era contains ample evidence of stories, games, and riddles from many cultures and has begun to explore the origins of those rhymes, stories, games, and riddles. The variety of books and materials available each year is beginning to represent the many cultures of the world.

The Image of African Americans in American Children's Literature. Children's books often reflect the social norms of their times. For instance, most senior adults in America can remember only three main children's books printed before the 1940s with African Americans as main characters. (Perhaps that is evidence of the way that the African American was often overlooked by society.) The various editions of those three books—*Uncle Remus Stories* (1883), *Little Black Sambo* (1899), and *Epaminondas and His Auntie* (1907, 1938)—did not always present the main characters in a favorable light. The "happy slave" image of Uncle Remus, the derogatory name of Sambo for the character in the book with the same title, the actions of Epaminondas suggesting that the character does "not have the sense you was born with," and the stereotyping in all three could create an unfavorable image of the African American for the young reader and listener. These books clearly promoted prejudice; no books with African Americans as positive role models existed at the time.

A few books of the late 1940s dared to break the mold. *Two Is a Team* (1945) by Lorraine and Jerrold Beim shows two boys playing together. The two children are almost identical in size, facial features, interests, and even hair styles; they are different, however, in that one of the boys is "shaded" a somewhat darker color than the other. This book, in particular, illustrates the idea that people are the same inside even though they might be different in color outside. Another book with that message is *Bright April* (1946), by Marguerite de Angeli. April is a member of a Brownie troop who, like the two boys in Beim's book, is almost identical in needs, interests, and physical appearance to the other girls in the troop. April's skin, however, is darker. Although both books focus on the similarities among all people, De Angeli also refers to some of the racial problems of the era.

A book for older readers, *Call Me Charley* (1945) by Jesse Jackson, shows the prejudice of the time and depicts the discrimination that Charley encounters from his peers and from adults. Charley's quiet resignation and his father's acceptance of their lot are often points of discussion among students today.

During the 1950s, "the focus was on racial balance and institutional change" (Finazzo 1997, 28), and children's books of that era often reflect those interests in balance and change. Books with African Americans as main characters and with interactions among African American and white characters became more common. Charming picture books portraying but never mentioning color began appearing for the youngest children. Some of the juvenile literature of the 1950s faces the controversy head-on from the African American point of view. Yet all too often authors resolve the terror and humiliation of racism too quickly and too easily (Arbuthnot 1964).

By the 1960s, most schools began to acknowledge the differences among people and the existence of distinct minority and ethnic experiences, literatures, histories, and traditions. The view of America as a melting pot was beginning to change for some people to the view of America as a salad bowl. Change came slowly, however. In a 1965 *Saturday Review* article, Nancy Larrick expressed her fear that even though the curriculum was changing, the students were still experiencing the "All-White World of Children's Books."

Even though more books with African Americans as main characters were appearing on children's book shelves by the mid-1960s, the words often did not indicate the race of the characters. For example, The Snowy Day (Keats 1962), Roosevelt Grady (Shotwell 1963), and Mississippi Possum (Miles 1965) received criticism "for 'whitewashing' blacks and attempting to make everyone the same" (Huck et al. 1993, 80). By contrast, Stevie (Steptoe 1969) "captured something of the special pride of the black experience in children's literature" (Huck et al. 1993, 80).

Books published after the sixties, like *Shawn Goes to School* (Breinburg 1974) and *Cornrows* (Yarbrough 1979), depict the uniqueness of the African American culture. Characters in these books are individuals; their facial features and the color of their skin emphasize their distinctiveness. Instead of trying to make all the characters look alike except for "shading," the books encourage pride in self and family.

Teaching Activities for the Elementary Classroom. Dolores B. Malcolm, president of the International Reading Association (IRA) in the late 1990s, stated, "Only through the acceptance of the presence of 'all' will the true concept of pluralism be realized . . . . Every culture has a heritage, and all children need to know and respect their own heritage and that of other people" (Micklos 1995, 8). Teachers can heighten students' appreciation for the importance of cultural pluralism—as opposed to separatism or elitism—using activities like the following:

1. Give students the opportunity to look at a situation through several viewpoints. *Faithful Elephants* (Tsuchiya 1988) requires the reader to consider war through its impact on animals, particularly the animals in Japan. *Sadako and the Thousand Paper Cranes* (Coerr 1977) enables the reader to consider war through the eyes of an innocent child. *Maniac Magee* (Spinelli 1990) asks the reader to consider prejudice in America through a child's eyes.

2. Invite members of the community to share their diverse backgrounds.

3. Establish a cooperative work environment in the classroom and the schools.

4. Explore the history of rhymes, riddles, superstitions ("unlucky 13"), customs, symbols (yule logs, menorahs), chants, songs ("Star-Spangled Banner"), foods, dances, and games.

5. Identify authors who present diverse cultures, like the Cuban writer Carmen Deedy.

6. Read books about various cultures, such as the southern African American community in *Roll of Thunder, Hear My Cry* (Taylor 1976).

7. Explore various family organizations.

8. Compare and contrast the "melting pot" view with the "salad bowl" view of American society.

9. Show successful individuals from various cultural groups.

10. Experiment with writing Haiku (an ancient Japanese verse form), make origami cranes after reading *Sadako and the Thousand Paper Cranes* (Coerr 1977), and experiment with rope rhymes after reading Eloise Greenfield's poem "Rope Rhyme."

Exceptionalities

Schools have progressed from ignoring children with special needs, to isolating children with special needs in special schools, to providing separate classrooms for exceptional students within the public schools, to mainstreaming the students into the classrooms, and finally to including those with exceptionalities into the "regular" class. Because biases and prejudices sometimes exist as a result of or even before this inclusion, teachers must help construct a working environment that meets each student's basic needs, including a feeling of belonging, a feeling of safety, and a place where each student feels loved and accepted.

Children's literature can show others how it feels to be different in some way and can emphasize that everyone has the same basic needs. For instance, *Crow Boy* (Yashima 1955) helps the students to see what it is like to be excluded because of being "different." *The Flunking of Joshua T. Bates* (Shreve 1984) explores the impact that failing a class has on a student. *Discoveries*, by Anita Price Davis and Katharine Slemenda, provides numerous biographical sketches of successful people who are deaf. The book establishes effective role models, discourages labeling, and presents individuals who have overcome obstacles in their lives.

Many activities are useful for encouraging the acceptance of others. For instance, teachers can have students role-play situations in which they feel different or in which they encounter another who feels different or left out of the activities. The students can model their responses and discuss their feelings when they respond. Teachers should encourage all students to express worries, fears, and concerns. The teacher could work toward a constructivist classroom.

Bibliotherapy—giving the right book to the right child at the right time, or treating problems with books—is particularly helpful in constructing a cooperative classroom. Students might read and discuss such books as *I Have a Sister; My Sister Is Deaf* (Peterson 1977), about deafness, and *The Summer of the Swans* (Byars 1970), about academic problems. These books and others can serve as springboards for discussions of exceptionalities. *The Bookfinder* (Dreyer 1977) is a particularly good source for locating books for bibliotherapy on individual topics.

Multicultural Poems and Poets. Although the poetry of Eloise Greenfield, Nikki Giovanni, Gwendolyn Brooks, and Lee Bennet Hopkins has not yet lasted a century, the quality of their works ensures that their poems will become classics. Their poems (and prose) honor and make others aware of their rich African American heritage.

In Daddy's Arms I Am Tall: African Americans Celebrating Fathers edited by Javaka Steptoe (1997) is a recent Coretta Scott King Award winner. The book of poetry emphasizes the African American experience. Javaka Steptoe's father was author/illustrator John Steptoe. The multicultural literature of father and son are important contributions to children's literature.

Teachers must make certain to include poetry of all cultures in their classrooms. Cynthia Rylant has written many poems on growing up in the Appalachian Mountains. Charlotte Pomerantz writes about her winters in Puerto Rico. Louise Bennett writes of Jamaica. The Japanese Haiku is a type of poetry specific to another culture. A Haiku poem has three lines with 6, 7, and 5 syllables, respectively. The teacher and students should research other poems about various cultures and experiences.

The twenty-first century promises to provide quality juvenile poetry and literature. Which poems will become classics, only time will tell (Davis 2000).

Sexism

Teaching Activities and Guidelines to Combat Sexism. Despite Title IX and much publicity, students—and adults—sometimes witness sex discrimination. To keep students from taking these actions for granted, it is often helpful to raise their consciousness of the existence of sexism in American society.

Role playing, having students look at a situation through several viewpoints, inviting successful members of the community of both sexes to visit the classroom, establishing a cooperative work environment in the classroom, and exploring the contributions of males and females in history are all useful activities to heighten students' awareness of sexism—whether subtle or blatant. Books like *Focus on Women* (Davis and Selvidge 1995) provide activities, biographical sketches, and insight into the contributions of women to America.

Exploring the contributions of individual women to society is another valuable tool in presenting women favorably. *Harriet Quimby: America's First Lady of the Air (An Intermediate Biography*; Davis and Hall 1998) is such a book. When coupled with the suggested activities in *Harriet Quimby: America's First Lady of the Air (An Activity Book for Children*; Davis and Hall 1993), the class can engage in some lively discussions and learning experiences. Using children's books as bibliotherapy may be helpful also, if the books themselves are not sexually biased.

Sexism in Children's Books. Are children's books biased? How do children's books themselves—particularly Caldecott Award–winning books—treat males and females? Do Caldecott-winning books, for example, present males and females in equal numbers? Has the presentation of males and females changed since the 1970s? Has sexism in children's literature abated?

In the early 1970s, Suzanne Czaplinski conducted a baseline study of picture books that won the Caldecott Award between 1940 and 1971, focusing on sex inequalities in both text and pictures. She published her findings in *Sexism in Award Winning Picture Books* (1972). The researcher counted each appearance of a male or female in the text and in the pictures and calculated the proportion of males and females in text. Among Czaplinski's findings were that males outnumbered females both in the text (65 percent to 35 percent) and in the pictures (63 percent to 37 percent). Surprisingly enough, however, the proportion of females in the books decreased from 1950 (51 percent) through the 1960s (23 percent).

To find out if there had been change since Czaplinski's study, Davis and McDaniel (1999), with the help of their students, conducted their own study. They predicted that females would appear more frequently in Caldecott winners after 1972. After all, that was the year Congress passed Title IX as a federal law to promote (if not guarantee) sex equity in education. Furthermore, sex discrimination was an emerging political issue in American life, feminism was on the rise, publishers were issuing guidelines for sex-neutral language, and women were outpacing men in college (and professional) school admissions, and academics. From Carol Gilligan (1982) to Deborah Tannen (1991) women were raising the sex equity banner. The United States Supreme Court had even required male military bastions like the Virginia Military Institute and The Citadel to accept women applicants. Surely, Caldecott winners from 1972 through 1997 would reflect a quarter century of social change.

When Davis, McDaniel, and their students compared their analyses of the contemporary period to the earlier period analyzed by Czaplinski, they discovered the following:

- In the text of Caldecott winners from 1972 through 1997, there were 803 instances of male appearances versus 550 instances of female appearances. This meant that 61 percent of the character appearances mentioned in text were male compared with 39 percent females. Czaplinski's earlier study had found 65 percent males compared with 35 percent females.

- In the pictures of Caldecott winners from 1972 through 1997, there were 1,426 instances of male appearances compared with 771 instances of female appearances. Males made up 65 percent of the instances of characters portrayed through pictures; females made up 35 percent of the instances of characters portrayed through pictures. Czaplinski's study had found 63 percent of the instances of character appearances in pictures in Caldecott winners had been males. This meant that by 1997, the percentage of females in pictures had dropped from 37 percent to 35 percent.

- Thirty-nine percent of the instances of characters appearing in texts of Caldecott winners were females in the decade of the 1990s, a slight decrease from the 1980s.

- The proportion of females appearing in texts of Caldecott winners never exceeded that of the decade of the 1950s, when 51 percent of the characters were females.

- The proportion of females appearing in pictures in Caldecott winners rose steadily from a low in the 1960s of 19 percent, to 31 percent in the 1970s, to a high of 40 percent in the 1980s, and then dropped back to 39 percent in the 1990s.

There were many more statistical conclusions, but the ones above generated the most interest.

Although the gains for females in the 1980s were encouraging, Davis, McDaniel, and their students were perplexed that the decade of the 1950s remained the golden era for females in the text of Caldecott winners, and they were concerned about the decrease in the percentage of females in the Caldecott-winning books of the 1990s. The findings showed that in some ways, sex bias in children's literature has not abated. Yet the mere awareness of this fact can raise people's consciousness and serve a purpose. The empowered teacher can help make students aware of sex bias, modify the curriculum, and teach acceptance of others (Davis and McDaniel 1999).

Summary

Children's literature that is truthful reflects the diversity of the nation's and the world's peoples. Children's books in America have changed through the years. The image of the African American in children's books has reflected the society, which has undergone a series of changes from ignoring and deprecating, to "whitewashing," to interacting, to recognizing as unique.

Cultural pluralism advocates the acceptance of differences and promotes the strength that comes from diversity. Multiculturalism advocates many cultures combining to form a better society and reflects both assimilationism (which supports the "national" culture) and pluralism (which advocates the recognition and acceptance of diverse groups). Teachers, literature, and activities are instrumental in helping students become more aware of the importance of cultural pluralism, as opposed to separatism and elitism.

Schools have progressed from ignoring children with special needs, to isolating them in special schools, to providing separate classrooms for exceptional students within the public schools, to mainstreaming the students into the classrooms, and finally to including those with exceptionalities into the "regular" class. Teachers must help construct a working environment that meets all students' basic needs, including a feeling of belonging.

Czaplinski conducted a 1972 study of Caldecott-winning books published from 1940 through 1971; she found that males outnumbered females both in the text (65 percent to 35 percent) and in the pictures (63 percent to 37 percent). Surprisingly, however, the proportion of females in the award-winning books decreased from 1950 (51 percent) through the 1960s (23 percent).

McDaniel, Davis, and their students attempted to replicate Czaplinski's study in the 1990s. Although the gains for females in the 1980s were encouraging, the class was perplexed that the decade of the 1950s remained the golden era for females in the text of Caldecott winners. They were concerned about the decrease in the percentage of females in the Caldecott-winning books of the 1990s (Davis and McDaniel 1999). The research project proved to be a valuable experience. The findings showed the class, McDaniel, and Davis that in some ways, sex bias in children's literature has not abated. Yet the awareness of this fact can raise one's consciousness and serve a purpose.

The empowered teacher must work to heighten students' awareness of prejudice and discrimination, modify the curriculum, bring about multiculturalism, and teach acceptance of others: a tall order (Davis 2000).

Skill Four

Identify Appropriate Techniques for Encouraging Students to Respond to Literature in a Variety of Ways

Reading literature requires students to make responses to the print.

Eight Comprehension Strategies. There are eight comprehension strategies that require students to respond to literature and will aid in their understanding what they read (Tompkins 2006):

Predicting. Requires readers to make guesses about what will happen; they can then confirm or decide whether their predictions were accurate or not.

Connecting. Requires students to relate the reading to their own lives, to the world, and to other materials.

Visualizing. Requires students to create mental images of the information that they are reading.

Questioning. Requires students to answer literal, interpretive, critical, and creative questions that they ask themselves or that their teachers might ask.

Identifying. Requires recognizing the major points of information as they read.

Summarizing. Requires restating the major points in concise statements, writing summaries, and/or depicting the story through book reports, dioramas, posters, plays, and other forms of expression.

Monitoring. Performed by the teachers and the students themselves to ensure that young readers understand what they are reading. An important part of helping students to monitor their understanding is helping them use the appropriate techniques (decoding, context clues, picture clues, sight words, etc.) if they are having difficulty.

Evaluating. The final stage of reading response. Evaluation questions are in the highest level of Bloom's *Taxonomy*. Ideally, the students will also evaluate their reading experience.

Competency 5: Knowledge of Writing

Ten test items relate to this competency.

Skill One

Demonstrate Knowledge of the Developmental Stages of Writing

For years, educators believed that reading preceded writing in the development of literacy. This belief has recently changed.

Stages in Writing Development

Emergent literacy research indicates that learning to write is an important part in a child's learning to read.

As children begin to name letters and read print, they also begin to write letters and words. Writing development seems to occur at about the same time as reading development—not afterward, as traditional reading readiness assumed. (Open Court Publishing Company has long recognized and encouraged this synonymous development in its reading programs.) Whole language seeks to integrate the language arts rather than sequencing them. Just as change has marked educators' beliefs about reading instruction and the way that reading develops, change has also marked the methods and philosophies behind the teaching of writing in the schools.

Children seem to progress through certain stages in their writing. Although many authorities have examined the stages in writing development, Alexander Luria presents the most thoroughly elaborated model (Klein 1985; Davis 2004). He cautions, however, that the stages are not entirely a function of age. Luria explains that it is not uncommon to find children from 3 to 6 years old who are the same age but are two to three stages apart in their writing. He also notes that children do not advance systematically through the stages. At times, a child may regress or "zigzag." At other times, the child may appear to remain at one level without progression or regression. Here is a summary of Luria's stages in writing:

Stage 1. The undifferentiated stage from ages 3 to 5 is a period that Luria defines as a prewriting or preinstrumental period. The child does not distinguish between marks written on a page. The marks (writing) seem merely random to the child and do not help the child recall information.

Stage 2. The differentiated stage from about age 4 is when the child intentionally builds a relationship between sounds and written expression. For instance, the child represents short words or short phrases with shorter marks and longer words, phrases, or sentences with longer marks. The child might use dark marks to help remember a sentence like "The sky was dark." Making such marks is an example of mnemonics, or associating symbols with information.

Stage 3. The pictographic stage from ages 4 to 6 is the period that Klein (1985) says is "the most important stage in the development of the child's perception of writing-as-a-conceptual-act."

Skill Two

Demonstrate Knowledge of the Writing Process

Skill Three

Distinguish Between Revising and Editing

Teachers in the early 1970s were very concerned with spelling and punctuation in students' papers. The teacher did all the "correcting" and watched carefully for grammatical, spelling, and punctuation errors. In the late 1970s, writing "experts" denounced students' compositions as being too dull. The schools began to foster creative writing and encouraged teachers to provide opportunities for creative writing each week. However, many teachers began to view the creative writing as lacking in structure. **Process writing** has since become the "buzz" word in writing. With process writing, students engage in several activities (Noyce and Christie, 1989):

Prewriting stage. During the first stage in the writing process, the students begin to collect information for the writing that they will do.

Composing or writing stage. The class resembles a laboratory. Students may consult with one another and use various books and materials to construct their papers. At this stage, the student-writers do not worry about spelling and mechanics.

Revising stage. Writers polish and improve their compositions.

Editing/evaluation/postwriting stage. Students read and correct their own writing and the works of others. The teacher does not have to do all the evaluating.

Rewrite stage. After their self-evaluations and after their classmates and teachers share praise and constructive criticisms, including spelling and punctuation, the students rewrite their compositions.

In some classes the students **publish** their own works and even have an **author's chair** from which the writers can tell some things about themselves, discuss their writing process, and read their compositions aloud (Noyce and Christie 1989). According to research, the most effective writing process includes at least the prewriting, composing, revising, and editing/evaluation/postwriting stages (Bennett 1987).

The way you speak can vary depending on whom you are speaking to—just as what you wear can vary depending on whom you are going to see. More commonly, language varies according to geographic region, ethnic group, social class, and educational level. The language used in U.S. schools is Standard American English. This formal language (dialect) is the language in texts, newspapers, magazines, and the news programs on television.

There are other forms of the English language beside Standard American English. Some variations are the forms spoken in Appalachia, in urban ghettos, and by Mexican Americans, particularly in the southwest. In all these variations, the syntax, phonology, and semantics differ from Standard American English. When instructing students who do not speak the standard dialect, teachers should not try to replace the culture or the language with Standard American English; the goal of school is to add Standard American English to students' language registers (Tompkins 2006).

Writing Standard American English requires the use of certain mechanics or conventions. Using the conventions in capitalization, punctuation, spellings, and formatting, among others, is a courtesy to readers of the written language (Tompkins 2006). With the Language Experience Approach, the teacher attempts to facilitate the students' language development through the use of experiences, rather than printed material alone. After the class participates in an experience or event, the students, as a group, record what happened (often with the help of the teacher). The teacher writes exactly what the students say—even if they do not use Standard American English. The idea is to enable each student to see that

- what I say, I can write;
- what I can write, I can read; and
- what others write, I can read (Davis 2004).

The teacher may talk at this time about alternative ways to say what the students do not say in Standard American English.

In summary, many forms of language exist, but the school should not try to eradicate the culture or the language of its students.

Skill Four
Identify Characteristics of the Modes of Writing

Writing serves many different functions. The main functions, however, are to narrate, to describe, to explain, and to persuade. Students need to be aware of each of these types of literature. In any event, the four categories are neither exhaustive nor mutually exclusive.

The **narrative** is a story or an account. It may recount an incident or a series of incidents. The account may be autobiographical to make a point, as in Orwell's short story "Shooting an Elephant." The narrative may be fiction or nonfiction.

The purpose of **descriptive** writing is to provide information about a person, place, or thing. Descriptive writing can be fiction or nonfiction. E. B. White uses description when he relates what the barn is like in *Charlotte's Web* (1952); the book itself, however, is fiction. Realtors use descriptive writing when they advertise a house in a local newspaper; the general public expects the descriptions of events in the local paper to be factual.

The purpose of **expository** writing is to explain and clarify ideas. Students are probably most familiar with this type of writing. While the expository essay may have narrative elements, the storytelling or recounting aspect is minor and subservient to that of the explanation element. Expository writing is typically found in many textbooks; for instance, a textbook on how to operate a computer would likely be expository.

The purpose of **persuasive** writing is to convince the reader of something. Persuasive writing fills current magazines, and newspapers and permeates the World Wide Web. The writer may be trying to push a political candidate, to convince someone to vote for a zoning ordinance, or even to promote a diet plan. Persuasive writing usually presents a point, provides evidence, which may be factual or anecdotal, and supports the point. The structure may be very formal, with counterpositions and counterarguments. Whatever the organizational pattern, the writer's intent is to persuade readers of the validity of some claim. Nearly all essays have some element of persuasion.

Authors choose their form of writing not necessarily just to tell a story but to present an idea. Whether writers choose the narrative, descriptive, expository, or persuasive format, they have something on their minds that they want to convey to their readers. When readers analyze writing, they often seek first to determine the its form.

There are other types of writing, of course. For instance, **speculative** writing is so named because, as the Latin root suggests, it looks at ideas and explores them rather than merely explaining them, as expository writing does. The speculative essay might be considered meditative; it often makes one or more points, and the thesis may not be as obvious or clear-cut as that in an expository essay. The writer deals with ideas in an associative manner and plays with ideas in a looser structure than the writer might do in an expository format. This "flow" may even produce intercalary paragraphs, which present alternately a narrative of sorts and thoughtful responses to the recounted events.

Skill Five

Select the Appropriate Mode of Writing for a Variety of Occasions, Purposes, and Audiences

The writer must consider the audience, the occasion, and the purpose when choosing the writing mode.

The writer's responsibility is to write clearly, honestly, and cleanly for the reader's sake; the **audience** is very important. After all, writing would be pointless without readers.

Why write? Why add evidence, organize your ideas, or correct bad grammar? The reason to do any of these things is that someone out there—an audience—needs to understand what you mean to say.

The teacher can designate an audience for students' writing. Knowing those who will read what their work, students can modify their writing to suit the intended readers. For instance, a fourth-grade teacher might suggest that the class take their compositions about a favorite animal to second graders and allow the younger children to read or listen to the works. The writers will realize that they need to use manuscript—not cursive—writing, to employ simple vocabulary, and to omit complex sentences when they write for their young audience.

The **occasion** helps to determine the elements of the writing. The language should fit the occasion; particular words may have certain effects: evoke sympathy or raise questions about an opposing point of view, for instance. The students and teacher might try to determine the likely effect on an audience of a writer's choice of a particular word or words.

The **purpose** helps to determine the format (narrative, expository, descriptive, persuasive) and the language of the writer. The students, for instance, might consider the appropriateness of written material for a specific purpose: a business letter, a communication with residents of a retirement center, or a thank-you note to parents. The teacher and students might try to identify persuasive techniques used by a writer in a passage.

In selecting the mode of writing and the content, the writer might ask the following:

- What would the audience need to know to believe you or to accept your position? Imagine someone you know (visualize her or him) listening to you declare your position or opinion and then saying, "Oh yeah? Prove it!"
- What evidence do you need to prove your idea to this skeptic?
- With what might the audience disagree?
- What common knowledge does the audience share with you?
- What information do you need to share with the audience?

The teacher might wish to have the students practice selecting the mode and the language by adapting forms, organizational strategies, and styles for different audiences and purposes.

Skill Six

Identify Elements and Appropriate Use of Rubrics to Assess Writing

A **rubric** is a checklist with point values. To construct a rubric, a teacher uses the lesson objectives. Students should receive an explanation of the rubric *before* starting to work on their writing assignment, and they can use the rubric as a guideline *while* they are preparing their writing assignment. The teacher can use the rubric to evaluate student work *after* the student has completed the assignment.

When teachers can provide clear, well-planned instructions and guidelines for activities, they can decrease student frustration. Rubrics can provide this valuable guidance. When teachers model what they expect and state clear objectives or goals for each assignment, students perform better. Accordingly, there should be a clear and obvious link between the assignment's goals and the students' achievement.

Competency 6: Knowledge and Use of Reading Assessment

Six skills are covered under this competency:

1. Identify measurement concepts, characteristics, and uses of norm-referenced, criterion-referenced, and performance-based assessments.

2. Identify oral and written methods for assessing student progress (e.g., informal reading inventories, fluency checks, think alouds, rubrics, running records, story retelling, portfolios).

3. Interpret assessment data (e.g., screening, progress monitoring, diagnostic) to guide instructional decisions.

4. Use individual student reading data to differentiate instruction.

5. Interpret a student's formal and informal assessment results to inform students and parents.

6. Evaluate the appropriateness (e.g., curriculum alignment, cultural bias) of assessment instruments and practices.

The two main types of assessment are formal and informal. Both have a place in the classroom, particularly in the reading class. The effective teacher understands the importance of ongoing assessment as an instructional tool for the classroom and uses both informal and formal assessment measures. There is never an occasion to group children permanently on the basis of one assessment—either formal or informal. Any grouping of students should come about after a consideration of *several* assessments, and the grouping should be flexible enough to consider individual differences among the students in each group.

Informal Assessment

Evaluation does not have to be expensive and purchased to be useful to the teacher and student alike. For instance, Clay (1985) developed a procedure for sampling the child's reading vocabulary and determining the extent of a child's print-related concepts. Her assessment checks whether children can find the title, show where to start reading a book, and locate the last page or the end of the book. As such, Clay's procedure is an informal way of **determining a child's readiness for reading** (Davis 2004).

Teachers can gain much valuable information by simply observing their students at work. Many school districts use a type of inventory/report card to inform adults in the home of the progress that the kindergartner or first grader is making. Long-time teachers usually develop, through trial and error, their own means of assessing the skills of students in their classes. Almost every book on teaching reading contains its own informal tests. The Southern Regional Education Board's Health and Human Services Commission (SREB 1994) cautions that assessment should be **ongoing** and **natural**. The commission has determined that **continual observation of the physical, social, emotional, and cognitive domains of students** by both parents and teachers is the most meaningful approach to assessing young children. To obtain a meaningful, complete view of a young child, the commission endorses portfolios of a child's progress and performance inventories rather than standardized test results. Similarly, letter grades and numeric grades are less likely to give a complete picture than narrative reports on the young child.

Teachers can also develop their own informal reading inventories. The purpose of these assessments is to collect meaningful information about what students can and cannot do. A **running record** is a way to assess students' word identification skills and fluency in oral reading. As the teacher listens to a student read a page, the teacher uses a copy of the page to mark each word the child mispronounces. The teacher will write the incorrect word over the printed word; draw a line through each word the child skips, and draw an arrow under repeated words.

If the student reads 95 percent of the words correctly, the book is easy for the child, or it is at the child's **independent level**. If the student reads 90 percent to 94 percent of the words correctly, the book is at the child's **instructional level**; this means the child can perform satisfactorily with help from the teacher. A book in which the student reads 89 percent or fewer words correctly is probably at the child's **frustration level**. In addition to assessing the student's reading skills, the teacher should ask some comprehension questions to be sure that the child understands (**comprehends**) the passage.

Asking a child to **retell** a story is another type of informal assessment. The ability to retell a story is an informal type of assessment that is useful to the teacher, parent, and—eventually—the child. Informal assessment measures can also include observations, journals, written drafts, and conversations.

The teacher may make **observations** for individual or group work. This method is very suitable for skills or for effective learning. Usually, the teacher makes a **checklist** of competencies, skills, or requirements and then uses the list to check off the ones a student or group displays. A teacher wishing to emphasize interviewing skills could devise a checklist that includes personal appearance, mannerisms, confidence, and addressing the questions asked. A teacher who wants to emphasize careful listening might observe a discussion with a checklist that includes paying attention, not interrupting, summarizing the ideas of other members of the group, and asking questions of others.

Advantages of checklists include the potential for capturing behaviors that cannot be accurately measured with a paper-and-pencil test, such as shooting free throws on the basketball court, following the correct sequence of steps in a science experiment, or including all important elements in a speech in class. One characteristic of a checklist that is both an advantage and a disadvantage is its structure, which provides consistency but inflexibility. An open-ended comment section at the end of a checklist can overcome this disadvantage.

Anecdotal records are helpful in some instances, such as capturing the process a group of students uses to solve a problem. This formative data can be useful during feedback to the group. Students can also be taught to write explanations of the procedures they use for their projects or science experiments. One advantage of an anecdotal record is that it can include all relevant information. Disadvantages include the amount of time necessary to complete the record and difficulty in assigning a grade. If the anecdotal record is used solely for feedback, no grade is necessary.

Portfolios are collections of students' best work. They can be used in any subject area where the teacher wants students to take more responsibility for planning, carrying out, and organizing their own learning. Like a portfolio created by an artist, model, or performer, a student portfolio provides a succinct picture of the child's achievements over a certain period. Portfolios may contain essays or articles written on paper, videotapes, multimedia presentations on computer disks, or a combination. Language arts teachers often use portfolios as a means of collecting the best samples of student writing over an entire year, and some teachers pass on the portfolios to the teacher next year to help in student assessment.

Teachers should provide or assist students in developing guidelines for what materials should go in their portfolios; it would be unrealistic to include every piece of work in one portfolio. Using portfolios requires the students to devise a means of evaluating their own work. A portfolio should not be a scrapbook for collecting handouts or work done by other individuals, but it can certainly include work by a group in which the student was a participant.

Some advantages of portfolios over testing are that they provide a clear picture of students' progress, they are not affected by one inferior test grade, and they help develop students' self-assessment skills.

One disadvantage is the amount of time required to teach students how to develop meaningful portfolios. However, the time is well spent if students learn valuable skills. Another concern is the amount of time teachers must spend to assess portfolios. However, as students become more proficient at self-assessment, the teacher can spend more time in coaching and advising students throughout the development of their portfolios. Another concern is that parents may not understand how the teacher will grade the portfolios. The effective teacher devises a system that the students and parents understand before work on the portfolios begins.

Through informal observations and through the use of inventories (formal and informal), teachers should determine the **learning styles** of their students. Student learning styles play an important role in determining classroom structure.

Formal Assessment

Formal measures may include teacher-made tests, district exams, and standardized tests.

Both formative and summative evaluations are part of effective teaching. **Formative evaluation** occurs during the process of learning when the teacher or the students monitor progress in obtaining outcomes and while it is still possible to modify instruction. **Summative evaluation** occurs at the end of a specific time or course of study. Usually, a summative evaluation applies a single grade to represent a student's performance.

The effective teacher uses a **variety of formal assessment techniques**. Teacher-made instruments are ideally developed at the same time as the planning of goals and outcomes, rather than at the last minute after the completion of the lessons. Carefully planned objectives and assessment instruments serve as lesson development guides for the teacher. Paper-and-pencil tests are the most common method for evaluating student progress.

Students in the classroom are diverse. The task of the teacher is to provide the best education possible to every individual. The students in a class may differ in culture, background, religion, economic level, social class, ethnic group, national origin, and learning style. They create within the classroom a microcosm reflective of American society at large.

The effective teacher appreciates human diversity. An empowered instructor recognizes how diversity in the classroom and the community can affect learning and creates a classroom environment in which everyone accepts and celebrates both the diversity and the uniqueness of individuals. In that environment, the teacher and the students view race, ethnicity, religion, national origin, learning style, and gender of learners as strengths that foster learning with and from each other.

Learning Diversity

Determining the learning styles of individuals and teaching to those styles transcends cultural boundaries and recognizes that all people have distinct learning preferences and tendencies. Furthermore, this approach acknowledges that all preferences and tendencies are equally valid and that each style of learning has strengths. The teacher who understands learning styles (auditory, visual, tactile, or kinesthetic) can validate all students in the class.

The obvious benefit of determining a student's learning style is not simply to cater to the learners' preferences or strengths; the significance is that once the teacher identifies strengths, the teacher can design instruction to teach students to use those strengths in situations that are not easy or natural. For example, students who are **tactile and kinesthetic** must often become responsible for their own learning; they must learn to become involved in lecture classes. Becoming involved means that they learn to take copious notes, participate in class discussions, ask questions, and answer questions posed by the teacher.

Visual learners must sit where they can see what's going on in class and where they can see the teacher and the board. They need opportunities to draw pictures, to diagram, to take good notes, to create mind maps, and to use flash cards. They must learn how to visualize abstract concepts, and they need opportunities to practice all these techniques. For visual learners who learn best by reading, teachers can provide adequate opportunities for them to read in class. All students need to learn specific note-taking methods as well as reading and comprehension strategies. They also need use supplemental readings, workbooks, and the library.

Auditory learners need to practice attention-directing activities. They can use audiocassettes as learning aids. They can learn to ask questions in class and to participate in class discussions. They must be taught how to summarize and paraphrase, especially how to state in their own words the concepts they are trying to master. They may need the teacher to repeat or to restate ideas. Auditory learners pay close attention to verbal cues, such as voice tone and inflection. Reciting what they have heard (or read) is an important strategy for auditory learners, as is finding someone to whom they can explain the information.

The teacher's goal should be to create a range of experiences and activities that embraces student diversity. Activities should make use of appropriate materials and resources that support a multicultural experience. While promoting and valuing the diverse cultures and linguistic backgrounds of the students, classroom experiences should maintain the equitable treatment of all students. Teachers should encourage (1) shared values and expectations that create a climate of mutual respect; (2) appropriate social behaviors that lead to acceptance, openness, and tolerance; and (3) a supportive climate of inquiry that helps students gain knowledge about the diversity of their school, families, and community.

Students who are not proficient in speaking English (limited English proficient, or LEP) require special consideration. The English language consists of many slang and multidefinitional words that can confuse students. To build their vocabulary, teachers need to employ such tactics as matching concrete pictures to vocabulary, rewording complex statements, simplifying instructions, and modeling correct vocabulary. It is important to remember that students learn to speak a language long before they are proficient at writing in that language.

Because multiculturalism and cultural diversity can be controversial issues with many sides to consider, a reasonable approach to diversity for the classroom teacher is to distinguish between cultural diversity and learning diversity and to focus on diversity in learning. This approach transcends cultural boundaries and recognizes that all people have distinct learning preferences and tendencies. Furthermore, this approach acknowledges that all preferences and tendencies are equally valid and that each style of learning has strengths. The teacher who understands learning styles can validate all students in the class.

Assessing Diverse Learners

The purpose of both formal and informal assessments in the classroom is to improve the instruction and the learning of the students—all the students. It is important for the teacher (1) to analyze and interpret the information gathered through informal and formal means and (2) to use test results professionally to help all students in the classroom to learn to the best of their ability.

The use of criterion-referenced, norm-referenced, performance-based, classroom, and authentic assessments is essential to giving the child, the teacher, and the parents a complete picture of the child and the child's progress.

Criterion-Referenced Tests. In **criterion-referenced tests (CRTs)**, the teacher attempts to measure each student against uniform objectives or criteria. CRTs allow the possibility that all students can score 100 percent because they understand the concepts being tested. Teacher-made tests should be criterion-referenced because the teacher should develop them to measure the achievement of predetermined outcomes for the course. If teachers have properly prepared lessons based on the outcomes and if students have mastered the outcomes, then scores should be high. This type of test is noncompetitive because students are not in competition with each other for a high score, and there is no limit to the number of students who can score well. Some commercially developed tests are criterion-referenced; however, most are norm-referenced.

Norm-Referenced Tests. The purpose of a **norm-referenced test (NRT)** is to compare the performance of groups of students. This type of test is competitive because a limited number of students can score well.

A plot of large numbers of NRT scores resembles a **bell-shaped curve**, with most scores clustering around the center and a few scores at each end. The **midpoint** is an average of data; therefore, by definition, half the population will score above average and half below average. The bell-shaped curve is a mathematical description of the results of tossing coins. As such, it represents the chance or normal distribution of skills, knowledge, or events across the general population. A survey of the height of sixth-grade boys will result in an average height, with half the boys above average and half below. There will be a very small number with heights far above average and a very small number with heights far below average; most heights will cluster around the average.

A **percentile score** (not to be confused with a percentage) is a way of reporting a student's NRT score; the percentile score indicates the percentage of the population whose scores fall at or below the student's score. For example, a group score at the eightieth percentile means that the group scored as well as or better than 80 percent of the students who took the test. A student with a score at the fiftieth percentile has an average score. Percentile scores rank students from highest to lowest. By themselves, percentile scores do not indicate how well the student has mastered the content objectives. **Raw scores** indicate how many questions the student answered correctly and are, therefore, useful in computing a percentage score.

A national test for biology would include objectives for the widest possible biology curriculum, for the broadest use of the test. Reported **normed scores** would enable schools to compare the performance of their students with the performance of students whom the test developers used as its norm group. The test would likely include more objectives than are in a particular school's curriculum; therefore, that school's students might score low in comparison to the norm group. A teacher must be very careful in selecting a norm-referenced test and should look for one with objectives that are the most congruent with the school's curriculum.

The teacher must also consider the test **reliability**, or whether the instrument will give consistent results with repeated measurements. A reliable bathroom scale,

for example, will give almost identical weights for the same person measured three times in a morning. An unreliable scale, however, may give weights that differ by 6 pounds. A teacher evaluates test reliability over time by giving the same, or almost the same, test to different groups of students. However, because many factors can affect reliability, teachers must be careful in evaluating test reliability.

Another aspect of a test that the teacher must carefully assess is the test's **validity**, or whether the test actually measures what it is supposed to measure. If students score low on a test because they could not understand the questions, the test is not valid because it measures reading ability instead of content knowledge. If students score low because the test covered material that was not taught, the test is not valid for that situation. A teacher assesses the validity of his or her own tests by examining the questions to see if they measure what was planned and taught in the classroom. **A test must be reliable before it can be valid.** However, measurements can be consistent without being valid. A scale can indicate identical weights for three weigh-ins of the same person during one morning but actually be 15 pounds in error. A history test may produce similar results each time the teacher administers it, but the test may not be a valid measure of what the teacher taught and what the students learned.

Tests should be both reliable and valid. If the test does not measure consistently, it cannot be accurate. If it does not measure what it is supposed to measure, then its reliability does not matter. Commercial test producers perform various statistical measures of the reliability and validity of their tests and provide the results in the test administrator's booklet.

Performance-Based Assessment. Some states and districts are moving toward performance-based tests, which assess students on how well they perform certain tasks. Students must use higher-level thinking skills to apply, analyze, synthesize, and evaluate ideas and data. For example, a biology performance-based assessment might require students to read a problem, design and carry out a laboratory experiment, and then write summaries of their findings. The performance-based assessment would evaluate both the processes students used and the output they produced. An English performance-based test might ask students to first read a selection of literature and then write a critical analysis. A mathematics performance-based test might state a general problem, require students to invent one or more methods of solving the problem, use one of the methods to arrive at a solution, and write the solution and an explanation of the processes they used.

Performance-based assessment allows students to be creative in solutions to problems or questions, and it requires them to use higher-level skills. Students work on content-related problems and use skills that are useful in various contexts. There are weaknesses, however. This type of assessment can be time consuming. Performance-based assessment often requires multiple resources, which can be expensive. Teachers must receive training in applying the test. Nonetheless, many schools consider performance-based testing to be a more authentic measure of student achievement than traditional tests.

Classroom Tests. Teachers must consider fundamental professional and technical factors to construct effective classroom tests. One of the first factors to recognize is that test construction is as creative, challenging, and important as any aspect of teaching. The planning and background that contribute to effective teaching are incomplete unless evaluation of student performance provides accurate feedback to the teacher and the student about the learning process.

Good tests are the product of careful planning, creative thinking, hard work, and technical knowledge about the various methods of measuring student knowledge and performance. Classroom tests that accomplish their purpose are the result of the development of a pool of items and refinement of those items based on feedback and constant revision. It is through this process that evaluation of students becomes valid and reliable.

Tests serve as a valuable instructional aid because they help determine pupil progress and also provide feedback to teachers regarding their own effectiveness. Student misunderstandings and problems that the tests reveal can help the teacher understand areas of special concern in providing instruction. This information also becomes the basis for the remediation of students and the revision of teaching procedures. Consequently, the construction, administration, and proper scoring of classroom tests are among the most important activities in teaching.

Authentic Assessments. Paper-and-pencil tests and essay tests are not the only methods of assessment. Other assessments include projects, observations, checklists, anecdotal records, portfolios, self-assessments, and peer assessments. Although these types of assessments often take more time and effort to plan and administer, they can often provide a more authentic measurement of student progress.

There are advantages and disadvantages to essay tests. Advantages of essay questions include the possibility for students to be creative in their answers, the opportunity for students to explain their responses, and the potential to test for higher-level thinking skills. Disadvantages of essay questions include the time students need to formulate meaningful responses and the time teachers need to evaluate the essays. In addition, language difficulties can make essay tests extremely difficult for some students, Consistency in evaluating essays can also be a problem for some teachers, but an outline of the acceptable answers—a scoring rubric—can help a teacher avoid inconsistency. Teachers who write specific questions and know what they are looking for are more likely to be consistent in grading. Also, if there are several essay questions, the effective teacher grades all student responses to the first question, then moves on to all responses to the second, and so on.

References

Ainsworth, Larry, and Jan Christinson. 1998. *Student-generated rubrics: An assessment model to help all students succeed.* Upper Saddle River, NJ: Pearson.

Arbuthnot, May Hill. 1964. *Children and books.* Glenview, IL: Scott, Foresman.

Bailey, Mildred Hart. 1967. The utility of phonic generalizations in grades one through six. *Reading teacher* 20 (February): 413–418.

Barry, Leasha M., et al. 2005. *The best teachers' test preparation for the FTCE.* Piscataway, NJ: Research and Education Association.

Bennett, William. 1987. *What works: Research about teaching and learning.* Washington, DC: U.S. Department of Education.

"Biography of Robert Frost." *http://ssl.pro-et.co.uk/home catalyst/RF/bio.html*

Breinburg, Petronella. 1974. *Shawn goes to school.* New York: Crowell.

Carbo, Marie. 1978. Teaching reading with talking books. *Reading teacher* 32 (December): 267–273.

_____. 1993. Reading styles and whole language. *Schools of thought II.* VHS. Bloomington, IN: Phi Delta Kappa.

Chudowsky, Naomi, and James W. Pellegrino. 2001. *Knowing what students know: The science and design of educational assessment.* Washington, DC: National Academy Press.

Clay, Marie M. *Emergent reading behavior.* 1966. PhD diss., University of Auckland, New Zealand.

_____. 1979. *Reading: The patterning of complex behavior.* Auckland, New Zealand: Heinemann.

_____. 1985. *The early detection of reading difficulties.* Portsmouth, NH: Heinemann.

Clymer, Theodore. 1963. The utility of phonic generalizations in the primary grades. *Reading teacher* 16 (January): 252–258.

Combs, Martha. 2006. *Readers and writers in primary grades: A balanced and integrated approach.* Upper Saddle River, NJ: Pearson.

Commission on Reading. 1986 (September). *Becoming a nation of readers.* Washington, DC: U.S. Department of Education.

Cook, Jimmie E., et al. 1980. Treating auditory perception problems: The NIM helps. *Academic therapy* 15 (March): 473–481.

Czaplinski, S. M. 1972. *Sexism in award winning picture books.* Pittsburgh: Know, Inc.

Davis, Anita P. 2000. *Children's literature essentials.* Boston: American Press.

_____. 2004. *Reading instruction essentials.* 3rd ed. Boston: American Press.

Davis, Anita P., and Thomas R. McDaniel. 1998. Essential vocabulary words. *Reading teacher* 52 (November): 308–309.

_____. 1999. You've come a long way, baby—or have you? *Reading teacher* 52 (February): 532–535.

Davis, Anita P., and Marla Selvidge. 1995. *Focus on women.* Westminster, CA: Teacher Created Materials, Inc.

Dolch, Edward William. 1960. *Dolch sight word list.* Champaign, IL: Garrard Press.

Dreyer, Sharon Spredemann. 1977. *The bookfinder: A guide to children's literature about the needs and problems of youth aged 2–15.* Circle Pines, MN: American Guidance Service.

Finazzo, Denise Ann. 1997. *All for the children.* Albany, NY: Delmar Press.

Finn, Patrick J. 1990. *Helping children learn to read.* New York: Longman.

Flesch, Rudolf Franz. 1955. *Why Johnny can't read—And what you can do about it.* New York: Harper.

Fry, Edward. 1980. The new instant word lists. *Reading teacher* 34 (December): 264–289.

Gilligan, C. 1982. *In a different voice: Psychological theory and women's development.* Cambridge, MA: Harvard University Press.

Goudvis, Anne, and Stephanie Harvey. 2000. *Strategies that work.* Portland, ME: Stenhouse.

Gunning, Thomas G. 1964. *Creating reading instruction for all children.* Boston: Allyn and Bacon.

Harmon, William, and C. Hugh Holman. 2002. *Handbook of literature.* Upper Saddle River, NJ: Prentice-Hall.

Hebert, Elizabeth A. 2001. *The power of portfolios: What children can teach us about learning and assessment.* Hoboken, NJ: Jossey-Bass.

Heckleman, R. G. 1969. A neurological-impress method of remedial-reading instruction. *Academic therapy* IV (Summer): 277–282.

Hildebrand, V., L. A. Phenice, M. M. Gray, and R. P. Hines. 2000. *Knowing and serving diverse families.* 2nd ed. Englewood Cliffs, NJ: Merrill.

Hollingsworth, Paul. 1978. An experimental approach to the impress method of teaching reading. *Reading teacher* 31 (March): 624–626.

Huck, Charlotte S., Susan Hepler, and Janet Hickman. 1993. *Children's literature in the elementary school.* Fort Worth, TX: Harcourt Brace Jovanovich.

IRA takes a stand on phonics. 1997. *Reading today* (April/May): 1–4.

Klein, Marvin L. 1985. *The development of writing in children pre-K through grade 8.* Englewood Cliffs, NJ: Prentice-Hall.

Krathwohl, David R., Benjamin S. Bloom, and Bertram B. Masia. 1964. *Taxonomy of educational objectives: The classification of educational goals.* Handbook II, *Affective domain.* New York: David McKay Co., Inc.

Larrick, Nancy. September 11, 1965. "The all-white world of children's books. *Saturday review,* 63-65.

Marzano, Robert J., and Daisy E. Arredondo. 1986. *Tactics for thinking*. Aurora, CO: Mid-Continent Regional Education Laboratories.

Merleau-Ponty, Maurice. 1973. *Consciousness and the acquisition of language*. Trans. Hugh J. Silverman. Evanston, IL: Northwestern University Press.

Michaelis, John U., and Jesus Garcia. 1996. *Social studies for children: A guide to basic instruction*. Boston: Allyn and Bacon.

Micklos, B., Jr. 1995–96. Multiculturalism and children's literature. *Reading today* (December/January): 1, 8.

Noyce, Ruth M., and James F. Christie. 1989. *Integrating reading and writing instruction in grades K–8*. Boston: Allyn and Bacon.

Partridge, Susan. 1979. *The neurological-impress method of teaching reading*. Opinion paper cited by ERIC.

Popham, W. James. 2001. *Classroom assessment: What teachers need to know*. 3rd ed. Upper Saddle River, NJ: Pearson, Allyn, and Bacon.

Pyles, Thomas, and John Algeo. 1982. *The origins and development of the English language*. New York: Harcourt Brace Jovanovich.

Richardson, Judy S., and Raymond F. Morgan. 1990. *Reading to learn in the content areas*. Belmont, CA: Wadsworth.

Southern Regional Education Board. Health and Human Services Commission. 1994. *Getting schools ready for children: The other side of the readiness goal*. Atlanta, GA.

Stiggins, Richard J. 2005. *Student involved assessment for learning*. 4th ed. Upper Saddle River, NJ: Prentice-Hall.

Tannen, D. 1991. *You just don't understand: Women and men in conversation*. New York: Ballantine Books.

Tompkins, Gail E. 2006. *Literacy for the twenty-first century: A balanced approach*. 4th ed. Upper Saddle River, NJ: Pearson.

Trelease, Jim. 1985. *The read-aloud handbook*. New York: Penguin Books.

Vacca, Richard T., and Jo Anne L. Vacca. 1989. *Content area reading*. 3rd ed. Glenview, IL: Scott, Foresman.

Wittgenstein, Ludwig. 1921/1974. *Tractatus logico-philosophicus*. Trans. D. F. Pears and B. F. McGuinness. London: Routledge.

_____. 1958. *Philosophical investigations*. 3rd ed. Eds. G. E. M. Anscombe and Rush Rhees. Trans. G. E. M. Anscombe. New York: Macmillan.

Children's Literature

Aesop. 1950. *The fables of Aesop: Selected, told anew, and their social history traced by Joseph Jacobs*. New York: Macmillan.

Afanas'ev, Aleksandr Nikolaevich. 1975. *Russian fairy tales*. Trans. Norbert Guterman. New York: Pantheon.

Alcott, Louisa Mae. 1868/1968. *Little women*. Boston: Little, Brown.

Asbjornsen, Peter, and Jorgen Moe. 1946. *East o' the sun and west o' the moon*. Evanston, IL: Row, Peterson.

Banks, Lynne Reid. 1980. *The Indian in the cupboard*. Garden City, NY: Doubleday.

Beim, Lorraine, and Jerrold Beim. 1945. *Two is a team*. New York: Harcourt, Brace.

Bonham, Frank. 1965/1975. *Durango Street*. New York: Dell.

Bryant, Sara Cone. 1938. *Epaminondas and his auntie*. Boston: Houghton.

Byars, Betsy. 1970. *The summer of the swans*. New York: Viking Press.

Capote, Truman. *Complete stories of Truman Capote*. 2004. New York: Random House.

Chase, Richard. 1943. *Jack tales*. New York: Houghton Mifflin.

_____. 1948. *Grandfather tales*. New York: Houghton Mifflin.

Cleaver, Vera, and Bill Cleaver. 1969. *Where the lilies bloom*. New York: Lippincott.

Coerr, Eleanor. 1977. *Sadako and the thousand paper cranes*. New York: Putnam.

Cormier, Robert. 1974/1977. *The chocolate war*. New York: Dell.

Dahl, Roald. 1972. *Charlie and the chocolate factory*. New York: Knopf.

Davis, Anita P. and Ed Y. Hall. 1993. *Harriet Quimby: First lady of the air (an activity book for children)*. Spartanburg, SC: Honoribus Press.

_____. 1998. Harriet Quimby: *First lady of the air (an intermediate biography)*. Spartanburg, SC: Honoribus Press.

Davis, Anita P., and Katharine Preston. 1996. *Discoveries*. Hillsborough, ID: Butte Publications.

De Angeli, Marguerite. 1946. *Bright April*. Garden City, NY: Doubleday.

Defoe, Daniel. 1719/1972. *Robinson Crusoe*. Boston: Houghton Mifflin.

Dodge, Mary Mapes. 1963. *Hans Brinker*. New York: Grosset and Dunlap.

Garis, Howard. 1912/1915. *Uncle Wiggly's adventures*. New York: Platt and Munk.

Gipson, Fred. 1956. *Old Yeller*. New York: Harper.

Golding, William. 1954. *Lord of the flies*. New York: Perigee.

Grimm, Jacob, and Wilhelm Grimm. 1968. *Grimm's fairy tales*. Chicago: Follett.

Henry, Marguerite. 1953/1967. *Brighty of the Grand Canyon*. New York: Scholastic.

Hesse, Karen. 1997/1999. *Out of the dust*. New York: Scholastic.

Hickam, Homer H., Jr. 1999. *October sky*. New York: Dell.(Originally published in 1998 as Rocket boys.)

Hinton, S. E. 1967/1983. *The outsiders*. New York: Dell.

Jackson, Jesse. 1945. *Call me Charley*. New York: Harper.

Jacobs, Joseph. 1959. *Favorite fairy tales told in England*. Boston: Little, Brown.

Keats, Ezra Jack. 1962. *The snowy day*. New York: Viking Press.

Kellogg, Steven. 1938/1986. *Paul Bunyan*. New York: Morrow.

Knight, Eric. 1938/1966. *Lassie come home*. New York: Scholastic.

Konigsburg, E. L. 1967. *From the mixed-up files of Mrs. Basil E. Frankweiler*. New York, Atheneum.

Lee, Harper. 1960/1982. *To kill a mockingbird*. New York: Warner Books.

Lewis, C. S. 1950/1988. *The lion, the witch, and the wardrobe*. New York: Macmillan.

Miles, Miska. 1965. *Mississippi possum*. Boston: Little, Brown.

Montgomery, L. M. 1908/1935. *Anne of Green Gables*. New York: Farrar, Straus, and Giroux.

Mowat, Farley. 1963/1984. *Never cry wolf*. Toronto: Bantam Books.

New testament. The good Samaritan. Luke 10:30–36. The lost coin. Luke 15:8–11.

_____. The seeds on rich and fallow ground. Mark 4:3–8; Luke 8:5–8.

_____. The prodigal son. Luke 16:11–32.

Norton, Mary. 1953. *The borrowers*. New York, Harcourt, Brace.

O'Dell, Scott. 1960. *Island of the blue dolphins*. New York: Houghton Mifflin.

Peck, Robert Newton. 1974. *Soup*. New York: Knopf.

Perrault, Charles, et al. 1959. *Favorite fairy tales told in France: Retold from Charles Perrault and other French storytellers*. Ed. Virginia Haviland. Boston: Little, Brown.

Peterson, Jeanne Whitehouse. 1977. *I have a sister—My sister is deaf*. New York: Harper and Row.

Rawlings, Marjorie Kinnan. 1938. *The yearling*. New York: Scribner.

Rawls, Wilson. 1961/1976. *Where the red fern grows*. New York: Bantam.

_____. 1977. *Summer of the monkeys*. New York: Dell.

Sanders, Dori. *Clover*. 1991. New York: Fawcett Columbine.

Shotwell, Louisa Rossiter. 1963. *Roosevelt Grady*. Cleveland: World.

Shreve, Susan. 1984. *The flunking of Joshua T. Bates*. New York: Knopf.

Singer, Isaac Bashevis. 1966. *Zlateh the goat and other stories*. New York: Harper.

Spinelli, Jerry. 1990. *Maniac Magee*. Boston: Little, Brown.

Spyri, Johanna. 1884/1982. *Heidi*. New York: Messner

Steinbeck, John. 1939. *The grapes of wrath*, New York: Viking.

Steptoe, Javaka (ed.). 1997. *In daddy's arms I am tall: African Americans celebrating fathers*. New York: Lee and Low Books.

Steptoe, John. 1969. *Stevie*. New York: Harper and Row.

Stevenson, Robert Louis. 1883/1981. *Treasure island*. New York: Scribner.

Swift, Jonathan. *Gulliver's travels*. 1726/1945. Garden City, NY: Doubleday.

Taylor, Mildred D. 1976. *Roll of thunder, hear my cry*. New York: Dial Press.

Tsuchiya, Yukio. 1988. *Faithful elephants: A true story of animals, people, and war*. Boston: Houghton Mifflin.

Twain, Mark. 1876/1989. *The adventures of Tom Sawyer*. New York: Morrow.

Twain, Mark. 1884/1991. *The adventures of Huckleberry Finn* (1991). New York: Knopf.

Ward, Lynd. 1952. *The biggest bear*. New York: Houghton Mifflin.

White, E. B. 1952. *Charlotte's web*. New York: Harper and Row.

Wilder, Laura Ingalls. 1953. *Little house in the big woods*. New York: Harper.

Wyss, Johann. 1814/1981. *Swiss family Robinson*. Sharon.

Yarbrough, Camille. 1979. *Cornrows*. New York: Coward, McCann, and Geoghegan.

Yashima, Taro. 1955. *Crow boy*. New York: Viking Press.

Mathematics

Chapter

3

Competency 7: Knowledge of Number Sense, Concepts, and Operations

Eleven test items relate to this competency.

Skill One

Associate Multiple Representations of Numbers Using Word Names, Standard Numerals, and Pictorial Models for Real Numbers

The representations for numbers include the following:

Word names. For example, *four, one hundred, thirty-five*

Standard numerals. For example, 4, 100, 35

Pictorial models. For students in the lower grades, the number 4 may be represented by the following four drawings of a bird:

For students in the upper grades, pie graphs like the following, bar graphs, charts, and other pictorial representations can represent numbers:

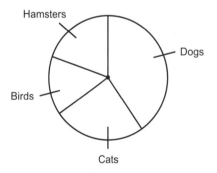

Counting numbers begin with the number 1 and continue 1, 2, 3, and so on.

Whole numbers are the counting numbers plus zero (0, 1, 2, 3, etc.).

A **common fraction** is a number in the form a/b, where a and b are whole numbers. In the expression a/b, the dividend a is called the **numerator**, and the divisor

107

b is called the **denominator**. A common fraction cannot have zero as a denominator, because **division by zero is undefined**.

Decimal numbers are fractions written in special notation. All decimal numbers are actually fractions whose denominators are powers of 10 (10, 100, 1,000, etc.). For instance, 0.25 can be thought of as the fraction ²⁵/₁₀₀, which reduces to ¼.

Integers are numbers preceded by either a positive (+) or negative (–) sign. An integer presented without a sign is assumed to be positive are negative and integers to the right of zero are positive.

Operations indicate what one is to do with numbers. There are four main operations: addition, subtraction, multiplication, and division. Multiplication is repeated addition. Division is repeated subtraction.

Skill Two
Compare the Relative Size of Integers, Fractions, Decimals, Numbers Expressed as Percents, Numbers with Exponents, and/or Numbers in Scientific Notation

Integers are numbers preceded by either a positive (+) or negative (–) sign. An integer presented without a sign is assumed to be positive (e.g., 4 means +4). On a number line, integers to the left of zero are negative and integers to the right of zero are positive. All integers can be written as fractions, but not all fractions can be written as integers. There are more fractions than integers.

Common **fractions** are in the form *a/b*, where *a* and *b* are whole numbers. Integers can be expressed as fractions, but not all fractions can be expressed as integers. For example, the number 4 can be expressed as ⁴/₁. However, the fraction ¼ cannot be expressed as an integer. There are more fractions than whole numbers; between every integer is a fraction. Between the fraction and the whole number is another fraction, between the fraction and the other fraction is another fraction, and so on. Negative and positive fractions are

not integers (unless they are equivalent to whole numbers or their negative counterparts).

Decimal numbers are fractions written in special notation. For instance, 0.25 can be thought of as the fraction ¼. All decimal numbers are actually fractions. When expressed as decimals, some fractions terminate and some do not. For instance, 0.315 is a terminating decimal; 0.0575757 . . . is a repeating (nonterminating) decimal. All fractions, however, can be written as decimals. There are more decimals than integers.

Fractions, decimal numbers, and percents are different ways of representing values. It is useful to be able to convert from one to the other. The following paragraphs provide some conversion tips.

The practical method for changing a fraction into a decimal is by **dividing the numerator by the denominator**. For example, ¼ becomes 0.25 when 1 is divided by 4, as follows:

$$
\begin{array}{r}
.25 \\
4\overline{)1.00} \\
\underline{-.08} \\
.20
\end{array}
$$

Naturally, this can be done longhand or with a calculator. (If the fraction includes a whole number, as in 2-3/5, the whole number is not a part of the division.) The decimal number may terminate or repeat. Converting a simple fraction to a decimal number never results in an irrational number.

To convert a nonrepeating (terminating) decimal number to a fraction in lowest terms, write the decimal as a fraction with the denominator a power of 10, and then reduce to lowest terms. For example, 0.125 can be written as ¹²⁵/₁,₀₀₀, which reduces to ⅛.

To convert a decimal number to a **percent**, shift the decimal point two places to the right and add the percent symbol (%). For instance, 0.135 becomes 13.5%. (If the number before the percent symbol is a whole number, there is no need to show the decimal point.)

To convert a percent to a decimal number, shift the decimal point two places to the left and drop the percent symbol. For example, 98% becomes 0.98 as a decimal.

To convert a percent to a fraction put the percent (without the percent symbol) over 100 and then reduce. In this way, 20% is represented as $^{20}/_{100}$, which reduces to $^1/_5$.

Exponential notation is a way to show repeated multiplication more simply. For example, $2 \times 2 \times 2$ in exponential notation is 2^3 and is equal to 8. (Note that 2^3 does *not* mean 2×3.)

Scientific notation is a method for showing any numbers using exponents (although it is most useful for very large and very small numbers). A number represented as between 1 and 10 times a power of 10 is in scientific notation. Thus, the number 75,000 in scientific notation is 7.5×10^4.

Skill Three

Apply Ratios, Proportions, and Percents in Real-World Situations

Ratio notation is an alternative method for showing fractions. For example, $^2/_5$ can be expressed as "the ratio of 2 to 5." The use of ratio notation emphasizes the relationship of one number to another. To show ratios, one may use numbers with a colon between them; 2:5 is the same ratio as 2 to 5 and $^2/_5$.

To illustrate the equivalencies and conversions above, consider the fraction $^{19}/_{20}$. As a decimal, it is 0.95. As a percent, it is 95%. As a ratio, it is 19 to 20, or 19:20.

The relationship between two ratios is one of equality; that is, they are equivalent ratios. An equation of two equivalent ratios is one of **proportion**.

Skill Four

Represent Numbers in a Variety of Equivalent Forms, Including Whole Numbers, Integers,

Fractions, Decimals, Percents, Scientific Notation, and Exponents

Numbers may be represented in many ways, as shown in the following chart:

Number Form	Two Blocks Can Be Represented As
Whole number	2
Integer	+2 or 2
Fraction	2/1
Decimal	2.0
Percent	200%

A real number expressed in scientific notation is written as the product of a real number n times an integral power of 10; the value of n is $1 \leq n \geq 10$. Some examples are shown in the following chart:

Number	Scientific Notation
1956	1.956×10^3
0.0036	3.6×10^{-3}
59600000	5.96×10^7

Exponential notation is a way to show repeated multiplication more simply. For example, $2 \times 2 \times 2$ can be shown as 2^3, and is equal to 8. (Note that 2^3 does *not* mean 2×3.)

Skill Five

Recognize the Effects of Operations on Rational Numbers and the Relationships among These Operations

Addition is an operation that, when performed on numbers of disjoint sets, results in a **sum**. One can show addition on a number line by counting forward. Addition is a **binary operation** on two numbers that results in a sum—or a third, unique number. Adding two whole numbers always results in a whole number.

The operation of **subtraction** is the inverse of addition. Like addition, subtraction is a binary operation; that is, we work on only two numbers at a time. The result is a third, unique number called the **difference**. Given two whole numbers, subtracting the smaller number from the larger one, results in a whole number. However, subtraction of whole numbers does not result in a whole number if the larger whole number is subtracted from the smaller one.

Multiplication, like addition, is a binary operation. We work on only two numbers at a time with multiplication. The result of the operation of multiplication is the **product**. The result of multiplying two whole numbers is always a whole number. Multiplication is repeated addition.

The operation of **division** has the same inverse relation to multiplication that subtraction has to addition. What multiplication does, division undoes. Teaching division should parallel teaching multiplication. Division is repeated subtraction.

Some pairs of operations are considered to be **inverse**. Addition and subtraction are inverse operations, as are multiplication and division. The operations "undo" one another. For example, multiplying 4 by 9 gives 36; dividing 36 by 9 "gives back" 4.

Skill Six

Select the Appropriate Operation(s) to Solve Problems Involving Ratios, Proportions, and Percents and the Addition, Subtraction, Multiplication, and Division of Rational Numbers

The key to converting word problems into mathematical problems is attention to **reasonableness,** with the choice of operations being crucial to success. Often,

individual words and phrases translate into numbers and operation symbols; making sure that the translations are reasonable is important. Consider this word problem:

Each word problem requires an individual approach, but keeping in mind the reasonableness of the computational setup should be helpful.

Most modern math programs introduce the concept of ratio and use ratio to solve various problems. For example:

Pencils are 2 for 25 cents. How many pencils can Teresa buy for 50 cents?

"Two pencils for 25 cents" suggests the fixed constant of 2/25:

$$\frac{2 \text{ (pencils)}}{25 \text{ (cents)}}$$

With a fixed ration, it should be possible to figure out how many pencils Teresa can buy for 50 cents by setting up an equivalent ratio:

$$\frac{x \text{ (number of pencils)}}{50 \text{ (cents)}}$$

The relationship between the two ratios is one of equality; that is, they are equivalent ratios. An equation of two equivalent ratios is one of **proportion**. There are several ways to solve the equivalent ratios problem with the pencils, but one way to do it is to use cross multiplication:

$$\frac{x}{50} \times \frac{2}{25}$$

Cross multiplication gives $25x = 100$. Solving for x requires dividing 100 by 25 to get 4. Thus, Teresa can buy 4 pencils for 50 cents.

Another way to solve the problem is to set up a chart:

Pencils	Cost
2	25 cents
4	50 cents
x	75 cents

In solving problems involving percents, the student must always consider reasonableness in their thinking and estimating. Mathematical reasoning includes analyzing problem situations, making conjectures, organizing information, and selecting strategies to solve problems. Problem-solvers must rely on both formal and informal *reasoning processes*. A key informal process relies on *reasonableness*. Consider this problem:

Center Town Middle School has an enrollment of 640 students. One day, 28 students were absent. What percent of the total number of students were absent?

    (A) 28%   (C) 4%
    (B) 1%   (D) 25%

Even if someone forgot how to compute percents, some possible answers could be rejected instantly: 28 is a "small-but-not-tiny" chunk of 640; answers like 1% and 25% are *unreasonable*.

Look for "key" words in solving problems. The words may provide a clue as to which operation to use. Some examples follow in the subsequent chart:

Operation	Key Words
Addition	Increased by More than Combined Together Total of Sum Added to
Subtraction	Decreased by Minus Less Difference of Difference between Less than Fewer than

Operation	Key Words
Multiplication	Of Times Multiplied by Product of Increased by a factor of Decreased by a factor of
Division	How many to each How many groups Share Separate Equal groups Divide Quotient

Skill Seven

Use Estimation in Problem-Solving Situations

Estimation is a useful tool in predicting and in checking the answer to a problem. Estimation is at the second level in Bloom's *Taxonomy*—the comprehension level. Thinking at the comprehension level requires students not only to recall or remember information but also to understand the meaning of information and to restate it in their own words.

The ability to render some real-life quandaries into mathematical or logical problems—workable using established procedures—is an important part of finding solutions. Because each quandary will be unique, so too will be students' problem-solving plans of attack. Still, many real-world problems that lend themselves to mathematical solutions are likely to require one of the following strategies:

Guess and check. This is not the same as "wild guessing." With this problem-solving strategy, students make their best guess and then check the answer to see whether it is right. Even if the guess does not immediately provide the solution, it may help to get students closer to it so that they can continue to work on it. For example:

Three persons' ages add up to 72, and each person is one year older than the last person. What are their ages?

Because the three ages must add up to 72, it is reasonable to take one-third of 72 (24) as the starting point. Of course, even though 24 + 24 + 24 gives a sum of 72, those numbers do not match the information ("each person is one year older"). So, students might guess that the ages are 24, 25, and 26. Checking that guess by addition, students would see that the sum of 75 is too high. Lowering their guesses by one each, they try 23, 24, and 25, which indeed add up to 72, giving students the solution. There are many variations of the guess-and-check method.

Make a sketch or a picture. Being able to visualize a problem can help to clarify it. Consider this problem:

Mr. Rosenberg plans to put a 4-foot-wide concrete sidewalk around his backyard pool. The pool is rectangular, with dimensions 12 ft. by 24 ft. The cost of the concrete is $1.28 per square foot. How much concrete is required for the job?

Students with exceptional visualization abilities will not need a sketch. For most, however, a drawing like the one shown here may be helpful in solving this and many other real-life problems.

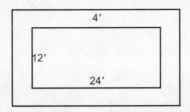

Make a table or a chart. Sometimes organizing the information from a problem makes it easier to find the solution; tables and charts can be helpful.

Make a list. Like a table or chart, a list can help organize information and perhaps provide or at least hint at a solution. The list-making strategy would work well for solving this problem: "How many different outcomes are there if you roll two regular six-sided dice?"

Act it out. Sometimes literally "doing" a problem—with physical objects or even their bodies—can help students produce a solution. A class problem that could be solved in this manner is the following: "If five strangers meet and everyone shakes everyone else's hand once, how many total handshakes will there be?"

Look for patterns. This technique encourages students to ask, "What's happening here?" Spotting a pattern would be helpful in solving a problem such as this: Nevin's weekly savings account balances for 15 weeks are as follows: $125, $135, $148, $72, $85, $96, $105, $50, $64, $74, $87, $42, $51, $60, $70. If the pattern holds, what might Nevin's balance be the next week?

Work a simpler problem. By finding the solution to a different but simpler problem, students might spot a way to solve the harder one. **Estimating** can be thought of as working a simpler problem. To find the product of 23 times 184 when no calculator or pencil and paper are handy, students could estimate the product by getting the exact answer to the simpler problem, 20 × 200.

Writing an open math sentence (an equation with one or more variables, or "unknowns") and then solving it. This is sometimes called "translating" a problem into mathematics. Here is a sample problem: "Tiana earned grades of 77%, 86%, 90%, and 83% on her first four weekly science quizzes. Assuming all grades are equally weighted, what score will she need on the fifth week's quiz to have an average (or mean) score of 88%?" Using the given information, students could set up and solve the following equation to answer the question:

$$\frac{(77 + 86 + 90 + 83 + x)}{5} = 88$$

Work backward. Consider this problem: "If you add 12 to some number and then multiply the sum by 4, you will get 60. What is the number?" Students could find a solution by *starting at the end*, with 60. The problem states that the 60 came from multiplying a sum by 4. When 15 is multiplied by 4, the result is 60. The sum must be 15; if 15 is the sum of 12 and something else, the "something else " can only be 3.

There are of course hybrid approaches to problem solving. Students can mix and match strategies wherever they think they are appropriate. In general, attention to *reasonableness* may be most crucial to problem-solving success, especially in real-life situations.

Skill Eight

Apply Number Theory Concepts

Factors, Primes, Composites, and Multiples

Factors are any of the numbers or symbols in mathematics that, when multiplied together, form a product. For example, the whole-number factors of 12 are 1, 2, 3, 4, 6, and 12. A number with exactly two whole-number factors—1 and the number itself—is a **prime number**. The first few primes are 2, 3, 5, 7, 11, 13, and 17. Most other whole numbers are **composite numbers** because they are *composed* of several whole-number factors. The number 1 is neither prime nor composite; it has only one whole-number factor.

The **multiples** of any whole number are the results of multiplying that whole number by the counting numbers. The multiples of 7 are 7, 14, 21, 28, and so on. Every whole number has an infinite number of multiples.

Number Properties

Key properties of whole numbers (and some related terms) include the following:

Multiplicative identity property of one. Any number multiplied by 1 remains the same. For instance, $34 \times 1 = 34$. The number 1 is called the **multiplicative identity**.

Property of reciprocals. Any number (except zero) multiplied by its reciprocal gives 1. The **reciprocal** of a number is 1 divided by that number. Remember that dividing by zero has no meaning; avoid dividing by zero when computing or solving equations and inequalities.

Additive identity property of zero. Adding zero to any number will not change the number. For instance, $87 + 0 = 87$. Zero is the **additive identity**.

Commutative property for addition and multiplication. The order of adding addends or multiplying factors does not determine the sum or product.

For example, 6×9 gives the same product as 9×6. Division and subtraction are not commutative.

Associative property for addition and multiplication. Associating, or grouping, three or more addends or factors in a different way does not change the sum or product. For example, $(3 + 7) + 5$ gives the same sum as $3 + (7 + 5)$. Division and subtraction are not associative.

Distributive property of multiplication over addition. A number multiplied by the sum of two other numbers can be handed out, or distributed, to both numbers, multiplied by each of them separately, and the products added together. For example, multiplying 6 by 47 gives the same result as multiplying 6 by 40, multiplying 6 by 7, and then adding the products. That is, $6 \times (47) = (6 \times 40) + (6 \times 7)$. The simple notation form of the distributive property is

$$a(b + c) = (a \times b) + (a \times c)$$

The definition of the distributive property of multiplication over addition can be stated simply: the product of a number and a sum can be expressed as a sum of two products.

$$4 \times (3 + 5) = (4 \times 3) + (4 \times 5)$$
$$a \times (b + c) = (a \times b) + (a \times c)$$

Pairs of operations which "undo" each other are **inverse**. Addition and subtraction are inverse operations, as are multiplication and division. Multiplication and division "undo" one another. That is, multiplying 4 by 9 gives 36; dividing 36 by 9 "gives back" 4.

Number Sequences

Many children start school with some knowledge of the number sequence. Their parents probably taught them in a rote manner to count from 1 to 10. These children have used the **counting numbers** (1, 2, 3, etc.). Early in school, children learn about other sets of numbers. The next set that they encounter is the set of **whole numbers** (0, 1, 2, 3, etc.).

Students discover a new sequence of numbers when they learn about **negative numbers**. Many teachers use a number line, a temperature thermometer, or even a countdown, such as the space controllers use at a satellite launch, to show the integers: . . . –5, –4, –3, –2, –1, 0, +1, +2. +3. +4 . . . .

Students also encounter fractions, or **rational numbers**. The sequence of rationals varies according to the starting fraction. For example, starting at ¼, the sequence of rationals is ²⁄₄, ³⁄₄, ⁴⁄₄ (1). All these sets of numbers can help children to see sequencing and patterning.

Divisibility

The **rules of divisibility** are as follows:

- Division by zero is not possible.

- Only whole numbers ending in 0, 2, 4, 6, and 8 are divisible by 2.

- Only whole numbers whose digits add up to a number divisible by 3 are divisible by 3. The following chart illustrates:

Number	Sum Of Digits	Divisible By 3?
12	3	Yes
21	3	Yes
44	8	No
56	11	No
158	14	No

- A number is divisible by 4 if the last two digits are divisible by 4. The following chart illustrates:

Number	Last Two Digits	Divisible By 4?
28	28	Yes
128	28	Yes
311	11	No
816	16	Yes

- A number is divisible by 5 if the ones place has a 5 or zero.

- A number is divisible by 6 if it is divisible by both 2 and 3. For example, 666 has digits that add to 18, which is divisible by 3; it ends in 6 so it is divisible by 2. Because it is divisible by both 2 and 3, it is also divisible by 6.

- A number is divisible by 8 if the last three digits are divisible by 8. For example, 99816 has 816 as its last digits; 800 can be divided evenly by 8, and 16 is divisible by 8. The number 8 is, therefore, a factor of 99816.

- A number is divisible by 9 if the sum of the digits is divisible by 9. The number 245 has digits that add to 11; 11 is not evenly divisible by 9, so 9 is not a divisor of 245. The number 333 has digits that add to the number 9; because 9 goes evenly into 9, 333 is divisible by 9.

- A number that has a 0 in the ones place is divisible by 10.

Skill Nine

Apply the Order of Operations

Some mathematical expressions indicate several operations. Simplifying that type of expression requires following a universally agreed-upon order for performing each operation:

- First, compute any multiplication or division, left to right.

- Second, compute any addition or subtraction, also left to right.

- If an expression contains any parentheses, complete all computations within the parentheses first.

- Treat exponential expressions ("powers") as multiplication.

Thus, solving the expression $3 + 7 \times 4 - 2$ requires multiplying 7 by 4 *before* doing the addition and subtraction to obtain the result of 29.

The rules for performing operations on integers (whole numbers and their negative counterparts) and on fractions and decimal numbers where at least one is negative are generally the same as the rules for performing operations on nonnegative numbers. The trick is to pay attention to the sign (the positive or negative value) of each answer.

The rules for both multiplication and division when at least one negative number is involved are as follows:

- Two positives or two negatives give a positive.

- "Mixing" a positive and a negative gives a negative. For example, $-5 \times 3 = -15$, and $-24 \div 3 = -8$.

For adding or subtracting when at least one negative number is involved, it may be useful to think of the values as money, considering adding as "gaining," subtracting as "losing," positive numbers as "credits," and negative numbers as "debts." Be careful, though: Adding or "gaining" –8 is actually losing 8.

Competency 8: Knowledge of Measurement

Eight test items relate to this competency.

Skill One

Apply Given Measurement Formulas for Perimeter, Circumference, Area, Volume, and Surface Area in Problem Situations

Perimeter of Rectangles, Squares, and Triangles

Perimeter refers to the measure of the distance around a figure. Perimeter is measured in linear units (e.g., inches, feet, meters). **Area** refers to the measure of the interior of a figure. The measurement of area is in square units (e.g., square inches, square feet, square meters).

The formula or the representation of the **perimeter of a rectangle** is:

$$P = 2l + 2w$$

where l is the measure of the length and w is the measure of the width. For example, if a rectangle has $l = 10$ m and $w = 5$ m, to determine the perimeter of the rectangle, one would solve in this manner:

$$P = 2(10 \text{ m}) + 2(5 \text{ m}) = 30 \text{ m}$$

The formula for the **perimeter of a square** is

$$P = 4s$$

where s is the measure of a side of the square. For example, if a square has $s = 5$ ft., one would determine the perimeter of the square in this manner:

$$P = 4(5 \text{ ft.}) = 20 \text{ ft.}$$

The formula for (method of determining) the **perimeter of a triangle** is:

$$P = s_1 + s_2 + s_3$$

where s_1, s_2, and s_3 are the measures of the sides of the triangle. For example, if a triangle has three sides measuring 3 in., 4 in., and 5 in., the perimeter of the triangle is give by

$$P = 3 \text{ in.} + 4 \text{ in.} + 5 \text{ in.} = 12 \text{ in.}$$

Area of Rectangles, Squares, and Triangles

The formula for (method of determining) the **area of a rectangle** is:

$$A = l \times w$$

where l is the measure of the length and w is the measure of the width. For example, if a rectangle has $l = 10$ m and $w = 5$ m, the area of the rectangle is

$$A = 10 \text{ m} \times 5 \text{ m} = 50 \text{ m}^2$$

The formula for (method of determining) the **area of a square** is:

$$A = s^2$$

where s is the measure of a side. For example, if a square has $s = 5$ ft., the area of the square is:

$$A = (5 \text{ ft.})^2 = 25 \text{ ft.}^2$$

The formula for (method of determining) the **area of a triangle** is;

$$A = \tfrac{1}{2}bh$$

where b is the base and h is the height. For example, if a triangle has a base of 3 in. and a height of 4 in., the area of the triangle is:

$$A = \tfrac{1}{2}(3 \text{ in.} \times 4 \text{ in.}) = \tfrac{1}{2}(12 \text{ in.}^2) = 6 \text{ in.}^2$$

Circumference and Area of Circles

The **radius of a circle** is the distance from the center of the circle to the edge of the circle. The **diameter of a circle** is a line segment that passes through the center of the circle, the end points of which lie on the circle. The measure of the diameter of a circle is twice the measure of the radius. The number **pi**, symbolized as π and approximately equal to 3.14, is often used in computations involving circles.

The formula for (method of determining) the **circumference of a circle** is:

$$C = \pi \times d, \text{ or}$$
$$C = 2 \times \pi \times r$$

where d is the diameter and r is the radius.

The formula for (method of determining) the **area of a circle** is:

$$A = \pi \times r^2$$

where r is the radius. For example, if a circle has a radius of 5 cm, the circumference and area are

$$C = \pi \times 10 \text{ cm} \approx 3.14 \times 10 \text{ cm} = 31.4 \text{ cm, and}$$
$$A = \pi \times (5 \text{ cm})^2 \approx 3.14 \times 25 \text{ cm}^2 = 78.50 \text{ cm}^2$$

Volume of Cubes and Rectangular Solids

Volume refers to the measure of the interior of a three-dimensional figure. A **rectangular solid** is a rectilinear (right-angled) figure that has length, width, and height. The formula for (method of determining) the volume of a rectangular solid is

$$V = l \times w \times h$$

where l is length, w is width, and h is height. For example, if a rectangular solid has $l = 5$ cm, $w = 4$ cm, and $h = 3$ cm, the volume is

$$V = 5 \text{ cm} \times 4 \text{ cm} \times 3 \text{ cm} = 60 \text{ cm}^3$$

A **cube** is a rectangular solid with the same measures of length, width, and height. That measure is the **edge** of the cube. The formula for (method of determining) the volume of a cube is

$$V = e^3$$

where e is the edge. For example, if a cube has $e = 5$ cm, the volume is

$$V = (5 \text{ cm})^3 = 125 \text{ cm}^3$$

Skill Two

Evaluate How a Change in Length, Width, Height, or Radius Affects Perimeter, Circumference, Area, Surface Area, or Volume

Changing even one number in a formula can affect the final result. Evaluating the effect of that change involves thinking at the highest level of Bloom's *Taxonomy*. By contrast, estimating is level 2 thinking (comprehension), which requires students to understand the meaning of the information and restate it in their own words; predicting that a perimeter, circumference, area, or volume will increase or decrease if a dimension becomes larger or smaller involves the third level of Bloom's *Taxonomy*: application. Having the class experiment with these numbers, make predictions, and then evaluate how and why the changes happened, takes the work with perimeter, circumference, area, and volume to a level higher than just "plugging in" numbers to a formula.

Skill Three

Within a Given System, Solve Real-World Problems Involving Measurement, with Both Direct and Indirect Measures, and Make Conversions to a Larger or Smaller Unit

Customary units are generally the same as **U.S. units**. Customary units of length include inches, feet, yards, and miles. Customary units of weight include ounces, pounds, and tons. Customary units of capacity (or volume) include teaspoons, tablespoons, cups, pints, quarts, and gallons.

The **metric system of measurement** relates to the base 10 place value scheme. The chart below lists the common metric prefixes:

Prefix	Meaning
Kilo-	Thousand (1,000)
Deci-	Tenth (0.1)
Centi-	Hundredth (0.01)
Milli-	Thousandth (0.001)

The basic unit of linear measure in the metric system is the **meter**, represented by **m**. The relationships among the commonly used linear units of measurement in the metric system are:

1 kilometer (km) = 1,000 m
1 meter (m) = 1.0 m

1 decimeter (dm) = 0.1 m
1 centimeter (cm) = 0.01 m
1 millimeter (mm) = 0.001 m

The basic unit of measurement for mass (or weight) in the metric system is the **gram**, represented by **g**. The relationships among the commonly used units of measurement for mass in the metric system include the following:

1 kilogram (kg) = 1,000 g
1 gram (g) = 1.0 g
1 milligram (mg) = 0.001 g

The basic unit of measurement for capacity (or volume) in the metric system is the **liter**, represented by **L** or **l**. The relationships among the most common metric units of capacity include:

1 liter (l) = 1,000 milliliters (ml)
1 deciliter (dl) = 100 ml; 10 cl
1 centiliter (cl) = 10 ml

Metric units of length include millimeters, centimeters, decimeters, meters, and kilometers. The centimeter is the basic metric unit of length, at least for short distances. About 2.5 centimeters are equal to 1 inch. The kilometer is a metric unit of length used for longer distances. It takes more than 1.5 kilometers to make a mile. A very fast adult runner could run a kilometer in about three minutes. Metric units of weight include grams and kilograms. The gram is the basic metric unit of mass (which for many purposes is the same as *weight*). A large paper clip weighs about 1 gram. It takes about 28 grams to make 1 ounce. Metric units of capacity include milliliters and liters. The liter is the basic metric unit of volume (or capacity). A liter is slightly smaller than a quart; it takes more than four liters to make a gallon.

Here are some frequently used customary-to-metric ratios. (Values are approximate.)

1 inch = 2.54 centimeters
1 yard = 0.91 meter
1 mile = 1.61 kilometers
1 ounce = 28.35 grams
1 pound = 2.2 kilograms
1 quart = 0.94 liter

One can determine the metric-to-customary conversions by taking the reciprocals of each of the factors noted above. For instance, 1 kilometer = 0.62 mile (computed by dividing 1 by 1.61).

An important step in solving problems involving measurement is to decide what is being measured. Generally, such problems will fall under one of these categories: length, area, angles, volume, mass, time, money, and temperature. Solving measurement problems will likely require knowledge in several other areas of mathematics, especially algebra.

The following is one example of a measurement problem that requires knowledge of several math topics (geometry, multiplication, conversions, estimation, etc.):

Sophie's Carpet Store charges $19.40 per square yard for the type of carpeting Tony would like in his bedroom (padding and labor included). How much would Tony pay to carpet his 9-by-12-foot room?

One way to find the solution is to convert the room dimensions to yards (3 yards by 4 yards) and then multiply to get 12 square yards. The final step is to multiply 12 by the price of $19.40 per square yard, for a total price of $232.80.

Skill Four

Solve Real-World Problems Involving Estimates and Exact Measurements

From the pencil and field notebook to modern instruments in the laboratory, science involves the tools of observation, measurement, and computational analysis. The microscope and telescope each extend the range of human observation beyond human physiology. The spectroscope separates visible light into its component colors, and the spectrophotometer measures the selective absorption of those colors as a function of some property of a solution, solid, or gas. Mathematics is a tool to evaluate the results of scientific observations, to organize large quantities of data into averages, ranges, and statistical probabilities.

The fundamental uncertainty of the measuring device limits all measurements. The concept of **significant figures** derives from the simple assumption that calculations using measurements cannot generate results that are more precise than the measurements themselves. For example, if one pie is divided into three pieces, a calculator might report that each piece is 0.33333333 of the pie (depending on the number of digits on the calculator display). However, because crumbs will undoubtedly remain in the pan, no amount of care in dividing the pieces will result in the level of accuracy the calculator suggests.

The presumption is that every measuring device is accurate to the smallest of the marked subdivisions, and every measurement with such a device should include one additional estimated digit. For instance, if one is using measurements made with a ruler whose smallest divisions are 1 centimeter apart, one should record the reading to the tenth of a centimeter, the smallest measured digit plus one estimated digit. When scientists read the results of measurements made by others, they therefore presume that the recorded values include a final digit that is an estimate based on the inherent accuracy of the instrument or device.

Sometimes finding the solution to a simpler problem helps reveal a way to solve a hard one. **Estimating** is one example of this technique of working a simpler problem. If students need to know the product of 43 times 284 and no calculator or pencil and paper are handy, they could estimate the product by getting the exact answer to the simpler problem: 40×300.

Skill Five

Select Appropriate Units to Solve Problems

Solving measurement problems requires first determining whether to use customary units or metric units. The next decision is whether the problem involves measurements of length, volume, mass, or temperature. The following chart summarizes the various units used in various types of measurement:

Measure	Metric Units	Customary Units
Length	Meter Centimeter Kilometer	Yard Inch Mile
Volume	Liter, dekaliter Deciliter	Quart, gallon Cup, teaspoon, tablespoon
Mass	Kilogram, gram	Ounce, pound, ton
Temperature	Kelvin*	Celsius, Fahrenheit

* Kelvin is not generally used in schools.

Using the metric system requires choosing the appropriate prefix to *meter*. The chart below explains those prefixes.

Metric Prefix	Meaning
Kilo-	10^3
Hecto-	10^2
Deka- (deca-)	10^1
Deci-	10^{-1}
Centi-	10^{-2}
Milli-	10^{-3}

Competency 9: Knowledge of Geometry and Spatial Sense

Eight test items relate to this competency.

Skill One

Identify Angles or Pairs of Angles as Adjacent, Complementary, Supplementary, Vertical, Corresponding, Alternate Interior, Alternate Exterior, Obtuse, Acute, or Right

An **angle** consists of all the points in two noncollinear rays that have the same vertex. More simply, an angle is commonly thought of as two "arrows" joined at their bases; the point at which they join is called the **vertex**. Two angles are **adjacent** if they share a common vertex, they share only one side, and one angle does not lie in the interior of the other.

Angles are usually measured in **degrees** (°). A circle has a measure of 360°, a half circle 180°, a quarter circle 90°, and so forth. If the sum of the measures of two angles is 90°, the two angles are **complementary**. If the sum of the measures of the two angles is 180°, the two angles are **supplementary**. If two lines intersect, they form two pairs of **vertical** angles.

If a third line intersects two intersecting lines at the same point of intersection, the third intersecting line is called a **transversal**. In the drawing below, *t* is the transversal.

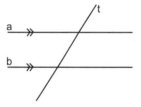

Two lines crossed by a transversal form eight angles. The four angles that lie between the two lines are called **interior angles**. In the following drawing, A and D are alternate interior angles. Angles B and C are alternate interior angles also. The interior angles that lie on the same side of the transversal are called **consecutive interior angles**. The interior angles that lie on opposite sides of the transversal are called **alternate interior angles**.

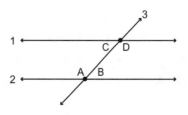

Consider the following drawing. The four angles that lie outside the two lines are called **exterior angles**. Exterior angles that lie on the same side of the transversal are called **consecutive exterior angles**, and those that lie on opposite sides of the transversal are called **alternate exterior angles**. Angles A and D are alternate exterior angles; they have the same degree measurement. Angles B and C are alternate exterior angles. An interior angle and an exterior angle that have different vertices and have sides on the same side of the transversal are called **corresponding angles**.

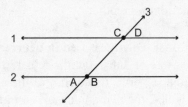

If the measures of two angles are the same, the angles are **congruent**. An angle with a measure of 90° is a **right angle**. An angle measuring less than 90° is called **acute**. An angle measuring more than 90° is called **obtuse**.

Skill Two

Identify Lines and Planes as Perpendicular, Intersecting, or Parallel

If lines have a point or points in common, they are said to **intersect**. Lines are **perpendicular** if they contain the sides of a right angle. Lines are **parallel** if they do not intersect.

Through any two points, there is exactly one straight **line**; straight lines are one dimensional. A **plane** is two dimensional (think of a surface without elevations or depressions). These concepts form the foundation of other important geometric terms and ideas.

Skill Three

Apply Geometric Properties and Relationships, Such as the Pythagorean Theorem, in Solving Problems

Triangles have various properties. One is that the sum of the measures of the three angles of any triangle is

180°. If one knows the measures of two angles, the third can be deduced using first addition and then subtraction. The **Pythagorean theorem** states that in any right triangle with legs (shorter sides) a and b and a hypotenuse (longest side) c, the sum of the squares of the sides equals the square of the hypotenuse. In algebraic notation, the Pythagorean theorem is given as

$$a^2 + b^2 = c^2$$

Skill Four

Identify the Basic Characteristics of, and Relationships Pertaining to, Regular and Irregular Geometric Shapes in Two and Three Dimensions

Regular Rectangle

A **polygon** is a simple closed curve formed by the union of three or more straight sides; this geometric figure is called a regular polygon if the angles suggested are equal in measure. Every polygon that is not regular is irregular.

A **regular rectangle** is a polygon with all sides of equal length. A square is the special case of a regular rectangle whose angles are equal (90°). If each side of a regular rectangle is of length s, the area would be given as $A = s^2$, and the perimeter would given as $P = 4s$.

Regular Triangle

The area of a triangle is the product of half its base multiplied by its height. Using either the Pythagorean theorem or trigonometric functions, one can assign each side a length of b and can describe the height of a **regular triangle** (an equilateral triangle) in terms of the length of its sides. The length is equal to b multiplied by the square root of ¾, so that the area and perimeter are as follows:

$$A = b^2 \frac{\sqrt{3}}{4}$$
$$P = 3b$$

Regular Hexagon

A **hexagon** circumscribed (surrounded) by a circle, its area is equivalent to the sums of the areas of six regular triangles a polygon with six sides; the six line segments lie in a plane and form a simple closed curve. If the sides are congruent (equal in length) and if the angles formed are all equal in measure, the figure is a **regular hexagon**, like some of the heads of bolts. If the angles are not all equal in measure, the figure is an **irregular hexagon**.

Regular Polygon

In an *n*-sided **regular polygon**, the sides are all the same length (**congruent)** and are symmetrically placed about a common center (i.e., the polygon is both equiangular and equilateral). Only certain regular polygons are "constructible" using the classical Greek tools of the compass and straightedge.

The terms **equilateral triangle** and **square** refer to regular polygons with three and four sides, respectively. The words for polygons with more than five sides (e.g., pentagon, hexagon, heptagon, etc.) can refer to either regular or nonregular polygons, although the terms generally refer to regular polygons unless otherwise specified. The sum of perpendiculars from any point to the sides of a regular polygon of *n* sides is *n* times the apothem.

Students in the elementary grades typically solve problems involving two- and three-dimensional geometric figures (e.g., perimeter and area problems, volume and surface area problems). A fundamental concept of geometry is the notion of a **point**. A point is a specific location, taking up no space, having no area, and frequently represented by a dot. A point is considered one dimensional. Through any two points, there is exactly one straight line; straight lines are one dimensional.

A **plane** is two dimensional (think of a surface without elevations or depressions). That definition forms the foundation for other important geometric terms and ideas. The **perimeter** of a two-dimensional (flat) shape or object is the distance around the object. **Volume** refers to how much space is inside a three-dimensional, closed container. It is useful to think of volume as how many cubic units fit into a solid. If the container is a rectangular solid, the volume is the product of width times length times height. If all six faces (sides) of a rectangular solid are squares, the object is a cube.

Skill Five

Apply the Geometric Concepts of Symmetry, Congruency, Similarity, Tessellations, Transformations, and Scaling

Polygons may have lines of **symmetry** that can be thought of as imaginary fold lines producing two congruent, mirror-image figures. Squares have four lines of symmetry, and nonsquare rectangles have two. Circles have an infinite number of lines of symmetry.

Geometric figures are **similar** if they have exactly the same shape, even if they are not the same size. In the figure that follows, triangles A and B are similar:

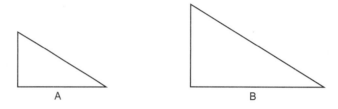

Corresponding angles of similar figures have the same measure, and the lengths of corresponding sides are proportional. In the similar triangles below, $\angle A \cong \angle D$ (meaning "angle A is **congruent** to angle D"), $\angle B \cong \angle E$, and $\angle C \cong \angle F$. The corresponding sides of the following triangles are proportional, meaning that

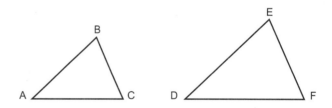

A **tessellation** is a collection of plane figures that fill the plane with no overlaps and no gaps. The following chart provides some examples:

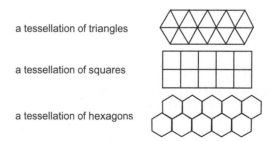

a tessellation of triangles

a tessellation of squares

a tessellation of hexagons

Scaling that is uniform is a linear transformation that enlarges or reduces an object; the scale factor is the same in all directions. The result of uniform scaling is similar (in the geometric sense) to the original. Scaling may be directional or may have a separate scale factor for each axis direction. This type of scaling may result in a change in shape.

Transformations include a variety of different operations from geometry; these operations can include rotations, reflections, and translations. Students will have experiences in such transformations as flips, turns, slides, and scaling. For example, the teacher might ask students to select a shape that is a parallelogram. Then the teacher might ask the students to do the following:

• Describe the original position and size of the parallelogram. Students can use labeled sketches if necessary.

• Rotate, translate, and reflect the parallelogram several times. Students should list the steps they followed.

• Challenge a friend to return the parallelogram to its original position.

• Determine if the friend used a reversal of the original steps or a different set of steps.

Skill Six

Determine and Locate Ordered Pairs in All Four Quadrants of a Rectangular Coordinate System

The **coordinate plane** is useful for graphing individual ordered pairs and relationships. The coordinate plane is divided into four quadrants by an x-axis (horizontal) and a y-axis (vertical). The upper-right quadrant is quadrant I, and the others (moving counterclockwise from quadrant I) are quadrants II, III and IV.

Ordered pairs indicate the locations of points on the plane. For instance, the ordered pair (–3,4) describes a point that is three units *left* from the center of the plane (the **origin**) and four units *up*, as shown in the following diagram:

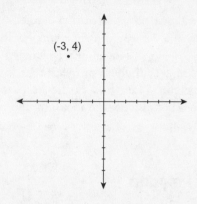

Ordered pairs are sets of data that one can display in a chart and graph on the coordinate plane. For example, the following set of data demonstrates four ordered pairs:

x	*y*
3	5
4	6
5	7
6	8

Competency 10: Knowledge of Algebraic Thinking

Six test items relate to this competency.

Skill One

Extend and Generalize Patterns of Functional Relationships

Algebraic expressions can represent relationships among numbers. For example, if *S* represents the number of students in a school and *T* represents the number of teachers, the total number of students and teachers in the school is *S* + *T*. If the school has 10 times as many students as teachers, an algebraic expression equating the number of students and teachers in the school is $S = 10T$. (Note that if either the number of students or the number of teachers is known, the other quantity can be found.)

Students should be able to generalize and extend patterns of functional relationships in algebra. This skill involves **synthesizing**, which is at the fifth level of thinking, according to Bloom's *Taxonomy*. Synthesizing involves putting information together in a new, creative way. An example of a synthesis question is, "Create a graph to illustrate what you think will be the total number of cars purchased in the year 2010 if purchases continue as they have in the years 2006 through 2008." Given the factual knowledge on the chart in their textbook, students should be able to develop or synthesize the information and generate reasonable numbers.

Skill Two

Interpret Tables, Graphs, Equations, and Verbal Descriptions to Explain Real-World Situations Involving Functional Relationships

Graphs and tables are visual aids for sets of information. Often, the impact of numbers and statistics written in text is diminished by an overabundance of tedious numbers. A graph or table helps students rapidly visualize, organize a myriad of information, and trace long periods of decline or increase. The principal graphic forms are line graphs, bar graphs, pie charts, and tables.

Line Graphs

A **line graph** is used to track one or more subjects. One element is usually time, over which the other element increases, decreases, or remains static. The lines are composed of connected points displayed on the graph through each period (e.g., years, days, seconds). The line graph in Fig. 3-1 depicts U.S. immigration statistics (from the United States Department of Justice Immigration and Naturalization Service).

This line graph is not meant to give a strictly accurate representation for every year between the two decades. If this were so, the line would hardly be straight at the beginning of the graph and the numbers might even progress from year to year. When dealing with more

than one subject, a line graph might use either different-colored lines or different types of lines if the graph is printed in black and white. On the immigration line graph, for instance, a solid line could represent immigration from northwestern Europe, and a broken line could represent immigration from southeastern Europe.

To read the line graph, students would first find the point of change that interests them. For example, if students wanted to determine immigration in 1861 at the outbreak of the Civil War, they would find the point 1861. Next, students would trace the position to the vertical information on the chart. In this instance, they would discover that approximately .1 million immigrants arrived in 1861; this was a decrease from recent years. If students wanted to discover when the number of immigrants reached 1.2 million, they would read and see that that number came in 1990.

Bar Graphs

A **bar graph** can plot one or more than one dynamic elements of a subject. Sometimes the graph is three dimensional, and the bars take on the dimension of depth; however, primary-level mathematics normally uses only two-dimensional, single-subject bar graphs.) For example, the following bar graph depicts inflation and deflation over a span of years:

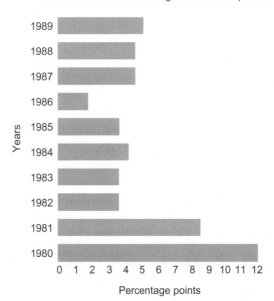

INFLATION

Inflation is a rise in the general level of prices.
Deflation is a decline in the general level of prices.

**FIG. 3-1. IMMIGRATION TO THE UNITED STATES: FISCAL YEARS
1820 TO 2001 (IN MILLIONS)**

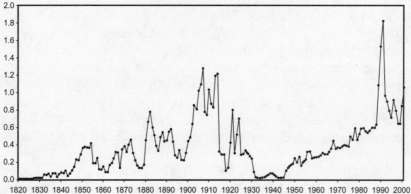

Percentage points indicate the level of prices in each year; percentage decreases (deflation) from 1980 to 1981 and from 1981 to 1982. The price level is static from 1982 to 1983. The price level then increases (inflation) from 1983 to 1984.

To read a bar graph, students begin at the base of a bar and trace the bar to its full length. Then students cross-reference the other element of information that matches the length of the bar.

Pie Charts

A pie chart helps a reader visualize percentages of a particular subject. An entire pie represents 100% of a given quantity. The measurement of the pie slices correspond to their respective shares of the 100%. For example, in the pie chart that follows, the slice representing Myrna's rent is a larger slice than any other in the pie; no other element equals or exceeds 25% of Myrna's monthly budget.

MYRNA'S MONTHLY BUDGET

Another aspect of a pie chart is the placement of the slices. The smaller-percentage elements move consecutively toward the larger elements. Therefore, the largest element in the chart will be next to the smallest element in the chart, and the line that separates them is the beginning or endpoint of the chart. From that point, the chart fans out to the other elements, going from the smallest percentages to the largest.

To read a pie chart, students choose the element of the subject that interests them and compare its size to those of the other elements. Students must be careful not to assume that elements that are similar in size are equal. The exact percentage of each element will be listed within that slice of the chart. For example, Myrna's budgeted amounts for utilities, savings, and spending are all similar in size, but it is clear from the labels on the chart that each possesses a different value.

Tables

A table is useful because it can convey large amounts of information within a confined area. To read a table, students cross-reference the column headings that run horizontally across the top of the table with the row headings that run vertically down the left side of the table. Students can scan the table for the information by reading line by line, as if reading regular text, while referring to the appropriate headings of the table to interpret the information listed. Note that some tables possess horizontal subheadings, which further ease the separation of different areas of information.

The following is an example of a unit conversion table that students might see in an elementary mathematics textbook:

Metric Units	Customary Units
1 meter	39.37 inches
1 meter	1.09 yards
1 kilometer	.62 mile
1 kilogram	2.2 pounds
1 liter	1.057 quarts

Skill Three

Selecting a Representation of an Algebraic Expression, Equation, or Inequality that Applies to a Real-World Situation

One helpful approach when attempting to solve an algebraic word problem is first to translate the problem into an equation (or, sometimes, an inequality). For example, consider this word problem:

The Acme Taxicab Company charges riders $3 just for getting into the cab, plus $2 for every mile or fraction of a mile driven. What would be the fare for a 10-mile ride?

Translating the word problem into math results in the following algebraic expression:

$$x = 3 + (2 \times 10)$$

The equation can be read as "the unknown fare (x) is equal to $3 dollars plus $2 dollars for each of the 10 miles driven." Solving the equation gives 23 for x, so $23 is the solution to the word problem.

Several common English-to-math translations are important to remember when solving word problems The word *is* often suggests an equal sign; *of* may suggest multiplication, as does *product. Sum* refers to addition; *difference* suggests subtraction; and a *quotient* is obtained after dividing. The key when translating

is to make sure that the equation accurately matches the information and relationships given in the word problem.

Competency 11: Knowledge of Data Analysis and Probability

Eight test items relate to this competency.

Skill One

Apply the Concepts of Range and Central Tendency (Mean, Median, and Mode)

Measures of central tendency of a set of values include the mean, median, and mode. The **mean** is found by adding all the values and then dividing the sum by the number of values. The **median** of a set is the middle number when the values are in numerical order. (If the set comprises an even number of values, and therefore no middle value, the mean of the middle two values gives the median.) The **mode** of a set is the value occurring most often. (Not all sets of values have a single mode; some sets have more than one.) Consider the following set:

$$6 \quad 8 \quad 14 \quad 5 \quad 6 \quad 5 \quad 5$$

The mean, median, and mode of the set are 7, 6, and 5, respectively. (Note that the mean is often referred to as the average, but all three measures are averages of sorts.)

The **range** of a set of numbers is a measure of the spread of, or variation in, the numbers.

Determining the Mean, Median, Mode, and Range

To determine the **mean** of a set of numbers add the set of numbers and divide by the total number of elements in the set. For example, the mean of 15, 10, 25, 5, 40 is $(15 + 10 + 25 + 5 + 40) \div 5 = 19$.

To find the **median,** order a given set of numbers from smallest to largest; the **median** is the "middle" number. That is, half the numbers in the set of numbers are below the median and half the numbers in the set are above the median. For example, to find the median of the set of whole numbers 15, 10, 25, 5, 40, the first step is to order the set of numbers to get 5, 10, 15, 25, 40. Because 15 is the middle number (half of the numbers are below 15, half are above 15), 15 is the median of this set of whole numbers. If the set has an even number of numbers, the median is the mean of the middle two numbers. For instance, in the set of numbers 2, 4, 6, and 8, the median is the mean of 4 and 6, or 5.

The **mode** of the set of numbers 15, 10, 25, 10, 5, 40, 10, 15 is the number 10 because it appears most frequently (three times).

The **range** of a set of numbers is obtained by subtracting the smallest number in the set from the largest number in the set. For example, the range of the set 15, 10, 25, 5, 40 is $40 - 5 = 35$.

Skill Two

Determine Probabilities of Dependent or Independent Events

Probability theory provides models for chance variations. The likelihood or chance that an event will take place is called the **probability** of the event. The probability of any event occurring is equal to the number of desired outcomes divided by the number of all possible events. Thus, the probability of blindly pulling a green ball out of a hat (in this case the desired outcome) if the hat contains two green and five yellow balls, is 2/7 (about 29%).

The probability of a particular event occurring is the ratio of the number of ways the particular event can occur to the number of possible events. We can express the ratio mathematically:

$$\text{Probability of a particular event occurring} = \frac{\text{Number of ways the event can occur}}{\text{Total number of possible events}}$$

Skill Three

Determine Odds for and Odds against a Given Situation

Odds are related to but different from probability. The odds that any given event *will* occur can be expressed as the ratio of the probability that the event will occur to the probability that the event *will not* occur. In the example from the previous section, the odds that a green ball will be drawn are 2:5, because two balls are green and five balls are not green.

If I have 4 marbles in a jar, 3 red and 1 blue, then the probability of drawing the blue is ¼. There is one chance of a blue marble, and there are 4 total chances (marbles). Odds are the number of chances for (or against) versus the number of chances against (or for). Since there is 1 chance of your picking the blue and 3 chances of your picking red, the odds are 3 to 1 AGAINST your picking the blue. For odds in favor, we just reverse them. The odds are 1 to 3 IN FAVOR of your picking the blue.

To repeat, if you express odds as AGAINST, you put the number of chances against first, versus the number of chances for. If you express odds as IN FAVOR OF, you put the number of chances for FIRST.

Note that this does not mean that the probability is 1/3 for or against. To convert odds to probability, we have to ADD the chances. So, if the odds against a horse winning are 4 to 1, this means that, out of 5 (4 + 1) chances, the horse has 1 chance in favor of winning; the PROBABILITY of the horse winning is 1/5 or 20% (*http://www.mathforum.org/library/drmath/view/56495.html*).

Skill Four

Apply Fundamental Counting Principles Such as Combinations to Solve Probability Problems

Probability is calculated as follows:

$$\text{Probability of a Particular Event Occurring} = \frac{\text{Number of Ways the Event Can Occur}}{\text{Total Number of Possible Events}}$$

Human sex type is determined by the genetic material in the sperm and egg. The genetic sex code for human females is XX. The genetic sex code for human males is XY. Eggs carry only X genes. Sperm carry both X and Y genes. The following chart helps determine the probability of a fertilized human egg being male or female:

	Female	Female
Male	X	X
X	XX	XX
Y	XY	XY

The table shows that the probability of a female (XX) is 2 out of 4, and the probability of a male (XY) is 2 out of 4. Therefore, there is a 50% chance of a boy and a 50% chance of a girl.

Skill Five

Interpret Information from Tables, Charts, Line Graphs, Bar Graphs, Circle Graphs, Box and Whisker Graphs, and Stem and Leaf Plots

Interpreting—rather than just reading—a table, chart, graph, or plot requires thinking at level 6 of Bloom's *Taxonomy*, the highest level. Students must not only read the data (numbers and words) on the visual but also comprehend what the data means. The interpretation of line graphs, bar graphs, pie charts, and tables was a topic in "Skill Two: Interpret Tables, Graphs, Equations, and Verbal Descriptions to Explain Real-World Situations Involving Functional Relationships" of Competency 10: Knowledge of Algebraic Thinking.

Two other types of visual representations are the **box-and-whisker graph** or plot and the **stem-and-leaf plot**. The box-and-whisker graph displays the range, quartiles, mean, and distribution. The following box-and-whisker graph displays the test scores of a teacher's mathematics class:

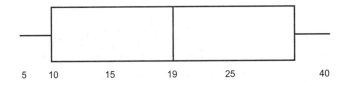

| 5 | 10 | 15 | 19 | 25 | 40 |

The data are split into four groups, called quartiles. The box represents the middle 50% of the scores. The "whiskers" extending from the left and right ends of the box represent the upper and lower quartiles. The test scores lie between 5 and 40. The upper quartile encompasses scores from about 30 to 40; the lower quartile encompasses the scores between 5 and 10. The vertical line in the box represents about 19, the mean of the scores.

A stem-and-leaf plot is an easy way to display raw data. The following example displays the ages of people attending a movie theater on a particular evening. The "stem" row lists the numbers in the tens place of each of the ages of the theatergoers, and the numbers in the "leaf" row show the digit in the ones place for each age group. For example, six people in the audience were in their thirties: two were 30, two were 33, one was 35, and one was 38.

Stem	Leaf
3	0 0 3 3 5 8
4	5 6
5	6 7
6	2 2
7	3 4

The plot makes it easy to see the range: 30 to 74. Modes (most frequent ages) are readily apparent: 30, 33, 62. There are fourteen ages—an even number; 45 and 46 are in the middle of the range. Halfway between 45 and 46 is 45.5—the **median**. The mean age (30 + 30 + 33 + 33 + 35 + 38 + 45 + 46 + 56 + 57 + 62 + 62 + 73 + 74 divided by 14) of the movie audience was about 48.

Skill Six

Make Accurate Predictions and Draw Conclusions about Data

Using the data that the students themselves assemble is an important part of their higher-level thinking.

According to Bloom's *Taxonomy*, using data in a new, creative way is a part of the synthesis level of thinking, level 5. For example, after studying the following graph of tar and nicotine in cigarettes, students would display synthesis by anticipating that a new cigarette with 10 mg of tar would have between 0.7 and 0.8 mg of nicotine:

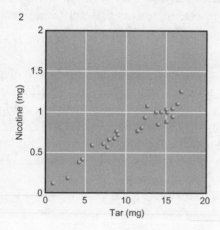

Correlation is the relationship between two variables. For example, in the graph of tar and nicotine, each dot represents one cigarette, and the placement of the dot depends on the amount of tar (x-axis) and nicotine (y-axis) the cigarette contains. Drawings like this are called **scatter plots**. If students drew a straight line through this scatter plot, it would go up and to the right, because in general the higher amount of tar, the higher amount of nicotine. The amounts of tar and nicotine are thus **positively correlated**. Some variables are negatively correlated; for instance, the weight of a vehicle would be **negatively correlated** with gas mileage if several models of vehicle were plotted in a scatter plot.

Competency 12: Knowledge of Instruction and Assessment

Four test items relate to this competency.

Skill One
Identify Alternative Instructional Strategies

Theory Behind Alternative Teaching Strategies

To design and deliver effective instruction, teachers need to understand the developmental processes common to all learners and how the varied and diverse environmental features and learning styles affect learning. Although there may be some intuitive aspects to teaching (and it seems that some people were born to teach), educators can acquire some skills through processes of introspection, observation, direct instruction, self-evaluation, and experimentation.

How teachers teach should be directly related to how learners learn. Theories of cognitive development describe how learners learn new information and acquire new skills. Among the many theories of cognitive development, one of the most influential is the Piagetian (and neo-Piagetian) theory. **Piagetian theory** describes learning in discrete and predictable stages. Therefore, teachers who understand this theory can provide students with developmentally appropriate instruction. This theory also describes learners moving from simpler ways of thinking to more complex ways of thinking and problem solving. For teachers, this theoretical perspective has many important implications. For example, teachers must create enriched environments that present learners with multiple opportunities to encounter new and unfamiliar stimuli—be they objects or ideas. Teachers must also provide learners with opportunities to engage in extended dialogue with adults; according to Piaget's theory, conversational interactions with adults are a key component of learning in the classroom.

The teacher considers environmental factors that may affect learning by designing a supportive and responsive classroom community that promotes all students' learning and self-esteem. This competency addresses the need that teachers have to be able to recognize and identify both external and internal factors that affect student learning.

The effective teacher who acknowledges the **internal factors** of all students may need to use alternative learning strategies. Internal factors, beyond the general characteristics that humans share as they grow and mature, include students' personality characteristics, their self-concept and sense of self-esteem, their self-discipline and self-control, their ability to cope with stress, their general outlook on life, their learning styles, etc.

The effective teacher also considers **external factors**. Although they are not individual traits, external factors do have an impact on student learning and progress and may necessitate alternative instructional strategies. External factors include the home environment and family relationships, peer relationships, community situations, and the school environment. In other words, external factors constitute the context in which the student lives and learns.

Effective teachers may need to use alternative learning strategies as they examine their classes in light of **Maslow's hierarchy of human needs**. Before attempting to encourage students to achieve higher levels of learning, effective instructors might use alternative instructional strategies to make sure that the classroom instruction satisfies the students' lower-level physiological, psychological, safety, and affiliation needs.

Educational **scaffolding** is a technique used to provide guidance to students as they conduct research, but the technique does not limit the student in the investigation. Ideally, educational scaffolding will

- provide direction,
- clarify purpose,
- keep students on task,
- offer the assessment (rubric) to clarify expectations,
- supply some suggestions for sources,
- make available a lesson or activity without problems,
- be an efficient instructional technique, and
- generate thinking.

Many teachers do not encourage students to question them. The teaching strategy that Marcia Baxter Magolda encourages, however, has teachers' acting as

examples to students of positive ways to question authority and teachers' letting students know that they can also question educators. This means that teachers model critical thinking skills in the classroom. One way teachers can question authority is by examining and evaluating readings—whether from textbooks or other sources. Teachers can also question authority by exposing advertising claims and gimmicks—particularly those that seem to manipulate numbers.

Moreover, by allowing students to question them, teachers acknowledge that everyone is a learner. Everyone should participate in a lifelong process of continuous learning. It is no shame or disgrace for a teacher to admit that sometimes he or she doesn't know the answer to every question. This gives the teacher the opportunity to show students how adults think, how they have a level of awareness (metacognition) even when they do not know something, and how they go about finding answers to their questions. A teacher who admits not to have all the answers has the opportunity to work with students to find answers and/or to help students realize that some of life's most difficult questions do not have easy answers.

By being open to questioning and encouraging investigation, effective teachers express their respect for students as learners. Teachers' affirmations include smiles and nods of approval, positive comments (such as, "That's a good answer"), and encouraging cues (such as, "That may seem like a reasonable answer, but can you think of a different answer?" or "Can you explain what you mean by that answer?"). Validating students as knowers also means supporting students' voices and giving them ample opportunities to express their ideas, share their opinions, and contribute to class discussions. These opportunities can include times of oral discussion as well as written assignments.

Some alternative instructional strategies reflect the instructional objectives that the teacher and students devise, desired learning outcomes, and students' needs as evidenced by preassessment. Regardless of which theoretical perspective teachers adopt—and even if at times they find themselves taking a rather eclectic approach and borrowing elements from several theoretical bases, it is helpful for teachers to consider whether they are structuring their classrooms to satisfy learners' needs or merely their own needs as teachers. Furthermore, if a teacher's goal is to become a more effective instructor by facilitating learners' knowledge and skill acquisition, then that teacher will engage continuously in a process of self-examination and self-evaluation.

Looking Outside the Classroom for Alternative Teaching Strategies

Parents and other members of the community can be excellent local experts from whom students can learn about any subject; for example, bankers and computer programmers can teach students practical applications of mathematics. The list can be endless. An effective teacher makes sure that any guest who is invited to speak to the class understands the purpose of the visit and the goals or objectives of the presentation. Preparation can make the class period more focused and meaningful.

Field trips are also excellent sources of information, especially about careers and current issues. One field trip can yield assignments in mathematics, science, and social science. Teachers can collaborate with each other to produce thematic assignments for the field trip or to coordinate the students' assignments. In math classes students can analyze data and present their analysis with the aid of computers.

Skill Two

Select Manipulatives, Mathematical and Physical Models, and Other Classroom Teaching Tools

Manipulatives are touchable, movable materials that enhance students' understanding of a concept. Particularly in mathematics and science classes manipulatives give students a concrete way of dealing with concepts, but tangible materials are appropriate and helpful in all subject areas. Math teachers use plastic shapes in studying geometry. Number lines, place value cubes, and tessellation blocks can help students understand math, not only in elementary classes but also in algebra, trigonometry, and calculus.

The effective teacher uses criteria to evaluate audiovisual, multimedia, models, and computer resources. The first thing to look for is congruence with lesson

goals. If the models, materials, manipulatives, and software do not reinforce student outcomes, then schools should not use them, no matter how flashy or well-made they are. A checklist for selecting the materials could include appropriate sequence of instruction, meaningful student interaction, pacing, motivation, clarity of purpose, and the potential for individual or group use.

When evaluating resources, teachers should also consider students' strengths and needs, learning styles or preferred modalities, and interests. Teachers can determine students' needs through formal or informal assessment. Most standardized tests include an indication of which objectives the student did not master. Mastering these objectives can be assisted with computer or multimedia aids.

The effective teacher evaluates resources well in advance of the lesson and before purchase whenever possible. The teacher also evaluates the materials as students use them. When students have finished using the materials, the teacher can assess material usefulness by considering students' achievement levels and/or by asking students to voice their opinions of the materials.

Skill Three

Identify Ways That Calculators, Computers, and Other Technology Can Be Used in Instruction

Calculators and computers are important problem-solving tools. Their effectiveness, however, depends on the accuracy of the input and the ability of the user to operate the devices correctly.

The effective teacher includes resources of all types in the curriculum planning process. The educator should be very familiar with the school library, the local library, education service center resources, and the library of any colleges or universities in the area. Another important set of resources is the audiovisual aids that the teacher can borrow: kits, films, filmstrips, videos, laser disks, and computer software, among others. All audiovisual aids relate to curricular objectives. Many librarians have keyed their resources to objectives in related subject areas and enable the teacher to incorporate library holdings with ease into the lessons. However, teachers should never use resources with a class unless they have previewed and approved them. The teacher should include the list of resources for a lesson or unit in the curriculum guide or the lesson plan to make use more efficient.

The effective teacher determines the appropriate place in the lesson for audiovisual aids. If the material is especially interesting and thought-provoking, the teacher can use it to introduce a unit. For example, a travel video on coral reefs or snorkeling might be an excellent introduction to the study of ocean depths and how to graph them.

Because textbooks do not stay up-to-date on batting averages and stock reports, local, state, and national newspapers and magazines are important resources for teaching mathematics. Figuring batting averages and watching the stock reports are practical lessons in mathematics. Some newspapers and magazines provide special programs to help teachers use their products in the classroom. Local newspapers may even be willing to send specialists to work with students or act as special resource persons.

Technology experts argue that tools, like the Internet, make available such a substantial amount of wide-ranging content that today's teachers have a greater role than ever helping students acquire process skills (such as critical and creative thinking) rather than merely teaching content skills. Content changes and expands, but thinking processes remain salient and necessary, regardless of the content.

On-line databases are essential tools for research. Chapter 5 provides more information on technology in the section titled "Skill One: Identify the Purposes and Functions of Common Computer Software" within Competency 26.

Spreadsheets are especially useful to the math classroom. The reader can see rows and columns of numbers linked to produce totals and averages. Formulas can connect information in one cell (the intersection of a row and column) to another cell. Teachers often keep grade books on spreadsheets because of the ease in updating information. Once formulas are in place, teach-ers can enter grades and have completely up-to-date averages for all students. Some spreadsheet programs also include charting functions that enable teachers to display class averages on a bar chart to provide visual comparisons of performance among various classes.

Students can use spreadsheets to collect and analyze numerical data and then sort the data in various orders. For example, students could enter population figures from various countries and then draw various types of graphs—lines, bars, pies, and scatter plots, for example—to convey information. This type of graphic information can also be used in multimedia presentations. Various stand-alone graphing and charting software packages are also available.

Graphics or paint programs allow users to draw freehand to produce any type of chart, graph, picture. In addition, many word-processing programs have some graphic functions. Students can use these programs to produce boxes, circles, or other shapes to illustrate classroom presentations or individual research projects. For teachers, these relatively simple tools make it easy to create handouts and instructional materials with a very professional and polished appearance.

Today's teachers also need to acquire and demonstrate skill in using presentation software (such as Microsoft PowerPoint) to prepare instructional lessons. In many classrooms, the use of presentation software makes the traditional use of transparencies on an overhead projector obsolete. Presentation software also makes it possible to provide students with instructional handouts and outlines to complement classroom instruction. In some situations and in some schools, Web authoring experience and skills will also prove useful.

Skill Four
Identify a Variety of Methods of Assessing Mathematical Knowledge, Including Analyzing Student Thinking to Determine Strengths and Weaknesses.

An acceptable testing environment requires the mathematics teachers to

- prepare students by emphasizing the critical knowledge they need to learn,

- establish a setting with clear instructions and fair tests for students to complete, and

- give feedback that praises correct responses and corrects errors and misunderstandings.

Assessment has many purposes. It provides proper feedback to the students about their progress in their academic program. Assessment can also determine the prior knowledge student possess before they begin a topic of discussion.

Assessment can help to determine behavioral issues that can disrupt the learning process. For instance, behavioral assessment may look at how students work together in groups, how they organize their work, or how they pay attention to details and instructions. In addition, asking students to self-assess their work can provide great insight into the attitudes, work patterns, and ethics the students are harboring inside.

Used daily as part of a sound instructional program, assessment can provide information about the effectiveness of the lesson, the method of delivery, the

Bloom's Taxonomy of Educational Objectives

Level of Question	Student Capability	Questioning Verbs
Level 1: Knowledge	Remembers, recalls learned (or memorized) information	define, describe, enumerate, identify, label, list, match, name, read, record, reproduce, select, state, view
Level 2: Comprehension	Understands the meaning of information and is able to restate in own words	classifiy, cite, convert, describe, discuss, estimate, explain, generalize, give examples, make sense out of, paraphrase, restate (in own words), summarize, trace, understand
Level 3: Application	Uses the information in new situations	act, administer, articulate, assess, chart, collect, compute, construct, contribute, control, determine, develop, discover, establish, extend, implement, include, inform, instruct, operationalize, participate, predict, prepare, preserve, produce, project, provide, relate, report, show, solve, teache, transfer, use, utilize
Level 4: Analysis	Breaks down information into component parts; examines parts for divergent thinking and inferences	break down, correlate, diagram, differentiate, discriminate, distinguish, focus, illustrate, infer, limit, outline, point out, prioritize, recognize, separate, subdivide
Level 5: Synthesis	Creates something new by divergently or creatively using information	adapt, anticipate, categorize, collaborate, combine, communicate, compare, compile, compose, contrast, create, designs, devise, express, facilitate, formulate, generate, incorporate, individualize, initiate, integrate, intervene, model, modify, negotiate, plan, progress, rearrange, reconstruct, reinforce, reorganize, revise, structure, substitute, validate
Level 6: Evaluation	Judges on the basis of informed criteria	appraise, compare and contrast, conclude, criticize, critique, decide, defend, interpret, judge, justify, reframe, support

curriculum (in terms of meeting district goals and expectations), and information on how students are learning. Effective teachers continually perceive assessment as a vital and integral part of their programs.

Assessing students using a variety of methods is an important part of every class, regardless of the subject matter. When preparing assessment techniques, the teacher must consider both the goals and purposes of assessment. Chapter 4 provides details on assessment techniques that apply to all subject areas in the section titled "Skill Two: Identify Appropriate Assessment Methods in Teaching Social Science Concepts" under Competency 17.

A teacher should use a variety of methods to assess mathematical knowledge. Previous chapters of this book have discussed such methods as the following:

- Teacher-made tests
- Paper-and-pencil tests
- Projects, papers, and portfolios
- Machine-scorable tests
- Essay tests
- Authentic assessments
- Observations

- Anecdotal records
- Self- and peer assessment
- Criterion-referenced tests
- Norm-referenced tests
- Performance-based assessment

Creating and using effective assessment tools requires an understanding of the six levels of thinking established by Benjamin Bloom in his *Taxonomy*. The following chart describes each level and list some verbs that teachers can use to formulate questions that will test at the appropriate level:

REFERENCES

United States Department of Justice Immigration and Naturalization Service. *Statistical yearbook of the immigration and naturalization service 2001.* Washington, DC: US Government Printing Office. *http://www.migrationinformation.org/Globaldata/charts/final.immigbyyear.shtml*

"Math Forum—Ask Dr. Math." *http://www.mathforum.org/library/drmath/view/56495.html*

Social Science

Competency 13: Knowledge of Time, Continuity, and Change (History)

Twelve test items relate to this competency.

Skill One

Identify Major Historical Events That Are Related by Cause and Effect

Knowledge of significant events, ideas, and people from the past is an important part of the social studies curriculum. This knowledge results from careful analysis of cause-and-effect relationships in the following chronological eras:

- Beginnings of civilization to 1620
- Colonization and settlement (1585–1763)
- Revolution and the new nation (1754–1815)
- Expansion and reform (1801–1861)
- Civil War and Reconstruction (1850–1877)
- Development of the industrial United States (1870–1900)
- Emergence of modern America (1890–1930)
- Great Depression and World War II (1929–1945)

- Postwar United States (1945–1970)
- Contemporary United States (1968–present)

According to Piaget, there are four stages of cognitive development, and it is during the fourth stage (formal operations) that students can begin to identify cause-and-effect relationships. The formal operations stage describes the way of thinking for learners between the ages of 11 and 15 years. Piaget explains that the stage constitutes the ultimate stage of cognitive development (thus also describing adult thinking).

Piaget's four stages of cognitive development are as follows:

Stage 1: The **sensorimotor stage** describes individuals from birth to around the age of 2.

Stage 2: The **preoperational stage** describes cognitive behavior between the ages of 2 and 7. Egocentrism, rigidity of thought, semilogical reasoning, and limited social cognition characterize the state. Some cognitive psychologists have observed that this stage seems to describe how individuals think more in terms of what they cannot do than what they can do. This stage is indicative of the way that children in preschool and kindergarten go about solving problems. Many children in the primary grades also may be at this stage in their cognitive development.

The next two stages may be most important for elementary and secondary school teachers because the stages describe cognitive development during the times that most students are in school.

Stage 3: The **concrete operations stage** is the beginning of operational thinking and describes the thinking of children between the ages of 7 and 11. Learners at this age begin to decenter; they are able to take into consideration viewpoints other than their own. They can perform transformations, meaning that they can understand reversibility, inversion, reciprocity, and conservation. Students at this stage can group items into categories, make inferences about reality, engage in inductive reasoning, increase their quantitative skills, and manipulate symbols if they have concrete examples with which to work. This stage of cognitive development is the threshold to higher-level learning for students.

Stage 4: The **formal operations stage** is the last stage of cognitive development and opens the door for high-level critical thinking. This stage describes adult thinking. Learners at this stage of cognitive development can engage in logical, abstract, and hypothetical thought; they can use the scientific method, meaning they can formulate hypotheses, isolate influences, and identify cause-and-effect relationships. They can plan and anticipate verbal cues. They can engage in both deductive and inductive reasoning, and they can operate on verbal statements exclusive of concrete experiences or examples. These cognitive abilities characterize the highest levels of thought.

Skill Two

Evaluate Examples of Primary Source Documents for Historical Perspective

Evaluating primary source documents to gain a historical perspective involves the ability to analyze and interpret the past. Analysis and interpretation result from an understanding that history is logically constructed; this conclusion results from careful analysis of documents, eyewitness accounts, letters, diaries, artifacts,

photos, historical sites, and other primary sources. It is through these primary source documents that history can come alive.

The Library of Congress has on-line a wide range of primary source documents, from the Declaration of Independence and the Constitution to recordings and photographs made during the Great Depression. Students can even conduct interviews with veterans and examine the diaries, letters, and discharge papers that veterans or members of their families or communities may possess. Visits to local museums, libraries, and courthouses can also uncover primary source documents.

Skill Three

Identify Cultural Contributions and Technological Developments of Africa; the Americas; Asia, including the Middle East; and Europe

Skill Four

Relate Physical and Human Geographic Factors to Major Historical Events and Movements

Skill Five

Identify Significant Historical Leaders and Events That Have Influenced Eastern and Western Civilizations

The earth is estimated to be approximately 6 billion years old. The earliest known humans, called **hominids**, lived in Africa 3 to 4 million years ago. Of the several species of hominids that developed, all modern humans descended from just one group, the *Homo sapiens sapiens*. *Homo sapiens sapiens* is a subspecies of *Homo sapiens* (along with Neanderthals, who became extinct) and appeared in Africa between 200,000 and 150,000 years ago.

Historians divide prehistory into three periods. The period from the emergence of the first-known hominids, or humans, around 2.5 million years ago until approximately 10,000 BCE is the **Paleolithic period**, or **Old Stone Age**. During that period, human beings lived in very small groups of perhaps 10 to 20 nomadic people, constantly moving from place to place. Human beings had the ability to **make tools and weapons** from stone and from the bones of animals they killed. Hunting large game such as mammoths, which were sometimes driven off cliffs in large numbers, was crucial to the survival of early humans, who used the meat, fur, and bones of the animals to survive. Early humans supplemented their diets by foraging for food. They took shelter in caves and other natural formations, and they **painted and drew on the walls of caves.** Cave paintings discovered in France and northern Spain, created during the prehistoric period, depict scenes of animals such as lions, owls, and oxen. Around 500,000 years ago, humans began to use **fire**, which provided light and warmth in shelters and caves, and cooked meat and other foods. Human beings developed **means of creating fire** and improved techniques of **producing tools and weapons**.

The **Mesolithic period**, or **Middle Stone Age**, from 10,000 to 7000 BCE, marks the beginning of a major transformation known as the Neolithic Revolution. Previously, historians and archeologists thought this change occurred later. Thus, they called it the Neolithic Revolution because they thought it took place entirely within the *Neolithic period*, or *New Stone Age*. Beginning in the Mesolithic Age, humans domesticated plants and began to shift away from a reliance on hunting large game and foraging. Human beings had previously relied on gathering food where they found it and had moved almost constantly in search of game and wild berries and other vegetation. During the Mesolithic age, humans were able to **plant and harvest** some crops and began to stay in one place for longer periods. Early humans also improved their tool-making techniques and developed various kinds of tools and weapons.

During the **Neolithic period**, or **New Stone Age**, this "revolution" was complete, and humans engaged in systematic agriculture and began domesticating animals. Although humans continued to hunt animals, to supplement their diet with **meat**, and to use the skins and bones to make clothing and weapons, major changes in society occurred. Human beings became settled and lived in farming villages or towns, the population increased, and people began to live in much larger communities. A more settled way of life led to a **more structured social system**; a higher level of organization within societies; the development of **crafts**, such as the production

of **pottery**; and a rise in **trade** or exchange of goods among groups.

Between 4000 and 3000 BCE, **writing** developed, and the towns and villages settled during the Neolithic period developed a more complex pattern of existence. The existence of written records marks the **end of the prehistoric period**. The beginning of history coincides with the emergence of the earliest societies that exhibit characteristics that enable them to be considered as civilizations. The first civilizations emerged in Mesopotamia and Egypt.

Ancient and Medieval Times

Appearance of Civilization and Related Cultural and Technological Developments. Between 6000 and 3000 BCE, humans invented the **plow**, developed the **wheel**, harnessed the **wind**, discovered how to smelt **copper ores**, and began to develop accurate **solar calendars**. Small villages gradually grew into populous cities. The **invention of writing** in 3500 BCE in Mesopotamia marks the beginning of civilization and divides prehistoric from historic times.

Mesopotamia. Sumer (4000–2000 BCE) included the city of Ur. The Sumerians constructed **dikes and reservoirs** and established a loose confederation of **city-states**. They probably invented writing (called **cuneiform** because of its wedge-shaped letters). After 538 BCE, the peoples of Mesopotamia, whose natural boundaries were insufficient to thwart invaders, were absorbed into other empires and dynasties.

Egypt. During the end of the Archaic period (5000–2685 BCE), in about 3200 BCE, Menes, or Narmer, probably unified upper and lower Egypt. The capital moved to Memphis during the Third Dynasty (ca. 2650 BCE). The **pyramids** were built during the Fourth Dynasty (ca. 2613–2494 BCE). After 1085 BCE, in the Post-Empire period, Egypt came under the successive control of the Assyrians, the Persians, Alexander the Great, and finally, in 30 BCE, the Roman Empire. The Egyptians developed papyrus and made many medical advances.

Palestine and the Hebrews. Phoenicians settled along the present-day Lebanon coast (Sidon, Tyre, Beirut, Byblos) and established colonies at Carthage and in Spain.

They spread **Mesopotamian culture** through their trade networks. The Hebrews probably moved to Egypt in about 1700 BCE and suffered enslavement in about 1500 BCE. The Hebrews fled Egypt under Moses and, around 1200 BCE, returned to Palestine. King David (reigned ca. 1012–972 BCE) defeated the Philistines and established Jerusalem as a capital. The poor and less attractive state of Judah continued until 586 BCE, when the Chaldeans transported the Jews to Chaldea as advisors and slaves (Babylonian captivity). The Persians conquered Babylon in 539 BCE and allowed the Jews to return to Palestine.

Greece. In the Archaic period (800–500 BCE), the Greeks organized around the *polis*, or **city-state**. Oligarchs controlled most of the *polis* until near the end of the sixth century, when individuals holding absolute power (tyrants) replaced them. By the end of the sixth century, **democratic governments** in turn replaced many tyrants.

The Classical Age. The fifth century BCE was the high point of Greek civilization. It opened with the Persian Wars (560–479 BCE), after which Athens organized the Delian League. Pericles (ca. 495–429 BCE) used money from the league to rebuild Athens, including construction of the Parthenon and other buildings on the Acropolis hill. Athens' dominance spurred war with Sparta. At the same time, a revolution in philosophy occurred in classical Athens. The **Sophists** emphasized the individual and the attainment of excellence through rhetoric, grammar, music, and mathematics. **Socrates** (ca. 470–399 BCE) criticized the Sophists' emphasis on rhetoric and emphasized a process of questioning, or dialogues, with his students. Like Socrates, **Plato** (ca. 428–348 BCE) emphasized ethics. Aristotle (ca. 384–322 BCE) was Plato's pupil. He criticized Plato and argued that ideas or forms did not exist outside of things. He contended that it was necessary to examine four factors in treating any object: its matter, its form, its cause of origin, and its end or purpose.

Rome. The traditional founding date for Rome is 753 BCE. Between 800 and 500 BCE, Greek tribes colonized southern Italy, bringing their alphabet and religious practices to Roman tribes. In the sixth and seventh centuries BCE, the Etruscans expanded southward and conquered Rome. In the early Republic, power was in the hands of the patricians (wealthy landowners).

During the 70s and 60s, **Pompey** (106–48 BCE) and **Julius Caesar** (100–44 BCE) emerged as the most powerful men.

In 60 BCE, Caesar convinced Pompey and Crassus (ca. 115–53 BCE) to form the First Triumvirate. When Crassus died, Caesar and Pompey fought for leadership. In 47 BCE, the Senate proclaimed Caesar dictator and later named him consul for life. **Brutus** and **Cassius** believed that Caesar had destroyed the Republic. They formed a conspiracy, and on March 15, 44 BCE (the Ides of March), Brutus and Cassius assassinated Caesar in the Roman forum. Caesar's 18-year-old nephew and adopted son, Octavian, succeeded him.

The Roman Empire. After a period of struggle, Octavian (reigned 27 BCE–14 CE), named as Caesar's heir, gained absolute control while maintaining the appearance of a republic. When he offered to relinquish his power in 27 BCE, the Senate gave him a vote of confidence and a new title, Augustus. He introduced many reforms, including new coinage, new tax collection, fire and police protection, and land for settlers in the provinces. By the first century CE, Christianity had spread throughout the Empire. Around 312 CE, Emperor Constantine converted to Christianity and ordered toleration in the Edict of Milan (ca. 313 CE). In 391 CE, Emperor Theodosius I (reigned 371–395 CE) proclaimed Christianity the empire's official religion.

The Byzantine Empire. Emperor Theodosius II (reigned 408–450 CE) divided his empire between his two sons, one ruling the East and the other ruling the West. After the Vandals sacked Rome in 455 CE, Constantinople was the undisputed leading city of the Byzantine Empire. In 1453 CE, Constantinople fell to the Ottoman Turks.

Islamic Civilization in the Middle Ages. **Mohammed** was born about 570 CE. In 630 CE, he marched into Mecca. The Sharia (code of law and theology) outlines five pillars of faith for Muslims to observe. The beliefs that there is one God and that Mohammed is his prophet form the first pillar. Second, the faithful must pray five times a day. Third, they must perform charitable acts. Fourth, they must fast from sunrise to sunset during the holy month of Ramadan. Finally, they must make a *haj*, or pilgrimage, to Mecca. The Koran, which consists of 114 *suras* (verses), contains Mohammed's teachings.

The Omayyad caliphs, with their base in Damascus, governed from 661–750 CE. They called themselves **Shiites** and believed they were Mohammed's true successors. (Most Muslims were **Sunnis**, from the word *sunna*, meaning "oral traditions about the prophet.")

The Abbasid caliphs ruled from 750–1258 CE. They moved the capital to Baghdad and treated Arab and non-Arab Muslims as equals. Genghis (or Chingis) Khan (reigned 1206–1227 CE) and his army invaded the Abbasids. In 1258 CE, they seized Baghdad and murdered the last caliph.

Feudalism in Japan. Feudalism in Japan began with the arrival of mounted nomadic warriors from throughout Asia during the Kofun Era (300–710 CE). Some members of the nomadic groups formed an elite class and became part of the court aristocracy in the capital city of Kyoto, in western Japan. During the Heian Era (794–1185 CE), a hereditary military aristocracy arose in the Japanese provinces; by the late Heian Era, many of these formerly nomadic warriors had established themselves as independent landowners, or as managers of landed estates, or *shoen* owned by Kyoto aristocrats. These aristocrats depended on the warriors to defend their *shoen*, and in response to this need, the warriors organized into small groups called *bushidan*.

After victory in the Taira-Minamoto War (1180–1185 CE), Minamoto no Yorimoto forced the emperor to award him the title of *shogun*, which is short for "barbarian-subduing generalissimo." Yorimoto used this power to found the Kamakura Shogunate, a feudal military dictatorship that survived for 148 years.

By the fourteenth century CE, the great military governors (*shugo*) had augmented their power enough to become a threat to the Kamakura, and in 1333 CE they led a rebellion that overthrew the shogunate. The Tokugawa shogunate was the final and most unified of the three shogunates. Under the Tokugawa, the *daimyo* were direct vassals of the shoguns and were under strict control. The warriors gradually became scholars and bureaucrats under the *bushido*, or code of chivalry, and

the principles of neo-Confucianism. Under the Meji Restoration of 1868, the emperor again received power and the samurai class lost its special privileges.

Chinese and Indian Empires. In the third century BCE, the Indian kingdoms fell under the Mauryan Empire. The grandson of the founder of this empire, named Ashoka, opened a new era in the cultural history of India by believing in the Buddhist religion.

Buddha had disregarded the Vedic gods and the institutions of caste and had preached a relatively simple ethical religion that advocated two levels of aspiration—a monastic life of renunciation of the world and a high, but not too difficult, morality for the layman. Although the two religions of Hinduism and Buddhism flourished together for centuries in a tolerant rivalry, Buddhism virtually disappeared from India by the thirteenth century CE.

Chinese civilization originated in the Yellow River Valley, only gradually extending to the southern regions. Three dynasties ruled early China: the Xia or Hsia, the Shang (ca. 1500 to 1122 BCE), and the Zhou (ca. 1122 to 211 BCE). After the Zhou Dynasty fell, China welcomed the teachings of **Confucius**; warfare between states and philosophical speculation created circumstances ripe for such teachings. Confucius made the good order of society depend on an ethical ruler, who would receive advice from scholar-moralists like Confucius himself. In contrast to the Confucians, the Chinese Taoists professed a kind of anarchism; the best kind of government was none at all. The wise man did not concern himself with political affairs but with mystical contemplation that identified him with the forces of nature.

African Kingdoms and Cultures. The **Bantu** peoples lived across large sections of Africa. Bantu societies lived in tiny chiefdoms, starting in the third millennium BCE, and each group developed its own version of the original Bantu language.

The **Nok** people lived in the area now known as Nigeria. Artifacts indicate that they were peaceful farmers who built small communities consisting of houses of wattle and daub (poles and sticks). The **Ghanaians** lived about 500 miles from what is now Ghana. Their kingdom fell to a Berber group in the late eleventh century CE, and

Mali emerged as the next great kingdom in the thirteenth century. The Malians lived in a huge kingdom that lay mostly on the savanna bordering the Sahara Desert. Timbuktu, built in the thirteenth century CE, was a thriving city of culture where traders visited **stone houses**, **shops**, **libraries**, and **mosques**.

The Songhai lived near the Niger River and gained their independence from the Mali in the early 1400s. The major growth of the empire came after 1464 CE, under the leadership of Sunni Ali, who devoted his reign to warfare and expansion of the empire.

Civilizations of the Americas. The great civilizations of early America were agricultural, and the foremost civilization was the Mayan in Yucatan, Guatemala, and eastern Honduras. Farther north in Mexico, a series of advanced cultures arose that derived much of their substance from the Maya. Peoples like the Zapotecs, Totonacs, Olmecs, and Toltecs evolved into a high level of civilization. By 500 BCE, agricultural peoples had begun to use a **ceremonial calendar** and had built **stone pyramids** on which they held religious observances.

The Aztecs then took over Mexican culture, and a major feature of their culture was human sacrifice in repeated propitiation of their chief god. Aztec government was centralized, with an elective king and a large army. Andean civilization was characterized by the evolution of **beautifully made pottery**, **intricate fabrics**, and **flat-topped mounds**, or *huacas*.

In the interior of South America, the Inca, who called themselves "Children of the Sun," controlled an area stretching from Ecuador to central Chile. Sun worshippers, they believed that they were the sun god's vice regents on Earth and more powerful than any other humans. They believed that every person's place in society was fixed and immutable and that the state and the army were supreme. They were at the apex of their power just before the Spanish conquest. In the present-day southwestern United States and northern Mexico, two varieties of ancient culture are still identifiable. The Anasazi developed **adobe architecture**, worked the land extensively, had a highly developed system of **irrigation**, and made cloth and baskets. The Hohokam built separate stone and timber houses around a central plaza.

Europe in Antiquity. The Frankish Kingdom was the most important medieval Germanic state. Under Clovis I (reigned 481–511 CE), the Franks finished conquering France and the Gauls in 486 CE. Clovis converted to Christianity and founded the Merovingian dynasty.

Charles the Great, or **Charlemagne** (reigned 768–814 CE), founded the Carolingian dynasty. In 800 CE, Pope Leo III named Charlemagne Emperor of the Holy Roman Empire. In the Treaty of Aix-la-Chapelle (812 CE), the Byzantine emperor recognized Charles's authority in the West. The purpose of the Holy Roman Empire was to reestablish the Roman Empire in the West. Charles's son, Louis the Pious (reigned 814–840 CE), succeeded him. On Louis's death, his three sons vied for control of the Empire. The three eventually signed the Treaty of Verdun in 843 CE. This gave Charles the Western Kingdom (France), Louis the Eastern Kingdom (Germany), and Lothair the Middle Kingdom, a narrow strip of land running from the North Sea to the Mediterranean.

In this period, **manorialism** developed as an economic system in which large estates, granted by the king to nobles, strove for self-sufficiency. The lord and his serfs (also called villeins) divided the ownership.

The church was the only institution to survive the Germanic invasions intact. The power of the popes grew in this period. **Gregory I** (reigned 590–604 CE) was the first member of a monastic order to rise to the papacy. He advanced the ideas of penance and purgatory. He centralized church administration and was the first pope to rule as the secular head of Rome. Monasteries preserved the few remnants that survived the decline of antiquity.

The year 1050 marked the beginning of the High Middle Ages. Europe was poised to emerge from five centuries of decline. Between 1000 and 1350, the population of Europe grew from 38 million to 75 million. New technologies, such as **heavy plows**, and a slight temperature rise produced a longer growing season and contributed to agricultural productivity.

The Holy Roman Empire. Charlemagne's grandson, Louis the German, became Holy Roman Emperor under the Treaty of Verdun. Otto became Holy Roman

Emperor in 962. His descendants governed the empire until 1024, when the Franconian dynasty assumed power, reigning until 1125. Under the leadership of **William the Conqueror** (reigned 1066–1087), the Normans conquered England in 1066. William stripped the Anglo-Saxon nobility of its privileges and instituted feudalism. He ordered a survey of all property of the realm; the Domesday Book (1086) records the findings.

William introduced feudalism to England. **Feudalism** was the decentralized political system of personal ties and obligations that bound vassals to their lords. Serfs were peasants who were bound to the land. They worked on the *demesne*, or lord's property, three or four days a week in return for the right to work their own land.

In 1215, the English barons forced King John I to sign the **Magna Carta Libertatum**, acknowledging their "ancient" privileges. The Magna Carta established the principle of a limited English monarchy.

In 710 to 711, the Moors conquered Spain from the Visigoths. Under the Moors, Spain enjoyed a stable, prosperous government. The caliphate of Córdoba became a center of scientific and intellectual activity. The Reconquista (1085–1340) wrested control from the Moors. The fall of Córdoba in 1234 completed the Reconquista, except for the small state of Granada.

Most of eastern Europe and Russia was never under Rome's control; Germanic invasions separated the areas from Western influence. In Russia, Vladimir I converted to Orthodox Christianity in 988. He established the basis of Kievian Russia. After 1054, Russia broke into competing principalities. The **Mongols (Tartars)** invaded in 1221. They completed their conquest in 1245 and cut Russia's contact with the West for almost a century.

The **Crusades** attempted to liberate the Holy Land from infidels. Seven major crusades occurred between 1096 and 1300. Urban II called Christians to the First Crusade (1096–1099) with the promise of a plenary indulgence (exemption from punishment in purgatory). Younger sons who would not inherit their fathers' lands were also attracted. The Crusades helped to renew interest in the ancient world. However, the Crusaders massacred thousands of Jews and Muslims, and relations between Europe and the Byzantine Empire collapsed.

Scholasticism. Scholasticism was an effort to reconcile reason and faith and to instruct Christians on how to make sense of the pagan tradition. The most influential proponent of this effort was Thomas Aquinas (ca. 1225–1274), who believed that there were two orders of truth. The lower level, reason, could demonstrate propositions such as the existence of God, but the higher level necessitated that some of God's mysteries, such as the nature of the Trinity, be accepted on faith. Aquinas viewed the universe as a great chain of being, with humans midway on the chain, between the material and the spiritual.

Late Middle Ages and the Renaissance

The Black Death. Conditions in Europe encouraged the quick spread of disease. Refuse, excrement, and dead animals filled the streets of the cities, which lacked any form of urban sanitation. Living conditions were overcrowded, with families often sleeping in one room or one bed; poor nutrition was rampant; and there was often little personal cleanliness. Merchants helped bring the plague to Asia; carried by fleas on rats, the disease arrived in Europe in 1347. By 1350, the disease had killed 25 percent to 40 percent of the European population.

Literature, Art, and Scholarship. Humanists, as both orators and poets, often imitated the classical works which inspired them. The literature of the period was more secular and wide ranging than that of the Middle Ages. **Dante Alighieri** (1265–1321) was a Florentine writer whose *Divine Comedy*, describing a journey through hell, purgatory, and heaven, shows that reason can take people only so far, and that attaining heaven requires God's grace and revelation. Francesco Petrarch (1304–1374) encouraged the study of ancient Rome, collected and preserved works of ancient writers, and produced a large body of work in the classical literary style.

Giovanni Boccaccio (1313–1375) wrote *The Decameron*, a collection of short stories that the Italian author meant to amuse, not edify, the reader. Artists also broke with the medieval past, in both technique and content. Renaissance art sometimes used religious topics but often dealt with secular themes or portraits of individuals.

Oil paints, chiaroscuro, and linear perspectives produced works of energy in three dimensions.

Leonardo da Vinci (1452–1519) produced numerous works, including *The Last Supper* and *Mona Lisa*. Raphael Santi (1483–1520), a master of Renaissance grace and style, theory, and technique, brought all his skills to his painting *The School of Athens*. Michelangelo Buonarroti (1475–1564) produced masterpieces in architecture, sculpture (*David*), and painting (the Sistine Chapel ceiling). His work was a bridge to a new, non-Renaissance style: mannerism.

Renaissance scholars were more practical and secular than medieval ones. **Manuscript collections** enabled scholars to study the primary sources and to reject traditions established since classical times. Also, scholars participated in the lives of their cities as active politicians. Leonardo Bruni (1370–1444), a civic humanist, served as chancellor of Florence, where he used his rhetorical skills to rouse the citizens against external enemies. Niccolo **Machiavelli** (1469–1527) wrote *The Prince*, which analyzed politics from the standpoint of expedience rising above morality in the name of maintaining political power.

The Reformation. The Reformation destroyed western Europe's religious unity and introduced new ideas about the relationships among God, the individual, and society. Politics greatly influenced the course of the Reformation and led, in most areas, to the subjection of the church to the political rulers.

Martin Luther (1483–1546), to his personal distress, could not reconcile the sinfulness of humans with the justice of God. During his studies of the Bible, Luther came to believe that personal efforts—good works such as a Christian life and attention to the sacraments of the church—could not "earn" the sinner salvation but that belief and faith were the only way to obtain grace. By 1515, Luther believed that "justification by faith alone" was the road to salvation.

On October 31, 1517, Luther nailed 95 theses, or statements, about **indulgences** (the cancellation of a sin in return for money) to the door of the Wittenberg church and challenged the practice of selling them. At this time

he was seeking to reform the church, not divide it. In 1519, Luther presented various criticisms of the church and declared that only the Bible, not religious traditions or papal statements, could determine correct religious practices and beliefs. In 1521, Pope Leo X excommunicated Luther for his beliefs.

In 1536 **John Calvin** (1509–1564), a Frenchman, arrived in Geneva, a Swiss city-state that had adopted an anti-Catholic position. In 1540, Geneva became the center of the Reformation. Calvin's *Institutes of the Christian Religion* (1536), a strictly logical analysis of Christianity, had a universal appeal. Calvin emphasized the doctrine of **predestination**, which indicated that God knew who would obtain salvation before those people were born. Calvin believed that church and state should unite. Calvinism triumphed as the majority religion in Scotland, under the leadership of John Knox (ca. 1514–1572), and in the United Provinces of the Netherlands. Puritans in England and New England also accepted Calvinism.

The Thirty Years' War. Between 1618 and 1648, the European powers fought a series of wars. The reasons for the wars varied; religious, dynastic, commercial, and territorial rivalries all played a part. The battles were fought over most of Europe and ended with the Treaty of Westphalia in 1648. The Thirty Years' War changed the boundaries of most European countries.

Explorations and Conquests. Between 1394 and 1460 (Prince Henry the Navigator's lifespan) and afterwards, a period of exploration and conquests characterized European history. "Skill Six: Identify the Causes and Consequences of Exploration, Settlement, and Growth" includes more information on the people and the explorations of the period.

Revolution and the New World Order

The Scientific Revolution. For the first time in human history, the eighteenth century saw the appearance of a secular worldview: the Age of Enlightenment. The philosophical starting point for the Enlightenment was the belief in the autonomy of man's intellect apart from God. The most basic assumption was faith in reason rather than faith in revelation. René Descartes (1596–1650) sought a basis for logic and believed he found it in man's ability to think. "I think; therefore, I am" was his most famous statement.

Benedict de Spinoza (1632–1677) developed a rational pantheism in which he equated God and nature. He denied all free will and ended up with an impersonal, mechanical universe. Gottfried Wilhelm Leibniz (1646–1716) worked on symbolic logic and calculus and invented a calculating machine. He, too, had a mechanistic view of the world and life and thought of God as a hypothetical abstraction rather than a persona.

John Locke (1632–1704) pioneered the empiricist approach to knowledge; he stressed the importance of the environment in human development. Locke classified knowledge as either (1) according to reason, (2) contrary to reason, or (3) above reason. Locke thought reason and revelation were complementary and from God.

The Enlightenment's Effect on Society. The Enlightenment affected more than science and religion. New political and economic theories originated as well. John Locke and **Jean-Jacques Rousseau** (1712–1778) believed that people were capable of governing themselves, either through a political (Locke) or social (Rousseau) contract forming the basis of society.

Most philosophers opposed democracy, preferring a limited monarchy that shared power with the nobility. The assault on mercantilist economic theory was begun by the physiocrats in France, who proposed a laissez-faire (minimal governmental interference) attitude toward land usage that culminated in the theory of economic capitalism associated with Adam Smith (1723–1790) and his notions of free trade, free enterprise, and the law of supply and demand.

The French Revolution. The increased criticism directed toward governmental inefficiency and corruption and toward the privileged classes demonstrated the rising expectations of "enlightened" society in France. The remainder of the population (called the Third Estate) consisted of the middle class, urban workers, and the mass of peasants, who bore the entire burden of taxation and the imposition of feudal obligations.

The most notorious event of the French Revolution was the so-called Reign of Terror (1793–1794), the government's campaign against its internal enemies and counterrevolutionaries. **Louis XVI** faced charges of treason, declared guilty, and executed on January 21, 1793. Later the same year, the queen, **Marie Antoinette**, met the same fate.

The middle class controlled the Directory (1795–1799). Members of the Directory believed that through peace they would gain more wealth and establish a society in which money and property would become the only requirements for prestige and power. Rising inflation and mass public dissatisfaction led to the downfall of the Directory.

The Era of Napoleon. On December 25, 1799, a new government and constitution concentrated supreme power in the hands of **Napoleon**. Napoleon's domestic reforms and policies affected every aspect of society.

French-ruled peoples viewed Napoleon as a tyrant who repressed and exploited them for France's glory and advantage. Enlightened reformers believed Napoleon had betrayed the ideals of the Revolution. The downfall of Napoleon resulted from his inability to conquer England, economic distress caused by the Continental System (boycott of British goods), the Peninsular War with Spain, the German War of Liberation, and the invasion of Russia. The actual defeat of Napoleon occurred at the **Battle of Waterloo** in 1815.

The Industrial Revolution. The term *Industrial Revolution* describes a period of transition, when machines began to significantly displace human and animal power in methods of producing and distributing goods and when an agricultural and commercial society became an industrial one.

Roots of the Industrial Revolution are evident in

- the Commercial Revolution (1500–1700) that spurred the great economic growth of Europe and brought about the Age of Discovery and Exploration, which in turn helped to solidify the economic doctrines of mercantilism;

- the effect of the Scientific Revolution, which produced the first wave of mechanical inventions and technological advances;

- the increase in population in Europe from 140 million people in 1750 to 266 million people by the mid-nineteenth century (more producers, more consumers); and

- the nineteenth century political and social revolutions that began the rise to power of the middle class and that provided leadership for the economic revolution.

A transportation revolution ensued to distribute the productivity of machinery and to deliver raw materials to the eager factories. This led to the growth of canal systems; the construction of hard-surfaced **"macadam" roads**; the commercial use of the **steamboat** that **Robert Fulton** (1765–1815) demonstrated; and the **railway locomotive**, that **George Stephenson** (1781–1848) made commercially successful.

The Industrial Revolution created a unique new category of people who depended on their jobs for income and who needed job security. Until 1850, workers as a whole did not share in the general wealth produced by the Industrial Revolution. Conditions improved as the century wore on. Union action combined with general prosperity and a developing social conscience to improve the working conditions, wages, and hours of skilled labor first and unskilled labor later.

Socialism. The Utopian Socialists were the earliest writers to propose an equitable solution to improve the distribution of society's wealth. The name of this group comes from *Utopia*, **Saint Thomas More**'s (1478–1535) book on a fictional ideal society. While they endorsed the productive capacity of industrialism, the Utopian Socialists denounced its mismanagement. Human society was ideally a community rather than a mixture of competing, selfish individuals. All the goods a person needed could be produced in one community.

Scientific socialism, or Marxism, was the creation of **Karl Marx** (1818–1883), a German scholar who, with the help of **Friedrich Engels** (1820–1895), intended to replace utopian hopes and dreams with a militant blueprint for socialist working-class success. The principal works of this revolutionary school of socialism were *The Communist Manifesto* and *Das Kapital*.

Marxism has four key propositions:

1. An economic interpretation of history that asserts that economic factors (mainly centered on who controls the means of production and distribution) determines all human history.

2. The belief that there has always been a class struggle between the rich and the poor (or the exploiters and the exploited).

3. The theory of surplus value, which holds that the true value of a product is labor; because workers receive a small portion of their just labor price, the difference is surplus value "stolen" from workers by capitalists.

4. The belief that socialism is inevitable because capitalism contains the seeds of its own destruction (overproduction, unemployment, etc.). The rich grow richer and the poor grow poorer until the gap between each class (proletariat and bourgeoisie) becomes so great that the working classes rise up in revolution and overthrow the elite bourgeoisie to install a "dictatorship of the proletariat." The creation of a classless society guided by the principle "from each according to his abilities, to each according to his needs" will be the result from dismantling capitalism.

Skill Six

Identify the Causes and Consequences of Exploration, Settlement, and Growth

Beginnings of European Exploration

Europeans were largely unaware of the existence of the American continent, even though a Norse seaman, **Leif Eriksson**, had sailed within sight of the continent in the eleventh century. Few other explorers ventured nearly as far as America. Before the fifteenth century, Europeans had little desire to explore and were not ready to face the many challenges of a long sea voyage. Just as developments led to changes and conflict in North America and produced an increasing number of distinct cultures and systems, developments in Europe were about to make possible the great voyages that led to contact between Europe and the Americas. In the fifteenth and sixteenth centuries, technological devices such as the **compass** and **astrolabe** freed explorers from some of the constraints that had limited early voyages. Three primary factors—God, gold, and glory—led to increased interest in exploration and eventually to a desire to settle in the newly discovered lands.

Although Europeans, such as Italians, participated in overland trade with the East and sailed through the Mediterranean and beyond, it was the Arabs who played the largest part in such trade and who benefited the most economically. **Prince Henry the Navigator**, ruler of Portugal, sponsored voyages aimed at adding territory and gaining control of trading routes to increase the power and wealth of Portugal. Prince Henry also wanted to spread Christianity and prevent the further expansion of Islam in Africa. Henry the Navigator brought a number of Italian merchant traders to his court at Cape St. Vincent, and subsequently they sailed in Portuguese ships down the western coast of Africa. The initial voyages were extremely difficult because they lacked navigational instruments and any kind of maps or charts. Europeans had charted the entire Mediterranean Sea, including harbors and the coastline, but they had no knowledge or maps of the African coast.

The first task of the explorers was to create accurate charts of the African shoreline. The crews on these initial voyages did not encounter horrible monsters or boiling water, which rumors had said existed in the ocean beyond Cape Bojador, the farthest point Europeans had previously reached. They did discover, however, that strong southward winds made it easy to sail out of the Mediterranean but difficult to return.

Most people believed that Africa and China were joined by a southern continent, eliminating any possibility of an eastern maritime route to the Indian Ocean. Prince Henry, however, sent ships along the coast of Africa because he believed it was possible to sail east through the Atlantic and reach the Indian Ocean.

Technical Innovations Aiding Exploration

One of the reasons that the explorers sailing from Portugal traveled along the coast was to avoid losing sight of land. By the thirteenth century, explorers were using the compass, borrowed from China, to determine direction; it was more difficult to determine the relative position from the North and South Poles and from landmasses or anything else. In the Northern Hemisphere, a navigator could determine the relative north-south position, or latitude, by calculating the height of the **Pole Star** from the horizon. South of the equator, one cannot see the Pole Star; until around 1460, captains had no way to determine their position if they sailed too far south.

Although longitude (relative east-west position) remained unknown until the eighteenth century, the introduction of the **astrolabe** allowed sailors to calculate their latitude south of the equator. Along with navigational aids, improvements in shipbuilding and in weaponry also facilitated exploration. Unlike the Mediterranean, it was not possible to use ships propelled only by oarsmen in the Atlantic because the waves were high and the currents and winds were strong. Europeans had initially used very broad sails on ships that went out into the Atlantic; the ships were heavy and often became stranded by the absence of the favorable tailwinds upon which the ships and sailors depended.

The Portuguese borrowed techniques from Arab and European shipbuilding and developed the Caravela Redondo. This ship proved to be more worthy of long voyages because it combined square rigging for speed with lateen sails that were more responsive and easier to handle. Other European states adopted the ship and also the practice of mounting artillery and other weapons on exploration vessels.

Main Elements of European Exploration

As the Portuguese began to trade and explore along the coast of Africa, they brought back slaves, ivory, gold, and knowledge of the African coast. It looked as though the Portuguese might find a route to the Indian Ocean, and it was clear that the voyages sponsored by Prince Henry were benefiting Portugal in many ways.

Other European states wanted to increase their territory and wealth and to establish trade routes to the East. Although the desire for control of trade routes and wealth was a primary motive in launching voyages of exploration, it was not the only incentive.

Europe in the fifteenth and sixteenth centuries, despite the increase in dissenting views, was still extremely religious. The Catholic Church continued to exert a tremendous influence, and some Christians were motivated to go on voyages of discovery to conduct missionary activities and spread the word of God.

After the beginning of the Reformation, many Lutherans, Calvinists, and other groups who had left the Catholic Church emigrated from Europe in the hopes of settling where they would be free from religious persecution or violent conflicts. Younger sons of families in Europe were able to secure prominent positions in the church; they were often not able to find lucrative opportunities at home, however, because the eldest son usually inherited lands and wealth.

The voyages of exploration, therefore, were a means of securing fame and fortune and of obtaining opportunities that would not be available otherwise. Other individuals sponsored or participated in voyages in the hope of gaining wealth or increased opportunities.

Although the motivation of fame and fortune was often secondary to God and glory, many individuals were attracted to exploration by the possibility of adventure and by their desire to explore uncharted territory. These three factors—gold, God, and glory—operated on both individual and state levels; kings and heads of states were as interested as the seamen were in spreading their faith and increasing the wealth and prestige of their states.

Portugal was the first European state to establish sugar plantations on an island off the west coast of Africa and to import slaves from Africa to labor there. It was the beginning of the slave trade. The level of trading was initially far less extensive and intense than during the later period of slave trade when Spain and England became involved. In an attempt to maintain control of the slave trade and of the eastern routes to India, the Portuguese appealed to the pope; he ruled in their favor and forbade the Spanish and others to sail south and east in an attempt to reach India or Asia.

When **Ferdinand and Isabella** married and united the two largest provinces in Spain, Castile and Aragon, they not only began the process of uniting all of Spain but also agreed to sponsor **Christopher Columbus** in his voyage of exploration. Only the heads of states had the necessary resources and could afford the risk involved in sponsoring a major voyage across the oceans of the world, but most monarchs were unwilling to take such a risk. Columbus was an Italian explorer looking for a sponsor and had approached Ferdinand and Isabella after being turned down by the English government. He convinced the Spanish monarchs that a western route to the Indian Ocean existed and that it would be possible to make the voyage.

However, Columbus had miscalculated the distance of the voyage from Europe to Asia. His estimate of the circumference of the earth was much less than it should have been for an accurate calculation, and no Europeans were aware of the existence of the American continents. One of the reasons that Ferdinand and Isabella were willing to support Columbus was that the previous agreements prevented all states but Portugal from sailing east to reach India. Therefore, the only chance for Spain to launch an expedition to India and to participate in trade and exploration was in the discovery of a western route to India.

European Contact with the Americas

In 1492, Columbus sailed from Spain with 90 men on three ships, the *Niña*, the *Pinta*, and the *Santa María*. After a 10-week voyage, they landed in the Bahamas. On his second trip, Columbus reached Cuba, and then in 1498, during his third trip, he reached the mainland and sailed along the northern coast of South America. Columbus originally thought he had reached India; he referred to the people he encountered in the Bahamas and on his second landing in Cuba as Indians.

There is considerable debate over whether Columbus realized, either during his third voyage or just before his death, that he had landed not in India but on an entirely unknown continent between Europe and Asia. Another question is whether Columbus, who died in obscurity despite his fame for having discovered America, should receive credit for this discovery; earlier explorers had reached the American continent.

However, because Columbus's voyages prompted extensive exploration and settlement of the Americas, it is accurate to state that he was responsible for the discovery of the New World by Europeans. Another result of Columbus's voyages was the increased focus of Spain on exploration and conquest. Nevertheless, the New World took its name from the Florentine merchant **Amerigo Vespucci**–not Columbus. Vespucci took part in several voyages to the New World and wrote a series of descriptions that not only gave Europeans an image of this "New World" but also spread the idea that the discovered lands were not a part of Asia or India. Vespucci, then, popularized the image of the Americas and the idea that the Americas were continents separate from those previously known.

It was a Portuguese navigator, **Vasco da Gama**, who crossed the Isthmus of Panama and came to another ocean, which separates the American continents from China. The Spanish sponsored another Portuguese sailor, **Ferdinand Magellan**, who discovered at the southern end of South America a strait that provided access to the ocean west of the Americas. Magellan named this ocean the Pacific because it was much calmer than the strait through which he had sailed to reach it. Later, he reached the Philippines and met his death in a conflict with the natives. Magellan's voyage, nevertheless, was the final stage of the process whereby Europeans completed the first-known circumnavigation of the globe. Although initially the Spanish were eager to find a route around the Americas that would enable them to sail on toward their original goal, the treasures of the Far East, they began to consider the Americas as a possible source of untapped wealth.

The Spanish claimed all the New World except Brazil, which papal decree gave to the Portuguese. The first Spanish settlements were on the islands of the Caribbean Sea. It was not until 1518 that Spain appointed Hernando Cortez as a government official in Cuba; Cortez led a small military expedition against the Aztecs in Mexico. Cortez and his men failed in their first attack on the Aztec capital city, Tenochtitlan but were ultimately successful.

A combination of factors allowed the small force of approximately 600 Spanish soldiers to overcome the extensive Aztec Empire. The Spanish were armed with rifles and bows, which provided an advantage over Aztec fighters armed only with spears. However, weapons and armor were not the main reason that the Spanish were able to overcome the military forces of the natives.

The Aztec ruler, Montezuma, allowed a delegation, which included Cortez, into the capital city because the description of the Spanish soldiers in their armor and with feathers in their helmets was similar to the description in Aztec legend of messengers who would be sent by the chief Aztec god, Quetzcoatl. The members of Cortez's expedition exposed the natives to smallpox and other diseases that devastated the native population. Finally, the Spanish expedition was also able to form alliances with other native tribes that the Aztecs had conquered; these tribes were willing to cooperate to defeat the Aztecs and thus break up their empire.

Twenty years after Cortez defeated the Aztecs, another conquistador, Francisco Pizarro, defeated the Incas in Peru. Pizarro's expedition enabled the Spanish to begin to explore and settle South America. Spain funded the conquistadors, or conquerors, who were the first Europeans to explore some areas of the Americas. However, the sole purpose of the conquistadors' explorations was defeating the natives to gain access to gold, silver, and other wealth. Spain established mines in the territory it claimed and produced a tremendous amount of gold and silver. In the 300 years after the Spanish conquest of the Americas in the sixteenth century, those mines produced 10 times more gold and silver than the total produced by all the mines in the rest of the world.

Spain had come to view the New World as more than an obstacle to voyages toward India; over time, Spain began to think that it might be possible to exploit this territory for more than just mining. It was the conquistadors who made it possible for the Spanish to settle the New World, but they were not responsible for forming settlements or for overseeing Spanish colonies in the New World. Instead, Spain sent officials and administrators from Spain to oversee settlements after their initial formation.

Spanish settlers came to the New World for various reasons: some went in search of land to settle or buy, others went looking for opportunities that were not available to them in Europe, and priests and missionaries went to spread Christianity to the natives. By the end of the sixteenth century, Spain had established firm control over not only the several islands in the Caribbean, Mexico, and southern North America but also in the territory currently within the modern states of Chile, Argentina, and Peru.

Spanish Settlements in the New World

The first permanent settlement established by the Spanish was the predominantly military fort of St. Augustine, located in Florida. In 1598, Don Juan de Onate led a group of 500 settlers north from Mexico and established a colony in what is now New Mexico.

Onate granted *encomiendas* to the most prominent Spaniards who had accompanied him. Under the *encomienda* system, that the Spanish in Mexico and parts of North America established, these distinguished individuals had the right to exact tribute and/or labor from the native population, which continued to live on the land in exchange for the services it provided.

Spanish colonists founded Santa Fe in 1609, and by 1680 about 2,000 Spaniards were living in New Mexico. Most of the colonists raised sheep and cattle on large ranches and lived among approximately 30,000 Pueblo Indians. The Spanish crushed a major revolt that threatened to destroy Santa Fe in 1680. Attempts to prevent the natives—both those who had converted to Catholicism and those who had not—from performing religious rituals that predated the Spaniards' arrival provoked the revolt. The natives drove the Spanish from Santa Fe, but they returned in 1696, crushed the Pueblos, and seizing the land. Although the Spanish ultimately quelled the revolt, they began to change their policies toward the natives, who still greatly outnumbered the Spanish settlers.

The Spanish continued to try to Christianize and civilize the native population, but they also began to allow the Pueblos to own land. In addition, the Spanish unofficially tolerated native religious rituals although Catholicism officially condemned all such practices. By 1700, the Spanish population in New Mexico had increased and reached about 4,000; the native population had decreased to about 13,000 and intermarriage between natives and Spaniards increased.

Nevertheless, disease, war, and migration resulted in the steady decline in the Pueblo population. New Mexico had become a prosperous and stable region, but it was still relatively weak and, as the only major Spanish settlement in northern Mexico, was isolated.

Effects of European-American Contact

One cannot underestimate the impact of Europeans on the New World, both before and after the arrival of the English and French. The most immediate effect was the spread of disease, which decimated the native population. In some areas of Mexico, 95 percent of the native population died as a result of contact with Europeans and the subsequent outbreaks of diseases like smallpox.

In South America, the native population was devastated not only by disease but also by deliberate policies instituted to control and in some cases eliminate native peoples. Although Europeans passed most diseases to the natives, the natives passed syphilis to the Europeans, who carried it back to Europe.

The European and American continents exchanged plants and animals. Europeans brought over animals to the New World, and they took plants like potatoes, corn, and squash back to Europe, where introduction of these crops led to an explosion of the European population. The decimation of the native population and the establishment of large plantations led to a shortage of workers, and Europeans began to transport slaves from Africa to the New World to fill the shortage.

Skill Seven

Identify Individuals and Events That Have Influenced Economic, Social, and Political Institutions in the United States

European Settlement and Development in North America

In 1497, King Henry VIII of England sponsored a voyage by **John Cabot** to try to discover a northwest passage through the New World to the Orient. However, the English made no real attempt to settle in the New World until nearly a century later. By the 1600s, the English became interested in colonizing the New World for several reasons. Many people in England emigrated overseas because the country's population was increasing and because of the use of the land for raising sheep for wool rather than for growing foodstuffs for survival. In England scarce opportunities, like the ability to buy land, were primary motivators for emigration from England.

Some people in England left their homeland because of the religious turmoil that engulfed England after the beginning of the Protestant Reformation. In addition to converts to Lutheranism and Calvinism, a major emigrating group was the Puritans, who called for reforms to "purify" the church. Mercantilism also provided a motive for exploration and for the establishment of colonies. According to mercantile theories, an industrialized nation needed an inexpensive source of raw materials and markets for finished products. Colonies provided a way to obtain raw materials and to guarantee a market for industrial goods.

Economic reasons, among others, motivated the French and the Dutch to explore and establish colonies in the New World. In 1609, the year after the first English settlement, the French established a colony in Quebec. Overall, far fewer French settlers traveled to the New World than did English settlers, but the French were able to exercise a tremendous influence through the establishment of strong ties with the natives. The French created trading partnerships and a vast trading network; they often intermarried with the local native population.

The Dutch financed an English explorer, **Henry Hudson**, who claimed for Holland the territory that is now New York. The Dutch settlements along the Hudson, Delaware, and Connecticut rivers developed into the colony of New Netherlands and established a vast trading network that effectively separated the English colonies of Jamestown and Plymouth.

One reason that English settlements began to become more prominent after 1600 was the defeat of the Spanish fleet, the supposedly invincible Armada, by the English in 1588. The changing power balance on the seas encouraged the English to increase their exploration and attempted colonization of the Americas. The first

few colonies founded by the English in America did not flourish.

Sir Humphrey Gilbert, who had obtained a six-year grant giving him the exclusive rights to settle any unclaimed land in America, was planning to establish a colony in Newfoundland, but a storm sank his ship. Instead, **Sir Walter Raleigh** received the six-year grant. Raleigh explored the North American coast and named the territory through which he traveled Virginia, in honor of the "Virgin Queen" Elizabeth I of England. In addition, Raleigh convinced his cousin, Sir Grenville, to establish a colony on the island of Roanoke.

Roanoke was off the coast of what later became North Carolina. The first settlers lived there for a year while Sir Grenville returned to England for supplies and additional settlers. However, when Sir Francis Drake arrived in Roanoke nearly a year later and found that Sir Grenville had not yet returned, the colonists left on his ship and abandoned the settlement. In 1587, Raleigh sent another group of colonists to Roanoke, but a war with Spain broke out in 1588 and kept him from returning until 1590. When Raleigh returned to Roanoke, the colonists had vanished. A single word, "Croatan," carved into a tree could have referred to a nearby settlement of natives. This suggested a number of possibilities in regard to the missing settlers; conclusive proof of their fate was never found.

Colonization: The Jamestown Settlement

In 1606, King James I of England granted to the Virginia Company a charter for exploration and colonization. This charter marked the beginning of ventures sponsored by merchants rather than directly by the Crown. The charter of the Virginia Company had two branches. James I gave one branch to the English city of Plymouth, which had the right to the northern portion of territory on the eastern coast of North America, and he granted the London branch of the company the right to the southern portion.

Considerable difficulties prevented the English from founding and maintaining a permanent settlement in North America. The Plymouth Company failed to establish a lasting settlement. The company itself ran out of money, and the settlers who had gone to the New World gave up and abandoned their established Sagadahoc Colony in Maine.

Having decided to colonize the Chesapeake Bay area, the London Company sent three ships with about 104 sailors to that area in 1607. The company's ships sailed up a river, which they named the James in honor of the English king, and they established the fort and permanent settlement of Jamestown. The London Company and the men who settled Jamestown were hoping to find a northwest passage to Asia, gold, and silver, or to be able to find lands capable of producing valuable goods, such as grapes, oranges, or silk.

The colony at Jamestown did not allow the settlers to accomplish any of those things, and its location on the river, which became contaminated every spring, led to the outbreak of diseases such as typhoid, dysentery, and malaria. Over half the colonists died the first year, and by the spring of 1609, only one-third of the total number of colonists who had joined the colony were still alive.

The survival of the colony initially was largely accomplished through the efforts of **Captain John Smith**. Smith was a soldier who turned the colony's focus from exploration to obtaining food. Initially, Smith was able to obtain corn from the local Indians led by **Powhatan** and his 12-year-old daughter **Pocahontas**. Smith also forced all able men in the colony to work four hours a day in the wheat fields. Attempts by the London Company to send additional settlers and supplies encountered troubles and delays.

Thomas Gates and some 600 settlers, who left for Jamestown in 1609, ran aground on Bermuda and had to build a new ship. Although some new settlers did arrive in Jamestown, disease continued to shrink the population. When seriously-injured Smith had to return to England. his departure deprived the colony of its most effective and resourceful leader.

It was not long after Smith left that the colonists provoked a war with Powhatan, who was beginning to tire of the colonists' demands for corn. Powhatan realized that the settlers intended to stay indefinitely and might challenge the Indians for control of the surrounding territory.

Gates finally arrived in June 1610 with only 175 of the original 600 settlers. He found only 60 colonists who had survived the war with the Indians and the harsh winter of 1610, during which they had minimal food and other resources. Gates decided to abandon Jamestown and was sailing down the river with the surviving colonists on board when he encountered the new governor from England, **Thomas West**, Baron de la Warr. Gates and West returned to Jamestown, imposed martial law, responded to Indian attacks, and survived a five-year war with the Indians. Although the war did not end until 1614, when the colonists were able to negotiate a settlement by holding Pocahontas hostage, the situation in Jamestown began to improve in 1610.

Some of the settlers went to healthier locations, and in 1613 one of them, **John Rolfe**, married Pocahontas. In 1614, the settlers planted a mild strain of tobacco, which gave them a crop they could sell for cash. The Crown issued two new charters that allowed Virginia to extend its borders all the way to the Pacific and made the London Company a joint-stock company. Changes in the company led to a new treasurer, **Sir Edwin Sandy**, who tried to reform Virginia.

Sandy encouraged settlers in Virginia to try to produce grapes and silkworms and to diversify the colony's economy in other ways. Sandy also replaced martial law with English common law. The colonists established a council to make laws, and settlers now had the right to own land. By 1623, about 4,000 additional settlers had arrived in Virginia. Attempts to produce and sell crops other than tobacco, however, failed, and the arrival of large numbers of new colonists provoked renewed conflict with the Indians. A major Indian attack launched in March 1622 killed 347 colonists.

Investors in the London Company withdrew their capital and appealed to the king, and a royal commission visited the colony. As a result of this investigation, the king declared the London Company bankrupt and assumed direct control of Virginia in 1624. Virginia became the first royal colony, and the Crown appointed a governor and a council to oversee its administration.

Three trends continued after the Crown assumed control. The first was unrelenting conflict with the Indians. Through war and raids, by 1632 the colonists had killed or driven out most of the Indians in the area immediately around Jamestown. The other two trends were the yearly influx of thousands of new settlers and the high death rate in the colony.

Despite the high mortality rate, the population of the colony began gradually to increase. The expansion of tobacco production led to a demand for labor, and thousands of the young men who came were indentured servants. In exchange for their passage to America and food and shelter during their terms of service, these men were bound to work for their masters for four or five years. After that time, they gained their freedom and often a small payment to help them become established. Most of these men were not able to participate in the running of the colony even after they became free, but some were able to acquire land.

In 1634, the Crown divided Virginia into counties, each with appointed justices and the right to fill all other positions. Under this type of system, individuals from a few wealthy families tended to dominate the government. Most of the counties became Anglican, and the colony continued to elect representatives to its House of Burgesses, an assembly that met with the governor to discuss issues of common law. The king, however, refused to recognize the colony's House of Burgesses. After 1660, the colony became even more dominated by the wealthiest 15 percent of the population, and these individuals and their sons continued to be the only colonists to serve as justices and burgesses. Settlement of the colonies continued, primarily for religious and economic reasons. Conflict between the colonists and the natives was a constant.

Growth of the Slave Trade

The shortage of labor in the southern colonies and a drop in the number of people coming to the colonies as indentured servants forced the colonists to search for other sources of labor. Although the colonists began using African servants and slaves almost immediately after settling in the New World, the slave trade and the slave population in British North America remained small in the first half of the seventeenth century. Toward the end of the seventeenth century, increasing numbers of slaves from Africa became available, and the demand for them in North America further stimulated the growth of the transatlantic slave trade.

By the nineteenth century, millions of Africans had been forcibly taken from their native lands and sold into perpetual slavery. The Europeans sold slaves at forts the slave traders had established on the African coast; the Europeans packed the slaves as closely as possible into the lower regions of ships for the long journey to the Americas. Chained slaves traveled in deplorably unsanitary conditions and received only enough food and water to keep them alive.

Many slaves died during this Middle Passage voyage. Plantation owners in the Caribbean, Brazil, or North America bought the slaves to do the work. It was only after 1697 that English colonists began to buy large numbers of slaves. By 1760, the slave population had reached approximately a quarter of a million with most of the slaves concentrated in the southern colonies. Slave labor replaced indentured servitude, and a race-based system of perpetual slavery developed. Colonial assemblies began to pass "slave codes" in the eighteenth century. These codes identified all nonwhites or dark-skinned people as slaves, made their condition permanent, and legalized slavery in British North America.

Salem Witch Trials

During this period of increasing tensions, several communities held witchcraft trials. In Salem, Massachusetts, a group of young girls accused servants from West India and older white members of the community, mostly women, of exercising powers that Satan had given to them. Other towns also experienced turmoil and charged residents with witchcraft. In Salem alone, the juries pronounced 19 people guilty; in 1692 after the execution of all 19 victims, the girls admitted their stories were not true.

The witchcraft trials illustrate the highly religious nature of the New England society, but they also suggest that individuals who did not conform to societal expectations were at risk. Most of the accused were outspoken women who were often critical of their communities, were older, and were either widows or unmarried. Some of these women had acquired property despite the accepted views and limitations regarding women's role in society.

Religion in the Colonies and the Great Awakening

The religious nature of colonial settlers did not lead to the kind of intolerance or persecution that had plagued Europe since the Reformation. Conflict among various religious groups did break out occasionally, but British North America enjoyed a far greater degree of religious toleration than anywhere else. Among the reasons this toleration existed were that several religious groups had immigrated to North America and that every colony, except Virginia and Maryland, ignored the laws establishing the Church of England as the official faith of the colony. Even among the Puritans, differences in religious opinion led to the establishment of different denominations.

Although there was some religious toleration, Protestants still tended to view Roman Catholics as a threatening rival. In Maryland, Catholics numbered about 3,000, the largest population of all the colonies, and were the victims of persecution. Jews were often victims of persecution; they could not vote or hold office in any of the colonies, and only in Rhode Island could they practice the Jewish religion openly.

The other main trends in addition to toleration were the westward spread of communities, the rise of cities, and a decline in religious piousness. This sense of the weakening of religious authority and faithfulness led to the Great Awakening.

The Great Awakening refers to a period beginning in the 1730s in which several well-known preachers traveled through British North America giving speeches and arguing for the need to revive religious piety and closer relationships with God. The main message of the preachers was that everyone has the potential, regardless of past behavior, to reestablish their relationship with God. This message appealed to many women and younger sons of landowners who stood to inherit very

little. The best-known preacher during this period was **Jonathan Edwards**. Edwards denounced some current beliefs as doctrines of easy salvation. At his church in Northampton, Edwards sermonized about the absolute sovereignty of God, predestination, and salvation by grace alone.

The Great Awakening further divided religion in America by creating distinctions among New Light groups (revivalists), Old Light groups (traditionalists), and new groups that incorporated elements of both. The various revivalists, or New Light groups, did not agree on every issue. Some revivalists denounced education and learning from books while others founded schools in the belief that education was a means of furthering religion. While some individuals were stressing a need for renewed spiritual focus, others were beginning to embrace the ideas of the Enlightenment.

The **Scientific Revolution** had demonstrated the existence of natural laws that operated in nature, and enlightened thinkers began to argue that man had the ability to improve his own situation through the use of rational thought and acquired knowledge. Intellectuals of the **Enlightenment** shifted the focus from God to man, introduced the idea of progress, and argued that people could improve their own situations and make decisions on how to live rather than just having faith in God and waiting for a better life after death and salvation.

Enlightenment thought had a tremendous impact on the North American colonists, who began to establish more schools, encourage the acquisition of knowledge, and become more interested in gaining scientific knowledge. The colleges founded in North America taught the scientific theories held by **Copernicus**, who argued that planets rotated around the sun not the earth, and Newton, who introduced the key principles of physics, including gravity.

The colonists did not just learn European theories. **Benjamin Franklin** was among the colonists who began to carry out their own experiments and form their own theories. Franklin experimented with electricity and was able to demonstrate in 1752, by using a kite, that electricity and lightning were the same.

Scientific theories also led to inoculations against smallpox. The Puritan theologian **Cotton Mather** convinced the population of Boston that injections with a small amount of the smallpox virus would build up their resistance to the disease and reduce the likelihood of reinfection. Leading theologians and scientists spread European scientific ideas and developed their own theories and applications using their acquired knowledge.

The American Revolution

The Coming of the American Revolution. In 1764, George Grenville pushed through Parliament the **Sugar Act** (the Revenue Act), which aimed at raising revenue by taxing goods imported by Americans. The **Stamp Act** (1765) imposed a direct tax on the colonists for the first time. By requiring Americans to purchase revenue stamps on everything from newspapers to legal documents, the Stamp Act would have created an impossible drain on hard currency in the colonies.

Americans reacted first with restrained and respectful petitions and pamphlets in which they pointed out that "taxation without representation is tyranny." The colonists began to limit their purchase of imported goods. From there, resistance progressed to stronger protests that eventually became violent. In October 1765, delegates from nine colonies met as the Stamp Act Congress and passed moderate resolutions against the act and asserted that Americans could not be taxed without the consent of their representatives. The colonists now ceased all importation.

In March 1766, Parliament repealed the Stamp Act. At the same time, however, it passed the **Declaratory Act**, which claimed the power to tax or make laws for the Americans "in all cases whatsoever." In 1766, Parliament passed a program of taxes on items imported into the colonies. The taxes came to be known as the Townsend duties, a name that came from Britain's chancellor of the exchequer, Charles Townsend. American reaction was at first slow, but the sending of troops aroused them to resistance.

Again the colonies halted importation, and soon British merchants were calling on Parliament to repeal the Townsend duties. In March 1770, Parliament repealed all the taxes except that on tea; Parliament wanted to prove that it had the right to tax the colonies if it so desired. When Parliament ended the **Tea Act** in 1773, a relative peace ensued.

In desperate financial condition—partially because the Americans were buying smuggled Dutch tea rather than the taxed British product—the British East India Company sought and obtained from Parliament concessions that allowed it to ship tea directly to the colonies rather than only by way of Britain. The result would be that the East India Company tea, even with the tax, would be cheaper than smuggled Dutch tea. The company hoped that the colonists would thus buy the tea–tax and all, save the East India Company, and tacitly accept Parliament's right to tax them.

The Americans, however, proved resistant to this approach. Rather than acknowledge Parliament's right to tax, they refused to buy the cheaper tea and resorted to various methods, including tar and feathers, to prevent the collection of the tax on tea. In most ports, Americans did not allow ships carrying the tea to land.

In Boston, however, the pro-British governor **Thomas Hutchinson** forced a confrontation by ordering Royal Navy vessels to prevent the tea ships from leaving the harbor. After 20 days, this would, by law, result in selling the cargoes at auction and paying the tax. The night before the time was to expire, December 16, 1773, Bostonians thinly disguised as Native Americans boarded the ships and threw the tea into the harbor. This was the **Boston Tea Party**.

The British responded with four acts collectively titled the **Coercive Acts** (1774), in which they strengthened their control over the colonists. The **First Continental Congress** (1774) met in response to the acts. The Congress called for strict nonimportation and rigorous preparation of local militia companies.

The War for Independence. British troops went to Massachusetts, which the Crown had officially declared to be in a state of rebellion. General Thomas Gage received orders to arrest the leaders of the resistance or, failing that, to provoke any sort of confrontation that would allow him to turn British military might loose on the Americans. Americans, however, detected the movement of Gage's troops toward Concord, and dispatch riders like **Paul Revere** and **William Dawes** spread the news throughout the countryside.

In Lexington, about **70 minutemen** (trained militiamen who would respond at a moment's notice) awaited the British on the village green. A shot was fired; it is unknown which side fired first. This became **"the shot heard 'round the world."**

The British opened fire and charged. Casualties occurred on both sides. The following month, the Americans tightened the noose around Boston by fortifying Breed's Hill (a spur of Bunker Hill). The British determined to remove them by a frontal attack. Twice thrown back, the British finally succeeded when the Americans ran out of ammunition. There were more than 1,000 British casualties in what turned out to be the bloodiest battle of the war (June 17, 1775), yet the British had gained very little and remained "bottled up" in Boston.

Congress put **George Washington** (1732–1799) in charge of the army, called for more troops, and adopted the Olive Branch Petition, which pleaded with **King George III** to intercede with Parliament to restore peace. However, the king gave his approval to the Prohibitory Act, declaring the colonies in rebellion and no longer under his protection. Preparations began for full-scale war against America.

In 1776, the colonists formed two committees to establish independence and a national government. One was to work out a framework for a national government. The other was to draft a statement of the reasons for declaring independence. The statement, called the **Declaration of Independence**, was primarily the work of Thomas Jefferson (1743–1826) of Virginia. It was a restatement of political ideas by then commonplace in America and showed why the former colonists felt justified in separating from Great Britain. Congress formally adopted the Declaration of Independence on **July 4, 1776**.

The British landed that summer at New York City. Washington, who had anticipated the move, was waiting for them. However, the undertrained, underequipped, and badly outnumbered American army was no match

for the British and had to retreat. By December, what was left of Washington's army had made it into Pennsylvania.

With his small army melting away as demoralized soldiers deserted, Washington decided on a bold stroke. On Christmas night, 1776, his army crossed the **Delaware River** and struck the Hessians at **Trenton**. Washington's troops easily defeated the Hessians, still groggy from their hard-drinking Christmas party.

A few days later, Washington defeated a British force at **Princeton**. The Americans regained much of New Jersey from the British and saved the American army from disintegration. Hoping to weaken Britain, France began making covert shipments of arms to the Americans early in the war. These French shipments were vital for the Americans. The American victory at Saratoga convinced the French to join openly in the war against England. Eventually, the Spanish (1779) and the Dutch (1780) joined as well.

The final agreement became known as the Treaty of Paris of 1783. Its terms stipulated the following:

1. The recognition by the major European powers, including Britain, of the United States as an independent nation.

2. The establishment of America's western boundary at the Mississippi River.

3. The establishment of America's southern boundary at 31 degrees north latitude (the northern boundary of Florida).

4. The surrender of Florida to Spain and the retainment of Canada by Britain.

5. The enablement of Private British creditors to collect any debts owed by United States citizens.

6. The recommendation of Congress that the states restore confiscated loyalist property.

The Creation of New Governments

After the adoption of the Articles of Confederation, Congress adopted a new constitution and the Americans elected George Washington as president under the guidelines.

The Federalist Era. George Washington received virtually all the votes of the presidential electors. **John Adams** (1735–1826) received the next highest number and became the vice president. After a triumphant journey from Mount Vernon, Washington attended his inauguration in New York City, the temporary seat of government.

To oppose the antifederalists, the states ratified 10 amendments—the Bill of Rights—by the end of 1791. The first nine spelled out specific guarantees of personal freedoms, and the Tenth Amendment reserved to the states all powers not specifically withheld or granted to the federal government.

Alexander Hamilton (1757–1804) interpreted the Constitution as having vested extensive powers in the federal government. This "implied powers" stance claimed that the government had all powers that the Constitution had not expressly denied it. Hamilton's was the "broad" interpretation of the Constitution.

By contrast, **Thomas Jefferson** and **James Madison** (1751–1836) held the view that the Constitution prohibited any action not specifically permitted in the Constitution. Based on this view of government, adherents of this "strict" interpretation opposed the establishment of Hamilton's national bank. The Jeffersonian supporters, primarily under the guidance of James Madison, began to organize political groups in opposition to Hamilton's program. The groups opposing Hamilton's view called themselves Democratic-Republicans or Jeffersonians.

The Federalists, Hamilton's supporters, received their strongest confirmation from the business and financial groups in the commercial centers of the Northeast and from the port cities of the South. The strength of the Democratic-Republicans lay primarily in the rural and frontier areas of the South and West. Federalist candidate John Adams won the election of 1796. The elections in 1798 increased the Federalists' majorities in both houses of Congress that used their "mandate" to enact legislation to stifle foreign influences.

The **Alien Act** raised new hurdles in the path of immigrants trying to obtain citizenship, and the **Sedition Act** widened the powers of the Adams administration to muzzle its newspaper critics. Democratic-Republicans were convinced that the Alien and Sedition Acts were unconstitutional, but the process of deciding on the constitutionality of federal laws was as yet undefined.

The Jeffersonian Era. **Thomas Jefferson** and **Aaron Burr** ran for the presidency on the Democratic-Republican ticket, though not together, against John Adams and Charles Pinckney for the Federalists. Both Jefferson and Burr received the same number of votes in the Electoral College, so the election went to the House of Representatives. After a lengthy deadlock, Alexander Hamilton threw his support to Jefferson. Burr had to accept the vice presidency, the result obviously intended by the electorate.

The adoption and ratification of the Twelfth Amendment in 1804 ensured that a tie vote between candidates of the same party could not again cause the confusion of the Jefferson-Burr affair. Following the constitutional mandate, an 1808 law prevented the importation of slaves. An American delegation purchased the trans-Mississippi territory from Napoleon for $15 million in April 1803 (the Louisiana Purchase), even though they had no authority to buy more than the city of New Orleans.

The War of 1812. Democratic-Republican **James Madison** won the election of 1808 over Federalist Charles Pinckney, but the Federalists gained seats in both houses of Congress.

The Native American tribes of the Northwest and the **Mississippi Valley** were resentful of the government's policy of pressured removal to the West, and the British authorities in Canada exploited their discontent by encouraging border raids against the American settlements. At the same time, the British interfered with American transatlantic shipping, including impressing sailors and capturing ships. On June 1, 1812, President Madison asked for a declaration of war, and Congress complied. After three years of inconclusive war, the British and Americans signed the Treaty of Ghent (1815). It provided for the acceptance of the status quo that had existed at the beginning of hostilities, and both sides restored their wartime conquests to the other.

The Monroe Doctrine. As Latin American nations began declaring independence, British and American leaders feared that European governments would try to restore the former New World colonies to their erstwhile royal owners. In December 1823, **President James Monroe** (1758–1831) included in his annual message to Congress a statement that the peoples of the American hemisphere were "henceforth not to be considered as subjects for future colonization by any European powers."

The Marshall Court. Chief Justice **John Marshall** (1755–1835) delivered the majority opinions in several critical decisions in the formative years of the U.S. Supreme Court. These decisions served to strengthen the power of the federal government (and of the court itself) and restrict the powers of state governments. Here are two key examples:

- *Marbury v. Madison* (1803) established the Supreme Court's power of judicial review over federal legislation.
- In *Gibbons v. Ogden* (1824), a case involving competing steamboat companies, Marshall ruled that commerce includes navigation and that only Congress has the right to regulate commerce among states. Marshall's ruling voided the state-granted monopoly.

The Missouri Compromise. The Missouri Territory, the first territory organized from the Louisiana Purchase, applied for statehood in 1819. Because the Senate membership was evenly divided between slaveholding and free states at that time, the admission of a new state would give the voting advantage to either the North or the South. As the debate dragged on, the northern territory of Massachusetts applied for admission as the state of Maine. By combining the two admission bills, Maine came in as a free and Missouri as a slave state. To make the Missouri Compromise palatable for the House of Representatives, an added provision prohibited slavery in the remainder of the Louisiana Territory north of the southern boundary of Missouri (latitude 36°30′).

Jacksonian Democracy. **Andrew Jackson** (1767–1845), the candidate of a faction of the emerging Democratic Party, won the election of 1828. Jackson was popular with the common man. He seemed to be the prototype of the self-made westerner: rough-hewn, violent, vindictive, with few ideas but strong convictions. He ignored his appointed cabinet officers and relied instead on the counsel of his "Kitchen Cabinet," a group of partisan supporters. He exercised his veto power more than any other president before him.

Jackson supported the removal of all Native American tribes to an area west of the Mississippi River. **The Indian Removal Act** of 1830 provided for the federal enforcement of that process. One of the results of this policy was the **Trail of Tears**, the forced march under U.S. Army escort of thousands of Cherokee Indians to the West. One-quarter or more of them, mostly women and children, perished on the journey.

The National Bank. The Bank of the United States had operated under the direction of Nicholas Biddle since 1823. He was a cautious man, and his conservative economic policy enforced conservatism among state and private banks—which many bankers resented. In 1832, Jackson vetoed the national bank's renewal, and it ceased being a federal institution in 1836.

The Antislavery Movement. In 1831, William Lloyd Garrison started his newspaper the *Liberator* and began to advocate total and immediate emancipation. He founded the New England Antislavery Society in 1832 and the American Antislavery Society in 1833. Theodore Weld pursued the same goals but advocated more gradual means.

The movement split into two wings: Garrison's radical followers and the moderates who favored "moral suasion" and petitions to Congress. In 1840, the Liberty Party, the first national antislavery party, fielded a presidential candidate on the platform of "free soil" (preventing the expansion of slavery into the new western territories).

The Role of Minorities. The women's rights movement focused on social and legal discrimination, and women like Lucretia Mott and Sojourner Truth became well-known figures on the speakers' circuit. By 1850, roughly 200,000 free blacks lived in the North and West. Prejudice restricted their lives, and "Jim Crow" laws separated the races.

Manifest Destiny and Westward Expansion. The coining of the term *Manifest Destiny* did not occur until 1844, but the belief that the destiny of the American nation was expansion all the way to the **Pacific Ocean**— and possibly even to Canada and Mexico—was older than that. A common conviction was that Americans should share American liberty and ideals with everyone possible, by force if necessary. In the 1830s, American missionaries followed the traders and trappers to the Oregon country and began to publicize the richness and beauty of the land. The result was the Oregon Fever of the 1840s, as thousands of settlers trekked across the Great Plains and the Rocky Mountains to settle the new Shangri-la.

Texas had been a state in the Republic of Mexico since 1822, following the Mexican revolution against Spanish control. The new Mexican government invited immigration from the North by offering land grants to Stephen Austin and other Americans. By 1835, approximately 35,000 "gringos" were homesteading on Texas land. When the Mexican officials saw their power base eroding as the foreigners flooded in, they moved to tighten control through restrictions on immigration and through tax increases. The Texans responded in 1836 by proclaiming independence and establishing a new republic. In 1845, after a series of failed attempts at annexation, the United States Congress admitted Texas to the Union.

The Mexican War. Though Mexico broke diplomatic relations with the United States immediately after Texas's admission to the Union, there was still hope of a peaceful settlement. In the fall of 1845, President **James K. Polk** (1795–1849) sent **John Slidell** to Mexico City with a proposal for a peaceful settlement, but like other attempts at negotiation, nothing came of it. Racked by coup and countercoup, the Mexican government refused even to receive Slidell. Polk responded by sending U.S. troops into the disputed territory. On April 5, 1846, Mexican troops attacked an American patrol. When news of the clash reached Washington, Polk sought and received from Congress a declaration of war against Mexico.

Negotiated peace came about with the signing of the Treaty of Guadalupe Hidalgo on February 2, 1848. Under the terms of the treaty, Mexico ceded to the United States the southwestern territory from Texas to the California coast.

Sectional Conflict and the Causes of the Civil War

The Crisis of 1850. The Mexican War had barely started when, on August 8, 1846, a freshman Democratic congressman, **David Wilmot** of Pennsylvania, introduced his **Wilmot Proviso** as a proposed amendment to a war appropriations bill. It stipulated that "neither slavery nor involuntary servitude shall ever exist" in any territory to be acquired from Mexico. The House passed the proviso, but the Senate did not; Wilmot introduced his provision again amidst increasingly acrimonious debate.

One compromise proposal called for the extension of the 36°30′ line of the Missouri Compromise westward through the Mexican cession to the Pacific, with territory north of the line closed to slavery. Another compromise solution was "popular sovereigntym" which held that the residents of each territory should decide for themselves whether to allow slavery.

Having more than the requisite population and being in need of better government, California petitioned in September 1849 for admission to the Union as a free state. Southerners were furious. Long outnumbered in the House of Representatives, the South would find itself, should Congress admit California as a free state, similarly outnumbered in the Senate. At this point, the aged **Henry Clay** proposed a compromise. For the North, Congress would admit California as a free state; the land in dispute between Texas and New Mexico would go to New Mexico; popular sovereignity would decide the issue of slavery in the New Mexico and Utah territories (all of the Mexican cession outside of California); and there would be no slave trade in the District of Columbia. For the South, Congress would enact a tougher Fugitive Slave Law, promise not to abolish slavery in the District of Columbia, and declare that it did not have jurisdiction over the interstate slave trade; the federal government would pay Texas's $10 million preannexation debt.

The Kansas-Nebraska Act. All illusion of sectional peace ended abruptly in 1854 when Senator

Stephen A. Douglas of Illinois introduced a bill in Congress to organize the area west of Missouri and Iowa as the territories of Kansas and Nebraska on the basis of popular sovereignty. The **Kansas-Nebraska Act** aroused a storm of outrage in the North, which viewed the repeal of the Missouri Compromise as the breaking of a solemn agreement, hastened the disintegration of the Whig Party, and divided the Democratic Party along North-South lines.

Springing to life almost overnight as a result of northern fury at the Kansas-Nebraska Act was the Republican Party. This party included diverse elements whose sole unifying principle was banning slavery from all the nation's territories, confining slavery to the states where it already existed, and preventing the further spread of slavery.

The Dred Scott Decision. In *Dred Scott v. Sanford* (1857), the Supreme Court attempted to settle the slavery question. The case involved a Missouri slave, **Dred Scott**, whom the abolitionists had encouraged to sue for his freedom on the basis that his owner had taken him to a free state, Illinois, for several years and then to a free territory, Wisconsin.

The Court attempted to read the extreme southern position on slavery into the Constitution, ruling not only that Scott had no standing to sue in federal court but also that temporary residence in a free state, even for several years, did not make a slave free. Additionally, the Court ruling signified that the Missouri Compromise (already a dead letter by that time) had been unconstitutional all along because Congress did not have the authority to exclude slavery from a territory, nor did territorial governments have the right to prohibit slavery.

The Election of 1860. As the 1860 presidential election approached, the Republicans met in Chicago, confident of victory and determined to do nothing to jeopardize their favorable position. Accordingly, they rejected as too radical the front-running candidate, New York Senator **William H. Seward**, in favor of Illinois' favorite son **Abraham Lincoln** (1809–1865). The platform called for federal support of a transcontinental railroad and for the containment of slavery. On election day,

the voting went along strictly sectional lines. Lincoln led in popular votes; though he was short of a majority of popular votes, he did have the needed majority in Electoral College votes and received election.

The Secession Crisis. On December 20, 1860, South Carolina, by vote of a special convention, seceded from the Union. By February 1, 1861, six more states (Alabama, Georgia, Florida, Mississippi, Louisiana, and Texas) had followed suit.

Representatives of the seceded states met in Montgomery, Alabama, in February 1861 and declared themselves to be the Confederate States of America. They elected former secretary of war and United States senator **Jefferson Davis** (1808–1889) of Mississippi as president and Alexander Stephens (1812–1883) of Georgia as vice president.

Civil War and Reconstruction

Hostilities Begin. In his inaugural address, Lincoln urged Southerners to reconsider their actions but warned that the Union was perpetual, that states could not secede, and that he would therefore hold the federal forts and installations in the South. Only two remained in federal hands: Fort Pickens, off Pensacola, Florida; and Fort Sumter, in the harbor of Charleston, South Carolina.

From **Major Robert Anderson**, commander of the small garrison at Sumter, Lincoln soon received word that supplies were running low. Desiring to send in the needed supplies, Lincoln informed the governor of South Carolina of his intention but promised that no attempt would be made to send arms, ammunition, or reinforcements unless Southerners initiated hostilities.

Confederate **General P. G. T. Beauregard**, acting on orders from President Davis, demanded Anderson's surrender. Anderson said he would surrender if not resupplied. Knowing supplies were on the way, the Confederates opened fire at 4:30 AM on April 12, 1861. The next day, the fort surrendered. The day following Sumter's surrender, Lincoln declared an insurrection and called for the states to provide 75,000 volunteers to put it down. In response, Virginia, Tennessee, North Carolina, and Arkansas declared their secession. The remaining slave states—Delaware, Kentucky, Maryland, and Missouri—wavered but stayed with the Union.

The North enjoyed many advantages over the South. It had the majority of wealth and was vastly superior in industry. The North also had an advantage of almost three to one in manpower; over one-third of the South's population was slaves, whom Southerners would not use as soldiers. Unlike the South, the North received large numbers of **immigrants** during the war. The North retained control of the U.S. Navy; it could command the sea and blockade the South. Finally, the North enjoyed a much superior system of railroads.

The South did, however, have some advantages. It was vast in size and difficult to conquer. In addition, its troops would be fighting on their own ground, a fact that would give them the advantage of familiarity with the terrain and the added motivation of defending their homes and families.

The Homestead Act and the Morrill Land Grant Act. In 1862, Congress passed two highly important acts dealing with domestic affairs in the North. The Homestead Act granted 160 acres of government land free of charge to any person who would farm it for at least five years. Many of the settlers of the West used the provisions of this act. The Morrill Land Grant Act offered large amounts of the federal government's land to states that would establish "agricultural and mechanical" colleges. The founding of many of the nation's large state universities was under the provisions of this act.

The Emancipation Proclamation. By mid-1862, Lincoln, under pressure from radical elements of his own party and hoping to create a favorable impression on foreign public opinion, determined to issue the **Emancipation Proclamation**, which declared free all slaves in areas still in rebellion as of January 1, 1863. At Seward's recommendation, Lincoln waited to announce the proclamation until the North won some sort of victory. The Battle of Antietam (September 17, 1862) provided this victory.

Northern Victory. Lincoln ran on the ticket of the National Union Party—essentially, the Republican Party with the addition of loyal or "war" Democrats.

His vice presidential candidate was **Andrew Johnson** (1808–1875), a loyal Democrat from Tennessee.

In September 1864, word came that **General William Sherman** (1820–1891) had taken Atlanta. The capture of this vital southern rail and manufacturing center brought an enormous boost to northern morale. Along with other northern victories that summer and fall, it ensured a resounding election victory for Lincoln and the continuation of the war to complete victory for the North.

General Robert E. Lee (1807–1870) abandoned Richmond on April 3, 1865, and attempted to escape with what was left of his army. Pursued by **Ulysses S. Grant** (1822–1885), Northern forces cornered Lee's troops and forced his surrender at Appomattox, Virginia, on April 9, 1865. Other Confederate troops still holding out in various parts of the South surrendered over the next few weeks.

Lincoln did not live to receive news of the final surrenders. On April 14, 1865, **John Wilkes Booth** shot Lincoln in the back of the head while the president was watching a play in Ford's Theater in Washington, D.C.

Reconstruction. In 1865, Congress created the **Freedman's Bureau** to provide food, clothing, and education and generally to look after the interests of former slaves. To restore legal governments in the seceded states, Lincoln developed a policy that made it relatively easy for southern states to enter the collateral process.

Congress passed a **Civil Rights Act** in 1866, declaring that all citizens born in the United States are, regardless of race, equal citizens under the law. This act became the model of the Fourteenth Amendment to the Constitution.

President Andrew Johnson obeyed the letter but not the spirit of the Reconstruction acts. Congress, angry at his refusal to cooperate, sought in vain for grounds to impeach him. In August 1867, Johnson violated the Tenure of Office Act, which forbade the president from removing from office officials who had been approved by the Senate. This test of the act's constitutionality took place not in the courts but in Congress. The House of Representatives impeached Johnson and came within one vote of being removed from office by the Senate.

The Fifteenth Amendment. In 1868, the Republicans nominated **Ulysses S. Grant** for president. His narrow victory prompted Republican leaders to decide that it would be politically expedient to give the vote to all blacks, northern as well as southern. For this purpose, leaders of the north drew up and submitted to the states the Fifteenth Amendment. Ironically, the idea was so unpopular in the North that it won the necessary three-fourths approval only because Congress required the southern states to ratify it.

Industrialism, War, and the Progressive Era

The Economy. Captains of industry—such as **John D. Rockefeller** in oil, **J. P. Morgan** in banking, **Gustavus Swift** in meat processing, **Andrew Carnegie** in steel, and **E. H. Harriman** in railroads—created major industrial empires. In 1886, **Samuel Gompers** and **Adolph Strasser** put together a combination of national craft unions, the **American Federation of Labor (AFL)**, to represent labor's concerns about wages, hours, and safety conditions. Although militant in its use of the strike and in its demand for collective bargaining in labor contracts with large corporations, the AFL did not promote violence or radicalism.

The Spanish-American War. The Cuban revolt against Spain in 1895 threatened American business interests in Cuba. Sensational "yellow" journalism and nationalistic statements from officials such as Assistant Secretary of the Navy **Theodore Roosevelt** (1858–1919) encouraged popular support for direct American military intervention on behalf of Cuban independence.

On March 27, 1897, President **William McKinley** (1843–1901) asked Spain to call an armistice, accept American mediation to end the war, and stop using concentration camps in Cuba. Spain refused to comply. On April 21, Congress declared war on Spain with the objective of establishing Cuban independence (Teller Amendment). The first U.S. forces landed in Cuba on June 22, 1898, and by July 17 had defeated the Spanish forces. Spain ceded the Philippines, Puerto Rico, and

Guam to the United States in return for a payment of $20 million to Spain for the Philippines.

Theodore Roosevelt and Progressive Reforms. On September 6, 1901, while attending the Pan American Exposition in Buffalo, New York, President McKinley was shot by Leon Czolgosz, an anarchist. The president died on September 14. Theodore Roosevelt, at age 42, became the nation's twenty-fifth president and its youngest president to date.

In accordance with the Antitrust Policy (1902), Roosevelt ordered the Justice Department to prosecute corporations pursuing monopolistic practices. Attorney General P. C. Knox first brought suit against the Northern Securities Company, a railroad holding corporation put together by J. P. Morgan, and then moved against Rockefeller's Standard Oil Company. By the time he left office in 1909, Roosevelt had indictments against 25 monopolies.

Roosevelt engineered the separation of Panama from Colombia and the recognition of Panama as an independent country. The **Hay-Bunau-Varilla Treaty** of 1903 granted the United States control of the Canal Zone in Panama for $10 million and an annual fee of $250,000; the control would begin nine years after ratification of the treaty by both parties. Construction of the **Panama Canal** began in 1904 and was completed in 1914.

In 1905, the African American intellectual and militant **W. E. B. DuBois** founded the **Niagara Movement**, which called for federal legislation to protect racial equality and to grant full citizenship rights. Formed in 1909, the **National Association for the Advancement of Colored People** pressed actively for the rights of the African Americans. A third organization of the time, the radical labor organization called the **Industrial Workers of the World** (IWW, or Wobblies; 1905–1924), promoted violence and revolution. The IWW organized effective strikes in the textile industry in 1912 and among a few western miners' groups, but it had little appeal to the average American worker. After the Red Scare of 1919, the government worked to smash the IWW and deported many of its immigrant leaders and members.

The Wilson Presidency. The nation elected Democratic candidate **Woodrow Wilson** (1856–1924) as president in 1912. Before the outbreak of World War I in 1914, Wilson, working with cooperative majorities in both houses of Congress, achieved much of the remaining progressive agenda, including lower tariff reform (Underwood-Simmons Act, 1913); the Sixteenth Amendment (graduated income tax, 1913); the Seventeenth Amendment (direct election of senators, 1913); the Federal Reserve banking system (that provided regulation and flexibility to monetary policy, 1913); the Federal Trade Commission (to investigate unfair business practices, 1914); and the Clayton Antitrust Act (improving the old Sherman Act and protecting labor unions and farm cooperatives from prosecution, 1914).

Wilson's Fourteen Points. When America entered World War I in 1917, President Wilson maintained that the war would make the world safe for democracy. In an address to Congress on January 8, 1918, he presented his specific peace plan in the form of the Fourteen Points. The first five points called for open rather than secret peace treaties, freedom of the seas, free trade, arms reduction, and a fair adjustment of colonial claims. The next eight points addressed national aspirations of various European peoples and the adjustment of boundaries. The fourteenth point, which he considered the most important and which he had espoused as early as 1916, called for a "general association of nations" to preserve the peace.

Social Conflicts. Although many Americans had called for immigration restriction since the late nineteenth century, the only major restriction imposed on immigration by 1920 had been the Chinese Exclusion Act of 1882. Labor leaders believed that immigrants depressed wages and impeded unionization. Some progressives believed that they created social problems. In June 1917, Congress, over Wilson's veto, imposed a **literacy test for immigrants** and **excluded many Asian nationalities**.

In 1921, Congress passed the **Emergency Quota Act**. In practice, the law admitted almost as many immigrants as the nation wanted from such nations as Britain, Ireland, and Germany but severely restricted Italians, Greeks, Poles, and eastern European Jews hoping to enter the country. The law became effective in 1922 and reduced the number of immigrants annually to about 40 percent of the 1921 total. Congress then passed the National Origins Act of 1924, which further reduced the number of southern and eastern European immigrants and cut the annual immigration total to 20 percent of the 1921 figure. In 1927, the nation set the annual maximum number of immigrants allowed into the United States to 150,000.

On Thanksgiving Day in 1915, **William J. Simmons** founded the **Knights of the Ku Klux Klan**. Its purpose was to intimidate African Americans, who were experiencing an apparent rise in status during World War I. The Klan's methods of repression included cross burnings, tar and featherings, kidnappings, lynchings, and burnings. The Klan was not a political party, but it endorsed and opposed candidates and exerted considerable control over elections and politicians in at least nine states.

Fundamentalist Protestants, under the leadership of **William Jennings Bryan**, began a campaign in 1921 to prohibit the teaching of evolution in the schools and protect the belief in the literal biblical account of creation. The South especially received the idea well.

The Great Depression and the New Deal

The Crash. Signs of recession were apparent before the market crash in 1929. The farm economy, which involved almost 25 percent of the population, coal, railroads, and New England textiles had not been prosperous during the 1920s.

After 1927, new construction declined and auto sales began to sag. Many workers lost their jobs before the crash of 1929. Stock prices increased throughout the decade. The boom in prices and volume of sales was especially active after 1925 and was intensive from 1928 to 1929. Careful investors recognized the overpricing of stocks and began to sell to take their profits.

During October 1929, prices declined as more people began to sell their stock. **"Black Thursday,"** October 24, 1929, saw the trading of almost 13 million shares; this was a large number for that time, and prices fell precipitously. Investment banks tried to boost the market by buying, but on October 29, **"Black Tuesday,"** the market fell about 40 points, with 16.5 million shares traded.

Hoover's Depression Policies. The nation had elected **Herbert Hoover** (1874–1964) to the presidency in 1928. In June 1929 Congress passed the Agricultural Marketing Act, which created the Federal Farm Board. The board had a revolving fund of $500 million to lend agricultural cooperatives to buy commodities, such as wheat and cotton, and hold them for higher prices.

The Hawley-Smoot Tariff of June 1930 raised duties on both agricultural and manufactured imports. Chartered by Congress in 1932, the Reconstruction Finance Corporation loaned money to railroads, banks, and other financial institutions. It prevented the failure of basic firms, on which many other elements of the economy depended, but many people criticized it as relief for the rich.

The Federal Home Loan Bank Act, passed in July 1932, created home loan banks, which made loans to building and loan associations, savings banks, and insurance companies. Its purpose was to help avoid foreclosures on homes.

The First New Deal. Franklin D. Roosevelt (1882–1945), governor of New York, easily defeated Hoover in the election of 1932. At his inauguration on March 4, 1933, the American economic system seemed to be on the verge of collapse. Roosevelt assured the nation that "the only thing we have to fear is fear itself," called for a special session of Congress to convene on March 9, and asked for "broad executive powers to wage war against the emergency." Two days later, he closed all banks for a brief time and forbade the export of gold or the redemption of currency in gold. A special session of Congress from March 9 to June 16, 1933 ("The Hundred Days") passed a great body of legislation that has left a lasting mark on the nation. Historians have divided Roosevelt's legislation into the First New Deal (1933–1935) and a new wave of programs beginning in 1935 called the Second New Deal.

Passed on March 9, the first day of the special session, the Emergency Banking Relief Act provided additional funds for banks from the Reconstruction Finance Corporation and the Federal Reserve, allowed the Treasury to open sound banks after 10 days and to merge or liquidate unsound ones, and forbade the hoarding or exporting of gold. Roosevelt, on March 12, assured the public of the soundness of the banks in the first of many "fireside chats," or radio addresses. People believed him, and most banks were soon open, with deposits outnumbering withdrawals.

The Banking Act of 1933, or the Glass-Steagall Act, established the Federal Deposit Insurance Corporation to insure individual deposits in commercial banks and to separate commercial banking from the more speculative activity of investment banking. The Federal Emergency Relief Act appropriated $500 million for state and local governments to distribute to aid the poor. The act also established the Federal Emergency Relief Administration under **Harry Hopkins** (1890–1946).

The **Civilian Conservation Corps** enrolled 250,000 young men aged 18 to 24 from families on relief to go to camps where they worked on flood control, soil conservation, and forest projects under the direction of the War Department. **The Public Works Administration** had $3.3 billion to distribute to state and local governments for building projects such as schools, highways, and hospitals. The Agricultural Adjustment Act of 1933 created the **Agricultural Adjustment Administration**. Farmers agreed to reduce production of principal farm commodities and received subsidies in return. Farm prices increased; when owners took land out of cultivation, however, tenants and sharecroppers suffered. The repeal of the law came in January 1936 on the grounds that the processing tax was not constitutional.

The National Industrial Recovery Act was the cornerstone of the recovery program. In June 1933, Congress passed the National Industrial Recovery Act and the National Recovery Administration (NRA); the goal was the self-regulation of business and the development of fair prices, wages, hours, and working conditions. Section 7-a of the NIRA permitted collective bargaining for workers; laborers would test the federal support for their bargaining in the days to come. The slogan of the NRA was, "We do our part." The economy improved but did not recover.

The Second New Deal. The **Works Progress Administration** (WPA) began in May 1935, following the passage of the Emergency Relief Appropriations Act of April 1935. The WPA employed people from the relief rolls for 30 hours of work a week at pay double that of the relief payment but less than private employment.

Created in May 1935, the **Rural Electrification Administration** provided loans and WPA labor to electric cooperatives so they could build lines into rural areas that the private companies did not serve. Passed in August of 1935 the **Social Security Act** established for persons over age 65 a retirement plan to be funded by a tax on wages paid equally by employee and employer. The government paid the first benefits, ranging from $10 to $85 per month in 1942. Another provision of the act forced states to initiate unemployment insurance programs.

Labor Unions. The 1935 passage of the National Labor Relations Act, or the **Wagner Act**, resulted in a massive growth of union membership but at the expense of bitter conflict within the labor movement. Primarily craft unions made up the **American Federation of Labor**, formed in 1886. Some leaders wanted to unionize the mass-production industries, such as automobiles and rubber, with industrial unions.

In November 1935, **John L. Lewis** formed the Committee for Industrial Organization (CIO) to unionize basic industries, presumably within the AFL. **President William Green** of the AFL ordered the CIO to disband in January 1936. When the rebels refused, the AFL expelled them. The insurgents then reorganized the CIO as the independent Congress of Industrial Organizations. Labor strikes, particularly in the textile mills, marked the end of the 1930s. Soon the nation would receive another test.

World War II

The American Response to the War in Europe. In August 1939, Roosevelt created the War Resources Board to develop a plan for industrial mobilization in the event of war. The next month, he established the Office of Emergency Management in the White House to centralize mobilization activities.

Roosevelt officially proclaimed the neutrality of the United States on September 5, 1939. The Democratic Congress, in a vote that followed party lines, passed a new Neutrality Act in November. It allowed the cash-and-carry sale of arms and short-term loans to belligerents but forbade American ships to trade with belligerents or Americans to travel on belligerent ships.

Roosevelt determined that to aid Britain in every way possible was the best way to avoid war with Germany. In September 1940, he signed an agreement to give Britain 50 American destroyers in return for a 99-year lease on air and naval bases in British territories in Newfoundland, Bermuda, and the Caribbean.

The Road to Pearl Harbor. In late July 1941, the United States placed an embargo on the export of aviation gasoline, lubricants, and scrap iron and steel to Japan and granted an additional loan to China. In December, additional articles—iron ore and pig iron, some chemicals, machine tools, and other products—fell under the embargo.

In October 1941, a new military cabinet headed by **General Hideki Tojo** took control of Japan. The Japanese secretly decided to make a final effort to negotiate and to go to war if there was no solution by November 25. A new round of talks followed in Washington, but neither side would make a substantive change in its position. The Japanese gave final approval on December 1 for an attack on the United States.

The Japanese planned a major offensive to take the Dutch East Indies, Malaya, and the Philippines and to obtain the oil, metals, and other raw materials they needed. At the same time, they would attack Pearl Harbor in Hawaii to destroy the American Pacific fleet to keep it from interfering with their plans.

At 7:55 AM on Sunday, December 7, 1941, the first wave of Japanese carrier-based planes attacked the American fleet in **Pearl Harbor**. A second wave followed at 8:50 AM. The United States suffered the loss of two battleships sunk, six damaged and out of action, three cruisers and three destroyers sunk or damaged, several lesser vessels destroyed or damaged, and the destruction of all the 150 aircraft on the ground at Pearl Harbor. Worst of all, 2,323 American servicemen were killed and about 1,100 were wounded. The Japanese lost 29 planes, five midget submarines, and one fleet submarine.

Declared War Begins. On December 8, 1941, Congress declared war on Japan, with one dissenting vote—Representative Jeanette Rankin of Montana. On December 11, Germany and Italy declared war on the United States. Great Britain and the United States then established the Combined Chiefs of Staff, headquartered in Washington, to direct Anglo-American military operations.

On January 1, 1942, representatives of 26 nations met in Washington, D.C., and signed the Declaration of the United Nations, pledged themselves to the principles of the Atlantic Charter, and promised not to make a separate peace with their common enemies.

The Home Front. In *Korematsu v. United States* (1944), the Supreme Court upheld sending the Issei (Japanese Americans from Japan) and Nisei (native-born Japanese Americans) to concentration camps. The camps did not close until March 1946. Roosevelt died on April 12, 1945, at Warm Springs, Georgia. **Harry S Truman** (1884–1972), formerly a senator from Missouri and vice president of the United States, became president on April 12, 1945.

The Atomic Bomb. The Army Corps of Engineers established the Manhattan Engineering District in August 1942 for the purpose of developing an atomic bomb; the program eventually took the name the **Manhattan Project. J. Robert Oppenheimer** directed the design and construction of a transportable atomic bomb at Los Alamos, New Mexico. On July 16, 1945, the Manhattan Project exploded the first atomic bomb at Alamogordo, New Mexico.

The *Enola Gay* dropped an atomic bomb on Hiroshima, Japan, on August 6, 1945, killed about 78,000 persons, and injured 100,000 more. On August 9, the United States dropped a second bomb on Nagasaki, Japan. Japan surrendered on August 14, 1945, and signed the formal surrender on September 2.

The Postwar Era

The Cold War and Containment. In February 1947, Great Britain notified the United States that it could no longer aid the Greek government in its war against Communist insurgents. The next month, President Truman asked Congress for $400 million in military and economic aid for Greece and Turkey. Truman argued that the United States must support free peoples who were resisting Communist domination in his **Truman Doctrine**.

Secretary of State George C. Marshall proposed in June 1947 that the United States provide economic aid to help rebuild Europe. The following March, Congress passed the European Recovery Program; popularly known as the **Marshall Plan**, the program provided more than $12 billion in aid.

Anticommunism. On February 9, 1950, Senator **Joseph R. McCarthy** of Wisconsin stated that he had a list of known Communists who were working in the State Department. He later expanded his attacks. After making charges against the army, the Senate censured and discredited him in 1954.

Korean War. On June 25, 1950, North Korea invaded South Korea. President Truman committed U.S. forces to the United Nations (UN) auspices; **General Douglas MacArthur** would command the troops. By October, UN forces (mostly American) had driven north of the thirty-eighth parallel, which divided North and South Korea.

Chinese troops attacked MacArthur's forces on November 26, pushing them south of the thirty-eighth parallel, but by spring 1951, UN forces had recovered their offensive. The armistice of June 1953 left Korea divided along virtually the same boundary that had existed before the war.

Eisenhower-Dulles Foreign Policy. Dwight D. Eisenhower (1890–1969), elected president in 1952, chose **John Foster Dulles** as secretary of state. Dulles talked of a more aggressive foreign policy, calling for "massive retaliation" and "liberation" rather than containment. He wished to emphasize nuclear deterrents rather than conventional armed forces.

After several years of nationalist war against French occupation, in July 1954 France, Great Britain, the Soviet Union, and China signed the Geneva Accords, which divided Vietnam along the seventeenth parallel. The north would be under the leadership of **Ho Chi Minh** and the South under **Emperor Bao Dai**. The purpose of the scheduled elections was to unify the country, but **Ngo Dinh Diem** overthrew Bao Dai and prevented the elections from taking place. The United States supplied economic aid to **South Vietnam**.

In January 1959, **Fidel Castro** overthrew the dictator of Cuba. Castro criticized the United States, moved closer to the Soviet Union, and signed a trade agreement with the Soviets in February 1960. The United States prohibited the importation of Cuban sugar in October 1960 and broke off diplomatic relations in January 1961.

Space Exploration. The launching of the Soviet space satellite *Sputnik* on October 4, 1957, created fear that America was falling behind technologically. Although the United States launched *Explorer I* on January 31, 1958, the concern continued. In 1958, Congress established the **National Aeronautics and Space Administration** to coordinate research and development and passed the National Defense Education Act to provide grants and loans for education.

Civil Rights. Eisenhower completed the formal integration of the armed forces; desegregated public services in Washington, D.C., naval yards, and veterans' hospitals; and appointed a civil rights commission. In *Brown v. Board of Education of Topeka* (1954), **Thurgood Marshall**, lawyer for the **National Association for the Advancement of Colored People,** challenged the doctrine of "separate but equal" (*Plessy v. Ferguson*, **1896**). The Court declared that separate educational facilities were inherently unequal. In 1955, the Court ordered states to integrate "with all deliberate speed."

On December 11, 1955, in Montgomery, Alabama, **Rosa Parks** refused to give up her seat on a city bus to a white man and faced arrest. Under the leadership of **Martin Luther King Jr.** (1929–1968), an African American pastor, African Americans of Montgomery organized a bus boycott that lasted for a year until, in December 1956, the Supreme Court refused to review

a lower-court ruling that stated that separate but equal was no longer legal.

In February 1960, a segregated lunch counter in Greensboro, North Carolina, denied four African American students service; the students staged a sit-in. This inspired sit-ins elsewhere in the South and led to the formation of the Student Nonviolent Coordinating Committee, which had a chief aim of ending segregation in public accommodations.

The New Frontier, Vietnam, and Social Upheaval

Kennedy's "New Frontier." Democratic Senator **John F. Kennedy** (1917–1963) won the presidential election of 1960. The Justice Department, under Attorney General **Robert F. Kennedy**, began to push for civil rights, including desegregation of interstate transportation in the South, integration of schools, and supervision of elections. President Kennedy presented a comprehensive civil rights bill to Congress in 1963. With the bill held up in Congress, 200,000 people marched and demonstrated on its behalf, and Martin Luther King Jr. gave his "I Have a Dream" speech.

Cuban Missile Crisis. Under Eisenhower, the **Central Intelligence Agency** had begun training some 2,000 men to invade Cuba and to overthrow Fidel Castro. On April 19, 1961, this force invaded at the **Bay of Pigs**; opposing forces pinned them down, demanded their surrender, and captured some 1,200 men.

On October 14, 1962, a U-2 reconnaissance plane brought photographic evidence of the construction of missile sites in Cuba. Kennedy, on October 22, announced a blockade of Cuba and called on the Soviet premier, **Nikita Khrushchev** (1894–1971), to dismantle the missile bases and remove all weapons capable of attacking the United States from Cuba. Six days later, Khrushchev backed down and withdrew the missiles. Kennedy lifted the blockade.

Johnson and the Great Society. On November 22, 1963, **Lee Harvey Oswald** assassinated President Kennedy in Dallas, Texas; **Jack Ruby** killed Oswald two days later. Debate still continues as to whether the assassination was a conspiracy. **Lyndon B. Johnson** (1908–1973) succeeded John Kennedy as president of the United States.

The **1964 Civil Rights Act** outlawed racial discrimination by employers and unions, created the Equal Employment Opportunity Commission to enforce the law, and eliminated the remaining restrictions on black voting.

Michael Harrington's *The Other America: Poverty in the United States* (1962) showed that 20 to 25 percent of American families were living below the governmentally defined poverty line. The Economic Opportunity Act of 1964 sought to address the problem by establishing a job corps, community action programs, educational programs, work-study programs, job training, loans for small businesses and farmers, and a "domestic peace corps" called Volunteers in Service to America. The Office of Economic Opportunity administered many of these programs.

Emergence of Black Power. In 1965, Martin Luther King Jr. announced a voter registration drive. With help from the federal courts, he dramatized his effort by leading a march from Selma, Alabama, to Montgomery, Alabama, between March 21 and 25. The Voting Rights Act of 1965 authorized the attorney general to appoint officials to register voters.

Seventy percent of African Americans lived in city ghettos. In 1966, New York and Chicago experienced riots, and the following year there were riots in Newark and Detroit. The Kerner Commission, appointed to investigate the riots, concluded that the focus of the riots was a social system that prevented African Americans from getting good jobs and crowded them into ghettos.

On April 4, 1968, **James Earl Ray** assassinated Martin Luther King Jr. in Memphis. Ray was an escaped convict; he pled guilty to the murder and received a sentence of 99 years in prison. Riots in more than 100 cities followed.

Vietnam. After the defeat of the French in Vietnam in 1954, the United States sent military advisors

to South Vietnam to aid the government of **Ngo Dinh Diem**. The pro-Communist Vietcong forces gradually grew in strength because Diem failed to follow through on promised reforms and because of the support from North Vietnam, the Soviet Union, and China.

"Hawks" defended the president's policy and, drawing on the containment theory, said that the nation had the responsibility to resist aggression. The claim was if Vietnam should fall, all Southeast Asia would eventually go. Antiwar demonstrations were attracting large crowds by 1967. "Doves" argued that the war was a civil war in which the United States should not meddle.

On January 31, 1968, the first day of the Vietnamese new year (Tet), the Vietcong attacked numerous cities and towns, American bases, and even Saigon. Although they suffered large losses, the Vietcong won a psychological victory as American opinion began turning against the war.

The Nixon Conservative Reaction. Republican **Richard M. Nixon** (1913–1994), emphasizing stability and order, defeated Democratic nominee Hubert Humphrey by a margin of one percentage point. The Nixon administration sought to block renewal of the Voting Rights Act and delay implementation of court-ordered school desegregation in Mississippi. In 1969, Nixon appointed **Warren E. Burger**, a conservative, as chief justice. Although more conservative than the Warren court, the Burger court did declare in 1972 that the death penalty in use at the time was unconstitutional in 1972; it struck down state antiabortion legislation in 1973.

The president turned to "Vietnamization," the effort to build up South Vietnamese forces while withdrawing American troops. In 1969, Nixon reduced American troop strength by 60,000 but at the same time ordered the bombing of Cambodia, a neutral country. In the summer of 1972, negotiations between the United States and North Vietnam began in Paris. A few days before the 1972 presidential election, **Henry Kissinger**, the president's national security advisor, announced that "peace was at hand."

Nixon resumed the bombing of North Vietnam in December 1972; he claimed that the North Vietnamese were not bargaining in good faith. In January 1973, the two sides reached a settlement in which the North Vietnamese retained control over large areas of the South and agreed to release American prisoners of war within 60 days. Nearly 60,000 Americans had been killed and 300,000 more wounded, and the war had cost American taxpayers $109 billion. On March 29, 1973, the last American combat troops left South Vietnam. The North Vietnamese forces continued to push back the South Vietnamese, and in April 1975, Saigon fell to the North.

Watergate, Carter, and the New Conservatism

Watergate. The Republicans renominated Nixon, who won a landslide victory over the Democratic nominee, Senator **George McGovern**. What became known as the Watergate crisis began during the 1972 presidential campaign. Early on the morning of June 17, a security officer for the Committee for the Reelection of the President, along with four other men, broke into Democratic headquarters at the Watergate apartment complex in Washington, D.C. The authorities caught the men going through files and installing electronic eavesdropping devices.

In March 1974, a grand jury indicted some of Nixon's top aides and named Nixon an unindicted co-conspirator. Meanwhile, the House Judiciary Committee televised its debate over impeachment. The committee charged the president with obstructing justice, misusing presidential power, and failing to obey the committee's subpoenas. Before the House began to debate impeachment, Nixon announced his resignation on August 8, 1974, to take effect at noon the following day.

Gerald Ford (1913–) then became president. Gerald Ford was in many respects the opposite of Nixon. Although a partisan Republican, he was well liked and free of any hint of scandal. Ford almost immediately encountered controversy when in September 1974 he offered to pardon Nixon. Nixon accepted the offer although he admitted no wrongdoing and had not yet received any charges of crime.

Carter's Moderate Liberalism. In 1976, the Democrats nominated **James Earl Carter** (1924–), formerly governor of Georgia, who ran on the basis of his integrity and lack of Washington connections. Carter narrowly defeated Ford in the election.

Carter offered amnesty to Americans who had fled the draft and gone to other countries during the Vietnam War. He established the departments of Energy and Education and placed the civil service on a merit basis. He created a "superfund" for cleanup of chemical waste dumps, established controls over strip mining, and protected 100 million acres of Alaskan wilderness from development.

Carter's Foreign Policy. Carter negotiated a controversial treaty with Panama, affirmed by the Senate in 1978, that provided for the transfer of ownership of the canal to Panama in 1999 and guaranteed its neutrality. In 1978, Carter negotiated the Camp David Accords between Israel and Egypt. Israel promised to return occupied land in the Sinai to Egypt in exchange for Egyptian recognition, a process completed in 1982. An agreement to negotiate the Palestinian refugee problem proved ineffective.

The Iranian Crisis. In 1978, a revolution forced the **shah of Iran** to flee the country and replaced him with a religious leader, **Ayatollah Ruhollah Khomeini** (ca. 1900–1989). Because the United States had supported the shah with arms and money, the revolutionaries were strongly anti-American, calling the United States the "Great Satan."

After Carter allowed the exiled shah to come to the United States for medical treatment in October 1979, some 400 Iranians broke into the American embassy in Teheran on November 4 and took the occupants captive. They demanded the return of the shah to Iran for trial, the confiscation of his wealth, and the presentation of his wealth to Iran. Carter rejected these demands; instead, he froze Iranian assets in the United States and established a trade embargo against Iran. After extensive negotiations with Iran, in which Algeria acted as an intermediary, the Iranians freed the American hostages on January 20, 1981.

Attacking Big Government. Republican **Ronald Reagan** (1911–2004) defeated Carter by a large electoral majority in 1980. Reagan placed priority on cutting taxes. He based his approach on "supply-side" economics, the idea that if government left more money in the hands of the people, they would invest rather then spend the excess on consumer goods. The results would be greater production, more jobs, and greater prosperity, resulting in more income for the government despite lower tax rates. However, from a deficit of $59 billion in 1980, the federal budget was running $195 billion in the red by 1983. Reagan ended ongoing antitrust suits against IBM and AT&T and fulfilled his promise to reduce government interference with business.

Iran-Contra. In 1985 and 1986, several Reagan officials sold arms to the Iranians in hopes of encouraging them to use their influence in obtaining the release of American hostages being held in Lebanon. Profits from these sales went to the Nicaraguan *contras*—a militant group opposed to the left-leaning elected government—in an attempt to get around congressional restrictions on funding the *contras*. The attorney general appointed a special prosecutor, and Congress held hearings on the affair in May 1987.

The Election of 1988. Vice President George H. W. Bush (1924–) won the Republican nomination. Bush defeated Democrat **Michael Dukakis**, but the Republicans were unable to make any inroads in Congress.

Operation Just Cause. Since coming to office, the Bush administration had been concerned that Panamanian dictator **Manuel Noriega** was providing an important link in the drug traffic between South America and the United States. After economic sanctions, diplomatic efforts, and an October 1989 coup failed to oust Noriega, Bush ordered 12,000 troops into Panama on December 20 for what became known as **Operation Just Cause**.

On January 3, 1990, Noriega surrendered to the Americans and faced drug-trafficking charges in the United States. Found guilty in 1992, his sentence was 40 years.

Persian Gulf Crisis. On August 2, 1990, Iraq invaded Kuwait, an act that Bush denounced as "naked aggression." The United States quickly banned most trade with Iraq, froze Iraq's and Kuwait's assets in the

United States, and sent aircraft carriers to the Persian Gulf. On August 6, after the UN Security Council condemned the invasion, Bush ordered the deployment of air, sea, and land forces to Saudi Arabia and dubbed the operation Desert Shield.

On February 23, the allied air assault began. Four days later, Bush announced the liberation of Kuwait, and ordered offensive operations to cease. The United Nations established the terms for the cease-fire, which Iraq accepted on April 6.

The Road to the Twenty-First Century

The Election of 1992. William Jefferson Clinton (1946–) won 43 percent of the popular vote and 370 electoral votes, while George H. W. Bush won 37 percent of the popular vote and 168 electoral votes. Although he won no electoral votes, the Independent Party candidate, Ross Perot (1930–), gained 19 percent of the popular vote.

Domestic Affairs. The **North American Free Trade Agreement (NAFTA)**, negotiated by the Bush administration, eliminated most tariffs and other trade barriers between the United States, Canada, and Mexico. Passed by Congress and signed by Clinton in 1993, NAFTA became law in January 1994.

In October 1993, the Clinton administration proposed legislation to reform the health care system, which included universal coverage with a guaranteed benefits package, managed competition through health care alliances that would bargain with insurance companies, and employer mandates to provide health insurance for employees. With most Republicans and small business, insurance, and medical business interests opposed to the legislation, the Democrats dropped their attempt at a compromise package in September 1994.

Impeachment and Acquittal. Clinton received criticism for alleged wrongdoing in connection with a real estate development called Whitewater. While governor of Arkansas, Clinton had invested in Whitewater, along with **James B. and Susan McDougal**, owners of a failed savings and loan institution. After Congress renewed the independent counsel law, a three-judge panel appointed Kenneth W. Starr to the new role of independent prosecutor.

The Starr investigation yielded massive findings in late 1998, roughly midway into Clinton's second term, including information on an adulterous affair that Clinton had had with Monica Lewinsky while she was an intern at the White House. It was on charges stemming from this report that the House of Representatives impeached Clinton in December 1998 for perjury and obstruction of justice. The Senate acquitted him of all charges in February 1999.

Continuing Crisis in the Balkans. During Clinton's second term, continued political unrest abroad and civil war in the Balkans continued to be a major foreign policy challenge. In 1999, the Serbian government attacked ethnic Albanians in Kosovo, a province of Serbia. In response, North Atlantic Treaty Organization (NATO) forces, led by the United States, bombed Serbia. Several weeks of bombing forced Serbian forces to withdraw from Kosovo.

The Election of 2000. Preelection polls indicated that the election would be close, and few ventured to predict the outcome. Indeed, the election outcome was much in doubt for several weeks after the election. Though Clinton's vice president, **Al Gore** (1948–), won the popular vote, the Electoral College was very close, and Florida (the state governed by George W. Bush's brother) was pivotal in deciding the election.

George W. Bush (1946–), son of the former president **George H. W. Bush**, appeared to win Florida, but by a very small margin; a recount began. Then, controversy over how to conduct the recount led to a series of court challenges, with the matter ultimately decided by the U.S. Supreme Court, which ruled in favor of Bush. George W. Bush thus became the forty-third President of the United States.

Terrorism Hits Home. The new president would soon face the grim task of dealing with a massive terrorist attack on major symbols of U.S. economic and military might. On the morning of September 11, 2001, hijackers deliberately crashed U.S. commercial jetliners into the World Trade Center in New York—toppling its 110-story twin towers—and the Pentagon, just outside Washington, D.C. Thousands died in the deadliest act of terrorism in American history.

Though the person or persons behind the attacks were not immediately known, Bush cast prime suspicion on the Saudi exile Osama bin Laden, the alleged mastermind of the bombings of two U.S. embassies in 1998 and of a U.S. naval destroyer in 2000. The United States had earlier seen terrorism on its home soil carried out by Islamic militants in the 1993 bombing of the World Trade Center and by a member of the American militia movement in the bombing of the Oklahoma City federal building in 1995. The dispute with Iraq continued, and George W. Bush declared war (a disputed option) with Iraq. The outcome of sending troops to Iraq is undetermined.

Skill Eight

Identify Immigration and Settlement Patterns That Have Shaped the History of the United States

"The United States is a nation of immigrants" is a frequently quoted remark. The quotation, however, may cause some to forget that the Europeans came to a country already occupied by Native Americans.

The New World that Columbus and other explorers discovered in the late fifteenth and early sixteenth centuries was neither recently formed nor recently settled. It had actually been settled between 15,000 and 35,000 years before. As in other areas of the world, the native peoples of the "New World" formed communities but did not immediately develop written languages. The lack of any kind of written record makes interpreting the prehistorical past more difficult. Archeologists and anthropologists working in North and South America have unearthed the remains of these early communities, and it is on this evidence that anthropologists base the earliest theories about the origins, movements, and lifestyles of native people.

It is important to remember that there is not one universally accepted theory regarding the earliest history of the people who settled North and South America. It is also important to remember that by the time Europeans came into contact with the indigenous peoples of the Americas, more than 2,000 distinct cultures and hundreds of distinct languages existed. It is therefore necessary to trace not just the origins but also the developments, affected by various factors such as the environment, that took place before the Europeans arrived. This will provide an understanding of the various Indian cultures and societies and the impact that contact with Europeans had on them.

Especially after 1697, the English colonies bought large numbers of slaves. By 1760, approximately a quarter of a million slaves populated the colonies, with the highest concentration in the South. The decimation of the native population, a declining number of indentured servants, and the establishment of large plantations led to a shortage of workers; slavery seemed to be the answer. Colonial assemblies began to pass "slave codes" in the eighteenth century. These codes identified all nonwhites or dark-skinned people as slaves, made their condition permanent, and legalized slavery in British North America.

The transporting of the slaves was cruel. Chained in the dark, unsanitary holds with little food and water, many died during the Middle Passage from Africa to the Americas. Slave traders sold the survivors to plantations owners in the Caribbean, Brazil, or North America.

By the late 1700s, the new government in America began to try to stifle foreign influences. The **Alien Act** raised new hurdles in the path of immigrants trying to obtain citizenship, and the **Sedition Act** widened the powers of the Adams administration to muzzle its newspaper critics. Members of the Democratic-Republican Party were convinced that the Alien and Sedition Acts were unconstitutional, but the process of deciding on the constitutionality of federal laws was as yet undefined.

Americans, too, immigrated to other countries in the early 1800s, primarily to Mexico. Texas had been a state in the Republic of Mexico since 1822, following the Mexican revolution against Spanish control. The new Mexican government invited immigration from the North by offering land grants to Stephen Austin and other Americans. By 1835, approximately 35,000 "gringos" were homesteading on Texas land. The Mexican officials saw their power base eroding as the foreigners flooded in, so Mexico moved to tighten control through restrictions on immigration and through tax increases. The Texans responded in 1836 by proclaiming independence and establishing a new republic. In 1845, after a series of failed attempts at annexation, Texas became a part of the Union.

During the period of Andrew Jackson's service as president, he supported the removal of all Native American tribes to an area west of the Mississippi River, even though the tribes had inhabited their lands since long before the Europeans arrived. **The Indian Removal Act** in 1830 provided for the federal enforcement of that process. One of the results of this policy was the **Trail of Tears**, the forced march under U.S. Army escort of thousands of Cherokee Indians to the West. One-quarter or more of them, mostly women and children, perished on the journey. Thus immigrant Americans were enacting policies affecting Native Americans who were on the land when the "gringos" arrived.

The presence of the slave population continued to be a debatable issue.

"Skill Seven: Identifying Individuals and Events That Have Influenced Economic, Social, and Political Institutions in the United States" traces some of the problems through the Missouri Compromise, the antislavery movement, the work of Lucretia Mott and Sojourner Truth, the Dred Scott Decision, the election of 1860, secession, the Civil War, the Emancipation Proclamation, and Reconstruction. Immigrants and emigrants arriving in the North contributed, in fact, to the North's victory over the South.

Human rights discussions have continued. The **National Association for the Advancement of Colored People** was organized in 1909. A radical labor organization called the **Industrial Workers of the World** (IWW, or Wobblies; 1905–1924) was active in promoting violence and revolution. The IWW organized effective strikes in the textile industry in 1912 and among a few western miners groups but had little appeal to the average American worker. After the Red Scare of 1919, the government worked to smash the IWW and deported many of its immigrant leaders and members.

Calls for immigration restriction had begun in the late nineteenth century, but the only major restriction imposed on immigration had been the Chinese Exclusion Act of 1882. Labor leaders believed that immigrants depressed wages and impeded unionization. Some progressives believed that they created social problems. In June 1917, Congress, over Wilson's veto, had imposed a **literacy test for immigrants** and **excluded** many Asian nationalities. In 1921, Congress passed the **Emergency Quota Act**.

In practice, the law admitted almost as many immigrants as wanted to come from such nations as Britain, Ireland, and Germany but severely restricted Italians, Greeks, Poles, and eastern European Jews wanting to enter the country. The law became effective in 1922 and reduced the number of immigrants annually to about 40 percent of the 1921 total. Congress then passed the National Origins Act of 1924, which further reduced the number of southern and eastern European immigrants and cut the annual immigration total to 20 percent of the 1921 figure. In 1927, the annual maximum number of immigrants allowed into the United States was reduced to 150,000.

On Thanksgiving Day in 1915, the **William J. Simmons** founded the **Knights of the Ku Klux Klan** to intimidate African Americans, who were experiencing an apparent rise in status during World War I. The Klan's methods of repression included cross burnings, tar and featherings, kidnappings, lynchings, and burnings. The Klan was not a political party, but it endorsed and opposed candidates and exerted considerable control over elections and politicians in at least nine states.

In *Korematsu v. United States* (1944), the Supreme Court upheld sending the Issei (Japanese Americans from Japan) and Nisei (native-born Japanese Americans) to concentration camps. The camps closed in March 1946.

Since the recording of the first arrivals in 1820, the United States has accepted 66 million legal immigrants, with 11 percent arriving from Germany and 10 percent from Mexico. However, two centuries of immigration and integration have not yielded consensus on the three major immigration questions: how many, from where, and in what status newcomers should arrive.

The U.S. immigration system in the early twenty-first century recognizes 800,000 to 900,000 foreigners a year as legal immigrants, admits 35 million nonimmigrant tourist and business visitors a year, and knows of another 300,000 to 400,000 unauthorized foreigners who settle in the country annually. Recent decades have witnessed contentious debates over the place of immigrants and their children in the educational, welfare, and political systems of the United States, or more broadly, whether the immigration system serves U.S. national interests (Martin 2002).

Martin (2002) predicts that immigration is likely to continue at current levels of 900,000 legal and 300,000 unauthorized a year. In the words of a former director of the U.S. Census Bureau, Kenneth Prewitt, America is "the first country in world history which is literally made up of every part of the world" (Alvarez 2001).

Skill Nine

Identify How Various Cultures Contributed to the Unique Social, Cultural, Economic, and Political Features of Florida

Florida celebrates its multitude of cultures and its diversity. The population breakdown reveals the state's diversity. In 2000, Florida was fourth among the states in terms of population, ranking behind California, Texas, and New York. The city with the highest population in 2000 was Jacksonville (736,000); the second most populous city was Miami (362,000). The population of Florida went up 23.5 percent from 1990 to 2000, and its population continues to increase. In 2000, persons over age 65 made up 17.6 percent of the 15,982,378 people in the state; persons 18 years and younger made up 28.7 percent of the population (Florida Smart). Thus, 46.3 percent of Floridians in 2000 were of an age that most people do not associate with employment.

During the 1930s the Works Progress Administration collected folklore from Florida. The collection documented African American, Arabic, Bahamian, British American, Cuban, Greek, Italian, Minorcan, Seminole, and Slavic cultures throughout Florida. The Library of Congress presents these documents as part of the record of the past.

In 2000, persons of Hispanic or Latino origin made up 16.8 percent of Florida's population; African Americans, 14.6 percent; Asians, 1.7 percent; American Indians and Alaska natives, 0.3 percent; white persons, 65.4 percent; two or more races, 2.4 percent; and other races, 3.0 percent. The average number of people per square mile in 2000 was 296.4 compared with 79.6 persons per square mile for the nation as a whole (U.S. Census Bureau).

The many cultural backgrounds of a population that originated from many countries make Florida unique (Florida Smart). Native Americans, descendants of the pioneering settlers, Cubans, Puerto Ricans, Greeks, Asians, African Americans, Caucasians, and dozens of other ethnic groups, old and young, are features throughout the Florida boundaries. This varied background began with the exploration and settlement of the state.

History

About 12,000 years ago, hunters and gatherers reached Florida and settled in areas with a water supply, stones for tools, and firewood. These Floridians created complex cultures. Before the arrival of Europeans, the native people developed cultivated agriculture, traded with groups in the southeastern United States, and expanded their social organization. Their temple mounds and villages reflect their complex social organization.

The Spanish explorer and adventurer Juan Ponce de León arrived near what is now St. Augustine in 1513. The written record of Florida began with his arrival. He called the land *la Florida*, in honor of the Feast of the Flowers, an Easter celebration in Spain. No evidence exists of other Europeans arriving before him, but it is a possibility. Eight years later Juan Ponce de León, 200 people, 50 horses, and other beasts of burden arrived on Florida's southwest coast. With attacks from the natives there, however, the colonization attempt failed. Still, Juan Ponce de León described the area as a suitable place for missionaries, explorers, and treasure seekers.

Hernando de Soto began another treasure hunting expedition in 1539. His travels through Florida and the southeastern United States took his group to what is now Tallahassee; they camped there for five months. Although de Soto died in 1542 near the Mississippi, some of his expedition reached Mexico.

The stories from these travelers reached others. Spain regularly shipped silver, gold, and other products from Cuba, Mexico, Central America, and South America; the accounts spread rapidly to others interested in exploration. In 1559 Tristán de Luna y Arellano led another group attempting to settle in Florida. After a series of misfortunes during a period of two years, however, they had to abandon the settlement. The French also arrived in Florida. In 1562, Jean Ribault explored the area near what is now Jacksonville, and in 1564, René Goulaine de Laudonnière established a colony there.

Spain accelerated its colonization plans. In 1565, Pedro Menéndez de Avilés settled near St. Augustine. This was the first permanent European settlement in what is now America. Pedro Menéndez de Avilés worked to remove all the French and to kill all French settlers except those who were Roman Catholic or noncombatants. Menéndez captured the Spanish Fort Caroline and renamed it San Mateo.

Two years later, the Frenchman Dominique de Gourgues captured San Mateo and killed the Spanish there. The Spanish, however, continued to explore, construct forts, and establish Roman Catholic missions among the Floridians. The English also continued to explore. Conflict frequently arose between the Spanish and the English. Sir Francis Drake and his crew burned the Spanish settlement of St. Augustine in 1586.

Spain's power in the southeastern part of the New World was without question in the 1600s. True, the English established colonies, but they were primarily in Jamestown, Virginia (1607); Plymouth, Massachusetts (1620); and Georgia (1733). French explorers continued to move down the Mississippi and along the Gulf Coast.

The feuds between Spain and England—particularly in Florida—continued. The Englishman Colonel

James Moore, along with the Carolinians and their Creek Indian allies, attacked Spanish Florida in 1702 and destroyed the town of St. Augustine. The fort Castillo de San Marcos remained uncaptured, however. In 1704, the English moved between Tallahassee and St. Augustine and destroyed the Spanish missions as they went. The French harassed the Spanish on the western side and captured Pensacola in 1719. Then Georgians attacked in 1740, but like the English, they were unable to take the Castillo de San Marcos at St. Augustine, even after a month.

In exchange for Havana (which the British had taken from Spain during the Seven Years' War of 1756–1763), the British took control of Florida. Spain evacuated Florida after the exchange, and British surveyors tried to establish relations with the Native Americans—Seminoles of Creek Indian descent—who were moving into the area. To attract other settlers, Britain offered land for settling and help if settlers produced exportable items. The plan, however, lasted only 20 years. Spain captured Pensacola from the British in 1781 and retained it as part of the peace treaty that ended the American Revolution.

Other Spanish colonists came pouring into the state after the British evacuation. Some came because of the favorable terms for obtaining property (land grants) that the Spanish offered to immigrants; some were escaped slaves trying to find freedom. Finally Spain ceded Florida to the United States in 1821. Andrew Jackson had been in Florida battling the Seminoles in 1818 (during the First Seminole War). Returning in 1821 to establish a new territorial government, he found Native Americans, African Americans, and Spaniards.

Many Southerners moved to Florida. A divided state became one with Tallahassee as capital. As the population increased through immigration, the residents began to pressure the federal government to remove the Creeks, the Miccosukees, and the African American refugees. The reason that the new immigrants wanted the three groups removed was to open up some prime land and because of the problems associated with runaway slaves.

Osceola, a Seminole war leader, refused to leave his Florida homeland. While waging the Seminole War of 1835–1842, President Andrew Jackson allocated $20 million and many U.S. soldiers to enforce the movement of the Seminoles to Oklahoma. The war ended, but not as the government had planned. Many Seminoles, private citizens, and soldiers lost their lives. Soldiers captured some of the Seminoles and sent them West under guard, others "volunteered" to go, but some fled into the Everglades and made a life for themselves there. The government eventually established reservations; many Native Americans still occupy portions of Florida.

By 1840, the population of Florida had reached 54,477, about half of which were African American slaves. The state had three parts: east, middle, and west. The middle area had many plantations, owned by men who set the political tone for the state until the Civil War. In 1845, Florida became the twenty-seventh state.

Slavery

Florida residents were concerned about the North's dislike of slavery. Most Florida voters, however, did not oppose slavery. Florida did not vote for Abraham Lincoln. On January 10, 1861, Florida seceded from the Union. No decisive battles occurred in Florida, but the state provided 15,000 soldiers and many supplies; 2,000 African Americans and whites from Florida joined the Union army.

The state and the lives of many of its residents changed after the Civil War. Although Tallahassee was the only southern capital east of the Mississippi River to avoid capture during the war, federal troops occupied Tallahassee on May 10, 1865. The ports of Jacksonville and Pensacola began to thrive. Slaves became free. Plantations did not regain their prewar levels; instead, tenant farmers and sharecroppers—white and African American—began to farm.

Beginning in 1868, the federal government began Reconstruction in Florida. Republicans in office tried to make many changes, including the improvement of conditions for African Americans. As the election year of 1876 began, federal troops were still in the state. African American voters and Republicans helped elect Rutherford B. Hayes. Democrats took control of enough states that Republican rule ended, and federal troops left Florida and other states.

Investors in industries brought more people to the state through the increased construction of roads and railroads. Citrus fruit cultivation, sponge harvesting, steamboat tours, and the tourist industry in general flourished.

The Internal Improvement Act (IIA) of 1855 hastened the growth of the state and its transportation system. Between the end of the Civil War and the beginning of World War I, Florida's offer of free or cheap public land to investors brought diverse cultures into the state. **Henry Flagler** and **Henry B. Plant** built lavish hotels for tourists near their railroad lines. The IIA encouraged the draining of land to make it usable. All these efforts resulted in a changed Florida, especially in increased shipping of citrus fruits to other parts of the nation.

Florida became the staging area for American troops bound for the war in Cuba during the Spanish-American War; many people came through the state. Florida supported Cuba's effort to free itself of Spanish rule.

By the beginning of the twentieth century, per capita income and population were rising in the Sunshine State. After World War I, increasing numbers of tourists and land developers came into the state (Florida Smart). The number of registered cars in the nation jumped from 548,000 in 1910 to 8,132,000 in 1920. That meant that in 1910, one of every 36.5 households owned an automobile; by 1920, one of every 3.0 households had a car. The number of cars registered in the United States in 1928 was 21,362,000—almost triple the number in 1920; the new average was one car for every 1.4 households—a sizable increase over just eight years (Davis 2003). Many of these car owners were coming to Florida to tour and purchase land. Prices and profits reached inflated levels.

Florida During the Great Depression

Hurricanes in 1926 and in 1928 helped hasten the bursting of Florida's economic bubble. Money and credit began to dry up, and the "paper" millionaires lost their credibility. By the time the rest of the nation felt the Great Depression, Florida was accustomed to "hard times." To add to Florida's troubles, the Mediterranean fruit fly invaded Florida in 1929 and caused citrus production to fall by 60 percent.

The face of Florida's voting population changed after women won the right to vote in 1920, after the repeal of the poll tax (a tax of a uniform, fixed amount per individual) in 1937, and after the U.S. Supreme Court outlawed a system of all-white primary elections in 1944. More "outsiders" entered the state when World War II began. With its mild climate, the state became a major training center for the military. Construction of highways and airports increased. It began to ready itself for residents and visitors.

Postwar Immigration and Migration

With the influx of large numbers of people from places within the United States and from countries within the Western Hemisphere (primarily Cuba and Haiti), Florida has experienced a surge in population in recent years. It is now the fourth most populous state in the nation.

The diverse population has worked to make the Sunshine State a place where all citizens have equal rights under the law. Many changes have occurred since the 1950s. Schools and other institutions are integrated. The economy has diversified. Electronics, plastics, construction, real estate, and international banking have recently joined tourism, citrus fruit cultivation, and phosphate production as major elements in Florida's economy. The U.S. space program located in Florida has attracted much media attention; the historic Cape Canaveral launches and the space shuttle program have brought tourists and employment to the state. The state's community colleges, technical colleges, and universities draw students to Florida each year. Millions of visitors come to its large theme parks and resorts.

A study of the state's history and its diverse population is useful to residents and others alike. Through studying the past, Floridians can create a better Florida for all its citizens (Florida Smart).

Competency 14: Knowledge of People, Places, and Environment (Geography)

Eleven test items relate to this competency.

Skill One

Identify the Five Themes of Geography, Including the Specific Terms for Each Theme

The five themes of geography are place; location; human-environmental interaction; movement and connections; and regions, patterns, and processes. An understanding of these themes would include the ability to use them to analyze regions, states, countries, and the world to gain a perspective about interrelationships among those areas. When a teacher uses the five themes, students should gain the ability to compare regions:

1. In this world of fast-breaking news from throughout the globe, students must be able to recognize the **place** names of continents, countries, and even cities. In addition to geography, the theme of place encompasses the fields of political science.

2. An understanding of the theme of **location** requires knowledge of both absolute and relative location. **Absolute location** is determined by longitude and latitude. **Relative location** deals with the interactions that occur between and among places. Relative location involves the interconnectedness among people because of land, water, and technology. For example, the Silver River brought commerce and steamboats to the Silver Springs area; the 99.8 percent pure artesian spring waters in one of the largest artesian spring formations in the world offered respite and beauty to settlers and tourists alike. Hullam Jones invented the glass-bottom boat there in 1878 and enabled visitors to view the underwater world of fish, turtles, crustaceans, and fossils more than 10,000 years old. The location of Silver Springs has contributed to the area's economic development and vitality. In addition to geography, the theme of

location encompasses the fields of technology, history, and economics.

3. An understanding of the theme of **human-environmental interaction** involves consideration of how people rely on the environment, how we alter it, and how the environment may limit what people are able to do. For example, Silver Springs is at the headwaters of the Silver River. In the 1850s barges carried cotton, lumber, and nonperishables up the Silver River to the area's growing population. The development of a stagecoach line and the bringing of conventional steamboats to Silver Springs in 1860 aided in the development of Silver Springs and the nearby areas. In addition to geography, the theme of human-environmental interaction encompasses the field of ecology.

4. An understanding of the theme of **movement and connections** requires identifying how people are connected through different forms of transportation and communication networks and how those networks have changed over time. This would include identifying channels of the movement of people, goods and information. For example, the automobile industry had a profound impact on the number of visitors to Silver Springs, Florida, and on the movement patterns of ideas, fashion, and people. In addition to geography, the theme of movement and connections encompasses the fields of communications, history, anthropology, economics, and sociology.

5. An understanding of the theme of **regions, patterns, and processes** involves identifying climatic, economic, political, and cultural patterns within regions. To comprehend why these patterns were created, students need to understand how climatic systems, communication networks, international trade, political systems, and population changes contributed to a region's development. With an understanding of a particular region, students can study its uniqueness and relationship to other regions. In addition to geography, the theme of regions, patterns, and processes encompasses the fields of economics, sociology, and politics.

The study of global issues and events includes comprehending the interconnectedness of peoples throughout the world (sociology and political science). For example, knowing the relationship between world oil consumption and oil production helps students understand the impact that increased demand for oil in China would have on the price of a barrel of oil, which in turn could affect the decisions of consumers of new vehicles in the United States.

Skill Two

Interpret Maps and Other Graphic Representations and Identify Tools and Technologies to Acquire, Process, and Report Information from a Spatial Perspective

Any study of maps should begin with a study of the globe—a model of the earth with a map on its surface. The globe is more accurate than a flat map. Constantly using the globe helps bring understanding of the earth's shape and structure.

Some of the points on the globe that students should be able to locate include the Equator, Antarctic Circle, Arctic Circle, Prime Meridian, International Date Line, North Pole, South Pole, meridians, parallels, the Great Circle Route, and time zones.

The use of maps requires students to identify four main types of map projections: conic, cylindrical, interrupted, and plane. Additional graphics that students use in geography include charts, graphs, and picture maps.

Skill Three

Identify the Factors That Influence the Selection of a Location for a Specific Activity

Factors that influence the location for a specific activity include the area's population density, government, latitude (distance from the equator), altitude (height above sea level), distance from bodies of water, culture, economics, landforms, sociology, vegetation, and climate (temperature, rainfall, etc.)

The human development of the area also affects selection. For instance, methods of transportation, highways, airports, communication, waterways, water travel, buildings, industries, and facilities are only a few of the factors that influence location for a specific activity. For some industries, nearness to sources of raw materials for

production and ways of transporting the goods after production may be important in selecting an area in which to locate.

There are two types of location—absolute and relative—that describe the positions of people and places on the earth's surface. Determining **absolute location** requires the use of longitude and latitude on a grid system. The longitude and latitude coordinates identify exact (absolute) location. **Relative location**, on the other hand, recognizes the interdependence of people and places. Places do not exist in isolation. Geographers attempt to identify relationships between or among places and to determine the factors that might encourage those relationships.

Skill Four

Identify the Relationship Between Natural Physical Processes and the Environment

As the study of places on the earth's surface, one can approach geography from various perspectives. One study approach is **physical geography**—locating and describing places according to physical features (climate, soils, landforms, vegetation, etc.). Physical geography must take into account how the earth's movements around the sun, the tilt of the earth, the sea, weather patterns, the distance from the equator, the altitude, and the air affect the earth's surface. The physical approach alone, however, is a narrow methodology from the social science point of view because it ignores the human factor.

Skill Five

Interpret Statistics That Show How Places Differ in Their Human and Physical Characteristics

For geography (the study of the earth) to be a true social science, there must be some attention to the human factor. Some notice of the interaction of the humans and animals that live on the earth—whether the interaction is deliberate or incidental—is an important part of the social sciences. The relationship between place and human/animal relationships is **cultural geography**.

Location affects both plant and animal life. The physical environment impinges on the life of people by affecting diet, shelter, clothing, accessibility, inventions, religion, resources, and prosperity; climate, resources, terrain, and location affect all of these. In fact, in pre-historic times—even before history, government, or economics—the earth (geography) was the most important element in human life. Geography is still important in our society today.

Studying a map of the rivers and the fall line (a physical feature that indicates the navigability of rivers) in North Carolina reveals why many people decided to settle there. In the late 1800s, textile mills were often built near the fall line so they could use water as a power source. Many people who needed employment and were not highly skilled sought work in the textile mills. This example shows how the physical characteristics of a place can affect the people who move there.

Skill Six

Identify How Conditions of the Past, Such as Wealth and Poverty, Land Tenure, Exploitation, Colonialism, and Independence, Affect Present Human Characteristics of Places

Three generalizations of geography relate the past to human characteristics of places:

1. Physical factors and cultural factors are related. For instance, the types of houses that families build reflect the available materials and climates. Therefore, physical differences can arise among houses in various places. The richness of the physical environment can affect the wealth of the people.

2. Change is a constant. The effects of change on people are both physical and cultural. For example, the people themselves bring about some changes; they may modify the environment by cutting trees and affecting the landscape now and in days to come.

3. People modify the environment to suit their changing needs and wants. When tenant farmers lived on another person's land, they had little say over the use of the land; planting gardens for their own families' uses may have been out of the question. Once they were able to purchase land, their use of the land changed; many began planting gardens and

fruit trees for their families. People living in an area damaged by a storm, for instance, can not only repair the damages but also change the place to suit their current needs and wants.

Skill Seven

Identify Ways in Which People Adapt to an Environment through the Production and Use of Clothing, Food, and Shelter

Although the environment can affect the way people live, people can change the environment to meet their wants and needs. For example, the jobs that people hold enable them to get money for food, clothing, and shelter. Some jobs—farming, logging, and mining, for example—have a profound effect on the environment. In parts of the world without adequate rainfall, farmers have to use irrigation to grow their crops. Through their adaptation of the environment, the farmers acquire the things they need to survive but, in the process, may damage their environment and ultimately threaten the survival of future generations.

Ideally, people will explore a damaged environment to determine the causes of water and air pollution. They will also decide if there is any harm to local plants and animals and ascertain the cause if there is damage. The people will ideally work to change damages to the environment and prevent further harm.

Skill Eight

Identify How Tools and Technology Affect the Environment

The period from the emergence of the first-known hominids, or humans, around 2.5 million years ago until approximately 10,000 BCE has been designated as the Paleolithic period, or the Old Stone Age. During that period, human beings lived in very small groups of perhaps 10 to 20 nomadic people who were constantly moving from place to place. Human beings had the ability to make tools and weapons from stone and the bones of animals they killed. Hunting large game such as mammoths, which the hunters sometimes drove off cliffs in large numbers, was crucial to the survival of early humans. The meat, fur, and bones of the hunted animals were essential to the survival of prehistoric people, who supplemented their diets by foraging for food.

Early human beings found shelter in caves and other natural formations and took the time to paint and draw on the walls of their shelters. Created during the prehistorical period, cave paintings in France and northern Spain depict scenes of animals, such as lions, owls, and oxen. Around 500,000 years ago, humans developed the means of creating fire and used it to provide light and warmth in shelters and to cook meat and other foods. They also developed improved techniques of producing tools and weapons.

Tools and technology can improve the lives of people; needless to say, tools and technology can also harm the lives of people. Likewise, people can use tools and technology both to improve their environment and to harm or even destroy their immediate areas or even the world. For example, as Alfred Nobel learned after he developed dynamite, escalating the power of weapons has never successfully prevented war. As weapons become more powerful, the danger from the technology increases.

Skill Nine

Identify Physical, Cultural, Economic, and Political Reasons for the Movement of People in the World, Nation, or State

The people living in a particular area determine the characteristics of that area. The physical characteristics, the cultural characteristics, the economic characteristics, and the political characteristics are important to most area residents and may affect their original decision to settle there.

If the characteristics of an area become unacceptable to residents, the inhabitants may consider moving to a different location. With the ease of transportation today, most people can move more easily than they could have a decade ago. The move may be to another region of their state, the nation, or the world.

Economic reasons for moving include the finances of an individual considering relocating and the economic level required to live comfortably in the area. Some residents may move to a more expensive area, but others may decide to go to a less expensive area. Many change their places of residence, therefore, to get ahead economically or to raise their standard of living.

Some people decide to relocate for **cultural reasons**. These people might consider their neighbors too similar to them and decide to move to an area with more diversity. On the other hand, some people would rather live with others who are similar to them.

Physical reasons can also affect a person's decision to relocate. An understanding of the theme of human-environmental interaction involves considering how people rely on the environment, how they alter it, and how the environment can limit what people are able to do. Sometimes people move to a place where they can satisfy their physical wants or needs. In some cases, people can modify their environment or bring the needed goods to their area without having to relocate.

For example, an adaptation of the environment that aided the Illinois's shipping industry was the development of the lock and dam system on the Mississippi. An understanding of the theme of location, movement, and connections involves identifying how people are connected through different forms of transportation and communication networks and how those networks have changed over time. This would include identifying the channels of movement of people, goods, and information. Another example is the steel industry in Chicago, which had a profound impact on the movement patterns of ideas and people in both the Chicago area and downstate.

Political reasons also compel the movement of peoples. Many people equate the political system with government. There is a distinction, however. Government carries out the decisions of the political system. The organizations and processes that contribute to the decision-making process make up the political system. Individuals may move to another region or area if they are unhappy with the government and/or political systems in their area and are unable to bring about change. On the other hand, an attractive system of government may bring people to an area.

Skill Ten

Identify How Transportation and Communication Networks Contribute to the Level of Economic Development in Different Regions

Economics is the study of society's choices among a limited amount of resources to attain the highest practical satisfaction. It is the allocation of scarce resources among competing ends. Because people across the globe can interact with each other almost instantly, the choices available to them throughout the world are more readily apparent.

Advances in communication—especially through the satellites—made it possible for someone in Los Angeles to witness the advances of Hurricane Katrina on the Gulf Coast and to become aware of the wants and needs there. Similarly, a person in Tokyo can see the goods and products readily available to American consumers in the newscasts and movies shown in Japan. People in New York can pick up the phone and call a person in London without delay to discuss the latest automobile styles. It is evident, then, that people can see and hear about the goods and services available in other parts of the world; such knowledge affects the needs and wants of the world's people.

Convenient transportation and even world travel is now possible for a large number of people throughout the world. Around the globe, people are becoming more aware of the world's products, services, and even clothing styles (blue jeans) as they see people an ocean away firsthand or in films. Even food chains are familiar throughout the globe.

As people become aware of lifestyles in other places, their wants and needs may change. People may aspire to what they perceive as a higher economic level. Transportation and communication networks, therefore, have helped initiate many changes in people's needs and wants and have ultimately contributed to the economic development of many regions.

Skill Eleven

Compare and Contrast Major Regions of the World

There are many ways of dividing the world into regions. Perhaps the simplest is to consider the equator as a dividing line between the Northern Hemisphere and the Southern Hemisphere. Another way of dividing the world in regions is to draw a line from pole to pole into the Eastern Hemisphere and Western Hemisphere.

Another way geographers might divide the world into regions is by landmasses, or continents. Using the continents as a way of dividing the earth results in the continents of Africa, Asia, Australia, Europe, North America, and South America; some geographers include Antarctica as a separate continent. Other geographers prefer to group the regions according to political characteristics. Still others prefer to designate regions by latitudes: low, middle, and high. It is possible, therefore, to divide our world in many different ways.

Two important higher-order thinking skills that teachers should encourage among their students are comparing and contrasting. The use of regions is an ideal place to work with these skills of contrasting two (or more) things (or concepts). Requiring deeper thought is the process of finding similarities between or among the things or concepts that appear dissimilar on the surface. Thomas Gordon has described a process of synectics, which forces students to make an analogy between two concepts, one familiar and the other new. At first, the concepts might seem completely different, but through a series of steps the students discover underlying similarities. By comparing something new with something familiar, students have a "hook" that will help them remember and understand the new information. (Huitt)

For example, a biology teacher might ask students to draw an analogy between a cell (new concept) and a city government (familiar concept). Although they seem impossibly different, both concepts involve systems for transportation, systems for disposing of unwanted materials, and parts that govern those systems. After discussion of this analogy, students trying to remember the functions of a cell would find help in remembering the systems of city government.

Competency 15: Knowledge of Government and the Citizen (Government and Civics)

Twelve test items relate to this competency.

Skill One

Identify the Structure, Functions, and Purposes of Government

As stated earlier, many people equate the terms *political system* and *government*, but the two concepts are distinct.

Definitions

Government is the agency for regulating the activities of people. It is the system that carries out the decisions of the political system or, in some countries, the decisions of the ruler. The organizations and processes that contribute to the decision-making process comprise the **political system**.

Structure

The distribution of power within the various **structures** of government is a key variable. Separation of powers among branches of the federal government is another aspect of structure useful in comparing political systems. The following are among the most important structures of government:

Confederation. A weak central government delegates principal authority to smaller units, such as states. The United States had this structure under the Articles of Confederation, before the Constitution was ratified in 1789.

Federal. Sovereignty is divided between a central government and a group of states. Contemporary examples of federal republics are the United States, Brazil, and India.

Unitary. The centralized government holds the concentration of power and authority. Examples include France and Japan.

Authoritarian. A government's central power is in a single or collective executive, with the legislative and judicial bodies having little input. Some examples of this include the former Soviet Union, the People's Republic of China, and Nazi Germany.

Parliamentary. The legislative and executive branches are combined, with a prime minister and cabinet selected from within the legislative body. They maintain control so long as the legislative assembly supports their major policies. Great Britain is an example of this form of government.

Presidential. The executive branch is clearly separate from the legislative and judicial branches. However, all three (particularly the executive and legislative branches) must cooperate for policy to be consistent and for smooth government operation. An example of this is the United States.

America has a federal system of government; it divides the sovereignty between the central government and the states. It is also a presidential form of government, with the executive branch clearly separated from the legislative and judicial branch. All countries, of course, do not have a division of power.

Functions

The *Merit Students Encyclopedia* (1991) notes that the **functions** of a government include (1) political functions, to maintain order within its territories and to protect its borders; (2) legal functions (in fact the word *anarchy*—lack of government—has come to mean lawlessness); (3) economic functions, or those concerned with the economic activity of citizens; and/or (4) social functions, which may include civil rights, religion, and education.

Purposes

The question of how to define the purpose of government has been puzzling scholars from Plato's time to the present day. Although some say that government's purpose is to protect all people's rights and preserve justice, others contend that its purpose is to preserve and protect the rights of the few. From these diverging definitions, myriad ideologies—like communism, liberalism, conservatism, and many others—have evolved. Although most thinkers agree that government is morally justified, they disagree on the role and form of government. News commentator Bob Schieffer stated boldly in 2005, following Hurricane Katrina, "There is no purpose for government except to improve the lives of its citizens."

Skill Two

Demonstrate Knowledge of the Rights and Responsibilities of a Citizen in the World, Nation, State, and/or Community

Essential democratic principles include those fundamental to the American judicial system, such as the right to due process of law, the right to a fair and speedy trial, protection from unlawful search and seizure, and the right to avoid self-incrimination. The democratic values include life, liberty, the pursuit of happiness, the common good, justice, equality, truth, diversity, popular sovereignty, and patriotism. Furthermore, the ideals of American democracy include the following essential constitutional principles: the rule of law, separation of powers, representative government, checks and balances, individual rights, freedom of religion, federalism, limited government, and civilian control of the military.

It is essential—indeed, a responsibility—for citizens to be active in maintaining a democratic society. Active citizens participate in the political process by voting, providing services to their communities, and regulating themselves in accordance with the law. Citizens of the United States need also to assume responsibilities to their communities, their states, the nation, and the world.

Skill Three

Identify Major Concepts of the U.S. Constitution and Other Historical Documents

Historical Documents

The **Articles of Confederation**, adopted in 1777 after the quarrel with Great Britain, provided for a **unicameral** Congress, in which each state would have one vote, as had been the case in the Continental Congress. Executive authority under the articles would be vested in a committee of 13, with one member from each state. Amending the articles required the unanimous consent of all the states. Under the Articles of Confederation, the government could declare war, make treaties, determine the number of troops and amount of money each state should contribute to a war effort, settle disputes between states, admit new states to the Union, and borrow money. It could not levy taxes, raise troops, or regulate commerce.

As time went on, the inadequacy of the Articles of Confederation became increasingly apparent. In 1787 there was a call for a convention of all the states in Philadelphia for the purpose of revising the Articles of Confederation. The assembly unanimously elected George Washington to preside, and the enormous respect that he commanded helped hold the convention together through difficult times.

The 55 delegates who met in Philadelphia in 1787 to draft a constitution drew on a variety of sources to shape the government that would be outlined in the document. Three British documents were important to the delegates' work: **the Magna Carta (1215), the Petition of Right (1628)**, and the **Bill of Rights (1689)**. These three documents promoted the concept of limited government and were influential in shaping the fundamental principles embodied in the Constitution. The British philosopher John Locke, who wrote about the social contract concept of government and the right of people to alter or abolish a government that did not protect their interests, was another guiding force in the drafting of the Constitution.

Crises in Establishing the U.S. Constitution

One major problem that the delegates faced involved the number of state representatives. With George Washington presiding over the discussions, the delegates finally adopted a proposal known as the **Great Compromise**, which provided for a president, two senators per state, and representatives elected to the House according to their states' populations.

Another major crisis involved disagreement between the North and the South over slavery. To reach a compromise this time, the delegates decided that each slave was to count as three-fifths of a person for purposes of apportioning representation and direct taxation on the states (the Three-Fifths Compromise). Before 1808 the federal government could not stop the importation of slaves.

The delegates had to compromise on the nature of the presidency. The result was a strong presidency with control over foreign policy and the power to veto Congress's legislation. Should the president commit an actual crime, Congress would have the power of impeachment. Otherwise, the president would serve for a term of four years and was eligible for reelection without limit. As a check to the possible excesses of democracy, an Electoral College elected the president; each state would have the same number of electors as it did senators and representatives combined.

The U.S. Constitution

The new Constitution was to take effect when nine states, through special state conventions, had ratified it. By June 21, 1788, the required nine states had ratified, but the crucial states of New York and Virginia still held out. Ultimately, the promise of the addition of a bill of rights helped win the final states. With the inauguration of March 1789, George Washington became the nation's first president.

One of the most significant principle embodied in the Constitution is the concept of a federal system that divides the powers of government between the states and the national government. The local level handles local matters, and those issues that affect all citizens are the responsibility of the federal government. Such a system was a natural outgrowth of the colonial relationship between the Americans and the mother country of England.

The Tenth Amendment declares: "Those powers not delegated to the United States by the Constitution, nor prohibited by it to the States, are reserved to the States respectively, or to the people." The federal government and those of the separate states have powers that may in practice overlap, but in cases where they conflict, the federal government is supreme.

In 1920, the passage of the Eighteenth Amendment prohibited the manufacture, transportation, and sale of alcoholic beverages in the United States. Speakeasies became popular, and bootlegging became a profitable underground business. The ratification of the Twenty-first Amendment repealed prohibition in 1933.

Congress approved the Nineteenth Amendment, providing for women's suffrage in 1919; the Senate had been defeated women's suffrage earlier in 1918. The states ratified the Nineteenth Amendment in time for the election of 1920.

Skill Four

Identify How the Legislative, Executive, and Judicial Branches Share Powers and Responsibility

A key principle of the U.S. Constitution is separation of powers. The national government is divided into three branches—legislative, executive, and judicial—with separate functions, but they are not entirely independent. Articles I, II, and III of the main body of the Constitution outline these functions.

The Legislative Branch

Legislative power is vested in a bicameral (two houses) Congress, which is the subject of Article I of the Constitution. The expressed or delegated powers are set forth in Section 8 and can be divided into several broad categories.

Economic powers are as follows:

1. Lay and collect taxes.
2. Borrow money.
3. Regulate foreign and interstate commerce.
4. Coin money and regulate its value.
5. Establish rules concerning bankruptcy.

Judicial powers comprise the following:

1. Establish courts inferior to the Supreme Court.
2. Provide punishment for counterfeiting.

3. Define and punish piracies and felonies committed on the high seas.

   War powers of Congress include:

1. Declare war.
2. Raise and support armies.
3. Provide and maintain a navy.
4. Provide for organizing, arming, and calling forth the militia.

   Other **general peace powers** include the following:

1. Establish uniform rules on naturalization.
2. Establish post offices and post roads.
3. Promote science and the arts by issuing patents and copyrights.
4. Exercise jurisdiction over the seat of the federal government (District of Columbia).

The Constitution also grants Congress the power to discipline federal officials through impeachment and removal from office. The House of Representatives has the power to charge officials (impeach), and the Senate has the power to conduct the trials. The first impeachment of a president was that of Andrew Johnson.

Significant also is the Senate's power to confirm presidential appointments (to the cabinet, federal judiciary, and major bureaucracies) and to ratify treaties. Both houses are involved in choosing a president and vice president if there is no majority in the Electoral College. The House of Representatives votes for the president from among the top three electoral candidates, with each state delegation casting one vote. The Senate votes for the vice president. This Senate has exercised this power only twice, in the disputed elections of 1800 and 1824.

The Executive Branch

Article II of the Constitution deals with the powers and duties of the president. The chief executive's constitutional responsibilities include the following:

1. Serve as commander in chief.
2. Negotiate treaties (with the approval of two-thirds of the Senate).
3. Appoint ambassadors, judges, and other high officials (with the consent of the Senate).

4. Grant pardons and reprieves for those convicted of federal crimes (except in impeachment cases).
5. Seek counsel of department heads (cabinet secretaries).
6. Recommend legislation.
7. Meet with representatives of foreign states.
8. See that federal laws are "faithfully executed."

The president's powers with respect to foreign policy are paramount. Civilian control of the military is a fundamental concept embodied in the naming of the president as commander in chief. In essence, the president is the nation's leading general. As such, the president can make battlefield decisions and shape the military policy.

The president also has broad powers in domestic policy. The most significant domestic policy tool is the president's budget, which he/she must submit to Congress. Though Congress must approve all spending, the president has a great deal of power in budget negotiations. The president can use considerable resources in persuading Congress to enact legislation, and the president also has opportunities, such as in the "State of the Union" address, to reach out directly to the American people to convince them to support presidential policies.

The Judicial Branch

Article III of the Constitution states that "the judicial power of the United States shall be vested in one Supreme Court and in such inferior courts as the Congress may from time to time ordain and establish." The Constitution makes two references to a trial by jury in criminal cases (in Article III and in the Sixth Amendment).

Skill Five

Demonstrate Knowledge of the U.S. Electoral System and the Election Process

To become president, a candidate must be (1) a natural-born United States citizen, (2) a resident of the United States for at least 14 years, and (3) at least 35 years old. Each political party must select a candidate as its representative in an upcoming election. At the end of the primaries and caucuses, each party holds a national convention and finalizes its selection of its presidential nominee. Each presidential candidate chooses a vice presidential candidate.

The candidates usually begin their campaign tours once they have the nomination of their parties. In November, U.S. citizens cast their votes, but they are not actually voting directly for the presidential candidate of their choice in the general election. Instead, voters cast their votes for **electors**, who are part of the Electoral College and who are supposed to vote for the candidate that their state prefers.

The 55 delegates who met in Philadelphia in 1787 to draft a constitution established the Electoral College originally as a compromise between electing the president by popular vote and by Congressional election. At first the legislators in some states chose the electors; some states had the people elect the electors.

In 1796, political parties started to operate. Each state would have the same number of electors as the state had senators and representatives. Each elector voted for two candidates. The person receiving the largest number of votes became the president, and the person receiving the second-highest number of votes became the vice president (as specified in Article II).

The Twelfth Amendment to the U.S. Constitution specifies that the electors must meet in their respective states and cast their votes for president and vice president. The slates of electors pledge to vote for the candidates of the parties that the people select. Each elector must have his/her vote signed and certified. The electors send the votes to the president of the Senate for counting in front of Congress. The person having the majority (two-thirds of the votes cast) is declared president. The House chooses the president from the top three if there is no majority. The Twentieth Amendment dictates the process that takes place if no president has qualified by the third day of January.

The president and vice president are the only two nationally elected officials. (The states elect their senators and representatives on a state-by-state basis.) Both houses of Congress are involved in choosing a president and vice president if no majority is achieved in the Electoral College. The House of Representatives votes for the president from among the top three electoral candidates, with each state delegation casting one vote. The Senate votes for the vice president. The Senate has exercised this power only twice: in the disputed elections of 1800 and 1824.

Skill Six
Identify the Structures and Functions of U.S. Federal, State, and Local Governments

Structures

According to the Constitution, all governmental powers ultimately stem from the people. Local governments generally handle local matters, and those issues that affect all citizens are the responsibility of the federal government. Such a system is a natural outgrowth of the colonial relationship between the Americans and the mother country of England.

The Tenth Amendment declares, "Those powers not delegated to the United States by the Constitution, nor prohibited by it to the States, are reserved to the States respectively, or to the people." The federal and state governments have powers that may in practice overlap, but when they conflict, the federal government is supreme.

Functions

The following powers are reserved for the federal government:

1. Regulate foreign commerce.
2. Regulate interstate commerce.
3. Mint money.
4. Regulate naturalization and immigration.
5. Grant copyrights and patents.
6. Declare and wage war and declare peace.
7. Admit new states.
8. Fix standards for weights and measures.
9. Raise and maintain an army and a navy.
10. Govern Washington, D.C.

11. Conduct relations with foreign powers.
12. Universalize bankruptcy laws.

The state governments have the following powers:

1. Conduct and monitor elections.
2. Establish voter qualifications within the guidelines established by the Constitution.
3. Provide for local governments.
4. Ratify proposed amendments to the Constitution.
5. Regulate contracts and wills.
6. Regulate intrastate commerce.
7. Provide for education for its citizens.
8. Levy direct taxes.

Skill Seven

Identify the Relationships between Social, Economic, and Political Rights and the Historical Documents That Secure These Rights

Throughout the summer and fall of 1787, the Constitutional Convention worked on the new Constitution. Of the 55 delegates, only 39 signed. George Mason of Virginia objected to the fact that the Constitution contained no bill of rights. Eventually, the Bill of Rights became the first ten amendments to the Constitution. As time passed, Congress ratified several other amendments. Various portions of the Constitution provided for social, economic, and political rights.

Articles I, II, and II provided for the legislative, executive, and judicial powers. Article IV guaranteed citizens of each state the privileges and immunities of the other states; this was to help prevent discrimination against visitors. If a person commits a crime in one state and escapes to another state, the state in which that person is hiding must give the person up to the state from which the criminal escaped. The Fourth Article also provides protection to the states.

The Bill of Rights

The first Congress met in 1789. On the agenda was the consideration of 12 amendments to the Constitution written by James Madison. The states approved 10 of the 12 on December 15, 1791. Those 10 amendments make up the Bill of Rights (Congress for Kids).

First Amendment. Right to freedom of worship, speech, press, and assembly.

Second Amendment. Right to keep and bear arms.

Third Amendment. Right against quartering of troops.

Fourth Amendment. Right against unreasonable searches and seizures.

Fifth Amendment. Rights of accused person: grand jury, due process, just compensation.

Sixth Amendment. Right to jury trial.

Seventh Amendment. Rights in suits; decisions of facts in case decided by jury; judge's role limited to questions about the law.

Eighth Amendment. Prohibition of cruel and unusual punishment.

Ninth Amendment. Rights retained by people.

Tenth Amendment. Rights retained by states.

Other Amendments to the Constitution

An amendment is either an addition to the Constitution or a change in the original text. Making additions or revisions to the Constitution is no small feat. Since 1787, more than 9,000 amendments have been proposed, but only 27 have been approved (Congress for Kids).

Eleventh Amendment. A citizen of one state may sue a citizen of another state only if that person has the state's permission.

Twelfth Amendment. Election of the president.

Thirteenth Amendment. Abolishment of slavery.

Fourteenth Amendment. Definition of *citizen*; protection of the citizen against states' abridging rights.

Fifteenth Amendment. Suffrage rights not denied or abridged by "race, color, or previous condition of servitude."

Sixteenth Amendment. Income tax.

Seventeenth Amendment. Senators elected by popular vote.

Eighteenth Amendment. Prohibition of intoxicating liquors.

Nineteenth Amendment. Women's suffrage.

Twentieth Amendment. Beginning and ending of terms of elected officials (members of Congress, vice president, president); presidential succession.

Twenty-first Amendment. Repeal of Eighteenth Amendment.

Twenty-second Amendment. Limitation of president to two terms in office.

Twenty-third Amendment. District of Columbia given vote in presidential elections.

Twenty-fourth Amendment. Repeal of poll tax in federal elections.

Twenty-fifth Amendment. Appointment of vice president if vacancy in that office occurs; procedure in case of presidential disability.

Twenty-sixth Amendment. Establishment of voting age at 18.

Twenty-seventh Amendment. No change in compensation for representatives and senators can take effect until an intervening election of representatives.

Skill Eight

Demonstrate Knowledge of the Processes of the U.S. Legal System

The contemporary judicial branch consists of thousands of courts and is, in essence, a dual system, with each state having its own judicial structure functioning simultaneously with a complete set of federal courts. The most significant piece of legislation with reference to establishing a federal court network was the Judiciary Act of 1789. That law organized the Supreme Court and set up the federal district courts (13) and the circuit (appeal) courts (3).

The Supreme Court today is made up of a chief justice and eight associate justices. The president with the approval of the Senate appoints the justices for life; the justices often come from the ranks of the federal judiciary. In recent years, the public has viewed the appointment of Supreme Court justices with intense scrutiny and in some cases, heated political controversy has accompanied the choices for appointment.

Understanding of the role of law in a democratic society results from a knowledge of the nature of civil, criminal, and constitutional law and how the organization of the judicial system serves to interpret and apply such laws. Essential judicial principles include

comprehension of rights, such as the right of due process, the right to a fair and speedy trial, and the right to a hearing before a jury of one's peers. Additional judicial principles include an understanding of the protections granted in the Constitution, which include protection from self-incrimination and unlawful searches and seizures.

The U.S. Constitution makes two references to trials by jury (Article III and the Sixth Amendment). The accused seems to benefit by the provision because a jury consists of 12 persons; the accused cannot receive a conviction unless all 12 agree that the defendant is guilty. There is mention of a speedy trial to prevent incarceration indefinitely unless the jury finds the accused guilty and the person receives such a sentence. The public trial statement ensures that the defendant receives just treatment. In 1968, the Supreme Court ruled that jury trials in criminal courts extended to the state courts as well as the federal courts. The Sixth Amendment uses the phrase "compulsory process for obtaining witnesses." This means that it is compulsory for witnesses for the defendant to appear in court.

Skill Nine

Identify the Roles of the United States in International Relations

The United States does not exist in isolation. Understanding global interdependence begins with recognition that world regions include economic, political, historical, ecological, linguistic, and cultural regions. This understanding should include knowledge of military alliances (like NATO), of economic alliances and cartels, and of their effects on political and economic policies within regions. World regions and alliances lead to issues that affect people worldwide. These common issues include food production, human rights, use of natural resources, prejudice, poverty, and trade.

A country with a true sense of global interdependence realizes that its actions can affect the world. For instance, continuing to allow the use of certain sprays in a country can damage the ozone layer and affect the entire world.

Competency 16: Knowledge of Production, Distribution, and Consumption (Economics)

Eight test items relate to this competency.

Skill One
Identify Ways That Limited Resources Affect the Choices Made by Government and Individuals

A basic understanding relating to economics is that wants are unlimited while resources are limited. When resources are limited, it affects prices (the amounts of money needed to buy goods, services, or resources). Individuals and institutions must, therefore, make choices when making purchases. These seemingly local decisions may affect other people and even other nations.

A true sense of global interdependence results from an understanding of the relationship between local decisions and global issues. For example, individual or community actions regarding waste disposal or recycling can affect the availability of resource worldwide. A country's fuel standards can affect air pollution, oil supplies, and gas prices. The government can provide the legal structure and help needed to maintain competition, redistribute income, reallocate resources, and promote stability.

There are two main types of resources:

Economic resources. The land (natural), labor (human), capital, and entrepreneurial ability used in the production of goods and services; productive agents; factors of production.

Human resources. The physical and mental talents and efforts of people; these resources are necessary to help produce goods and services.

The result of combining resources may be entrepreneurship. As a human resource that also takes advantage of economic resources to create a product, **entrepreneurship** is characterized by nonroutine decisions, innovation, and the willingness to take risks.

Skill Two
Compare and Contrast the Characteristics of Different Economic Institutions

Two important higher-order thinking skills that teachers should encourage in their students are comparing and contrasting. The study of various economic institutions is an ideal place to work with the skills of comparing and contrasting. The following are the main economic institutions of the United States:

Banks. Serve anyone in the general public. Small groups of investors who expect a certain return on their investments own the banks. Only the investors have voting privileges; customers do not have voting rights, cannot be elected board members, and do not participate in governing the institution. The Federal Deposit Insurance Corporation (FDIC) insures the banks. Typically, banks do not share information, ideas, or resources.

Credit unions. Owned by members. Each person who deposits money is a member, not a customer. Surplus earnings go to the members in higher dividends, low-cost or free services, and lower loan rates. The National Credit Union Share Insurance Fund insures credit unions. All credit unions share ideas, information, and resources.

Federal Reserve System. The central banking system of the United States. It has a central board of governors in Washington, D.C. There are 12 Federal Reserve Bank districts in major cities throughout the nation. The district banks issue bank notes, lend money to member banks, maintain reserves, supervise member banks, and help set the national monetary policy. Alan Greenspan served as the chairman of the board of governors for 18 years. On Greenspan's retirement on January 31, 2005, Ben Bernanke succeeded him.

Stock market. An abstract concept. It is the mechanism that enables the trading of company stocks. It is different from the **stock exchange**, which is a corporation in the business of bringing together stock buyers and sellers.

Skill Three

Identify the Role of Markets from Production, through Distribution, to Consumption

A **market** is the interaction between potential buyers and sellers of goods and services. Money is the usual medium of exchange. **Market economies** have no central authority; custom plays a very small role. Every consumer makes buying decisions based on his or her own needs, desires, and income; individual self-interest rules.

Every producer decides personally what goods or services to produce, what price to charge, what resources to employ, and what production methods to use. Profits motivate the producers. There is vigorous competition in a market economy. **Supply** and **demand** may affect the availability of resources needed for production, distribution, and consumption.

After production, the producer ideally distributes the product to the places where consumers need/want the product—and have the money to pay for the goods or services. In the United States, there is a large and active government (command) sector, but there is a greater emphasis on the market economy.

The following are the major types of economies in world today:

Command economies. Rely on a central authority to make decisions. The central authority may be a dictator or a democratically constituted government. The Soviet economy relies mainly on the government to direct economic activity; there is a small market sector as well.

Traditional economies. Largely rely on custom to determine production and distribution issues. While not static, traditional systems are slow to change and are not well equipped to propel a society into sustained growth. Many of the poorer countries of the developing world have traditional systems.

Mixed economies. Contains elements of each of the two previously defined systems. All real-world economies are mixed economies, but the proportions of the mixture can vary greatly.

Capitalist economies. Produce resources owned by individuals.

Socialist economies. Produce resources owned collectively by society. In other words, resources are under the control of the government.

Efficiency occurs when a society produces the types and quantities of goods and services that most satisfy its people. Failure to do so wastes resources. **Technical efficiency** occurs when a society produces the greatest types and quantities of goods and services from its resources. Again, failure to do so wastes resources. **Equity** occurs when the distribution of goods and services conforms to a society's notions of "fairness." These goals often determine the type of economic system that a country has.

Skill Four

Identify Factors to Consider When Making Consumer Decisions

Adam Smith (1723–1790) was a Scottish economist whose writing may have inaugurated the modern era of economic analysis. Published in 1776, *The Wealth of Nations* is Smith's analysis of a market economy.

Smith believed that a market economy was a superior form of organization from the standpoint of both economic progress and human liberty. Smith acknowledged that **self-interest** was a dominant motivating force in a market economy; this self-interest, he said, was ultimately consistent with the **public interest**. An "invisible hand" guided market participants to act in ways that promoted the public interest. **Profits** may be the main concern of firms, but only firms that **satisfy** consumer demand and offer **suitable prices** earn profits.

Goods and services refer to things that satisfy human **needs, wants**, or **desires**. **Goods** are tangible items, such as food, cars, and clothing; **services** are intangible items such as education and health care. A market is the interaction between potential buyers and sellers of goods and services. **Money** is usually the medium of exchange. The **supply** of a good is the quantity of that good that producers offer at a certain price. The collection of all such points for every price is the **supply curve**. **Demand** for a good is the quantity of a good that consumers are willing and able to purchase at a certain price. The **demand curve** is the combination of quantity and price, at all price levels.

Skill Five

Identify the Economic Interdependence among Nations

Understanding global interdependence begins with recognizing that world regions include economic, political, historical, ecological, linguistic, and cultural regions. This understanding should include knowledge of military and economic alliances such as NATO, of cartels, and of how their existence affects political and economic policies within regions. Knowledge of world regions and alliances leads to identification of issues that affect people worldwide. Common issues that affect people everywhere include **finances**, **movement of labor**, **trade**, food production, human rights, use of natural resource, prejudice, poverty, and trade.

A true sense of global interdependence results from an understanding of the relationship between local decisions and global issues—for example, how individual or community actions regarding waste disposal or recycling can affect the availability of resources worldwide. Fuel emission standards, for example, can affect air pollution, oil supplies, and gas prices.

Microeconomics focuses on problems specific to a household, firm, or industry, rather than national or global issues. Microeconomics gives particular emphasis to how these units make decisions and the consequences of those decisions.

Macroeconomics is the study of the economy as a whole. Some of the topics considered include inflation, unemployment, and economic growth. **Economic theory** is an explanation of why certain economic phenomena occur. For example, there are theories explaining the rate of inflation, how many hours people choose to work, and the amount of goods and services a specific country will import. Economic theory is essentially a set of statements about cause-and-effect relationships in the economy.

Skill Six

Identify Human, Natural, and Capital Resources and How These Resources Are Used in the Production of Goods and Services

Goods and services are the things that generally satisfy human needs, wants, or desires. **Goods** are tangible items, such as food, cars, and clothing; **services** are intangible items such as education and health care. A **market** is the interaction between potential buyers and sellers of goods and services, where money is usually the medium of exchange. **Supply** of a good is the quantity of that good that producers offer at a certain price. The collection of all such points for every price is the **supply curve**. **Demand** for a good is the quantity of a good that consumers are willing and able to purchase at a certain price. The **demand curve** is the combination of quantity and price, at all price levels.

Necessary for the production of goods and services are human resources, natural resources, and capital resources. **Human resources** are the persons employed in a business or organization; in other words, a firm's human resources are its personnel. Originally, the term for human resources was labor. **Natural resources** are the material source of wealth. Examples of natural or material resources are timber, fresh water, and mineral deposits that occur in a natural state and have economic value.

The word *capital* comes from the Latin word *caput*, which means "head." In economics, capital originally meant the profit that one made; the measure of profit was probably heads (caput) of cattle. In finance and economics today, **capital** means how much real, usable money a person or a company has.

Competency 17: Knowledge of Instruction and Assessment of the Social Sciences

Two test items relate to this competency.

Skill One

Identify Appropriate Resources for Teaching Social Science Concepts

The ability to understand and apply skills and procedures related to the study of social sciences involves knowledge of the use of **systematic inquiry**. Inquiry is essential for use in examining single social sciences topics or integrated social sciences. Being able to engage in inquiry involves the ability to acquire information from a variety of resources, and to organize and interpret that information. The process of inquiry begins with **designing and conducting investigations** that lead to the identification and analysis of social sciences issues.

Systematic social science inquiry uses various resources. Among the most commonly used resources are **the Internet, primary and secondary sources, encyclopedias, almanacs, atlases, government documents, artifacts,** and **oral histories**.

The effective teacher uses a variety of educational resources (including people and technology) to enhance both individual and group learning. Resources of all types are also key elements of the **curriculum planning process**. The effective teacher should be very familiar with the school library, the local public library, education service center resources, and the library of any college or university in the area. Another important set of resources is all the audiovisual aids the teacher can borrow: kits, films, filmstrips, videos, laser disks, and computer software, among others. All used audiovisual aids should relate to curricular objectives.

Many librarians have keyed their resources to objectives in related subject areas, enabling the teacher to incorporate them with ease into the lessons. However, teachers should never use resources with a class without previewing them and approving their use. The curriculum guide or the lesson plan should ideally include the list of resources the teacher might use.

The effective teacher determines the appropriate place in the lesson for audiovisual aids. If the material is especially interesting and thought provoking, the teacher can use it to introduce a unit or to summarize it.

Throughout the unit, the teacher and students may use the Internet for research.

Print Resources

The most common print material is the textbook, which teachers on the campus usually select from a list of books approved by the state. There are disadvantages to the use of textbooks. The cost of textbooks has increased drastically in recent years and some do not match curriculum guidelines. The adoption process is a long one, and textbooks (particularly for history) can become out-of-date quickly; therefore, the teacher must use additional resources with recent dates.

Another limitation of textbooks is their tendency to provide sketchy or minimal information, partly because publishers must include such a broad range of topics. An ineffective teacher may use the "chapter a week" theory of "covering" a textbook. This method gives no consideration to the importance of information in each chapter or its relevance to the overall district curriculum. Merely covering the material does not promote critical thinking on the part of the teacher or the student. Students tend to believe the textbook is something they must endure and not necessarily employ as a tool for learning. The effective teacher chooses sections from the textbook that are relevant to the learning goals and omits the rest. The teacher may supplement the sketchy textbook treatments by using an abundance of other resources.

Local, state, and national newspapers and magazines are important sources of up-to-date information not available in textbooks. Some newspapers and magazines have special programs to help teachers use their products in the classroom as sources of information and for reading and writing opportunities. Local newspapers may even be willing to send specialists to work with students or act as special resource persons.

Visual Materials

The most available visual tools in classrooms are the chalkboard and the overhead projector. There are several principles that apply to both. The teacher must write clearly and in large letters. Overhead transparencies should never be typed on a regular typewriter because the print is too small. Computers allow type sizes of at least 18 points, which is the minimum readable size. Also, both boards and transparencies should be free of clutter. Teachers must remove old information from the board or screen before adding new information. These tools work more effectively if the teacher plans their use ahead of time. Using different colors emphasizes relationships or differences.

Posters and charts can complement lessons, but they should not clutter the walls so that students are unable to focus on what's important for the current lesson. Teachers may display posters and charts on a rotating basis.

The Internet is essential to the students and the teachers in gathering information. Computer programs, filmstrips, films, and videos are appealing to students because visual images on television, computers, and video games already surround them. Films, computer displays, and filmstrips have the advantage of large screen projection so all students can see clearly, but many projection devices are expensive.

Teachers may stop videos, films, and filmstrips for discussion. Students comprehend better and remember longer if the teacher introduces a video or film appropriately and stops it frequently to discuss it with the students. This method also helps keep students' attention focused and assists them in learning note-taking skills.

Some of the best graphic aids are those that individual students or by groups of students develop. While learning about subject area concepts, students become familiar with the design and presentation of information. Students can take pictures of their products to put in a portfolio or scrapbook.

Compact Discs and Interactive Video

Compact discs (CDs) provide a sturdy, condensed system of storage for pictures and sound. These discs can store many separate frames of still images, up to 2 hours of music, or 2 hours of motion pictures with sound. An advantage of a CD rather than videotape is that one can assess each frame separately and quickly

by inputting its number. The simplest level of use involves commands to play, pause, forward, or reverse.

A CD or video program can become interactive with a computer link. The teacher can then access individual images, sequence images, and pace the information from the interactive system. A social studies teacher with a collection of pictures of the world's art treasures can choose which pictures to use, order the images, and design custom-made lessons for repeated use or for easy revision. The teacher can develop numerous lessons from one CD or videotape. More comprehensive interactive programs use the computer to present information, access a disc to illustrate main points, and ask for responses from the student.

A multimedia production can include images, text, and sound from a videodisc, CD-ROM, graphics software, word processing software, and a sound effects program. Teachers can develop classroom presentations, but students can also develop learning units as part of a research or inquiry project. The cost of a multimedia system remains relatively high, but students can use it to develop high-level thought processes, collaborative work, research skills, content knowledge, and understanding.

Human Resources

Parents and other members of the community can be excellent local experts from whom students can learn about any subject: economics from bankers, history from veterans, music from a specific period from local musicians or recording collectors, community history from local historians or librarians, business from owners of companies—the list of possibilities is endless. Effective teachers make sure that any invited guest understands the purpose of the visit and the goals or objectives of the presentation. Preparation can make the class period more focused and meaningful.

Field trips are excellent sources of information, especially about careers and current issues like pollution control. One field trip can yield assignments in mathematics, history, science, English, art, architecture, music, or health. Teachers can collaborate with each other to produce thematic assignments for the field trip or simply to coordinate the students' assignments.

Often a history report can serve as an English paper as well. Data can be analyzed in math classes and presented with the aid of computers.

Skill Two
Identify Appropriate Assessment Methods in Teaching Social Science Concepts

The basic goals of assessment are to enhance teachers' knowledge of learners and their needs, to monitor students' progress toward goals and outcomes, and to modify instruction when progress is not sufficient.

Purposes of Assessment

The effective teacher understands the importance of ongoing assessment as an instructional tool for the classroom and uses both informal and formal assessment measures. Informal measures can include observation, journals, written drafts, and conversations. Formal measures can include teacher-made tests, district exams, and standardized tests.

Both formative and summative evaluations are part of effective teaching. **Formative** evaluation occurs during the process of learning, when the teacher or the students monitor progress in obtaining outcomes and while it is still possible to modify instruction. **Summative** evaluation occurs at the end of a specific time or course of study. Usually, a summative evaluation applies a single grade to represent a student's performance.

Teacher-Made Tests

At the same time that they plan goals and outcomes, teachers should develop assessments—not after they have taught all the lessons. Carefully planned objectives and assessment instruments serve as lesson development guides for the teacher.

Paper-and-pencil tests are the most common method for evaluation of student progress. Among the various types of questions are multiple-choice, true/false, matching, fill-in-the-blank, short answer, and essay questions. The first five types tend to test students'

knowledge or comprehension levels. Essays may test at the lower levels but can be suitable for assessing learning at higher levels. **Projects**, **papers**, and **portfolios** can assess higher-level thinking skills.

To test students' recall of factual information, a short objective test (with multiple-choice, true/false, matching, fill-in-the blank questions) might be most effective and efficient. Students can answer the first three types of questions on machine-scorable scan sheets for quick and accurate scoring. Disadvantages are that these questions generally test lower levels of knowledge and do not provide an opportunity for an explanation of answers.

To test students' ability to analyze an event, compare and contrast two concepts, make predictions about an experiment, or evaluate a character's actions, an **essay** question may provide the best opportunity for the students to show what they can do. The teacher should make the question explicit enough for students to know exactly what is expected. For example, "Explain the results of World War II" is too broad; students do not know the teacher's expectations. A more explicit question is, "Explain the three results of World War II that you think had the most impact on participating nations. Explain the criteria you used in selecting these results."

Advantages of an essay include the possibility for students to be creative in their answers, the opportunity for students to explain their responses, and the potential to test for higher-level thinking skills. Disadvantages of essay questions include the time needed for students to formulate meaningful responses, language difficulties of some students, and the time needed to evaluate the essays.

Consistency in evaluating essays can also be a problem for some teachers, but an outline of the acceptable answers—a scoring *rubric*—can help a teacher avoid inconsistency. Teachers who write specific questions and know what they are looking for are more likely to be consistent in grading. Also, if there are several essay questions, the effective teacher grades all student responses to the first question, then moves on to all responses to the second, and so on.

Authentic Assessments

Paper-and-pencil tests or essays are not the only methods of assessment. Others include projects, observation, checklists, anecdotal records, portfolios, self-assessments, and peer assessments. Although these types of assessment often take more time and effort to plan and administer, they can often provide a more authentic assessment of student progress.

Projects are common in almost all subject areas. Projects promote student control of learning experiences and provide opportunities for research into various topics and the chance to use visuals, graphics, videos, or multimedia presentations in place of, or in addition to, written reports. Projects also promote student self-assessment because students must evaluate their progress at each step of the project. Many schools have history fairs for which students plan and develop projects to display. Projects can also be part of economics and other areas of the social sciences.

Effective teachers must make clear the requirements and the criteria for evaluation of projects before students begin work. Teachers must also assist students in selecting projects that are feasible, for which the school has learning resources, and that do not require an exorbitant investment of time and expense.

The advantages of **projects** are that students can use visuals, graphics, art, or even music abilities; students can be creative in their topics and research; and the projects can appeal to various learning styles. The primary disadvantage is difficulty with grading, although this can be overcome by devising a checklist for required elements and a rating scale for quality.

Observation is another assessment method for individual or group work. Observation is very suitable for skills or for effective learning. Usually, the teacher makes a **checklist** of competencies, skills, or requirements and checks off the ones the student or group displays. A teacher who wants to emphasize careful listening might observe a discussion with a checklist that includes paying attention, not interrupting, summarizing the ideas of other members of the group, and asking questions of others.

Advantages of checklists include the potential for capturing behavior that a paper and pencil test cannot accurately measure, such as important elements in a speech in class. One characteristic of a checklist that is both an advantage and a disadvantage is its structure, which provides consistency but inflexibility. An open-ended comment section at the end of a checklist can overcome this disadvantage.

Anecdotal records are helpful in some instances, such as capturing the process a group of students uses to solve a problem. This formative data can be useful during feedback to the group. Students can also be taught to write explanations of the procedures they use for their projects. One advantage of an anecdotal record is that it can include all relevant information. Disadvantages include the amount of time necessary to complete the record and difficulty in assigning a grade. If the anecdotal record is solely for feedback, no grade is necessary.

Portfolios are collections of students' best work and can be useful in any subject area where the teacher wants students to take more responsibility for planning, carrying out, and organizing their own learning. Like a portfolio that an artist, model, or performer creates, a student portfolio provides a succinct picture of the child's achievements over a certain period. Portfolios may contain essays or articles written on paper, videotapes, multimedia presentations on computer disks, or a combination. Teachers often use portfolios as a means of collecting the best samples of student writing over an entire year, and some teachers pass on the portfolios to the next teacher to help in student assessment.

Teachers should provide or assist students in developing guidelines for what materials should go in their portfolios because it would be unrealistic to include every piece of work in one portfolio. Using portfolios requires the students to devise a means of evaluating their own work. A portfolio should not be a scrapbook for collecting handouts or work done by other individuals although it can certainly include work by a group in which the student was a participant.

Some advantages of portfolios over testing are that they provide a clear picture of a student's progress, they are not affected by one inferior test grade, and they help develop students' self-assessment skills. One disadvantage is the amount of time required to teach students how to develop meaningful portfolios. However, the time is well spent if students learn valuable skills. Another concern is the amount of time teachers must spend to assess portfolios. As students become more proficient at self-assessment, however, the teacher can spend more time in coaching and advising students throughout the development of their portfolios. Another concern is that parents may not understand the grading of portfolios. The effective teacher devises a system that the students and parents understand before work on the portfolio begins.

Self- and Peer Assessment

One goal of an assessment system is to promote student self-assessment. Because most careers require employees or managers to evaluate their own productivity as well as that of others, self-assessment and peer assessment are important lifelong skills. Effective teachers use a structured approach to teach self-assessment, help students set standards at first by making recommendations about standards, and then have students gradually move toward developing their own criteria and applying those criteria to their work.

One method of developing self-assessment is to ask students to apply the teacher's own standards to a product. For example, a history teacher who uses a rating scale for essays might have students use that scale on their own papers and compare their evaluations with those of the teacher. A science teacher who uses a checklist while observing an experiment might ask students to use the checklist; students can compare their scores with the teacher's. The class can set standards for evaluating group work and individual work. Collaborative groups are effective vehicles for practicing the skills involved in self- and peer assessment.

Performance-Based Assessment

Some states and districts are moving toward performance-based tests, which assess students on how well they perform certain tasks. Performance-based tests allow students to use higher-level thinking skills to apply, analyze, synthesize, and evaluate ideas and data. Performance-based testing evaluates process and output.

A history performance-based assessment might require students to research a specific topic over a period of several days, make presentations of their findings to the rest of the class, and write a response that uses what they have learned from their own research and from that of their classmates. Again, the candidate should the section on assessment in Chapter 2 of this book for more details.

Testing Measurements

There are primarily two types of assessment. In **criterion-referenced** tests, the teacher measures each student against uniform objectives or criteria. Teacher-made tests should be criterion-referenced because the teacher should develop them to measure the achievement of predetermined outcomes for the course.

The purpose of a **norm-referenced test (NRT)** is to compare the performance of groups of students. This type of test is competitive because a limited number of students can score well. A plot of large numbers of NRT scores resembles a bell-shaped curve. Interpretation involves using terms like **percentile scores** (which rank students from highest to lowest), **normed scores** (which can help compare the performance of test-takers with the performance of a norm group), **reliability** (whether the instrument will give consistent results with the repetition of the measurement), **validity** (whether the test actually measures what it is supposed to measure), and other related terms and measures discussed in Chapter 2 under competency 6, skill 2. To prepare for the Florida Teacher Certification Examination: Elementary Education, Kindergarten–Grade 6, the candidate should thoroughly review that section.

References

Alvarez, Lizette. 2001. Census director marvels at the new portrait of America. *New York Times*. January 1.

Cayne, Bernard S., ed. 1969. *Merit students encyclopedia*. Chicago: Crowell-Collier.

Congress for Kids. *http://congressforkids.net/Constitution_amendments.htm.*

Davis, Anita Price. 2003. *North Carolina during the Great Depression: A documentary portrait of a decade.* Jefferson, NC: McFarland.

Florida Smart. Florida population and demographics. *http://www.floridasmart.com/facts/demographics.htm.*

Halsey, William D., and Bernard Johnston, eds. 1991. *Merit students encyclopedia.* New York: Macmillan.

Harrington, Michael. 1962. *The Other America: Poverty in the United States.* New York: Macmillan.

Huitt, W. 1998. Critical thinking: An overview. *Educational psychology interactive.*

Valdosta, Georgia: Valdosta State University. *http://chiron.valdosta.edu/whuitt/col/cogsys/critthnk.html*

Martin, Philip L. 2002. Immigration in the United States. *http://ies.berkeley.edu/pubs/workingpapers/ay0102.html.*

Schieffer, Bob. 2005 (September 4). Government failed the people. *CBS News. http://www.cbsnews.com/stories/2005/09/06/opinion/schieffer/main818486.html.*

Schuncke, George M. 1988. *Elementary social studies: Knowing, doing, caring.* New York: Macmillan.

U.S. Census Bureau. Florida quickfacts. *http://quickfacts.census.gov/qfd/states/12000.html.*

Science and Technology

Competency 18: Knowledge of the Nature of Matter

Three test items relate to this competency.

Skill One

Identify the Physical and Chemical Properties of Matter

Matter is everything that has mass and volume. **Mass** is the amount of matter in an object; one way to measure mass is by using a lever arm balance. **Volume** is the amount of space an object occupies. Water is matter because it takes up space (i.e., it has volume), whereas light is not matter because it does not take up space.

Weight, although sometimes incorrectly interchanged with mass, is a measure of the force of gravity on an object; a spring scale can determine weight. An electronic scale may display an object's mass in grams, but it is dependent on gravity for its operation. An electronic scale, such as some butchers use, is only accurate when an expert (usually with the state trade agency) has adjusted the electronics for the local gravitational force.

Although an object appears "weightless" as it floats inside the space shuttle, it is not; gravitational forces from both the earth and the sun keep it in orbit and affect the object. The force of gravity is proportional to the product of the masses of the two objects under consideration divided by the square of the distance between them. Earth, being larger and more massive than Mars, has proportionally higher gravitational forces. This is the basis of the observation in H. G. Wells's *The War of the Worlds*; he said that the Martian invaders were "the most sluggish things I ever saw crawl."

Density is the ratio of mass to volume. An intrinsic property, density depends on the type of matter but not the amount of matter. Thus, the density of a 5-ton cube of pure copper is the same as that of a small copper penny. However, the modern penny is a thin shell of copper over a zinc plug, and the density of the coin may be significantly lower than that of the older pure copper coin.

Density is related to **buoyancy**. Objects sink in liquids or gases alike if they are denser than the material that surrounds them. Archimedes's principle, also related to density, states that an object is buoyed up by a force equal to the mass of the material the object displaces. Thus, a 160-pound concrete canoe will easily float in water if the volume of the submerged portion of the canoe is equal to the volume of 20 gallons of water.

(The weight of water is approximately 8 pounds per gallon; therefore, 8 lbs/gal × 20 gal = 160 lbs.)

Density is not the same as **viscosity**, a measure of thickness or flowability. The strength of intermolecular forces between molecules determines, for example, that molasses will be slow in January or that hydrogen bromide is a gas in any season.

Matter can undergo chemical and physical changes. A **physical change** affects the size, form, or appearance of a material. These changes can include melting, bending, or cracking. Physical changes do not alter the molecular structure of a material. **Chemical changes** do alter the molecular structure of matter. Examples of chemical changes are burning, rusting, and digestion. Under the right conditions, compounds can break apart, combine, or recombine to form new compounds; this process is **chemical reaction**. Chemical equations can describe chemical reactions. For instance, sodium hydroxide and hydrochloride combine to form sodium chloride and water. The chemical equation for that reaction is

$$NaOH + HCl \rightarrow NaCl + H_2O$$

The materials to the left of the arrow are **reactants**, and materials to the right of the arrow are **products**.

Skill Two

Identify the Characteristics of Elements, Compounds, and Mixtures and Distinguish Among the Three Main States of Matter

Classifications of matter also include elements, compounds, mixtures, or solutions. An **element** consists of only one type of atom. An example is iron. A symbol of one or two letters, such as Fe (iron) or C (carbon), represents an element. A **compound** is matter that comprises atoms chemically combined in definite weight proportions. An example of a compound is water, which is oxygen and hydrogen combined in the ratio of two hydrogen molecules to one oxygen molecule.

A **mixture** is made up of one or more types of molecules, not chemically combined and without any definite weight proportions. For example, milk is a mixture of water and butterfat particles. Mixtures can be separated by either physical or chemical means. An example of a physical means would be straining the butterfat from milk to make skim milk. **Solutions** are **homogeneous** mixtures—that is, mixtures with evenly distributed substances. An example of a solution is seawater. Separating the salt from seawater requires the process of evaporation.

The three main **states of matter** are solids, liquids, and gases. A **solid** has a definite volume and a definite shape (e.g., ice). A **liquid** has a definite volume but has no definite shape (e.g., water). A **gas** has no definite volume or shape (e.g., water vapor or steam).

Skill Three

Identify the Basic Components of the Atom

Atoms are the basic building blocks of matter. Three types of subatomic particles, which have mass and charge, make up atoms. The three components of atoms are protons, neutrons, and electrons. **Protons** and **neutrons** are in the **nucleus**, or solid center of an atom. **Electrons** are in the outer portion of an atom.

Under most conditions, atoms are indivisible. However, during atomic reactions atoms may split or combine to form new atoms. Atomic reactions occur deep inside the sun, in nuclear power reactors, in nuclear bombs, and in radioactive decay.

A symbol of one or two letters, such as K (potassium) or Na (sodium), represents an element. Atoms of the same element have the same number of protons in their nuclei. An atom is the smallest particle of an element that retains the characteristics of that element. Each element has an atomic number, which is equal to the number of protons in an atom of that element. The periodic table is an arrangement of all the elements in order according to their atomic number. The periodic table is a reference tool and summarizes the atomic structure, mass, and reactive tendencies of elements; the periodic table groups elements vertically according to their chemical properties. Two or more atoms may combine to form molecules.

Competency 19: Knowledge of Forces, Motion, and Energy

Ten test items relate to this competency.

Skill One
Apply Knowledge of Temperature and Heat

Energy is the ability of matter to move other matter or to produce a chemical change in other matter. Scientists also define energy as the ability to do work. There are many forms of energy, which scientists divide into six main groups: (1) heat energy, (2) mechanical energy, (3) electrical energy, (4) wave energy, (5) chemical energy, and (6) nuclear energy.

Heat is the energy of moving molecules. **Temperature** describes how hot or cold a material is. Temperature has nothing to do with the amount of heat a material has; it only has to do with the degree of "hotness" or "coldness" of the material. Temperature depends on the speed that the molecules in a material are moving. The faster the molecules are moving, the hotter the temperature becomes.

A **thermometer** measures temperature. There are several types of thermometers, but the most common ones are glass tubes containing mercury or a liquid, such as colored alcohol. Thermometers usually use the Fahrenheit scale or the Celsius scale.

Skill Two
Identify the Types and Characteristics of Contact Forces and At-a-Distance Forces

A **force** is a push or a pull. A force is necessary to make a machine work. If the force is unbalanced, the object will accelerate. A good example of an unbalanced force is the thrust of a rocket engine moving the rocket upward at ever-increasing speeds from a launch pad. If, however, there is a balanced net force on an object, the object will not accelerate. It will either remain still or continue to move at a constant speed.

There are two main types of force: **contact** and **at-a-distance**. Within both of the primary types of force are many subtypes. One type of contact force is **mechanical force**. Machines in general multiply force or change the direction of force. For perfect (frictionless) machines, the work that the user does is equal to the work that the machine does.

The following are types of at-a-distance force:

Magnetic force. Magnets are materials that will pick up or attract materials made of iron, steel, cobalt, or nickel; such materials are **magnetic materials**. The force (push or pull) of a magnet is strongest at its ends, or poles. The space around which the magnetic force of a magnet acts is the magnetic field.

Gravitational force. Gravitational force is the attraction or pull that every body in the universe has for every other body.

Electrostatic force. Two negatively charged materials will repel, or move away from, each other. Two positively charged materials also will repel each other. This is the law of **electrostatic repulsion**. The law of **electrostatic attraction** states that a positively-charged material and a negatively-charged material will attract each other.

Skill Three
Apply Knowledge of Simple Machines to Solve Problems Involving Work

Simple machines include the lever, ramp (inclined plane), pulley, wheel-and-axle, wedge, and screw. A good example of a **lever** is the nail puller on a hammer. The user exerts a small force at a large distance, while the hammer exerts a larger (multiplied) force over a short distance. **Ramps (inclined planes)** enable users to push horizontally to move objects upward with relatively small amounts of applied force compared with direct lifting. **Pulleys** change the direction of a form; a user pulls down to move an object up. The **wheel-and-axle** is a variation on the lever. The **wedge** and the **screw** (an inclined plane wrapped around a cylinder) are different forms of the inclined plane.

These machines do not save work. They make work easier; in other words, they provide **mechanical advantage**. One way to define **work** is to say it occurs when an effort or a resistance moves through a distance. The **effort** is the force exerted on a machine. The object that the machine lifts or moves is the **resistance**. Two formulas apply:

Mechanical advantage = Resistance ÷ Effort

Mechanical advantage = Effort distance ÷ Resistance distance

Another way to define **work** is to say it occurs when applied force (push or pull) to an object results in movement of the object. The formula for work is:

Work = Force × Distance

The greater the force applied, or the longer the distance traveled, the greater the work done.

Energy is the ability to do work. Energy comes in many forms, such as heat, light, and sound. All energy is potential or kinetic. **Potential energy** is stored energy through chemical structure, position, or physical configuration. **Kinetic energy** is energy of motion. Light, sound, and heat are kinetic energy, as is the energy possessed by a moving object. Energy transformation from one type to another is possible, but energy is never created or destroyed.

Skill Four

Identify the Properties and Characteristics of Sounds as They Apply to Everyday Situations

Sound is a form of energy. Sound results when an object **vibrates** rapidly. Plucking, stroking, blowing, or hitting causes vibrations. When an object vibrates, the vibrations travel as **waves** in all directions. The waves stop when the vibration stops.

When a guitar string vibrates, it rapidly moves back and forth. The string pushes against the air molecules in front of it; it presses the air molecules in front of it together. The compacted molecules create a space called **compression**. The space behind the strings is a **rarefaction**. A rarefaction and a compression compose a complete vibration.

When vibrations, or **sound waves**, reach the ear, the auditory nerve carries the result to the brain. This is a sensation of sound. Most of us hear the sounds after they travel through the air, which is a gas. The speed is about 1,100 feet a second. When the air is warm, the molecules move faster, and the vibrations will reach our ears sooner. Vibrations travel better through liquids because the molecules are closer together. They travel even better through solids. Vibrations do not carry well in a vacuum without molecules.

Sound can differ in pitch, intensity, and quality. **Pitch** is the highness or lowness of a sound. The faster an object vibrates, the higher the sound it makes. Sounds vary in **intensity** (loudness or softness). The stronger is the vibration, the louder is the sound. It is possible to differentiate between voices and musical instruments because of the **quality** of the sounds. When an object vibrates, it can vibrate as a whole or in parts; the resulting sound is the quality.

Another aspect of sound is **reflection**. An echo is the result of a sound wave that reflects. Reflection means that the sound wave bounced.

Skill Five

Apply Knowledge of Light and Optics to Practical Applications

Light is a form of energy. The sun and other bodies radiate or give out light (radiant energy). Light is in the form of waves and is one of a group of waves—the **electromagnetic waves**. Among the other kinds of electromagnetic waves are X-rays, radio waves, and ultraviolet rays.

Light rays travel at 186,000 miles each second. That is considerably faster than the speed of sound (about 1,100 feet per second). Therefore, we see a bolt of lightning before we hear the clap of thunder. Light travels in a straight line.

Light can pass through some materials but other materials stop its passage. Materials like air, water, and clear glass are **transparent**. Most light rays pass through transparent materials. Frosted glass is **translucent**. Only some of the light passes through a translucent substance. It is not possible to see through **opaque** materials, like a brick wall, because none of the light passes through.

Light can change direction, but it still travels in a straight line. When a light ray strikes a mirror, for instance, the light changes direction, but it continues traveling in a straight line. The mirror **reflects** the light.

Light passes through a transparent material, like water, at a slant or angle. The bending of light rays is called **refraction**. For example, if you try to use your hands to catch a fish that appears in the clear water of a stream, you find that the fish is not where it appears to be. The refracted light gives a distorted view.

A **lens** is a piece of transparent material, like glass, that is curved. When the light passes through the curved lens, the light bends. A **convex lens** is thicker in the middle. It acts as a magnifying glass and can help a far-sighted person's ability to focus on a near object. A convex lens bends the light inward before it enters the eyes; the rays come together and form sharper, clearer images on the retina. Projectors use a convex lens to change a small photograph into a larger picture on the screen.

A lens that is thinner in the middle is a **concave lens**. Concave lenses can help a nearsighted person to see better at a distance. The concave lens spreads the light rays before they enter the eyes, and the rays merge farther back in the eye to form a clear image on the retina.

A beam of light may pass through a triangular material called a **prism**. When light passes through a prism, the prism may diffuse (or break apart) the light ray into its parts. The white light is really a mixture of seven colored lights: red, orange, yellow, green, blue, indigo, and violet. Diffusion—the breaking of the white light into a rainbow—reverses when the rainbow of colors passes through another prism; the second result is white light.

Skill Six

Identify the Regions of the Electromagnetic Spectrum and the Relative Wavelengths and Energy Associated with Each Region

Both light and sound travel; light travels at about 186,000 miles per second—about 1 million times as fast as sound, which travels at 1,100 feet per second. Both light and sound appear to be wave phenomena. The length of a wave can vary in both sound and light. In sound, different wavelengths produce different pitches. In light, different wavelengths produce different colors in light. Just as each note has a different wavelength in sound, each color in light has a different wavelength. The deepest red visible to the eye has a 1/30,000-inch wavelength; at the other end of the spectrum, the deepest violet has a 1/60,000-inch wavelength.

Just as some sound waves (ultrasonic) are inaudible to the human ear, some waves of light are invisible to the human eye. Beyond the deepest violet wave with its 1/60,000-inch spectrum is the **ultraviolet** wave. Invisible to the human eye, the ultraviolet wavelength is shorter than violet. The ultraviolet wavelength is important to human health because it stimulates the production of vitamin D. Ultraviolet radiation is responsible for the sun tanning—or sun burning—of human skin.

At the other end of the color spectrum, just beyond the deepest red, is the **infrared** wave. Infrared waves are the radiant waves that warm the earth. Sunlight and all warm bodies radiate infrared light. Long in wavelength and low in frequency, infrared waves are useful in photography in the dark, in fingerprint detection, and in medicine.

Beyond the reds and the blues is a larger spectrum of waves: the **electromagnetic** spectrum. Visible light forms only one-tenth of the length of the electromagnetic spectrum. Radio, television, radar, visible light, X-rays, cosmic rays, and gamma rays are some of the effects of the electromagnetic spectrum. The wavelengths vary from 2 miles (radio wave) to 1 millionth of 1 millionth of an inch (gamma ray). X-rays have a shorter wavelength and a higher frequency compared with ultraviolet rays. X-rays can pass through nonmetals, are useful in taking pictures of the human body, and can help to inspect fruit for frostbite damage.

James Maxwell first described electromagnetic waves in 1865. These waves illustrate the basic unity of nature. Just as all matter consists of the same fundamental parts (protons, neutron, electrons, etc.), many forms of radiation consist of the waves that travel at 186,000 miles per second.

Skill Seven

Identify Characteristics and Examples of Static Electricity

Friction can produce **static electricity**. For instance when two different materials—particularly nonmetals—rub together, they can attract light objects. These materials have become **electrically charged**. This kind of electricity is nonmoving, or **static**. By contrast, moving electricity is **current electricity**.

Tiny particles, or atoms, make up all things. Inside each atom are electrons, a neutron, and protons. Each **proton** has a positive charge; each **electron** has a negative charge. The **neutron** is neither positive nor negative. Usually, the atom has the same number of electrons and protons; it is, therefore electrically neutral.

Some materials hold their electrons very tightly, and electrons do not move through them very well. These things are **insulators**; some examples of insulators are glass, cloth, dry air, and plastic. Other materials (**conductors**) have loosely held electrons; a metal is good conductor.

It is possible to remove electrons from a material by rubbing it against another material. The electrons then move from one material to the other and alter the balance of protons and electrons in both materials. The material that loses electrons is left with more positive protons than negative electrons. The material that gains electrons is left with more negative electrons than positive protons.

For instance, if you rub a piece of wool against a rubber comb, the comb gains electrons from the wool and thus has more negative electrons than positive protons.

The wool, on the other hand, has lost electrons and has more protons than negative electrons. A material stays charged only as long as electrons do not have a way to enter or leave the material.

When a negatively charged comb is brought near some small bits of paper, the comb attracts the bits of paper, and they will stick to the comb. This is the law of **electrostatic attraction**. The attraction results because the negative electrons on the paper are repelled by the negative electrons on the comb; the negative electrons on the paper move, and the positive protons are attracted to the negative electrons on the comb. The paper drops off the comb when the paper has the same electrical charge as the comb.

When two negatively charged combs are brought close to each other, they repel each other. Likewise, two positively charged materials repel each other. This is the law of **electrostatic repulsion**. Materials that are not charged electrically are said to be neutral.

Most of us have experienced static electricity when we have slid across a car seat and touched the door handle in cool weather, have tried to brush our hair on a cool day, or have had our clothing stick to us when the day is cold. We might even see the sparks of static electricity if there is no light.

Skill Eight

Apply Knowledge of Currents, Circuits, Conductors, and Insulators to Everyday Situations

Atoms may carry electrical charges. A neutral atom has an equal number of protons and electrons in it. The charges of the protons and electrons cancel each other, so the atom has no net charge. If an atom has more electrons than protons, the atom has a negative charge. If an atom has fewer electrons than protons, the atom has a positive charge.

If two objects are rubbed together, electrons—the lightest stable subatomic particles known—move from one object to the other, leaving both charged. Electrons can also flow through certain materials. The flow of electrons produces an **electric current**. Insulators are materials that do not allow electrons to flow freely; examples are glass, rubber, and air. Copper, on the other hand, allows the electric current to flow easily through it; copper is a good **conductor** of electricity. An electric wire is often made of copper to allow the current to flow easily, but it has a covering of rubber (**insulator**) to help prevent electric shock if someone touches the wire.

Circuits are paths through which electric current flows. A circuit can comprise one or more complete paths made up of connections of electrical elements through which current flows. Circuits can be in series or parallel. **Series circuits** are made of a single path through which all current must flow. If any part of a series circuit breaks, the circuit is "opened," and the flow of the current must stop. Some sets of Christmas tree lights are designed in series. If one bulb in the string of lights burns out, none of the lights in the string will work; the current is disrupted for the entire string.

Parallel circuits provide more than one path for current to flow. When one pathway opens so that current cannot flow in it, the current continues to move through the other paths. Wired homes use parallel circuits so that burned-out lightbulbs and turned-off television sets do not disrupt electricity used in other parts of the house.

Skill Nine

Identify Types of Magnets, Their Characteristics, and Their Applications to Everyday Situations

Magnets are solids that attract iron. **Lodestones** are naturally occurring magnets. Magnetic forces make magnets attract or repel each other. Regions in magnets that create magnetic forces are **magnetic poles**. All magnets have a north and a south pole. The north pole of one magnet will **repel** the north pole of another magnet; the same holds true for south poles. The south pole of one magnet will **attract** the north pole of another magnet.

A **magnetic field** is the area that the magnetic force affects. A magnetic field surrounds both poles of a magnet; an electric current can create a magnetic field. **Electromagnets** create large magnetic fields with electric

current. Similarly, moving a wire through a magnetic field produces a current. The earth has a magnetic field. Compasses are magnets that align themselves with the earth's magnetic field.

Skill Ten

Identify Types of Energy

Energy is the ability to do work. **Kinetic energy** is the energy of motion. The formula for kinetic energy is

$$KE = \frac{1}{2}mv^2$$

where m is the mass and v is the velocity of an object. Our food stores **chemical energy** for later conversion to kinetic energy and heat in our bodies.

An icicle hanging off the roof is an example of **potential energy**. The formula for potential energy is

$$PE = mgh$$

where m is mass, g is the gravitational force constant, and h is the height. When the icicle falls, there is a conversion of its potential energy to kinetic energy, to sound energy as it hits the pavement, and to kinetic energy again as the fragments skitter off.

Electrical energy is the energy that moving electrons produce. A stream of electrons moving through a substance is an **electric current**. Electrical energy enables us to light our homes and operate our telephones, televisions, and computers.

Nuclear energy results when the nucleus of an atom splits in two or when the nuclei of atoms become fused together; both cases produce great amounts of energy. **Mechanical energy** is the form of energy most evident in the world. All moving bodies produce mechanical energy. The energy that machines create is mechanical energy.

Magnetic energy is the force (pull or push) of a magnet. When the poles of two magnets are near each other, they repel each other if the poles are alike and attract each other if the poles are different. The space around a magnet can also act like a magnet; this is the magnetic field.

Radiant energy is a form of wave energy. X-rays, infrared rays, radio waves, and ultraviolet rays are a few of the many types of radiant energy. The sun produces **solar energy**. All heat on the earth—except that from the interior of atoms—comes from the sun. The sun warms the earth, and energy from the sun enables plants to synthesize the food that provides food for their needs and for the animals that eat them. The heat from the sun allows for evaporation. The sun is vital to survival.

Competency 20: Knowledge of Processes That Shape the Earth

Seven test items relate to this competency.

Skill One

Identify Characteristics of Geologic Formations, the Mechanisms by Which They Were Formed, and Their Relationship to the Movement of Tectonic Plates

Geology is the study of the structure and composition of the earth. The three layers that compose the earth are the core, mantle, and crust. It is made of solid iron and nickel make up the **core**, which is about 7,000 kilometers in diameter. The **mantle** is the semimolten layer between the crust and the core. It is about 3,000 kilometers thick. The **crust** is the solid outermost layer, composed of bedrock overlaid with mineral and/or organic sediment (soil) and ranging from 5 to 40 kilometers thick.

At times, large sections of the earth's crust move and create faults, earthquakes, volcanoes, and mountains. These moving sections of the earth are **plates**, and the study of their movements is **plate tectonics**.

Faults are cracks in the crust and are the results of the movements of plates. **Earthquakes** occur when plates slide past one another quickly. Volcanoes may also cause earthquakes. A seismograph measures earthquakes and uses the Richter scale.

Volcanoes are mountains that form when two plates move away from one another to let magma reach the crust. **Magma** is molten rock beneath the earth's crust. **Lava** is molten rock on the earth's surface. A volcano shoots out magma, which eventually hardens into lava, and releases ash. Sometimes the erupting volcano forms rivers of lava.

All over the world there are volcanoes—for example, the Pacific Ocean, the Hawaiian Islands, and the southeastern border of Asia. The composition of volcanoes is fiery igneous rock, ash, and many layers of dirt and mud that have hardened from previous eruptions. Volcanic activity, or the collision of plates, causes the crust of the earth to buckle upward and form mountains.

Plate tectonics is a relatively new theory that has revolutionized the way geologists think about the earth. According to the theory, large lithospheric plates form the surface of the earth. The size and position of these plates change over time. The edges of the plates, where they move against each other, are sites of intense geologic activity such as earthquakes, volcanoes, and mountain building. Plate tectonics is a combination of two earlier ideas: continental drift and seafloor spreading. **Continental drift** is the movement of continents over the earth's surface and their change in position relative to each other. **Seafloor spreading** is the creation of new oceanic crust at midocean ridges and movement of the crust away from the midocean ridges.

The following is some of the evidence of continental drift and the underlying plate tectonics:

- The shapes of many continents are such that they look like they are separate pieces of a jigsaw puzzle. For example, the east coasts of North America and South America and the west coasts of Africa and Europe appear to fit together.

- Many fossil comparisons along the edges of continents that look like they fit together suggest species similarities that would only make sense if the two continents were joined at some point in the past.

- Much seismic, volcanic, and geothermal activity occurs more frequently along plate boundaries than in sites far from boundaries.

- There are ridges, such as the Mid-Atlantic Ridge; these occur where plates are separating because of lava welling up from between the plates as they pull apart. Likewise, there are mountain ranges forming where plates are pushing against each other (e.g., the Himalayas, which are still growing).

Skill Two

Identify How Fossils are Formed and How Fossils Are Used in Interpreting the Past and Extrapolating to the Future

Fossils are preserved remnants of or marks made by plants and animals that were once alive. As such, fossils are one source of information about changes in the environment over time. Finding fossils of marine organisms in what is now a desert is an opportunity to discuss scientific ways of knowing, how science forms and tests hypotheses, and how theories develop to explain the reasons behind observations.

There are several ways that fossils formed. When sediment covered some animals and then hardened into rock, the hard parts of the animal remained preserved in the rock. Some animals fell into tar pits, swamps, or quicksand; when the tar hardened, bones and teeth remained. Ice and mud preserved some animals in their entirety. The sticky sap from trees trapped some insects and later hardened; when oceans and sediment eventually covered the trees and sap, the sap became amber, and some parts of the insects remained preserved as fossils. Some animals left casts of their remains; some became petrified. Some plants and animals left prints. Coal also retained the prints of plants and animals pressed into it.

Scientifically literate individuals understand the concepts of uncertainty in measurement and the basis of scientific theories. Such an understanding may lead the teacher in an elementary classroom to refer to fossils and rocks simply as "very old," to say that dinosaurs

"lived long ago," and to preface statements of scientific theory with the observation, "Many scientists believe."

Skill Three

Interpret Geologic Maps, Including Topographic and Weather Maps That Contain Symbols, Scales, Legends, Directions, Latitudes, and Longitudes

Geologic maps provide much information about the earth. By reading a **topographical map**, a student can find out about **altitudes** (heights above and below sea level) and landforms. **Symbols** on the map may represent rivers, lakes, rapids, and forests. Map **scales** allow the student to determine distances. The **legends** of a map furnish additional information, including the locations of mineral deposits and quarries, dams and boat ramps, fire and ranger stations, and more. Often a map displays a **compass rose**, which gives the cardinal directions: north, south, east, and west.

Parallels and meridians grid the earth. **Meridians** run from pole to pole, and 360 of them surround the earth in 1-degree increment. Every hour, a given location on the earth's surface rotates through 15 degrees of longitude. Meridians help measure longitude, the distance east and west of the Prime Meridian, which has a measurement of 0 degrees E-W. **Parallels** are the lines that run in an east-west direction; parallels help measure **latitude**, the distance north and south of the Equator.

Geologic maps often contain all this information. A geologic map usually differs from a political map, which shows political boundaries, counties, cities, towns, churches, schools, and other representations of government and people.

Skill Four

Identify the Major Groups of Rocks, Examples of Each, and the Processes of Their Formation

Rocks are naturally occurring solids found on or below the earth's surface. One or more minerals, which are pure substances made of just one element or chemical compound, compose the rocks. There are three groups of rocks, according to their method of formation:

1. **Igneous rocks** are fire rocks; their place of formation can be either under or above ground. Sometimes melted rock, called magma, becomes trapped in small pockets deep within the earth. As these pockets of magma slowly cool underground, the magma becomes igneous rocks. When volcanoes erupt and the magma rises above the earth's surface, it is called lava. Igneous rocks are the result of the lava cooling aboveground. Examples include granite and obsidian.

2. **Sedimentary rocks** are the result of wind or water breaking down or wearing little pieces of earth; often the bits of earth settle to the bottom of rivers, lakes, and oceans. Over the course of thousands or even millions of years this layer after layer of eroded earth, silt, or deposited rock fragments by compaction at high pressures and/or cementation forms rock. This formed sedimentary rock includes shale and limestone.

3. **Metamorphic rocks** are rocks that have "morphed," or changed into other kinds of rocks. Igneous or sedimentary rocks heated under tons of pressure change into metamorphic rocks. Geologists examining metamorphic rock samples have found that some of the grains in the rocks are flattened. Marble and slate are two examples of metamorphic rocks.

Weathering is the breaking down of rock into small pieces. Acid rain, freezing, wind abrasion, glacier scouring, and running water weathers rock. Erosion transports rock or sediment to new areas. Agents of erosion include wind, running water, and glaciers.

Skill Five

Identify Atmospheric Conditions and Properties of Air

An **air mass** is a huge body of air that may cover a large portion of the earth's surface and may be high and wide. The temperature and the humidity are relatively constant throughout the air mass. The weather that can result from an air mass depends mostly on the humidity and the temperature of that air mass. An air mass forms when the largely undisturbed atmosphere over one part of the earth's surface picks up the temperature and

humidity of that part of the earth. The condition of an air mass may change when the mass moves from one place to another. When two air masses meet, the boundary between them is called a **front**. Most stormy weather occurs at these fronts.

Differences in pressure governs air movement, or **wind**, in the atmosphere. In general, high pressure and low moisture content characterize air masses at the poles. Air masses near the equator usually have low pressure and high moisture content. (Heating decreases the density of air at the equator and increases it at the poles.) Therefore, wind tends to flow **from high to low pressure** regions. The rotation of the earth affects the picture, however. In addition, belts of high-speed winds in the upper troposphere (the lowest layer of the earth's atmosphere) complicate the scene further; these winds are the **jet streams**. A jet stream is like a narrow current flowing around the earth. The two jet streams in the Northern Hemisphere are near the pole and near the middle latitudes; similar ones are apparent below the equator.

Clouds help predict the weather. The three main types of clouds are stratus, cumulus, and cirrus, as described in Table 5-1.

Students are most familiar with three main types of **storms**: hurricanes, tornadoes, and thunderstorms. **Hurricanes** are cyclones (or intense lows) that form over the oceans in the tropics—usually between June and November. The large amounts of heat energy created during these months cause ocean waters to evaporate and to form warm moist air. When cooler air pushes on the warm air, a violent storm with much rain often results.

Table 5-1. Clouds and the Weather They Cause

Type	Appearance		Weather
Stratus	Flat	Light	Stable weather
		Dark	Rain expected soon
Cumulus	Fluffy	Solid, light	Good weather
		Dark	Heavy rain, perhaps a thunderstorm
Cirrus	Thin	Wispy	Changes in weather expected

A hurricane has no front, but it does have an "eye," which is a calm area. The winds in a hurricane move swiftly, but the hurricane itself moves slowly. The waves that a hurricane produces usually cause much damage. Hurricanes in the western Pacific Ocean are typhoons. In the Indian Ocean, they are cyclones; in Australia, they are willy-willies; and in the Philippines they are baguios.

Tornadoes are violent, small, short-lived storms. They occur almost exclusively in the United States. The tornado cloud is very thick, black, and funnel-shaped. A deafening roar accompanies the tornado, which usually travels about 15 miles in about 8 minutes. If the tornado passes over a body of water, it becomes a **waterspout**.

Dark cumulus clouds are often a predictor of strong **thunderstorms**. Lightning, heavy rain, gusts of wind, and thunder accompany a thunderstorm. Sometimes hail forms. A thunderstorm rarely lasts more than 2 hours; it is possible, however, to have more than one thunderstorm a day. A frontal thunderstorm forms when a cold front pushes warm air ahead of it. An air-mass thunderstorm (summer thunderstorm) forms within an air mass—usually on a hot summer afternoon.

Gases that are colorless, tasteless, and odorless form **air**. Air is all around us, but it is invisible and has no shape of its own; it conforms to the shape of its container. Air does have weight, however; 1 liter of air weighs 1.2 grams. Air also has **pressure**, which means its weight presses against things. The pressure air exerts on the surface of the earth is **air pressure**. Air pressure decreases as the distance from the earth increases. Air presses in all directions: upward, sideways, and downward. Moving air also exerts pressure.

Skill Six

Identify the Movement of Water in the Water Cycle, Including Types of Precipitation and Causes of Condensation

The hydrologic cycle, or **water cycle**, is a series of movements of water above, on, and below the surface of the earth. The sun's energy is a key component of the process of transporting, through the atmosphere, water from the oceans to the landmasses. The water cycle consists of four stages: evaporation, condensation, precipitation,

and collection. **Evaporation** occurs when the sun heats up water and turns it into water or steam; this water vapor leaves the river, lake, or ocean and goes into the air. This water vapor in the air may get colder and change back into liquid and form clouds; this is **condensation. Precipitation** occurs when so much water has condensed that the air cannot hold it anymore; the clouds get heavy and water falls back to the earth in the form of rain, hail, sleet, or snow. When the moisture falls back to the earth as precipitation, **collection** occurs when the water falls back into the oceans, lake or rivers or it may end up on land. When it ends up on land, it will soak into the earth and become part of the "ground water" or it may run over the soil and collect in the oceans, lakes, or rivers.

Differences in pressure govern air movement in the atmosphere. In general, air masses at the poles have high pressures and low moisture content. Air masses near the equator have low pressures and high moisture content. (Heating decreases the density of air at the equator and increases it at the poles.) Therefore, wind tends to flow from high to low pressure regions, although the rotation of the earth can complicate the picture.

The concept of cycle reappears in the discussion of the recurring patterns of weather. **Weather** is the local, short-term condition of the atmosphere. The factors that affect weather most are the amounts of energy and water present.

Water covers about 70 percent of the earth's surface. As that water slowly evaporates, the atmosphere holds some of the vapor. It is the water vapor in the earth's atmosphere that causes humidity, fog, clouds, and precipitation.

Heat energy warms the air and increases water evaporation; warm air expands and rises above cooler surrounding air. When the rising air cools and water vapor condenses, clouds form, and the result is usually precipitation. If the surrounding air is above 32° Fahrenheit, the precipitation may be in the form of **rain**.

Snow comes from cooled droplets of water that the clouds or the upper air holds. Snow consists of crystals of water. Crystals formed in the low clouds are usually large and branching; those formed in the high clouds are small and compact.

The white, rolling cloud that often appears at the beginning of a thunderstorm is typically where **hail** forms. The air in the cloud is whirling parallel to the earth. A raindrop caught in the cloud and carried up high in the atmosphere turns to snow. When it comes down, water might coat it again. Then it might rise again and freeze. The longer the hailstone travels, the larger it gets, the more violent the whirl of air becomes, and the larger the hailstone is before it hits the earth. Hail is a part of a thunderstorm, and it usually occurs in the summer. Frozen rain is **sleet**.

Warm air holds moisture. In the summer, the warm, moist air may cool when it comes in contact with the ground. This cooling on the ground, the grass, and items near the ground may result in the collection of drops of moisture, or **dew**.

Fog is a large mass of water vapor that has condensed to fine particles. These fine drops often attach to particles in the air—like dust—just as drops near the earth attach to grass, rocks, and other objects to form dew. Fog is often at or just above the earth's surface.

Skill Seven

Identify Ways in Which Land and Water Interact

An **aquifer** is an underground layer of water-bearing, permeable (porous) rock. In fact, the earth may have an entire aquifer stratum that is porous and bears water or other liquids or matter, like oil or gas. The water or other matter in the rock may pass gradually through porous stone or a bed of sand down to another level; this filtering process is **percolation**. When the matter percolates to another level, it may carry with it materials and minerals it has taken (leached) from the area above. **Leaching** is the extracting of a substance from a solid by dissolving it in a liquid.

A **reservoir** is a container for storing something, like water. On the earth, a reservoir is an artificial lake that natural acts, like flooding, may create or that people may construct to collect and store water for public use. When beavers build a dam, the land behind the dam becomes a reservoir; the halting of the water flow, the collection of rainfall, and flooding may increase the depth of the water.

Sinkholes occur in nature in low areas, but some sinkholes are the result of human activity. For example, in underground mines, the upper level may collapse into the cavity underneath. Viewed from above, the collapsed earth looks like a huge hole—a sinkhole. Sinkholes can form when drainage pipes collapse under the ground or even under a roadway.

Precipitation falls on the land; flows overland as **runoff**; and runs into creeks, rivers, and eventually the ocean. Rivers also gain and lose water to the ground, but most of the water in rivers seems to come from runoff from the land surface. Human activities can affect runoff: parking lots, shopping centers, buildings, roads, and other constructions reduce the infiltration of water into the ground, producing more runoff. An increase in runoff can also result from the removal of vegetation, grading, and the construction of drainage networks. Flooding frequently occurs in urban areas because of the increased runoff resulting from human actions.

Soil is a mixture of water, air, mineral, and organic materials. Although the content of soil varies in different locations and is constantly changing, there are three main components of **soil**: these components give soil its texture (Table 5-2). The three main mineral-based components are **sand, silt,** and **clay**. **Sand** is the largest particle in soil; sand does not hold many nutrients. **Silt** particles are smaller than sand but larger than clay. **Silt** feels smooth and powdery when dry; when set, it feels smooth and not sticky. **Clay** is the smallest of particles; it is smooth when dry and sticky when wet. Clay holds nutrients well. Clay soil takes in and holds more water than does sand or loam; its **absorption level** is, therefore, higher, and it has less runoff because of its high absorption capabilities.

Table 5-2. Composition of Soil

Categories Of Soil	Sand Content	Silt Content	Clay Content
Sand	90%	10%	0%
Silt	10%	90%	0%
Clay	20%	30%	50%

Competency 21: Knowledge of Earth and Space

Four test items relate to this competency.

Skill One

Identify the Components of Earth's Solar System and Compare Their Individual Characteristics

The solar system is the sun and its nine orbiting planets. The sun, composed of hydrogen, has a mass 750 times that of all the planets combined. The names of the planets in order from the sun are Mercury, Venus, Earth, Mars, Jupiter, Saturn, Uranus, Neptune, and Pluto. Rocky, metallic materials primarily compose the innermost planets of Mercury, Venus, Earth, and Mars; hydrogen, helium, and ices of ammonia and methane compose the outermost planets of Jupiter, Saturn, Uranus, Neptune, and Pluto. Composed largely of hydrogen gas, Jupiter—a giant, half-formed sun—is an exception among the planets.

Many of the planets have satellite moons, including Earth (1), Mars (2), Jupiter (8), and Pluto (2). Saturn has the distinguishing feature of rings. Both the Earth and Venus have significant atmospheres. Jupiter has a giant red spot.

To express distances from the sun, an accepted measurement is the **astronomical unit (AU)**, with 1 AU equal to the distance from the sun to Earth. The planet closest to the sun is Mercury at 0.39 AU, and the planet farthest from the sun is Pluto at 39.4 AU.

Skill Two

Demonstrate Knowledge of Space Exploration

During and after World War II, scientists began to study rockets and make great advances. They sent rockets—often containing instruments, cameras, and recording devices—to greater heights than ever before. Next, scientists experimented with keeping rockets in space for extended periods. The nations involved in space exploration, primarily the United States and Russia, hoped to learn more about space, observe Earth from a different perspective, set up weather satellite stations in space, establish sky laboratories, and prepare for the possibility of warfare in space. In the course of setting and accomplishing these goals, the two nations learned the importance of cooperation to success.

The launching of the Soviet space satellite *Sputnik* on October 4, 1957, created fear that America was falling behind technologically. *Sputnik* was the first satellite to travel in space around Earth. Although the United States launched *Explorer I* on January 31, 1958, the concern continued. In 1958, Congress established the **National Aeronautics and Space Administration (NASA)** to coordinate space research and development. In another important action, Congress passed the National Defense Education Act to provide grants and loans for education. The explosion of *Pioneer 0* and the failure of *Pioneer 1* and *Pioneer 3* to reach escape velocity heightened concern among Americans. At last, in 1959, the *Pioneer 4* reached solar orbit.

Both the Union of Soviet Socialist Republics (USSR; now the Commonwealth of Independent States) and the United States continued with their space exploration programs. The United States launched *Ranger 7* on July 31, 1964, to send back pictures from the moon. In January 1966 the USSR's *Luna 9* managed to achieve a soft landing on the moon and send pictures from the surface. The United States followed that lead the following April with the soft landing of *Surveyor 1* on the lunar surface. Four months later, America's *Lunar Orbiter 1* orbited the moon, photographed the far side, and landed on command.

The USSR and the United States continued to compete in space exploration, focusing on the moon and Venus. The *Mariner 5* flew by Venus's surface (June 14 to November 1967), studied the Venusian magnetic field, and discovered that the atmosphere was 85 percent to 99 perce)nt carbon dioxide.

On December 24, 1967, Frank Borman, James A. Lovell Jr., and William Anders made 10 orbits of the moon. They became the first people to fly around the moon and return. Their success was followed by explorations of Mars (*Mariner 6* and *Mariner 7*) and manned lunar orbits. Then on July 20, 1969, two men (Neil A. Armstrong and Edwin E. Aldrin Jr.), left their ship, *Apollo 11,* which had launched from the Kennedy Space Center four days earlier, to walk on the moon and gather samples.

Apollo 12 was another successful manned lunar landing for the United States in November 1969. The nation held its breath, however, in April of the following year when an explosion destroyed the power and the propulsion systems of the command service module of the *Apollo 13*. James A. Lovell Jr., Fred W. Haise Jr., and John L. Swigert Jr. used the lunar module as a lifeboat and safely returned to Earth. Other successful manned lunar landings for the United States followed in early 1971 (*Apollo 14*), the summer of 1971 (*Apollo 15*), and April 1972 (*Apollo 16*). It was the USSR, however, that landed the first spacecraft on another planet; the *Venera 7* landed on Venus on December 15, 1970. Japan, the USSR, and the United States continued their flybys and orbits of the planets and even explored comets and the sun.

One important result of space exploration occurred on May 26, 1973, when America established *Skylab*, its first space station, and manned it for 171 days. Another major achievement was the space weather satellite that the United States established in 2000. IMAGE is the first weather satellite to study the global response to changes in the solar wind by Earth's magnetosphere. In January 2006, the return capsule from the rendezvous with comet P/Wild 2 returned to Earth with samples from the comet. For budgetary reasons, NASA has curtailed many of its programs, but NASA scientists still believe much exploration of our solar system remains and is worth doing.

Skill Three

Identify the Phases of the Moon and the Moon's Effect on Earth

The moon is a satellite of Earth; the moon orbits the Earth at the rate of one revolution every 29½ days.

Although it is the second brightest heavenly body, the moon does not give off its own light. Rather, it reflects the sun's light. The amount of lighted moon we see on Earth changes, however. When the moon is becoming brighter, it is waxing. When the moon is growing less bright, it is waning. These changes in the amount of the lighted surface that is visible are the **phases** of the moon.

When the moon is between Earth and the sun, the dark side of the moon is turned toward Earth. It is difficult to see the moon from Earth; this phase has the name **new moon**. As the moon revolves around Earth (west to east), a little more of the lighted side is visible from Earth. The part of the moon that is visible is crescent-shaped; this is the **crescent moon**. About a week after the crescent moon, about one-half of the moon is visible. This is the **half moon (first quarter)**. Almost all the moon is visible a few days later. This phase is the **gibbous moon**.

About two weeks after the new moon, almost all the lighted side of the moon is visible from Earth. At this phase—the **full moon phase**—the Earth is between the sun and the moon. After the full-moon phase, the moon moves to its **half-moon phase (last quarter)**. The phases of the moon begin again and repeat.

When Earth blocks sunlight from reaching the moon, it creates a shadow on the moon's surface, known as a **lunar eclipse**. If the moon blocks sunlight from hitting Earth, a **solar eclipse** is created.

The moon exerts a **gravitational pull** on Earth. This pull causes **tides**, or periodic changes in the ocean depths.

Skill Four

Identify Earth's Orbital Pattern and Its Effect on the Seasons

Earth revolves around the sun. The axis of Earth is tilted at a 23½-degree angle, and the axis always points toward the North Star (Polaris). It is the tilt and revolution about the sun that causes the seasons. **It is not** the distance from the sun that causes the seasons. In fact, the Northern Hemisphere is closer to the sun in the winter—not in the summer.

The Northern Hemisphere experiences **summer** when the Northern Hemisphere tilts toward the sun. Summer begins in the Northern Hemisphere on June 21, when the rays of the sun shine directly on the area. The rays of the sun are stronger and cover a smaller part of this surface of Earth in the summer. In the summer, therefore, the Northern Hemisphere has hot surface temperatures and, because of the tilt of Earth, more hours of sunlight than darkness. This means that the longer direct rays of the sun last longer in the summer.

When the Northern Hemisphere tilts away from the sun, the Northern Hemisphere experiences **winter**. Winter begins in the Northern Hemisphere on December 22. During this season, the days are shorter, fewer direct rays from the sun reach the Northern Hemisphere, and the hours of night are longer than in the summer.

When it is summer in the Northern Hemisphere, it is winter in the Southern Hemisphere. When it is winter in the Northern Hemisphere, it is summer in the Southern Hemisphere. In the **fall** and **spring**, Earth is not tilted toward or away from the sun; is the Earth's tilt is somewhere between being toward or away from the sun. The days and nights have an almost equal number of hours in the spring and fall. The Northern Hemisphere has equal days and nights at the **vernal equinox** (March 21) and at the **autumnal equinox** (September 23). Earth's orbital pattern and its tilt toward the sun, again, results in the season.

Competency 22: Knowledge of the Processes of Life

Six test items relate to this competency.

Table 5-3. Required Activities of Living Things

Activity	Description
Food getting	Procuring the food needed to sustain life by eating, absorption, or photosynthesis
Respiration	Exchanging of gases
Excretion	Eliminating wastes
Growth	Increasing in size over part or all of a life span
Repair	Repairing damaged tissue
Movement	Willfully moving a portion of a living thing's body, or channeling growth in a particular direction
Response	Reacting to events or things in the environment
Secretion	Producing and distributing chemicals that aid digestion, growth, metabolism, etc.
Reproduction	Making new living things similar to the parent

Skill One

Compare and Contrast Living and Nonliving Things

Biology is the study of living things. A specific set of life activities at some point in a normal life span differentiate living things from nonliving things. Table 5-3 describes the activities that define life.

It is important to note that living things *must*, during a typical life span, be able to perform *all* these activities. It is quite common for nonliving things to perform one or more of these activities (e.g., robots can move, respond, and repair; and crystals can grow).

A **cell** is the basic structural unit of living things. In a living thing, a cell is the smallest component that can, by itself, be considered living. Plant cells and animal cells, though generally similar, are distinctly different because of the unique plant structures, cell walls, and chloroplasts.

Skill Two

Distinguish Among Microorganisms

Bacteria are single-celled living organisms. They can reproduce by themselves and do so by duplicating. They do not need a host for survival. Bacteria are responsive to antibiotics.

A **virus** is smaller than one cell. It lives and multiplies within a cell for survival; therefore, a virus is **intracellular** and not a living thing. Antibiotics intended to kill living things are not effective against viruses. The only way to treat a person with a virus is to provide supportive therapy that may help the body fight off the virus. The only way to protect a person against viruses is through vaccines. Vaccines help the body build up antibodies against viruses. Vaccines are not available for every virus, however, and do not cure viruses. Some biologists believe that a virus is a living organism; they believe that the virus has a protein coat surrounding strands of nuclear material.

Protozoans are one-celled living organisms. Protozoans can live inside or outside a cell. Although most antibiotics are not effective against protozoans, some protozoans are susceptible to antibiotics.

Skill Three

Differentiate Structures and Functions of Plant and Animal Cells

A **cell** is the basic structural unit of living things and the smallest unit that can, by itself, be considered living. Plant cells and animal cells, though generally similar, are distinctly different because of the unique plant structures, cell walls, and chloroplasts. Figure 5-1 illustrates the structures of animal and plant cells.

Several smaller structures called **organelles**, make up cells. Cell fluid, or cytoplasm, surrounds organellas. Table 5-4 lists the functions of several cell structures.

Skill Four

Identify the Major Steps of the Plant Physiological Processes of Photosynthesis, Transpiration, Reproduction, and Respiration

Cells perform several chemical processes to maintain essential life activities. The sum of these necessary chemical processes is **metabolism**. Table 5-5 lists the processes related to metabolism and the organelles involved.

Cells need to move materials into their structures to get energy and to grow. The cell **membrane** allows certain small molecules to flow freely across it. This flow

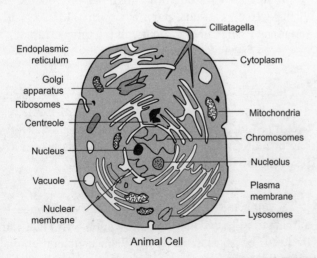

Animal Cell

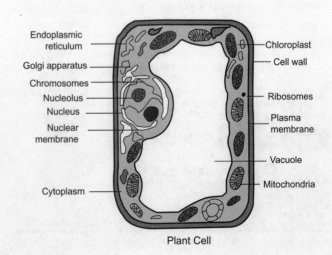

Plant Cell

Figure 5-1. Typical Animal and Plant Cells

Table 5-4. Cell Structures and Their Functions

Organelle	Function
Cell membrane	Controls movement of materials into and out of cells
Cell wall	Gives rigid structure to plant cells
Chloroplast	Contains chlorophyll, which enables green plants to make their own food
Cytoplasm	Comprises the cytosol and organelles but not the nucleus; a jellylike substance within a cell
Mitochondrion	Liberates energy from glucose in cells for use in cellular activities
Nucleus	Directs cell activities; holds DNA (genetic material)
Ribosome	Makes proteins from amino acids vacuole stores materials in a cell

Table 5-5. Processes of Cell Metabolism

Process	Organelle	Life Activity
Diffusion	Cell membrane	Food getting, respiration, excretion
Osmosis	Cell membrane	Food getting, excretion
Phagocytosis	Cell membrane	Food getting
Photosynthesis	Chloroplasts	Food getting
Respiration (aerobic)	Mitochondrion	Provides energy
Fermentation	Mitochondrion	Provides energy

of chemicals from areas of high concentration to areas of low concentration is **diffusion**. **Osmosis** is diffusion of water across a semipermeable membrane. The cell membrane may engulf and store particles too large to pass through the cell membranes in vacuoles until the

digestion of the particles. This engulfing process is called **phagocytosis**.

All cells need energy to survive. Sunlight energy can be made biologically available During photosynthesis sunlight energy is converted to chemical energy and **becomes biologically available**. Photosynthesis occurs in the **chloroplasts** of green cells. **Chlorophyll**, the pigment found in chloroplasts, catalyzes (causes or accelerates) the photosynthetic reaction that turns carbon dioxide and water into glucose (sugar) and oxygen. Sunlight and chlorophyll are necessary for the reaction to occur. Chlorophyll, because it is a catalyst, is still available after the reaction and is accessible for repeated use.

The term **respiration** has two distinct meanings in the field of biology. As a life activity, respiration is the exchange of gases in living things. As a metabolic process, respiration is the release of energy from sugars for use in life activities. All living things get their energy from the digestion (respiration) of glucose (sugar). Respiration may occur with oxygen (aerobic respiration) or without oxygen (anaerobic respiration, or fermentation). Most often the term *respiration* refers to aerobic respiration. Aerobic respiration occurs in most plant and animal cells.

Fermentation occurs in yeast cells and other cells in the absence of oxygen. Fermentation by yeast produces the alcohol in alcoholic beverages and the gases that make yeast breads rise and have a light texture.

Reproduction is a process whereby organisms or living plant or animal cells produce offspring. Inherited characteristics and environmental conditions may impose growth limitations on individual plants. In plants, reproduction may be either sexual or asexual.

Asexual plant propagation, also known as vegetative reproduction, is the method by which plants reproduce without the union of cells or nuclei of cells. The product of asexual plant propagation is genetically identical to the parent. Asexual propagation takes place either by **fragmentation** or by special asexual structures. An example of fragmentation is growing new plants from cuttings.

Sexual plant propagation almost always involves seeds produced by two individuals: male and female. Most plant propagation is, in fact, from seed, including all annual and biennial plants. Seed **germination** begins when a sufficient amount of water is absorbed by the seed, precipitating biochemical changes that initiate cell division.

Water is essential for plant life. The plant needs the water to make food, among other uses. A plant usually takes in more water than it needs. To get rid of excess water, the stomata of the leaves allow the water to pass out as water vapor. This evaporation of water from the plant is **transpiration**.

Skill Five
Identify the Structures and Functions of Organs and Systems of Animals, Including Humans

Not all cells are alike. Cells that perform different functions differ in size and shape. A group of the same kind of cells is a **tissue**. A group of the same kind of tissues working together is an **organ**. Examples of animal organs are the brain, stomach, heart, liver, and kidneys. A group of organs that work together to accomplish a special activity is a **system**. The complex organism of the human body is made up of several organ systems.

Bones, cartilage, and ligaments compose the **skeletal system**. The area where two or more bones come together is a joint. Cartilage, which reduces friction in the joint, often covers bone surfaces in a joint. Ligaments are connective tissues that hold bones together. The human skeleton consists of more than 200 bones; ligaments connect the bones at joints. Contractions of the skeletal muscles, to which the bones are attached by tendons, bring about movements. The nervous system controls muscular contractions.

The **muscular system** controls movement of the skeleton and movement within organs. There are three types of muscle: striated (voluntary), smooth (involuntary), and cardiac, and tendons attach muscles to bone. Skeletal muscles work in pairs. The alternating contractions of muscles within a pair cause movement in joints.

The **nervous system** has two divisions: the somatic, allowing voluntary control over skeletal muscle, and the autonomic, or involuntary, controlling cardiac and glandular functions. Nerve impulses arising in the brain, carried by cranial or spinal chord nerves connecting to skeletal muscles cause voluntary movement. Involuntary movement occurs in direct response to outside stimulus. Involuntary responses are **reflexes**. Various nerve terminals, which are **receptors**, constantly send impulses to the central nervous system. As discussed in Chapter 4, there are three types of receptors:

Exteroceptors. Pain, temperature, touch, and pressure receptors

Interoceptors. Internal environment receptors

Proprioceptors. Movement, position, and tension receptors

Each receptor routes nerve impulses to specialized areas of the brain for processing.

Food supplies the energy required for sustenance of the human body. The **digestive system** receives and processes food. The digestive system includes the mouth, esophagus, stomach, large intestine, and small intestine.

The **excretory system** eliminates wastes from the body. Excretory organs include the lungs, kidneys, bladder, large intestine, rectum, and skin. The lungs excrete gaseous waste. The kidneys filter blood and excrete wastes, mostly in the form of urea. The bladder holds liquid wastes until their elimination through the urethra. The large intestine absorbs water from solid food waste, and the rectum stores solid waste until its elimination. The skin excretes waste through perspiration.

The **circulatory system** is responsible for internal transport in the body. The system includes the heart, blood vessels, lymph vessels, blood, and lymph. The **immune system** is important for health and indeed life. The body defends itself against foreign proteins and infectious microorganisms by means of a complex dual system that depends on recognizing a portion of the surface pattern of the invader. The human body generates lymphocytes and antibody molecules to destroy the invader molecules.

The **respiratory system** performs the essential process of respiration. In humans, respiration involves the expansion and contraction of the lungs. Some animals, however, make use of gills and other means of respiration. The **reproductive system** is essential for the continuance of life in animals and in humans.

Skill Six
Identify the Major Steps of the Animal Physiological Processes

The expansion and contraction of the lungs produces the essential process of **respiration** in humans. In the lungs, oxygen enters tiny capillaries, where it combines with hemoglobin in the red blood cells; the capillaries help carry the red blood cells to the tissues. At the same time, carbon dioxide passes through capillaries into the air contained within the lungs. Inhaling draws air that is higher in oxygen and lower in carbon dioxide into the lungs; exhaling forces air from the lungs that is high in carbon dioxide and low in oxygen. Some animals, however, make use of gills and other means of respiration.

Reproduction is the process whereby living plant or animal cells or organisms produce offspring. In almost all animal organisms, reproduction occurs during or after the period of maximum growth. Reproduction in animals is either asexual or sexual.

Asexual animal propagation occurs primarily in single-celled organisms. Through the process of **fission**, the parent organism splits into two or more daughter organisms, thereby losing its original identity. In some instances, cell division results in the production of buds that arise from the body of the parent and then later separate to develop into a new organism identical to the parent. A reproductive process in which only one parent gives rise to the offspring is asexual reproduction. The offspring produced are identical with the parent.

Sexual animal propagation results from sperm uniting with ova for fertilization. The primary means of this kind of reproduction are insemination (copulation between a male and female vertebrate) and cross-fertilization (the depositing of ova and sperm in water at some distance from each other, most commonly by fish).

Digestion is the process of receiving and processing food. Food supplies the energy required for sustenance of the human body. The digestive system receives and processes food. The digestive system includes the mouth, stomach, large intestine, and small intestine. Digestion begins when mastication, or chewing, breaks down the food physically and mixes it with saliva. Next, the stomach chemically breaks down food; the gastric and intestinal juices continue to break down the food. Thereafter, the mixture of food and secretions makes its way down the alimentary canal by peristalsis, the rhythmic contractions of the smooth muscle of the gastrointestinal system. The small intestine absorbs nutrients from food, and the large intestine absorbs water from solid food waste.

The **excretory system** eliminates wastes from the body. Excretory organs include the lungs, kidneys, bladder, large intestine, rectum, and skin. The lungs excrete gaseous waste. The kidneys filter blood and excrete wastes, mostly in the form of urea. The bladder holds liquid wastes until their elimination through the urethra. The large intestine absorbs water from solid food waste, and the rectum stores solid waste until its elimination. The skin excretes waste through perspiration.

The **immune system** is important for health and indeed life. The body defends itself against foreign proteins and infectious microorganisms by means of a complex dual system that depends on recognizing a portion of the surface pattern of the invader. The human body generates lympthocytes and antibody molecules to destroy the invader molecules.

Circulation is the internal transportation system of the body. The circulatory system includes the heart, blood vessels, lymph vessels, blood, and lymph. The heart is a muscular four-chambered pump. The upper chambers are the atria and the lower chambers are the ventricles. In the circulatory system, the heart pumps blood through the right chambers of the heart and through the lungs, where it acquires oxygen. From there it is pumped back into the left chambers of the heart. Next, it is pumped into the main artery, the aorta, which branches into increasingly smaller arteries. Beyond that, blood passes through tiny, thin-walled structures called capillaries. In the capillaries, the blood gives up oxygen and nutrients to tissues and absorbs a metabolic waste product containing carbon dioxide. Finally, blood completes the circuit by passing through small veins, joining to form increasingly larger vessels until it reaches the largest veins that return it to the right side of the heart.

Competency 23: Knowledge of How Living Things Interact with the Environment

Four test items relate to this competency.

Skill One

Identify Parts and Sequences of Biogeochemical Cycles of Common Elements in the Environment

The amount of oxygen and carbon dioxide in the air remains the same as a result of the **carbon dioxide–oxygen cycle**. To make food, green plants take in carbon dioxide from the air. The waste product that plants give off in the process is oxygen. When animals breathe in oxygen to digest their food, they give off carbon dioxide as a waste product.

The amount of nitrogen in the air remains constant as a result of the **nitrogen cycle**. Nitrogen-fixing bacteria live in the soil and in the roots of legumes (e.g., beans, peas, and clover). Bacteria change the nitrogen in the air (that plants cannot use) into nitrogen materials that plants can use. After animals eat plants, they give off waste materials that contain nitrogen.

Bacteria in the soil act on the animals' waste materials and on dead plants and animals. Bacteria break down the waste materials and dead remains and make the remaining nitrogen available. **Nitrifying bacteria** return the nitrogen to the soil for plants to use. **Denitrifying bacteria** change some of the nitrogen in the materials

and the dead plants and animals to free nitrogen, which returns to the air and continues the nitrogen cycle.

The air today is different in composition from what it was at the time of the formation of the earth. Large amounts of hydrogen and helium characterized the composition of air millions of years ago. As the earth cooled, water vapor, carbon dioxide, and nitrogen became components of the air. When the water vapor condensed, carbon dioxide and nitrogen remained. The plants reduced the amount of carbon dioxide in the air and increased the amount of oxygen in the air. Today pollution is changing the composition of the air.

Skill Two

Identify Causes and Effects of Pollution

Any material added to an ecosystem that disrupts its normal functioning is **pollution**. Typical pollutants are excess fertilizers or other waste materials that factories and manufacturing plants dump into the water or onto the ground, and industrial emissions into the air. Pollution generates large quantities of gases and solids every day. Smokestacks, chimneys, and car exhaust pipes are some sources of air pollutants. Some pollutants are simply annoying, but others are dangerous to the health of those exposed. Continuous exposure to polluting materials discharged into the air can cause lung diseases or aggravate existing health conditions. Bomb tests (hydrogen and atom) add radioactive particles to the air, and if more testing occurs, the particles may accumulate and become increasingly dangerous.

If weather conditions prevent the distribution of polluting materials, air pollution can become increasingly severe. When cold air is next to the ground with warm air lying on top, polluting materials remain concentrated in one area. The warm air acts as a blanket, and the cold air remains stationary. This is a **temperature inversion.**

A recent phenomenon (since 1950) is **acid rain**— a form of precipitation that contains high levels of sulfuric or nitric acid. Acid rain occurs when sulfur dioxide and nitrogen oxide combine with moisture. Acid rain can pollute drinking water, damage plant and animal life and even erode monuments and buildings. Among the primary causes of acid rain are forest fires, volcanic eruptions, and the burning of certain fuels, including the gas used to power automobiles.

Skill Three

Identify the Living and Nonliving Factors That Influence Population Density

Our surroundings form a complex, interconnected system in which living organisms exist in relationship with the soil, water, and air. Earth's inhabitants are in states of continual change or dynamic equilibrium.

Ecosystem is the term for all the living and nonliving things in a given environment and how they interact. Scientifically literate individuals are aware of their surroundings, the interdependence of every aspect of those surroundings, and the impact of human activities. Mutualistic and competitive relationships also exist among the organisms in an ecosystem, determining how organisms rely on each other and how they exist in competition and conflict with each other.

Energy transformations are the driving force within an ecosystem. Many organisms obtain energy from light. For example, light drives the process of photosynthesis in green plants. Solar energy also provides the heat that cold-blooded animals require. Another source of energy for organisms is other organisms, including other plants and animals.

When one source of energy is depleted in an ecosystem, many organisms must shift their attention to other sources of energy. For example, a bear derives energy primarily from berries, fish, or nuts, depending on the season. The **energy pyramid** for an ecosystem illustrates these relationships and identifies the organisms most dependent on the other organisms in the system. Higher-order organisms cannot survive for long without the other organisms beneath them in the energy pyramid.

The availability of adequate food within an ecosystem helps to explain the system's functioning, the size of an animal's territory, or the effects of a single species preying too heavily on organisms above it in the food chain.

Ecosystems change over time, both from natural processes and from the activities of man. Scientifically literate individuals can identify how the environment changes, how those changes impact the organisms that live there, and what the differences are between long-term and short-term variation. Natural succession occurs when one community replaces another—for example, the colonies of fungus that grow, thrive, and are replaced by different colonies on rodent droppings held under ideal conditions.

Ecology is the study of the relationship between living things and their environment. An **environment** is all the living and nonliving things surrounding an organism. A **population** is a group of similar organisms, like a herd of deer. A **community** is a group of populations that interact with one another. A pond community, for example, consists of all the plants and animals in the pond. An **ecosystem** is a group of populations that shares a common pool of resources and a common physical or geographical area.

Each population lives in a particular area and serves a special role in the community. This combination of defined role and living areas is the concept of **niche**. The niche of a pond snail, for example, is to decompose materials in ponds. The niche of a field mouse is to eat seeds in fields. When two populations try to fill the same niche, **competition** occurs. If one population replaces another in a niche, **succession** occurs. Succession is the orderly and predictable change of communities as a result of population replacement in niches.

Skill Four

Analyze Various Conservation Methods and Their Effectiveness in Relation to Renewable and Nonrenewable Natural Resources

Conservation is the practice of using natural areas without disrupting their ecosystems. This definition suggests **interdependence** among people and the world and **practices** or actions to improve or maintain the world. These practices must recognize that there are both renewable and nonrenewable resources. **Renewable resources** are those that can endure indefinitely under wise practices; examples of renewable resources are soil, vegetation, animals, and fresh water. On the other hand, it is possible to deplete **nonrenewable natural resources**; examples of nonrenewable resources are coal, oil, and metals.

Laws to manage the mining and drilling of natural resources and laws on the use and recycling of natural resources are among the efforts to conserve nonrenewable resources. A major component of conservation is educating people on the importance of managing nonrenewable natural resources.

Renewable resources are dependent on each other—they are **interdependent**. Crops cannot grow in the soil without water. Bees play a part in the life cycle of many plants, and animals help provide carbon dioxide for photosynthesis. Forests management ensures a supply of wood, a steady flow of water, and protection of the soil against wind and water damage. Enforced laws governing hunting and fishing are effective in ensuring that game and other animals can renew themselves and continue their role in the web of life.

In the 1930s, the Civilian Conservation Corps enrolled 250,000 men aged 18 to 24 from families on relief; these men went to camps where they worked on flood control, soil conservation, park development, and forest projects under the direction of the federal government. Conservation is not a new concept, but it is still not as effective as it could be. Again, education is the key.

Competency 24: Knowledge of the Nature and History of Science

Five test items relate to this competency.

Skill One

Demonstrate Knowledge of Basic Science Processes

The **scientific method** is *not* a specific set of steps requiring rigorous adherence whenever a question arises involving the knowledge and techniques of science.

Rather, the scientific method is a process of observation and analysis; it can help to develop a reliable, consistent, and objective representation and understanding of our world. The scientific method is useful for answering many but not all questions. The processes that make up the scientific method are observing and describing, formulating hypotheses, making predictions based on the hypotheses and testing those predictions (experimenting), and deriving conclusions.

Scientists—and students—must carefully observe their surroundings and consider the data available. The scientific method is best applied to situations in which the experimenter can control the variables, eliminate or account for all extraneous factors, and perform repeated independent tests that change only one variable at a time. Students and scientists must be able to find similarities and differences and to classify the information, objects, plants, and animals accordingly.

Scientists and students must be able to communicate and share their observations and their questions. This communication can be either written or oral. To communicate data clearly enough to foster sound interpretation, the students or scientists can present the information in various formats: graphs, diagrams, maps, concrete models, role playing, and charts, among others.

Quantifying the results of observing and classifying is part of effective communication. Effective quantifying requires scientists and students to select appropriate tools for observing, describing, measuring, comparing, and computing. The **microscope** and **telescope** extend the range of human observation beyond human physiology. The **spectroscope** separates visible light into its component colors, and the **spectrophotometer** measures the selective absorption of those colors as a function of some property of a solution, solid, or gas. **Mathematics** is a tool to evaluate the results of the observations and to organize large quantities of data into averages, ranges, and statistical probabilities. The fundamental uncertainty of the measuring device, however, limits all quantifying and measurements.

The simple assumption that calculations on measurements cannot generate results that are more precise than the measurements themselves produces the concept of significant figures. For example, if you divide one pie into three pieces, a calculator might report that each piece represents 0.33333333 (depending on the number of digits on the calculator display). You know from experience that there will be crumbs left in the pan and that no amount of care in dividing the pieces will result in the level of accuracy the calculation suggests. Every measuring device is presumed to be accurate to the smallest of the subdivisions marked, and every measurement with such a device should include one additional estimated digit. For example, when you use a ruler with one centimeter as its smallest division, you should record your measurements to the tenth of a centimeter, the smallest measured digit plus one estimated digit.

The following terms are an indispensable part of the vocabulary of scientific experimentation:

Observation. Sensing some measurable phenomenon.

Organization. Relating parts to a coherent whole.

Experimental. Testing the effect of an independent variable on a dependent variable in a controlled environment.

Inference. Deducing a conclusion from a measurement or observation that is not explicit to either. For example, you can infer that a classroom of 30 students has 16 girls if you know that there are 14 boys. Here one makes the inference by subtracting 14 from 30.

Prediction. Stating the outcome of an experiment in advance of doing it. An example would be predicting that a plot of velocity versus time for a freely falling object will be a straight line.

Skill Two

Apply Knowledge of the Integrated Science Processes of Manipulating Variables, Defining Operationally, Forming Hypotheses, Measuring (Metric) and Graphing, and Interpreting Data

As stated in Skill One of Competency 7, the **scientific method** is a process of observation and analysis

for developing a reliable, consistent, and objective representation and understanding of the world. The scientific method is useful for answering many but not all questions and is not a regimen that the user must follow rigorously.

In planning experiments, the scientist or student is generally attempting to test a hypothesis. A **hypothesis** is an educated guess about the relationship between two variables; the hypothesis is subject to testing and verification. The outcome of the test in a well-designed experiment answers questions suggested by the hypothesis in a clear and unambiguous way.

In planning and conducting an experiment, the scientist or student must (1) identify relevant variables, (2) identify necessary equipment and apparatus for measuring and recording the variables, (3) eliminate or suppress any other factors that could influence measured variables, and (4) decide on a means of analyzing the data obtained. In conducting experiments, it is imperative that questions raised by the hypotheses be testable and that the data recorded be sufficiently accurate and repeatable.

Testable Questions

An example of a testable question might be, "Does mass have an influence on acceleration for bodies subjected to unbalanced forces?" This question is testable because it identifies specific variables (force, mass, and acceleration) that can be measured and controlled in any experiment that seeks to establish a connection. Thus, testable questions must specify variables that are subject to both measurement and control.

Data Representation

One way of representing data is in a graphical form, which shows the plotting of raw data. The independent (controlled) variable is usually on the x-axis of a graph (horizontal), and the dependent variable is usually on the y-axis (vertical). Graphs can either be linear (a straight line) or nonlinear. Graphs can display equations and can aid in finder analyses. Use of a graphing calculator and specialized software can facilitate both the data collection and data representation in graphical form. The x-y plots, however, are not the only means of data representation. Charts, diagrams, and tables can display results also.

Interpreting Experimental Results

Sometimes experimental work involves measurements that do not directly yield the desired variable value but interpretation or reduction can provide the desired value. The experimental approach in that case is indirect.

An example is the measurement of acceleration of gravity, or *g*, a fundamental gravitational constant. One common method is to measure displacement over time for a falling body. Reducing (interpreting) the resulting graph yields a plot of velocity versus time. In turn, reducing (interpreting) this plot yields a plot of acceleration versus time;one can read the acceleration of gravity, *g*, from the plot. Inherent to each of the reductions was finding the slope (the rise divided by the run) at various points, which is a mathematical technique that enables interpretation of the results.

Variables

The science fair project is a common tool for instruction in the scientific method. Many formal and informal sources, often Web based, provide lists of suggested science fair topics, but not all the topics are experiments. For the youngest students, it is appropriate and useful for the focus to be on models and demonstrations—for example, a model of the solar system, a volcano, or a clay cross section of an egg. Older students should move to true experiments that focus on identifying a testable hypothesis and controlling all experimental variables but the one of interest.

It is possible to elevate many projects that begin as models or demonstrations to experiments. One can develop a demonstration on how windmills work into an experiment when the student adds quantitative measurements of one variable against variations in one other variable; the student must hold all other variables constant. For example, using an electric fan, the student could measure the number of rotations per minute as a function of the fan setting (low, medium, or high). Then, while keeping the fan setting constant, the student could conduct several experiments that vary the number of fans, the sizes of fans, or the shapes of fans and measure the rotational speed at each variation.

Collecting and Presenting Data

Scientifically literate individuals have detailed and accurate content knowledge that is the basis of their scientific knowledge. They do not try to recall every detail of that knowledge but build conceptual frameworks on which they can add both prior knowledge and new learning. From this framework of facts, concepts, and theories, scientifically literate individuals can reconstruct forgotten facts and use them to answer new questions not previously considered. Scientifically literate individuals are lifelong learners who ask questions that scientific knowledge and techniques can answer.

Reasons for communicating scientific information to nonscientific audiences are to inform, guide policy, and influence the practices that affect all of society. Text, tables, charts, figures, pictures, models, and other representations that require interpretation and analysis can present the information. Scientifically literate individuals can (1) read and interpret these representations and (2) select appropriate tools to present the information they gather.

Experimentation is the basis of science, but individuals cannot gain all knowledge daily from first principles. Scientifically literate individuals base their information on existing knowledge and are aware of the sources, accuracy, and value of each source. Not every source is equally reliable, accurate, or valid. Classroom teachers should use trusted educational sites such as those that their state board of education sponsors.

Scientifically literate individuals can evaluate critically the information and evidence they collect and the conclusions or theories to which that information and evidence leads. Such analysis incorporates an understanding of the limitations of knowledge in general and, more specifically, the limitations of all measurements and information based on the quality of the experimental design. Scientifically literate individuals can evaluate claims for scientific merit, identify conflicting evidence and weigh the value and credibility of conflicting information. They can also recognize that even using scientific knowledge, valuing the contributions of other cultures, and employing other ways of knowing, including art, philosophy, and theology, will not enable them to answer every question.

Measurement

Measurement includes (1) estimating and converting measurements within the customary and metric systems; (2) applying procedures for using measurement to describe and compare phenomena; (3) identifying appropriate measurement instruments, units, and procedures for problems involving length, area, angles, volume, mass, time, money, and temperature; and (4) using a variety of materials, models, and methods to explore concepts and solve problems involving measurement.

Skill Three

Apply Knowledge of Inquiry Approaches to Learning Science Concepts

Effective teachers use not one but many methods and strategies to enhance student learning. Teachers choose various strategies to meet both content- and student-driven purposes. If the purpose is to investigate current problems without specific answers, the teacher might choose an inquiry lesson.

To engage in **inquiry**, a student must be able to acquire information from a variety of resources and then organize and interpret that information. Inquiry may involve designing and conducting investigations that lead to the identification of issues to analyze. Inquiry is essential for examining single topics or integrated sciences.

Scientists and students should understand the principles and processes of scientific investigation and how to promote the development of scientific knowledge and skills, including the use of scientific thinking, inquiry, reasoning, and investigation. Effective science-teaching methods include the following:

- Determining the type of scientific investigation (e.g., experimentation, systematic observation) that best addresses a given question or hypothesis.

- Demonstrating a knowledge of considerations and procedures, including safety practices, related to designing and conducting experiments (e.g., formulation of hypotheses; use of control and experimental groups; and recognition of variables being held constant, those being manipulated, and those responding in an experiment).

- Recognizing how to use methods, tools, technologies, and measurement units to gather and organize data, compare and evaluate data, and describe and communicate the results of investigations in various formats.

- Understanding concepts, skills, and processes of inquiry in the social sciences (e.g., locating, gathering, organizing, formulating hypotheses) and how to promote students' development of knowledge and skills in this area.

There are two main categories of teaching methods: deductive and inductive. Using **inductive** methods, teachers encourage students to study, conduct research, collect and analyze data, and then develop generalizations and rules based on their findings. During inductive lessons, the teacher first introduces a hypothesis or concept, and using inferences from the data, the students develop generalizations.

Inquiry or discovery lessons are inductive in nature. An inquiry lesson starts with a thought-provoking question for which students are interested in finding an explanation. After posing the question, the teacher guides students in brainstorming a list of what they already know about the topic and then categorizing the information. Students use these categories as topics for group or individual research. The lesson typically ends with students presenting their research to the class (a form of deductive learning, as discussed later).

A teacher who uses inquiry strategies takes the role of a facilitator who plans outcomes and provides resources for students as they work. In their role as inquirers, students must take responsibility for their own learning by planning, carrying out, and presenting research and projects.

Some advantages of inductive lessons are that they generally require higher-level thinking by both teacher and students, and they usually result in higher student motivation, interest, and retention. They are also more interesting to the teacher, who deals with the same concepts year after year. Disadvantages of inductive lessons include the need for additional preparation by the teacher, access to numerous resources, and additional time for students to conduct research.

Generally, the more planning, predicting, and preparing the teacher does for an inductive lesson, the more successful the students will be. This does not mean that the teacher must use only tightly-structured or rigid activities but that the effective teacher tries to predict students' responses and their reactions to them. Teachers do not have to purchase as many additional resources with the Internet, computerized bibliographic services, interlibrary loans, and CD-ROMs with all types of information. Because inductive, research-oriented units require more class time, subject-area teachers must work together to determine which concepts are essential for students to understand, which are nonessential, and which ones they can omit.

An effective teacher plays many roles in the classroom. The teacher who uses lecture is in the role of information provider. Students listening to the lecture are usually in the passive, often inattentive, role of listener. The teacher who uses cooperative strategies takes on the roles of a coach, encouraging students to work together, and a facilitator, smoothing students' way through activities and providing resources. Students in a collaborative role must learn social and group roles as well as content to accomplish learning tasks. The teacher who listens to student discussions and presentations and evaluates student papers and projects assumes the role of an audience providing constructive feedback. Students in a discussion role must prepare carefully and think seriously about the topic under discussion.

Using **deductive** methods, teachers present material through lectures, and students teach each other through presentations. In deductive lessons, the teacher first teaches the generalizations or rules and then develops examples and elaboration to support the generalizations or rules. Deductive thinking often requires students to

make assessments based on specific criteria that they or others develop.

The **mastery lecture** is a deductive method whereby the teacher presents information to students. New teachers are especially attuned to lecturing because that is the usual mode of instruction in college classes. An advantage of the mastery lecture is that teachers can present large amounts of information in an efficient manner; however, teachers should avoid giving students too much information through lectures. To be most effective, mastery lectures should be short, usually no more than 10 or 15 minutes, and frequently interrupted by questions to and from students. The effective teacher uses both lower- and higher-level questions during lectures.

Teachers must supplement lectures with an array of visual materials that will appeal to both visual and auditory learners. Putting words or outlines on the board or a transparency is very helpful; however, this is still basically a verbal strategy. Drawings, diagrams, cartoons, pictures, caricatures, and graphs are attention-getting visual aids for lectures. Teacher drawings need not be highly artistic, merely memorable. Often a rough or humorous sketch will be more firmly etched in students' minds than elaborate drawings. Using a very simple sketch is a better means of teaching the most critical information than is a complicated drawing. The major points stand out in a simple sketch; the teacher can add details once students understand the basic concepts.

Teachers should also be careful to instruct students on how to take notes while listening to a speaker; note-taking skills will be useful during every student's career, whether educational or professional. Teachers can teach note-taking skills by showing students notes or an outline from the lecture they are about to hear, writing notes or an outline on the board or on a transparency while they are presenting the information, or using a projector to display the organization while they speak. This activity requires careful planning by the teacher and will result in a more organized lecture. A well-structured lecture is especially helpful for sequential learners, who like organization. It also helps random learners develop organizational skills. A web, map, or cluster is a more creative method of connecting important points in a lecture or a chapter. The effective teacher will use both systems and teach both to students in order to provice students a choice of strategies.

Skill Four

Identify the Appropriate Laboratory Equipment for Specific Activities

Scientific experimentation uses a variety of tools or instruments. These include microscopes, graduated cylinders, scales, voltmeters, ammeters, meter sticks, and micrometers. In general, these devices measure mass, volume, length, and voltage.

Inherent to the proper use of measuring devices is recognition of their limitations in accuracy and precision. Precision concerns the number of places that can be reliably read from any measurement device. For example, a meter stick is generally good to three-place precision, the first two places being determined by scale markings and the third place determined by the estimated position between scale markings.

Scientific process skills, including the proper and accurate use of laboratory equipment, are an important component of science education. Instruction is necessary to guide the effective use of each measurement or observationl tool: rulers, microscopes, balances, laboratory glassware, and so forth. As students develop their measuring skills, they move from simple observations and conformist activities to using these tools to find answers to questions that they develop themselves.

Skill Five

Identify State Safety Procedures for Teaching Science, Including the Care of Living Organisms and the Accepted Procedures for the Safe Preparation, Use, Storage, and Disposal of Chemicals and Other Materials

Florida rules and regulations on safety procedures for teaching science may change. It is important to review the current rules and regulations. The rules listed here are current as of November 2005.

Handling Living Organisms Safely

- Live vertebrates are not appropriate for elementary students, except for observation.

- Students should not touch or handle reptiles; the animals may carry *Salmonella* bacteria.

- Some plants may be toxic.

- Students and teachers should wash hands after handling plants and animals.

- Both students and teachers should use gloves when handling animals that might bite or scratch.

- Children should not bring pets to class. If the students do bring animals, only the owner should handle the animal.

- The teacher and students should treat animals with care and respect.

- The teacher should remember that animal hair, scales, and waste can cause allergies.

- Plant and animal specimens from ponds, ditches, canals, and other bodies of water may contain microorganism that can cause disease. Suppliers can provide cultures that are safer.

- Set aquariums on stable furniture out of traffic ways. Be sure electrical accessories are plugged into a GFI (ground-fault interrupter) outlet.

- The teacher should ensure that thermostats and heating elements are working correctly.

Safe Preparation, Use, Storage, and Disposal of Chemicals and Other Materials

- Teachers and students must wear eye-protective devices when using hazardous materials in activities such as treating materials with heat, tempering a metal, working with caustic or explosive materials, and working with hot liquids or solids.

- School boards should give out or sell plano glasses to students. visitors, and teachers.

- Fire extinguishers must be available to classrooms.

- Fire blankets must be available in each classroom where a fire hazard exists.

- Fire alarms, detector systems, lighting, and electrical outlets should be in operating condition, even in storage rooms.

- The teachers should make sure that the outlets are grounded.

- Outlets within two feet (six feet for new constructions) of water supplies must have a ground fault circuit interrupt protection device.

- All buildings must have ground fault circuit interrupt protected outlets.

- The teacher should make sure that there are no stapled, spliced, or taped extension cords.

- The teacher should make sure that there are no extension cords run through or over doors, windows or walls.

- Extension cords must be in only continuous lengths.

- Adapters must be UL-approved.

- Adapters must have overcurrent protection with a total rating of no more than 15 amperes.

- Every classroom with electrical receptacles at student workstations should have an emergency, unobstructed shut-off switch within 15 feet of the teacher's workstation.

An elementary classroom usually does not contain hazardous chemicals or equipment. The following rules are necessary for classrooms where hazardous chemicals are present.

- Rooms where students handle materials or chemicals that are harmful to human tissue must have a dousing shower, a floor drain, and an eye-washing facility.

- Rooms where students handle materials or chemicals that are harmful should have emergency exhaust systems, fume hoods, and fume hood supply fans that shut down when emergency exhaust fans are operating.

- There must be lockable cabinets for hazardous materials or hazardous chemicals.

Monitoring Guide for Chemical Storage

- Secured chemical storage areas with lock and key and limited student access are necessary.

- There must be clearly posted signs prohibiting student access.

- Chemical storage areas must be well lighted to avoid mix-ups.

- The floor space must not be cluttered.

- The area must be inventoried at least once a year. The chemical labels and the inventory list must have the name, supplier, date of purchase of mix, the concentration, and the amount available.

- Chemicals must be purged at least once a year.

- Chemical storage must use recognized storage patterns and chemicals should be in compatible groups—not in alphabetical order.

- There must be materials to dilute and absorb a large-volume (one-gallon) chemical spill.

- Certain chemicals that present a potential for explosion are not permitted in science classrooms or storage areas. These chemicals include benzoyl peroxide, phosphorus, carbon disulfide, ethyl ether, disopropyl ether, picric acid, perchloric acid, potassium chlorate, and potassium metal.

- Some chemicals present a danger as a human carcinogen and are not allowed in science classrooms or chemical storage areas. These include arsenic compounds, benzene, chloroform, nickel powder, asbestos, acrylonitrile, benzidine, chromium compound, ortho-toluidine, cadmium compounds, and ethylene oxide.

Tables 5-6 and 5-7 are checklists for teachers to use to ensure that their classrooms are safe places for students to learn science.

Through active, hands-on activities, science instruction is richer and more meaningful. From simple observations and activities at early grades to detailed controlled experiments at higher grades, students who do science to learn science understand science better. While students are engaged in the process of discovery and exploration, the teacher must be engaged in protecting students' health and safety. The hazards vary with the discipline; thoughtful planning and management of the activities will significantly reduce the risks to students. In all cases, students must use appropriate personal hygiene (hand washing) and wear personal protective equipment (goggles, gloves) while engaged in laboratory or field activities.

Table 5-6. Checklist for Chemical Storage in Schools According to Florida Law

Ventilation	
Temperature	
Heat detector	
Secured	
Well illuminated	
Uncluttered floor	
Chemical inventory	
Chemicals purged annually	
Chemicals grouped correctly	
Labels on chemical containers	
Flammables cabinet	
Spill protection	
No explosives	
No carcinogens	

Table 5-7. Checklist for Science Classrooms According to Florida Law in 2006

Fire extinguisher	
Fire blanket	
Gas cut-off (present and labeled)	
Water cut-off (present and labeled)	
Electrical cut-off (present and labeled)	
Dousing shower	
Floor drain	
Eye-washing facility	
Room ventilation adequate	
Fume hood	
Grounded receptacles	
Ground fault circuit interrupters within 2 inches of water	
No flammable storage	
Face protection that meets standards	
Face protection in sufficient numbers	

Substitution of less hazardous materials whenever possible is a high priority. For example, in the physical sciences, teachers can (1) replace mercury thermometers with alcohol or electronic ones, (2) replace glass beakers and graduated cylinders with durable polyethylene containers, and (3) eliminate or reduce the use of hazardous chemicals. In the earth sciences, (1) rocks and minerals used in class should not contain inherently hazardous materials, (2) students should not taste the minerals, and (3) teachers should dispense reagents like hydrochloric acid used for identification of carbonate minerals from spill-proof plastic containers. In the life sciences, the teacher should give special care to (1) safe practices with sharp objects, (2) the safe handling of living organisms, and (3) the care and use of microscopes. The teacher should discourage experiments or activities involving the collection or culture of human cells or fluids; the teacher should make sure to use proper sterilization procedures to prevent the growth or spread of disease agents. When possible, field activities like visiting nature centers or other outdoor facilities or museums can bring valuable enrichment to the science curriculum in all disciplines. However, the teacher must assume responsibility for planning and implementing activities that not only increase students' learning but also maintain their health and safety.

Competency 25: Knowledge of the Relationship of Science and Technology

Two test items relate to this competency.

Skill One

Identify the Interrelationship of Science and Technology

Technology is, loosely, the application of science for the benefit of mankind. From science and technology our society now has the knowledge and tools to understand some of nature's principles and to apply that knowledge for some useful purpose. Few would debate the benefits of the wheel and axle, the electric light, the polio vaccine, and plastic. The benefits of science and technology become more complicated to evaluate, however, when discussing the applications of gene splicing for genetically modified foods, of cloning, of nuclear energy to replace fossil fuels, or the application of atomic energy to weapons of mass destruction. Science can tell us how to do something, not whether we should.

Scientific literacy helps us participate in the decision-making process of our society as well-informed and contributing members. Real-world decisions have social, political, and economic dimensions, and scientific information is often used to both support and refute those decisions. Understanding that the inherent nature of scientific information is unbiased and based on experimental evidence that can be reproduced by any laboratory under the same conditions can help us all make better decisions, recognize false arguments, and participate fully as active and responsible citizens.

The science teacher should incorporate the effective use of technology to plan, organize, deliver, and evaluate instruction for all students. Moreover, the effective

From the pencil and field notebook to modern instruments in the laboratory, science involves the tools of observation, measurement, and computational analysis. The microscope and telescope each extend the range of human observation beyond human physiology. The spectroscope separates visible light into its component colors, and the spectrophotometer measures the selective absorption of those colors as a function of some property of a solution, solid, or gas. Mathematics is a tool to evaluate the results of the observations and to organize large quantities of scientific data into averages, ranges, and statistical probabilities.

Compared to the goose quill, the modern mechanical pencil is a dramatic advancement in the technology of written communication. However, neither the quill nor the pencil replaces the critical, analytical, and creative act of authorship. Many technological tools are available to assist in the observation, collection of data, analysis, and presentation of scientific information, yet none replaces the role of the investigator who must

formulate meaningful questions that the tools of science can answer. The bases of modern science include the application of technology. Some of these technological tools should be available in the classrooms to give students the opportunity to participate firsthand in the process of inquiry and discovery.

The technology that students and teachers employ in this context must facilitate student learning, remove barriers to understanding, and not create new barriers to delay and obscure the scientific concepts that we want to teach.

Scientific process skills, including the proper and accurate use of laboratory equipment, are an important component of science education. Instruction is necessary to guide the effective use of each measurement or observational tool: rulers, microscopes, balances, laboratory glassware, and so forth. As students develop these skills, they move from simple observations and confirmatory activities to using these tools to find answers to questions that they develop themselves. Through active, hands-on activities, science instruction becomes a richer and more meaningful experience. From simple observations and activities at early grades, through detailed controlled experiments at higher grades, students who do science to learn science understand science better.

Computers

When computers first appeared in classrooms, their initial purpose was to give students drill and practice in simple skills, like arithmetic operations. As the technology advanced, programmers developed elaborate systems of practice and testing, with management capabilities that enabled teachers to track student achievement.

Drill-and-practice software is useful for students who need considerable practice in certain skills because it gives students immediate feedback; they need not wait for the teacher to correct their papers to know if they chose the correct answers. Many of these programs have game formats to make the practice more interesting. One disadvantage of drill-and-practice software is they generally they are limited to lower-level learning.

Skill Two

Identify the Tools and Techniques of Science and Technology Used for Data Collection and Problem Solving

Reliability of data obtained in any experiment is always a concern. At issue is reproducibility and accuracy. In general, data must be **reproducible** not only by the experimenter but others using the same apparatus. Results that cannot be reproduced are suspect. **Accuracy** is often limited by the measurement instruments used in the experiment. Any reported numerical result must always be qualified by the uncertainty in its value. A typical example might be a voltage meter readout of 3.0 volts. If the meter has a full-scale reading of 10 volts and accuracy of 3 percent, the actual value could be anywhere between 2.7 volts and 3.3 volts.

Computer programs and on-line resources make data collection and problem solving easier and more accurate. Neither, however, replaces the critical, analytical, and creative investigator. Likewise, although many tools are available to assist in observation, data collection, analysis, and the presentation of scientific information, no technology can replace the role of the investigator who must formulate meaningful questions, perform critical analyses, analyze the information, reach meaningful conclusions, and recognize how to use scientific tools effectively. Technology provides the tools on which all of modern science is based. By making some of these tools available in their classrooms, teachers give students the opportunity to participate firsthand in the process of inquiry and discovery.

Technology used in the classroom must facilitate student learning, remove barriers to understanding, and prevent the creation of new barriers that might delay or obscure the scientific concepts being taught. Scientific process skills, including the proper and accurate use of laboratory equipment, are an important component of science education. Instruction is necessary to guide the effective use of each measurement or observational tool: rulers, microscopes, balances, laboratory glassware, telescopes, and so forth. As students develop these skills, they move from simple observations to using these tools to find answers to questions that they develop themselves.

Competency 26: Knowledge of Technology Processes and Applications

Four test items relate to this competency.

Skill One

Identify the Purposes and Functions of Common Computer Software

Many software tools for the computer are extremely useful for teachers and students. **Word-processing programs** allow students to write, edit, and polish written assignments like term papers and research reports. Most programs include spelling and grammar checkers that enable students to enhance the quality of their written assignments. With most word processors, students can put the text into columns topped by headlines of varying sizes to produce periodic newsletters. For example, a class could write a series of reviews of scientific articles and add information about class activities in science. **Desktop publishing programs** allow students to integrate text and graphics to produce more complex publications like a school newspaper or yearbook.

Databases are like electronic file cards; they allow students to input data and then retrieve it in various formats and arrangements. For example, science students can input data about an experiment on temperature, volume, or time, for instance, and then manipulate the data to call out information in a variety of ways. The most important step in learning about databases is dealing with huge quantities of information. Students need to learn how to analyze and interpret the data to discover connections among isolated facts and figures and how to eliminate unnecessary information.

On-line databases are essential tools for research. Students can access databases related to science and other subject areas. Through electronic mail (e-mail), students can communicate over the computer with scientific associations and scientists from around the world. Massive bibliographic databases are also available to help students and teachers find the resources they need. Many of the print materials can then be borrowed through interlibrary loan. The use of electronic systems can geometrically increase the materials available to students.

Spreadsheets are similar to teacher grade books. Rows and columns of numbers can be linked to produce totals and averages. Formulas can connect information in one cell (the intersection of a row and column) to another cell. Teachers often keep grade books on a spreadsheet because of the ease in updating information. Once formulas are in place, teachers can enter grades and have completely up-to-date averages for all students. Some spreadsheet programs also include charting functions that enable teachers to display class averages on a bar chart and thus provide a visual comparisons of performance among various classes. Several stand-alone graphing and charting software packages are also available.

Students can use spreadsheets to collect and analyze numerical data, sort the data in various orders, and create various types of graphs, bars, columns, scatters, histograms, and pies to convey information. Students can use the graphics they produce to enhance written reports or in multimedia presentations.

Computer-Assisted Instruction

In the past, teachers used computers strictly for **drill-and-practice** lessons, giving students an alternative to printed worksheets to practice simple skills like arithmetic operations. Programmers have since developed many elaborate systems of practice and testing and have often included management systems that enabled teachers to keep track of students' progress. Drill-and-practice software is still useful for students who need to hone basic skills. One advantage of these programs is the immediate feedback they provide to students; students know at once if they chose the correct answer and do not have to wait for the teacher to correct their papers. Many drill-and-practice programs have game formats to make students' practice sessions more interesting. One disadvantage of the programs is they generally require low-level thinking skills.

Tutorials are a step above drill-and-practice programs because they also include explanations and information. A student makes a response, and the program branches to the most appropriate section based on the student's answer. Tutorials help with remedial work but can also be useful for instruction in any topic—for instance, the metric system. Improved graphics and sound allow non-English-speaking students to listen to correct pronunciation while viewing pictures of words. Tutorials should supplement, not supplant, teacher instruction.

Selection and Evaluation Criteria

The effective teacher uses criteria to evaluate audiovisual, multimedia, and computer resources. The first thing to look for is congruence with lesson goals. If the software does not reinforce student outcomes, the teacher should not use it in the classroom no matter how flashy or well-crafted it is. A checklist for instructional computer software could include appropriate sequence of instruction, meaningful student interaction with the software, learner control of screens and pacing, and motivation. Other factors to consider are the ability to control sound and progress, effective use of color, clarity of text and graphics, and potential as an individual or group assignment.

In addition to congruence with curriculum goals, the teacher needs to consider students' strengths and needs, their learning styles or preferred modalities, and their interests. Formal and informal assessment can help to determine students' needs. Most standardized tests include an indication of which objectives the student did not master. Students can receive help in mastering these objectives from computer or multimedia aids.

Skill Two
Identify Ways Technology Can Be Used by Students to Represent Understanding of Science Concepts

Graphics or paint programs allow students to produce freehand drawings of cells viewed under a microscope, plants or animals observed outdoors, or other images. Students can use these programs to illustrate classroom presentations, individual research projects, or multimedia presentations. Many word-processing programs have some graphic functions.

Simulations or **problem-solving programs** provide opportunities for students to have experiences that otherwise could not take place in the classroom because of time or cost constraints or simply because the classroom setting does not allow for such experiences. For example, several simulation programs available give students the opportunity to "dissect" animals. Using the program rather than attempting to perform real dissections saves time and materials, is less messy, and allows students who might be reluctant to dissect real animals to learn about them. Other software might explore the effects of weightlessness on plant growth, a situation that would be impossible to set up in the classroom lab.

Students may even teach each other through multimedia presentations. Students in an inquirer role often take responsibility for their own learning by planning, carrying out, and presenting research and projects.

Skill Three
Identify Telecommunications Terminology, Processes, and Procedures

Communication across long distances is **telecommunication**. Telecommunications can include computer networking, telephones, telegraphy, radio, television, and data communications. These forms of communication can play an important role in science classroom instruction.

A telecommunication system has several components. The **transmitter** changes or encodes the message into a physical result called the **signal**. The transmission **channel** is the medium the message travels through and may modify or degrade the signal while it is on its way from the transmitter to the receiver. The **receiver** recovers and decodes the message within certain limits. The human eye, ear, and brain examples of receivers.

Telecommunications can be in point-to-point, point-to-multipoint, or broadcast form. Broadcast

telecommunications is a particular form of point-to-multipoint telecommunication that goes directly from the transmitter to the receivers without passing through intermediaries. A telecommunications engineer analyzes both the statistical properties of the message and the physical properties of the transmission medium or the line. The engineer must design effective encoding and decoding mechanisms.

When designing a system, a telecommunications engineer must consider the human sensory organs (especially the eyes and ears) and both the physiological and psychological characteristics of human perception. The engineer must research defects in the signal and determine the ones that are tolerable and will not significantly impair the hearing or the viewing of the message. Economics also plays an important role in establishing a telecommunications system.

In a conversation between two people, the message is the information that one person wants to communicate to the other. The sender's brain, vocal cords, larynx, and mouth produce the sounds (speech). The spoken result—the sound waves or the pressure fluctuations in the air—is the signal.

The channel is composed of the air carrying sound waves and all the properties of the sound, including echoes, reverberations, and ambient noise. All channels have noise. An important aspect to consider in the channel is the **bandwidth**. A telephone, with its low bandwidth channel, cannot carry all the audio information that the sender transmits in the conversation. Some distortion and irregularities in the speaker's voice that would not be as evident in normal speech can occur in a telephone conversation.

The receiver is the listener's auditory system, including the ear and the auditory nerve, and the brain, which receives and decodes auditory signals. The receiver must also filter out background noise. Devices like radios and telephones that come between the speaker and the listener can distort the original vocal signal.

The fax machine and email have definitely affected written communications in the new century.

Skill Four

Demonstrate Knowledge of Legal and Ethical Practices as They Relate to Information and Technological Systems

Computer technology is becoming a larger focus of the classroom. In addition to being part of the curriculum, educators frequently used computers as aids in storing information and developing lesson materials. Computer software programs fall under the domain of copyright law. As defined by federal law, computer programs, such as word-processing software or graphic design programs, are "a set of statements or instructions to be used directly in a computer in order to bring about a certain result" (P.L. 96-517, Section 117).

Often a teacher will make a backup, or copy of a computer program, in case the original disk containing the program becomes damaged. A backup copy is not considered an infringement of the copyright law as long as the teacher follows these rules when creating the backup:

1. The teacher must make the new copy or adaptation only to facilitate use of the program in conjunction with the machine.

2. The new copy or adaptation must be for archival purposes only, and all archival copies must be destroyed in the event that continued possession of the computer program should cease to be rightful.

3. If a teacher prepares or adapts any copies of a software program, the educators may not lease, sell, or otherwise transfer without the authorization of the software copyright owner the copies; sharing or borrowing copies of a computer program is illegal.

4. The educator should not use the original disk to install a program on more than one machine unless the owner has a license to do so from the computer software company. If unsure about the licensing status of a computer program, the teacher can check with the media specialist or school administrator.

Teachers are role models for their communities; therefore, all educators must be aware of the software copyright law and be in complete compliance.

Protecting Children Accessing the Internet

As teachers discover more ways to use the Internet as an instructing tool, they must also be mindful of the Children's Internet Protection Act (CIPA) and the Neighborhood Children's Internet Protection Act (N-CIPA), which passed Congress in December 2000. Both were part of a large federal appropriations measure (P.L. 106-554).

The legislation established three basic requirements that schools and libraries using the Internet must meet, or be "undertaking actions" to meet:

1. The school or library must use blocking or filtering technology on all computers with Internet access. The blocking or filtering must protect against access to certain visual depictions, including obscenity, child pornography, and materials harmful to minors. The law does not require the filtering of text.

2. The school or library must adopt and implement an Internet safety policy that addresses the key criteria, including
   a. access by minors to inappropriate matter on the Internet and the Web;
   b. the safety and security of minors when using electronic mail, chat rooms, and other forms of direct electronic communications;
   c. unauthorized access, including so-called hacking, and other unlawful activities by minors online;
   d. unauthorized disclosure, use, and dissemination of personal identification information regarding minors; and
   e. measures designed to restrict minors' access to materials harmful to minors.

3. The school or library must hold a public meeting to discuss the Internet safety policy; specifically, the law requires that the school or library "provide reasonable public notice and hold at least one public hearing or meeting to address the proposed Internet safety policy."

Technology and Copyright Issues

Copyright is a form of protection provided by the laws of the United States (U.S. Code, Title 17) to the authors of "original works of authorship," including literary, dramatic, musical, artistic, and certain other intellectual works. The protection applies to both published and unpublished works. It is illegal for anyone to violate any of the rights provided by copyright law to the owner of the copyright. These rights, however, are not unlimited. Sections 107 through 121 of the **1976 Copyright Act** establish limitations on the rights of copyright holders. In some cases, these limitations are specified exemptions from copyright liability. One major limitation is the doctrine of fair use, which is given a statutory basis in Section 107 of the 1976 Copyright Act.

The **fair use doctrine** allows limited reproduction of copyrighted works for educational and research purposes. In general, a teacher can copy a chapter from a book; an article from a periodical or newspaper; a short story, short essay, or short poem, whether or not from a collective work; and/or a chart, graph, diagram, drawing, cartoon, or picture from a book, periodical, or newspaper. For a classroom, a teacher can make multiple copies (not to exceed the number of students in the class) as long as the copying meets the following tests of brevity, spontaneity, and cumulative effect, and as long as each copy includes a notice of copyright.

Brevity generally refers to a poem of 250 words or less or a prose passage less than 2,500 words. **Spontaneity** refers to the need for a teacher to use a work without undertaking the normal time to obtain copyright permission. Finally, the **cumulative effect** test refers to copying material for only one class, from a single author, and no more than nine times during a term. Regarding the fair use of multimedia materials, it is generally acceptable for teachers and students to incorporate others' work into a multimedia presentation and display or perform it as long as the presentation is for a class assignment. It is suggested that educators be conservative in the use of such materials, using only small amounts of others' works and not making unnecessary copies of such works. Teachers can access the December 2005 fair use regulations at *http://www.copyright.gov/fls/fl102.html*. Complete information about copyright can be found at the official Web site of the United States Library of Congress Copyright Office: *http://www.loc.gov/copyright*.

Teachers must monitor student performance to ensure that the students uphold the highest standards of academic integrity are upheld; teachers should not allow cheating. In addition, teachers should make students aware of the consequences and penalties for academic dishonesty (including plagiarism).

The Internet

The Internet and the World Wide Web are having a profound effect on students and teachers alike. This very powerful learning tool is a source of information. By linking computers around the world, the Internet serves as a network of networks. From 500 hosts in 1983, the Internet has rapidly grown to about 30 million hosts in 1998, and the number continues to mount at a dramatic rate. At the start of the twenty-first century, an estimated 360 million people had access to the Internet.

Oscar Wilde once argued that there is no such thing as a good or bad book and that a work of literature exists apart from issues of morality. One can apply the same logic to the Internet. Like any source of information, students can use the Internet well or badly. The amount of information available is so enormous that people often have difficulty finding the exact information they are seeking. Moreover, with no form quality control to filter the massive amounts of information posted on the Internet, much of what is available is inaccurate, misleading, or false. Consequently, teachers must instruct students in using critical thinking skills to judge the accuracy of information, look for evidence and substantiation of claims, and separate facts from opinions. Educators and parents alike must also be concerned about the appropriateness of the information accessed by students; a wide range of material is available and some of it is unsuitable for children.

To safeguard children and provide some kind of quality control, many public schools use Internet filters. These tools limit access to unsuitable material; however, some of the filters do not discriminate adequately. Sometimes students can access questionable material and cannot access appropriate material. Teachers must carefully supervise students' use of this powerful resource.

The Internet offers many tools that classroom teachers will find valuable. Basically, teachers should be familiar with common Internet browsers (such as

Microsoft Explorer and Netscape) and popular search engines (such as Yahoo, Excite, Lycos, and Google) that make it possible to research any topic. Many Web sites offer teaching tips and tools, so teachers will want to investigate these and bookmark the ones that are most pertinent and reliable to their classrooms. Communicating with colleagues, parents, and even students is made convenient through e-mail.

The Internet, then, is a common tool for teachers and students of the twenty-first century. The Internet sites, however, are changing constantly; sites that are popular today may not be here tomorrow. However, the following sites have endured with teachers for many years:

• U.S. Department of Education: *http://www.ed.gov/*

• Education World: *http://www.education-world.com/*

• National Education Association: *http://www.nea.org/*

• Discovery Channel/Education: *http://school.discovery.com/teachingtools/teachingtools.html*

• Florida Department of Education *http://www.firn.edu/doe/sas/ftcehome.htm*

• TeachersFirst: *http://www.teachersfirst.com.*

References

Blough, Glenn O., and Julius Schwartz. 1969. *Elementary school science and how to teach it.* New York: Rhinehart and Winston.

Victor, Edward. 1975. *Science for the elementary school.* New York: Macmillan.

Chapter

Music, Visual Arts, Physical Education, and Health

Competency 27: Knowledge of Skills and Techniques in Music and Visual Arts

Six test items relate to this competency.

Skill One

Identify Appropriate Vocal Literature

Children's **vocal ranges** vary from one child to the next. However, Wassum found that 67% of first-grade children had a vocal range on one octave; 64% were able to sing as high as C_5 (C_4 is middle C), and 90% can sing as low as C_4. In sixth grade 98% of the singers had a vocal range of an octave or more; 52% could vocalize two octaves or more.

The voice ranges of girls and boys remain about the same until the boys' voices begin to change—usually, sometime during junior high. When selecting vocal literature (music for singing), the teacher must consider the age-appropriate range of the students and their vocal abilities.

The materials used for a quality music program in any grade should reflect various musical periods and styles, cultural and ethnic diversity, and a gender balance. The goal of a quality music program is to make students aware that music is both a part of and a reflection of many cultures and many ethnic groups. The teacher should provide and encourage students to sing, play, and listen to music of many cultural and ethnic groups.

The teacher should include diverse **styles** (basic musical languages) and **genres** (categories). Dividing music into categories is difficult. Styles are constantly emerging. Many songs include multiple genres. Nevertheless, the main groupings are classical, gospel, jazz, Latin American, blues, rhythm and blues, rock, country, electronic, electronic dance, electronica, melodic music, hip hop, rap, punk, reggae, contemporary African music, and dub.

Skill Two

Identify Developmentally Appropriate Singing Techniques

The voices of singing children should sound as if they are "floating out" rather than forced. To help students achieve the preferred sound, the teacher might ask students to imagine trying to support a feather fluttering a few inches from their mouths.

Posture is an important part of good singing. Children should stand or sit erectly, not slouch, as they sing. An excellent way to attain the desired straight spine is to have the students stand. Standing helps to allow for sufficient breath.

Inhaling the **breath** should mimic directing it to the area just below the rib cage; as the child takes in a breath, the wall of the child's abdomen should move out. The expansion that is necessary for the inhalation should not come from raising the shoulders or from puffing up the chest; instead, the inhalation should result from the diaphragm moving toward the waistline. Because the flow of air should be steady, the child's mouth should remain open. The child should not try to manipulate the voice box; the idea is not to sing *with* the larynx but to sing *through* the larynx (Hoffer 1982). Whether standing or sitting, children should make sure that both feet are flat on the floor. When standing, children should be certain that their hands are down at their sides or clasped loosely in front; children should not clasp their hands tightly in the back or place their hands in their pockets.

The **tone** is the musical sound of the voice; it may describe the quality of the musical sound. For instance, one might say that someone sings with a "nasal tone," a "thin tone," or a "full tone." A synonym for tone is *timbre*.

The voice of the average child is similar to the voice of the adult in terms of range but not quality. The teacher should not encourage children to imitate the heavier and fuller quality of the mature adult voice. Children can sing high, but like the adult, tension results when the pitch is too high.

The average voice range is from around middle C to F (fifth line); D and E-flat (fourth line and space) are, however, far more comfortable. For the beginner, a very comfortable range is from E-flat (first line) to B-flat or C.

Skill Three

Identify Correct Performance Techniques for Rhythmic and Melodic Classroom Instruments

Music is the arrangement of sounds for voice and musical instruments and, like dance, requires training and repetitive practice. Making music is a basic experience. Mothers sing to their babies. Children beat sticks together, make drums, and sing during their play. Adults whistle or sing along with tunes on the radio. Sound and music naturally draw people; music is an important part of culture, religious practice, and personal experience for all people. Some people become professional musicians, whereas others whistle, sing, or play for their own enjoyment and nothing more.

It is important that students have the opportunity to experience as many ways to make music as possible. It is through the acquisition of basic skills in singing and playing instruments that people grow in their ability to express themselves through music. As students develop skills, they are also exposed to basic musical concepts such as melody, harmony, rhythm, pitch, and timbre (tone). With experience, students come to make decisions about what is acceptable or not acceptable within a given cultural or historical context and thereby develop their own aesthetic awareness. Only a very small segment of society does not make music. These people would likely choose to make music if they could but are unable as a result of a physical impairment or personal choice (e.g., a vow of silence). Music making is a natural part of human experience.

There is a distinction between the study of simple instruments and the study of orchestral instruments. The child does not usually begin the study of orchestral instruments until the fourth or fifth grade; a music teacher—not the classroom teacher—gives instruction in orchestral instruments.

The instruments that the classroom teacher normally teaches include the **rhythmic instruments** (e.g., triangle, tambourine, blocks, and sticks); **melodic instruments** (e.g., melody bells and simple flutes); and **harmonic instruments** (e.g., chording instruments, like the autoharp).

Rhythmic Instruments

After the students have a chance to move with the music in the manner that the music suggests and after singing games and action songs, they may be ready to try rhythmic instruments. The students will need opportunities to experiment with triangles, tambourines, sticks, and blocks, among others, to experience the sounds they make; students might try striking the tambourine with the hand to get one sound and with the knee to get another, for instance. After this experimentation, the teacher and class will be ready to try something new.

If the teacher decides on the instruments the class will use, who will use them, and when, music instruction becomes a teacher-directed activity that can stifle the children's creativity. Superior to the teacher-directed approach is allowing the students to make decisions about what and when to play. For example, the teacher might write out a piece of music on a large sheet of paper and allow the students to draw pictures where they should play their instruments.

Another student-directed approach to music instruction is having students first listen to a piece of music and then allowing them to decide on the instruments they want to play and when it seems right to play them. This more creative approach is appropriate for young children who cannot read music or even for music readers who want to produce their own performance techniques. Upper-grade students can even try making their own instruments.

Melodic Instruments

Melodic bells are melodic instruments that the child strikes with a mallet. The child may use the bells before the flutes. The simple flutes include the trade names of Flutophone, Song Flute, and Tonette. Teachers usually include these melodic instruments with the music instruction at about the fifth grade. For most of the instruments, the right thumb supports the flute; to play the notes, the fingers cover the various holes. The use of the fingers to help attain the sounds varies from one instrument to the other. The melodic instruments are helpful to use as the children are learning to read music.

Harmonic Instruments

The wooden base of an autoharp (which is approximately rectangular in shape) has wire strings stretched across it. The child can press the wooden bars attached at right angles; when the child presses the bars and strums the wires, the instrument produces chords. Students can experiment with harmony using the autoharp. They will find that sometimes a variety of choices of chords "sound right" but that at other times only one choice works.

Skill Four

Read and Interpret Simple, Traditional, and Nontraditional Music Notation

Music notation is a way of writing music. Teaching students to use, read, and interpret music notation will heighten their enjoyment of music. Students can begin with **simple music notation**. For example, students might try listening to a simple melody and making dashes on the board or on their papers to indicate the length the notes are held. As they sing "Three Blind Mice," for instance, they would mark dashes of similar length for the words/notes *three* and *blind*.

With **traditional music notation**, the students use the lines and spaces on the staff. They observe that there are four spaces and five lines, for instance. They also notice that the appearance of the notes indicates the length and the placement of the notes on the staff indicates the various tones.

Nontraditional music notation is something that many students in the upper grades may have noticed in their books. In the South, for example, many of the hymnals use a nontraditional type of music notation called shape notes. Instead of the elliptical note head in the traditional notation, the heads of the notes are in various shapes to show the position of the notes on the major scale. Another nontraditional music notation is Braille notation.

Rhythm is the contrast among the various lengths of musical tones. For instance, in *The Star-Spangled Banner,* the rhythm is short, short, medium, medium, medium, long. To indicate the lengths of the tones, musical notation uses various types of notes and rests.

The sheet music uses simultaneous combinations of musical tones to indicate **harmony**. Harmony is the vertical aspect of the groups of notes. **Melody**, on the other hand, is the succession of the notes. Melody is the horizontal aspect of the notes. Sometimes the teacher may refer to the melody as the *tune*.

Skill Five

Select Safe and Developmentally Appropriate Media, Techniques, and Tools to Create Both Two-Dimensional and Three-Dimensional Works of Art

The art room is the scene for many activities. There should be one art room for every 400 to 500 elementary school students. At least 55 square feet of workspace—excluding storage and teacher workspace—per student is necessary for safety. The room should allow for individual seating arrangements as well as small-group and large-group arrangements. There should be areas for the teacher to lecture and display students' work; space for learning centers; and areas for drawing and painting, printmaking, creating computer graphics, working with ceramics, modeling, assembling crafts, and sculpting.

Ideally, the art room is near the service entrance to make deliveries easier. There should be both natural and artificial lighting in the room. Locked storage is necessary for hazardous materials. At least 45 square feet of space is essential for the kiln room, and venting is necessary.

Safety guidelines are critical, and following them is mandatory. Proper ventilation is essential, especially in the kiln room and in areas devoted to printmaking, ceramics, and spraying. Ease of cleanup is a requirement; sinks and surfaces must have durable, cleanable finishes (South Carolina Visual and Performing Arts Curriculum Framework Writing Team, 1993).

Skill Six

Identify Appropriate Uses of Art Materials and Tools for Developing Basic Processes and Motor Skills

Throughout the lower elementary grades, students should engage in drawing, painting, designing, constructing, crafts, sculpting, weaving, finger painting, and Styrofoam carving. In grades 3 through 5, students should continue to work with drawing, painting, designing, constructing, crafts, and sculpting and should start new techniques like printmaking, sponge painting, graphics, film animation, and environmental design. In the upper-elementary grades, students continue with the earlier activities and add jewelry making and intaglio.

Both large and small motor skills are involved in art activities. Larger motor skills might be involved in painting a mural on a cement-block fence than in painting a small clay figure.

Art materials for the elementary art program include scissors, wet and dry brushes, fabrics, wrapping papers, film, computers, clay, glue, Styrofoam, construction paper, crayons, beads, and much more (South Carolina Visual and Performing Arts Curriculum Framework Writing Team. 1993).

Competency 28: Knowledge of Creation and Communication in Music and Visual Arts

Six test items relate to this competency.

Skill One

Identify the Elements of Music and Ways They Are Used in Expressing Text; Ideas; Emotions; and Settings, Time, and Place

There are several elements of music:

Rhythm. The contrast among the various lengths of musical tones. For instance, in "The Star-Spangled Banner," the rhythm is short, short, medium, medium, medium, long.

Melody. The succession of the notes. Melody is the horizontal aspect of the notes. Sometimes the teacher may refer to the melody as the *tune.*

Form. The structure of the song, or the way that it is put together. Sometimes there is a refrain that is repeated; sometimes there is a chorus that is used after each verse.

Texture. The context in which simultaneous sounds occur. The sounds can be chords (harmony) or even counterpoint (concurrent melodies of equal importance).

Timbre or tone. The quality of the musical sound.

Dynamics. Refers to the volume or the loudness of the sound or the note. The two basic dynamic indications are *p* (for *piano,* meaning softly or quietly) and *f* (for *forte,* meaning loudly or strong).

These elements work together to express a text, ideas, certain emotions, settings, time, and place through music.

Skill Two

Demonstrate Knowledge of Strategies to Develop Creative Responses Through Music to Ideas Drawn from Text, Speech, Movement, and Visual Images

Skill Three

Demonstrate Knowledge of Strategies to Develop Creative Responses through Art to Ideas Drawn from Text, Music, Speech, Movement, and Visual Images

To respond creatively through art to text images, music and visual suggestions, and speech and movement ideas, students need a variety of techniques and media. This means that they must work with many art forms. Ideally, even the child in the earliest grades engages in drawing, painting, designing, constructing, crafts, sculpting, weaving, finger painting, and—to a limited extent—Styrofoam carving. In grades 3 through 5, students should work further with drawing, painting, designing, constructing, crafts, and sculpting and should start new techniques like printmaking, sponge painting, graphics, film animation, and environmental design. In the upper-elementary grades, students should have continued with the earlier activities/media/techniques and add jewelry making and intaglio.

Skill Four

Identify the Elements of Art and Principles of Design and Ways They Are Used in Expressing Text, Ideas, Meanings, and Emotions

Ideas, meanings, and human emotions are varied and numerous. To respond to these many stimulations, students must have knowledge of and be able to use many of the elements of art (the things that make up a painting, drawing, or design) and the basic principles of design (what one does with the elements of design). The basic principles follow:

Line. A linear mark from a pen or brush; the edge created where two shapes meet.

Color. Hue. There are three primary colors (red, yellow, blue); three secondary colors (green, orange, violet); tertiary colors (colors that fall between primary and secondary colors); and compound colors (colors containing a mixture of the three primary colors). In addition, there are complimentary colors (colors opposite each other on the color wheel) and saturated colors (colors around the outside of the color wheel).

Shape. A self-contained, defined area of a form (geometric or organic). A positive shape in a painting automatically results in a negative shape.

Form. A total structure; a synthesis of all the visible aspects of a structure or design; all the elements of a work of art independent of their meaning.

Texture. The surface quality of a shape. A shape's qualities: rough, smooth, soft, hard, and glossy. Texture can be physical (felt with the hand; e.g., a buildup of paint, layering, etc.) or visual (giving the illusion of texture; e.g., the paint gives the impression of texture, but the surface remains smooth and flat).

Balance. Similar to balance in physics. A large shape, for example, close to the center can be balanced by a smaller shape that is close to the edge; a large light-toned shape can be balanced on the surface by a small dark-toned shape.

Movement. A way of combining elements of art to produce the appearance of action; a representation of or suggestion of motion; implied motion.

Competency 29: Knowledge of Cultural and Historical Connections in Music and Visual Arts

Four test items relate to this competency.

Skill One
Identify Characteristics of Style in Musical Selections

Often, after listening to a piece of music, a person might be able to determine the specific artist by putting several clues together, as in a detective story. To help students reach this level of discernment, the teacher should expose them to diverse **styles** (basic musical languages) and **genres** (categories). Dividing music into categories is difficult. Styles are constantly emerging. Many songs include multiple genres. Nevertheless, the main groupings are as follows:

- Classical
- Gospel
- Jazz
- Latin American
- Blues
- Rhythm and blues
- Rock
- Country
- Electronic
- Electronic dance
- Electronica
- Melodic
- Hip hop
- Rap
- Contemporary African
- Punk
- Reggae
- Dub

Skill Two
Demonstrate Knowledge of How Music Reflects Particular Cultures, Historical Periods, and Places

Music is the arrangement of sounds for voice and musical instruments and, like dance, requires training and repetitive practice. Throughout most of history, music has been an outgrowth of a community or an ethnic group (**culture**) feeling the need to celebrate and is often linked to storytelling or poetry.

By having students listen to music from China, Japan, Germany, Australia, or Africa when they are studying those cultures, the teacher enriches students' learning experience and make it more memorable for them. Even more valuable for students is viewing live or videotaped performances of the music and dance of these cultures because often the performers dress in traditional costume with traditional instruments (sometimes very different from modern instruments). Seeing the costumes and the movement is an important part of understanding the culture.

In music, the system of tonal scales and preferences is often unique to a culture: for example, the Chinese prefer the pentatonic scale of five notes while the West has primarily used a scale of seven notes (eight with the repeated first note for an octave). Indian musical pieces use *ragas* (meaning "mood" or "color"), which are melodic patterns of five to seven tones. Indian compositions feature repetitive patterns and use scales whose octaves have 22 intervals, or steps.

Merely experiencing the music is not enough. The students must be able to recognize the music or art as part of its **historical context**; through discussion or written exercises, they must demonstrate an understanding of the music's place in the historical context and be able to note things that are common and things that are different from context to context—period to period, culture to culture, and so forth. The activities must be appropriate to the developmental age of the students.

For example, Joseph Haydn, Wolfgang Amadeus Mozart, and William Billings were composers of the late-eighteenth to early-nineteenth centuries. These composers used simple melodies in their works. However, Haydn and Mozart wrote many large works, like symphonies and operas, and Billings wrote short choral pieces. Students must be aware of these facts and then consider why more highly developed forms were preferred in the "Old World," while basic psalms and songs were more common in the American colonies. The obvious answer is that colonists did not have the time or the resources to encourage or produce larger musical works. However, the discussion could go further, depending on the sophistication of the students.

Historical Periods and Places

In the ancient world, Egyptian, Sumerian, and Hebrew cultures used song and such instruments as lyres, harps, drums, flutes, cymbals, and trumpets. The ancient Greeks accompanied the recitation of poetry with the stringed lyre,; Athenian drama was accompanied by The *aulos*, or double-piped oboe (an instrument used in the worship of Dionysus) often accompanied Athenian drama; between recited passages the audience often heard choral songs.

In the early Christian era (the late sixth century), Pope Gregory the Great often codified and arranged the **plainsong**, or unaccompanied religious chant, using early forms of music notation. This is the origin of **Gregorian chant**.

By the twelfth and thirteenth centuries, the important form of **polyphony**, which is the basis of the distinctive art music of the West, enabled supportive melodies to be added to the main chant. The Italian Benedictine monk Guido d'Arezzo invented the basic form of music notation, representing pitch through the use of a staff. The later Middle Ages saw the compostion of both religious and secular polyphonic music. Melodies and rhythms became more diversified.

During the Renaissance, with the resolution of many technical problems, the spirit of humanism and rationalism pervaded polyphonic music, and music became a mark of culture. There was more and more emphasis on secular music, dance, instrumental music ensembles, and on complex combinations of voices and instruments.

Baroque music of the seventeenth and early eighteenth centuries employed a greater complexity of melodies, forms, the beginnings of harmony, the use of colorful instrumental ensembles, and great drama and emotion. The new dramatic forms became popular entertainment. Other innovative forms included the oratorio, the cantata, the sonata, the suite, the concerto, and the fugue. Composers of some of the great works of baroque music included Johann Pachelbel, Antonio Vivaldi, Henry Purcell, George Frideric Handel (*The Messiah*), and Johann Sebastian Bach.

A clarity of form, logical thematic development, and strict adherence to sonata form marked the music of the classical period (the latter half of the eighteenth century). The greatest composers of the classical period were Ludwig van Beethoven, Franz Joseph Haydn, and Wolfgang Amadeus Mozart. Mozart's structurally exquisite works approach perfection of form while adding inventive melodic diversity. Mozart wrote 41 symphonies and 22 operas, including innovative works like *The Marriage of Figaro* and *The Magic Flute*.

The German composer Ludwig van Beethoven ushered in the romantic school of symphonic music. His symphonies and piano sonatas, concertos, and string quartets explode with dramatic passion, expressive melodies and harmonies, and complex thematic development. His most famous works are the Fifth and Ninth symphonies and the *Moonlight* sonata.

Much of the romantic music that followed was less formal and more expressive, often associated with grandiose concepts and literary themes and colorful instrumentation. Art songs, piano concertos and sonatas, and symphonic poems (which try to paint a musical picture or tell a story) became important forms for romantic composers. These included Frédéric Chopin (mainly piano music, some of which he called nocturnes); Franz Liszt (*Mephisto* Waltz, piano concertos); Richard Strauss (the orchestral piece *Don Juan*, the operas *Salome* and *Elektra*); and Felix Mendelssohn (four symphonies, incidental music to *A Midsummer Night's Dream*). Other important symphonic composers of the nineteenth century were Robert Schumann, Johannes Brahms, Pyotr Ilich Tchaikovsky, and Gustav Mahler. Throughout the century, musical development continued in the direction of a greater richness of harmony, a more varied use of musical instruments and orchestral color, and increased employment of *chromaticism* (the freedom to use tones not related to the key of the composition).

Other important influences in nineteenth-century music are the use of ethnic influences or folk melodies, music of a nationalistic vein, and popular songs—often linked to composers who were outstanding melodists and harmonic innovator. Composers who wrote in these styles include Giacomo Rossini (*The Barber of Seville, William Tell*); Georges Bizet (*Carmen*); Giuseppe Verdi (*Aida, La Traviata*); Giacomo Puccini (*La Boheme, Tosca*); and the Russians, including Modest Mussorgsky (*A Night on Bald Mountain*) and Nicholas Rimsky-Korsakov (*Scheherazade*).

Mussorgsky and Wagner's idiomatic and chromatic harmonies greatly influenced the French "impressionist" composers Claude Debussy (*Prelude to the Afternoon of a Faun*) and Maurice Ravel (*Mother Goose* Suite, *Bolero*). Debussy, Mussorgsky, and Wagner for the most part eschewed the traditional larger forms and wrote emotional, dramatic, and colorful sonatas and tone poems (one-movement orchestral pieces based on poems, novels, or other nonmusical sources); they used oriental tonalities and free rhapsodic forms freely. One of the great innovators in opera, Richard Wagner, sought to create a new form of music drama, using continuous music and relentless, swirling harmonies to underlie massive spectacle and recitative, or sung dialogue.

The concert music of the twentieth century increasingly sought to enlarge the boundaries of rhythm, form, and harmony; the music was seemingly parallel to the direction in the visual arts, moved away from traditional structure and melodic-harmonic connections with listeners; and shifted the emphasis more personal or intellectual experiments in abstraction. Thus, Igor Stravinsky, a composer who, during the years before World War I, broke apart rhythms and introduced radical harmonies in works like *Firebird* Suite, seems the musical equivalent of Pablo Picasso. He sought to use the new rhythms

and harmonies in more structurally clear, and less orchestrally dense, neoclassical pieces.

Ethnic and popular influences continued to exert an important pull in the creation of twentieth-century music. Folk music was a major element in the works of the English composers and often in the music of Stravinsky and the Soviet Union's Sergei Prokofiev.

Ragtime, blues, jazz, and other popular folk, dance, and commercial music provided material for some of the most innovative and exciting work in twentieth-century music, including Stravinsky's *Ragtime for Eleven Instruments*, George Gershwin's *Rhapsody in Blue* and *Porgy and Bess*, and many pieces by Leonard Bernstein. Composers after World War II continued to experiment with tape-recorded sound.

Skill Three
Identify Characteristics of Style in Works of Art

A **style** is an artist's manner of expression. When a group of artists during a specific period (usually a few months, years, or decades) have a common style, it is called an **art movement**. Art movements seem to occur only in the West and may occur in both visual art and architecture.

There are eight historical periods, with various styles and movements within each. Although some periods have only one or two styles, the twentieth century has 36 unique styles. Some of the best-known styles throughout history are:

Prehistoric
   Cave painting

Ancient

Medieval
   Gothic architecture: ribbed vaulting, pointed roofs, flying buttresses
   Panel painting: painting (often oil) on a thin board

Renaissance
   Early Renaissance: religious themes
   Renaissance classicism: realistic painting

Baroque

Early baroque: detailed, elaborate; often sculpture, painting

Eighteenth century

Rococo: opulence, grace, lightness (in contrast to baroque)

Nineteenth century

Romanticism: idealistic

Realism: everyday characters, situations, dilemmas

Naturalism: realistic subjects in natural settings

Impressionism: visible brushstrokes, emphasis on light colors; layers of oil paints added without waiting for the other oil paints to dry

Twentieth century

Cubism: the most direct call for the total destruction of realistic depiction; taking objects apart and reassembling them, showing a subject's multiplicity of aspects and dissolving time and space

Photorealism: art resembles photos, lifelike; often portraits, still lifes, and landscapes

Graffiti; marking on surfaces, private and public; scratching used before spray paints

Skill Four

Demonstrate Knowledge of How Visual Arts Reflect Particular Cultures, Historical Periods, and Places

Paleolithic people in Europe painted animal pictures on the cave walls at Lascaux and Altimira from about 15,000 to 13,000 BCE. Some examples of even older art, dating from 30,000 to 20,000 BCE, are the various "Venuses"—small stylized stone carvings of women–often in modern France, Italy, and Austria–as symbols of fertility. The artists of the ancient civilizations of Sumer, Babylon, and Assyria skillfully carved even the hardest rocks, such as granite and basalt, into narratives of battles and historical records. Egyptian statues—like their architectural monuments, the pyramids—were often of colossal size to exalt further the power of the society's leaders and gods.

The art of ancient Greece has its roots in the Minoan civilization on the island of Crete, which flourished from about 2500 to 1400 BCE. The palace at Knossos held characteristic wall paintings revealing a people enamored of games, leisure, and the beauty of the sea. The mainland Greeks of the classical period, about 1,000 years later, were fascinated by physical beauty. Fashioned in the human image, with a universe of perfection and guided by a master plan, the Greeks recreated their Olympian gods in their idealized and gracefully proportioned sculptures, architecture, and paintings.

In the Hellenistic period, the populace appreciated these various objects of art for their beauty alone. The culture of Rome excelled in engineering and building, skills intended to organize efficiently a vast empire and provide an aesthetic environment for private and public use. The Romans built temples, roads, bathing complexes, civic buildings, palaces, and aqueducts. One of the greatest of their artistic and engineering accomplishments was the massive-domed temple of all the gods, the Pantheon, which is today one of the most perfectly preserved of all buildings from the classical period.

The early Christian era borrowed the basilica form of Roman architecture for its churches, particularly evident in churches in the town of Ravenna in northeastern Italy. The seventh-century church of San Vitale echoes the mosaic mastery of the Byzantine Empire in Constantinople (which flourished as a center of civilization for a thousand years after the decline of Rome). Its grandiose apse mosaic depicts Emperor Justinian and Empress Theodora.

The Romanesque style of art and architecture was preeminent from about 800 to 1200. By then many local styles, including the decorative arts of the Byzantine Empire, the Near East, and the German and Celtic tribes, were contributing to European culture. Common features of Romanesque churches are round arches, vaulted ceilings, and heavy walls that are ornately decorated—primarily with symbolic figures of Christianity, realism had become less important than the message.

Gothic art flourished in Europe for 300 years. The cathedrals in this style are some of the purest expressions of an age. They combine a continued search for engineering and structural improvement with stylistic features that convey a relentless verticality, a reach toward heaven, and the unbridled adoration of God. Soaring and airy, the construction of the Gothic cathedrals employed such elements as flying buttresses and pointed arches and vaults; a profusion of sculptures and stained-glass windows that were, for the worshippers, visual encyclopedias of Christian teachings and stories decorated these structures.

When the painter Giotto began to compose his figures into groups and depict expressive human gestures, he laid the cornerstone of the Italian Renaissance. The fifteenth century saw the invigoration of art, architecture, literature, and music.

Renaissance artists developed new forms and revived classical styles and values, with the belief in the importance of the human experience on Earth. Great sculptors approached true human characterization and realism. Lorenzo Ghiberti created the bronze doors of the Florence Baptistry (early fifteenth century), and Donatello produced *Gattamelata*, the first equestrian statue since the Roman era. Architecture, in the hands of Filippo Brunelleschi and Leon Battista Alberti, revived elements of Greek architecture. Like the painters of the period, Renaissance architects took a scientific, ordered approach and emphasized perspective and the calculated composition of figures in space.

The Renaissance artists sought to produce works of perfect beauty and engaged in a constant search for knowledge, most often portraying religious subjects and wealthy patrons. The stylistic innovations of such fifteenth-century painters as Masaccio, Paolo Uccello, Fra Angelico, Piero della Francesca, Andrea Mantegna, and Sandro Botticelli formed the basis of the High Renaissance of the next century.

Art became more emotional and dramatic, the use of color and movement increased, compositions were more vigorous, and references to classical iconography and the pleasures of an idyllic golden age increased. Typical examples of this emotional, dramatic art are Michelangelo's magnificent Sistine Chapel frescoes and his powerful sculptures of David and Moses, Leonardo's *Mona Lisa*, Raphael's *School of Athens* fresco, and the increasingly dramatic and colorful works of the

Venetian and northern Italian masters Titian, Correggio, Giorgione, and Bellini.

The northern European Renaissance emphasized also a renewed interest in the visible world. For example the works by Albrecht Dürer (*Praying Hands*), Lucas Cranach, Matthias Grünewald, and Albrecht Altdorfer typify an emphasis on the symbolism of minutely observed details and accurate realism based on observation of reality rather than prescribed rules.

Presaged by the works of the Venetian artist Tintoretto (*The Last Supper*) and El Greco in Spain (*View of Toledo, The Immaculate Conception*), the baroque period of the seventeenth century produced artists who added heightened drama to the forms of Renaissance art. Caravaggio (*The Calling of Saint Matthew, The Conversion of Saint Paul*), the sculptor Gianlorenzo Bernini (*Saint Teresa in Ecstasy*) in Italy, the Flemish masters Peter Paul Rubens (*Marie de Medici Lands at Marseilles*) and Jacob Jordaens all portrayed figures in constant motion, draperies of agitated angles, and effects of lighting and shadow that amplified emotional impact and mystery.

In this spirit followed such painters of court life and middle-class portraiture as Velazquez, Rembrandt, Anthony Van Dyck, and Frans Hals. Rembrandt used expressive brushwork and mysterious light contrasts to enliven genre painting and portraiture, particularly of groups. Rembrandt's influence has remained potent because his art appears to impart universal truths, and sections of his compositions glow with a mysterious inner light often unrelated to realistic effects (*The Night Watch*, many self-portraits).

Rococo art characterizes the art of the early eighteenth century. Painters like Jean-Antoine Watteau (*Embarkation for Cythera*), Giambattista Tiepolo (*Wurzberg Residenz* frescoes), François Boucher, and Jean-Honore Fragonard, often with walls or ceilings as their canvases, turned the agitated drama of the baroque style into light, pastel-toned, swirling compositions that seem placed in an idyllic land of a golden age.

In the seventeenth and eighteenth centuries, European artists responded to both middle-class life and everyday objects and created genre paintings (Jan Vermeer, Adriaen van Ostade, Jean-Baptiste Chardin). Jean-Baptiste Greuze in France and William Hogarth in England endowed their everyday subjects with a wealth of narrative detail that aimed to impart a specific moral message. Such narrative art combined in the nineteenth century with political events and romantic literature—Goethe, Byron, Shelley, Scott, Wordsworth, and others—to produce works in a variety of styles with political points of view or stories to tell.

Jacques-Louis David used a severe classical sculptural style (neoclassical) in his paintings to revive classical art and ennoble images of the French Revolution and Napoleon's empire (*The Death of Marat, The Oath of the Horatii, Napoleon in His Study*). Neoclassical sculpture revived the aloof severity and perfection of form of ancient art (Jean-Antoine Houdon, Antonio Canova, Bertel Thorvaldsen, Horatio Greenough)—a style also reflected in Thomas Jefferson's architectural designs for his Monticello home and the University of Virginia.

The Spanish painter Francisco de Goya commented powerfully on the atrocities of war in his painting *May 3, 1808*. In France, Eugene Delacroix (*The Death of Sardanapalus, Liberty Leading the People*) and Theodore Gericault (*The Raft of the Medusa*) imbued subjects from literature, the Bible, exotic lands, and current events with dramatic and heroic intensity. The grandeur and transcendence of nature, the emotional reaction to inner dreams and metaphysical truths of romanticism are evident in the work of such mystical artists as England's William Blake, Henry Fuselli, and John Martin and in America's Thomas Cole. Caspar David Friedrich in Germany and the English Pre-Raphaelites (William Holman Hunt, John Everett Millais, Dante Gabriel Rossetti, Ford Madox Brown, Arthur Hughes, and others) accurately re-created the natural world in brilliantly colored landscapes; the artists had keenly observed, minutely detailed, and fully imbued these works with a romantic spirit of poetic yearning and literary references.

In the first half of the nineteenth century, landscape painting in England reached a zenith with the works of John Constable and Joseph Mallord William Turner.

Turner's awe-inspiring landscapes form a bridge between the spirit of romanticism and the expressionistic brushwork and realism of the Barbizon School in France, whose chief painters were Charles Daubigny and Jean-Baptiste-Camille Corot. Beginning with Barbizon, the French painters of the nineteenth century concentrated increasingly on the reporter-like depiction of everyday life and the natural environment in a free, painterly (gesture and brushwork) style.

The realist pioneers were Gustave Courbet (*The Stone Breakers, A Burial at Ormans*), Jean-Francois Millet (*The Sower, The Angelus*), and Honoré Daumier (*The Third-Class Carriage*). Renowned as a political caricaturist, Daumier made the lithograph his chief medium and paved the way for the stylistic and subject innovations of the impressionists. Realists rejected traditional means of composing a picture, academic methods of figure modeling and color relations, and accurate and exact rendering of people and objects in favor of an art that emphasized quickly observed and sketched moments from life, the relation of shapes and forms and colors, the effects of light, and the act of painting itself.

Beginning with Edouard Manet (*Le Déjeuner sur l'Herbe, Olympia*) in the 1860s, French artists continually blurred the boundaries of realism and abstraction; the landscapes and everyday-life paintings of impressionist artists like Claude Monet, Camille Pissarro, Auguste Renoir, Alfred Sisley, and Edgar Degas gave way to the more experimental arrangements of form and color of the great postimpressionists: Paul Gauguin, Vincent Van Gogh, Georges Seurat, and Henri de Toulouse-Lautrec. Auguste Rodin produced powerful sculptures with the freedom of impressionist style.

Japanese art and particularly the flattened space, distinctive shapes, and strong colors of Japanese woodblock prints influenced art. Artists from Manet and Degas to the American impressionist Mary Cassatt and from Toulouse-Lautrec to the Nabis (Edouard Vuillard, Pierre Bonnard, and Maurice Denis) used paintings, pastels, and lithography to break down the boundaries between representational art and abstraction. The new, freer form of art, centered around the personality of the artist, celebrated personal style and the manipulation of form and color, and evolved in a number of directions in the late nineteenth and early twentieth centuries.

Some artists—symbolists, expressionists, and exponents of art nouveau like Odilon Redon, Jan Toorop, Edvard Munch (*The Scream*), James Ensor (*The Entry of Christ into Brussels*), Gustav Klimt (*The Kiss*), Ernst Kirchner, and Max Pechstein–turned inward to explore mystical, symbolic, and psychological truths. Others, among them Paul Cézanne, Henri Matisse, Pablo Picasso, Georges Braque, and Juan Gris, pursued formal innovations. Picasso's cubism (*Les Demoiselles d'Avignon*) seemed the most direct call for the total destruction of realistic depiction; his use of African and Oceanic tribal art and his emphasis on taking objects apart and reassembling them—thus showing a subject's multiplicity of aspects and dissolving time and space—led to similar experiments by Fernand Leger, Marcel Duchamp, the sculptors Alexander Archipenko and Jacques Lipchitz, and the Italian futurist Umberto Boccioni (*Unique Forms of Continuity in Space*).

The more emotional, expressionistic, and color-oriented paintings of Wassily Kandinsky, Roger Delauney, and Paul Klee approached pure abstraction with little or no relation to the outside world. More cerebral arrangements of abstract geometrical shapes and colors were the mark of Kasimir Malevich, Piet Mondrian, and the Bauhaus School of Design in Germany, whose stripped-down, simplified, and usually geometrically oriented aesthetics influenced architecture, industrial and commercial design, sculpture, and the graphic arts for half a century.

Architecture displays the most obvious effect of the move toward abstraction, from the simplified, sleek structures of Le Corbusier and Walter Gropius to the boxlike glass skyscrapers of Philip Johnson. The pioneering giant of twentieth-century architecture was the American Frank Lloyd Wright, whose rejection of eclectic decorative styles of the previous century's architecture and use of new engineering techniques paralleled the German Bauhaus aesthetic. From the early 1900s, Wright's buildings (the Robie House, Fallingwater, and Tokyo's Imperial Hotel) exhibited a personal and bold originality based on a philosophy of "organic architecture," or the belief that natural surroundings,

purpose, and building materials should dictate the form of a structure.

Inspired by the psychoanalytic writings of Sigmund Freud and Carl Jung, artists made the subconscious and the metaphysical important elements in their work. The influence of psychology is especially evident in the work of the surrealist artists Salvador Dali (*The Persistence of Memory*), Giorgio de Chirico, Max Ernst, René Magritte, Joan Miro, and Yves Tanguy. Important sculptors who manipulated abstract shapes and looked to the tribal arts in the twentieth century include Constantin Brancusi, Henry Moore, Hans Arp, and Alberto Giacometti. Alexander Calder created floating assemblies called mobiles, and Louise Nevelson made constructions and wall sculptures from scraps of everyday objects.

Obsession with the self and abstraction also led to abstract expressionism, the major American art movement after World War II. The chief proponents of this style were Clifford Still, Jackson Pollock, Willem de Kooning, and Robert Motherwell. Other Americans took this movement into the area of color-field painting, a cooler, more reserved formalism of simple shapes and experimental color relationships. Artists in this movement include Mark Rothko, Barnett Newman, Joseph Albers, and Ad Reinhardt.

Other important trends in American art in the twentieth century were reflective of a democratic and consumer society. The muralists and social realists between the wars created art that was physically interesting and whose subjects were accessible to the average person. John Sloan, George Bellows, Edward Hopper, Thomas Hart Benton, Grant Wood, and John Stuart Curry were among those who celebrated the American scene in paintings, frequently in murals for public buildings, and through widely available fine prints. The great Mexican muralists, who usually concentrated on political themes—Diego Rivera, José Clemente Orozco, and David Siqueiros—brought their work to the public both in Mexico and in the United States. The icons of American popular culture found their way, in the movement known as pop art, onto canvases by Andy Warhol, Robert Indiana, Larry Rivers, Jasper Johns, Roy Lichtenstein, and Robert Rauschenberg.

Competency 30: Knowledge of Aesthetic and Critical Analysis of Music and Visual Arts

Two test items relate to this competency.

Skill One

Identify Strategies for Developing Students' Analytical Skills to Evaluate Musical Performance

Any work to encourage the thinking skills of children can help develop the analytical skills needed to evaluate musical performance. The thinking skills, according to Benjamin Bloom's *Taxonomy*, proceed from knowledge, comprehension, application, analysis, and synthesis to evaluation. The skill of **analysis** requires looking at the parts that make up the whole.

For example, a teacher might ask young children, after they played "Here We Go 'Round the Mulberry Bush," some questions requiring them to perform some very basic analysis of the music. A simple question might be, "Do you think this song would be good to march to on the playground?" Upper-elementary students might listen to *Peter and the Wolf,* by Sergei Prokofiev, and try to identify the instruments in the recording. The students might talk about why the composer used certain instruments for a character, suggest other instrument sounds for the characters, and give their justifications for the new instrument. Because these activities involve analysis, they help develop the upper-level thinking skills needed to evaluate musical performance.

Skill Two

Identify Strategies for Developing Students' Analytical Skills to Evaluate Works of Art

To judge the quality of a work of visual art—whether it is or is not good art—students need to consider the following questions:

1. Does the work achieve its purpose?

2. Has the artist has spoken with a unique voice, regardless of style, or could this artwork just as easily be the work of someone else?

3. Is the style appropriate to the expressed purpose of the work?

4. Is the work memorable and distinctive?

5. Has the artist used all the technical elements available to the particular discipline with accomplished skill?

As with analyzing music skills, any activity that encourages children to use their thinking skills can help students develop the analytical skills needed to evaluate visual arts. The thinking skills, according to Bloom's *Taxonomy*, proceed from knowledge, comprehension, application, analysis, and synthesis to evaluation. The skill of analysis requires looking at the parts that make up the whole.

Viewing many types of art, examining the works of many artists, and experimenting with various media themselves help students to analyze art forms. Using the vocabulary associated with art helps them form and express their opinions.

Competency 31: Knowledge of Appropriate Assessment Strategies in Music and Visual Arts

Four test items relate to this competency.

Skill One

Identify a Variety of Developmentally Appropriate Strategies and Materials to Assess Skills, Techniques, Creativity, and Communication in Music

The overall goals of music education include

- encouraging responsiveness to music,

- increasing involvement in music,

- aiding in music discrimination,

- promoting understanding of music and music structure,

- increasing listening awareness, and

- developing sensitivity to the expressive qualities of music.

Table 6-1 describes the elements of elementary school music curriculum.

Although students can experience music and find it satisfying, challenging, or beautiful without prior knowledge of a piece or an understanding of its form, cultural significance, and so forth, those things can enrich the experience. People respond to music naturally. They do not need prompting or help to respond. However, to share their thoughts and feelings about music, students must learn how to put their responses into musical terminology. Some people call music a language, but it does not function as a spoken language. It does not provide specific information, instructions, or reactions.

Rather, music sparks thoughts, feelings and emotions. To put their experiences into words, musicians and artists have developed vocabularies and approaches to discussing music and art. This does not mean there is only one way to respond to or talk about music or art. However, it is easier to understand music and musicians, art and artists, if the students understand and can use the kind of vocabulary and approaches that musicians or artists use to discuss their work. This includes terms as basic as melody and harmony and as profound as the aesthetic experience.

People cannot express themselves or effectively communicate if they do not understand the structures and rules that underlie the "language" that they are trying to use. Although music does not provide the kind of specific communication that spoken language does, it has structures. When students are able to think about and discuss music, they gain a deeper understanding of the music and can better express their responses to the music.

The aesthetic experience is what draws people to music. The experience is one that most people have had but one that some people cannot describe. In fact, words seem clumsy when it comes to something that can be so profound and wonderful.

The type of music, the period, or the performer does not necessarily limit the aesthetic experience. It is equally as possible to have an aesthetic experience when listening to a child sing a simple melody as it is when listening to a professional orchestra performing a symphony by Beethoven. The important thing is to share that aesthetic experience. It is part of what makes music and art special.

There are many ways to encourage exploration of and growth through aesthetic responsiveness. A common experience is a crucial starting point. After students listen attentively to several pieces of music, the teacher might ask them to describe how each piece made them feel. It is often best to write their responses down before starting a discussion. Then, the teacher might ask them to explain why each piece of music made them feel the way they indicated.

Young students will likely provide simple, straightforward emotional responses to music (e.g., "It made me feel happy!"). Older students should explore why the music affected the feelings that it did and use both musical concepts (e.g., "It made me feel happy because it was in a major key") and nonmusical associations (e.g., "It made me feel happy because it sounded like a circus, and I like to go to the circus"). Through this kind of sharing, along with teacher insights and readings about how other people have responded to music, students can explore and come to a deeper understanding of their personal responses to music, other art forms, and possibly the world. In addition, it should provide them with practical ways to express their responses or reactions to what they experience in life.

In addition to having aesthetic experiences, recognizing their value, and being able to grapple with discussing or sharing those experiences, teachers and students must attempt to foster an appreciation for the arts and their ability to create meaning. The arts provide an opportunity to explore and express ideas and emotions through a unique view of life experiences. It is

Table 6–1. Music Strategies, Material, Skills, Techniques, Creativity, and Communication

Grades	Strategies	Materials	Skills	Techniques	Creativity	Communication
K–2	**a.** Provide exposure to a wide variety of sounds: recorded music, sheet music, live performances. **b.** Experiment with ways to change sounds. **c.** Use simple instruments in the classroom.	**a.** Simple instruments. **b.** Compact discs (CDs), tapes, records. **c.** Attend programs.	**a.** Classify sounds as high and low; use body to show high and low. **b.** Play simple rhythm instruments.	**a.** Play simple rhythm instruments. **b.** Sing, especially rote songs. **c.** Move in time with the music.	**a.** Walk, run, jump to music. **b.** Create simple songs.	**a.** Create symbols to notate sounds of music. **b.** Use musical terms and concepts to express thoughts about music.
3–5	**a.** Provide experiences with music of many periods and many cultures. **b.** Experiment with ways to change sounds. **c.** Use simple instruments in the classroom. **d.** Move to music.	**a.** Simple instruments. **b.** CDs, tapes, records. **c.** Attend programs and study written programs.	**a.** Sing rounds. **b.** Sing two-part songs by rote. **c.** Conduct simple songs. **d.** Move to music. **e.** Distinguish between classical and popular music.	**a.** Play music. **b.** Dance to music. **c.** Conduct duple and triple meter.	**a.** Encourage students to express themselves through music. **b.** Encourage students to create sounds. **c.** Encourage students to improvise.	**a.** Sing and play instruments from written notation. **b.** Create own notation system. **c.** Hear, read, and learn about careers in music. **d.** Notate a simple phrase. **e.** Create a simple phrase. **f.** Practice basic etiquette for performing and as audience. **g.** Read music notation. **h.** Express ideas about origin, culture, etc., of music listened to in class.
6–8	**a.** Provide occasions to listen to music of many cultures and many periods. **b.** Encourage students to respond to music and create their own music. **c.** Provide opportunities for students to communicate with notation. **d.** Use a range of instruments and types of music.	**a.** Simple instruments. **b.** CDs, tapes, records. **c.** Programs. **d.** Autoharp and/or guitar.	**a.** Sing rounds. **b.** Sing three-part songs by rote. **c.** Conduct simple songs. **d.** Move to music. **e.** Identify major and minor scales. **f.** Dance.	**a.** Play simple accompaniment on autoharp, guitar, etc. **b.** Read some music. **c.** Use correct terminology **d.** Perform dance steps.	**a.** Create some simple songs. **b.** Create an accompaniment. **c.** Create a dance.	**a.** Write notation for original song. **b.** Write own idea of notation for song heard. **c.** Read notation.

through the experience of music, or any art form, that people begin to transcend the mundane day-to-day experience and reach beyond to a richer life experience.

When preparing for this part of the exam, it is important to understand that the primary objectives of music education are teaching the contexts of music, the concepts and skills involved in experiencing music, and the aesthetic and personal dimensions of music. These constitute a broad overview of the field of music and the musical experience.

Music does not exist in a vacuum. The historical or cultural context of a piece of music is very important. Students should know and be able to discuss the context of music by making connections among social studies, reading or language arts, and the fine arts. For example, when students are reading stories about the American Revolution, they should be aware that it occurred during the period known as the classical period in music history. Listening to a piece by Haydn or Mozart, talking about how they reacted to the Old World, and comparing their works to a colonial American tune by Billings is an effective way to understand the historical, cultural, and societal contexts of music.

Similarly, the visual art of Andy Warhol, the music of the Beatles, the assassination of John F. Kennedy, and the war in Vietnam all took place within the same approximate time frame. The teacher can ask students to find contrasts and similarities among these artistic and social events; students can attempt to find ways that the historical context affected music and ways that music affected and reflected history.

These examples from American history are easy for most to grasp quickly. However, the objective seeks to have teachers and students consider the role of music in history and culture beyond the American experience. By having students listen to music from China, Japan, Germany, Australia, or Africa when they are studying those cultures, the teacher enriches the students' learning experience and makes it more memorable for them. It is even more valuable for students to view live or videotaped performances of the music and dance of these cultures because often the music is performed in traditional costume with traditional instruments

(sometimes very different from modern instruments). Seeing the costumes and the movement are an important part of understanding the culture.

Skill Two

Identify a Variety of Developmentally Appropriate Strategies and Materials to Assess Skills, Techniques, Creativity, and Communication in Art

The overall goals of art education include

- developing aesthetic perception;

- providing opportunities to examine many art forms of both natural and human in form;

- providing opportunities to reflect on and discuss observations and reactions;

- providing opportunities to develop and extend their own art abilities;

- providing opportunities to identify symbols and characteristics of art, objects of arts, and natural art forms;

- increasing awareness of tactile art;

- fostering the ability to select and enjoy arts (natural and human made); and

- promoting the ability to analyze and enjoy forms based on informed judgments.

Table 6-2 summarizes an elementary school art curriculum.

Students should be able to describe a work of art using terms like *line, color, value, shape, balance, texture, repetition, rhythm,* and *shape.* Students should be able to discuss some of the major periods in the history of the visual arts. It is important that students be able to confront a work and judge its aesthetic merits, regardless of their ability to recognize it from memory. Analytical questions a teacher might ask include the following:

- What is the purpose of the work? Religious? Entertainment? Philosophical? Emotional? Didactic? Pure form? Social or political commentary?

- To what culture does it belong, and to what geographical region and period? How does it reflect that context?

Table 6-2. Art Strategies, Materials, Skills, Techniques, Creativity, and Communication

Grade	Strategies	Materials	Skills	Techniques	Creativity	Communication
K–2	**a.** Provide a wide variety of art: natural and human-made forms. **b.** Experiment with art materials. **c.** Provide opportunities to view art in the classroom, the art room, and elsewhere.	**a.** Art materials to use in the art room and classroom. **b.** Art forms from nature and humans, slides, art shows, visiting guests, trips, the computer, etc.	**a.** Use terms like *line, color, value, shape, balance, texture, repetition, rhythm,* and *shape.* **b.** Respond to art. **c.** Describe feelings and ideas while viewing art. **d.** Use various art materials to produce art in the art room and classroom. **e.** Use a program from an art exhibit. **f.** Practice acceptable behavior at an art exhibit or as a member of an audience.	**a.** Try various art media and produce art forms. **b.** Behave as a responsible member of an audience. **c.** Use an art program to locate exhibits at an art show.	**a.** Experiment with various art supplies. **b.** Create simple art projects. **c.** Respond to art in an individual way.	**a.** Create feelings, ideas, and impressions through art products. **b.** Use art terms and concepts to express thoughts about art.
3–5	**a.** Experience art of many periods and many cultures through art exhibits, computer, slides, speakers, etc. **b.** Experiment with ways to produce art using many media.	**a.** Actual art materials to use in the classroom and art room. **b.** Actual art forms from speakers and teacher. **c.** Slides, computer programs, etc. **d.** Attend programs and study written programs.	**a.** Continue to use terms like *line, color, value, shape, balance, texture, repetition, rhythm,* and *shape.* **b.** Continue to respond to art. **c.** Become more adept at describing feelings and ideas while producing and viewing art. **d.** Continue to use various art materials to produce art in the art room and classroom. **e.** Use a program from an art exhibit. **f.** Practice acceptable behavior at an art exhibit or as a member of an audience. **g.** Distinguish between classical and popular art.	**a.** Try various art media and produce art forms. **b.** Behave as a responsible member of an audience. **c.** Use an art program to locate exhibits at an art show. **d.** Describe feelings about own art and the art of others.	**a.** Encouraged to express self through art. **b.** Encouraged to create art. **c.** Encouraged to improvise. **d.** Encouraged to respond to art.	**a.** Create art using various materials to express self. **b.** Create original art. **c.** Hear, read, and learn about careers in art. **d.** Practice basic etiquette for showing own art and as a member of an audience. **e.** Read art programs. **f.** Express ideas about origin, culture, etc., of art.

Grade	Strategies	Materials	Skills	Techniques	Creativity	Communication
6–8	**a.** Provide occasions to view art of many cultures and many periods through exhibits, slides, books, computer searches, speakers, etc. **b.** Encourage students to respond to art and create own art. **c.** Give chances to communicate orally and in written form. **d.** Use a range of types of art.	**a.** Many art media, including weaving, film, crafts, etc **b.** CDs, Internet searches, media, slides, books. **c.** Programs for art shows. **d.** Exhibits and guest speakers.	**a.** Use art to express self. **b.** Use many different art media to produce many art forms. **c.** Identify major artists, media, and periods.	**a.** Produce simple art products. **b.** Demonstrate understanding of terms when others use them. **c.** Use correct terminology. **d.** Read about art.	**a.** Create some simple art. **b.** Explain the art and the feelings it produces.	**a.** Realize that art can be a career. **b.** Produce an original art piece for display. **c.** Express a feeling for an event by producing art. **d.** Analyze art. **e.** Talk about ways that art can be used as a career.

- Is its origin and/or function popular or commercial?

- Does it derive organically from the needs or celebratory functions of a community, or is it a self-conscious artistic creation of one individual?

- What style is it in? For example, is the music baroque, classical, or romantic? Is it influenced by ethnic or popular music?

Often after answering such questions, some student might be able to determine the specific artist by putting all the clues together, as in a detective story.

Competency 32: Knowledge of Personal Health and Wellness

Six test items relate to this competency.

Skill One

Demonstrate Knowledge of the Interrelatedness of Physical Activity, Fitness, and Health

The axiom "Use it or lose it" certainly holds for the human body. Our bodies thrive on **physical activity**, which is any bodily movement produced by skeletal muscles and resulting in energy expenditure. Unfortunately, Americans tend to be relatively inactive. In a recent survey, 25 percent of adult Americans had not participated in any leisure-time physical activities in the past month; in 2003, 38 percent of students in grades 9 through 12 viewed television 3 hours or more per day (Centers for Disease Control and Prevention).

Physical fitness enables a person to meet the physical demands of work and leisure comfortably. It is a multicomponent trait related to the ability to perform physical activity. A person with a high level of physical fitness is also at lower risk of developing chronic disease.

Lack of activity can cause many problems, including flabby muscles, a weak heart, poor circulation, shortness of breath, obesity, coronary artery disease,

hypertension, type 2 diabetes, osteoporosis, and certain types of cancer. Overall, mortality rates from all causes are lower in physically active people than in sedentary people. In addition, physical activity can help people manage mild-to-moderate depression, control anxiety, and prevent weakening of the skeletal system.

By **increasing physical activity**, a person may improve heart function and circulation, respiratory function, and overall strength and endurance. All of these lead to improved vigor and vitality. Exercise also lowers the risk of heart disease by strengthening the heart muscle, lowering pulse and blood pressure, and lowering the concentration of fat in both the body and the blood. It can also improve appearance, increase range of motion, and lessen the risk of back problems associated with weak bones and osteoporosis.

Each person should engage in regular physical activity and reduce sedentary activities to promote health, psychological well-being, and a healthy body weight. On most days of the week, children should engage in at least 60 minutes of physical activity.

Proper hydration is important during physical activity. Two steps that help prevent dehydration during prolonged physical activity or when it is hot are (1) consuming fluid regularly during the activity and (2) drinking several glasses of water or other fluid after the physical activity is completed (U.S. Department of Agriculture).

Skill Two

Demonstrate Basic Knowledge of Nutrition and Its Role in Promoting Health

Along with exercise, a knowledge of and a participation in a healthy lifestyle are vital to good health and longevity. The elements of good nutrition, the role of vitamins, elimination of risk factors, and strategies to control weight are all part of a healthy lifestyle.

In the spring of 2005, the U. S. Department of Agriculture (USDA) changed the food pyramid to guide Americans in how to eat healthily. As shown in the figure, the food pyramid has six rainbow-colored divisions. The climbing figure reminds us all to be active.

USDA Food Pyramid

Source: U.S. Department of Agriculture, Steps to a Healthier You, *http://www.mypyramid.gov.*

The food groups indicated on the pyramid are as follows:

1. Grains (orange).
2. Vegetables (green).
3. Fruits (red).
4. Fats and oils (yellow, the smallest group).
5. Milk and dairy products (blue).
6. Meat, beans, fish, and nuts (purple).

Complex carbohydrates—vegetables, fruits, high-fiber breads, and cereals—should comprise at least one-half of the diet. These foods provide fiber, which helps digestion, reduces constipation, and reduces the risk of colon cancer. Complex carbohydrates also provide water, which is vital to the entire body.

Proteins should make up about one-fifth of the diet. Proteins build and repair the body. Protein sources include fish, beans, peas, lentils, peanuts, and other pod plants; red meat also contains protein, but because it is high in saturated fat, one should eat it less often.

Saturated fat is present also in cocoa butter, palm oil, and coconut oil.

There is a link between high-fat diets and many types of cancer. Diets high in saturated fats cause the body to produce too much **low-density lipoprotein (LDL)**, which is one type of **cholesterol**. The other type of cholesterol is **high-density lipoprotein (HDL)**. Some cholesterol is essential to the brain functions and to the production of certain hormones, but too much LDL cholesterol encourages the buildup of plaque in the arteries. LDL cholesterol can be controlled through proper diet, and HDL cholesterol levels can be raised by exercise. **Triglycerides** are other types of fat in the blood that are important to monitor; triglycerides seem to be inversely proportional to HDLs.

Unsaturated vegetable fats are preferable to saturated fats. Unsaturated fats appear to offset the rise in blood pressure that accompanies too much saturated fat and may lower cholesterol and help with weight loss. Unsaturated fats are present in vegetable products. Although whole milk products contain saturated fat, the calcium they contain is vital to health. For this reason, weight-loss diets still recommend dairy products but in the form of skim milk and low-fat cheese.

Vitamins are essential to good health; however, a person must be careful not to take too much of certain vitamins. The fat-soluble vitamins, A, D, E, and K, are stored in the body, and excessive amounts will cause some dangerous side effects. All other vitamins are water-soluble and are generally excreted through the urinary system and the skin when taken in excess. A brief synopsis of the vitamins and minerals needed by the body follows:

Vitamin A. Needed for normal vision, prevention of night blindness, healthy skin, resistance to disease, and tissue growth and repair. Found in spinach, carrots, broccoli, and other dark green or yellow-orange fruits and vegetables; also found in liver and plums.

Vitamin D. Promotes absorption of calcium and phosphorus and the normal growth of healthy bones, teeth, and nails. Formed by the action of the sun on the skin. Present in halibut liver oil, herring, cod liver oil, mackerel, salmon, and tuna and is an additive to many milk products.

Vitamin E. Protects cell membranes, seems to improve elasticity in blood vessels, and may prevent the formation of blood clots and protect red blood cells from damage by oxidation. Found in wheat germ oil, sunflower seeds, raw wheat germ, almonds, pecans, peanut oil, and cod liver oil.

Vitamin B$_1$ (thiamin). Helps with the functioning of nerves, muscle growth, and fertility. Also aids in the production of energy, appetite, and digestion. Found in pork, legumes, nuts, enriched and fortified whole grains, and liver.

Vitamin B$_2$ (riboflavin). Aids in the production of red blood cells, good vision, healthy skin, mouth tissue, and energy. Found in lean meat, dairy products, liver, eggs, enriched and fortified whole grains, and green leafy vegetables.

Vitamin B$_3$ (niacin). Promotes the production of energy and appetite, aids the functioning of the digestive and nervous systems, and promotes healthy skin and tongue. Present in beef liver, peanuts, chicken, salmon, and tuna.

Vitamin B$_6$ (pyridoxine). Promotes red blood cell formation and growth. Found in liver, beans, pork, fish, legumes, enriched and fortified whole grains, and green leafy vegetables.

Vitamin B$_{12}$. Promotes healthy nerve tissue, production of energy, utilization of folic acid, aids in the formation of healthy red blood cells. Found in dairy products, liver, meat, poultry, fish, and eggs.

Vitamin C. Promotes healing and growth, resists infection, increases iron absorption, and aids in bone and tooth formation and repair. Found in citrus fruits, cantaloupe, potatoes, strawberries, tomatoes, and green vegetables.

Minerals. Essential to good health. Several necessary:

Sodium. Maintains normal water balance inside and outside cells, regulates blood pressure, and balances electrolytes and chemicals. Found in salt, processed foods, bread, and bakery products.

Potassium. Maintains the volume and balance of body fluids, prevents muscle weakness and cramping, and is important for normal heart rhythm and electrolyte balance in the blood. Found in citrus fruits, leafy green vegetables, potatoes, and tomatoes.

Zinc. Promotes taste, appetite, healthy skin, and wound healing. Found in lean meat, liver, milk, fish, poultry, whole grain cereals, and shellfish.

Iron. Promotes red blood cell formation, oxygen transport to the cells, and prevents nutritional anemia. Found in liver, lean meats, dried beans, peas, eggs, dark green leafy vegetables, and whole grain cereals.

Calcium. Promotes strong bones, teeth, and nails. Helps maintain muscle tone, prevents osteoporosis and muscle cramping, and promotes sound nerve function and heart beat. Found in milk, yogurt, and other dairy products, and dark leafy vegetables.

Phosphorus. Regulates blood chemistry and internal processes, strong bones and teeth. Found in meat, fish, poultry, and dairy products.

Magnesium. Promotes energy production, helps maintain normal heart rhythm ensures nerve and muscle function, and prevents muscle cramps. Found in dried beans, nuts, whole grains, bananas, and leafy green vegetables.

Skill Three

Identify the Process of Decision Making and Goal Setting in Promoting Individual Health and Wellness

One of the primary reasons for the teaching of physical education is to instill a willingness to exercise and to encourage students to make good decisions about their health. To that end, it is important to understand the benefits of participating in a lifelong program of exercise and physical fitness and of avoiding the risks of choosing an unhealthy lifestyle.

Reaping the Benefits, Avoiding the Risks

Fortunately, it is not difficult to find justification for exercising and maintaining a consistently high level of fitness. The benefits of a consistent program of diet and exercise are many. Improvements in cardiac output, maximum oxygen intake, and enhancing the blood's ability to carry oxygen are just a few of these benefits.

Another aspect of physical education concerns awareness and avoidance of the risks that are present in our everyday lives. Some risk factors include being overweight, smoking, using drugs, having unprotected sex, and not eliminating excessive stress. Education is the key to minimizing the presence of these risk factors. Unfortunately, because of the presence of peer pressure and the lack of parental control, the effect of education is sometimes not enough.

Weight Control Strategies

Statistics show that Americans get fatter every year. Even though countless books and magazine articles are available on the subject of weight control, often the only place a student gets reliable information about diet is in a classroom. The unfortunate reality is that people who are fat do not live as long, on average, as those who are thin. Being overweight has been isolated as a

risk factor in various cancers, heart disease, gall bladder problems, and kidney disease. Chronic diseases such as diabetes and high blood pressure are also aggravated by, or caused by, being overweight.

Conversely, being underweight presents a great many problems. Our society often places too much emphasis on losing weight. Women are especially prone to measuring their self-worth by the numbers they read on the bathroom scale. Ideal weight and a good body fat ratio are the goals when losing weight. A correlation may exist between body fat and high cholesterol. Exercise is the key to a good body fat ratio. Exercise helps keep the ratio low, improve cholesterol levels, and prevent heart disease.

To lose weight, calories burned must exceed calories consumed. No matter what kind of diet is tried, that principle applies. There is no easy way to maintain a healthy weight. Again, the key is exercise. If calorie intake is restricted too much, the body goes into starvation mode and operates by burning fewer calories. Just a 250-calorie drop a day combined with a 250-calorie burn will result in a loss of one pound a week. Crash diets, which bring about rapid weight loss, are not only unhealthy but also ineffective. Slower weight loss is more lasting. Aerobic exercise is the key to successful weight loss. Exercise speeds up metabolism and causes the body to burn calories. Timing of exercise will improve the benefits. Exercise before meals speeds up metabolism and helps suppress appetite. Losing and maintaining weight is not easy. Through education, people will be better able to realize that maintaining a healthy weight is crucial to a healthy life and should be a constant consideration.

Skill Four

Demonstrate Knowledge of Common Health Problems and Risk Behaviors Associated with Them

The health of students and their families depends not only on individual and family decisions about diet and exercise but also on various social factors. For example, advertising often encourages children to make unhealthy decisions.

Students as young as kindergarten and first grade can learn how to recognize advertisements (e.g., for candy or sugar-laden cereal) that might lead them to unhealthy behavior. By third or fourth grade, children should be able to demonstrate that they are able to make health-related decisions regarding advertisements in various media. Teachers can encourage students (1) to avoid alcohol, tobacco, stimulants, and narcotics; (2) to get plenty of sleep and exercise; (3) to eat a well-balanced diet; (4) to receive the proper immunizations; and (5) to avoid sharing toothbrushes, combs, hats, beverages, and food with others.

In addition, any study of the physical environment—in science, social studies, or other subjects—should relate to health whenever possible. Examples include

- the effects of pollution on health;

- occupational-related disease (e.g., "black lung" disease and the effects of chemicals on soldiers);

- the different health care options available to people in different parts of the world and in different economic circumstances;

- differentiation between communicable and noncommunicable diseases; and

- the importance of even very young children washing their hands frequently.

Older children should be able to explain the transmission and prevention of communicable diseases, and all children should learn which diseases cannot be transmitted through casual contact.

Competency 33: Knowledge of Physical, Social, and Emotional Growth and Development

Nine test items relate to this competency.

Skill One

Identify the Structure, Function, and Interrelatedness of the Systems of the Human Body

Cells are the building blocks of the human body. **Tissues** are groups of similar cells working together to perform a specific job. Different kinds of tissues may work together for a larger purpose; a group of tissues working together is called an **organ**. A group of organs working together in a special activity is a **system**. There are several organ systems in humans.

Musculoskeletal System

The human skeleton consists of more than 200 **bones** held together by connective tissues called **ligaments**. Contractions of the **skeletal muscles**, to which the bones are attached by **tendons, affect movements**. The nervous system controls muscular contractions.

Nervous System

The nervous system has two divisions: the **somatic**, allowing voluntary control over skeletal muscle, and the **autonomic**, or involuntary, controlling cardiac and glandular functions. Nerve impulses arising in the brain, carried by cranial or spinal chord nerves connecting to skeletal muscles, causes **voluntary movement**. **Involuntary movement**, or reflex movement, occurs in direct response to outside stimulus. Various nerve terminals, called **receptors**, constantly send impulses to the central nervous system. There are three types of receptors:

Exteroceptors. Pain, temperature, touch, and pressure receptors.

Interoceptors. Internal environment receptors.

Proprioceptors. Movement, position, and tension receptors.

Each type of receptor routes nerve impulses to specialized areas of the brain for processing.

Circulatory System

The **heart** pumps blood in the circulatory system. The blood passes through the right chambers of the heart and through the lungs, where it acquires oxygen, and back into the left chambers of the heart. Next, is the heart pumps the blood into the main artery, the **aorta**, which branches into increasingly smaller arteries. Beyond that, blood passes through tiny, thin-walled structures called **capillaries**. In the capillaries, the blood gives up oxygen and nutrients to tissues and absorbs a metabolic waste product containing carbon dioxide. Finally, blood completes the circuit by passing through small **veins**, joining to form increasingly larger vessels until it reaches the largest veins, which return it to the right side of the heart.

Immune System

The body defends itself against foreign proteins and infectious microorganisms by means of a complex dual system that depends on recognizing a portion of the surface pattern of the invader and the generation of **lymphocytes** and **antibody** molecules to destroy the invader molecules.

Respiratory System

Respiration results from the expansion and contraction of the **lungs**. In the lungs, oxygen enters tiny capillaries, where it combines with hemoglobin in the red blood cells and goes to the tissues. At the same time, carbon dioxide passes through capillaries into the air contained within the lungs. Inhaling draws air that is higher in oxygen and lower in carbon dioxide into the lungs; exhaling forces air that is high in carbon dioxide and low in oxygen from the lungs.

Digestive and Excretory Systems

Food supplies the energy required for sustenance of the human body. After the fragmenting of food by chewing and mixing with **saliva**, digestion begins. Chewed food passes down the gullet into the **stomach**, where gastric and intestinal juices continue the process. Thereafter, the mixture of food and secretions makes its way down the **alimentary canal** by **peristalsis**, which is the rhythmic contraction of the smooth muscle of the **gastrointestinal tract**.

Skill Two

Identify the Principles of Sequential Progression of Motor Skill Development

Physical changes play a significant role in the development of children as they gradually gain control of the movements and functions of their bodies. As they

develop physically, children refine their motor skills, enabling them to engage in increasingly complex lessons and activities. For teachers to be able to identify patterns of physical development, they must create educational activities that are developmentally appropriate for their students' physical abilities.

Children between the ages of 3 and 4 have mastered standing and walking. At this stage, children are developing **gross motor skills**, including the ability to hop on one foot and balance, climb stairs without support, kick a ball, throw overhand, catch a ball that has bounced, move forward and backward, and ride a tricycle. Children between the ages of 3 and 4 are also developing fine motor skills, such as using scissors, drawing single shapes, and copying shapes like capital letters.

By age 4 or 5, when most children enter school, they are developing the gross motor ability to do somersaults, swing, climb, and skip. These skills require increasing coordination. In addition, children at this age can begin to dress themselves using zippers, buttons, and possibly tying shoes. They can eat independently using utensils. Children at this age are increasingly capable of copying shapes, including letters and numbers. They can cut and paste and draw a person with a head, body, arms, and legs. These **fine motor skills** develop quickly.

By age 6, children can bounce a ball, skate, ride a bike, skip with both feet, and dress themselves independently. As the student develops year by year, the physical skills, both fine and gross motor, become increasingly complex and involve more muscles and more coordination. By age 9, children can complete a model kit, learn to sew, and cook simple recipes. By age 10, children can catch fly balls and participate in all elements of a softball game.

Recognizing the basic milestones that most children will achieve by a certain age will assist teachers in making decisions about academic lessons and tasks. In addition, teachers may be able to identify children who may not be reaching their developmental milestones with the rest of the class.

In sum, the physical ability of students to engage in simple to complex activities in school gradually increases as they develop. Teachers must adjust and adapt classroom and playground activities to be developmentally appropriate for the specific skill levels of students. To this end, it is important for teachers to be able to identify the physical development patterns of their students.

Skill Three
Demonstrate Knowledge of Human Growth and Development and Its Relationship to Physical, Social, and Emotional Well-Being

A teacher does not have to be an expert in anatomy and physiology to see the physical changes that accompany students' growth and maturity. The preschool child has trouble grasping pencils and crayons in a manner that facilitates handwriting; however, even most 2-year-olds can grasp crayons sufficiently to make marks on papers and thus enjoy the creative excitement of art.

Physiological changes play a significant role in the development of children as they increase their control of bodily movements and functions and refine their motor skills. Their ability to engage in simple to complex classroom and playground activities increases as they develop. Teachers must adjust and adapt classroom and playground activities to be developmentally appropriate for students' various skill levels.

As students enter junior high or begin their secondary education, they again experience important physiological changes. With puberty comes changes in primary sexual characteristics and the emergence of secondary sexual characteristics. In addition to changes in bodily features, changes occur in bodily feelings, and students experience an increasing sex drive.

Girls, on average, reach maturational milestones before boys. Physical changes may cause embarrassment to both females and males when they draw unwelcome attention; moreover, these changes almost always create some discomfort as adolescents find the body they were familiar and comfortable with to be quite different, sometimes seemingly overnight.

Another theoretical approach to understanding human development is offered by Erik Erikson, who described the stages of psychosocial development. For each of eight stages, he identified a developmental task and explained it in terms of two polarities. This guide discusses only the stages describing school-aged individuals.

According to Erikson, preschoolers and primary grade students must be able to function in the outside world independent of parents. When children are able to do this, they achieve a sense of **initiative**. When children are not able to move away from total parental attachment and control, they experience a sense of guilt. Thus, this stage of psychosocial development is the stage of initiative versus guilt. The child's first venture away from home and into the world of school has considerable significance in light of Erikson's theory. It is imperative that teachers assist students in their first experiences on their own, away from parental control.

Erikson's next stage of development involves a tension between **industry** and **inferiority**. For example, if a child who enters school (thus achieving initiative) acquires the skills necessary for success in school (including academic skills like reading, writing, and computation and social skills like playing with others, communicating, and forming friendships), the child achieves a sense of industry. Failure to achieve these skills leads to a sense of inferiority.

Around the time students enter junior high, they begin the developmental task of achieving identity. According to Erikson, the struggle to achieve identity is one of the most important developmental tasks and can create serious psychosocial problems for adolescents. For example, even the individual who has successfully achieved all the important developmental milestones (such as initiative and industry) will be in a state of flux. Everything is changing—physically, emotionally, and psychologically. The adolescent starts to ask, "Who am I?" Erikson theorized that once adolescents find out what they believe in—what their goals, ideas, and values are—they can attain identity achievement. Failure to discover these things leads to identity diffusion.

By the time many students reach high school, they are entering a stage of young adulthood. Erikson described this as a psychosocial stage characterized by the polarities of intimacy and isolation. Individuals at this stage of development begin to think about forming lasting friendships, even marital unions. Erikson argued that many psychosocial problems experienced by young adults have their origin in the individual's failure to achieve identity during the preceding stage; the young men and women who do not know who they really are cannot achieve true intimacy.

For the classroom teacher, knowledge of psychosocial stages of human development can result in greater effectiveness. For example, the effective teacher realizes the importance of helping students to achieve the skills necessary to accomplish crucial developmental tasks. According to Erikson's theory, teachers of elementary school learners would do well to focus on teaching academic and social skills and to help students gain proficiency in skills that will enable learners to be productive members of society. As teachers engage students in higher-order thinking activities appropriate to their stage of cognitive development, teachers (typically at the secondary school level) should remember that students have pressing psychological and social needs in their struggle to achieve identity and attain intimacy. By understanding the key principles of human development in its multiple dimensions, effective teachers provide students with both age-appropriate and developmentally-appropriate instruction. The best instruction addresses all the needs of students—physical, emotional, social, and cognitive (intellectual).

Effective teachers help to bring about self-efficacy. **Self-efficacy** is the confidence you have in your ability to cope with life's challenges. Self-efficacy refers to your sense of control over life or over your responses to life. Experts say that ideas about self-efficacy are established by the time children reach age 4. Because of this early establishment of either a feeling of control or no control, classroom teachers may find that even primary grade students believe that they have no control over their life—that it makes no difference what they do or how they act. Therefore, it is all the more important that teachers attempt to help all students achieve coping skills and a sense of self-efficacy.

Skill Four

Identify Major Factors Associated with Social and Emotional Health

Many major factors relate to and are necessary to build both social and emotional health. For teachers, having a basic understanding of the principles of human development in its many dimensions—physical, mental, emotional, and social—is critically important. Additionally, teachers must appreciate a dynamic and interactive view of human development.

This approach to understanding human development is one that recognizes that human beings do not develop in a vacuum. People exist in an environment that, friendly or unfriendly, supportive or nonsupportive, evokes and provokes reactions from individuals. Moreover, human development is not a one-way street with the environment doing all the driving. People also act in certain ways to shape and form their environment.

A constant interaction or interplay occurs between people and their environments. Thus, effective teachers must be sensitive to and knowledgeable of both personal characteristics of students (internal factors) and characteristics of their environment. Internal factors, beyond the general characteristics that humans share as they grow and mature, also include factors like students' personality characteristics, their self-concept and sense of self-esteem, their self-discipline and self-control, their ability to cope with stress, and their general outlook on life.

Communication Skills

Communication with others is important to academic and social development. James Cummins (1981), a leader in the field of second-language acquisition, makes a distinction between social language and academic language. Basic interpersonal communication skills, or social language, deals with the here-and-now language that is context embedded, supported by the use of illustrations, realia, demonstrations, and so forth. Second-language learners acquire social language in approximately two years.

Cognitive academic language proficiency skills (academic language) are the language of school tasks, which is more abstract and decontextualized. Academic language is harder to acquire because it is context reduced, with little or no context clues. It takes second-language learners five to seven years to become proficient in the academic language.

Self-Concept

Empowerment has many components, one of which is **self-concept**, or self-esteem. A good definition of *self-concept* is that it is my opinion of me, your opinion of you. It is what we think and believe to be true about ourselves, not what we think about others and not what they think about us.

Related to self-concept is self-efficacy. Simply stated, **self-efficacy** is the confidence you have in your ability to cope with life's challenges. Self-efficacy refers to your sense of control over life or over your responses to life. Experts say that ideas about self-efficacy get established by the time children reach age 4. Because of this early establishment of either a feeling of control or no control, classroom teachers may find that even primary grade students believe that they have no control over their lives, that it makes no difference what they do or how they act. Therefore, it is all the more important that teachers attempt to help all students achieve coping skills and a sense of self-efficacy. Self-concept appears to be a combination of self-efficacy and self-respect as seen against a background of self-knowledge.

In this definition of self-efficacy, **control** can have external or internal motivators. **External motivators** include factors like luck and the roles that other people play in influencing outcomes. **Internal motivators** are variables within the individual. For example, consider a group of students who have done well on a test and whose teacher asks, "Why did you do so well on that test?" Students who rely on external motivators might reply, "Well, I just got lucky." A student who relies on internal motivators might explain the success by saying, "I studied hard." On the other hand, a student who relies on internal motivators and does poorly on tests would explain their performance by saying, "I'm dumb and that's why I don't do well," or "I didn't think the test was important and I didn't try very hard."

Although students may have similar experiences, the ways they explain those experiences relate to issues of control. Students with external motivators are likely either to dismiss their performance (success or failure) as matters of luck or to credit or blame the influence of others. Students with internal motivators are likely to attribute their performance either to their level of intelligence and skill or to their effort.

Students who have external motivators need help understanding how their behavior contributes to and influences their outcomes in school. These students need clarification as to how teachers determine grades and precise information about how teachers evaluate their work. Students who have internal motivators but low self-esteem (such as thinking, "I'm dumb") need help identifying their strengths and assets (something that can be accomplished when students are given information about learning styles). Self-efficacy can be enhanced.

Another component of empowerment is self-respect. **Self-respect** is believing that you deserve happiness, achievement, and love. Self-respect is treating yourself at least as nicely as you treat other people. Many students are not aware of their internal voices (established at an early age). Internal voices are constantly sending messages, either positive or negative. Psychologists say that most of us have either a generally positive outlook on life, which causes our inner voice to send positive messages ("You're okay," "People like you," "Things will be all right," etc.) or a generally negative outlook on life, which causes our inner voice to send negative messages ("You're not okay," "You're too fat, skinny, ugly, stupid," etc.).

Two tools that can help students "reprogram" their inner voices are affirmations and visualizations (Ellis 1991). Affirmations are statements describing what students want. Affirmations must be personal, positive, and written in the present tense. What makes affirmations effective are details. For example, instead of saying, "I am stupid," the teacher can encourage students to say, "I am capable. I do well in school because I am organized, I study daily, I get all my work completed on time, and I take my schoolwork seriously." Students must repeat these affirmations must until they say them with total conviction.

Visualizations are images students can create whereby they see themselves the way they want to be. For example, students wanting to improve their typing skills would evaluate what it would look like, sound like, and feel like to be better typists. Once the students identify the images, they have to rehearse those images in their minds.

Fair Play and Character Development

With regard to moral development, teachers should be familiar with the concepts of Lawrence Kohlberg. Following the example of Piaget, Kohlberg developed a scenario to quiz children and teens. Kohlberg told a story about a man whose wife was so seriously ill that she would die without medication, yet her husband had no money to buy her medicine. After trying various legal means to get the drug, her husband considered stealing it. After telling the story, Kohlberg asked the child or teen if it would be wrong or right to steal the drug and to explain why. Kohlberg did not evaluate whether the respondent said it was wrong or right to steal the medicine; he was interested in the reasons given to justify the actions.

On the basis of the responses he received, Kohlberg proposed six stages of moral development. Stage 1, **punishment and obedience**, describes children who follow the rules simply to escape punishment. If teachers tell these children, for example kindergarteners, not to talk or they will lose their chance to go outside for recess, they will not want to lose their playground privileges, so they will not talk.

On the other hand, stage 2, **individualism and change**, refers to children who follow the rules not only to escape punishment but also to receive a reward for following the rules. These children, for example older primary grade children, seek not only to escape punishment but also to receive a reward or benefit for their good behavior.

Kohlberg's stage 3 includes **mutual interpersonal expectations and interpersonal conformity**. At this stage, children want to please the people who are important to them. Junior high students, for example, may behave in a manner that gains the approval of their peers or their idols. At stage 4, Kohlberg believed, adolescents become oriented to conscience, and they recognize the importance of established social order. Teens at this stage **obey the rules** (**fair play**), unless those rules contradict higher social responsibilities. In other words, most high school students realize that rules are necessary, and they will obey most rules reflecting basic social values, such as honesty, mutual respect, courtesy, and so forth.

Postconventional morality was the term Kohlberg gave to stages 5 and 6. At stage 5, individuals recognize the importance of both **individual rights** and **social contracts** and believe that people should generally abide by the rules to bring the greatest good to the majority. Kohlberg believed that about one-fifth of adolescents reach stage 5. Therefore, Kohlberg expected few high school students to be operating at this level.

Finally, Kohlberg did not expect high school students to reach stage 6, because he believed that very few individuals ever reach this stage. Universal principles of justice characterize stage 6. Individuals at this stage believe that citizens should obey most rules based on just principles. However, if rules violate ethical principles, individuals have a greater obligation to follow their conscience even if that means breaking the rules. Social reformers, such as Martin Luther King Jr., would be examples of individuals with stage 6 moral reasoning.

Kohlberg's theory describes the progression of children's moral reasoning from school entry at kindergarten (stage 1) to graduation from high school (stage 4 and, for some, stage 5). Kohlberg's theory is not without controversy. Some describe Kohlberg's theory as limited and biased because of his research techniques (getting reactions to a scenario) and because he based his theory on a study of white, middle-class males under age 17. Many would say that his ideas have limited application to other ethnic or socioeconomic groups or females.

Conflict Resolution

Violence prevention strategies at school range from adding social skills training to the curriculum to installing metal detectors at the entrances to buildings. Educational experts recommend that schools teach all students procedures in conflict resolution and anger management, in addition to explaining the school's rules, expectations, and disciplinary policies.

The U.S. Department of Education and the Department of Justice have produced a joint report recommending actions to promote school safety. First, an open discussion of safety issues is essential. The report advises schools to instruct in the dangers of firearms, in the proper strategies for addressing feelings, and ways to settle conflicts. Furthermore, the report cautions that students must realize that they are responsible for actions, choices, and decisions; they are accountable for the choices. The report recommends treating students with equal respect, creating ways for students to share their concerns, and helping children feel safe when expressing their feelings.

Stress Management

Stress is the product of any change, either negative or positive. Environmental factors such as noise, air pollution, and crowding; physiological factors such as sickness and physical injuries; and, finally, psychological factors such as self-deprecating thoughts and negative self-image cause stress. In addition to the normal stressors that everyone experiences, some students may be living in dysfunctional families, some may be dealing with substance abuse and addictions, and some may be experiencing sexual abuse. Students have numerous sources of stress in their lives.

Because life is a stressful process, it is important that students and faculty learn acceptable ways to cope with stress. The first step in coping with stress is to recognize the role that stress plays in our lives. A teacher might lead a class through a brainstorming activity to help the students become aware of the various sources of stress affecting them. Next, the teacher could identify positive ways of coping with stress, including positive self-talk, physical exercise, proper nutrition, adequate sleep, balanced activities, time management techniques, good study habits, and relaxation exercises.

Students face stress often experience a wide range of emotions. They may be sad, depressed, frustrated, or afraid; on the positive side, they may be happy or surprised. Effective teachers realize that students' emotions, as explained in this section and the preceding section on human development, play a significant role in students' classroom performance and achievement. Thus, effective teachers seek to create a classroom environment supportive of students' emotional needs. They have appropriate empathy and compassion for the emotional conflicts facing students; a realistic awareness that students need to attain crucial academic and

social skills that will give them some control over their environment as they become increasingly independent individuals and, eventually, productive citizens should temper their concern.

Skill Five

Identify Problems Associated with Physical, Social, and Emotional Health

If a student continually misbehaves or behaves in a disturbing manner, the effective teacher tries to determine if any external influences are causing the misbehavior; the school may request additional intervention from the teacher and/or family. When under emotional stress, students may act out or behave differently for the duration of the stress-inducing event.

Teachers should also be concerned about the physical, social, and emotional health of their students. For instance, nervousness caused by a test or a school play audition may cause a student to speak out of turn or appear skittish. The loss of a loved one may cause a student to become depressed. Such behaviors are normal reactions to stress. However, teachers must pay attention to these situations and observe if the misbehavior occurs for an extended period. Unusual and/or aggressive student behavior may indicate that the student is suffering from severe emotional distress. Teachers must be careful to note the frequency, duration, and intensity of the student's misconduct.

The teacher should record atypical behaviors, such as lying, stealing, and fighting, and should attempt to determine the motivation behind the behavior. Is the child lying to avoid a reprimand? Is the student telling false stories to hide feelings of insecurity? Does the student cry during a particular subject or at random moments during the school day? These are some of the many questions the teacher needs to consider.

Misbehaving may be a sign that a student is losing control of his or her actions and is looking for help. The role of the teacher in these situations is to help determine if the student is acting out as a reaction to a particular issue or if there is a deeper emotional problem. Some students may require various forms of therapy to treat the emotional disturbances that cause the misbehavior. Therapy may determine if there is a more severe cause for the student's behavior. The teacher and appropriate school personnel may need to be in constant discussion with the student's parents and to establish an open dialogue with the student's family to facilitate the student's treatment. Together, the parents and teacher may provide important and unique insights into the student's situation.

School professionals are a valuable resource for advice, assistance, and support when treating students' emotional disturbances. Guidance counselors, school psychiatrists, and other specialists are able to aid in the counseling of these students and make recommendations for the parents and teacher. With the student's family, these professionals may develop or recommend a particular program or therapy for treatment.

When working with a class of students with emotional disorders, the management of the classroom must be flexible to aid in the students' development. While the goal of any management system is to prevent misbehavior, the teacher must be prepared to provide an area or opportunity for the students to regain control should emotional episodes occur.

Teachers should also be aware that drug therapy is often a form of treatment. Prescribed by medical doctors, the drug treatments that are available can help students gain independence from their disorder. However, these drugs treat the symptoms rather than the cause of the disorder and can have severe side effects. The classroom teacher and the school nurse must help to monitor the drug treatments.

Behavior Patterns

Established behavior patterns that teachers must be aware of include neurotic disorders, psychotic disorders, and autism.

Neurotic disorders, or neuroses, manifest various emotional and physical signs. **Depression** can manifest itself in an overall lack of interest in activities, constant crying, or talk of suicide. **Anxiety** or obsessive thoughts are another indication of a possible neurotic disorder. Physical signs include a disruption in eating or sleeping patterns, headaches, nausea and stomach pain, or diarrhea. The teacher needs to consider these neuroses as a cause for serious concern and treatment.

Psychotic disorders, such as schizophrenia, are serious emotional disorders. These disorders are rare in young children and difficult to diagnose. One of the warning signs for psychotic disorders is that the student experiences a complete break from the reality of his or her surroundings. Schizophrenics may have difficulty expressing themselves, resulting in unusual speech patterns or even muteness. Schizophrenics, who are more likely to be boys than girls, may also exhibit facial expressions that are either markedly absent of emotion or overly active.

Infantile autism is a serious emotional disorder that appears in early childhood. Characteristics include withdrawn behavior and delayed or absent language and communication skills.

Symptoms of autism can appear in children between four and eighteen months of age. Autistic children will usually distance themselves from others and may be unable to experience empathy. In addition, they often cannot distinguish or appreciate humor. Autistic children may have a preoccupation with particular objects or may perform particular activities repeatedly. While autistic children can range in all levels of intelligence, some children may have particular skills and in focused areas, such as music or math. Diagnosis might inaccurately determine mental retardation, hearing/auditory impairment, or brain damage. Treatment for autistic children may involve therapy, drugs, or residential living. However, only five percent of autistic children ever becomes socially well-adjusted adults.

Substance Abuse and the Law

Teachers should be aware of suspicious behaviors that might indicate substance abuse. Such abuse affects physical, social, and emotional health. Florida state law requires that school personnel report suspicions of use, possession, or sale of any controlled substance, model glue, or alcoholic beverage to the appropriate school authorities. More about the law and substance abuse is a part of Competency 3 (Knowledge of Community

Health and Safety Issues): Skill One (Identifying Factors Contributing to Substance Use and Abuse and Identifying Signs, Symptoms, Effects, and Prevention Strategies) below.

Schools as Social Places

Schools, regardless of grade level, are social places. Students form social relationships with adults, with peers who are their own age, and with students in different age and developmental groups. In the social environment of a school, teachers can encourage social development through their interactions with students.

Eric Erikson's theory of social development, or psychosocial theory, is commonly used in education to provide us with a way to think about the social and emotional development of students. Erikson used stages to describe social development. Knowing these stages and the approximate age ranges in which children struggle with each stage can help teachers identify the patterns of social development of their students.

From birth to about age 1, children develop a sense of **trust** and benevolence of society. While this stage occurs long before a child enters the classroom, it is important for teachers to recognize it as a stage of social development.

When children reach about 1 to 3 years of age, they develop a sense of **autonomy**. Autonomy can be seen in any typically developing 2-year-old who insists on accomplishing a task independently. Children at this stage of social development begin to refuse help and try to accomplish tasks on their own that previously were done for them. Teachers can encourage autonomy in their students by allowing students to try new things, make mistakes, and make messes as they try to accomplish tasks so that students can learn from those experiences.

As children enter school, at 3 to 6 years of age, they are developing a sense of **initiative**. Initiative can be seen in children who independently explore, make decisions, and investigate their world. Teachers can encourage initiative by providing positive feedback for student attempts at taking initiative regardless of the outcome. The social interaction of a teacher acknowledging a student's attempt or initiative is what motivates the student at this stage.

As children progress through elementary school, from 6 to 12 years of age, they develop a sense of **industry** or a need for mastery and competence in tasks they face. At this stage of social development, students seek out challenges and enjoy accomplishing tasks. Teachers can encourage industry by engaging students in tasks that are challenging, but not so challenging that the student always fails. Students are motivated by their successes when they have a healthy sense of industry. As with initiative, students who are developing a sense of industry are motivated by teachers who acknowledge their accomplishments.

During adolescence, from 12 to 18 years of age, children are developing their identity. Students in this stage of social development often rebel against society in an effort to define their identity. Teachers can encourage students to develop their sense of identity by offering a stable and consistent learning environment. They should encourage discussion and activities that facilitate the student to think about their role in society, societal affiliations such as political groups, education or career goals, and family or cultural values.

In summary, teachers should be concerned about the physical, social, and emotional health of their students. When problems arise, teachers can use appropriate school personnel and the administration for help.

Skill Six

Identify Factors Related to Responsible Sexual Behavior

Preventing substance abuse is a way to promote responsible sexual behavior. Successful prevention programs have led to more responsible sexual behavior. Teachers must be aware of children who are prematurely interested in sex acts. Children who are prepubertal and act in a sexual manner often have learned this behavior by example. They are possible victims of sexual abuse. For example, young children who masturbate in the classroom or attempt to foist sexual behavior on their classmates are neither sexually developed nor mature enough to understand the consequences of their actions.

A sudden show of promiscuity may follow molestation. Kissing, usually seen as a positive interaction between parent and child, is abuse if done in a sexual manner, as are leers and sexual stares. Parents are not the only ones to commit sexual abuse of children; other family members, including siblings or grandparents, or even family friends may also be the perpetrators of criminal abuse.

How to Report Suspicions of Abuse

A teacher may want to comfort a child who admits to being sexually abused. However, the teacher must be careful not to interview the child but to wait for the trained professional to deal with abuse; otherwise, the teacher might inadvertently delay or even damage the possibility of a conviction and potentially cause more harm to the child. A state-licensed teacher must report any suspicion of child abuse or neglect. Anyone—especially educators—must report these suspicions. Reports are required of anyone—but especially educators—in such cases.

Teachers must report suspicions to enable investigations. Failure to report suspected abuse might adversely affect the child's life. A teacher has the right to have the report kept confidential, but including the teacher's name could save time and effort if more information becomes necessary. Failure to file a report of suspicion of child abuse or neglect has consequences; it can result in a fine, criminal charges, or revocation of teacher certification or license to teach.

A delay in reporting solid suspicions of child abuse or neglect may be cause for action against the teacher. Solid suspicion does not mean proof; it means that the suspicion is reasonable. Once again, the onus of deciding if the suspected child abuse or neglect is real is on the counselor, not the teacher. If it is deemed necessary, the counselor—not the teacher who reports the suspicion—initiates an investigation immediately. If there is no immediate threat to the child, an investigatory team begins to collect further evidence within 24 hours.

After the report, the teacher should realize that the child—already needing support—may feel that the educator has exposed the child's private life. While accepting the child's feeling of betrayal, the teacher can explain that the report was necessary and assure the child of protection against reprisals for telling about the abuse. Sometimes the child benefits from just knowing that others do care about his or her well-being.

After the filing of the report, the teacher should avoid the person suspected of the abuse or neglect. Should the teacher experience harassment or persecution from this person, the teacher should go to the police. If the report turns into a legal issue, the teacher should retain an attorney. Although there should be protection for the teacher as the reporter, legal matters can take unusual directions, and a teacher may need legal advice to avoid becoming another victim of criminal behavior.

Every teacher needs to know that suspected sexual abuse creates special situations. The teacher should ask for permission before patting a student on the back or holding a student's hand. The student has the right to decide whether he or she wants the teacher's touch, and the teacher must acknowledge that decision. Often, the most important action for the teacher to take after reporting suspected abuse is to offer support to the student.

Puberty

As students enter junior high or begin their secondary education, they experience important physiological changes with the onset of puberty. With puberty come changes in primary sexual characteristics and the emergence of secondary sexual characteristics. In addition to a physical transformation, the student entering puberty experiences a number of bodily feelings and an increase in sex drive.

Girls, on average, reach maturational milestones before boys. Physical changes may cause embarrassment to both females and males when they draw unwelcome attention; moreover, these changes almost always create some discomfort as adolescents find the body they were familiar and comfortable with to be quite different, sometimes seemingly overnight. Teachers should be aware of the changes in the students and should not be afraid to use the professional resources available.

Competency 34: Knowledge of Community Health and Safety Issues

Four test items relate to this competency.

Skill One

Identify Factors Contributing to Substance Use and Abuse and Identify Signs, Symptoms, Effects, and Prevention Strategies

Factors That Contribute to Substance Use and Abuse

Drug and alcohol problems can affect anyone, regardless of age, sex, race, marital status, place of residence, income level, or lifestyle. However, there are certain identifiable risk factors for substance abuse. **Risk factors** are characteristics that occur statistically more often for those who develop alcohol and drug problems, as either adolescents or adults, than for those who do not develop substance abuse problems. These factors, include individual, familial, social, and cultural characteristics.

Individual Characteristics

These personality characteristics include the following:

- Aggressiveness
- Aggressiveness combined with shyness
- Decreased social inhibition
- Emotional problems
- Inability to express feelings appropriately
- Hypersensitivity

- Inability to cope with stress
- Problems with relationships
- Cognitive problems
- Low self-esteem
- Difficult temperament
- Overreaction

Other important personal factors are whether the individual is the child of an alcoholic or abuser of other drugs; whether there is less than two years between the child and older or younger siblings; and whether the child has any birth defects, including possible neurological and neurochemical dysfunctions. The presence of physical disabilities, physical or mental health problems, or learning disabilities can add to the student's vulnerability to substance abuse. In many ways, students who are at risk for academic problems are also susceptible to substance abuse problems.

In adolescence, other factors that are statistically related to problems with substance abuse emerge. These factors are school failure and attrition (dropping out); delinquency; violence; early, unprotected sexual activity; teen pregnancy or parenthood; unemployment or underemployment; mental health problems; and suicidal tendencies. Teachers should be alert to these factors; they can be signs of a number of negative adolescent behaviors and experiences, including a failure to bond with society through family, school, or community; rebellion and nonconformity; resistance to authority; a strong need for independence; cultural alienation; feelings of failure and a fragile ego; lack of self-confidence and low self-esteem; and the inability to form positive, close relationships and/or an increased vulnerability to negative peer pressure.

Family Characteristics

Associated with substance abuse among youth are several family characteristics. First, and perhaps most important, is the alcohol or other drug dependency of a parent or both parents. This characteristic might relate to another significant factor: parental abuse and neglect of children. Antisocial and/or mentally ill parents are factors that put children at risk for drug and/or alcohol abuse. In addition, high levels of family stress (including financial strain); large, overcrowded family conditions; family unemployment or underemployment; and parents who have little education or who are socially isolated are also risk factors. Single parents without family or other support; family instability; a high level of marital and family conflict or violence; and parental absenteeism due to separation, divorce, or death can also increase children's vulnerability. Finally, other important factors to consider are the lack of family rituals, inadequate parenting, little child-to-parent interaction, and frequent family moves. These factors describe children without affiliation or a sense of identity with their families or community. Any of these family factors could lead to a substance abuse problem in a student.

Social and Cultural Characteristics

Living in an economically depressed area with high unemployment, inadequate housing, a high crime rate, and a prevalence of illegal drug use are social characteristics that can put an individual at risk for substance abuse. Cultural risk factors include minority status involving racial discrimination, differing generational levels of assimilation, low levels of education, and low achievement expectations from society at large.

All the recognized risk factors are only indicators of the potential for substance abuse. They are not necessarily predictive of an individual's proclivity to drug or alcohol abuse. Some children who are exposed to very adverse conditions grow up to be healthy, productive, and well-functioning adults. Yet, knowing the risk factors, teachers are better able to identify children vulnerable to substance abuse and develop prevention education strategies. If teachers recognize these risk factors in some of their students, there are certain things that teachers possibly can do to increase the chances that the youngster or adolescent will resist the lures of illegal and dangerous alcohol and drug abuse.

Fetal Alcohol Syndrome

Another problem that merits teachers' attention is the effect of drug use. This can take many forms. A child may show developmental delays (cognitively, socially, physically, and psychologically) because of prenatal drug abuse by parents. Mothers who drink alcohol during pregnancy may give birth to infants with fetal alcohol syndrome (FAS). Children with FAS have a distinct pattern of facial abnormalities, growth retardation, and evidence of central nervous system dysfunction. Even those who do not have the characteristic facial abnormalities and growth retardation associated with FAS have brain and other neurological deficits, such as poor motor skills, hand-eye coordination problems, and complex behavioral and learning problems, including difficulties with memory, attention, and judgment. The National Organization on Fetal Alcohol Syndrome provides extensive information about individuals with FAS and effective strategies for working with these individuals.

Identify Signs and Symptoms of Substance Use and Abuse

Sometimes it can be difficult to tell if someone is using illegal drugs or alcohol. Usually, people who abuse drugs or alcohol (including young people) go to great lengths to keep their behavior a secret. They deny and/or try to hide the problem. However, certain warning signs can indicate that someone is using drugs or drinking too much alcohol:

- Lying about things

- Avoiding people who are longtime friends or associates

- Giving up activities that once brought pleasure and positive feedback (ranging from failing to turn in homework assignments to giving up extracurricular activities such as sports, drama, band, and so forth)

- Getting into legal trouble

- Taking risks (including sexual risks and driving under the influence of alcohol and/or drugs)

- Feeling run-down, hopeless, depressed, even suicidal

- Suspension from school for an alcohol- or drug-related incident

- Missing classes or performing poorly

Other suspicious behaviors are not making eye contact; having slurred speech; smelling of alcohol or drugs (such as marijuana); complaining of headaches, nausea, or dizziness; having difficulty staying awake; and difficulty in participating in class activities. These examples, in and of themselves, are insufficient to confirm a substance abuse problem, but in combination and when displayed consistently over time, they are strong indicators. Teachers should record their observations and keep written reports of the behavioral changes they witness. Moreover, they should report their suspicions to the appropriate school authorities.

Effects of Substance Use and Abuse

Dr. Elaine M. Johnson, director of the Center for Substance Abuse Prevention, believes that preventing substance abuse would reduce crime, violence, school failure, teen pregnancy, unemployment, homelessness, HIV/AIDS, accidental deaths, and the costs of health care. The focus of the schools and educators should be on promoting healthy, constructive lifestyles for drug-free individuals.

Prevention and Treatment of Drug Users

Prevention reduces the risk of danger in society and fosters a safer environment. Successful prevention programs have led to reductions in traffic fatalities, violence, HIV/AIDS and other sexually transmitted diseases, rape, teen pregnancy, child abuse, cancer and heart disease, injuries and trauma, and many other problems associated with drug abuse.

The backbone of substance abuse prevention is education. Every professional educator should be aware of the behaviors and characteristics that indicate a tendency toward the use of drugs and/or alcohol and that indicate that students are under the influence of drugs and/or alcohol. Moreover, to protect other students and to secure assistance for the abuser, teachers must be able to make immediate referrals when there is an indication that a student may be using drugs and/or alcohol. Finally, teachers must provide accurate information to students concerning substance abuse.

Experts suggest that children have a better chance to grow up as healthy adults if they can learn to do one thing well that they, their friends, or their community members value. Teachers certainly can help ensure that students achieve this goal by teaching them the crucial reading, writing, and math skills that will enable them to become independent learners. By presenting lessons that require the development of effective communication and critical thinking skills, teachers can help students acquire important life skills. Other important strategies for educators to consider are:

- Require children to be helpful as they grow up.

- Help children learn how to ask for help themselves (develop assertiveness skills).

- Help children elicit positive responses from others in their environment.

- Enable children to develop a sense of community in their classrooms and to work collaboratively and/or in cooperation.

- Assist children in developing a healthy distance from their dysfunctional families so family members are not their sole frame of reference.

- Encourage children to form bonds with the school and to identify with the school as an important and integral part of the community.

- Act as a caring adult who provides students with consistent caring responses and messages. (This is a crucial element in preventing substance abuse among children exposed to multiple risk factors.)

In addition to school resources, students with substance abuse problems can find help in a number of community resources, including community drug hotlines, community treatment centers, emergency health care clinics, local health departments, Alcoholics Anonymous, Narcotics Anonymous, Al-Anon, Alateen, and hospitals.

Schools should adopt zero-tolerance policies for guns and drugs. For safer schools and a higher quality of education, schools should provide effective anti-drug and substance abuse prevention programs, including those that teach responsible decision-making, mentoring, mediation, and other activities aimed at changing unsafe, harmful, or destructive behaviors.

Florida State Law Concerning Substance Abuse and Use in Schools

Teachers should report suspicious behaviors to the appropriate school authorities. Florida state law requires that school personnel "report to the principal or the principal's designee any suspected unlawful use, possession, or sale by a student of any controlled substance, any alcoholic beverage, or model glue."

The law further states:

> School personnel are exempt from civil liability when reporting in good faith to the proper school authority such suspected unlawful use, possession or sale by a student. Only a principal or the principal's designee is authorized to contact a parent or legal guardian of a student regarding this situation. (Florida Statute, Chapter 232.277, Item 1)

Teachers should not delay in taking action. Substance abuse has the potential for great harm. Authorities can investigate and verify or allay the teacher's concerns.

Skill Two

Demonstrate Knowledge of Resources from Home, School, and Community That Provide Valid Health Information, Products, and Services

Teachers can find a number of helpful resources for teaching students about the dangers of substance abuse and for promoting prevention by contacting agencies or organizations like the following:

American Council for Drug Education
164 West 74th Street
New York, NY 10023
(800) 488-3784
http://www.acde.org/

National Center on Addiction and Substance Abuse at Columbia University
633 Third Avenue, 19th Floor
New York, NY 10017-6706
(212) 841-5200
http://www.casacolumbia.org/

National Clearinghouse for Alcohol and Drug Information
11420 Rockville Pike
Rockville, MD 20852
(800) 729-6686
http://www.ncadi.samhsa.gov/

In addition, the Internet offers a number of sites with useful information. The Substance Abuse and Mental Health Services Administration (*http://www.samhsa.gov/*) and the National Institute on Drug Abuse (*http://www.nida.nih.gov/*) have excellent Web sites with links to updated statistics, reports, and educational materials. Prevention education promotes healthy and constructive lifestyles that discourage drug abuse and fosters the development of social environments that facilitate and support drug-free lifestyles.

Successful prevention means that underage youth, pregnant women, and others at high risk do not use alcohol, tobacco, or other drugs. Education for prevention is necessary. Alcohol is the drug of choice by teenagers in America. Those under 21 consume 25 percent of the alcohol in the nation. More than 31.5 percent of high school students binge drink once a month. The proportion of those who begin drinking in eighth grade jumped from 27% in 1975 to 36% in 2002. Male (40.2%) and female (41%) ninth graders are equally as likely to drink. The proportion of children who begin drinking in the eighth grade (or earlier) increased from 27 in 1975 to 36% in 2002. These numbers are disturbing. Eighty percent of high school students have tried alcohol while 70% have tried cigarettes (Califano, Joseph A. Jr.). Teachers and parents should play an important role in drug and alcohol education and abuse prevention.

Skill Three

Identify Appropriate Violence Prevention Strategies in the Home, School, and Community

Warning Signs of Violence

Experts tend to agree that drug use (including alcohol use) and other high-risk behaviors are inextricably linked to violence. Because of events like the shootings in Columbine, Colorado, teachers must be ever vigilant. These are some of the common warning signs that students could be at risk for violent behavior in the home, school, or community:

- History of being violent toward his/her peers
- Access to firearms
- Involvement in drinking alcohol or taking other drugs

- Caregivers with a history of drug or alcohol involvement

- Peer group that reinforces antisocial behaviors

- Learned attitudes of accepting aggressive behavior as "normal" and an effective way to solve problems

- High level of violence in the home, in the neighborhood, and in the media

- School history that includes aggressive and disruptive classroom behavior

- Poor school achievement, poor school attendance, and numerous school suspensions

- Difficulty with social skills and poor peer relations

- Difficulty controlling impulses and emotions

- History of parental rejection, inconsistent discipline, and lack of supervision

Of course, the parallel between the warning signs of potentially violent behavior and those of potential drug use is obvious. Often, although not always, the students with drug problems are the same ones with a proclivity for violent behavior.

Even though there is no precise way to predict when a person will become violent, there are some "triggers" that should cause teachers, caregivers, and people in the community to be alert and pay close attention. These include the following:

- Irrational beliefs and ideas

- Verbal, nonverbal, or written threats or intimidation

- Fascination with weaponry and/or acts of violence

- Expressions of a plan to hurt oneself or others

- Externalization of blame

- Unreciprocated romantic obsession

- Taking up much of a teacher's time with behavior or performance problems

- Fear reaction among fellow students or family

- Drastic change in belief systems

- Displays of unwarranted anger

- New or increased source(s) of stress at home or school

- Inability to take criticism

- Feelings of being victimized

- Intoxication from alcohol or other substances

- Expressions of hopelessness or heightened anxiety

- Productivity and/or attendance problems

- Violence toward inanimate objects

- Stealing or sabotaging projects or equipment

- Lack of concern for the safety of others

When teachers observe these "triggers," they must be increasingly aware of the possibility of a crisis situation. Experts on coping with school crises say educators must accept reality:

- Violence can occur.

- Violence can happen to you and your school.

- Teachers and administrators must be alert and aware.

- Safety is an "inside issue."

- Safety must involve a committed student body, school faculty, staff, and community.

If a crisis does occur, teachers should do certain things as part of the school response team. These include the following (Southeastern Regional Vision for Education, 2002):

- Provide accurate information to students.

- Lead class discussions to give everyone the opportunity to express personal feelings, ideas, and concerns.

- Dispel rumors by truthfully answering questions.

- Model appropriate responses of care and concern.

- Give permission for a range of emotions.

- Identify students who need counseling.

- Provide activities to reduce trauma and express emotions through artwork, music, and writing.

- Set aside curriculum as needed.

- Discuss funeral procedures, including customs and etiquette.

- Encourage parents to accompany their children to funerals.

Teachers can either be part of the solution or part of the problem. Armed with information and taking the time to contemplate their role in a crisis, teachers can provide students with important support and guidance in worst-case scenarios.

School Safety

The U.S. Department of Education, in its publication for *Creating Safe and Drug-Free Schools: An Action Guide* (1996), provides suggestions of ways schools can ensure safety and combat drug use. Among the recommendations are the following:

- Establish a team of educators, students, parents, law enforcement, juvenile justice officials, and community leaders to develop a plan for a safe and drug-free school.

- Ensure that students are engaged in schoolwork that is challenging, informative, and rewarding.

- Establish, publish, publicize, and enforce policies that clearly define acceptable and unacceptable behavior with zero tolerance for weapons, violence, gangs, and use or sale of alcohol and drugs.

- Take immediate action on all reports of drug use or sales, threats, bullying, gang activity, or victimization.

- Create an environment that encourages parents and other adults to visit the school and participate in activities.

- Encourage staff to treat students and each other with respect.

- Involve youth in policy and program development.

- Offer programs that teach peaceful, nonviolent conflict-management methods to students, their families, and school staff.

- Work with the media to increase public awareness of safety issues.

Although the concepts in this section have to do with student behaviors, these ideas are equally important to creating safe environments for learning. This, again, is an example of how teaching is not only a set of discrete skills but also the interplay and interconnectedness of skills, abilities, attitudes, and competencies that al-

low teachers to deal successfully with all elements of teaching effectiveness. The importance of a safe school environment for promoting good behavior is apparent; statistics indicate that school safety is a vital concern for all educators.

More than 100,000 students bring weapons to school each day. Every day, 40 students are killed or wounded with these weapons. One out of every five students is afraid to go the restroom at school for fear of victimization. In addition, more than 6,000 teachers are threatened by students each year.

Factors contributing to school violence and antisocial behaviors include (1) overcrowding, (2) poor design and use of school space, (3) lack of disciplinary procedures, (4) student alienation, (4) multicultural insensitivity, (5) rejection of at-risk students by teachers and peers, and (6) anger or resentment at school routines. On the other hand, **factors contributing to school safety** include (1) a positive school climate and atmosphere, (2) clear and high performance expectations for all students, (3) practices and values that promote inclusion, (4) bonding of the students to the school, (5) high levels of student participation and parent involvement in school activities, and (6) opportunities to acquire academic skills and develop socially.

Effective teachers need to be alert to the signs of potentially violent behavior, acknowledging that signs can easily be misinterpreted and misunderstood. Warning signs should be used to get help for children, not to exclude, punish, or isolate them. Experts also emphasize 1) that warning signs are not a checklist for identifying, labeling, or stereotyping children; 2) that referrals based on early warning signals must be kept confidential; and 3) that except for those suspected of child abuse or neglect, referrals to outside agencies must have parental consent.

The Prevention Institute has determined links to the high-risk behaviors among youth. These links to 20–50% of all the high-risk behaviors among youth include (1) poor academic performance; (2) unstructured free time; (3) delinquent peers; (4) media violence; (5) stressful family environments; (6) early involvement with drugs and alcohol; (7) easy access to weapons, especially handguns; (8) large, urban schools with gangs and drugs (particularly in deteriorating communities); and (9) especially males who have witnessed violence and who may have mental illness and poverty.

Longitudinal studies (studies following groups over time) have shown youth violence and delinquency to be linked with situations in which (1) one or more parents have been arrested; (2) the child has been the client of a child-protection agency; (3) the child's family has experienced death, divorce, or another serious transition; (4) the child has received special education services; and/or (5) the youth exhibits severe antisocial behavior.

Along somewhat parallel lines, the U.S. Department of Education and Department of Justice compiled a long list of **possible early warning signs of violent behavior**. Among these signs are the following:

- Social withdrawal (often associated with feelings of depression, rejection, persecution, unworthiness, and lack of confidence)

- Excessive feelings of isolation and being alone

- Excessive feelings of rejection

- Being a victim of violence—including physical or sexual abuse

- Feelings of being picked on and persecuted

- Low school interest and poor academic performance

- Expression of violence in writings and drawings

- Uncontrolled anger

- Patterns of impulsive and chronic hitting, intimidating, and bullying behaviors

- History of discipline problems

- History of violent and aggressive behaviors

- Intolerance for differences and prejudicial attitudes

- Drug use and alcohol use

- Affiliation with gangs

- Inappropriate access to, possession of, and use of firearms

- Serious threats of violence

In addition to these early warning signs are what the departments of Education and Justice call **imminent warning signs**, requiring an immediate response: (1) serious physical fighting with peers or family members; (2) serious destruction of property; (3) rage for seemingly minor reasons; (4) detailed threats of lethal violence; (5) possession and/or use of firearms and weapons; and (6) other self-injurious behaviors or threats of suicide.

Immediate intervention by school authorities and possibly law enforcement officials is required if a child has presented a detailed plan to harm or kill others or is carrying a weapon, particularly a firearm, and has threatened to use it. When students present other threatening behaviors, the schools should inform the parents immediately.

Violence prevention strategies at school range from adding social skills training to the curriculum to installing metal detectors at the entrances to buildings. Schools should teach all students procedures in conflict resolution and anger management and should explain the school rules, expectations, and disciplinary policies.

The federal **Gun-Free Schools Act of 1994** mandates that every state pass zero-tolerance laws on weapons at school or face the loss of federal funds. Every state has complied with this law and requires school districts to expel students for at least a year if they bring weapons to school.

In review, effective and safe schools develop and enforce consistent rules that are clear, broad-based, and fair. Effective schoolwide disciplinary policies include a code of conduct, specific rules, and consequences that can accommodate student differences on a case-by-case basis when necessary. School policies need to include antiharassment and antiviolence policies and due process rights.

Rules should reflect the cultural values and educational goals of the community. School staff, students, and families should develop, discuss, and implement fair rules, Written and applied in a nondiscriminatory manner, these rules should accommodate cultural diversity. Consequences for violating rules must be commensurate with the offenses, and negative consequences must be accompanied by positive teaching for socially appropriate behaviors. Finally, schools must have zero tolerance for illegal possession of weapons, drugs, or alcohol.

Skill Four

Identify Appropriate Safety and Injury Prevention Strategies in the Home, School, and Community

A feeling of safety at home, at school, and in the community is vital for self-actualization, according to Abraham Maslow. Maslow's hierarchy of human needs illustrates a model of self-actualization that is applicable to many fields, including education, business, industry, health, the medical professions, and more.

Maslow identified levels of needs in a hierarchical sequence; this order suggests the satisfaction of lower-level needs must come before individuals can ascend to higher levels of achievement. Maslow identified the fulfillment of basic physiological needs as fundamental to an individuals' sense of well-being and ability to engage in any meaningful activity. Simply stated, the satisfaction of students' physiological needs (to have hunger and thirst satisfied, to have sleep needs met, to be adequately warm, and so forth) is necessary before they can perform school tasks. Many schools provide nutritious meals for students who do not get breakfast at home in an effort to meet the physiological needs; the schools expend great effort and expense to install heating and cooling school buildings.

Maslow's second level of need concerns safety. Again, students must feel safe from harm and danger at home, at school, and in the community before they are ready to learn. Today, metal detectors in the schools increase students' sense of safety. In some schools, guards and security officers patrol the halls.

The third level of need, according to Maslow's theory, is the need for affiliation, or the need for belonging and acceptance by others. Children must feel accepted by their families, their peers, and their communities. Although this need may, at first glance, seem less related to the student's environment, it does, indeed, refer to the student's social environment. Students need

the opportunity to develop social relationships and to establish friendships among their peers. In essence, Maslow determined that environmental factors are important in education.

First Aid

First aid is the immediate, temporary care of an injured or ill person. Occasionally, during physical education classes or during the school hours, injuries and illnesses occur. Therefore, a basic knowledge of first aid is important for physical education teachers and other instructors. However, a teacher should not attempt first aid if the procedures are unclear. A first aid course is important to the classroom teacher.

The following are some common injuries and a brief description of their emergency treatments:

Fracture. Break in a bone. Fractures can be **simple** (a break in the bone, comminuted or shattered); multiple (many breaks in the bone); or **compound** (a break in the bone and the skin). First aid: Immobilize, use ice to control swelling, and seek medical aid. In the case of a compound fracture, it is important to stop the bleeding.

Traumatic shock. Severe compression of circulation caused by injury or illness. Symptoms include cool clammy skin and a rapid weak pulse. First aid: Minimize heat loss, and elevate the legs without disturbing the rest of the body. Seek medical help.

Sprain. Injury to a joint caused by the joint being moved too far or away from its range of motion. Both ligaments and tendons can be injured. Ligaments join bone to bone, and tendons join muscle to bone. First aid: Rest, ice, compression, and elevation (RICE).

Strain. Muscle injury caused by overwork. First aid: Use ice to lessen the swelling. Applying some heat after icing can be beneficial although opinion on the value of heat varies.

Dislocation. Joint injury; bone ends out of place at the joints; holding ligaments severely stretched and torn. First aid: Immobilize and seek medical help. Some people advocate "popping" the dislocation back into place, but this can be risky for both the injured person and for the person giving the first aid (liability).

Heat exhaustion. Cold and clammy skin, nausea, dizziness, and paleness; not as severe as heat stroke. First aid: Increase water intake, replace salt, and get out of the heat.

Heat stroke. High fever, dry skin, and possible unconsciousness. First aid: Attempt to cool off gradually, get into the shade, and seek medical attention immediately.

Heart attack. Shortness of breath, pain in the left arm, pain in the chest, nausea, and sweating. First aid: Elevate the head and chest, give cardiopulmonary resuscitation if indicated, and seek medical assistance.

Seizures. Cause often epilepsy. First aid: Clear the area around the victim to avoid injury during the seizure. Do not place anything in the victim's mouth; seek medical help after the seizure if necessary.

Resuscitation is a first-aid technique that provides artificial circulation and respiration. Remember the ABCs: A is for "airway," B is for "breathing," and C is for "circulation." Check the airway to make sure it is open, and check breathing and circulation.

Recognizing Abuse and Neglect

Consider the following scenario: During an observation, you see that the teacher, Mr. Smith, is getting nowhere with Belinda, the child who sits in the center of the third row of the classroom. No matter how many times Mr. Smith smiles at her, she flinches. If he waves his hands while illustrating a point, she flinches. If he raises his voice to ask for quiet, she flinches. You observe him taking a few spare minutes in his teaching day to sit with her independently, but she does not appear to want this. Is it his fault? Is it the child's? Maybe there is another question to ask: Is it the fault of another who may be abusing or neglecting her?

Despite all the media attention given to child abuse and neglect, many teachers still believe that it cannot happen to one of their students. They may think, "This is a nice neighborhood," or "Most of these students have both a mother and a father living at home."

However, abuse and neglect may happen to children, possibly even to one of your students.

Abuse can sometimes cause modifications in both the chemistry of the brain and a child's neurological structure. Worse yet, the effects may be permanent. The child suffers from chronic shock, which is a result of increased hormones and electrical impulses. Many doctors believe that each time the child suffers abuse, a modification in the child's brain and its systems may occur. It is the stress accompanying the abuse that causes the child to become hypersensitized to the abuse; this hypersensitizing causes brain and body modifications.

These modifications may explain why Belinda involuntarily flinches when Mr. Smith smiles at her. She may believe he is singling her out, and, based on her past experience, being singled out leads to being treated in a negative way. When Mr. Smith makes sudden motions with his hands, as is done when striking a person, or raises his voice, which can also be a precursor to rage, Belinda associates the teacher's behaviors with patterns of abuse. With older children, the effects of child abuse may not be as evident (possibly as a result of being told the child "asked for it" or being threatened with dire consequences if the child tells). The effects of child abuse in older children may be more apparent in their interactions with peers. At times, the teacher may become overly sensitive and may see child abuse or neglect in every bruise and mood change. Through practice and by discussing their suspicions with appropriate school personnel, teachers can become adept at recognizing signs of child abuse or neglect.

Abused children typically show signs of **overstimulation**: being "wired," unruly, and/or belligerent. By contrast, the behaviors of neglected children point to understimulation: all they want is to be left alone, and typically they are unsociable, sedate, and withdrawn; the child learns this behavior at home during periods of neglect. The neglect may change the child's behaviors from almost flat—registering no emotion—to anger. Although poor attention, tears, violence, and languid behavior may be indicators of either abuse or neglect, neglected children usually have feelings of hopelessness and cannot adequately control their thoughts. Students either become obsessed by the neglect or refuse to acknowledge that the neglect is really happening.

Consider another situation: Darnell looks as if he is not getting enough to eat, even though he eats everything, including the other children's leftovers at lunch. He is a shy loner who always looks rundown and seems oblivious to his appearance. The teacher notices he is often absent because of colds and other minor ailments. What the teacher may not know is that these are symptoms of neglect; Darnell's poor nutrition causes his illnesses. Because he is so susceptible to illness, it is important for the teacher to confirm that Darnell's immunizations are up-to-date. Darnell's sad affect may be another clue that he has experienced neglect.

Visible Signs of Abuse

One of the most obvious visible signs of child abuse is red welts caused by being hit. The appearance of welts on a child may be proof of **child abuse**, and the teacher must report the evidence. It is also one way teachers separate real abuse cases from unfounded ones. While marks from the hand, fist, or belt are usually recognizable, other marks in geometric shapes—from eating utensils, paddles, coat hangers, or extension cords—can signify child abuse.

If, for example, a boy in your class has unrecognizable bruises on his arms and legs, they could be the result of whippings. Furthermore, if he constantly has bruises on his neck and head and always tells you they are from falling, be prepared to report suspicion of child abuse; this could be the result of hitting, possibly even choking. Teachers need a basis for their reports. They must notice capillary ruptures (reddened areas) in any bruise, which indicate a strong hit; if a bruise is shaded on its outer borders, it may still be a result of a softer hit, but hitting nonetheless.

It may help to establish the charge of abuse if the teacher also reports the size and shape of the bruises; they brusies may indicate the object that created such bruises. Teachers should be alert to any suspicious marks or signs of abuse and neglect.

Teachers must be aware of children who are prematurely interested in sex acts. Children who are prepubertal and act in a sexual manner have been taught, by example, to act that way. A state-licensed teacher must report any suspicion of child abuse or neglect.

Homes, Schools, and Community

Outside support is a vital asset to any teacher and especially in the case of solicitation. As Hillary Clinton said, quoting an African proverb, "It takes a village to raise a child." The community should be a part of the educational process. Parent Teacher Associations, school improvement teams, colleague networking teams, and community volunteers can all work together to ensure a safe, nurturing climate where all students can bloom to their full potential. In addition, the teacher should become a vital part of the community outside the school system. Students who see their teachers actively involved in their communities gain a respect for their teachers and perceive their teachers as positive role models in their lives.

Competency 35: Knowledge of Subject Content and Appropriate Curriculum Design

Four test items relate to this competency.

Skill One

Distinguish between Developmentally Appropriate and Inappropriate Instructional Practices That Consider the Interaction of Cognitive, Affective, and Psychomotor Domains

There are three areas or domains of learning:

Psychomotor domain. Pertains especially to physical activities or skills that the individual masters. For example, playing basketball demands many physical skills, including dribbling, making free throws from the free throw line, and doing a lay-up shot.

Affective domain. Pertains to feelings and attitudes. If a basketball player enjoys playing with the other team members, it increases the positive feelings that player has about the practices and games. The coach certainly wants the players to feel joy in the game they are playing.

Cognitive domain. Pertains to thinking. Some basketball coaches administer paper-and-pencil tests to be certain that the players understand the rules.

Of course physical activities or instructional activities in the elementary school must be developmentally appropriate. The characteristics of children in grades 1 through 3 suggest that throwing the ball is easier than catching a ball; therefore, dodgeball is popular. Other characteristics of children age 6 through 8 indicate that they like large-muscle activities, games in which they can shout and chase each other, repetition of favorite games, and free play. Children in the upper-elementary grades are ready for increasing skill development, more games with rules, and activities involving tossing and catching balls.

Skill Two

Identify Various Factors to Consider When Planning Physical Activities

When planning physical activities—or any classroom activity, for that matter—the teacher should attempt to do the following:

- Create and sustain a safe, efficient, supportive learning environment.

- Evaluate the appropriateness of the physical environment for facilitating student learning and promoting safety.

- Identify a repertoire of techniques for establishing smooth, efficient, and well-paced routines.

- Involve students in establishing rules and standards for behavior.

- Identify emergency procedures for student and campus safety.

While there are certain physical aspects of the classroom that are permanent (e.g., size and shape of the room, number of windows, type of lighting, etc.),

others are changeable. Windows can have shades or blinds that distribute light correctly and allow for a darkened room for video or computer viewing. If the light switches do not allow part of the lights to remain on, sometimes schools will change the wiring system. If not, teachers can use a lamp to provide minimum lighting for monitoring students during videos or films.

Schools often schedule maintenance, such as painting and floor cleaning, during the summer. Often school administrators will comply with teachers' requests for specific colors of paint if the maintenance department has sufficient time for planning.

Most classrooms have movable desks, which allow for varied seating arrangements and for opening areas of the classroom up for group games or activities. However, the teacher should ensure that students cannot fall over or bump against furniture and receive injuries.

The equipment used in physical activities should vary according to the age of the students. For instance, large balls are better for young children than are small balls.

Skill Three

Analyzing the Influence of Culture, Media, Technology, and Other Factors When Planning Health and Wellness Instruction

All classrooms should have a bulletin board for the teacher and the students. The effective teacher has plans for changing the board according to units of study. Space for displaying students' work, either on the bulletin board, the wall, or in the hallway, is necessary.

Bare walls can be depressing; however, covering the walls with too many posters can be visually distracting. Posters with sayings that promote cooperation, rules for games, diagrams for warm-up drills, study skills, and content ideas are helpful. Teachers should change the displays several times during the school year because students will ignore the displays when they become too familiar.

Some physical activities require technological equipment. For instance, a dance class might need a compact disc (CD) player to play music and a video player to watch a film of a finished dance; a softball team might need a computer to check the rules of the game. Technology contributes to effective instruction.

Physical education—on the playground or in the classroom—has definite association with almost every subject in the curriculum. The opportunities for integrating physical education with other subjects in the curriculum are many.

An appreciation for other cultures and for other ways of life may be an outcome of including games and dances from other cultures and other nations. Teachers can integrate these activities into the curriculum or employ them in isolation during the physical education periods.

Using advertisements, public health brochures, and Web sites can help teachers when planning wellness and health instruction. Students, too, may receive or be able locate pertinent materials; the teacher can use them as a springboard to instruction.

References

Califano, Joseph A. Jr. "Teen Tipplers: America's Underage Drinking Epidemic." February 26, 2002. Washington, D. C.: National Press Club. *http://www.casacolumbia.org/absolutenm/templates/articles.asp?articleid=247&zoneid=31*

Cummins, J. "The Role of Primary Language Development in Promoting Educational Success for Language Minority Students." In *Schooling and Language Minority Students: A Theoretical Rationale* (3-49), ed. by California State Department of Education. Los Angeles, CA: California State University, 1981.

Cummins, J. "Tests, Achievement, and Bilingual Students." Focus, No. 9. February 1, 1982. Wheaton, MD: National Clearinghouse for Bilingual Education.

Centers for Disease Control and Prevention. *Physical activity for everyone: Physical activity terms. http://www.cdc.gov/nccdphp/dnpa/physical/terms/index.htm.*

Erikson, E. (1963). *Childhood and society*. New York: Horton.

Goplerud E. N., ed. 1990. *Breaking new ground for youth at risk: Program summaries*. Rockville, MD: Alcohol, Drug Abuse, and Mental Health Administration, Office for Substance Abuse Prevention. Report No. DHHS-ADM-89-1658 (OSAP technical report 1).

Elliott, Raymond. 1960. *Teaching music*. Columbus, Ohio: Charles E. Merrill.

Florida State Law, Chapter 232.277.

Ellis, D. (1991). *Becoming a master student*. Rapid City, SD: College Survival.

Hoffer, Charles R. 1982. *Teaching music in the elementary classroom*. New York: Harcourt Brace Jovanovich.

Johnson, Elaine M. 1998. *Making prevention work*. Rockville, MD: Center for Substance Abuse Prevention.

Kaufman, P., Chen, X., Choy, S. P., Ruddy, S. A., Miller, A. K., Chandler, K. A., Chapman, C. D., Rand, M. R., and Klaus, P. *Indicators of School Crime and Safety, 1999*. U.S. Departments of Education and Justice, National Center for Education Statistics and Bureau of Justice Statistics, Washington, D.C.: 1999.

Kohlberg, L. "The Psychology of Moral Development: The Nature and Validity of Moral Stages." *Essays on Moral Development* Vol. 2, 1984.

National Clearinghouse for Alcohol and Drug Information. 1998. *Straight facts about drugs and alcohol*. Rockville, MD: National Clearinghouse for Alcohol and Drug Information.

National Organization for Fetal Alcohol Syndrome (NO-FAS). *http://www.nofas.org/main/what_is_FAS.htm*

Piaget, J. The Psychology of Intelligence. London: Routledge and Kegan Paul, 1950. Prevention Institute. No date. "What Factors Increase the Risk of Being Involved in Violence?" *http://www.preventioninstitute.org/schoolvio14.html*

South Carolina Visual and Performing Arts Curriculum Framework Writing Team. 1993. *South Carolina visual and performing arts framework*. Columbia: South Carolina State Board of Education.

U.S. Department of Agriculture. *Steps to a healthier you. http://www.mypyramid.gov.*

U.S. Department of Education. 1996 (September). *Creating safe and drug-free schools: An action guide.* *http://www.ncjrs.org/pdffiles/safescho.pdf.*

U.S. Departments of Education and Justice. *Early Warning, Timely Response.* Washington, D.C.: U.S. Government Printing Office, 1998.

Wassum, S. (1979) "Elementary school children's vocal range." *Journal of Research in Music Education.* 27, 214–226.

FTCE

Florida Teacher Certification Examinations
Elementary Education K–6

Practice Test

Answer Sheet

1. Ⓐ Ⓑ Ⓒ Ⓓ
2. Ⓐ Ⓑ Ⓒ Ⓓ
3. Ⓐ Ⓑ Ⓒ Ⓓ
4. Ⓐ Ⓑ Ⓒ Ⓓ
5. Ⓐ Ⓑ Ⓒ Ⓓ
6. Ⓐ Ⓑ Ⓒ Ⓓ
7. Ⓐ Ⓑ Ⓒ Ⓓ
8. Ⓐ Ⓑ Ⓒ Ⓓ
9. Ⓐ Ⓑ Ⓒ Ⓓ
10. Ⓐ Ⓑ Ⓒ Ⓓ
11. Ⓐ Ⓑ Ⓒ Ⓓ
12. Ⓐ Ⓑ Ⓒ Ⓓ
13. Ⓐ Ⓑ Ⓒ Ⓓ
14. Ⓐ Ⓑ Ⓒ Ⓓ
15. Ⓐ Ⓑ Ⓒ Ⓓ
16. Ⓐ Ⓑ Ⓒ Ⓓ
17. Ⓐ Ⓑ Ⓒ Ⓓ
18. Ⓐ Ⓑ Ⓒ Ⓓ
19. Ⓐ Ⓑ Ⓒ Ⓓ
20. Ⓐ Ⓑ Ⓒ Ⓓ
21. Ⓐ Ⓑ Ⓒ Ⓓ
22. Ⓐ Ⓑ Ⓒ Ⓓ
23. Ⓐ Ⓑ Ⓒ Ⓓ
24. Ⓐ Ⓑ Ⓒ Ⓓ
25. Ⓐ Ⓑ Ⓒ Ⓓ
26. Ⓐ Ⓑ Ⓒ Ⓓ
27. Ⓐ Ⓑ Ⓒ Ⓓ
28. Ⓐ Ⓑ Ⓒ Ⓓ

29. Ⓐ Ⓑ Ⓒ Ⓓ
30. Ⓐ Ⓑ Ⓒ Ⓓ
31. Ⓐ Ⓑ Ⓒ Ⓓ
32. Ⓐ Ⓑ Ⓒ Ⓓ
33. Ⓐ Ⓑ Ⓒ Ⓓ
34. Ⓐ Ⓑ Ⓒ Ⓓ
35. Ⓐ Ⓑ Ⓒ Ⓓ
36. Ⓐ Ⓑ Ⓒ Ⓓ
37. Ⓐ Ⓑ Ⓒ Ⓓ
38. Ⓐ Ⓑ Ⓒ Ⓓ
39. Ⓐ Ⓑ Ⓒ Ⓓ
40. Ⓐ Ⓑ Ⓒ Ⓓ
41. Ⓐ Ⓑ Ⓒ Ⓓ
42. Ⓐ Ⓑ Ⓒ Ⓓ
43. Ⓐ Ⓑ Ⓒ Ⓓ
44. Ⓐ Ⓑ Ⓒ Ⓓ
45. Ⓐ Ⓑ Ⓒ Ⓓ
46. Ⓐ Ⓑ Ⓒ Ⓓ
47. Ⓐ Ⓑ Ⓒ Ⓓ
48. Ⓐ Ⓑ Ⓒ Ⓓ
49. Ⓐ Ⓑ Ⓒ Ⓓ
50. Ⓐ Ⓑ Ⓒ Ⓓ
51. Ⓐ Ⓑ Ⓒ Ⓓ
52. Ⓐ Ⓑ Ⓒ Ⓓ
53. Ⓐ Ⓑ Ⓒ Ⓓ
54. Ⓐ Ⓑ Ⓒ Ⓓ
55. Ⓐ Ⓑ Ⓒ Ⓓ
56. Ⓐ Ⓑ Ⓒ Ⓓ

57. Ⓐ Ⓑ Ⓒ Ⓓ
58. Ⓐ Ⓑ Ⓒ Ⓓ
59. Ⓐ Ⓑ Ⓒ Ⓓ
60. Ⓐ Ⓑ Ⓒ Ⓓ
61. Ⓐ Ⓑ Ⓒ Ⓓ
62. Ⓐ Ⓑ Ⓒ Ⓓ
63. Ⓐ Ⓑ Ⓒ Ⓓ
64. Ⓐ Ⓑ Ⓒ Ⓓ
65. Ⓐ Ⓑ Ⓒ Ⓓ
66. Ⓐ Ⓑ Ⓒ Ⓓ
67. Ⓐ Ⓑ Ⓒ Ⓓ
68. Ⓐ Ⓑ Ⓒ Ⓓ
69. Ⓐ Ⓑ Ⓒ Ⓓ
70. Ⓐ Ⓑ Ⓒ Ⓓ
71. Ⓐ Ⓑ Ⓒ Ⓓ
72. Ⓐ Ⓑ Ⓒ Ⓓ
73. Ⓐ Ⓑ Ⓒ Ⓓ
74. Ⓐ Ⓑ Ⓒ Ⓓ
75. Ⓐ Ⓑ Ⓒ Ⓓ
76. Ⓐ Ⓑ Ⓒ Ⓓ
77. Ⓐ Ⓑ Ⓒ Ⓓ
78. Ⓐ Ⓑ Ⓒ Ⓓ
79. Ⓐ Ⓑ Ⓒ Ⓓ
80. Ⓐ Ⓑ Ⓒ Ⓓ
81. Ⓐ Ⓑ Ⓒ Ⓓ
82. Ⓐ Ⓑ Ⓒ Ⓓ
83. Ⓐ Ⓑ Ⓒ Ⓓ
84. Ⓐ Ⓑ Ⓒ Ⓓ

85. Ⓐ Ⓑ Ⓒ Ⓓ
86. Ⓐ Ⓑ Ⓒ Ⓓ
87. Ⓐ Ⓑ Ⓒ Ⓓ
88. Ⓐ Ⓑ Ⓒ Ⓓ
89. Ⓐ Ⓑ Ⓒ Ⓓ
90. Ⓐ Ⓑ Ⓒ Ⓓ
91. Ⓐ Ⓑ Ⓒ Ⓓ
92. Ⓐ Ⓑ Ⓒ Ⓓ
93. Ⓐ Ⓑ Ⓒ Ⓓ
94. Ⓐ Ⓑ Ⓒ Ⓓ
95. Ⓐ Ⓑ Ⓒ Ⓓ
96. Ⓐ Ⓑ Ⓒ Ⓓ
97. Ⓐ Ⓑ Ⓒ Ⓓ
98. Ⓐ Ⓑ Ⓒ Ⓓ
99. Ⓐ Ⓑ Ⓒ Ⓓ
100. Ⓐ Ⓑ Ⓒ Ⓓ
101. Ⓐ Ⓑ Ⓒ Ⓓ
102. Ⓐ Ⓑ Ⓒ Ⓓ
103. Ⓐ Ⓑ Ⓒ Ⓓ
104. Ⓐ Ⓑ Ⓒ Ⓓ
105. Ⓐ Ⓑ Ⓒ Ⓓ
106. Ⓐ Ⓑ Ⓒ Ⓓ
107. Ⓐ Ⓑ Ⓒ Ⓓ
108. Ⓐ Ⓑ Ⓒ Ⓓ
109. Ⓐ Ⓑ Ⓒ Ⓓ
110. Ⓐ Ⓑ Ⓒ Ⓓ
111. Ⓐ Ⓑ Ⓒ Ⓓ
112. Ⓐ Ⓑ Ⓒ Ⓓ

Continued

113. (A) (B) (C) (D)
114. (A) (B) (C) (D)
115. (A) (B) (C) (D)
116. (A) (B) (C) (D)
117. (A) (B) (C) (D)
118. (A) (B) (C) (D)
119. (A) (B) (C) (D)
120. (A) (B) (C) (D)
121. (A) (B) (C) (D)
122. (A) (B) (C) (D)
123. (A) (B) (C) (D)
124. (A) (B) (C) (D)
125. (A) (B) (C) (D)
126. (A) (B) (C) (D)
127. (A) (B) (C) (D)
128. (A) (B) (C) (D)
129. (A) (B) (C) (D)
130. (A) (B) (C) (D)
131. (A) (B) (C) (D)
132. (A) (B) (C) (D)
133. (A) (B) (C) (D)
134. (A) (B) (C) (D)
135. (A) (B) (C) (D)
136. (A) (B) (C) (D)
137. (A) (B) (C) (D)
138. (A) (B) (C) (D)
139. (A) (B) (C) (D)
140. (A) (B) (C) (D)

141. (A) (B) (C) (D)
142. (A) (B) (C) (D)
143. (A) (B) (C) (D)
144. (A) (B) (C) (D)
145. (A) (B) (C) (D)
146. (A) (B) (C) (D)
147. (A) (B) (C) (D)
148. (A) (B) (C) (D)
149. (A) (B) (C) (D)
150. (A) (B) (C) (D)
151. (A) (B) (C) (D)
152. (A) (B) (C) (D)
153. (A) (B) (C) (D)
154. (A) (B) (C) (D)
155. (A) (B) (C) (D)
156. (A) (B) (C) (D)
157. (A) (B) (C) (D)
158. (A) (B) (C) (D)
159. (A) (B) (C) (D)
160. (A) (B) (C) (D)
161. (A) (B) (C) (D)
162. (A) (B) (C) (D)
163. (A) (B) (C) (D)
164. (A) (B) (C) (D)
165. (A) (B) (C) (D)
166. (A) (B) (C) (D)
167. (A) (B) (C) (D)
168. (A) (B) (C) (D)

169. (A) (B) (C) (D)
170. (A) (B) (C) (D)
171. (A) (B) (C) (D)
172. (A) (B) (C) (D)
173. (A) (B) (C) (D)
174. (A) (B) (C) (D)
175. (A) (B) (C) (D)
176. (A) (B) (C) (D)
177. (A) (B) (C) (D)
178. (A) (B) (C) (D)
179. (A) (B) (C) (D)
180. (A) (B) (C) (D)
181. (A) (B) (C) (D)
182. (A) (B) (C) (D)
183. (A) (B) (C) (D)
184. (A) (B) (C) (D)
185. (A) (B) (C) (D)
186. (A) (B) (C) (D)
187. (A) (B) (C) (D)
188. (A) (B) (C) (D)
189. (A) (B) (C) (D)
190. (A) (B) (C) (D)
191. (A) (B) (C) (D)
192. (A) (B) (C) (D)
193. (A) (B) (C) (D)
194. (A) (B) (C) (D)
195. (A) (B) (C) (D)
196. (A) (B) (C) (D)

197. (A) (B) (C) (D)
198. (A) (B) (C) (D)
199. (A) (B) (C) (D)
200. (A) (B) (C) (D)
201. (A) (B) (C) (D)
202. (A) (B) (C) (D)
203. (A) (B) (C) (D)
204. (A) (B) (C) (D)
205. (A) (B) (C) (D)
206. (A) (B) (C) (D)
207. (A) (B) (C) (D)
208. (A) (B) (C) (D)
209. (A) (B) (C) (D)
210. (A) (B) (C) (D)
211. (A) (B) (C) (D)
212. (A) (B) (C) (D)
213. (A) (B) (C) (D)
214. (A) (B) (C) (D)
215. (A) (B) (C) (D)
216. (A) (B) (C) (D)
217. (A) (B) (C) (D)
218. (A) (B) (C) (D)
219. (A) (B) (C) (D)
220. (A) (B) (C) (D)
221. (A) (B) (C) (D)
222. (A) (B) (C) (D)
223. (A) (B) (C) (D)
224. (A) (B) (C) (D)

Practice Test

1. Teachers can provide a positive testing environment by

   (A) encouraging students to be anxious about a test.
   (B) providing a comfortable physical setting.
   (C) surprising students with disruptions and distractions.
   (D) emphasizing the consequences for poor performance.

2. If mastery level for a skill is set at 75 percent, what does the student need to accomplish to exhibit mastery?

   (A) A grade of "C" or higher
   (B) A grade of "B" or higher
   (C) Answer correctly 75 percent of all the questions on that particular skill
   (D) Answer correctly 75 percent of all the questions on all skills

3. When a teacher asks students if they agree or disagree with a classmate's response, the teacher is using

   (A) redirect.
   (B) corrective.
   (C) positive feedback.
   (D) direct response.

4. Written academic feedback is most productive when it

   (A) is delayed by a day.
   (B) is uniform.

   (C) includes at least one positive remark.
   (D) is not specific.

5. Before working with mathematical word problems, a teacher needs to determine that

   (A) the student can complete the math unit.
   (B) the student is at a high enough reading level to understand the problems.
   (C) the math textbook mirrors the skills used in the word problems.
   (D) the class will be on-task for the problems.

6. Goals for individual students

   (A) should be based on the student's academic record.
   (B) should be the same for all students.
   (C) are created from individual observations only.
   (D) are developed after considering the student's history and motivation.

7. Feedback sessions for a test are most effective

   (A) when they are immediate.
   (B) when they are delayed by a day or so.
   (C) when they are delayed for a few weeks.
   (D) only when the feedback is recorded in writing.

8. Best practices indicate that effective teachers review

   (A) verbally.
   (B) at the end of a lesson.

(C) as students showed weaknesses in specific areas.

(D) daily, weekly, and monthly.

9. A student presents an analysis of a recent presidential address for the class. The teacher replies, "You have provided us with a most interesting way of looking at this issue!" The teacher is using

(A) a simple positive response.
(B) a negative response.
(C) redirect.
(D) academic praise.

10. Effective praise should be

(A) authentic and low key.
(B) used sparingly.
(C) composed of simple, positive responses.
(D) used to encourage high-achieving students.

11. While waiting for students to formulate their responses to a question, a student blurts out an answer. The teacher should

(A) ignore the answer entirely.
(B) respond immediately to the student's answer.
(C) silently acknowledge the student's response and then address the response after another student has answered the question.
(D) move on to another question without comment.

12. What is one way of incorporating nonperformers into a discussion?

(A) Ask a student to respond to a previous student's statement.
(B) Name a student to answer a question.
(C) Only call on students with their hands raised.
(D) Allow off-topic conversations.

13. A teacher who leads choral chants is

(A) practicing aural skills.
(B) practicing vocal exercises.
(C) having students repeat basic skills orally.
(D) repeating what the students answer.

14. A lesson in which students are given a tankful of water and various objects and are asked to order the objects by weight would be considered

(A) a science lesson.
(B) a discovery learning lesson.
(C) an inductive reasoning lesson.
(D) a waste of time because weight could be determined more quickly with bathroom scales.

Mr. Drake is teaching his first-grade class about animals. Questions 15–19 relate to Mr. Drake's teaching methods.

15. Mr. Drake is using the whole language method in his first-grade class. Before reading a story to the students, Mr. Drake tells them what he expects them to learn from the story. What is his reason for doing this?

(A) The students should know why the instructor chose this particular book.
(B) It is important for teachers to share personal ideas with their students to foster an environment of confidence and understanding.
(C) Mr. Drake wants to verify that all students are on-task before he begins the story.
(D) Mr. Drake is modeling a vital prereading skill he plans to teach to the young readers.

16. Mr. Drake wants to ensure that the class will have a quality discussion on the needs of house pets. In response to a student who said that her family abandoned their cat in a field because it ate too much, Mr. Drake asks, "What is one way to save pets that are no longer wanted." This exercise involves what level of questioning?

(A) Evaluation
(B) Analysis
(C) Comprehension
(D) Synthesis

17. Mr. Drake has a heterogeneously grouped reading class. He has the students in groups of two—one skilled reader and one remedial reader—reading selected stories to one another. The students read the story and question each other until they feel that they both understand the story. By planning the lesson this way, Mr. Drake has

(A) set a goal for his students.

(B) condensed the number of observations necessary, thereby creating more time for class instruction.

(C) made it possible for another teacher to use the school's limited materials.

(D) used the students' strengths and weaknesses to maximize time, materials, and the learning environment.

18. Mr. Drake is continuing his lesson on the animal kingdom. He wants to ensure that the students learn as much as they can about animals, so he incorporates information they are familiar with into the new information. Knowing that these are first-grade learners, what should Mr. Drake consider when contemplating their learning experience?

(A) The students will know how much information they can retrieve from memory.

(B) The students will overestimate how much information they can retrieve from memory.

(C) The students will be able to differentiate between the information they need to study and the information they have already mastered and thus do not need to study.

(D) The students will estimate how much they can learn in one period.

19. Before reading a story about a veterinary hospital, Mr. Drake constructs a semantic map of related words and terms using the students' input. What is his main intention for doing this?

(A) Demonstrate a meaningful relationship between the concepts of the story and the prior knowledge of the students

(B) Serve as a visual means of learning

(C) Determine the level of understanding the students will have at the conclusion of the topic being covered

(D) Model proper writing using whole words

20. Student data such as scores on tests and assignments would be the best criteria for determining which of the following?

(A) Only the students' academic grades

(B) Behavior assessment

(C) Student grades and the teacher's quality of instruction

(D) Student grades and behavior assessment

21. Results of a standardized test indicate that students in one classroom did poorly on the mathematics problem-solving section, while students in another classroom in the same school did much better. What is the best course of action for the teacher of the students who did poorly?

(A) Look at students' scores from last year to justify their poor achievement.

(B) Tell future students to study harder because that section is hard.

(C) Suggest that parents hire math tutors for their children.

(D) Ask the other teacher to share strategies that she used to help her students succeed.

22. Mr. Joseph is a fifth-grade math and science teacher working in a large suburban middle school. At the beginning of each class, he stands outside his classroom and greets his students as they enter. Mr. Joseph notices students coming into his classroom who appear upset or angry and show signs of poor self-esteem; and sometimes he overhears his students arguing with other students before class. Often these same students seem to "shut down" during lessons and do not follow along with the work. He knows this is a problem, but he is not sure what he should do to solve it. He wants to keep these students from getting behind in their learning. The best action for Mr. Joseph to take is to

(A) inform the school counselor of the problem and send each student with these symptoms to see the counselor as soon as class starts.

(B) call the parents of students who seem upset or angry and try to persuade them to fix the problem.

(C) send students with these kinds of problems out in the hall so they can get themselves together and learn.

(D) create an environment in his classroom where students feel safe and let them know he is aware of their problems and will do all he can to help them learn.

23. Teachers, researchers, and policymakers have indicated the greatest challenge to implementing effective professional development is the lack of

    (A) presenters.
    (B) time.
    (C) resources.
    (D) interested teachers.

24. The question "What was the name of Hamlet's father?" is

    (A) a high-order question of evaluation.
    (B) a low-order question that can be used to begin a discussion.
    (C) a transition.
    (D) questioning a skill.

25. Piaget's theory of cognitive development states that

    (A) children should be able to understand complex directions.
    (B) younger children are unable to understand complex language.
    (C) younger children will be unable to understand directions, even in simple language.
    (D) directions should not be given to young children.

26. Children under the age of 8

    (A) are unable to answer questions.
    (B) process information more slowly than older children.
    (C) can answer the same questions as slightly older children.
    (D) cannot learn in a cooperative environment.

27. Benjamin Rodriguez teaches a fifth-period class of 20 academically gifted, fifth-graders. Having recently read about the bell-shaped curve, Mr. Rodriguez tells his class that he will be using it for grading. "This means," he tells them, "that only about 2% will be making A's, 2% will fail the class, 13% will make D's, 13% will make B's, and the rest of you will be making C's." (Note that .02 of 20 is less than 1.) What is your professional opinion of his decision?

    (A) The decision on how to grade the class is a decision of the teacher; if a teacher sets the standards high and only gives 2% A's, the students will all stretch to get the one A.
    (B) The students should make the decision on how the teacher should grade them and the grading scale; the teacher should hand the decision down to the students.
    (C) Mr. Rodriguez doesn't seem to understand the bell-shaped curve; because it is for use with the general population, it is not suitable for application to a group of above-average students.
    (D) Fifth-graders have no business knowing how the teacher will determine the grades; grading is a decision of the teacher, and students are not a part of it.

28. Inductive thinking can be fostered through which activity?

    (A) Choral chanting of skill tables
    (B) Computer experience
    (C) Multiple-choice questions
    (D) Personal-discovery activities

29. How can a teacher elicit a high-order response from a student who provides simple responses?

    (A) Ask follow-up questions.
    (B) Repeat the questions.
    (C) Ask the same questions of a different student.
    (D) Ask another student to elaborate on the original response.

30. Bloom divided educational objectives into which of the following domains?

    (A) Knowledge, affective, and evaluation
    (B) Cognitive, affective, and psychomotor
    (C) Affective, value judgments, and psychomotor
    (D) Knowledge, comprehension, and application

Scenario: Mr. Owen, a third-grade teacher, has been teaching in a small rural district for three years. He enjoys the slow pace of the community and the fact that he knows most of his students' families relatively well. He is a member of the Lions Club, plays on the church basketball team, and volunteers at the animal shelter.

His class this year is made up of 21 eight- and nine-year-olds. Most of the students are of average ability, two receive special services for learning disabilities, and one receives speech therapy. Mr. Owen works hard to make his classroom an exciting place to learn with lots of hands-on, problem-based cooperative group projects. In the past, students have had difficulty grasping relationships between math concepts and economics. Mr. Owen has decided to offer a savings program with the help of local banks. Once a week, students will make deposits into their savings accounts. Periodically, they will figure interest at different rates, class totals saved, and other aspects of their accounts. As part of the social science curriculum, he encourages them to do chores at home and in their neighborhoods to earn the money for their savings.

31. Mr. Owen's approach in this project is evidence that he understands the importance of

    (A) relevance and authenticity in planning instructional activities for students.
    (B) integrating curriculum concepts across disciplines that support learning.
    (C) saving money.
    (D) all of the above.

32. Students are presented with the following problem: "Bill is taller than Ann, but Ann is taller than Grace. Is Ann the tallest child or is Bill the tallest?" This question requires students to use

    (A) inductive reasoning.
    (B) deductive reasoning.
    (C) hypothesis formation.
    (D) pattern identification.

33. Which of the following is the correct chronological order for the following events in history?

    I.   Puritans arrive in New England
    II. Protestant Reformation begins
    III. Columbus sets sail across the Atlantic
    IV. Magna Carta is signed in England

    (A) IV, III, II, I
    (B) IV, III, I, II
    (C) III, IV, II, I
    (D) III, II, I, IV

34. The intellectual movement that encouraged the use of reason and science and anticipated human progress was called the

    (A) American system.
    (B) mercantilism.
    (C) Enlightenment.
    (D) Age of Belief.

35. In American government, a system of checks and balances was developed to

    (A) regulate the amount of control each branch of government has.
    (B) make each branch of government independent from one another.
    (C) give the president control.
    (D) give the Supreme Court control.

36. Which of the following groups did *not* play a role in the settlement of the English colonies in America?

    (A) Roman Catholics
    (B) Puritans
    (C) Mormons
    (D) Quakers

37. On the following map, which letter represents the Philippines?

    (A) K
    (B) D
    (C) I
    (D) M

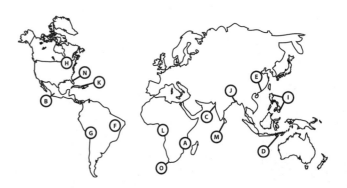

38. The Bill of Rights

    (A) listed the grievances of the colonists against the British.
    (B) forbade the federal government from encroaching on the rights of citizens.
    (C) gave all white males the right to vote.
    (D) specified the rights of slaves.

39. A teacher asks her eighth-grade English students to select careers they would enjoy when they grow up and then find three sources on the World Wide Web with information about their chosen careers. Students must find out how much education is required for their career choices. If the career requires postsecondary education, the student must find a school or college that provides that education and find out how long it would take to be educated or trained for this career. Through this assignment, the teacher is helping her students to

    (A) explore short-term personal and academic goals.
    (B) explore long-term personal and academic goals.
    (C) evaluate short-term personal and academic goals.
    (D) synthesize long-term personal and academic goals.

40. A teacher asks a student, "When you were studying for your spelling test, did you remember a mnemonic we talked about in class for spelling *principal*, that "a principal is your pal"? The teacher is

    (A) leading the student in a divergent thinking exercise.
    (B) teaching the student mnemonics, or memory devices.
    (C) asking questions to guide the student in correcting an error.
    (D) modeling inductive reasoning skills for the student.

41. Using student ideas and interests in a lesson

    (A) takes students off-task.
    (B) detracts from the subject content.
    (C) does not allow for evaluation of students' prior knowledge.
    (D) increases learning and student motivation.

42. If a child in your class suffers from serious emotional disturbances, it is important to

    (A) maintain open communication with the parents.
    (B) keep the child separate from the other students.
    (C) only discuss the student with other teachers.
    (D) keep an eye on attendance.

43. When working with ESL students, the teacher should be aware that

    (A) students should only speak English in class.
    (B) an accepting classroom and encouraging lessons will foster learning.
    (C) the student should be referred to a specialist.
    (D) limiting the number of resources available is beneficial to the students.

44. Ms. Borders, a second-year third-grade teacher, is preparing a theme study on water and the related concepts of conservation, ecology, and human needs. One of her instructional outcomes deals with students' abilities to demonstrate their new learning in a variety of ways. As she plans her unit of study, Ms. Borders first needs to consider

    (A) the strengths and needs of the diverse learners in her classroom.
    (B) the amount of reading material she assigns.
    (C) how the theme connects to other academic disciplines.
    (D) inviting guest speakers to the classroom.

45. Sequential language acquisition occurs when students

    (A) learn a second language after mastery of the first.
    (B) learn a second language at the same time as the first.
    (C) learn two languages in parts.
    (D) develop language skills.

46. Teachers should provide various experiences and concrete examples for children with reading difficulties because some children

(A) come from environments with limited language exposure.

(B) have poor learning habits.

(C) have trouble distinguishing letters.

(D) can speak well but have difficulty reading.

47. A teacher writes on the board "All men are created equal" and asks each student to explain the meaning of the statement. One student says that it means that all people are equal, but another student says that it just applies to men, and a third student says that it is a lie because not all people are equally good at all things; for example, some people can run faster than others and some can sing better than others. The teacher's instructional aim is to

(A) see if students can reach consensus on the meaning of the statement.

(B) see how well students can defend their beliefs.

(C) provoke the students to disagree with the statement.

(D) engage the students in critical thinking and allow them to express their opinions.

48. If the other students laugh when a first-grade girl says, "I want to be a truck driver when I grow up" and tell her that "Girls can't drive big trucks," what should the teacher do?

(A) Tell the class to quiet down, that the student can be whatever she wants to be when she grows up.

(B) Tell the class that most truck drivers are men.

(C) Tell the class that women and men can both be truck drivers, depending on their skills.

(D) Ask the class to vote on whether women should be truck drivers.

49. According to the following bar graph, the unemployment rate was highest in

(A) 1929.

(B) 1933.

(C) 1938.

(D) 1944.

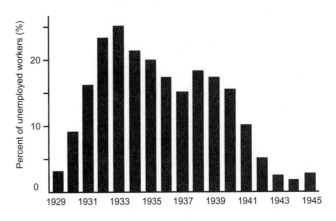

Unemployment, 1929–1945

50. According to the graph, the unemployment rate was lowest in

(A) 1929.

(B) 1933.

(C) 1938.

(D) 1944.

51. According to the graph titled "Households by Income Class," which one of the following statements is true?

(A) About 50 percent of households had annual incomes less than $15,000.

(B) Almost 75 percent of households had annual incomes of $50,000 or more.

(C) About 78 percent of households had annual incomes of $50,000 or more.

(D) About 20 percent of households had annual incomes between $15,000 and $25,000.

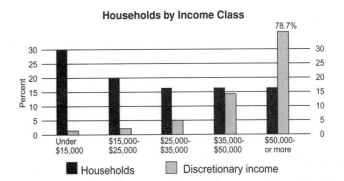

Households by Income Class

Percentage Distribution of Households and Discretionary Income (Total U.S. = 100 percent)

52. According to the graph titled "Age of Household Head," which one of the following statements is true?

(A) Middle-aged households tend to have greater discretionary income.
(B) The youngest have the most discretionary income.
(C) The oldest have the most discretionary income.
(D) The older people get, the less discretionary income they have.

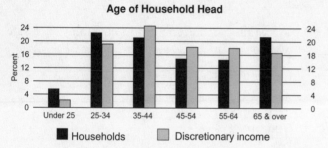

Age of Household Head

Percentage Distribution of Households and Discretionary Income (Total U.S. = 100%)

53. When a student writes about attempting suicide in a journal, the best way for the teacher to deal with the situation is to

(A) write encouraging notes to the student in the margins of the journal.
(B) ask the student to come over to his or her house after school to spend some time together.
(C) suggest that the student read some inspirational and motivational books.
(D) take the student's threats of suicide seriously and report the situation to the appropriate school authorities.

54. While the teacher is reading aloud to the class, Linda is telling jokes to get her peers to laugh. According to behavioral theory, what is a possible reason for Linda's behavior?

(A) Linda tells jokes to make her peers laugh, which may serve to gain attention for Linda or may serve to distract the teacher from the lesson, which allows Linda to escape academic tasks.
(B) Linda tells jokes to make the teacher angry.
(C) Linda obviously has trouble at home; therefore, this is an issue her parents need to deal with.
(D) Linda enjoys the performing arts.

55. According to the operant model in behavioral theory, negative reinforcement is

(A) operant behavior.
(B) stimulus for operant behavior.
(C) unknowingly strengthening negative behavior.
(D) removing a stimulus, which causes a behavior to increase.

56. Two children are fighting. The best approach for the teacher to take first is which of the following?

(A) Send another person for an administrator, separate the two, turn the aggressor over to the administrator, and then deal personally with the victim.
(B) Separate the two and take both to the guidance counselor for a conference.
(C) Separate the two and attend first to the victim.
(D) A teacher of young children should not attempt to separate the two unless an adult witness is present.

57. According to the Socratic method, teachers should

(A) impart all their knowledge to their students in ways they deem most appropriate.
(B) ask questions to get students to think about universal truths.
(C) ask questions so that students can show how much they know.
(D) encourage students to ask questions, which will enable them to learn.

58. All the following were true of education in the southern colonies *except*

(A) private tutors were used to educate the sons of wealthy plantation owners.
(B) the education of girls was limited to the knowledge of how to manage a household.

(C) slaves were taught to read so they could study the Bible.

(D) teaching a slave to read or write was a criminal act.

59. A student in the English for Speakers of Other Languages Program is proficient in oral language; however, he continues to experience difficulty with the academic language used in science and social studies classes. The teacher believes academic language proficiency correlates with oral language proficiency. What has the teacher failed to acknowledge in her analysis of the student's language proficiency?

(A) Both basic interpersonal communication skills and academic language proficiency are needed for successful academic performance.

(B) Basic interpersonal communication skills develop equally with academic language proficiency.

(C) Basic interpersonal communication skills are criteria for successful academic performance.

(D) Academic language proficiency is primary to basic interpersonal communication skills.

60. The atmospheres of the moon and other planets were studied using telescopes and spectrophotometers long before the deployment of interplanetary space probes. Scientists studied the spectral patterns of sunlight that passed through the atmosphere of distant objects to learn what elements make up those atmospheres. Which of the following explains the source of the black-line spectral patterns?

(A) When an element is excited, it gives off light in a characteristic spectral pattern.

(B) When light strikes an object, some wavelengths of light are absorbed by the surface and others are reflected to give the object its color.

(C) When light passes through a gas, light is absorbed at wavelengths characteristic of the elements in the gas.

(D) The black lines are the spectra of ultraviolet light, which is called black light because it cannot be seen with human eyes.

61. A student making top grades in class has received a percentile score of 63 on a nationally standardized math test. Which of the following is the best explanation of the student's score?

(A) A percentile score of 63 means that on a scale of 1 to 100, the student is 37 points from the top.

(B) A percentile score of 63 means that out of a group of 100 students, 37 would score higher and 62 would score lower, meaning that the student has done well by scoring in the top half of all students taking the test.

(C) A percentile score of 63 is just like a grade of 63 on a test; it means that the student made a low "D" on the test.

(D) A percentile score of 63 means that out of a group of 100 students, 37 would score higher and 62 would score lower, showing a big difference between the student's performance on the standardized test and in class.

62. The launching of *Sputnik* by the Soviet Union in 1957 triggered increased emphasis on all of the following areas of study *except*

(A) world history.
(B) math.
(C) science.
(D) foreign language.

63. The ruling of the Supreme Court in *Brown v. Board of Education of Topeka* (1954) was that

(A) separate educational facilities could offer equal educational opportunities to students.

(B) students could be placed in segregated tracks within desegregated schools.

(C) segregated schools resulted in unequal educational opportunity but caused no psychological effects.

(D) separate educational facilities were inherently unequal and violated the equal protection clause of the Fourteenth Amendment.

64. President Lyndon B. Johnson's "War on Poverty" resulted in all of the following *except* the

(A) Peace Corps.
(B) Head Start program.

(C) VISTA program.
(D) Elementary and Secondary Education Act.

65. The Education for All Handicapped Children Act of 1975 mandates that schools provide free and appropriate education for all the following *except*

(A) mentally handicapped children.
(B) physically handicapped children.
(C) socially–emotionally handicapped children.
(D) learning-disabled children.

66. The pose of the horse in the sculpture pictured below serves to express

(A) physical aging and decay.
(B) massiveness and stability.
(C) lightness and motion.
(D) military prowess.

***Flying Horse.* 2nd Century Han. Wuwie Tomb, Gansu.**

Source: Erich Lessing/Art Resource, NY

67. Mr. Stein is a middle school teacher who wants his class to learn about the classification system in the animal kingdom. He decides to introduce the subject to his class by having the students engage in general classification activities. He brings to class a paper bag filled with 30 household items. He dumps the contents of the bag onto a table and then asks the students, in groups of three or four, to put like items into piles and explain why they

made each particular pile. By assigning this task to his students, Mr. Stein is providing his students with a developmentally appropriate task because

(A) middle school students like to work in groups.
(B) the items in the bag are household items with which most students will be familiar.
(C) the assignment gives students the opportunity to practice their skills at categorizing.
(D) the assignment will give students a task to perform while the teacher finishes grading papers.

68. Ms. Smith is a sixth-grade teacher who is concerned about a student who is failing English class. The student has not turned in any outside assignments, and Ms. Smith has noticed a definite decline in the quality of work the student completes in class. Ms. Smith also has observed that the student has great difficulty staying awake in class and that she seems irritable and distracted most of the time. In her efforts to help the student, Ms. Smith decides to ask the student

(A) if she has been having family problems.
(B) if she realizes that the quality of her classwork is suffering and if she knows of any reasons for the decline.
(C) to work on better time management skills.
(D) to start coming in early or to stay after class to receive extra help with her work.

69. Mr. Rodriguez teaches fourth grade. He has structured his class so that students can spend 30 minutes daily, after lunch, in sustained, silent reading activities with books and reading materials of their own choosing. To maximize this reading opportunity and to recognize differences among learners, Mr. Rodriguez

(A) allows some students to sit quietly at their desks while others are allowed to move to a reading area where they sit on floor cushions or recline on floor mats.
(B) makes sure that all students have selected appropriate reading materials.
(C) plays classical music on a tape player to enhance student learning.
(D) dims the lights in the classroom to increase students' reading comprehension.

70. Ms. Dixon is a second-grade teacher who has selected a book to read to her class after lunch. She shows the students the picture on the cover of the book and reads the title of the book to them. She then asks, "What do you think this book is about?" By asking this question, Ms. Dixon is

    (A) learning which students are interested in reading strategies.
    (B) trying to keep the students awake since she knows they usually get sleepy after lunch.
    (C) encouraging students to make a prediction, a precursor of hypothetical thinking.
    (D) finding out which students are good readers.

71. Ms. Johnson teaches middle school reading. She teaches reading skills and comprehension through workbooks and through reading and class discussion of specific plays, short stories, and novels. She also allows students to make some selections according to their own interests. Because she believes there is a strong connection between reading and writing, her students are required to write their responses to literature in a variety of ways. Some of her students have heard their high school brothers and sisters discuss portfolios, and they have asked Ms. Johnson if they can use them. Which of the following statements are appropriate for Ms. Johnson to consider in deciding whether to agree to the students' request?

    I.   Portfolios will develop skills her student can use in high school.
    II. Portfolios will make Ms. Johnson's students feel more mature because they would be making the same product as their older brothers and sisters.
    III. Portfolios will assist her students in meeting course outcomes relating to reading and writing.
    IV. Portfolios will make grading easier because there will be fewer papers and projects to evaluate.

    (A) I, II, and IV
    (B) I and III
    (C) II and III
    (D) II and IV

72. Ms. Bailey teaches fifth-grade social studies in a self-contained classroom with 25 students of various achievement levels. She is starting a unit on the history of their local community and wants to stimulate the students' thinking. She also wants to encourage students to develop a project as a result of their study. Which type of project would encourage the highest level of thinking by the students?

    (A) Giving students a list of questions about people, dates, and events and then having them put the answers on a poster, with appropriate pictures, to display in class
    (B) Giving students questions to use to interview older members of the community and then having them write articles based on the interviews and publish them in a booklet
    (C) Discussing the influence of the past on the present community and then asking students to project what the community might be like in 100 years
    (D) Using archived newspapers to collect data and then having them draw a timeline that includes the major events of the community from its beginning to the current date

73. Mr. Roberts's sixth-grade social studies class has developed a research project to survey student use of various types of video games. They designed a questionnaire and then administered it to all fourth-, fifth-, and sixth-grade students on their campus. The students plan to analyze their data and develop a presentation to show at the next parent–teacher meeting. Which types of computer software would be helpful for this class project?

    I.   Word processing
    II. Database
    III. Simulation
    IV. Graphing and charting

    (A) I, II, III, and IV
    (B) I, II, and IV
    (C) I and III
    (D) III and IV

Scenario: Ms. Tillerson is an art teacher at McGregor High School, where she has taught successfully for several years. She is respected by her students as well as her fellow teachers. This year, the new director of instruction for the McGregor Independent School District has introduced several curriculum ideas, one of which is the concept of authentic assessment. All curriculum areas have had one or more staff development sessions on this concept. The idea will be incorporated into the curriculum as one of the strategies for assessment in each discipline and at each grade level. Ms. Tillerson has just received a request from the chairperson of the fine arts department to submit an example of a lesson involving authentic assessment. Accompanying the request are a form to complete that outlines the teacher's example, a review of the authentic assessment concept, a model of a completed example, and a deadline for submitting the example.

Ms. Tillerson's general response to the entire focus on authentic assessment has been that everything she does in her classroom is based on the authentic assessment philosophy. She really sees no need for making any changes in the curriculum guide or for preparing the assignment sent to her. On the other hand, Ms. Tillerson is an excellent teacher and generally cooperates in the various curriculum tasks requested of her. She has been a leader of staff development sessions within the district and has shared her innovative ideas with fellow professionals at both regional and state meetings of art educators.

74. Which of the following responses is the most appropriate for Ms. Tillerson to make to the department chairperson's request?

 (A) Ms. Tillerson files the request under things to do and forgets about it.
 (B) Ms. Tillerson writes a passionate letter in response to the chairperson's request, explaining how she feels about the proposed example of an authentic assessment in art. In addition to sending the letter to the chairperson, she sends a copy to the school district's director of instruction and then takes no further action.
 (C) Ms. Tillerson writes a passionate letter in response to the chairperson's request, explaining how she feels about the proposed example of an authentic assessment in art. She attaches to the letter a model unit of study she has used in her classes, including an authentic assessment project described in detail but not submitted on the form provided by the chairperson. Ms. Tillerson sends copies of these items to both the chairperson and the school district's director of instruction.

 (D) Ms. Tillerson uses the form provided by the chairperson to show an idea for an authentic assessment project. She submits this idea with supplementary photographs of student projects and a copy of the grading rubric returned to the students for each project photographed. She also sends a videotape of a student discussing the project he has submitted for the unit of study.

Use the diagram below to answer the question that follows.

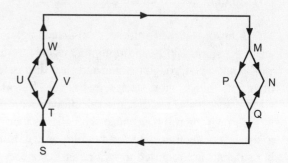

75. The diagram shows a path for electric flow. As the electrically charged particle flow moves through one complete circuit, it would *not* have go through

 (A) V to get to W.
 (B) W to get to M.
 (C) Q to get to T.
 (D) T to get to S.

Use the diagram below to answer the question that follows.

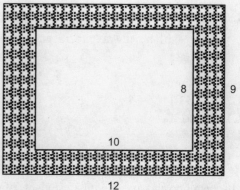

76. The floor of the rectangular room depicted is to be covered in two different types of material. The total cost of covering the entire room is $136.00. The cost of covering the inner rectangle is $80.00. The cost of covering the shaded area is $56.00. To determine the cost of material per square foot used to cover the shaded area, which of the following pieces of information is (are) *not* necessary?

    I.   The total cost of covering the entire room
    II.   The cost of covering the inner rectangle
    III. The cost of covering the shaded area

    (A) I only
    (B) II only
    (C) I and II
    (D) I and III

Use the picture below to answer the question that follows.

The Death of Socrates, Jacques-Louis David,
1789

Source: Metropolitan Museum of Art, New York

77. Who is the central focus in the picture and why?

    (A) The man on the left, with his hands and face pressed against the wall, because he is separate and thus draws the viewer's attention
    (B) The man sitting at the foot of the bed, because he is at the lowest elevation
    (C) The man standing beside the bed, because he is standing alone

    (D) The man sitting on the bed, because the other men are focused on him

78. The drop in temperature that occurs when sugar is added to coffee is the result of

    I.   sugar passing from a solid to a liquid state.
    II.   sugar absorbing calories from the water.
    III. heat becoming latent when it was sensible.

    (A) I only
    (B) I and II
    (C) I, II, and III
    (D) I and III

79. Ms. Thompson wants to teach her students about methods of collecting data in science. Which of the following describes the most appropriate method of teaching students about collecting data in science?

    (A) Ms. Thompson should arrange the students into groups of four. She should then have each group observe while she gently touches the class's pet mouse with a feather. The students should record how many times out of 10 the pet mouse moves away from the feather. Then Ms. Thompson should gently touch the class's philodendron 10 times with a feather. The students should record how many out of 10 times the philodendron moves away from the feather.
    (B) Ms. Thompson should arrange the students into groups of four. She should give each group five solid balls made of materials that will float and five solid balls made of materials that will not float. She should have the students drop the balls into a bowl of water and record how many float and how many do not.
    (C) Ms. Thompson should show the students a video about scientific methods of gathering data.
    (D) Ms. Thompson should have a scientist come and talk to the class about methods of collecting data. If she cannot get a scientist, she should have a science teacher from the high school come and speak about scientific methods of data collection.

Use the picture below to answer the question that follows.

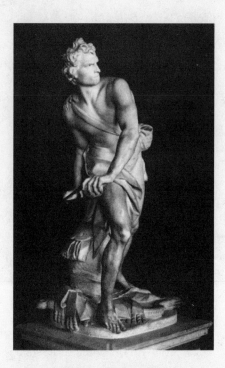

David, Gianlorenza Bernini,
1623

Source: Galleria Borghese, Rome

80. Which of the following seems most true of the sculpture?

   (A) The statue is conceived as a decorative work without a narrative function.
   (B) The figure seems to be static, passive, and introverted.
   (C) The figure is depicted as though frozen in a moment of action.
   (D) The figure's garments indicate that he is a soldier or warrior.

81. A positive condition depending on the absence of cold is

   (A) Fahrenheit.
   (B) intense artificial cold.
   (C) heat.
   (D) Celsius.

82. In the following lines of dialogue, what does the stage direction "*(Aside)*" mean?

   > King: Take thy fair hour, Laertes; time be thine,
   >
   > And thy best graces spend it at thy will!
   >
   > But now, my cousin Hamlet, and my son,—
   >
   > Hamlet: (Aside) A little more than kin, and less than kind.

   (A) The actor steps aside to make room for other action on stage.
   (B) The actor directly addresses only one particular actor on stage.
   (C) The actor directly addresses the audience while out of hearing of the other actors.
   (D) The previous speaker steps aside to make room for this actor.

Questions 83–85 refer to the following short passages.

   (A) Once upon a time, and a very good time it was, there was a moocow coming down along the road, and this moocow that was coming down along the road met a nicens little boy named baby tuckoo.
   (B) And thus have these naked Nantucketers, these sea hermits, issuing from their ant-hill in the sea, overrun and conquered the watery world like so many Alexanders.
   (C) A large rose tree stood near the entrance of the garden: the roses growing on it were white, but there were three gardeners at it, busily painting them red. Alice thought this a very curious thing, and she went nearer to watch them, and, just as she came up to them, she heard one of them say "Look out now, Five!"
   (D) Emma was not required, by any subsequent discovery, to retract her ill opinion of Ms. Elton. Her observation had been pretty correct. Such as Ms. Elton appeared to her on this second interview, such she appeared whenever they met again: self-important, presuming, familiar, ignorant, and ill-bred. She had a little beauty and a little accomplishment, but so

little judgment that she thought herself coming with superior knowledge of the world, to
enliven and improve a country neighborhood.

83. Which passage makes use of allusion?

84. Which passage employs a distinct voice to imitate
the speech of a character?

85. Which passage is most likely taken from a
nineteenth-century novel of manners?

Questions 86–89 refer to the following passage.

The issue of adult literacy has finally received recognition in the media
as a major social problem. It is more
important that the politicians themselves recognize the seriousness of the
problem and support increased funding
for literacy programs.

Literacy education programs need
to be directed at two different groups of
people with very different needs. The first
group is composed of people who have
very limited reading and writing skills.
These people are complete illiterates.
A second group is composed of people
who can read and write but whose skills
are not sufficient to meet their needs.
This second group is called functionally
illiterate. Successful literacy programs
must meet the needs of both groups

Instructors in literacy programs
have three main responsibilities. First,
the educational needs of the illiterates
and functional illiterates must be met.
Second, the instructors must approach
the participants in the program with
empathy, not sympathy. Third, all participants must experience success in the
program and must perceive their efforts
as worthwhile.

86. What is the difference between illiteracy and functional illiteracy?

(A) There is no difference.
(B) A functional illiterate is enrolled in a literacy
education program, whereas an illiterate is
not.
(C) An illiterate cannot read or write, whereas
a functional illiterate can read and write but
not at a very high skill level.
(D) There are more illiterates than functional
illiterates in the United States today.

87. What is the purpose of the passage?

(A) To discuss the characteristics of successful
literacy programs
(B) To discuss the manner in which literacy programs are viewed by the media
(C) To discuss some of the reasons for increased
attention to literacy as a social issue
(D) All of the above

88. According to the passage, which of the following
is *not* a characteristic of successful literacy programs?

(A) Participants should receive free transportation.
(B) Participants should experience success in the
program.
(C) Instructors must have empathy, not sympathy.
(D) Programs must meet the educational needs
of illiterates.

89. What is the author's opinion of the funding for literacy programs?

(A) Too much
(B) Too little
(C) About right
(D) Too much for illiterates and not enough for
functional illiterates

90. Mr. Dobson teaches fifth-grade mathematics at
Valverde Elementary. He encourages students to
work in groups of two or three as they begin homework assignments so they can answer questions for
each other. Mr. Dobson notices immediately that
some of his students choose to work alone, even

though they had been asked to work in groups. He also notices that some students are easily distracted, even though the other members of their group are working on the assignment as directed. Which of the following is the most likely explanation for the students' different types of behavior?

(A) Fifth-grade students are not physically or mentally capable of working in small groups; small groups are more suitable for older students.

(B) Fifth-grade students vary greatly in their physical development and maturity; this variance influences the students' interests and attitudes.

(C) Fifth-grade students lack the ability for internal control and therefore learn best in structured settings. It is usually best to seat fifth graders in single rows.

(D) Mr. Dobson needs to be more specific in his expectations for student behavior.

91. Mr. Dobson wants to encourage all his students to participate in discussions related to the use of math in the real world. Five students in one class are very shy and introverted. Which of the following would most likely be the best way to encourage these students to participate in the discussion?

(A) Mr. Dobson should call on these students by name at least once each day and give participation grades.

(B) Mr. Dobson should not be concerned about these students because they will become less shy and introverted as they mature during the year.

(C) Mr. Dobson should divide the class into small groups for discussion so these students will not be overwhelmed by speaking in front of the whole class.

(D) Mr. Dobson should speak with these students individually and encourage them to participate more in class discussions.

92. Ms. Kresmeier teaches sixth-grade language arts classes. One of her curriculum goals is to help students improve their spelling. As one of her techniques, she has developed a number of special mnemonic devices that she uses with the students,

getting the idea from the old teaching rhymes like "I before E except after C or when sounding like A as in neighbor or weigh." Her own memory tricks—"The moose can't get loose from the noose" or "Spell rhyme? Why me?"—have caught the interest of her students. Now, besides Ms. Kresmeier's memory tricks for better spelling, her students are developing and sharing their own creative ways to memorize more effectively. To improve her students' spelling, Ms. Kresmeier's method has been successful primarily because of which of the following factors related to student achievement?

(A) The students are not relying on phonics or sight words to spell difficult words.

(B) Ms. Kresmeier has impressed her students with the need to learn to spell.

(C) The ideas are effective with many students and help create a learning environment that is open to student interaction.

(D) Ms. Kresmeier teaches spelling using only words that can be adapted to mnemonic clues.

93. Mr. Freeman is preparing a year-long unit on process writing for his fifth-grade class. He plans for each student to write about a series of topics over each six-week grading period. At the end of each grading period, students will select three completed writing assignments that reflect their best work. Mr. Freeman will review the assignments and conference with each student. During the conference, Mr. Freeman will assist the students with preparing a list of writing goals for the next grading term. Which of the following best describes Mr. Freeman's plan for reviewing student writing assignments, conferencing with each student, and helping each student set specific goals for writing to be accomplished during the next grading period?

(A) Summative evaluation
(B) Summative assessment
(C) Formative assessment
(D) Peer evaluation

94. Mr. Freeman's goal in planning to conference with each student about his/her writing could be described as

(A) creating a climate of trust and encouraging a positive attitude toward writing.

(B) an efficient process for grading student writing assignments.

(C) an opportunity to stress the importance of careful editing of completed writing assignments.

(D) an opportunity to stress the value of prewriting in producing a final product.

95. Philip is a student in Mr. Freeman's class who receives services from a resource teacher for a learning disability that affects his reading and writing. Which of the following is the most appropriate request that Mr. Freeman should make of the resource teacher to help Philip complete the writing unit?

(A) Mr. Freeman should ask the resource teacher to provide writing instruction for Philip.

(B) Mr. Freeman should excuse Philip from writing assignments.

(C) Mr. Freeman should ask the resource teacher for help in modifying the writing unit to match Philip's needs.

(D) Mr. Freeman should ask the resource teacher to schedule extra tutoring sessions to help Philip with the writing assignments.

96. Mr. Dobson, the fifth-grade mathematics teacher at Valverde Elementary, and Mr. Lowery, the school's fifth-grade science teacher, are planning a celebration of Galileo's birthday. The students will research Galileo's discoveries, draw posters of those discoveries, and prepare short plays depicting important events in his life. They will present the plays and display the posters for grades 1 through 4. This is an example of

(A) an end-of-the-year project.

(B) problem-solving and inquiry teaching.

(C) working with other teachers to plan instructions.

(D) teachers preparing to ask the parent–teacher group for science lab equipment.

97. Mr. Dobson uses a variety of grouping strategies during the year. Sometimes he groups students with others of similar ability; sometimes he groups students with varying ability. Sometimes he permits students to choose their own groupings. Sometimes he suggests that students work with a particular partner; sometimes he assigns a partner. Sometimes he allows students to elect to work individually. This flexibility in grouping strategies indicates Mr. Dobson recognizes that

(A) fifth graders like surprises and unpredictable teacher behavior.

(B) grouping patterns affect students' perceptions of self-esteem and competence.

(C) frequent changes in the classroom keep students alert and interested.

(D) it is not fair to place the worst students in the same group consistently.

98. The principal asks Mr. Dobson and Ms. Gonzalez, another fifth-grade math teacher in the school, to visit the math classes and the computer lab in the middle school that most of the students at Valverde will attend. By asking Mr. Dobson and Ms. Gonzalez to visit the middle school, the principal is most likely encouraging

(A) collaboration among the math teachers at Valverde and the middle school.

(B) Mr. Dobson and Ms. Gonzalez to consider applying for a job at the middle school.

(C) the use of computers in math classes at Valverde.

(D) the use of the middle school math curriculum in the fifth-grade classes.

Scenario: The social studies teachers of an inner city school wanted to change to a more relevant curriculum. The department wanted to have units on economics throughout the world instead of only regions of the U.S. Ms. Dunn was asked to submit a proposal for the new curriculum, related activities, sequencing, themes, and materials. In consultation with the other teachers in the department, a needs assessment was planned.

99. The teachers believed that the needs assessment would

(A) help the students make a connection between their current skills and those that will be new to them.

(B) reveal community problems that may affect the students' lives and their performance in school.

(C) foster a view of learning as a purposeful pursuit, promoting a sense of responsibility for one's own learning.

(D) engage students in learning activities and help them to develop the motivation to achieve.

100. When the needs assessment was evaluated, it revealed an ethnically diverse community. Student interests and parental expectations varied, different language backgrounds existed, student exceptionalities were common, and academic motivation was low. The question confronting the teachers was how to bridge the gap from where the students were to where they should have been. The available choices were to

(A) change the textbook only.

(B) relate the lessons to the students' personal interests.

(C) create a positive environment to minimize the effects of the negative external factors.

(D) help students to learn and to monitor their own performance.

101. At the end of a question-and-answer period, the group of teachers, headed by Ms. Dunn, set a goal of having the students gain an awareness of the correlation between their skills or lack of skills and their salaries. A parent/guardian support group would be established to enhance the students' motivation to master new skills. Strategies to use at home and in the classroom would be developed. Ms. Dunn felt that, with the aid of parents, this plan would enable her to

(A) promote her own professional growth as she worked cooperatively with professionals to create a school culture that would enhance learning and result in positive change.

(B) meet the expectations associated with teaching.

(C) foster strong home relationships that support student achievement of desired outcomes.

(D) exhibit her understanding of the principles of conducting parent–teacher conferences and working cooperatively with parents.

102. During a period of field experiences in the community, Ms. Parks continually directs her students' attention to science as a way of solving problems. Following the period of field experiences, Ms. Parks asks her students to identify a problem in their school and to devise a scientific way of studying and solving that problem. The students work in groups for two class periods and select the following problem for investigation: It is late spring, and the classroom gets so hot during the afternoon that most students are uncomfortable. Their research questions are, "Why is it hotter in our classroom than in the music room, art room, or library?" and "How can we make our classroom cooler?" Which of the following is the most important benefit of allowing the students to select their own problem to investigate rather than having the teacher assign a problem?

(A) Students become self-directed problem solvers who can structure their own learning experiences.

(B) The teacher can best assess each student's academic and affective needs in a naturalistic setting.

(C) Students will have the opportunity to work with a wide variety of instructional materials.

(D) Students will learn to appreciate opposing viewpoints.

103. Which of the following is the most important force at work when students are allowed to select their own problem for investigation?

(A) Increased student motivation
(B) Increased student diversity
(C) Increased structure of student groups
(D) Increased use of self-assessment

104. What might Ms. Walker, a sixth-grade teacher of world history, include in her planning to challenge gifted students?

(A) Having them write an extra report on the history of the Greeks

(B) Letting them tutor unmotivated students

(C) Encouraging them to plan learning activities of their own

(D) Creating a tightly organized and well-designed unit

105. Ms. Carter is a second-grade social studies teacher at a small rural school in southern Florida. Several times during the semester, she has found herself in conversations with colleagues in the school and with various community members regarding concerns about a program initiated by the school librarian who is active in the wildlife refuge program in the county. The librarian often brings hurt or orphaned animals to the library to care for them during the day. Several parents are concerned about issues of hygiene and students with allergies. As a member of the site-based decision-making (SBDM) committee, Ms. Carter's best course of action is to

    (A) tell the librarian to remove the animals at once.
    (B) submit an agenda item to the principal to discuss the concerns at the next meeting.
    (C) call the Health Department for a surprise inspection.
    (D) take up for the librarian and praise her efforts to expose students to the issues of wildlife preservation.

Scenario: Mr. Brown feels very uncomfortable when he has to make decisions about the assessment of students. He has had some difficulty with various types of assessment. He decides it is time to talk to Mr. Williams, the principal.

106. Which of the following would be the most effective way for Mr. Brown to document his teaching in an authentic setting and to be aware of students' efforts, progress, and achievements in one or more areas?

    (A) Standardized tests
    (B) Teacher-made tests
    (C) Observations
    (D) Portfolios

107. Which would be the most effective way to evaluate specific objectives and specific content in Mr. Brown's course?

    (A) Self- and peer evaluations
    (B) Portfolios
    (C) Teacher-made tests
    (D) Observations

108. Mr. Williams asks Mr. Brown what type of test scores are rated against the performance of other students and are reported in terms of percentiles, stanines, and scaled scores. Mr. Brown should give which response?

    (A) Portfolios
    (B) Teacher-made tests
    (C) Observations
    (D) Standardized tests

Scenario: Mr. Jones was asked to improve the remedial reading curriculum for upper elementary students. He found that the students were continually tested and evaluated on reading, that the current objectives were unclear, and that the teaching materials were inappropriate. Following a lengthy observation of Ms. Ratu's teaching strategies, Mr. Jones concluded that she was teaching basic reading skills in the same manner as did the lower elementary teachers. The teaching materials used a controlled vocabulary and simple sentences. The students were being taught to rely heavily on pictures and illustrations for the story. Most of the material was fictional in genre. Rote was Ms. Ratu's preference for learning. Mr. Jones analyzed the test results and found that many of the students in Ms. Ratu's class had average scores in the areas of art, math, and music. He concluded that, with the exception of reading, most were normal students and would be successful when their remediation was complete. Mr. Jones made several decisions:

- The students would be evaluated annually with an achievement test.
- Reading materials of interest to upper elementary students would be substituted for elementary materials.
- Each student would be encouraged to read about the subject of his or her choice.
- Roundtable discussions would be developed for each "favorite subject."

109. Having reviewed the students' scores in other classes, Mr. Jones can justify his decisions with all of the following reasons *except*

    (A) development in one area can foster development in another area.
    (B) using a variety of techniques helps develop intrinsic and extrinsic motivation.
    (C) allowing students to have choices in their learning will create camaraderie.
    (D) roundtable discussions will increase student

interactions and help develop oral language skills.

110. Ms. Ratu's method of teaching remedial reading focused on

I. the level at which the students should have learned the basic reading skills.

II. her own minimal competency in instructional design and evaluation.

III. her lack of understanding of the learners in her class.

IV. her desire to make remedial reading easy for the students.

(A) I only
(B) I and IV
(C) II and III
(D) II only

Scenario: Students in a social studies class decide that they would like to read about an American they admire. Ms. Ruiz requests that the students use the library to find a magazine article about the person they have chosen and to work in pairs.

111. The approach that Ms. Ruiz decides will allow students to be most productive is to assign the student pairs, thus ensuring that learning preferences and learner characteristics are compatible for each pair of students. In choosing this approach, Ms. Ruiz

(A) avoids having students form their own groups so that the students simply end up working with friends.

(B) takes advantage of the information she has about students' individual learning styles, thus maximizing student learning effectiveness and efficiency.

(C) avoids randomly assigning students to pairs.

(D) risks having incompatible students working together in pairs.

112. Before the class goes to the library, Ms. Ruiz asks the students to predict how they will find the information they will need for the assignment. By doing this, Ms. Ruiz is

(A) engaging the students in hypothetical thinking and inductive reasoning.

(B) saving time so that the students will be able to go straight to work once they get to the library.

(C) helping her students acquire good self-management skills.

(D) assisting the librarian by covering important information in class.

DIRECTIONS: You may now take a 10-minute break before returning to finish the final 112 questions. After the break, you still have 2 hours and 10 minutes of testing to complete.

Scenario: Ms. Woods has two years of teaching experience at a large urban high school. This is her first year teaching at a small, suburban, ethnically mixed high school.

113. Ms. Woods wants to take advantage of the week of faculty meetings before school opens to become better acquainted with the school grounds, faculty, curriculum, and available materials. How could she best use her time?

(A) Tour the school while noting the teacher's room, materials room, and other important rooms.

(B) Talk to the principal about what is expected of her.

(C) Talk with a willing teacher who has spent several years at the school about community characteristics and available materials as they apply to the curriculum.

(D) Obtain a copy of the curriculum to take to the materials room where she can determine what materials are available for classroom use.

114. Three months have passed, and Ms. Woods is preparing to submit grades and conference request forms. Although students have done well in reading, writing grades seem to be low. Ms. Woods has come to the conclusion that her students are having trouble assessing their own writing strengths and weaknesses. Which of the following would be appropriate ways of monitoring and improving the students' writing?

I. Have each student submit an original work on a topic the student chooses every day to be graded.

II. Have each student identify, with the help of the teacher, one area of writing the student feels needs improvement; students focus on their chosen areas until they have reached their goals and are ready to identify new areas.

III. Keep all draft and final copies in a portfolio; the student will pick a piece to discuss with the teacher at a teacher–student conference.

IV. Once a week, the teacher will read a quality composition written by a class member.

(A) II and III
(B) I and III
(C) I, III, and IV
(D) II, III, and IV

Questions 115–117 refer to the following passage.

Reducing the amount of fat in the foods we eat is the goal of an ever-increasing number of people. Many restaurants are responding to the demand for low-fat foods by adding "Light" or "Good for You" entrées to their menus. These entrées are usually traditional foods prepared without added fat. Cooking methods that require little or no fat include steaming, poaching, broiling, and searing. Stir-fried vegetables and chicken dishes are especially popular with diet-conscious people. Almost all fried foods should be avoided when eating out, and it is best to avoid foods in cream sauces or gravies. Although salads are very healthful foods, the value of the salad can be ruined by the addition of a thick, creamy salad dressing. Desserts based on fresh fruit are usually a better choice than desserts thick with cream, butter, or sugar. If you are concerned about the content or preparation of any food on a restaurant menu, the best way to make an intelligent choice is to ask questions about ingredients and methods of preparation.

115. What is the author's purpose in this passage?

(A) To warn people of the dangers of fat in the diet

(B) To suggest ways to avoid excessive fat when eating out
(C) To discourage eating in restaurants
(D) To encourage the use of broiling, searing, and steaming to cook food

116. Which of the following should be avoided by diet-conscious diners?

(A) Salads
(B) Cream sauces or gravies
(C) Stir-fried vegetables and chicken
(D) Fresh-fruit desserts

117. According to the passage, the label "Light" or "Good for You" on a restaurant menu means that the foods

(A) are not deep-fat fried.
(B) have reduced salt.
(C) are especially good tasting.
(D) are prepared without added fat.

Questions 118–121 refer to the following passage.

The pituitary is a very small gland about the size of a marble. Located at the base of the brain, the pituitary produces many different hormones that are released into the blood. Hormones produced by the pituitary control the growth of bones and the function of the kidneys. The pituitary also controls the thyroid, a gland located in the throat, which is essential in regulating metabolism. The parathyroids, four tiny glands at the back of the thyroid, control the amount of calcium and phosphate in the blood. The parathyroids are also controlled by the pituitary. The adrenal glands, also controlled by the pituitary, are located on top of the kidneys. The adrenals have many functions, including controlling the amount of sodium and potassium in the body and producing hormones used in the metabolism of food. Another important function of the adrenal glands is the production of a hormone to help people cope with stress.

118. According to the passage, which of the following is *not* controlled by the pituitary?

(A) Growth of bones
(B) Adrenal glands
(C) Parathyroids
(D) Blood circulation

119. What do the parathyroids control?

(A) Metabolism
(B) Calcium and phosphate in the blood
(C) Sodium and potassium in the blood
(D) Kidneys

120. Where are the adrenals located?

(A) Near the pituitary
(B) At the back of the thyroid
(C) Near the liver
(D) On top of the kidneys

121. If a child is not growing at a normal rate, what glands discussed in the passage might be responsible?

(A) Adrenals
(B) Kidneys
(C) Pituitary
(D) Parathyroids

122. When a member of the House of Representatives helps a citizen from his or her district receive federal aid to which that citizen is entitled, the representative's action is referred to as

(A) casework.
(B) pork barrel legislation.
(C) lobbying.
(D) logrolling.

123. The probability of parents' offspring showing particular traits can be predicted by using

(A) the Linnaean system.
(B) DNA tests.
(C) the Punnett square.
(D) none of the above.

124. An acidic solution can have a pH of

(A) 20.
(B) 10.
(C) 8.
(D) 5.

125. A material with definite volume but no definite shape is called a

(A) titanium.
(B) gas.
(C) liquid.
(D) solid.

126. The intensity of an earthquake is measured by

(A) a thermograph.
(B) a seismograph.
(C) a telegraph.
(D) an odometer.

127. _____ is the ability to do work.

(A) Force
(B) Energy
(C) Speed
(D) Distance

Read the following passage and answer the question that follows.

Creating an English garden on a mountainside in the Ouachita Mountains in central Arkansas may sound like an impossible endeavor, but after two years the dream is becoming reality. Digging up the rocks and replacing them with bags of topsoil, humus, and peat, the persistent gardener now has sprouts that are not all weeds. Gravel paths meander through the beds of shasta daisies, marigolds, lavender, valerian, iris, daylilies, Mexican heather, and other flowers. Ornamental grasses, dogwood trees, and shrubs back up the flowers. Along the periodic waterway created by an underground spring, swamp hibiscus, helenium, hosta, and umbrella plants display their colorful and seasonal blooms. The flower beds are outlined by large rocks dug up by a pickax. Blistered hands are worth the effort when people stop by to view the mountainside beauty.

128. The purpose of this essay is

    (A) speculative.
    (B) argumentative.
    (C) narrative.
    (D) expository.

Use the pie chart below to answer the question that follows.

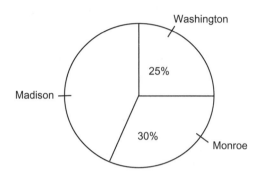

Votes for City Council

129. If the total number of people voting was 600, which of the following statements are true?

    I.   Madison received more votes than Monroe and Washington combined.
    II. Madison received 45 percent of the votes.
    III. Monroe received 180 votes.
    IV. Madison received 180 votes.

    (A) I and III
    (B) I and IV
    (C) II and III
    (D) II and IV

Use the graph below to answer the question that follows.

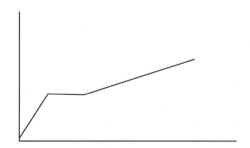

130. Which of the following scenarios could be represented by the graph?

    (A) Mr. Cain mowed grass at a steady rate for a while, took a short break, and then finished the job at a steady but slower rate.
    (B) Mr. Cain mowed grass at a steady rate for a while, mowed at a steady but slower rate and then took a break.
    (C) Mr. Cain mowed grass at a variable rate for a while, took a short break, and then finished the job at a variable rate.
    (D) Mr. Cain mowed grass at a steady rate for a while, took a short break, and then finished the job at a steady but faster pace.

Use the bar graph below to answer the question that follows.

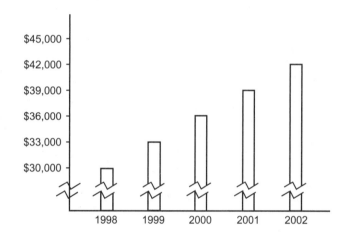

Ms. Patton's Earnings, 1998–2002

131. Which of the statements below is true?

    (A) The range of Ms. Patton's earnings for the years shown is $15,000.
    (B) Ms. Patton's annual pay increases were consistent over the years shown.
    (C) Ms. Patton earned $45,000 in 2003.
    (D) Ms. Patton's average income for the years shown was $38,000.

The following graph shows the distribution of test scores in Ms. Alvarez's class.

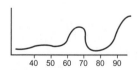

132. Which of the following statements do you know to be true?

    I.   The majority of students scored higher than 60.
    II.   The test was a fair measure of ability.
    III. The mean score is probably higher than the median.
    IV. The test divided the class into distinct groups.

    (A) I and II
    (B) I and IV
    (C) I, III, and IV
    (D) IV only

Use the graph below to answer the question that follows.

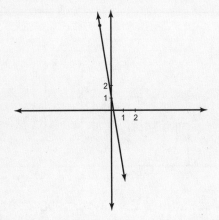

133. Which equation best describes the graph?

    (A) $y = 0x$
    (B) $y = x + 0$
    (C) $y = -8x$
    (D) $y = 8x$

134. What is the solution to the equation $x/3 - 9 = 15$?

    (A) 18
    (B) 8
    (C) 36
    (D) 72

135. There are 10 vehicles parked in parking lot. Each is either a car with four tires or a motorcycle with two tires. (Do not count any spare tires.) There are 26 wheels in the lot. Use a one-variable equation to find out how many cars are there in the lot.

    (A) 8
    (B) 6
    (C) 5
    (D) 3

136. Which equation could be used to solve the following problem?

    Three consecutive odd numbers add up to 117. What are they?

    (A) $x + (x + 2) + (x + 4) = 117$
    (B) $1x + 3x + 5x = 117$
    (C) $x + x + x = 117$
    (D) $x + (x + 1) + (x + 3) = 117$

137. Which equation could be used to solve the following problem?

    Here is how the Acme Taxicab Company computes fares for riders: People are charged three dollars for just getting into the cab, then they are charged two dollars more for every mile or fraction of a mile of the ride. What would be the fare for a ride of 10.2 miles?

    (A) $3 \times (2 \times 10.2) = y$
    (B) $3 + (2 + 11) = y$
    (C) $3 \times (2 + 10.2) = y$
    (D) $3 + (2 \times 11) = y$

138. Simplify the following expression.

$$\frac{2}{3}x^2 + 7x + 9 + \frac{1}{3}x^2 - 12x + 1$$

    (A) $x^2 - 5x + 10$
    (B) $6x^3 + 10$
    (C) $6x^2 + 10$
    (D) $x^4 - 5x + 10$

139. Use the Pythagorean theorem to answer this question: Which of the following comes closest to the actual length of side x in the triangle below?

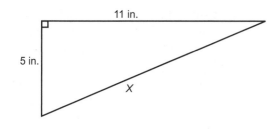

(A) 14 in.
(B) 12 in.
(C) 11 in.
(D) 13 in.

Use the figures below to answer the question that follows.

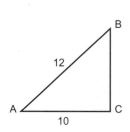 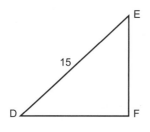

140. If the two triangles are similar, what is the length of side DF?

(A) 12.5 units
(B) 13 units
(C) 12 units
(D) 13.5 units

Use the figure below to answer the question that follows.

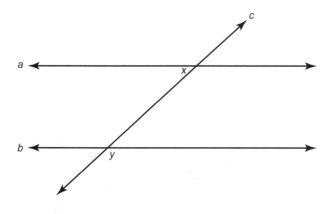

141. What is the measure of angle *y*, given the following?

> Lines *a* and *b* are parallel.
> *c* is a line.
> The measure of angle *x* is 50°.

(A) 50°
(B) 100°
(C) 130°
(D) 80°

Use the figure below to answer the question that follows. Assume that AD is a line.

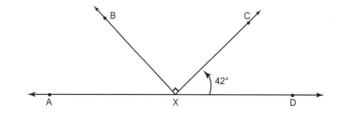

142. What is the measure of angle AXB?

(A) 48°
(B) 90°
(C) 42°
(D) There is not enough information to answer the question.

Use the figures below to answer the question that follows.

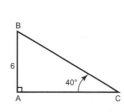 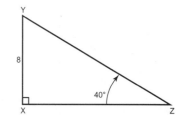

143. Which of the following statements about the two triangles are true?

I.   The triangles are similar.
II. The triangles are congruent.
III. The measures of angles ABC and XYZ are the same.

IV. The lengths of sides BC and YZ are the same.

(A) I and III
(B) I and IV
(C) II and III
(D) II and IV

Use the figure below to answer the question that follows.

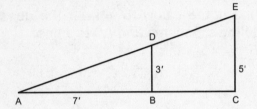

144. The figure is a sketch of a ramp. Given that the two ramp supports (DB and EC) are perpendicular to the ground and the dimensions of the various parts are as noted, what is the approximate distance from point B to point C?

(A) 4.7 feet
(B) 4.5 feet
(C) 4.3 feet
(D) 4.1 feet

145. Which is the national professional organization that represents teachers of mathematics (arithmetic)?

(A) IRA
(B) NATM
(C) NASDTEC
(D) TESOL

146. What does it mean that multiplication and division are *inverse operations*?

(A) Multiplication is commutative, whereas division is not. For example, 4×2 gives the same product as 2×4, but $4 \div 2$ is not the same as $2 \div 4$.
(B) Whether multiplying or dividing a value by 1, the value remains the same. For example, 9×1 equals 9, and $9 \div 1$ also equals 9.

(C) When performing complex calculations involving several operations, as in $8 \div 2 \times 4 + 7 - 1$, all multiplication must be completed before any division is performed.
(D) The operations "undo" each other. For example, multiplying 11 by 3 gives 33, and dividing 33 by 3 takes you back to 11.

Use the figure below to answer the question that follows.

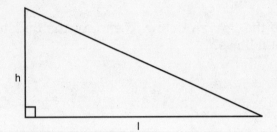

147. Which formula can be used to find the area of the triangle?

(A) $A = \dfrac{(l \times h)}{2}$

(B) $A = \dfrac{(l + h)}{2}$

(C) $A = 2(l + h)$
(D) $A = 2(l \times h)$

Use the figure below to answer the question that follows.

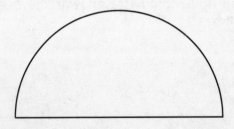

148. Which formula can be used to find the area of the figure? (Assume the curve is *half* of a circle.)

(A) $A = \pi r$
(B) $A = 2\pi r^2$
(C) $A = \pi r^2$
(D) $A = \pi r^2/2$

Use the figure below to answer the question that follows. Assume the following:

Point C is the center of the circle.
Angles XYZ and XCZ intercept minor arc XZ.
The measure of angle XYZ is 40°.

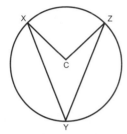

149. What is the measure of the major arc XYZ?

  (A)   140°
  (B)   280°
  (C)   160°
  (D)   320°

150. What is the volume of the following cylinder?

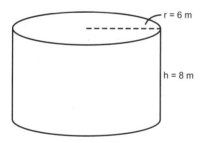

  (A)   904 cm³
  (B)   301 cm³
  (C)   151 cm³
  (D)   452 cm³

151. Listening is a process students use to extract meaning out of oral speech. Activities teachers can engage in to assist students in becoming more effective listeners include

  I.   clearly setting a purpose for listening.
  II.   allowing children to relax by chewing gum during listening.
  III.   asking questions about the selection.

  IV.   encouraging students to forge links between the new information and knowledge already in place.

  (A)   I and II
  (B)   II, III, and IV
  (C)   I, III, and IV
  (D)   I, II, III, and IV

152. Why should children be encouraged to figure out the structure and the features of the text they are attempting to comprehend and remember?

  I.   It helps the students to understand the way the author organized the material to be presented.
  II.   It helps the students to look at the features of the text.
  III.   Talking about the structure of the text provides an opportunity for the teacher to point out the most salient features to the students.
  IV.   The discussions may help the child make connections between the new material in the chapter and what is already known about the topic.

  (A)   I and III
  (B)   II and IV
  (C)   I and IV
  (D)   I, II, III, and IV

153. Dance can be a mirror of culture. Which of the following is not an illustration of this statement?

  (A)   Women in the Cook Islands dance with their feet together and sway while the men take a wide stance and flap their knees.
  (B)   Movement basics include body, space, time, and relationship.
  (C)   In Africa, the birth of a child is an occasion for a dance that asks for divine blessings.
  (D)   The court dancers of Bali study for many years to achieve the balance, beauty, and serenity of their dance.

154. Flying buttresses, pointed arches, and stained glass windows are characteristic of which historic style of architecture?

  (A)   Romanesque
  (B)   Byzantine

(C) Renaissance

(D) Gothic

155. Ms. Smith decided to stage three different versions of *Cinderella* with her students. Knowing that this is one of the world's most famous fairy tales, she located Chinese, Native American, and Russian versions of the story. She found age-appropriate plays of each that can be staged in her classroom. In addition to acting in these plays, her students are creating scenery, costumes, and props to use in their performances. Which of the following best describes what Ms. Smith primarily expects her students to achieve through these activities?

I.   Understanding cultural similarities and differences through dramatic literature

II.   Understanding theatrical practices

III.   Gaining experience with creative drama practices

IV.   Gaining experience with adapting stories into plays

(A) I only

(B) I and II

(C) III and IV

(D) I, II, and IV

156. A teacher tells her class that 1 meter equals 39.37 inches or 3.28 feet or 1.09 yard. The teacher has

(A) taught her class the principle of cause-and-effect.

(B) provided her class with a stated principle or law.

(C) connected cause-and-effect principles.

(D) provided applications of a law.

157. Ms. Gettler teaches 26 third graders in a large inner city school. About one-third of her students participate in the ESL program at the school. Ms. Gettler suspects that some of the students' parents are unable to read or write in English. Four of the students receive services from the learning resource teacher. At the beginning of the year, none of the students read above the 2.0 grade level, and some of the students did not know all the letters of the alphabet. Which of the following describes the instructional strategy that is most likely to improve the reading levels of Ms. Gettler's students?

(A) An intensive phonics program that includes drill and practice work on basic sight words

(B) An emergent literacy program emphasizing pattern books and journal writing using invented spelling

(C) An instructional program that closely follows the third-grade basal reader

(D) Participation by all students in the school's ESL program so they can receive services from the learning resource center

Scenario: Ms. Doe began planning a two-week unit of study of Native Americans for her fifth-grade class. To begin the unit, she chose a movie on Native Americans in the twenty-first century. As Ms. Doe reflectively listened, key questions were asked.

The following day, Ms. Doe reviewed the use of encyclopedias, indexes, and atlases. The students were divided into groups and taken to the library. Each group was responsible for locating information on one topic. The topics were maps showing the topography of the land, charts illustrating the climate, plants and animals, a map showing migration routes, and a map showing the general areas where the Native Americans settled.

158. The students' involvement in the unit of study is a result of

I.   the teacher's reflective listening during the discussion.

II.   the available resources and materials.

III.   careful planning and its relationship to success in the classroom.

IV.   the students' personal acquaintance with Native Americans.

(A) I only

(B) I and II

(C) II and III

(D) I and IV

159. Days 3 and 4 were spent with each group being involved in library research. Information was written on index cards. Each group prepared a presentation that included a written explanation of an

assigned topic, a shadow box, and a sawdust map or models of Native American clothing. A pictograph was to be used in the telling of a legend or folktale. The presentation was concluded with a collage depicting the Native American way of life. Multiple strategies and techniques were used for

I. motivation of the group and its effects on individual behavior and learning.
II. allowing each student regardless of ability to participate in the project.
III. integrating the project with other subjects.
IV. developing a foundation for teaching American history.

(A) I, II, and III
(B) I and II
(C) III only
(D) IV only

160. On day 8, Ms. Doe arranged a display of Native American artifacts and crafts in the hallway. Having collaborated with the music teacher at the onset of her planning and arranging for a general assembly of the entire student body, she took her students to the auditorium. The general assembly consisted of Native American poetry read by Fawn Lonewolf, with Native American music and dance performed by the school chorus. At the conclusion of the assembly, the class was invited to view the video *The Trail of Tears*. Native American refreshments, including fried bread, were served to the students. As the students ate, *Knots on a Counting Rope* was read orally by the reading teacher. Following the reading, the physical education teacher taught the students several games that had been played by Native American children. The planning of the assembly and the following activities required

I. risk-taking by both the teacher and the students.
II. stimulating the curiosity of the student body.
III. recognizing individual talents among the students.
IV. using the collaborative process of working with other teachers.

(A) I only
(B) II only

(C) II and III
(D) II, III, and IV

161. Day 10 of the unit was a field trip day. The students were given a choice of museums to visit. Whatever the student's choice, he or she was to take notes of what was seen, heard, and experienced. These would be shared with the remainder of the class on the following day. The field trip and its experiences

I. allowed the students to make connections between their current skills and those that were new to them.
II. allowed external factors to create a learning environment that would take advantage of positive factors.
III. allowed a sense of community to be nurtured.
IV. allowed the students to take responsibility for their own learning.

(A) I and II
(B) III only
(C) IV only
(D) III and IV

162. The choice of field trip locations

I. was to enhance the students' self-concept.
II. was to respect differences and enhance the students' understanding of the society in which they live.
III. was to foster the view of learning as a purposeful pursuit.
IV. was an example of using an array of instructional strategies.

(A) II only
(B) II and IV
(C) I and II
(D) III only

163. Troubled by what seems to be an increase in gang-type activity among younger and younger children, Mr. Billings wants to find out what his students think and know about gangs. He wants to learn the most he can about the students' thinking about this

topic in the least amount of time. Additionally, he wants to give all students the chance to share what they think and know while maximizing interaction among students. The students will spend the entire morning reading, talking, and writing a group report about this subject. Which of the following seating arrangements would best help Mr. Billings meet his objectives?

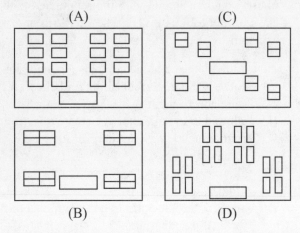

(A)   (C)

(B)   (D)

164. The strength of requiring a cognitive objective and a performance objective is that

(A) some students are not test takers and do poorly on paper-and-pencil tests.

(B) the score for one objective could offset the score for the other objective.

(C) the developmental level in one domain may affect performance in another domain.

(D) the teacher is matching the students' learning styles to her or his teaching style.

165. When developing a unit about the Erie Canal for elementary students, what would you do to assess student performance?

(A) Explain to the students that the unit will cover various projects; therefore, you will be using different assessment tools.

(B) Explain each project in the unit to the students and then describe what they will be asked to do.

(C) Give a list of new vocabulary words that they will need to know for the final test.

(D) Explain to the students that they will need to hand in their notebooks at the end of the unit.

166. Rubrics are used by many teachers in elementary schools for the purposes of assessment. What criteria should be used when creating a rubric?

I. Set clearly defined criteria for each assessment.

II. Include a rating scale.

III. Use only one idea at a time so that students are not confused.

IV. Tell students that they can rate themselves and determine their own grades.

(A) III and IV

(B) II and III

(C) I and II

(D) None of the above

167. Mr. O'Brien ends the class by telling students that over the next few weeks they will be required to keep a communications journal. Every time they have an eventful exchange—either positive or negative—they are to record the details of the exchange in their journals. This assignment is given as

(A) a way to help students improve their composition and rhetorical skills.

(B) a way of understanding individual students, monitoring instructional effectiveness, and shaping instruction.

(C) a way of helping students become more accountable for the way they manage their time.

(D) the basis for giving daily grades to students.

168. By requiring that students write about themselves, Mr. O'Brien is

(A) fulfilling his responsibilities as an English teacher.

(B) preparing his class to create autobiographies.

(C) relying on the Language Experience Approach for instruction.

(D) preparing his class to read biographies about great Americans from diverse cultural backgrounds.

169. Mr. O'Brien collects the students' papers at the end of class. As he reads the papers, he decides

that the best way to give his students positive feedback is

(A) not to mark errors on the paper so as not to discourage or inhibit their creativity.

(B) to make at least one positive comment about each paragraph.

(C) to begin with one or two positive comments about the paper and then suggest how students could improve their writing.

(D) to give everyone a high grade on the paper for participating in the assignment.

170. After Mr. O'Brien finishes reading all the students' papers, he observes that some of the students had difficulty identifying and describing their strengths, whether in class or outside class. He believes that all his students have strengths, and he wants to help them see the assets they possess. He decides that in the next class, students will

(A) take a learning style assessment to uncover their particular learning strengths and characteristics.

(B) listen to a lecture about how everyone possesses special skills and strengths.

(C) read a chapter from a book about Guilford's Structure of Intellect as a precursor to a discussion about how intelligence is specialized and diverse.

(D) rewrite their papers, correcting their errors and revising their paragraphs to name at least two additional classroom strengths they possess and at least two additional interpersonal skills they possess.

171. Mr. Swenson teaches mathematics in high school. He is planning a unit on fractal geometry for his advanced math students, using the computer lab for demonstrations and exploration. The students have used various computer programs to solve algebra and calculus problems. As Mr. Swenson plans a unit of study, he determines that a cognitive outcome will be that students will design and produce fractals using a computer program. An affective outcome is that students will become excited about investigating a new field of mathematics and will show this interest by choosing to devel-

op a math project relating to fractals. The most appropriate strategy to use first would be

(A) explaining the exciting development of fractal geometry over the past 10 to 15 years.

(B) demonstrating on the computer the way to input values into formulas to produce fractal designs.

(C) giving students a few simple fractal designs and asking them to figure out the formulas for producing them.

(D) showing students color pictures of complex fractals and asking them for ideas about how they could be drawn mathematically.

172. $\sqrt{100} =$

(A) 10
(B) 50
(C) 200
(D) 500

173. $(2^2)^4 =$

(A) $\sqrt{2}$
(B) 2^6
(C) 2^7
(D) 2^8

174. $3/4 \times 8/9 =$

(A) 24/9
(B) 32/3
(C) 2/3
(D) 11/13

175. Change the fraction 7/8 to a decimal.

(A) 0.666
(B) 0.75
(C) 0.777
(D) 0.875

176. $7.04 \times 2.5 =$

(A) 17.6
(B) 176
(C) 9.25
(D) 1.76

177. A quiet classroom is

(A) a good classroom.
(B) a negative learning environment
(C) inappropriate for some learning activities.
(D) the classroom of a teacher who has appropriate control of his/her students.

178. The characteristics of fascism include all the following *except*

(A) totalitarianism.
(B) democracy.
(C) romanticism.
(D) militarism.

179. The industrial economy of the nineteenth century was based on all of the following *except*

(A) the availability of raw materials.
(B) an equitable distribution of profits among those involved in production.
(C) the availability of capital.
(D) a distribution system to market finished products.

180. "Jim Crow" laws were laws that

(A) effectively prohibited blacks from voting in state and local elections.
(B) restricted American Indians to U.S. government reservations.
(C) restricted open-range ranching in the Great Plains.
(D) established separate segregated facilities for blacks and whites.

181. Which of the following is used to effect the release of a person from improper imprisonment?

(A) A writ of mandamus
(B) A writ of habeas corpus
(C) The Fourth Amendment requirement that police have probable cause to obtain a search warrant
(D) The Supreme Court's decision in *Roe v. Wade*

182. Which of the following defines a salt?

(A) A reactant product of an acid and a base
(B) A reactant product of a base and water

(C) A reactant product of an acid and water
(D) A reactant product of a phase transformation

183. The atomic number for a neutral (unionized) atom, as listed in the periodic table, refers to

(A) the number of neutrons in the atom.
(B) the number of protons in the atom.
(C) the number of electrons in the atom.
(D) both B and C.

184. Which of the following is a phenomenon involving the physical properties of a substance?

(A) Corrosion of iron
(B) Burning of wood
(C) Igniting of a rocket engine
(D) Melting of ice

185. Isotopes of a given element contain

(A) more electrons than protons, with equal numbers of neutrons.
(B) more protons than electrons, with equal numbers of neutrons.
(C) equal numbers of protons and electrons, with differing numbers of neutrons.
(D) unequal numbers of protons and electrons, with differing numbers of neutrons.

186. Newton's second law of motion states that "the summation of forces acting on a body is equal to the product of mass and acceleration." Which of the following is a good example of the law's application?

(A) Decreased friction between surfaces by means of lubrication
(B) Potential energy stored in a compressed spring
(C) A rocket lifting off at Cape Canaveral with increasing speed
(D) Using a claw hammer to pull a nail out with multiplied force

187. Which of the following is most likely to contain the greatest thermal energy?

(A) The Pacific Ocean, with an average temperature of 50°F

(B) A 1 g sample of molten metal at 2,000°F

(C) A bucket of water at 75°F

(D) Lake Michigan, with an average temperature of 50°F

188. Which cellular component is responsible for the regulation of exchanges of substances between a cell and its environment?

(A) Endoplasmic reticulum

(B) Cell nucleus

(C) Cytoplasm

(D) Cell membrane

189. Humans have 46 chromosomes in their body cells. How many chromosomes are found in the zygote?

(A) 2

(B) 10

(C) 23

(D) 46

190. Human body temperature regulation through the skin involves

(A) respiration.

(B) transpiration.

(C) perspiration.

(D) sensation.

191. Darwin's original theory of natural selection asserts that

(A) all organisms have descended with modification from a common ancestor.

(B) random genetic drift plays a major role in speciation.

(C) species characteristics are inherited by means of genes.

(D) speciation is usually a result of a gradual accumulation of small genetic changes.

192. The lunar period is nearest in length to

(A) 24 hours.

(B) 30 days.

(C) 365 days.

(D) 1 week.

193. A supernova normally occurs when

(A) a star first initiates fusion.

(B) galaxies collide.

(C) the end of a star's lifetime nears, with its nuclear fuel exhausted.

(D) a wandering comet plunges into the stars interior.

194. The most important factor in the earth's seasonal patterns is the

(A) distance from the sun to the earth.

(B) earth's rotation period of 24 hours.

(C) tilting of the earth's axis.

(D) moon and associated tides.

195. Metamorphic rocks are

(A) derived from igneous rocks.

(B) unrelated to igneous rocks.

(C) a type of sedimentary rock.

(D) a type of rock not found on this planet.

196. Which of the following is considered to be evidence for plate tectonics?

(A) Continental coastline "fit"

(B) Identical fossil evidence at fit locations

(C) Intense geological activity in mountainous regions

(D) All of the above

197. Seafloor spreading is characterized as

(A) plate spreading with upwelling magma-forming ridges.

(B) plate collisions with associated ridge formation.

(C) plate spreading with no ridge formation.

(D) plate collisions with no ridge formation.

198. Igneous rocks are formed by

(A) magma cooling in underground cells and pockets.

(B) magma ejected aboveground as lava, which cools.

(C) layers of sediment collecting and compacting at the bottom of lakes and seas.

(D) both A and B.

199. In descending order of abundance, what is the composition of the earth's atmosphere?

    (A) Oxygen, nitrogen, carbon dioxide, trace gases
    (B) Nitrogen, oxygen, carbon dioxide, trace gases
    (C) Nitrogen, carbon dioxide, oxygen, trace gases
    (D) Carbon dioxide, oxygen, nitrogen, trace gases

200. What is the greatest common divisor of 120 and 252?

    (A) 2
    (B) 3
    (C) 6
    (D) 12

201. How many odd prime numbers are there between 1 and 20?

    (A) 7
    (B) 8
    (C) 9
    (D) 10

202. Round 287.416 to the nearest hundredths place.

    (A) 300
    (B) 290
    (C) 287.42
    (D) 287.4159

203. In the number 72,104.58, what is the place value of the 2?

    (A) Thousands
    (B) Millions
    (C) Ten-thousands
    (D) Tenths

204. Until recently, a very quiet, reserved student had completed all her work on time and was making satisfactory progress. Lately, however, she has been erratic in her school attendance, and when she comes to school, she appears distracted. She is having trouble staying on-task and finishing her work. She has failed to turn in several recent assignments. On the last writing assignment, she wrote a very graphic poem about a girl who is sexually assaulted. The level of details used in the poem was shocking to the teacher. The teacher should

    (A) ignore the topic of the poem, grade it on its poetic merit only, and return it to the student, waiting to see what will happen with the next assignment.
    (B) grade the poem on its poetic merit and return it to the student with a written comment that she would like to talk to her about the poem.
    (C) ask the student to stay after class, return the poem, and ask the student about it.
    (D) make a copy of the poem and distribute it to other teachers to solicit their opinions about the poem.

205. To encourage students to read more books on their own time, a teacher develops a reward system to give students tokens for the books they read depending on the difficulty and the length of the book. At the end of the semester, students will be able to use their tokens to purchase "rewards" from the school store (pens, pencils, erasers, notebooks, and so forth). This reward system appeals to students who are

    (A) intrinsically motivated.
    (B) extrinsically motivated.
    (C) reading below grade level.
    (D) able to purchase their own school supplies.

206. Which of the following is NOT an example of a closed question?

    (A) Which bear's bed was too soft?
    (B) What was the name of the girl who went to the three bears' house?
    (C) Why did the girl go to the three bears' house?
    (D) What happened when the girl sat in little bear's chair?

207. A music teacher plays several recordings. Which would *not* be an appropriate follow-up activity?

    (A) Ask students to guess the decade that the music reflects and continue the guessing until a student gives the correct decade; justification of the guess is not necessary.

(B) Ask students to predict how music will sound in the year 2050.

(C) Have students use tempera paint to show the mood and feelings that they believe the music is expressing.

(D) Relate the music to the historical period that the composer reflects in the composition.

208. Certain rules and regulations must accompany the use of the Internet in the schools and libraries. These rules and regulations do *not* include

(A) the use of blocking or filtering technology to protect students against access to certain visual depictions on all school and library computers with Internet access.

(B) the filtering of text.

(C) disclosing personal identification about minors.

(D) unauthorized access, including so-called hacking, by minors on-line.

209. Certain copyright laws govern the use of materials in the classroom. Which of the following is *not* true?

(A) The fair use doctrine prohibits even limited reproduction of copyrighted works for educational and research purposes.

(B) A teacher can copy a chapter from a book; an article from a periodical or newspaper; and/or a chart, graph, diagram, drawing, cartoon, or picture from a book, periodical, or newspaper.

(C) A teacher can make copies of a short story, a short essay, or a short poem, whether or not from a collective work.

(D) For the classroom, a teacher can make multiple copies (not to exceed the number of students in the class) as long as the copying meets the tests of brevity, spontaneity, and cumulative effect and each copy includes a notice of copyright.

210. Which composer is best known for his technique of popularizing patriotic marches?

(A) Sousa
(B) Bernstein
(C) Stravinsky
(D) Haydn

211. Which jazz saxophonist was nicknamed "Bird"?

(A) John Coltrane
(B) Charlie Parker
(C) Dizzy Gillespie
(D) Stan Getz

212. Sergei Prokofiev's classical musical tale with a song or theme for each character is

(A) the *Nutcracker* Suite.
(B) the *Firebird* Suite.
(C) *Peter and the Wolf.*
(D) *West Side Story.*

213. In the picture below, which of the following contributes most to an effect of stability and changeless grandeur?

Pylon Temple of Horus in Edfu, Egypt

(A) The strong horizontal thrust of the architecture
(B) The wealth of elaborate ornamental detail
(C) The vast open courtyard with its surrounding columns
(D) The simplified geometry of the massive forms and the sloping diagonal walls

214. The figure pictured was most likely which of the following?

(A) a slave or menial servant
(B) a knight's page
(C) a religious novice
(D) a farmer.

215. Which of the following is the most important artistic device in the artwork shown below?

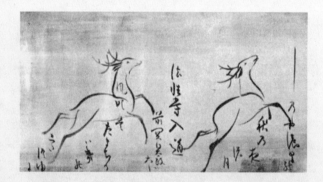

Deer Scroll, Tawaraya Sotatsu and Hon-Ami Koetsu, early Edo period

Source: Seattle Art Museum, Seattle

(A) Line
(B) Tone
(C) Color
(D) Volume

Questions 216–218 refer to the following passages.

(A) That's my last duchess painted on the wall,
Looking as if she were alive. I call
That piece a wonder, now: Fra Pandolf's hands
Worked busily a day, and there she stands.

(B) *Nov. 24.* A rainy morning. We were all well except that my head ached a little and I took my breakfast in bed. I read a little of Chaucer, prepared the goose for dinner, and then we all walked out. I was obliged to return for my fur tippet and Spenser it was so cold.

(C) There were times in early autumn—in September—when the greater circuses would come to town—the Ringling Brothers, Robinson's, and Barnum and Bailey shows, and when I was a route-boy on the morning paper, on those mornings when the circus would be coming in, I would rush madly through my route in the cool and thrilling darkness that comes before the break of day, and then I would go back home and get my brother out of bed.

(D) This American government—what is it but a tradition, though a recent one, endeavoring to transmit itself unimpaired to posterity, but each instant losing some of its integrity? It has not the vitality and force of a single living man; for a single man can bend it to his will. It is a sort of wooden gun to the people themselves; and, if ever they should use it in earnest as a real one against each other, it will surely split.

216. Which passage creates a mood of strange excitement?

217. Which passage is most likely taken from a dramatic monologue?

218. Which passage uses a metaphor to make a point?

219. Which of the following is the national professional organization that represents teachers of students who speak another language?

(A) IRA
(B) NATM
(C) NASDTEC
(D) TESOL

220. In a barn, there were lambs and people. If 30 heads and 104 legs were counted in the barn, how many lambs and how many people were in the barn?

    (A) 10 lambs and 20 people
    (B) 16 lambs and 14 people
    (C) 18 lambs and 16 people
    (D) 22 lambs and 8 people

221. Mr. Stephens, a science teacher, has the students in Ms. Allen's second-period social studies class during first-period physical science. He tells Ms. Allen and Mr. Ramirez, the other social studies teacher, that he would like to collaborate with them by integrating some science topics into their unit on the American Revolution. This will most likely

    (A) frustrate Ms. Allen and Mr. Ramirez because they will now have to discuss science.
    (B) cause the students to develop a broader view of the Revolutionary War period.
    (C) irritate the school librarian, who must put all the books related to the American Revolution on reserve.
    (D) cause the students to do English homework in science class and science homework in history class.

222. Ms. Fisher notices that one of her female ninth-grade students, Lisa, always asks to go to the restroom during class, which is immediately following lunch. Lisa typically makes good grades, and she is active in extra-curricular activities. Ms. Fisher also notices that Lisa has been more conscious of her weight lately, making comments like "if I weren't so fat" and "if I were skinny." Ms. Fisher suspects that Lisa has an eating disorder and is going to the restroom to purge. Based on this suspicion, Ms. Fisher should

    (A) share her concerns with the school counselor.

    (B) send another student to check on Lisa the next time she is in the restroom.
    (C) call Lisa's parents to express her concerns.
    (D) confront Lisa with her suspicions to find out the truth.

223. Mr. Shahid wants his students to understand how water is formed from the two elements of hydrogen and oxygen. He uses a manipulative of two blue balls labeled hydrogen and one white ball labeled oxygen. The balls are connected with wooden rods. Mr. Shahid briefly uses this manipulative but then continues his explanation with an in-depth description of how water is formed and the theoretical underpinnings for this scientific discovery. For students to understand this lesson, they must be at Piaget's_____ stage of development.

    (A) concrete operational
    (B) formal operational
    (C) preoperational
    (D) sensorimotor

224. Ms. Eagleton has noticed that during class discussions, many students answer her questions with one or two words or a short phrase. She makes certain that she provides enough time for students to consider the question and prepare an answer before calling on a student to respond. Which of the following is probably the cause of the students' short answers?

    (A) The students are too intimidated to provide lengthy answers.
    (B) The questions usually require factual recall.
    (C) The students are uncertain about the answer, so they keep their comments short.
    (D) The questions are probably too difficult for these students.

Answer Key

1. (B)	39. (B)	77. (D)	115. (B)	153. (B)	191. (A)
2. (C)	40. (C)	78. (C)	116. (B)	154. (D)	192. (B)
3. (A)	41. (D)	79. (B)	117. (D)	155. (B)	193. (C)
4. (C)	42. (A)	80. (C)	118. (D)	156. (B)	194. (C)
5. (B)	43. (B)	81. (C)	119. (B)	157. (B)	195. (A)
6. (D)	44. (A)	82. (C)	120. (D)	158. (C)	196. (D)
7. (B)	45. (A)	83. (B)	121. (C)	159. (A)	197. (A)
8. (D)	46. (A)	84. (A)	122. (A)	160. (D)	198. (D)
9. (D)	47. (D)	85. (D)	123. (C)	161. (A)	199. (B)
10. (A)	48. (C)	86. (C)	124. (D)	162. (B)	200. (D)
11. (C)	49. (B)	87. (D)	125. (C)	163. (B)	201. (A)
12. (A)	50. (D)	88. (A)	126. (B)	164. (C)	202. (C)
13. (C)	51. (D)	89. (B)	127. (B)	165. (B)	203. (A)
14. (B)	52. (A)	90. (B)	128. (C)	166. (C)	204. (C)
15. (D)	53 (D)	91. (C)	129. (C)	167. (B)	205. (B)
16. (D)	54. (A)	92. (C)	130. (A)	168. (C)	206. (C)
17. (D)	55. (D)	93. (C)	131. (B)	169. (C)	207. (A)
18. (B)	56. (C)	94. (A)	132. (B)	170. (A)	208. (B)
19. (A)	57. (B)	95. (C)	133. (C)	171. (D)	209. (A)
20. (C)	58. (C)	96. (C)	134. (D)	172. (A)	210. (A)
21. (D)	59. (D)	97. (B)	135. (D)	173. (D)	211. (B)
22. (D)	60. (C)	98. (A)	136. (A)	174. (C)	212. (C)
23. (B)	61. (D)	99. (A)	137. (D)	175. (D)	213. (D)
24. (B)	62. (A)	100. (C)	138. (A)	176. (A)	214. (A)
25. (B)	63. (D)	101. (C)	139. (B)	177. (C)	215. (A)
26. (B)	64. (A)	102. (A)	140. (A)	178. (B)	216. (C)
27. (C)	65. (C)	103. (A)	141. (C)	179. (B)	217. (A)
28. (D)	66. (C)	104. (C)	142. (A)	180. (D)	218. (D)
29. (A)	67. (C)	105. (B)	143. (A)	181. (B)	219. (D)
30. (B)	68. (B)	106. (D)	144. (A)	182. (A)	220. (D)
31. (D)	69. (A)	107. (C)	145. (B)	183. (D)	221. (B)
32. (B)	70. (C)	108. (D)	146. (D)	184. (D)	222. (A)
33. (A)	71. (B)	109. (C)	147. (A)	185. (C)	223. (B)
34. (C)	72. (C)	110. (C)	148. (D)	186. (C)	224. (B)
35. (A)	73. (B)	111. (B)	149. (B)	187. (A)	
36. (C)	74. (D)	112. (A)	150. (A)	188. (D)	
37. (C)	75. (A)	113. (C)	151. (C)	189. (D)	
38. (B)	76. (C)	114. (D)	152. (D)	190. (C)	

Detailed Explanations of Answers

1. (B)

Students are able to perform better on tests when their physical setting, which includes lighting, temperature, and seating, is favorable. When students feel anxious about a test (A) or when teachers threaten repercussions for poor performances (D), students do not perform as well. Outside disruptions (C) can break the concentration of students, especially younger children.

2. (C)

When a teacher sets a mastery level at a certain percentage and the student reaches that percentage, he or she is considered to have mastered that skill and receives a grade of "A" for his or her efforts. Therefore, choices A and B are incorrect. Answering correctly 75 percent of the questions on all the skills (D) is also incorrect because to master one skill, the student does not need to master all the skills.

3. (A)

A redirect occurs when a teacher asks one student to react to the response of another student. A corrective (B) occurs when a teacher responds to a student error by explaining why it is an error and then providing a correct answer. When teachers are redirecting, they are neither giving any feedback (C) nor directly responding to the student comments (D).

4. (C)

Written academic feedback should contain specific comments on errors and how to improve them. It should also contain a positive remark that notes an aspect of the assignment that was done well. Therefore, delaying feedback by a day (A), specifying uniform guidelines (B), and presenting feedback in a vague manner (D) are not aspects of productive feedback.

5. (B)

It is important to ensure that the word problems given to students are at their reading level; otherwise, a teacher will be unable to evaluate their successes with these problems accurately.

6. (D)

Goals for a student should be developed after reviewing both the student's history and assessing the student's motivation. This will ensure that the student can meet the goals. Goals should not be based solely on the student's academic record (A) or created from individual observations only (C). They also should not be the same for all students (B), because students learn at different levels and aim for different goals.

7. (B)

Research has shown that it is favorable to provide feedback in test situations when the feedback is delayed by a day or so, rather than giving immediate feedback (A). Delaying the feedback session for a few weeks is not beneficial to the students because too much time has elapsed (C). A class review of the test has been shown to be more beneficial in clearing up misunderstandings than handwritten notations (D).

8. (D)

Best teaching practices indicate that effective teachers conducted reviews as part of their daily, weekly, and monthly routines.

9. (D)

Academic praise is composed of specific statements that give information about the value of the object or about its implications. A simple positive response (A) does not provide any information other than the praise, such as the example, "That's a good answer!" There is nothing negative (B) about the teacher's response. A redirect (C) occurs when a teacher asks a student to react to the response of another student.

10. (A)

Praise has been shown to be the most effective when it is authentic and low key. It should be used frequently rather than sparingly (B) and should consist not of simple, positive responses (C) but of complex responses that provide information about the reasons for the quality of the student response. It should be used to provide positive experiences for all students, not a specific group (D).

11. (C)

If the teacher ignores the answer entirely (A) or moves on to another question (D), it devalues the student's response. If the teacher responds immediately to the digression (B), the disruptive behavior has been rewarded.

12. (A)

Nonperformers are students who are not involved in the class discussion at that particular moment. Asking students to respond to student statements is one way of incorporating nonperformers into a class discussion.

13. (C)

When students repeat basic facts, spellings, and laws, it is called a choral chant.

14. (B)

In a discovery learning lesson, students are organized to learn through their own active involvement in the lesson. In inductive reasoning lessons (C), the students are provided with examples for comparison and contrast and are expected to derive definitions from this information. The lesson is not a waste of time; the teacher has a different purpose in mind that students could not meet with bathroom scales alone. The lesson could take place in a science class (A) but could just as well be part of a mathematics lesson.

15. (D)

Readers display comprehension by questioning their intent for reading. For example, a student might read a story to find out what terrible things befall the main character. The rationale for choosing a book might be an interesting bit of information (A), but it is not a major topic of discussion with the students. Sharing personal information (B) creates a certain bond but is not directly relevant to the question. It is also important that all students are on-task before the beginning of a lesson, but that is a smaller part of the skill modeled in choice D.

16. (D)

A question that requires students to synthesize information also includes the need to make predictions or solve problems. An evaluation question (A) requires a judgment of the quality of an idea or solution. To involve real analysis (B), the question would have to ask students to analyze given information to draw a conclusion or find support for a given idea. Comprehension questions (C) require the rephrasing of an idea in the student's own words and then using the rephrased idea for comparison.

17. (D)

By having a mixed-level pair read together, the remedial student receives instruction and the skilled student receives reinforcement. It uses alternative teaching resources, the students themselves, to enhance the learning environment. A certain goal, comprehension, has been set (A), but that is not the most important outcome. The teacher will need to observe fewer groups (B), but it is unlikely that this will change the time needed to work with all groups as long as quality is to be maintained. Although students read in pairs, each student should have a book, and it would be impractical to permit another teacher to use the books while one teacher is using them (C).

18. (B)

Students at this age do not have the cognitive skills to realize how much they have actually learned, or how much they will actually be able to retain (A). At this stage in their intellectual development, students cannot differentiate between material they understand completely and that which they have not thoroughly comprehended (C). Students will generally feel that they are capable of learning much more than they will actually retain (D).

19. (A)

By mapping previous knowledge, information already known can be transferred to support new information. Although words on the board are visual (B), that is not the underlying motive. Semantic mapping done at the beginning of a story tests how much knowledge the students have about the topic at the outset, not the conclusion (C). This does model proper use of words (D), but that is not the main intent of the exercise.

20. (C)

Data gathered within the learning environment resulting from day-to-day activities could provide a means for reflection and discussion. This includes using students' scores not only for their most recognized use, student academic grades, but also to guide the teacher's professional development plan. Looking for inconsistencies in grading can be a basis for the teacher to explore teaching practices while looking for new and more effective methods. Student academic grades should never be used in behavior assessment (B and D).

21. (D)

Every teacher has unique strengths and weaknesses. By working collaboratively, teachers can share and thus increase their strengths while reducing weaknesses. If a teacher has found a method of teaching a concept that is successful, it is worth trying. Viewing the students' scores from the previous year would assist in seeing if they had made any progress since their last test but should not be used to justify their poor scores (A). That does nothing to assist students in improving their academic achievement. Telling future students to study harder (B) or suggesting math tutors (C) is always good advice but should not be the only method of helping students improve in a certain area.

22. (D)

During late childhood and early adolescence, students often exhibit problems with self-image, physical appearance, eating disorders, feelings of rebelliousness, and other similar problems. Teachers of students at this stage of development should be aware of the problems students face and do all they can to minimize them in their classrooms. Providing a safe learning environment and letting students know that the teacher is aware of these issues will assist in keeping these students on-task. Because many students at this age exhibit these kinds of problems, counselors do not have time to address them all (A), and sending each student to the counselor would cause a major disruption in the learning process. Although parents can sometimes help (B), this solution should be used only for the most severe cases. Calling attention to students with these kinds of problems by isolating and ostracizing them (C) often only makes the problems worse.

23. (B)

School schedules do not usually include time for teachers to engage in professional development activities such as consulting, observing colleagues, engaging in research, learning and practicing new skills, curriculum development, and professional reading. Contributing to this lack of time given to teachers for professional development is the prevailing school culture, which considers a teacher's proper place during school hours to be in front of the class. This isolates teachers from one another and discourages collaborative work. Presenters (A) for professional developments are plentiful, and creative school administrators can even use their own cache of teachers to deliver very effective in-service and workshops. Also, there are plenty of interested teachers (D), provided the professional development activities correspond to the needs of the teachers. Finally, although a lack of resources will always be an issue in education (C), that problem is not as pronounced as the lack of time.

24. (B)

A high-order question (A) tests the student's ability to apply information, evaluate information, and create new information, among other things, rather than simply to recall content. Transitions (C) are used to connect different ideas and tasks. The information that the question is looking for is one of content, not skill (D). The question presented here is a low-order question that ensures that a student is focused on the task at hand and can be used to develop into higher questioning.

25. (B)

Piaget developed four stages of cognitive development. As children go through each stage, new abilities will have been developed, but they will be unable to have this ability until they reach that particular stage. Children under the age of 8 do not have the understanding of language that grasps complexities (A). Accordingly, teachers should use simple language when working with these children (C and D).

26. (B)

When designing learning activities, teachers should be aware that younger students process information more slowly than their older counterparts. Activities for younger children should be simple and short.

27. (C)

The bell-shaped curve is for application to the general population. A teacher of an academically-gifted group and a teacher of a resource class should not use the bell-shaped curve; they are not working with the general population. Choice C implies all of this. Choice A is not a satisfactory answer; it is not acceptable for a teacher to pre-determine that in the gifted class, there will be only one grade of A. If the students achieve the grade, most teachers would say that they should receive it. Choice B is not a good answer because it is usually not acceptable for the students to dispense their own grades; the teacher is responsible for the grading, but the students can conceivably meet the criteria that the teacher—perhaps with their input—set. Fifth-graders do need to know the manner in which the teacher determines grades; choice D, therefore, is not an acceptable answer.

28. (D)

In inductive thinking, students derive concepts and definitions based on the information provided to them, which can be fostered through personal-discovery activities, in which students try to determine the relationships between the objects given to them. Choral chanting (A) practices skills; general computer experience (B) fosters computer knowledge; and multiple-choice questions (C) test objective knowledge.

29. (A)

A teacher can guide a student to a higher-level answer through questioning. Repeating the question (B) would probably elicit the same response, and asking a different student (C and D) would not help the original student who provided the simple response.

30. (B)

Bloom grouped educational objectives into a classification system that was divided into three domains: cognitive (memory and reasoning), affective (emotions), and psychomotor (physical abilities).

31. (D)

The integrated, real-life nature of this project builds deeper understandings of the economic concept of work and wages, saving versus spending, and banking. While providing the authentic experience of working and saving, the project also builds children's capacity to complete mathematical functions like figuring interest rates and compounding interest. In addition, the idea of saving money has been communicated.

32. (B)

The example illustrates a deductive reasoning task. Inductive reasoning (A) would be giving the class some information and asking them to form a rule or generalization. Choices C and D are examples of inductive tasks.

33. (A)

The Magna Carta was signed in 1215. Columbus's voyages began in the fifteenth century. The Protestant

Reformation occurred in the sixteenth century. The Puritans came to America in the seventeenth century.

34. (C)

The American system (A), as conceived by Henry Clay, referred to the nationalist policy of uniting the three economic sections of the United States in the time following the War of 1812. Mercantilism (B) was an economic theory whose principal doctrine was the belief that the wealth of nations was based on the possession of gold. The Age of Belief (D) is tied to tradition and emotion. The Enlightenment (C) is the best possible answer.

35. (A)

Checks and balances provide each of the branches with the ability to limit the actions of the other branches. Choice B is incorrect because the branches of the federal government do not achieve independence from each other due to checks and balances. Choices C and D are also incorrect because they deal with only one branch, whereas the system of checks and balances involves the manner in which the three branches interrelate.

36. (C)

Choices A, B, and D all played a role in the early settlements of the English colonies in America. The correct answer is choice C, because Joseph Smith founded Mormonism in Fayette, New York, in 1830. *The Book of Mormon*, first published in 1830, describes the establishment of an American colony from the Tower of Babel.

37. (C)

The letter *K* represents Cuba, *D* represents Indonesia, and *M* represents Sri Lanka. The correct answer is C, because the letter *I* represents the Philippine Islands.

38. (B)

The Bill of Rights clearly states that Congress may not make laws abridging citizens' rights and liberties.

Choices C and D are incorrect because the document does not talk about voting rights or slaves. A list of grievances (A) is contained in the Declaration of Independence.

39. (B)

This assignment asks students to gather information and explore long-term goals—goals that may be achieved many years in the future. Short-term goals (A and C) are those that can be achieved in days, weeks, or maybe months. Synthesizing goals (D) requires a more complicated process than merely gathering information.

40. (C)

The teacher is asking the student questions to allow the student to correct a spelling error. Spelling does not allow for divergent or creative thinking (A). Although the teacher reminds the student of a mnemonic, the teacher is not teaching the mnemonic (B). Applying spelling rules or guides to improve spelling would be an example of deductive reasoning, not inductive reasoning (D).

41. (D)

Students are more likely to be more enthusiastic when things that they enjoy are the subject or focus of a lesson, which in turn helps to build the academic success of the lesson.

42. (A)

It is important to keep strong communication lines open with the parents so that the child can get the best possible care and understanding from both the parents and the teacher.

43. (B)

It is very important that all students feel welcome, but it is especially helpful for ESL students to feel comfortable and welcomed in the classroom.

44. (A)

Ms. Borders must consider the learning preferences and emotional factors of her learners as she constructs learning activities for the study. To consider cooperative group projects versus independent work is one aspect of her preparation. Another would be the range of products deemed acceptable as demonstrations of knowledge (written or spoken, visual or performed art, technology based, etc.). Choices B, C, and D might be considerations once she plans the study, but they are unrelated to the issue of preparing for the stated instructional outcomes.

45. (A)

Students speaking two languages learn one of two ways: sequentially, in which one language is mastered before the study of the second language has begun (A), or simultaneously, in which both languages are learned concurrently (B). Sequential language acquisition does not mean a student learns two languages in parts (C) or develops language skills (D).

46. (A)

Some students may not speak English at home or may have limited exposure to the vocabulary of the classroom. It is important to be aware of these factors and provide the materials appropriate to help guide mastery.

47. (D)

The teacher hopes to engage the students in critical thinking, allowing them to express their opinions and realizing that students will have different interpretations of the statement. Choices A, B, and C are possible outcomes, but choice D is the best answer because it relates specifically to the teacher's aim.

48. (C)

The best response is to emphasize that occupations are open to both men and women and that most people make career choices based on their abilities and their preferences. Choices A and B fail to take advantage of the opportunity to teach the class about equal opportunity in career choices, and choice D implies that popular opinion determines career choices.

49. (B)

The 1933 bar is highest, and the graph represents the percentage of unemployment by the height of the bars. The bars for 1929 (A), 1938 (C), and 1944 (D) are all lower than the bar for 1933, the year in which unemployment was the highest.

50. (D)

The bar for 1944 is the lowest on the graph. As in the previous question, the graph depicts the percentage of unemployment. The bars for 1929 (A), 1933 (B), and 1938 (C) are all higher than the bar for 1944.

51. (D)

Choice A is incorrect because about 30 percent of households had annual incomes less than $15,000. Choices B and C are also incorrect, because slightly more than 15 percent of households fell into the $50,000-or-more category.

52. (A)

Graph reading and interpretation is the primary focus of this question. Choice B is incorrect because the youngest households have the least discretionary income. Choices C and D are also incorrect. The oldest group has less discretionary income than those between 25 and 65 but more than those under 25.

53. (D)

Students' threats of suicide must be taken seriously, and teachers must refer to trained professionals to take action in the face of such threats. Choices A, B, and C are inadequate responses to threats of suicide.

54. (A)

Linda's behavior serves a purpose or function. To assess the purpose or function of a behavior, teachers can use a functional behavioral assessment. Students normally do not exhibit behaviors for the purpose of making others angry (B). Telling jokes in class does not necessarily imply that Linda has trouble at home; the teacher should try to deal with the problem first before asking the parents to help with the problem so (C) is not the best choice. Although it is possible that Linda just simply enjoys telling jokes, it is unlikely that she chooses to do so in the midst of a class lesson for the sheer enjoyment of performing (D). Hypotheses about the functions of behavior address why a person might be exhibiting a particular behavior and what that person is accomplishing or avoiding by exhibiting it.

55. (D)

According to the operant model in behavioral theory, negative reinforcement is removing a stimulus, which causes a behavior to increase. Reinforcement can be positive or negative in that it is applied or removed. All reinforcement, positive or negative, increases the likelihood that the behavior will occur again. Likewise, punishment can be positive or negative, but all punishment decreases the likelihood that the behavior will occur again.

56. (C)

The teacher should attend first to the victim after separating the two. Choice C is the best answer. If the teacher responds first to the aggressor, it conveys that he/she is more important. After separating the two, the teacher should attend to the victim and, if possible, deal with the situation himself/herself; the guidance counselor may be consulted if it is a school rule as in choice B, but the teacher may handle the situation more easily. The teacher should not wait for a witness before separating the two children; harm could come to either or both. Choice D is not an appropriate answer. Again, the teacher should separate the two, not send someone for the administrator first as choice A states. Separating the two by having the aggressor dealt with by the administrator and the victim dealt with by the teacher is not the best approach. (A) is not the best answer.

57. (B)

According to the Socratic method, teachers should ask questions that allow students to find the truth within themselves.

58. (C)

Most people in the colonial South believed that slaves would be more submissive if they remained illiterate, so most enslaved blacks were never taught to read or write. Teaching a slave to read or write was, in fact, a criminal act.

59. (D)

In general, teachers believe that oral language proficiency correlates with academic proficiency. However, research indicates that oral language proficiency is easily acquired through daily living experiences, whereas academic language proficiency requires an academic setting with context-reduced activities.

60. (C)

Black-line spectra are formed when the continuous spectra of the sun pass through the atmosphere. The elements in the atmosphere absorb wavelengths of light characteristic of their spectra (these are the same wavelengths given off when the element is excited—for example, the red color of a neon light). By examining the line spectral gaps, scientists can deduce the elements that make up the distant atmosphere. Choice A is true, but it explains the source of a line spectrum. Choice B is true, but it explains why a blue shirt is blue when placed under a white or blue light source. A blue shirt under a red light source will appear black because there are no blue wavelengths to be reflected. Choice D is only a partial truth, because black lights do give off ultraviolet light that the human eye cannot see.

61. (D)

Choice D is the best answer because it contains information that is technically correct and expresses a concern about the difference in the student's standardized test score and usual performance in math class. Choice A is technically correct; however, it does not provide as much information as choice D. Choice B tends to provide the student with a false impression; although it is true that the student scored in the top half, as one of the best students in class, the student could have expected to score in the top 10 percent, or at least the top quartile. Choice C is a false statement.

62. (A)

The United States was shocked by the launching of *Sputnik* by the Soviet Union in 1957. Comparisons between Soviet education and that available in the public schools of the United States indicated a need to emphasize math (B), science (C), and foreign language (D) for us to compete with other countries and to remain a world power.

63. (D)

In handing down its decision in *Brown v. Board of Education of Topeka* in 1954, the Supreme Court stated, "Separate but equal has no place . . . . Separate educational facilities are inherently unequal and violate the equal protection clause of the Fourteenth Amendment."

64. (A)

The Peace Corps was established by President John F. Kennedy. Johnson's VISTA program (C) was modeled after it. Head Start (B) and the Elementary and Secondary Education Act (D) were also put into effect as part of Johnson's "War on Poverty."

65. (C)

The Education for All Handicapped Children Act of 1975 provides for mentally (A) and physically (B) handicapped as well as learning disabled children (D). It does not include socially–emotionally handicapped youngsters.

66. (C)

The horse shows motion and lightness. Notice, for instance, the tail and feet, which seem to imply movement. The horse is obviously young and spry, so choice A cannot be true. The horse does not suggest warlike attitudes, so choice D is not appropriate. The horse appears light on its feet, so massiveness (B) is not one of its qualities.

67. (C)

According to Piaget's theory of cognitive development, students in middle school would be at the stage of concrete operational thought. Students at that stage of cognitive development are able to categorize items. Choice A is a false statement because although some students like to work in groups, some students prefer to work alone—at this or any age or cognitive stage. Preferring to learn in groups (or socially) or to learn alone (or independently) is a characteristic of learning style or preference, not a characteristic of cognitive or affective development. Choice B is irrelevant to the teacher's intent in assigning the task. Students could just as easily work with unfamiliar items, grouping them by observable features independent of their use or function. Choice D is not a good choice under any circumstances. Teachers should assiduously avoid giving students any assignments merely to keep them busy while the teacher does something else. All assignments should have an instructional purpose.

68. (B)

This situation opens the door for dialogue with the student about a range of possible problems. Choice B shows that the teacher is concerned about the student and her welfare without making assumptions, jumping to conclusions, and/or intruding into the private affairs of the student. Choice A presumes that the source of all problems is the family. Although the student may be having family-related difficulties, it is unwise for the teacher to conclude that the student is having family problems. Among the other possibilities the teacher must consider is that the student has a job that is taking too much of her time away from her studies or that the student is having health problems.

Choice C is inappropriate because it too narrowly identifies one possible coping mechanism as the solution to the student's problem. Although the student may benefit from acquiring better time management skills, it also is possible that the student's present problems have little or nothing to do with time management. Choice D is equally inappropriate in that it demands that the student devote even more time to school, even though she currently is having trouble with present demands. If the student is unwell, then certainly spending more time at school is not the solution to her problem. Clearly, choice B is the best alternative to helping the student identify her problem and find a solution.

69. (A)

Only choice A takes into account differences among learners by giving them options as to how and where they will read. Choice B violates the students' freedom to select reading materials they find interesting and wish to read. When allowed to choose their own reading materials, some students might select materials beyond their present reading comprehension. However, reading research indicates that students can comprehend difficult material when their interest level is high. Therefore, any efforts by the teacher to interfere with students' selection of their own reading material would be ill advised.

Choices C and D are equally poor in that they both describe a concession to only one group of learners. For example, with choice C, while some students might prefer to read with music playing in the background, other students might find music distracting. The best action for the teacher to take would be to allow some students to listen to music on earphones while others read in quiet. In regard to choice D, some students might prefer bright illumination while others read better with the lights dimmed. Mr. Rodriguez would do well to attempt to accommodate various learner needs by having one area of the room more brightly illuminated than the other.

70. (C)

The teacher is encouraging students to become actively engaged in the learning process by making a prediction based on limited information given in the book title and cover illustration. When students can generate their own predictions or formulate hypotheses about possible outcomes on the basis of available (although limited) data, they are gaining preparatory skills for formal operations (or abstract thinking). Although second-grade students would not be expected to be at the level of cognitive development characterized by formal operations, Piagetian theory would indicate that teachers who model appropriate behaviors and who give students opportunities to reach or stretch for new cognitive skills are fostering students' cognitive growth. Choice A is a poor choice because students' responses to this one question posed by the teacher cannot be used to assess adequately their interest in reading activities. Choice B, likewise, is a poor choice in that it implies

no instructional intent for asking the question. Choice D is incorrect because students' responses to a single question cannot allow the instructor to determine which students are good readers and which ones are not.

71. (B)

The question asks for appropriate questions for Ms. Johnson to consider in making an instructional decision. Choice I is a valid reason for teaching students how to develop portfolios. Teachers constantly teach students the skills that will be useful in school and in their careers. Although choice II may produce positive affective results, students' feeling mature because they are imitating older siblings is not a sufficient reason to choose portfolios. Choice III is the most appropriate reason to decide whether to use portfolios. Most activities and projects that promote achievement of course outcomes would be considered appropriate strategies. Choice IV is not necessarily true; portfolio assessment can result in more written work, which can be more time consuming. Even if it were true, emphasizing student achievement is more important than easing the workload of teachers.

72. (C)

The question asks for work on the analysis, synthesis, or evaluation level. Choice C is the best answer because it asks the students to analyze how past causes have produced current effects and then to predict what future effects might be based on what they have learned about cause–effect relationships. It requires students to put information together in a new way. Choice A may involve some creativity in putting the information on a poster, but in general, answering factual questions calls for lower-level (knowledge or comprehension) thinking. Choice B may involve some degree of creativity, but giving students prepared questions requires thinking at a lower level than having students develop their own questions and then determining which answers to write about. Choice D is a lower-level activity, although there may be a great deal of research for factual information. All options may be good learning activities, but choices A, B, and D do not require as much deep thinking as choice C. Depending on the depth of the study, a teacher might want to include several of these activities.

73. (B)

This question asks for an evaluation of which software programs will help the students achieve their goals of analyzing data and presenting the results. Choice I, word processing, would be used in developing and printing the questionnaire, as well as writing a report on the results. Choice II, a database, would be used to sort and print information in various categories so students could organize and analyze their data. Choice III, a simulation, would not be appropriate here because the students' basic purpose is to collect data and analyze it. The project does not call for a program to simulate a situation or event. Choice IV, graphing and charting software, would be very useful in analyzing information and in presenting it to others.

74. (D)

Ms. Tillerson, as an effective teacher and respected professional in her school as well as beyond her district, realizes that the intent of central office curriculum efforts is to raise the standards of instruction throughout the district. She is a team player in the educational process and understands that though she may be performing at the highest level, other teachers need boosting. The work that Ms. Tillerson submits will probably be used as a model for other teachers throughout the district. The thoroughness of her response indicates that she will be invited to make other presentations at area and state professional meetings, perhaps on the topic of authentic assessment. Choice A would be an unprofessional action by Ms. Tillerson. It could indicate that she is forgetful or lazy, and she certainly would be expressing rudeness and lack of cooperation if she ignored the request made of her and all teachers in the district. None of these characteristics represents a teacher who is effective in the classroom and highly respected by her students and peers.

Choice B would indicate that Ms. Tillerson is unaware or resentful of the role she plays as a curriculum developer within her teaching assignment. Her decision to write a "passionate letter in response" to the request would be somewhat immature. The professional teacher who seriously questions a curricular approach from central office would discuss the situation reasonably, calmly, and privately with the new director of instruction. Of course, the very fact that Ms. Tillerson feels she has been incorporating authentic assessment ideas in her teaching for some time indicates that she values the concept. Therefore, her role should be one of support to get other teachers to value authentic assessment as well.

Choice C is incorrect because Ms. Tillerson, although showing support for the concept of authentic assessment, would still be blocking the central office efforts to get some degree of uniformity in preparing curriculum material. Again, her "passionate letter in response" to the request for an authentic assessment sample would indicate poor judgment on Ms. Tillerson's part. Would the strong expression of her feelings indicate an independent nature or a rebel in regards to teamwork? Would her refusal to rewrite her model unit of study to conform to the district format be laziness, a rejection of authority, or some other indicator of malcontent? The effective professional would find some other way to communicate her concerns if the provided format for the model of authentic assessment could be improved.

75. (A)

Notice that the particle flow divides at two points, T and M. At these points, the flow has two paths to reach either point W or point Q. Thus, the correct choice is A. Particle flow can reach point W by going through point U rather than V. It would have to flow through all other points listed to make a complete circuit or total clockwise path.

76. (C)

The total area of the larger rectangle is the base times the height, 12 ft. × 9 ft., which equals 108 sq. ft. Therefore, the area of the shaded portion surrounding the inner rectangle is

$$108 \text{ sq. ft.} - 80 \text{ sq. ft.} = 28 \text{ sq. ft.}$$

If the total cost of material is $56 to cover the shaded area of 28 sq. ft., the cost per square foot is $56/28 sq. ft. = $2.00/sq. ft. Choices A, B, and D are incorrect. Neither I nor II is necessary to determine the cost per square foot of the shaded area. D is incorrect because III is needed to determine the cost per square foot.

77. (D)

This question tests your ability to determine the central focus in a staged dramatic production and to explain why there is such a focus. The central attraction in this picture is the man on the bed. Many eyes are turned to him, and he appears to be speaking. The other men in the picture are either turned away from the viewers or directing their attention toward the man on the bed. Because this character is in a full-front position, he will draw more attention than those in profile or full back, which are weaker positions.

78. (C)

The best answer is C because it includes three correct statements. The sugar does pass from a solid to a liquid state, the sugar does absorb calories from the water, and the heat does become latent when it is sensible. Because statements I, II, and III are all causes of the drop of temperature when sugar is added to coffee, all three must be included when choosing an answer. Choice A states that sugar passes from a solid to a liquid state (I), but no other information is given. Choice B includes two true statements (I and II), but it does not include all the information; there is no mention of heat becoming latent when it was sensible (III). Choice D is not correct because it excludes statement II—that sugar absorbs calories from the water. Although choices A, B, and D each contain one or more of these statements, none contains all three; therefore, each of these choices is incorrect.

79. (B)

A hands-on activity would best help students learn about data collection. Because choice B is the only one that describes a hands-on activity, it is the best answer. The students would learn about direct observation by watching Ms. Thompson tickle the mouse and the philodendron (A); however, that method would not be as effective as allowing the students to conduct their own data collection. Research suggests that viewing a video is an inefficient method of learning (C). Having a guest speaker tell the students about data collection (D) is not a good choice for first graders.

80. (C)

Bernini's *David* of 1623 is a perfect example of the Baroque sculptor's wish to express movement and action and to capture a fleeting moment in time. Here, the figure's twisting posture and intense facial expression create a dynamic, not a static, character (B) as David begins the violent twisting motion in which he will hurl the stone from his sling. His gaze is directed outward at an unseen adversary, implying interaction with another character and denying any purely ornamental conception behind this work (A). The figure's meager garments, far from identifying him as a warrior (D), emphasize both his physical vulnerability and his idealized, heroic beauty.

81. (C)

Because heat is a positive condition depending on the absence of cold, C is the best answer. Fahrenheit is a measure of temperature, not a condition; therefore, choice A is incorrect. Heat is the opposite of intense artificial cold; therefore, choice B is not acceptable. Because Celsius is a measure of temperature, not a condition, choice D is not correct.

82. (C)

An aside is a comment spoken directly to the audience that the other actors on stage are supposedly unable to hear.

83. (B)

This passage from Melville's *Moby Dick* contains an allusion in the phrase, "like so many Alexanders." Melville is illustrating the strength and power of whalers ("naked Nantucketers") by alluding and comparing them to Alexander the Great, the famous conqueror who died in 323 BCE.

84. (A)

This passage, which opens James Joyce's *A Portrait of the Artist as a Young Man*, is written in "baby talk" ("moocow," "nicens," "baby tuckoo") to convey to readers the age, speech, and mental state of the narrator.

85. (D)

Nineteenth-century novels of manners employed such themes as the importance (or unimportance) of "good breeding," the elation (and suffocation) caused by society, and the interaction of individuals within the confines of a closed country community (to name just a few). This passage, taken from Jane Austen's *Emma*, mentions Emma's "opinion" of another character, the importance of "beauty" and "accomplishment" (notice how Emma sees them as almost saving graces for Ms. Elton), and the "improvement" of a "country neighborhood."

86. (C)

Choice C is correct because it restates the definitions of *illiterate* and *functional illiterate* given in the second paragraph. Choice A cannot be correct because the passage clearly distinguishes between illiterates and functional illiterates. Choice B is not correct because the definition stated is not related to participation in a program. The relative number of illiterates and functional illiterates is not discussed, so choice D is incorrect.

87. (D)

The passage has several purposes. First, the author complains about the way literacy issues are presented in the media (B). The author also discusses the increased attention given to literacy by society (C). Third, the author discusses many aspects of successful literacy programs (A). Therefore, choice D, which includes all these purposes, is correct.

88. (A)

This question must be answered using the process of elimination. You are asked to select a statement that names a possible program component that is not characteristic of successful literacy programs. Choice A is correct because choices B, C, and D are specifically mentioned in the passage.

89. (B)

Choice B is correct because the author specifically states that politicians should support increased funding for literacy programs. Choices A and C are incorrect because the author states that funding should be increased. There is no discussion of funding for different programs, so choice D is incorrect.

90. (B)

The variance in fifth graders' physical size and development has a direct influence on their interests and attitudes, including their willingness to work with others and a possible preference for working alone. Choice A is incorrect because fifth graders do have the physical and mental maturity to work in small groups. Choice C is incorrect because not all fifth-grade students lack internal control. Choice D is incorrect because although Mr. Dobson might need to be more specific in his directions to the students, that was not the main reason for their behavior.

91. (C)

Students who are shy are usually more willing to participate in small groups than in discussions involving the entire class. Choice A is incorrect because calling on each student once per day will not necessarily assist shy students to participate in class discussions, even if participation grades are assigned. Choice B is incorrect because although students may become less shy as the year progresses, the teacher still has a responsibility to encourage students to participate. Choice D is incorrect because although speaking to each student individually may help some students participate, it is likely more students will participate if the procedure outlined in choice C is implemented.

92. (C)

Ms. Kresmeier uses effective communication strategies to teach students and encourages them to interact for the same purposes. Mnemonic devices are apparently a new technique for most of the students; the teacher's own creative spelling clues are often new ones matching the age-level, interests, and patterns of humor enjoyed by her students. The most success is probably derived from her encouraging students to examine the words to find a feature that can be turned into a mnemonic device. Choice A is incorrect because Ms. Kresmeier has made no attempt to rule out other techniques of learning to spell. Choice B is incorrect because other teachers have undoubtedly impressed on the students that spelling is important. The creative methodology is probably the major difference between Ms. Kresmeier's method and those that students have encountered in the past. Choice D is incorrect because no evidence exists to show that Ms. Kresmeier is especially selective in choosing her spelling lessons.

93. (C)

Formative assessment is continuous and intended to serve as a guide to future learning and instruction. Summative evaluation (A) and summative assessment (B) are both used to put a final critique or grade on an activity or assignment with no real link to the future. Peer evaluation (D) would require students to critique each other.

94. (A)

Meeting with each student individually to discuss the student's strengths and weaknesses creates a feeling of trust and confidence. Grading papers solely on the content of a conference (B) is not an efficient means of grading. The student–teacher conference should not focus on only one part of the writing process, such as careful editing (C) or prewriting (D).

95. (C)

The role of the resource teacher is to provide individual instruction for students who qualify for services and, through collaborative consultation, work with the classroom teacher to adapt instruction to match student needs. A resource teacher should not be entirely responsible for teaching a learning-disabled student (A) and is also not responsible for tutoring outside the scheduled class meetings (D). A learning-disabled student should not be totally excused from assignments (B).

96. (C)

This is an example of working with other teachers to plan instruction. Choice A is incorrect because it is incomplete. This activity may complete the school year but is not necessarily an end-of-the-year project. Choice B is incorrect because problem-solving and inquiry teaching are only small components of the activity. Choice D is incorrect because asking students to research Galileo and asking the parent–teacher groups to buy science equipment are not necessarily related.

97. (B)

Grouping patterns affect a student's perceptions of self-esteem and competence. Maintaining the same groups throughout the year encourages students in the average group to view themselves as average, students in the above-average group to view themselves as above average, and students in the below-average group to view themselves as below average. Choice A is incorrect because most students do not like unpredictable teacher behavior. Choice C is incorrect because changes in the classroom often create an atmosphere of mistrust and uneasiness and do not cause students to be more alert.

Choice D is incorrect because although the explanation is correct, it is incomplete compared with the choice B.

98. (A)

Visiting other teachers in other schools will promote collaboration and cooperation. Choice B is incorrect because there is no reason to believe that the principal is encouraging these teachers to apply for a job in the middle school. Choice C is incorrect because although using computers in math classes may be a topic on which teachers choose to collaborate, choice A is more complete. Choice D is incorrect because the middle school math curriculum is not intended for use in the fifth grade.

99. (A)

A needs assessment will help students make the connection between their current skills and those that will be new to them. Choice B is incorrect because a needs assessment focuses on the skills a student currently possesses. Choice C is incorrect because the needs assessment is designed to determine what needs to be taught that is not currently in the curriculum. Choice D is a false statement; a needs assessment is not designed to motivate students.

100. (C)

A positive environment must be created to minimize the effects of negative external factors. Choice A is inappropriate because changing the textbook but allowing the environment to remain the same only results in maintaining the status quo. Choice B is incorrect because relating the students' personal interests to the new material is only part of creating a positive environment. Choice D is incorrect because again it is only a small part of maximizing the effects of a positive learning environment.

101. (C)

The teacher would be fostering strong home relationships that support student achievement of desired outcomes. Choice A is a result of choice C; as the teacher interacts with professionals in the community, her own professional growth would be promoted. Choice B is also the result of choice C; all teachers are expected to interact with the community to help meet the expectations associated with teaching. Choice D is incomplete, because strong home relationships are developed through the principles of conferences, trust, and cooperation.

102. (A)

When students are allowed to select their own problems for study, they become self-directed problem solvers. As such, they have the opportunity to structure their own learning experiences. Assessing students' needs in a naturalistic setting is highly time consuming and not an important benefit of having students select their own problem to investigate (B). There may or may not be a wide variety of instructional materials available to the students as they engage in studying the temperature problem (C); this is not likely to be a major benefit. Learning to appreciate opposing viewpoints is a competency that would be better addressed in social studies and language arts rather than in an activity that deals with a natural empirical science (D).

103. (A)

People are more highly motivated to solve problems that they choose, rather than problems that are chosen for them. Choosing a problem for investigation does not increase student diversity (B). Problem selection has nothing to do with the structure of student groups (C). Although students may engage in more self-assessment, this is not the most important force at work (D).

104. (C)

This question relates to human diversity and the knowledge that each student brings to the classroom a constellation of personal and social characteristics related to a variety of factors such as exceptionality. Choice A is simply more of the same kind of schoolwork and not an acceptable answer. Being intrinsically motivated, exceptional students often find unmotivated students difficult to tutor, making choice B incorrect. Teacher-made, tightly organized units do not allow the

exceptional student the opportunity to experience the learning situation (D).

105. (B)

Choice B describes the procedure in place at the campus level to deal with this type of issue. It respects the processes and oversight authority of the SBDM while addressing the concern of faculty and community. Choice A is incorrect because Ms. Carter does not have the authority to enforce the removal of the animals. Choice C is incorrect because the issue should remain at the campus until the SBDM and the principal have an opportunity to consider the concerns. Choice D is incorrect because even though Ms. Carter may appreciate the librarian's efforts, the health concerns are legitimate. Ms. Carter should remain neutral until the campus can act on the issue.

106. (D)

This question relates to enabling teachers to document their teaching and to be aware of students' efforts, progress, and achievements. Portfolios are purposeful collections of work that exhibit the efforts, progress, and achievement of students and enable teachers to document teaching in an authentic setting. Standardized tests (A) are commercially developed and are used for specific events. Teacher-made tests (B) are used to evaluate specific objectives of the course. Observations (C) are used only to explain what students do in classrooms and to indicate some of their capabilities.

107. (C)

This question relates to evaluating specific objectives and content. Teacher-made tests are designed to evaluate the specific objectives and specific content of a course. Self- and peer evaluations (A) utilize students' knowledge according to evaluation criteria that is understood by the students. Portfolios (B) are purposeful collections of work that exhibit the effort, progress, and achievement of students and enable teachers to document teaching in an authentic setting. Observations (D) are used to explain what students do in classrooms and to indicate to some degree their capabilities.

108. (D)

Standardized tests rate student performance against the performance of other students and report the scores in terms of percentiles, stanines, and scaled scores. Portfolios (A) are collections of student effort, progress, and achievement. Teacher-made tests (B) evaluate specific objectives and content. Students' classroom behaviors and capabilities are evaluated through observations (C).

109. (C)

Camaraderie cannot be fostered by choice alone. However, roundtable discussions will increase student interaction and help each student develop oral language skills (D). A variety of techniques can promote student motivation (B), and the finding that students have average scores in many areas emphasizes the importance of development in one area transferring to another (A).

110. (C)

Ms. Ratu's lack of competency is exhibited in her lack of understanding of her students and in her teaching at the elementary level. Ms. Ratu was not teaching her students at the appropriate level (A). Although she may have desired to make reading easy for her students (B), she was not going about it correctly. When appropriate techniques are used, teaching ninth graders to read is no more difficult than teaching third graders to read.

111. (B)

Although choices A, C, and D are possible, they are basically restatements of the idea that the teacher forms the groups instead of the students, which was specified in the context of the question. The only option that gives a rationale for the teacher choosing her action is choice B.

112. (A)

Only choice A recognizes the cognitive principle underlying the teacher's assignment. Choices B and D are essentially the same; although the assignment may result in these timesaving features, they are not the

instructional principle guiding the teacher's practice. Choice C is irrelevant. Asking students to hypothesize is not directly related to inculcating self-management skills in learners.

113. (C)

The most efficient way to gain information about a new setting is to speak with someone who is familiar with the circumstances. Orienting herself with the physical layout (A) might be helpful but cannot tell Ms. Woods about the student population or materials. Although communication with the principal (B) is always a good idea, the principal in this scenario probably will have little time to engage in an in-depth discussion and will not be able to tell Ms. Woods specifically which books are available for her use. Eventually, Ms. Woods will need to match curriculum guidelines to the material available (D), but sitting in a closet will not introduce her to staff and student characteristics.

114. (D)

Choice D includes all the techniques that would be useful in improving and monitoring writing. The students have set goals toward which they will strive, bit by bit, until they reach them (II). The teacher and students have an opportunity to discuss the good and bad points of the students' writing in a nonthreatening atmosphere (III). It is always helpful to have a model of good writing (IV), and by choosing students' papers, self-esteem is enhanced. Forcing a student to write every night (I) will do little to create quality work. Therefore choices B and C are incorrect.

115. (B)

The passage suggests several ways to reduce the total fat in what we eat. Choice A is incorrect because the author of the passage does not try to convince readers that too much fat in the diet is bad. The author is assuming that reducing fat consumption is the goal of many people, as stated in the first sentence. Choice C is incorrect because the author states that you can reduce fat in your diet and still eat in restaurants. Choice D is incorrect because, although these cooking methods are recommended, that is not the main purpose of the passage.

116. (B)

The suggestion to avoid creamy sauces and gravies is in the sixth sentence. Choice A is incorrect because the author states that salads are healthful. Choice C is incorrect because stir-frying is listed as a preferred cooking method. Choice D is incorrect because the author suggests fresh-fruit desserts.

117. (D)

The author states the meaning of the labels in the third sentence. Choice A is probably a true statement, but the meaning is too narrow. It does not specify what cooking method is used, only that the food is not deep-fat fried.

118. (D)

This question requires you to use the process of elimination. The passage specifically mentions the growth of bones (A), the adrenal glands (B), and parathyroids (C) as being controlled by the pituitary. Blood circulation is not mentioned, so choice D is the correct answer.

119. (B)

The fifth sentence specifically states that the parathyroids control the amount of calcium and phosphate in the blood. Choice A is incorrect because the thyroid and adrenals control metabolism. Choice C is incorrect because the adrenals control sodium and potassium. Choice D is incorrect because the pituitary controls the kidneys.

120. (D)

The adrenal glands are located on top of the kidneys. Choice A is incorrect because the passage does not discuss anything that is located near the pituitary. Choice B is incorrect because the parathyroids are located at the back of the thyroids. Choice C is incorrect because the liver is not mentioned in the passage.

121. (C)

The pituitary controls the growth of bones. Choice A is incorrect because the adrenals control responses to stress and metabolism. Choice B is incorrect because the kidneys function to clean the body of waste products. Choice D is incorrect because the parathyroids control the amount of calcium and phosphate in the blood.

122. (A)

The term *casework* is used by political scientists to describe the activities of members of Congress (the House and the Senate) on behalf of individual constituents. These activities might include helping an elderly person receive Social Security benefits or helping a veteran obtain medical services. Most casework is actually done by congressional staff and may take as much as one-third of the staff's time. Members of Congress supply this type of assistance for the good public relations it provides.

Choice B fails because pork barrel legislation is rarely, if ever, intended to help individual citizens. Pork barrel legislation authorizes federal spending for special projects, such as airports, roads, or dams, in the home state or district of a congressperson. It is meant to help the entire district or state. Also, there is no legal entitlement on the part of a citizen to a pork barrel project, as there is with Social Security benefits. Choice C is not the answer because lobbying is an activity directed toward, rather than done by, members of Congress. A lobbyist attempts to get congresspeople to support legislation that will benefit the group that the lobbyist represents.

Logrolling, choice D, is incorrect because it does not refer to a congressional service for constituents. It refers instead to the congressional practice of trading votes on different bills. Congressman A will vote for Congresswoman B's pork barrel project and in return B will vote for A's pork barrel project.

123. (C)

All known living things are grouped in categories according to shared physical traits. The process of grouping organisms is called classification. Carl Linné, also known as Linnaeus, devised the classification system used in biology today. In the Linnaean system (A), all organisms are given a two-word name (binomial nomenclature). The name consists of a genus (e.g. *Canis*) and a species (e.g. *lupus*) designation. DNA (B) holds the genetic materials of a cell.

When the genetic type of parents is known, the probability of the offspring showing particular traits can be predicted using the Punnett square (C). A Punnett square is a large square divided into four small boxes. The genetic symbol of each parent for a particular trait is written alongside the square, one parent along the top and one parent along the left side, as shown in the following figure.

Parent Aa
(A)   (a)

Parent Aa
(A) | AA | Aa
(a) | Aa | aa

Each gene symbol is written in both boxes below or to the right of the symbol. This results in each box containing two gene symbols. The genetic symbols in the boxes are all the possible genetic combinations for a particular trait of the offspring of these parents. Each box has a 25 percent probability of being the actual genetic representation for a given child. Because this question does have a correct answer, choice D is not correct.

124. (D)

Acid and *base* are terms used to describe solutions of differing pH. The concentration of hydrogen ions in a solution determines its pH. Solutions having pH 0 to 7 are called acids and have hydrogen ions (H$^+$) present. Common acids include lemon juice, vinegar, and battery acid. Acids are corrosive and taste sour. Solutions having pH 7 to 14 are called bases (or alkaline) and have hydroxide ions (OH$^-$) present. Bases are caustic and feel slippery in solution. Common bases include baking soda and lye. Solutions of pH 7 are called neutral and have both ions present in equal but small amounts. The only choice that was a number between 0 and 7 (acids) was choice D.

125. (C)

A liquid has a definite volume but molds to the shape of the container holding it. Titanium (A) is a solid (D); solids have a definite shape and volume. A gas will expand to fit the container in volume and shape.

126. (B)

The instrument for measuring the intensity of an earthquake is a seismograph. A thermograph (A) measures temperature, a telegraph (C) is a communication device, and an odometer (D) measures distance traveled.

127. (B)

Energy is the ability to do work. Work occurs when a force (push or pull) is applied to an object, resulting in movement. Work = force × distance. The greater the force applied, or the longer the distance traveled, the greater the work done. Therefore, force (A) is a factor of work but is not the ability to do work. Speed (C) is rate of movement, and distance (D) is the interval between two points.

128. (C)

The purpose of this essay is narrative. Narrative and expository essays have elements of both the speculative and argumentative modes. The narrative essay may recount an incident or a series of incidents to make a point and is almost always autobiographical. The informality of the storytelling makes the narrative essay less insistent than the argumentative essay (B) but more directed than the speculative essay (A). However, the thesis of a narrative may not be as obvious or clear-cut as that of an expository (D) or argumentative essay.

Essays fall roughly into four categories based on the writer's purpose: speculative, argumentative, narrative, and expository. The speculative essay is so named because, as its Latin root suggests, it looks at ideas; it explores them rather than explains them. Although the speculative essay may be said to be meditative, it often poses one or more questions.

Students are probably most familiar with the expository essay, the primary purpose of which is to explain and clarify ideas. Although the expository essay may have narrative elements, that aspect is minor and subservient to that of explanation. Furthermore, while nearly all essays have some element of persuasion, argumentation is incidental in the expository essay.

The purposes of the argumentative essay are always clear: to present a point, provide evidence, which may be factual or anecdotal, and support the point. The structure is usually very formal, as in a debate, with counterpositions and counterarguments.

129. (C)

The chart shows that Madison received less than half of the votes (his slice takes up less than half of the pie), so statement I cannot be true. Washington and Monroe together received 55 percent of the votes, and everyone else voted for Madison, so Madison must have received 45 percent of the votes (all the candidates' percentages must add up to 100). Statement II is therefore true. Monroe received 30 percent of the 600 votes; $0.30 \times 600 = 180$, so statement III is true. Madison received 45 percent of the vote, and 45 percent of 600 is 270, so statement IV is false.

130. (A)

The somewhat steep straight line to the left tells you that Mr. Cain worked at a steady rate for a while. The completely flat line in the middle tells you he stopped for a while—the line does not go up because Mr. Cain did not cut grass then. Finally, the line continues upward (after his break) less steeply (therefore more flatly), indicating that he was working at a slower rate.

131. (B)

Because Ms. Patton's increases were consistent ($3,000 annually), and because the directions tell you that only one statement is true, choice B must be the correct answer. To be more confident, however, you can examine the other statements. The range of Ms. Patton's earnings is $12,000 (the jump from $30,000 to $42,000), not $15,000, so choice A cannot be correct. Although Ms. Patton may have earned $45,000 in 2003, you do not know that, so choice C cannot be correct. Choice D gives the incorrect earnings average; it was $36,000, not $38,000.

132. (B)

Because most of the space under the curve is past the 60 mark on the x-axis, statement I is true and choice D is eliminated. The truth of statement II cannot be determined by the graph. It appears possible that certain questions were too hard for many in the class and that there were not enough questions to differentiate "B" students from "C" students, but perhaps the class performed exactly as it should have, given the students' abilities and Ms. Alvarez's teaching. The distribution can give a teacher many clues about the text and the students and

even herself, but by itself tells us nothing about the fairness of the test. Thus, choice A can be eliminated.

Statement III is also false; in left-skewed distributions such as this, the median is higher than the mean. This is true because the mean is lowered by the lowest scores while the median is relatively unaffected by them. Statement IV is true: one fairly large group has scored in the high 80s and 90s and another discernible group in the low to mid-60s, whereas few students fall outside these two groups. Thus, the answer has to be choice B.

133. (C)

There are several ways to determine which equation matches the line. An easy way is to decide first whether the line has a positive or negative slope. Because the line moves from the upper left to the lower right, it has a negative slope. In a linear equation of the form $y = mx + b$ (where y is isolated on the left side of the equation), the coefficient of x is the slope of the line. The only equation with a negative slope (-8) is choice C, so that is the correct answer. Another clue that choice C is correct is that the line appears fairly steep, and a slope of -8 (or 8) is considered fairly steep, too.

134. (D)

Using the rules for solving one-variable equations, the original equation is transformed as follows:

$$x/3 - 9 = 15.$$

Adding 9 to each side of the equation gives

$$x/3 = 24.$$

Multiplying both sides by 3 gives

$$x = 72.$$

135. (D)

One way to solve the problem is by writing a one-variable equation that matches the information given:

$$4x + 2(10 - x) = 26$$

The $4x$ represents four tires for each car. You use x for the number of cars because at first you do not know how many cars there are. $(10 - x)$ represents the number of motorcycle in the lot. (If there are 10 vehicles total, and x of them are cars, you subtract x from 10 to get the number of "leftover" motorcycles.) Then $2(10 - x)$ stands for the number of motorcycle tires in the lot. You know that the sum of the values $4x$ and $2(10 - x)$ is 26, and that gives you your equation. Using the standard rules for solving a one-variable equation, you find that x (the number of cars in the lot) equals 3. Another approach to answering a multiple-choice question is to try substituting each choice for the unknown variable in the problem to see which one makes sense.

136. (A)

You know that the correct equation must show three consecutive odd numbers being added to give 117. Odd numbers (just like even numbers) are each two apart. Only the three values given in choice A are each two apart. Because the numbers being sought are odd, one might be tempted to choose D. However, the second value in choice D $(x + 1)$ is not two numbers apart from the first value (x); it is different by only one.

137. (D)

All riders must pay at least three dollars, so 3 will be added to something else in the correct equation. Only choices B and D meet that requirement. The additional fare of two dollars "for every mile or fraction of a mile" tells you that you will need to multiply the number of miles driven (you use 11 because of the extra fraction of a mile) by 2, leading you to the answer, D.

138. (A)

The key to simplifying expressions such as these is to combine only like terms. Like terms are those with identical bases. $4x^2$ and $\frac{3}{5}x^2$, for instance, have like bases. So do $9x$ and $\frac{1}{5}x$. Real numbers without attached variables are like terms; thus, 4, −21, 0, 12, and $\frac{5}{8}$ are all like terms. In the expression, $\frac{2}{3}x^2$ and $\frac{1}{3}x^2$ are like terms; their sum is $\frac{3}{3}x^2$, or $1x^2$, or just x^2. The terms $-12x$ and $7x$ are like terms that add up to $5x$; and 9 and 1 are like terms with a sum of 10. Those three terms—x^2, $-5x$, and

10—are then separated by addition symbols to give the simplified version of the original expression.

139. (B)

You can use the Pythagorean theorem to compute the length of any side of any right triangle, as long as you know the lengths of the other two sides. Here is the theorem: For any right triangle with side lengths a, b, and c, and where c is the length of the hypotenuse (the longest side, and the one opposite the right angle), $c^2 = a^2 + b^2$. Substituting the real values for a and b from the problem, you get

$$c^2 = 11^2 + 5^2$$

or

$$c^2 = 146.$$

To complete the work, you take the (positive) square root of 146, which is slightly more than 12 ($12 \times 12 = 144$).

140. (A)

If two triangles are similar, they have the exact same shape (although not necessarily the same size). In addition, the corresponding angles of two similar triangles have the same measure, and their corresponding sides are proportionate. One way then to find the solution to this problem is to set up a proportion:

$$\frac{12}{10} = \frac{15}{x}$$

This can be read as "12 is to 10 as 15 is to x." The problem can be solved using cross-multiplication. Thus, $12x = 150$, leading to the solution $x = 12.5$.

141. (C)

When two parallel lines are crossed by another line (called a transversal), eight angles are formed. However, there are only two angle measures among the eight angles, and the sum of the two measures is 180°. All the smaller angles will have the same measure, and all the larger angles will have the same measure. In this case, the smaller angles all measure 50°, so the larger angles (including angle y) all measure 130°.

142. (A)

There are two things you must know to answer the question. One is the meaning of the small square at the vertex of angle BXC. That symbol tells you that angle BXC is a right angle (one that measures 90°). You must also understand that a straight line can be thought of as an angle that measures 180°. The sum of the angles DXC (42°) and BXC (90°) is 132°. Therefore, the remaining angle on the line must measure 48° (180° − 132°).

143. (A)

The triangles are similar (i.e., they have the same shape but not the same size), so statement I is true. If you know the measures of two angles of any triangle, you can compute the measure of the third angle. (The sum of the three angles is always 180°.) So the measure of the third angle in both of the triangles is 50°, and statement III is true. Thus, choice A is correct.

144. (B)

To answer the question, you must recognize that triangles ADB and AEC are similar triangles, meaning that they have the same shape. That means that the corresponding angles of the two triangles are the same, or congruent, and that corresponding sides of the two triangles are proportional. Given that, you can set up the following proportion, where x is the distance from point A to point C:

$$\frac{3}{7} = \frac{5}{x}$$

Solving the proportion by cross-multiplication, you find that the length of segment AC is about 11.7. Knowing that the length of segment AB is 7 feet, you subtract to find the length of BC (11.7 − 7 = 4.7).

145. (B)

NATM stands for the National Association of Teachers of Mathematics. Among all of the nationally recognized professional organizations, Teachers of Eng-

lish to Speakers of Other Languages, or TESOL (D), is identified as the organization that provides professional support for educators; it is not the best choice here. *IRA* stands for the International Reading Association; (A) is not the best choice. NASDTEC is the abbreviation of the National Association of State Directors of Teacher Education and Certification.

146. (D)

It is true that multiplication is commutative and division is not, but that is not relevant to their being inverse operations. Choice A does not address the property of being inverse. Choice B also contains a true statement, but again, the statement is not about inverse operations. Choice C gives a false statement; in the example shown, the order of operations tells you to compute 8 ÷ 2 before any multiplication. As noted in choice D, the inverseness of two operations indeed depends on their ability to undo each other.

147. (A)

The area of any rectangle is equal to the measure of its length times the measure of its width (or to say it differently, the measure of its base times the measure of its height). A right triangle can be seen as half of a rectangle (sliced diagonally). Choice A represents, in effect, a rectangle's area cut in half (i.e., divided by 2).

148. (D)

The formula for finding the area of any circle is $A = \pi r^2$ (about 3.14 times the length of the radius times itself). In this case, you need to take half of πr^2, as shown in choice D.

149. (B)

Angle XYZ is an inscribed angle (its vertex is on the circle). Angle XCZ is a central angle (its vertex is at the circle's center). When two such angles intercept (or cut off) the same arc of the circle, there exists a specific size relationship between the two angles. The measure of the central angle will always be double the measure of the inscribed angle. In this case, that means that the measure of angle XCZ must be 80°. That means that minor arc XZ also has measure 80°. Every circle (considered an arc) has measure 360°. That means that major arc XYZ has measure 280° (360° − 80°).

150. (A)

The formula for finding the volume of a cylinder is

$$V = \pi r^2 h.$$

That means the volume is equal to pi (about 3.14) times the measure of the radius squared times the height of the cylinder. In this case, that is

$$3.14 \times 6^2 \times 8$$

or

$$3.14 \times 36 \times 8$$

or about 904. (Notice that the final answer is given in cubic centimeters.)

151. (C)

Clearly setting a purpose for listening, asking questions about the selection, and encouraging students to forge links between the new information and knowledge already in place are all supported by research as effective strategies.

152. (D)

Children learn more from a text if the teacher helps them figure out how the book was put together and how the author organized the material. It can make the text more understandable. It also helps them to read the text critically because part of the conversation can address the issue of what is missing in the text and encourage the students to consider what they already know. All the answers, therefore, are correct so D is the best choice.

153. (B)

The statement "Movement basics include body, space, time, and relationship" describes only the dimensions of dance movement and does not speak to how

dance reflects the culture of which it is part. Choice B, then, is the best choice because the test taker is looking for the item that is *not* correct.

154. (D)

Flying buttresses, pointed arches, and stained glass windows appear together only on Gothic-style buildings, most of which were built between 1150 and 1500. Buildings of the Romanesque period (ca. 1050–1150) usually employ wall buttresses and rounded arches; only a few employ pointed arches. The flying buttress was a device invented specifically to support the high vaults of Gothic churches. Byzantine buildings, like the famous Hagia Sophia in Istanbul, are characterized by domes and rounded arches, among other things. The same is true for Renaissance and Baroque architecture.

155. (B)

In using three different versions of this well-known story, Ms. Smith is creating an opportunity to bring a multicultural perspective to the drama activity. In versions of *Cinderella* from around the world, the story of the mistreated but kindhearted protagonist is basically the same, but the characters, settings, and ways in which the plot unfolds are culturally centered. Furthermore, because Ms. Smith is using scripted versions of the story and staging these plays with costumes, scenery, and props, she is making theatrical elements integral to the performances. Because the students are engaging in formal dramatic activity that will result in a theatrical product, rather than informal, process-centered drama, choice III is incorrect. Choice IV is incorrect because the students are not the ones who have adapted the stories and, therefore, they are not having firsthand experience with that process.

156. (B)

By telling her students about equivalent measurements, she has stated a principle or law. She has not taught cause-and-effect (A, C) or provided applications of the principle (D).

157. (B)

The best way to teach children to read, regardless of grade level, is to use a program of emergent literacy, which includes pattern books and journal writing with invented spelling. Choice A is incorrect because although an intensive phonics program that includes drill and practice work may be effective with some students, it is not the most effective way to teach all students to read. Choice D is incorrect because an ESL program is intended to provide assistance to only those students who are learning English as a second language. Additionally, the learning resource teacher should provide assistance to only those students who have been identified as having a learning disability that qualifies them to receive services.

158. (C)

Careful planning includes checking the availability of resources and materials (II). Ms. Doe did reflective listening during the discussion (I). However, reflective listening is only one component of communication and is included in careful planning and its correlation to success in the classroom (III). Personal acquaintance with a Native American (IV) would have helped shape the students' attitudes, but it is not necessary for student involvement.

159. (A)

Multiple strategies were planned for the motivation of the students (I), and a result of the strategies was that each student participated in some way regardless of ability (II) and the unit was integrated into other subjects through library assignments, reading, writing, and so on (III). Developing a foundation for teaching American history (IV) is not even a long-range goal, although the attitudes and beliefs developed in the project may become the foundation on which the students will build their philosophy of American history.

160. (D)

Working collaboratively with other teachers, the teacher was able to identify the talents of the students and stimulate their curiosity. No risks were taken, so choice I is incorrect.

161. (A)

The external factors of the field trip could create a positive motivation and allow the students to make the connection between their old skills and the new skills they were learning. No mention is made of community involvement in the field trip (III), and the students did not take responsibility for their own learning (IV) because they were given instructions concerning what they were to do before they left for the field trip.

162. (B)

The teacher showed respect to the children by allowing them a choice of field trips (II). The trip is one of an array of instructional strategies used by Ms. Doe (IV). A is not correct because, while the students are to decide where they wish to go, this is not a part of the instructional objective. C is incorrect since the decision allowed through this strategy does not limit the view of learning as a purposeful pursuit. D is inaccurate because direct instructional strategies are not utilized here.

163. (B)

Placing the students in small groups in which they meet face to face will allow Mr. Billings to maximize the students' interaction while giving each student the maximum opportunity to speak. Placing students in the traditional rows facing the front (A) discourages student interaction and minimizes each student's opportunities to speak. Although placing students in pairs (C) maximizes each student's opportunity to speak, it limits the sources of interaction; each student may share thoughts with only one other student. In contrast, a group of four allows the student to interact as part of three dyads, two triads, and a quadrat. When placing the students in cooperative groups, it is wise to arrange the desks within the physical space of the classroom in such a way that each group's talking does not distract the members of other groups. The seating arrangement in choice D places groups close to one another, compared with the arrangement in choice B.

164. (C)

By requiring both a cognitive and a performance objective, the student was required to show that he or she not only had the knowledge but also could apply that knowledge to a life situation. Although choice A is true, it is not the foundation for developing specific objectives. Choice B is an assumption and not relevant to the setting of certain objectives. Teaching style and learning styles (D) are not relevant to the behavioral objectives.

165. (B)

This question is designed to demonstrate an understanding that the performance objective should directly tie into the assessment. Students need to know what the expectation is for them to complete the necessary assignments. Students do not understand what assessment tools are. Therefore, rather than explaining how they will be assessed (A), the teacher needs to give students clear directions and a list of explanations. Although the unit may have many new vocabulary words, students need to learn them within the context of the unit rather than from a random list (C); they should not feel threatened when learning to prepare for a test. There is no connection between notebooks and learning (D).

166. (C)

Rubrics are designed to help teachers assess student achievement and the quality of student responses. Therefore, a rubric should have clearly defined criteria (I), and each criterion needs to have a quality point (II); for example, excellent (5–4), good (3–2), and fair (1–0). Rubrics need to cover several subject areas to allow for a fair assessment of the student's work (III). Students may not grade/rate themselves (IV); the teacher needs to work with them as they complete the ratings. Teachers have the ultimate task for grading—not the student.

167. (B)

Students often disclose more personal information in journals than when speaking in class. The teacher can also check for comprehension of content and the success or failure of class objectives. Journals typically are not graded with consideration to standard usage or grammatical constructions; therefore, choice A is incorrect. The assignment has no direct bearing on time management skills; therefore, choice C is incorrect. Choice D is irrelevant: no mention is made of giving daily grades on the journal writing.

168. (C)

The Language Experience Approach is a proven method of increasing students' reading and writing proficiency and their overall language competency. It requires that students write about what they know. Choices A, B, and D are irrelevant. Choice A superficially addresses that Ms. Johnson is an English teacher, and choice B refers to autobiographies, something that is not mentioned in the preceding information. Choice D foreshadows the library project, but it has not yet been introduced into the context of these questions.

169. (C)

A basic principle in providing students with appropriate feedback is to first note the student's strengths (or positive aspects of the student's work and/or performance) and then to note specific ways the student can improve his or her work and/or performance. Choices A and B are in essence the same; both indicate that only students' strengths would be acknowledged, omitting the important aspect of addressing ways students could improve. Neither action would enhance students' cognitive skills or their metacognitive skills (or self-awareness). Choice D is unacceptable because it denigrates the teacher's responsibility to evaluate students' performance on the basis of individual merit against the standards established by particular disciplines.

170. (A)

Choice A is the best answer of the four options for the following reasons. First, learning style information acknowledges that although learners acquire knowledge in different ways, those differences can lead to effective learning when students are taught cognitive strategies that complement their natural learning tendencies; basically, teaching students about various learning styles and enabling each student to recognize her or his own learning style is a recognition of human diversity. Second, knowing about learning styles reveals the legitimacy of different approaches to learning. Every student can perform at a level of proficiency, although not every student will attain that level in the same manner; in other words, learning styles validate students as learners and promote high standards for academic achievement.

Third, when students are taught not only about learning styles in general but also about their own learning style specifically, they are empowered to take responsibility for their own learning. Fourth, of the four options, only choices A and D are tasks actively engaging the students. Choices B and C are passive activities and are therefore poor choices. Choice D requires that students perform a task without any discussion or assistance (direct instruction); simply asking students to name additional strengths without giving them an opportunity to self-examine, self-assess, and explore their strengths will not produce the desired outcome. Only choice A gives students the information they require to accomplish the task the teacher has identified as important.

171. (D)

The question relates to appropriate sequencing of activities. Choice D is the best introductory activity to generate student interest in this new field of mathematics and to get students thinking about how to produce fractals. It would stimulate students to use higher-level thinking skills to make predictions by drawing on their knowledge of how to solve problems mathematically. Choice A would be the least appropriate to begin the study. Students who want to learn more could research this topic after they have developed an interest in fractals. Choice B would be appropriate as a later step, after students are interested in the process and are ready to learn how to produce fractals. Choice C would be appropriate as a step in the process of learning how to produce fractals. Choice B requires students to use pre-planned formulas, whereas choice C allows them to develop their own formulas, a very high-level activity.

172. (A)

Finding the square root of 100 means finding the number that, when multiplied by itself, gives 100. Choice A is the correct answer because 10 times 10 does yield 100.

173. (D)

The exponent (the superscript 4) on the outside of the parenthesis indicates multiplication. Because 4 times 2 equals 8, the answer is D.

174. (C)

To solve the multiplication problem, you need to multiply the numerators (3×8) and multiply the denominators (4×9). The answer is 24/36. To simplify, you divide the numerator and the denominator by 12. The answer is, therefore, 2/3.

175. (D)

To change the fraction to a decimal, you divide 7 by 8. This will give the decimal answer 0.875.

176. (A)

The easiest way to find the answer is to estimate: $7 \times 2 = 14$. The answer closest to 14 is 17.6 (A).

177. (C)

A quiet classroom may be appropriate for some learning activities and inappropriate for others. It is not necessarily a good or bad learning environment (A), (B), nor does it demonstrate that the teacher has appropriate control of the students, (D)—e.g., the students might all be asleep.

178. (B)

Democracy is the antithesis of the authoritarianism of fascism. Indeed, the totalitarian, romantic, militaristic, and nationalistic characteristics of fascism were, in large part, a reaction against the perceived inadequacies of democracy.

179. (B)

The industrial economy of the nineteenth century was not based on an equitable distribution of profits among all those who were involved in production. Marxists and other critics of capitalism condemned the creed of capitalists and the abhorrent conditions of the industrial proletariat. Raw materials (A), a constant labor supply, capital (C), and an expanding marketplace (D) were critical elements in the development of the industrial economy.

180. (D)

In the 1880s and 1890s, the U.S. Supreme Court struck down desegregation laws and upheld the doctrine of segregated "separate but equal" facilities for blacks and whites. These laws became known as "Jim Crow" laws. Their impact was to allow racist governments in the South to set up "separate but unequal" facilities in which blacks were forced to sit in the rear of streetcars and buses and in the back rooms of restaurants, were excluded completely from white businesses, and had to use separate and usually inferior public restroom facilities. These laws allowed white supremacists to "put blacks in their place" and effectively kept blacks from achieving anything near equal status. It was not until the 1950s and 1960s that new Supreme Court decisions finally forced the repeal of Jim Crow laws.

181. (B)

A writ of habeas corpus is a court order that directs an official who is detaining someone to produce the person before the court so that the legality of the detention may be determined. The primary function of the writ is to effect the release of someone who has been imprisoned without due process of law. For example, if the police detained a suspect for an unreasonable time without officially charging the person with a crime, the person could seek relief from a court in the form of a writ of habeas corpus. Choice A is incorrect because a writ of mandamus is a court order commanding an official to perform a legal duty of his or her office. It is not used to prevent persons from being improperly imprisoned. The Fourth Amendment requirement that police have probable cause to obtain a search warrant (C) regulates police procedure; it is not itself a mechanism for affecting release of a person for improper imprisonment. Choice D is incorrect because the decision in *Roe v. Wade* dealt with a woman's right to have an abortion; it had nothing to do with improper imprisonment.

182. (A)

By definition, an acid and a base combine to produce a salt and water. An example is HCl (hydrochloric acid) and NaOH (sodium hydroxide) reacting to form NaCl (salt) and water.

183. (D)

A neutral atom has a net charge of zero, which means that the number of negative particles (electrons) equals the number of positive particles (protons).

184. (D)

Choices A, B, and C involve chemical changes in which iron, wood, and rocket fuel react with other substances to produce a reactant product with different chemical properties. When ice melts to form water, its chemical formula does not change.

185. (C)

Isotopes of a given element all have the same chemical properties, differing only in their atomic weights, which are based on the numbers of neutrons.

186. (C)

Newton's second law states that an unbalanced force acting on a mass will cause the mass to accelerate. In equation form, $F = ma$, where F is force, m is mass, and a is acceleration. Only choice C involves a mass that is being accelerated by an unbalanced force.

187. (A)

Thermal energy is the total amount of internal energy of a given body, while temperature is a measure of the vibrational activity of atoms or molecules comprising the material. Therefore, thermal energy involves both the mass and temperature of a given body. Choice A is the best answer because the mass of the Pacific Ocean far exceeds 1 g (B), a bucket of water (C), and Lake Michigan (D). Choice B is ruled out because even though the metal's temperature is very high, its mass is extremely small.

188. (D)

The cell membrane is a selectively permeable barrier that permits some substances to pass through while forming a barrier for others. None of the other choices has this property.

189. (D)

The zygote of a human is a cell derived from a sperm containing 23 chromosomes and an egg containing 23 chromosomes. Choices A and B are incorrect because they represents too few chromosome for either a haploid sex cell or a diploid body cell. Choice C cannot be the correct answer because it represents the number of chromosomes in a sperm or an egg.

190. (C)

The body regulates water and heat through perspiration. Transpiration (B) describes a process not involving humans. Respiration (A) is breathing in humans and will cause some water loss. However, the question asks how the body regulates substances through the skin. Sensation (D) is the ability to process or perceive. The skin does have nerve endings that can sense, but that does not involve temperature or water regulation.

191. (A)

Choices B, C, and D are ruled out because Darwin could not have been aware of the genetic work that was done by Mendel. Darwin and most other nineteenth-century biologists never knew of Mendel and his research. It was not until the beginning of the twentieth century that Mendel's pioneering research into genetic inheritance was rediscovered.

192. (B)

The lunar period is about 30 days, or one month, which is the time it takes for the moon to orbit the earth one time.

193. (C)

A star that becomes a nova is presumed to be at the end of its life. As hydrogen (or sometimes helium) is depleted, the fusion reaction becomes incapable of sustaining the pressures required to push the star's mass outward against the pull of gravity. The star then collapses, resulting in a gigantic explosion known as a supernova. Choice A is neither observed nor possible. Choice B is not observed. Choice D, although occasionally observed, does not trigger nova-sized explosions.

194. (C)

Choice A is ruled out because the earth is actually somewhat closer to the sun from December through January than it is from June through July, which is winter for the Northern Hemisphere. Choice B is ruled out because the rotation period is the same from season to season. Choice D is ruled out because it describes a daily not seasonal phenomena. Choice C is the answer because the tilting of the earth's axis causes the Northern Hemisphere to point toward the sun in the summer months and away from the sun in the winter months (with the reverse being true for the Southern Hemisphere).

195. (A)

Igneous rocks are transformed, or "metamorphed," into metamorphic rocks. Thus, they are not unrelated to igneous (B), not sedimentary (C), and not impossible to find on this planet (D).

196. (D)

The east coast of South America and the west coast of Africa fit together like pieces of a jig-saw puzzle (A). Fossil remains in locations where "fit" is observed to be too well matched to be coincidental (B). Earthquakes and volcanism are more prevalent in mountainous regions, where plates collided, than in other regions (C). Thus, all the choices support the theory of plate tectonics.

197. (A)

According to the theory of plate tectonics, plate spreading is associated with magma up welling to fill the vacated space, which forms ridges at those locations.

198. (D)

Raw material for igneous rock formation is magma that, when cooled either above or below ground, becomes igneous rock.

199. (B)

Multiple investigators have confirmed the order given in choice B: nitrogen, oxygen, carbon dioxide, trace gases.

200. (D)

The greatest common divisor (GCD) is the greatest integer that divides both 120 and 252. To find the GCD, you factor both numbers and look for common factors.

$$120 = 2^3 \times 3 \times 5$$

and

$$252 = 2^2 \times 3^2 \times 7$$

The common factors are 2^2 and 3, so the GCD = $2^2 \times 3 = 12$.

201. (A)

A prime number is an integer that is greater than one and that has no integer divisors other than 1 and itself. The prime numbers between 1 and 20 (not including 1 and 20) are 2, 3, 5, 7, 11, 13, 17, 19. However, 2 is not an odd number, so there are seven odd prime numbers between 1 and 20.

202. (C)

The 1 is in the hundredths place. If the number to the immediate right of the 1 (i.e., the number in the thousandths place) is greater than or equal to 5, you increase 1 to 2; otherwise, you do not change the 1. Then you leave off all the numbers to the right of the 1. In this problem, a 6 is in the thousandths place, so you change the 1 to a 2 to get 287.42.

203. (A)

The number 72,104.58 is read "seventy-two thousand, one hundred four and fifty-eight hundredths." Thus, the 2 is in the thousands place.

204. (C)

There is sufficient evidence to suggest that the student is a victim of sexual abuse. The situation is too serious to delay action (A) or to remain passive (B). In no case would it be appropriate to copy and distribute the poem to other teachers (D).

205. (B)

Providing external rewards (such as tokens and prizes) for reading appeals to students who are extrinsically motivated. Intrinsically motivated students read for the pleasure and self-satisfaction of reading (A). Students who read below, at, and above grade level may be motivated extrinsically or intrinsically (C). Some students may be uninterested in earning tokens to acquire school supplies whether or not they are able to purchase their own supplies (D).

206. (C)

This is not a closed question, but an open question, requiring some thoughtful reflecting and speculation to answer. Answers (A), (B), and (D) are examples of closed questions, requiring a simple statement of recall to answer the question.

207. (A)

Just guessing the decade that the composition reflects does not require the students to use their knowledge of music and the periods. Therefore, choice A is *not* a good activity, whereas the others are.

208. (B)

Rules and regulations for schools and libraries that make use of the Internet available to students do *not* currently include the filtering of text. On the other hand, these computers must provide the use of blocking or filtering technology to protect students against access to certain visual depictions (A). The rules also require that personal information about the students must not be disclosed (C) and prohibit the use of the computers for "hacking" (D).

209. (A)

Choice A is not true; the fair use doctrine *does* allow limited reproduction of copyrighted works for educational and research purposes. Choices B, C, and D are all true. Teachers can copy chapters, articles, and visual materials (e.g., charts, graphs, diagrams, cartoons) for the classroom (B). Regardless of whether the copy is from a collective work, an educator may make copies of a short story, essay, or poem for the classroom (C). Teachers can make multiple copies (not to exceed the number of students in the class) for the class, as long as the copying meets the tests of brevity and spontaneity (D).

210. (A)

John Philip Sousa popularized patriotic marches. Leonard Bernstein (B) worked in many genres using classical and jazz elements. Igor Stravinsky (C) explored primitivism and tonalities. Franz Joseph Haydn (D) was a composer of the classical period.

211. (B)

Charlie Parker had the nickname "Bird" because of his rapid alto saxophone bebop figures. John Coltrane (A) was master of the tenor and soprano saxophones. Dizzy Gillespie (C) was a master of the trumpet, and Stan Getz (D) was a tenor saxophonist of the "cool" jazz style.

212. (C)

Prokofiev is the composer of *Peter and the Wolf,* which had a unique theme for each character. Pyotr Ilyich Tchaikovsky is the composer of the ballet *The Nutcracker* from which the *Nutcracker* Suite (A) is extracted. Igor Stravinsky composed the *Firebird* Suite (B), another composition often used in the classroom. Leonard Bernstein is the composer of West Side Story (D).

213. (D)

The Egyptian Temple of Horus, ca. 212 BCE, pictured in the example, displays elements typical of the monumental architecture which developed during Egypt's Old Kingdom period (ca. 2600–2100 BCE) and continued until Egypt became a province of the Roman Empire (ca. 31 BCE). This architecture achieved an effect of imposing grandeur and durability through the use of simple, solid geometric forms constructed on an overwhelming scale and laid out with exacting symmetry. The Temple of Horus avoids any emphasis on horizontal lines (A), relying instead on the sloping outer walls to visually "pull" the massive building to the ground and make it seem immovable and eternal. Additionally, although the temple carries minor ornamental detail (B), displays huge reliefs of figures, and is set within a large open courtyard (C), all these elements are secondary to the massive character of the building itself.

214. (A)

The squatting position of the figure is indicative of a low position, like that of a slave (A). Since he is wearing only a cloak thrown back over one shoulder, this, too, indicates the clothing of a commoner or a person of low status. The action, that of sharpening of a knife, is a job that would be designated to a slave. The muscle structure of the figure would not really indicate a social level, making choices B, C, and D unlikely choices.

215. (A)

The seventeenth-century Japanese ink-on-paper scroll painting shown in the example relies almost exclusively on the qualities of line to convey the graceful forms of two leaping deer. In this painting, called *Deer Scroll,* both the animals and the scripted characters share the quality of fluid, rhythmic, spontaneous "writing." Gradations of tone (B) and color (C) are unimportant here because the images are defined by black line on white. Volume (D) is also absent because these forms show no shading or modulation of tone.

216. (C)

This question asks you to read and determine the mood created by an author in a short selection. Choice C, taken from Thomas Wolfe's "Circuses at Dawn," uses such words and phrases as "thrilling darkness" and "rushing madly" to let the reader share the narrator's strange excitement as he anticipates the circus.

217. (A)

A dramatic monologue is a poem in the form of an extended speech by an identifiable character. Choice A, the beginning of Robert Browning's poem "My Last Duchess," is unquestionably spoken by one character to another.

218. (D)

A metaphor is a literary device whereby an author compares two seemingly unlike things to achieve an effect. Choice D, taken from Henry David Thoreau's essay "Civil Disobedience," compares two seemingly unlike things—the American government and a wooden gun—to make a point.

219. (D)

Among all of the nationally recognized professional organizations, Teachers of English to Speakers of Other Languages (TESOL) is identified as the organization that provides professional support for educators. IRA (A) stands for the International Reading Association, NATM (B) is the National Association of Teachers of Mathematics, and NASDTEC (C) is the acronym for the National Association of State Directors of Teacher Education and Certification.

220. (D)

Let x be the number of people in the barn. Then, because each person and lamb has only one head, the number of lambs must be $30 - x$. People have two legs, so the number of human legs totals $2x$. Similarly, since each lamb has 4 legs, the total number of lamb legs in the barn is $4(30 - x)$. Thus, you have this equation:

$$2x + 4(30 - x) = 104$$

To solve this equation, you use the distributive property, which states

$$a(b - c) = ab - ac.$$

Using the distributive property for $4(30 - x)$, you get

$$(4 \times 30) - (4 \times x) = 120 - 4x.$$

Putting this back into the equation gives you

$$2x + 120 - 4x = 104$$

which reduces to

$$120 - 2x = 104.$$

Now you subtract 120 from both sides of the equation to get $-2x = 104 - 120 = -16$. Dividing both sides of the equation by -2 gives you $x = 8$. Therefore, there were 8 people and $30 - 8 = 22$ lambs in the barn.

221. (B)

Integrating another content area into the students' study of the American Revolution will develop a broader view of that period in history. Choice A is incorrect because although the teachers are integrating their lessons, each is responsible for his or her own subject area. Choice C is incorrect because librarians are usually pleased when books are used by teachers and students. Choice D is incorrect because teaching integrated units does not necessarily lead students to do homework for one subject during another's class period.

222. (A)

Ms. Fisher's best option is to express her concerns and the reasons for those concerns with the school counselor, who is trained to help in matters of student concern such as this. Involving another student (B) is a poor choice in this instance: it places a large emotional burden on the second student. In addition, it makes the teacher's concern public rather than keeping it confidential among school officials. As choice C suggests, Lisa's parents do need to be notified soon. However, that call should be made by the counselor because he or she is a professional trained to deal with these types of concerns. Confronting Lisa directly (D) could cause her to be defensive about her actions and, if there is indeed an eating disorder, could cause her to hide her symptoms to avoid further detection.

223. (B)

Students at the formal operational stage can understand complex theoretical descriptions with little or no direct observation. Students at the concrete observational stage (A) must have direct observation to reach understanding and have trouble with complex theoretical descriptions. The sensorimotor stage (D) applies to infants, and the preoperational stage (C) applies to children ages 2 to 7.

224. (B)

Questions that demand recall of factual information can be answered in one or two words or in a short phrase. If lengthy answers are desired, then the question format must change. There is no information to indicate that students are intimidated, therefore choice A is incorrect. Uncertainty about answers usually causes students to provide long, rambling responses, so choice C is incorrect. Choice D is incorrect because the students are providing answers, so it does not seem reasonable that the questions are too difficult.

INDEX

Index

Available at your local bookstore or order directly from us by sending in coupon below.

REA's Test Preps
The Best in Test Preparation

- REA "Test Preps" are **far more** comprehensive than any other test preparation series
- Each book contains up to **eight** full-length practice tests based on the most recent exams
- **Every** type of question likely to be given on the exams is included
- Answers are accompanied by **full** and **detailed** explanations

REA publishes over 70 Test Preparation volumes in several series. They include:

Advanced Placement Exams (APs)
Art History
Biology
Calculus AB & BC
Chemistry
Economics
English Language & Composition
English Literature & Composition
European History
French Language
Government & Politics
Latin
Physics B & C
Psychology
Spanish Language
Statistics
United States History
World History

**College-Level Examination
Program (CLEP)**
Analyzing and Interpreting Literature
College Algebra
Freshman College Composition
General Examinations
General Examinations Review
History of the United States I
History of the United States II
Introduction to Educational
   Psychology
Human Growth and Development
Introductory Psychology
Introductory Sociology
Precalculus
Principles of Management
Principles of Marketing
Spanish
Western Civilization I
Western Civilization II

SAT Subject Tests
Biology E/M
Chemistry
French
German
Literature
Mathematics Level 1, 2
Physics
Spanish
United States History

Graduate Record Exams (GREs)
Biology
Chemistry
Computer Science
General
Literature in English
Mathematics
Physics
Psychology

ACT - ACT Assessment

ASVAB - Armed Services Vocational
   Aptitude Battery

CBEST - California Basic Educational
   Skills Test

CDL - Commercial Driver License Exam

CLAST - College Level Academic
   Skills Test

COOP & HSPT - Catholic High School
   Admission Tests

ELM - California State University
   Entry Level Mathematics Exam

FE (EIT) - Fundamentals of
   Engineering AM Exam

FTCE - Florida Teacher Certification
   Examinations

GED - (U.S. Edition)

GMAT - Graduate Management
   Admission Test

LSAT - Law School Admission Test

MAT - Miller Analogies Test

MCAT - Medical College Admission
   Test

MTEL - Massachusetts Tests for
   Educator Licensure

NJ HSPA - New Jersey High School
   Proficiency Assessment

NYSTCE - New York State Teacher
   Certification Examinations

PRAXIS PLT - Principles of Learning
   & Teaching Tests

PRAXIS PPST - Pre-Professional
   Skills Tests

PSAT/NMSQT

SAT

TExES - Texas Examinations of
   Educator Standards

THEA - Texas Higher Education
   Assessment

TOEFL - Test of English as a Foreign
   Language

TOEIC - Test of English for
   International Communication

USMLE Steps 1,2,3 - U.S. Medical
   Licensing Exams

*If you would like more information about any of these books,
complete the coupon below and return it to us or visit your local bookstore.*

Research & Education Association
61 Ethel Road W., Piscataway, NJ 08854
Phone: (732) 819-8880   **website: www.rea.com**

Please send me more information about your Test Prep books.

Name _____

Address _____

City _____ State _____ Zip _____